Intellectual and Industrial Property Law

3rd Edition

My thanks go to Rhiannon Hough and Bernadette Favis, who capably assisted with the research for the first edition of this book, to Paris Gray for her sterling work on the second edition, and to Violet Atkinson for her assistance with the third edition.

Intellectual and Industrial Property Law

3rd Edition

William van Caenegem
LLM, PhD (Cantab)
Professor, Faculty of Law, Bond University

LexisNexis Butterworths
Australia
2019

	LexisNexis
AUSTRALIA	LexisNexis Butterworths 475–495 Victoria Avenue, Chatswood NSW 2067 On the internet at: www.lexisnexis.com.au
ARGENTINA	LexisNexis Argentina, Buenos Aires
AUSTRIA	LexisNexis Verlag ARD Orac GmbH & Co KG, Vienna
BRAZIL	LexisNexis Latin America, Sao Paulo
CANADA	LexisNexis Canada, Markham, Ontario
CHILE	LexisNexis Chile, Santiago
CHINA	LexisNexis China, Beijing, Shanghai
CZECH REPUBLIC	Nakladatelství Orac sro, Prague
FRANCE	LexisNexis SA, Paris
GERMANY	LexisNexis Germany, Frankfurt
HONG KONG	LexisNexis Hong Kong, Hong Kong
HUNGARY	HVG-Orac, Budapest
INDIA	LexisNexis, New Delhi
ITALY	Dott A Giuffrè Editore SpA, Milan
JAPAN	LexisNexis Japan KK, Tokyo
KOREA	LexisNexis, Seoul
MALAYSIA	LexisNexis Malaysia Sdn Bhd, Petaling Jaya, Selangor
NEW ZEALAND	LexisNexis, Wellington
POLAND	Wydawnictwo Prawnicze LexisNexis, Warsaw
SINGAPORE	LexisNexis, Singapore
SOUTH AFRICA	LexisNexis Butterworths, Durban
SWITZERLAND	Staempfli Verlag AG, Berne
TAIWAN	LexisNexis, Taiwan
UNITED KINGDOM	LexisNexis UK, London, Edinburgh
USA	LexisNexis Group, New York, New York LexisNexis, Miamisburg, Ohio

NATIONAL LIBRARY OF AUSTRALIA

A catalogue record for this book is available from the National Library of Australia

ISBN: 9780409350159 (pbk).
9780409350166 (ebk).

First edition, 2009. Second edition, 2015.

Typeset in Myriad Pro and Minion Pro.

Printed in Australia.

Visit LexisNexis Butterworths at www.lexisnexis.com.au

Contents

Detailed Contents

Preface

This book aims to introduce students to the diverse regimes that together make up contemporary Australian intellectual property law. The subject matter is vast and fluid, so coverage remains unavoidably selective, focusing on major principles as well as issues commonly addressed in IP courses. The text does not deal extensively with procedural issues relating to applications in the various regimes.

The underlying approach is doctrinal and domestic rather than policy orientated and international. Relevant international treaties are not dealt with separately or in any great detail; rather, Australian provisions and cases formed the main source material. Policy and theory are covered to a degree in the introduction chapter, but not extensively in others.

The choice of cases in this book reflects a search for illustrative recent IP examples, rather than a desire to provide the chronological chain of precedent for every legal principle. For the latter, a suitable commentary and materials book is a useful further source of reference. The reasons for decisions published by courts also commonly provide chronological surveys of binding and persuasive precedent.

Each regime is generally dealt with in a number of shorter chapters, to provide more digestible bites for the reader. A separate chapter on remedies in intellectual property law canvasses some issues of practical importance to IP disputes, including typical remedies and orders sought. Legal questions resulting from digitisation have also been compiled into a distinct chapter, because computers and the internet give rise to a myriad of distinct *but interconnected* issues. However, the chapter remains unavoidably selective, and new questions constantly arise in this sphere.

The limited bibliography in each chapter reflects doctrinal commentary or case comments published in Australia in recent years, and is intended to alert students to some publications that go into particular legal issues in more detail. It is not intended to provide a comprehensive reading list covering all policy, doctrinal and theoretical aspects of a given topic. The volume of publications about IP law in recent times is, in any case, so vast that the latter would require an impractically long list.

The bulk of the work on the first edition of this book was completed by December 2008, the second edition by mid-September 2014, and the third edition by September 2019.

William van Caenegem
Gold Coast
January 2009; September 2014; September 2019

Table of Cases

References are to paragraph numbers

E

F

G

I

L

M

N

O

P

T

U

Y

Z

Table of Statutes

References are to paragraph numbers

NEW SOUTH WALES

VICTORIA

GERMANY

NEW ZEALAND

UNITED KINGDOM

UNITED STATES

Chapter 1

Themes and Concepts in Intellectual Property Law

What is Intellectual Property?

1.1 In accordance with art 2(viii) of the Convention Establishing the World Intellectual Property Organization (WIPO), 14 July 1967, which Australia has ratified, intellectual property includes the rights relating to:

- literary, artistic and scientific works;
- performances of performing artists, phonograms and broadcasts;
- inventions in all fields of human endeavour;
- scientific discoveries;
- industrial designs;
- trade marks, service marks, and commercial names and designations;
- protection against unfair competition;

and all other rights resulting from intellectual activity in the industrial, scientific, literary or artistic fields.

It is immediately apparent that the term 'intellectual property' covers a broad and diverse field. In fact, the legal actions and remedies covered by the term 'intellectual property' are so varied in policy goals and structure that it is questionable whether they should be grouped together. The individual regimes such as copyright or patents law had a considerable history before the term 'intellectual property' was ever coined: see L Bently and B Sherman, *The Making of Modern Intellectual Property Law*, Cambridge University Press, Cambridge, 1999. The WIPO definition has a settled air about it, although this is perhaps misleading. First, the closing phrase hints at the open-ended nature of intellectual property; second, although the list suggests a universal consensus about the confines of intellectual property, such a consensus does not, in fact, exist. For instance, in Australia there is no general tort of unfair competition (see *Victoria Park Racing Recreation Grounds Co Ltd v Taylor* (1937) 58 CLR 479), and scientific discoveries (as opposed to 'inventions') are not, in fact, the subject of intellectual property rights. Conversely, plant variety rights (or 'plant breeder's rights'), geographical indications of origin and domain names are not referred to at all, although they are proving to be valuable forms of intellectual property.

Obviously, the WIPO definition identifies the objects of intellectual property rights but not the essential nature and structure of those rights. In various jurisdictions, despite recent attempts at harmonisation, these are still quite divergent.

In Australia, s 51(xviii) of the Commonwealth Constitution confers power over 'copyrights, patents of inventions and designs, and trade marks' on the Commonwealth Parliament. In *Grain Pool of WA v Commonwealth* (2000) 202 CLR 479; 46 IPR 515, the High Court effectively held that this was intended to cover the whole evolving area of intellectual property law, and therefore the legislation concerning plant varieties under consideration (the Plant Breeder's Rights Act 1994 (Cth)) was within power. Kirby J (at IPR 547) said:

> Each of the categories mentioned in the paragraph must be given its full meaning. However, the appearance of each category (including 'patents') within the context of other kinds of rights sharing in common temporary, monopolistic or oligopolistic characteristics, reinforces the amplitude of the grant. It is not unlimited. But neither is it narrow. And the collection of rights mentioned in the grant strengthens the pre-supposition that the Federal Parliament in Australia is to enjoy a most ample lawmaking power in respect of 'products of intellectual effort' as that notion may itself expand, in part as a by-product to the very inventiveness which it empowers the Parliament to protect.

Intellectual property law is marked by a dynamic relationship between recognised principles and policies, social and commercial trends, and changing technologies. While seeking to apply the law to new realities, existing principles themselves come under close scrutiny, adjust and mutate. Since the WIPO definition was formulated, intellectual property law has had to adapt to such major social and technological changes as the development of computers and digital data storage, the emergence of the internet, mobile telephony, computer games and the commercial application of biotechnology and genetic engineering. This process of adaptation is complex, since the law of intellectual property does not simply reflect but also moulds technical, commercial and social reality.

Physical and intellectual property

1.2 The separation of physical and intellectual ownership lies at the heart of the notion of intellectual property. The words 'intellectual property law' conceal a great variety of subject matter, but common to all is the notion that something has a value beyond its immediate worth as a physical article. It has an 'intangible' as well as a tangible aspect, which can be conceptually separated. Thus, the sheet of paper on which the score for the Beatles song 'Let it Be' was first written has little value as physical property (although it may now have some value as a historical document), yet the song expressed on it has great value as intellectual property; and an empty plastic bottle with a 'Coca-Cola' trade mark is worth very little, yet the trade mark on it is of inestimable commercial value. Furthermore, if I simply sell the sheet of paper or the bottle, I do not part with any intellectual property interest in either. The dealing in the 'intellectual property' is thus legally separate from the dealing in the 'physical property'. Authority to deal with physical property in a certain way (eg, to sell a canvas as owner) does not coincide with or imply authority to deal with the intellectual property (eg, the right to copy the painting on the canvas).

What gives the trade mark and the song value as legal objects is that a person or corporation has a legally sanctioned right to control, use or exploit it in certain commercially significant ways to the exclusion of all others within the jurisdiction. The rules of intellectual property law safeguard that exclusivity, either by statute or through the application of principles of equity (as is the case with confidential information) or of the common law (as is the case for passing off). The word 'property' is routinely used as a shorthand designation for the bundle of exclusive rights that intellectual property law vests in relation to certain subject matter. Nonetheless, the use of the term 'property' in this context is somewhat distorted: the rights are generally carefully limited and circumscribed in legislation or precedent, both in substance and in term; intellectual property is a purely legal construct, without an element of physical 'possession'; and intellectual property does not deplete nor deteriorate with use as does physical property.[1] There is thus no element of deprivation associated with the unauthorised exploitation of somebody else's intellectual property; for example, if somebody illegally downloads a song for which I own copyright, this does not reduce my ability to enjoy the song. Nonetheless, the criminal law has made inroads into intellectual property, with gradually more severe penalties being imposed on certain deliberate misappropriations. Some statutes expressly constitute the rights vested in their subject matter as personal property; for example, s 196(1) of the Copyright Act 1968 (Cth) ('Copyright is personal property and, subject to this section, is transmissible by assignment, by will and by devolution by operation of law.'). Other subject matter, such as trade secrets, is commonly referred to or dealt with as 'property', 'owned' and 'assigned', but is, in truth, based on equitable remedies rather than legal property rights. In fact, no property rights in information, intangibles or intellectual creations exist outside statute in Australia.

The Personal Properties Securities Act 2009 (Cth) (PSSA) creates and facilitates security interests in personal property through a system of registration. Section 10 of the PPSA defines 'intellectual property' as personal property by reference to common property rights being: design rights, patents, trade marks, plant breeder's rights, circuit layout rights and copyright: A Duggan and D Brown, *Australian Personal Property Securities Law*, LexisNexis, Sydney, 2013, 33 [2.34].

Creation and reputation

1.3 Two crucial processes result in intellectual property value: one is the creative operation of the mind, the external record or embodiment of which bears the resulting stamp of originality or novelty. The value derives from the fact that the creation differs from what has existed before, and from the fact that it has some sort of practical use or appeal to the senses. However, creative processes do not occur in a vacuum. As we shall see, creation always involves an element of imitation or reuse of existing ideas and forms of expression, requiring a fine balance to be struck by the law between rewarding creativity and permitting imitation and re-use.

---

1. Concerning the sometimes difficult notion of 'property' in intellectual property law, see P Drahos, *A Philosophy of Intellectual Property*, Dartmouth, Brookfield, 1996; see also Bently and Sherman, above.

The second process is that by which reputation or 'goodwill' becomes established. This is a predominantly commercial or industrial rather than a creative process, although it has elements of both. Thus, the reputation of the Coca-Cola trade mark is established and then maintained because the law enforces the exclusive user right of the person who through promotion, advertising and commercial dealing develops the reputation of the mark among consumers. The exclusivity of the legal right to use the mark in commerce gives it its value, because others cannot profit from consumers' recognition of or familiarity with it. However, not all marks are equal. Some are more striking, memorable and effective in distinguishing one person's goods or services from those of another, so devising a successful trade mark will also require skill and creativity.

Copyright law, the law of designs, patents law and the law of trade secrets are concerned largely, although not exclusively, with the creative process; that is, that process whereby the human mind blends existing information, themes and ideas with an element of autonomous creation, individuality or originality to arrive at some new form of expression or creation.

Those regimes grant a bundle of exclusive rights in various original emanations of the mind — for instance, in musical scores, paintings or multimedia works through copyright law, or in inventions through patent law. Trade marks law and the law of passing off (as well as s 18 of the Australian Consumer Law: see Competition and Consumer Act 2010 (Cth), Sch 2), on the other hand, are concerned with protecting goodwill or reputation that inheres in some distinctive aspect of the name, get-up or appearance of a product or service; for instance, a word mark (such as MERCEDES), a device (such as the Nike Swoosh) or a distinctive shape (eg, of a Coke bottle: see *Coca-Cola Co v All-Fect Distributors Ltd (t/a Millers Distributing Co)* (1998) 43 IPR 47 and (1999) 96 FCR 107; 47 IPR 481 (on appeal)). The word 'incentive' is often associated with intellectual property, but bestowal of legal rights does not, in itself, constitute a reward or incentive (quite the contrary in some areas, since an upfront registration cost will apply; eg, for the processing of a patent or trade mark application). All the law does is enable a rights holder to reduce the risk of others free-riding on their intellectual creations or goodwill by arming the rights holder with specific legal remedies.[2]

Inspiration and perspiration

1.4 Intellectual property is often associated with creativity and artistic originality. It conjures up the image of the brilliant inventor in the backyard shed or the artistic genius slaving away in a garret whose works or ideas are justifiably and fairly protected by the law from exploitation, appropriation or imitation by others. But, in fact, intellectual property law grants exclusive rights in a whole spectrum of subject matter — from 'high art' to the very mundane, and from historic inventions to trivial contraptions. For instance, in *Lincoln Industries Ltd v Wham-O Manufacturing Co* [1984] 1 NZLR 641; (1984) 3 IPR 115 at 131, the New Zealand Court of Appeal held that the wooden

---

2. Although not all intellectual property rights are concerned with protection of commercial interests: see, for instance, the moral rights regime in Chapter 5 Copyright: Other Rights and Exceptions.

model for a frisbee amounted to a sculpture protected by the New Zealand Copyright Act, a decision subsequently approved in Australia: see *Greenfield Products Pty Ltd v Rover-Scott Bonnar Ltd* (1990) 17 IPR 417 at 427 per Pincus J. James Watt's steam engine was a significant invention granted a famous patent, but patents have also been granted in relation to less momentous things, such as a prize-awarding system used in electronic gaming machines (see *Neurizon Pty Ltd v Jupiters Ltd* (2005) 67 IPR 33).

Although usually at least a minimal level of novelty or originality is required, proof of inspiration, genius, creative content or artistic merit plays only a minimal role in setting threshold conditions for the granting of exclusive rights. In a general sense, it may be said that where the rights granted are the broadest, the standard set for the granting of exclusive rights is the highest. Thus, to qualify for the granting of a patent, which confers a monopolistic exploitation right with few derogations, an invention must be novel and disclose an inventive step; that is, one not obvious to the average person who knows the relevant technical field. But to attract copyright protection — not a monopoly but only an anti-copying right — little more is required than showing that it has not been copied from some existing source work (see the requirement of 'originality' in Chapter 2 Copyright) and involves some mental activity of the author. In a sense, then, intellectual property law reflects the kernel of truth in what Thomas Alva Edison (the great inventor) is reputed to have said in a newspaper interview: 'Genius is 1 per cent inspiration and 99 per cent perspiration.' Intellectual property law straddles the policy goals of protecting the individual results of effort, skill and investment from unfair competition, and of empowering creators to make a return from the commercial exploitation of their intangible creations.

Intellectual property, imitation and culture

1.5 In any case, some notion of untrammelled creativity would be an unhelpful starting point for the consideration of intellectual property law. Virtually all new knowledge or artistic creation relies in some way or another on what has gone before, and arises in a particular cultural and social context. Anything creative is, in other words, to some degree also derivative and constrained. The human mind is not an empty vat but contains pre-existing knowledge, learning, information, skill and so on that is in part generic, rather than specific or exclusive to any one person. Forms of expression themselves tend to be generic and thus circumscribed by past practices (a good example is traditional indigenous art, which, although strictly circumscribed with regard to technique and theme, allows room for individual skill and originality). But in spite of the difficulty of drawing a clear distinction, be it practically or philosophically, between imitation and creation — and thus between the social and historical on the one hand, and the individual and novel on the other hand — the notion of inspired individual creativity continues to be central to intellectual property law's principles. Thus, rights are mostly vested in, or derived from, an identified creator and not a social group. Intellectual property struggles to deal with more social and historical notions of creativity and creation. For instance, in copyright law, earlier efforts to vest rights of action in indigenous communities as distinct from individual artists have been shelved (see the Copyright Amendment (Indigenous Communal Moral Rights) Bill 2003). In the area of patents law, the notion of reward for individual inventiveness arguably conflicts with the more modern need for protection of huge investments in the systematic and collaborative, rather than personal and idiosyncratic, search for new knowledge. For an example of courts struggling with these issues at a practical level, see *Genentech v The Wellcome Foundation Ltd* (1988) 15 IPR 423.

This leads us to the important insight that the whole concept of intellectual property as it has become known is, in fact, culturally determined. It is firmly anchored in a liberal, individualistic and free market social system and historical tradition. It is based on private rights and determination of value through the operation of more or less free markets. The effect of intellectual property rights is to turn knowledge and art into a commodity that can be traded. But this is not the only way knowledge and culture are dispersed, nor the way they are dealt with by all cultures. The whole notion of intellectual property also fits in with a technically innovative society interested in knowledge accumulation, rather than one predominantly concerned with tradition or adherence to spirituality, immutable norms or established patterns of exchange. In global terms, only a limited number of nations or communities have historically elevated levels of new knowledge generation and accumulation. Nonetheless, the global integration of markets and the acute decline of socialist models of ownership and trade have resulted in the extension of these culturally specific notions regarding intellectual property to virtually every society on the globe — the World Trade Organization (WTO) Trade-Related Aspects of Intellectual Property Rights (TRIPS) Agreement is the clearest manifestation of this trend. This has inevitably led to cultural clashes and international disputes opposing the dominant exporters of knowledge goods to more dependent nations in the developing world. However, recent times have seen a greater openness to balancing intellectual property rights with a 'development agenda' in multilateral international institutions such as the WIPO and the WTO/TRIPS.[3]

But the shape and extent of intellectual property protection have always been contested, even within industrialised countries. This may result from cultural divergence within national borders; for instance, in Australia, the interest of some indigenous people in seeing their traditional cultural expressions and knowledge governed by distinct rules and beliefs has found expression both at the political level and at the legal level. Courts have attempted to accommodate Aboriginal concerns, notably related to ownership, inevitably constrained as it is by the existing structures of copyright. In *Bulun Bulun v R & T Textiles Pty Ltd* (1998) 86 FCR 244; 41 IPR 513, von Doussa J called equity in aid to find that a fiduciary relationship existed between an artist and his clan, requiring the artist to restrain and remedy a copyright infringement that threatened traditional culture. In *Milpurrurru v Indofurn Pty Ltd* (1994) 54 FCR 240; 30 IPR 209, attenuation of the cultural values associated with Aboriginal artwork was remedied by an award of additional damages in copyright. At the political level, a previous government considered introducing legislation to protect the interests of communities in the art produced by their members: the Indigenous Communal Moral Rights Bill 2003 (see also above). Recently, the government also introduced a resale royalties scheme for artistic works, particularly intended to benefit indigenous artists: see the Resale Royalty

3. Development Agenda for WIPO: see http://www.wipo.int/ip-development/en/agenda/.

Right for Visual Artists Act 2009 (Cth). A most contested area of intellectual property has been copyright on the internet, with amendments to legislation to protect owners' rights attracting widespread interest.[4]

Creation, imitation and competition

1.6 The relationship between imitation and inspiration is a practical as well as a theoretical issue. Courts applying the rules of intellectual property law attempt to strike a balance between permissible imitation, a driver of competition, and unfair or misleading practices that distort the normal operation of markets: see *Campomar Sociedad, Limitada v Nike International* (2000) 202 CLR 45. At the same time, the law must strike a balance between diffusion of new ideas and information through processes of copying, improvement and further development and providing adequate safeguards against free-riding for those who invest talent and resources in the production of new intellectual creations.

For instance, in copyright law, a distinction is commonly drawn between the idea behind a work and the particular way it is expressed — although this distinction is often criticised for its vagueness (eg, see the famous statement by Judge Learned Hand in *Nichols v Universal Pictures Corp* (1930) 45 F 2d 119 at 121: 'Nobody has ever been able to fix that boundary, and nobody ever can.'). An idea may be copied or extracted from a copyright work but not the particular form of expression or presentation of that idea. The idea–expression dichotomy is a judicial device developed to patrol the boundaries of permissible copying.

An example from the sphere of commerce is the protection of reputation through the action of passing off. The line between acceptable imitation by competitors and unfair competition is drawn by reference to the concept of 'misrepresentation', the extent to which the commercial conduct misleads consumers. For instance, in the *Doc Martens* case (*Dr Martens Australia Pty Ltd v Bata Shoe Co of Australia Pty Ltd* (1997) 75 FCR 230; 38 IPR 163), the court found that closely imitating the appearance of the 'original' English Doc Martens shoes (heavy boots with striking coloured stitching and a z-welt and so on) was permissible. In coming to that decision, Goldberg J cited much authority, and stated (inter alia) that Lord Jauncey addressed the issue of copying get-up in the following terms in *Reckitt & Colman Products Ltd v Borden Inc* [1990] RPC 341 at 418:

> However, although the common law will protect goodwill against misrepresentation by recognising a monopoly in a particular get-up, it will not recognise a monopoly in the article itself. Thus A can compete with B by copying his goods provided that he does not do so in such a way as to suggest that his goods are those of B. Lawful competition will not be restricted by the common law.

Again, manipulation of legal categories and concepts ('misrepresentation', 'get-up', 'monopoly in the article') is employed to arrive at an acceptable balance between

4. Australian Law Reform Commission, *Copyright and the Digital Economy*, Report 122, 2014; the Copyright Amendment (Online Infringement) Act 2015 (Cth) and Review of the Copyright Online Infringement Amendment (https://www.communications.gov.au/have-your-say/review-copyright-online-infringement-amendment).

beneficial competition, including imitation, and deceptive and unfair practices: see, for example, *Bodum v DKSH Australia Pty Ltd* [2011] FCAFC 98; and *Sydneywide Distributors Pty Ltd v Red Bull Australia Pty Ltd* [2002] FCAFC 157.

Information and transformation

1.7 A strong theme underlying all areas of intellectual property law is the informative or communicative function of the subject matter of exclusive rights. For instance, trade marks immediately alert consumers to the origin and qualities of the goods or services they are using (the so-called search cost reduction function of trade marks). Copyright encourages the widest possible distribution of literary, dramatic, musical and artistic works by linking levels of remuneration to scope of distribution. Patents law makes the granting of a monopoly dependent upon publication of information about the invention; the only alternative for the inventor is to keep the invention secret, which does not serve the public interest in information sharing. Such sharing enables others to ascertain how an invention works and to build on that knowledge.

In the current information age, more than ever before, intellectual property law transforms amorphous information into an identifiable, itemised and tradable commodity. Intellectual property law may be said to enhance the efficiency of the exchange of information by creating a market for it that would not function efficiently in the absence of secure property rights. Nonetheless, paradoxically, intellectual property law achieves this aim at the cost of granting — at least in theory — greater control over information to private interests. This contradiction is well illustrated by a case involving the granting of patents in methods of medical treatment. Some judges held that the granting of a patent would constitute a restriction on the traditional free exchange of information between doctors concerning the best therapies to alleviate human suffering and would be against the public interest. But others stressed that in the area of human treatment, as in any other, the granting of a patent would have the ultimately beneficial effect of encouraging greater investment in research and innovation: see *Anaesthetic Supplies Pty Ltd v Rescare Ltd* (1994) 50 FCR 1; 28 IPR 383, particularly per Sheppard J (at 421–22) and Lockhart J (at 397ff).

Market value and inherent value

1.8 Much subject matter protected by intellectual property law has inherent value that is not quantifiable (ie, able to be expressed in terms of *monetary* value). Neither quantitative nor qualitative value is a pre-condition of protection, but both are important. The traditional English view of intellectual property law emphasises its economic purpose rather than the inherent value of intellectual creations (to cultural development or personal fulfilment); it is thus an instrumental view of the law. In contrast, the continental European tradition displays a greater regard for the inherent value of intellectual property.

A good illustration of this difference lies in the area of copyright law. Traditional civilian intellectual property law grants authors certain non-commercial inalienable rights, known as moral rights, such as the right to integrity and the right to attribution. This is a notion only recently introduced into Australian intellectual property law. Moral rights are based on a different justification for the granting of exclusive rights; that is, that works protected by copyright law (and arguably some other areas of intellectual property law) are expressions of the personality of the author and thus inherently deserving of legal protection. The common law tends to accentuate that intellectual property rights serve to ensure that creators can turn their efforts to account, and discounts the view that they serve some higher purpose. They are instruments serving a particular economic goal, rather than a vindication of meritorious creation or personal connection with a work.

Theories of Intellectual Property

History and theory

1.9 Theoretical justifications for the granting of intellectual property rights can inform our understanding of the law. But any theoretical analysis is tempered by the knowledge that most of the intellectual property regimes, whether statutory or case based, have distant historical roots that continue to mark their broad characteristics (there are exceptions, of course, such as the computer chip legislation: the Circuit Layouts Act 1989 (Cth)). That fact encourages us to treat any theoretical construct imposed on the law with some circumspection. The introduction of statutory intellectual property regimes by parliaments past hardly came about on the basis of exhaustive policy research or economic and social modelling. Rather, it resulted partly from historical accident (temporary political imperatives) and partly from crude or tangential policy formulation. For instance, parliament in the United Kingdom passed the Statute of Monopolies 1623 (UK), the precursor of our patent system, to abolish the detrimental monopolies that had proliferated in England. The parliament excepted inventions with a view to attracting skilled foreign craftsmen and to set up factories to provide local employment and training in new techniques. At that time, England's economy lagged behind the European continent in technology. This monopoly grant in inventions was a small exception in a broader political move to abolish the Crown practice of granting, for financial reward, trading monopolies in virtually every available commodity.

Perhaps the main impact of various theoretical, economic, sociological and political theories results from their use and manipulation by various interest groups in the context of law reform. An interesting example of this is provided by the report into the reform of design law that preceded the replacement of the Designs Act 1906 (Cth) with the current Designs Act 2003 (Cth): Australian Law Reform Commission (ALRC) Report 74, *Designs*. One of the main points of difference between various groups interested in design law reform was design registration for spare parts. Each side of the debate justified its position on the basis of complex and contradictory economic arguments. As a result, the ALRC proposed a tortuous compromise system for the review on anti-competition grounds of applications for design registration for spare parts: see Chapter 6 Registered Designs. The government rejected these recommendations and instead introduced a repair exception, as also exists in other jurisdictions: see Designs Act 2003, s 72. On other occasions, complex theoretical issues have been resolved by expeditious political compromise; for instance, the amendments to journalists' copyright relating to electronic distribution of copyright works came about through an agreement between the government and the journalists union: see Copyright Amendment Act 1998 (Cth) and the resulting s 35(4) of the Copyright Act 1968 (Cth). Furthermore, the policy space within which the Commonwealth Parliament can operate in matters of intellectual property is now severely restricted by the international obligations flowing from various multilateral and bilateral treaties. In recent times, intellectual property has been only one part of wider trade liberalisation agreements, which has tended to result in compromise, skewed policy direction and introduction of foreign transplants of sometimes uneasy fit.

Exclusive rights as incentives for creation

1.10 At the most basic level, intellectual property rights (at least when it comes to copyright and patents protection) are said to provide an incentive for the production of intellectual goods that are of cultural or practical value to society. The products of the arts and of science and technology arguably enrich society. The pursuit of knowledge and artistic expression enhances quality of life, as well as opportunities for self-expression, and should therefore be encouraged. Alternatively, the production of new intellectual goods is an integral part of Western cultural belief in progress and in our ability to improve the human condition. With either view, intellectual property serves an essentially non-economic purpose. In this context, the bestowal of property rights is symbolic of the importance that society attaches to the accumulation of practical knowledge and of cultural goods. However, at the outset of the 21st century, in an age of economic rationalism, more economic rationales have a wider appeal. From a modern economic perspective, intangible goods are integral to the economy and are simply another commodity. Indeed, much economically inspired political rhetoric promotes the view that intellectual goods are the vital motor of a successful economy in the post-Industrial Age (the 'knowledge economy', the 'information age', etc). In this view, 'successful' economies are those with a high rate of production of intellectual goods (in particular, technology) and innovation. The arts also become pursuits valued not necessarily for their own sake but for their contribution to economic activity. High rates of production of cultural and intellectual goods are then an important policy goal from the perspective of economic growth. Artistic expression is important for the 'copyright industries' or the 'cultural sector' of the economy. The creative and research and development (R&D) industries benefit from tax concessions.

Property rights as a response to market failure

1.11 A handy theoretical justification for the granting of property rights in intangible goods lies in the concept of market failure. Because intellectual goods are social goods and non-excludable, there will be a sub-optimal level of production unless those who invest in the production of such goods are granted exclusive rights against imitators. Why produce intellectual goods if others can simply reproduce and sell them at a lower marginal cost because they avoid the sunk costs of creation (the so-called free-rider problem)? Property rights preserve creators' competitive position by allowing them to drive up the marginal cost of imitation. The key is then to calibrate property rights in such a manner that they provide adequate protection against free-riding but do not result in overly broad monopolies that restrict derivation too much.[5] There are many difficulties with this theoretical justification. First, it is not empirically proven and may not lend itself ever to be. In other words, there are few forensic or historical data that support the thesis of sub-optimal knowledge production levels without intellectual property rights.

Second, it begs the question as to what are optimal levels of knowledge production, a question whose answer is arguably socially and culturally, rather than economically, determined.

Third, there are quite obviously a number of alternative mechanisms that could and do function to provide incentives for the production of intellectual goods; for instance, academic peer recognition and popular acclaim, prizes, salary bonuses and others. These incentives operate not only at the personal level but also at the level of the firm engaged in economic activity. A firm may wish to invest in innovation even in the absence of intellectual property rights, because it can then portray itself as a technological market leader, because there is a valuable time lag that protects it from imitators or because an innovative firm attracts the most capable employees. Further, innovators can use various strategies to prevent or reduce imitation or increase 'imitation lag', such as 'first-mover advantage', network control, market size, secrecy, etc.

In light of the inconclusive evidence, it may be that the effect of intellectual property rights is less to increase the production of intellectual goods but more to shift it; that is, to move it into areas in which the most advantage can be derived from intellectual property laws. As an illustration, the availability of proprietary rights in medical drugs through the patents system is said to result in the 'orphan drug' problem; that is, the diversion of investment away from the treatment of uncommon, though traumatic, diseases because of the limited size of the 'market'. Another difficulty with the thesis that property rights correct market failure is that it contradicts the traditional argument that requires property rights (in terms of physical property) to ensure optimal allocation of scarce resources. *Intellectual* property is not a scarce but an inexhaustible resource (ideas will never run out and copying does not deplete knowledge), and thus property rights are arguably *not* here required to optimise the allocation of a scarce resource.

Monopoly theory

1.12 Policy issues in intellectual property law are often addressed in terms of monopolies and, in particular, in terms of monopoly rights in information. Two questions arise:

- First, *are* intellectual property rights monopoly rights?
- Second, if a monopoly is detrimental to the public interest, in that it restricts competition and distorts price formation and the competitive functioning of a market, how can monopoly rights in intellectual goods be justified?

5. See, for instance, Posner's analysis of the economics of imitation in copyright law: W Landes and R Posner, 'An Economic Analysis of Copyright Law' (1989) 18 *J Leg Stud* 325.

To assert that intellectual property law grants monopolies in information is questionable. In one sense, if intellectual property is truly analogous to other forms of property, one might as well refer to real property rights as 'monopolies' in land and improvements. Why see intellectual property rights as a monopoly problem at all? Furthermore, although some regimes provide broad exploitation rights with monopolistic characteristics (such as patents), others bestow only anti-copying rights (such as copyright). In those areas that are not concerned with the protection of reputation, the rights are limited in time, and in all cases they are restricted in nature and subject to exceptions and derogations. But even accepting, for argument's sake, that the bestowal of an intellectual property right (eg, a patent) constitutes a monopoly grant, a detrimental restraint on competition does not necessarily follow. It may constitute a benign monopoly. For instance, a competitor may not exploit a patented invention but is free to use any substantially different way to obtain the same result (inventing around); and different substitute products may be marketed that have the same or similar effect. The essential issue is the definition of the relevant market; for instance, if the invention is a new HIV/AIDS treatment drug, and the relevant market is the market for that drug, then the owner of the patent has monopoly power in that market; if the relevant market is that for HIV/AIDS treatment drugs in general, then, depending on the alternatives available, the owner of the patent may not be a monopolist. Any person may apply for a patent on a different drug for the treatment of HIV/AIDS, and any person may engage in research and development for an alternative HIV/AIDS drug, as long as the patent is not infringed in the process or in the result.

Another approach to the question holds that the granting of a monopoly is the whole aim of the patent legislation, since only such a grant will allow the monopolist to ensure an adequate return on investment in research and development. It is therefore a benign monopoly or, in other words, it represents a necessary and appropriate impost, as it, in fact, corrects a deficiency in the market (as explained above), rather than generating a distorted market. It is a monopoly grant that enhances competition rather than reduces it by encouraging new products and processes to enter the market. The only alternative response would be some more direct intervention by the government in the production of knowledge. While there is little doubt that the state plays an important corrective role in the market, few would assert that it can direct the production of information and ideas with universal efficiency and regard for consumer preference.

Use and abuse of intellectual property rights

1.13 All this is not to say that private ownership, control and monopoly power over intellectual property cannot have deleterious effects on competition. This can be the case, not only where there is a clear legal abuse of such rights but even where the rights are exercised in the manner contemplated by law. In fact, there is a growing understanding of the need to apply the full force of anti-trust or trade practices rules and principles to intellectual property: see, for instance, Intellectual Property and Competition Law Review Committee, *Review of Intellectual Property Legislation Under the Competition Principles Agreement, Final Report*, September 2000; and the recommendations to repeal s 51(3) of the Competition and Consumer Act 2010 (Cth) (CCA) by the Competition Policy Review (March 2015) and the Productivity

Commission (PC) report of 2016 on intellectual property (PC Report).[6] Section 51(3) of the CCA previously exempted certain agreements relating to intellectual property, but the repeal of that section (by the Treasury Laws Amendment (2018 Measures No 5) Act 2019 (Cth), Sch 4) means that no conduct involving intellectual property rights is to be exempt from any provisions in Pt IV of the CCA from the commencement date of 13 September 2019.

Legitimate enforcement of intellectual property rights may have deleterious effects not on the market for the protected goods themselves but on subsidiary or related markets. A prime example (now addressed in the amendments introduced by the Copyright Amendments (Digital Agenda) Act 2000 (Cth)) is afforded by the issue of reverse engineering or decompilation of computer programs protected by copyright. Reverse engineering (simply put, in this context, working backwards from a computer program in object, machine-readable code to a computer program in source, human-readable code) necessarily entails a reproduction of a substantial part of the computer program, and thus amounts to an infringement of the copyright in the program. This means that reverse engineering software normally requires the licence of the copyright owner. Competitors wishing to ascertain the ideas, general structure and form of a program, which themselves are not copyrighted, may be restrained from obtaining that information and therefore from developing a rival program with the same functionality but expressed in different code. They may also be unable to legitimately ascertain details of the copyrighted program for the purpose of interoperability. The owner of copyright in a ubiquitous operating system may therefore be able to control the downstream market for applications software as well. A related example is how ownership of intellectual property rights in digital vehicle diagnostic systems may permit corporations to control the market for vehicle repairs for certain car brands.

At the level of global competition, anti-trust concerns are centred upon the accumulation of intellectual property by transnational mega corporations, which also have considerable power to influence or 'capture' policymakers to permit expansion of private property rights in intellectual property to the detriment of the 'public domain'. One concern is that ownership of intellectual property does not necessarily equate to exploitation of intellectual property, and that corporations may accumulate intellectual property rights for the strategic purpose of suppressing rival technologies. Economists also worry about patent thickets, patent 'trolls' and 'evergreening' of medical patents. Further concerns are expressed about developing nations largely dependent on agriculture where transnational corporations obtain ownership both of plant varieties (often through the new mechanisms of biotechnology, such as gene cloning and DNA technology) vital to the country's rural populations and of patents in agrochemicals and fertilisers required to be used in conjunction with those plant varieties, resulting in total dependence on foreign corporate interests. Similar concerns about the cost of access to vital technologies also exist in the medical field, where the expansion of patent protection for pharmaceuticals across the globe has the potential effect of driving up the cost of crucial healthcare in developing and least developed countries

6. Productivity Commission, *Intellectual Property Arrangements*, Inquiry Report No 78, Canberra, September 2016.

(LDCs) (although in reality LDCs are not obliged to implement patent protection for pharmaceuticals before 2033). On 23 January 2017 an amendments to TRIPS came into force enabling the export of generic equivalents of patented drugs to countries without drug manufacturing capacity. The Australian legislation amending the Patents Act 1990 (Cth) to enable export of drugs in such cases is the Intellectual Property Laws Amendment Act 2015 (Cth), which came into effect on 25 August 2015.

Commodification and the public domain

1.14 The possible deleterious effect of accumulation of private power over knowledge assets leads us to the issue of commodification of knowledge and information. The essential characteristic of the information age is that knowledge and information are treated as tradable commodities whose efficient production and exchange are a vital aspect of market dynamics. Quite clearly, intellectual property law is the vehicle by which the commodification of information operates. Equally clearly, as the value of information increases, there is considerable pressure from the production side of the information economy (those corporations that are knowledge, information or technology producers) to expand the pool of knowledge and information available for appropriation. To this end, those interests will attempt to 'capture' the process of policymaking and law reform to obtain the expansion of private rights. This is commonly said to be detrimental to the 'public domain' which is constituted by the knowledge and information freely circulating and available for everybody's use. For instance, there has been a steady increase both in subject matter and in rights granted under the Copyright Act 1968 over the past 50 years. Arguably, some of this growth may simply reflect the arrival of new exploitation technologies (such as CDs, DVDs, the internet, etc) and is thus not a true crimping of the public domain, but other aspects (extension of the term of protection to 70 years after the death of the author, for instance) directly affect public availability of intellectual goods. In other areas too the expansion of the rights owners' domain is incontrovertible; for instance, in trade marks law, where the categories of 'signs' that may be registered have been extended now to include colours as such and product shapes, or in the growth of the 'extended action in passing off', or where patents are now available for genetically modified organisms and other living things.

Various and diverse factors play a role in accelerating commodification. One important underlying influence is the changing nature of society. As industrialised nations move into the post-industrial, service-based age, information simply becomes more valuable. In such a context, firms will seek greater rights in intellectual goods to protect their increased interests in and dependence on them. Information enhances productivity when increases of input in materials and working hours become impossible due to their inherent scarcity. Knowledge and information are arguably resources whose potential expansion is limitless, as is illustrated by the current interest in the potential effect of artificial intelligence (AI) and 'big data' on intellectual property.

Not only have the number and extent of rights steadily increased but so have the potential adverse consequences faced by alleged infringers. There has been an increasing tendency to criminalise infringement of intellectual property law. It is questionable whether this trend, and the impost on the public purse that it implies, is desirable in the context of purely private rights and given the availability of monetary and other remedies, some of which are arguably punitive in nature anyway; for example, additional damages in copyright under s 115(4) of the Copyright Act 1968, as illustrated by the decision in *Milpurrurru v Indofurn Pty Ltd* (1994) 54 FCR 240; 30 IPR 209. Nevertheless, the Australia–United States Free Trade Agreement 2004 (AUSFTA) again resulted in further increases in penalties for infringement of intellectual property laws: see Chapter 19 Remedies in Intellectual Property Law. This is irrespective of the fact that the theft of intellectual property is not the same as that of personal property. Illegal copying does not deprive an intellectual property owner of any property, nor is the damage and social impact caused by intellectual property offences of the same order as offences against physical property. Nonetheless, infringement of intellectual property rights does need to be effectively deterred, and this may in some cases be difficult to achieve without the intervention of the state at some level. Furthermore, societal damage can be associated with intellectual or domain name property infringement; for instance, where counterfeit pharmaceuticals are sold under infringing trade marks or by way of fake domain names, or where large-scale piracy is undertaken by crime syndicates also engaged in other illegal activities.

Intellectual property has paradoxically also been the subject of both international regulatory competition and international coordination between industrialised nations (on the whole, 'net information producers' rather than consumers). If one country or bloc increases its levels of protection for intellectual property, others must or will follow, either through inherently dominating international treaty systems, such as the WTO, through bare competitive necessity or through bilateral pressures (historically exerted by the USA and to some extent also the European Union). This grand game bypasses much of the developing world because, far from moving into an information age, many societies remain largely dependent on subsistence farming and have barely entered the first stages of industrialisation. In fact, much of the international debate concerning intellectual property revolves around the diverging interests of net information-producing (developed or post-industrial) nations and information-consuming societies (less developed nations). Some champions for poorer nations argue that high standards of protection (and consequent high cost) of intellectual property are detrimental to the global economic development that free trade is meant to promote. They will not allow countries to escape penury but consign them to an information poverty trap because they drive up the cost of imitation and education.

Warnings about the expansion of intellectual property rights have emanated not only from poorer nations but also from within post-industrial societies like Australia and New Zealand; opposition is motivated by social, economic and philosophical concerns. Economists point to the dangers inherent in over-regulation and in excessively broad rights with increased transaction and acquisition costs and greater regulatory burdens. Progress in most areas of the arts and knowledge-based industries is at least partially based on the use of pre-existing materials and is substantially a process of imitation and modification. Thus, the greater the amount of pre-existing material that is subject to private rights and the higher the level of those rights, the greater the cost of creation.

The increased protection of intellectual property obtained by knowledge producers through lobbying or the capture of legislative, administrative or judicial processes may paradoxically reap undesirable consequences in the form of higher costs of the necessary inputs the same producers must use.

From a social perspective, there is the danger that more pervasive and all-encompassing intellectual property rights will accelerate the emergence of a social underclass of information-poor. Information as property is unavoidably exclusionary of those who cannot pay even to gain access, let alone to use, intellectual goods (which are now, in theory at least, mostly free to access, if not always to use). From a philosophical perspective, the extension of economic rights over intellectual goods arguably comes at the expense of more important values of community, social cohesion and personal autonomy. The proprietisation of information cannot be justified on moral or ethical grounds where it may permit private rights over essential building blocks of nature, culture or humankind itself. Private property rights may clash with the communal sharing of knowledge, information and art of less exclusionary (eg, tribal) cultures.

These various arguments may amount to no more than a detailed restatement of a common theme: growth of rights in information depletes the intellectual commons (the public domain), that wealth of information that *is* society, that *is* culture and that *is* free for everyone to learn and pass on.[7] An important illustration of this trend is provided by the recent tendency in universities (traditionally, vital contributors to the intellectual commons both in Australia and in other industrialised nations) to treat academic knowledge as their property. As a result, information and knowledge are arguably not produced freely for the common good or in the public interest but are subject to universities' exclusive rights and driven by a need to generate commercial returns: see A Monnotti, 'Ownership of Copyright in Traditional Literary Works within Universities' (1994) 22(2) *FLR* 1. This has been an area of considerable controversy with some high-profile litigation.[8]

Law Reform

1.15 Law is a permanent dialectic between the past and the future, and intellectual property law is no exception. The one constant in this area of the law is its inconstancy. Both rules and rationales are subjected to unrelenting review, whether as a consequence of the imperatives imposed by major multilateral treaty systems (such as the WIPO treaties and TRIPS) or other agreements (such as AUSFTA) or because of internal demands (such as those from indigenous communities for copyright reform, or copyright industries for reform of internet-related rights (see *Copyright and the Digital Economy*, ALRC Report 122, 2014).

As a discipline arguably concerned with monopolies, even if benign, it is perhaps not surprising that intellectual property law is regularly required to justify its existence

7. See, in this regard, P Drahos, *A Philosophy of Intellectual Property*, Dartmouth, Brookfield, 1996; see also P Drahos and J Braithwaite, *Information Feudalism: Who Controls the Knowledge Economy?*, Earthscan Publications, 2002.
8. See *University of Western Australia v Gray (No 20)* (2008) 76 IPR 222.

and universality. One example is the debate concerning the application of intellectual property law in the internet environment. At one stage it was advocated that the web become a giant public domain. With commercialisation of the cybersphere, this has not come to pass, even though the open source movement enjoys a considerable following.[9] As another example, the very existence of the registered designs regime is also questioned from the perspective of its relationship with copyright. Why not simply have unregistered designs as a category of subject matter protected by copyright? Less radically, extension of intellectual property rights to new areas is often very contested, and calls for the imposition of limitations, exceptions and derogations abound (see, eg, in relation to patents law, resulting in amendments introducing an 'experimental use exception';[10] in copyright, resulting in the introduction of 'format shifting' and 'time shifting' exceptions in relation to sound files (see Copyright Amendment Act 2006 (Cth); and the adoption of a new fair dealing defence for parody and satire: see further Chapter 5 Copyright: Other Rights and Exceptions).

Indeed, the complete abolition of intellectual property law as it exists has been suggested, to be replaced with a single action for unjust enrichment (see B Fitzgerald and L Gamertsfelder, 'A Conceptual Framework for Protecting Value of Informational Products Through Unjust Enrichment Law' (1998) *EIPR* 244) or an unfair competition tort. Such a solution is said to have the admirable qualities of consistency and simplicity, which existing intellectual property regimes lack. Arguably such simplicity would come at the cost of predictability. Nonetheless, apparent complexity is a constant motivation for reform aimed at streamlining regimes that have grown by piecemeal accretion – for example, the Patents Act 1990, which was intended to simplify patents law with clearer language and fewer sections; the Designs Act 2003; and the historical attempts to rewrite the Copyright Act 1968: see Copyright Law Review Committee (CLRC), *Simplification of the Copyright Act: Part 1* (1998) and *Simplification of the Copyright Act: Part 2* (1999).

The subject matter of many regimes has varied and expanded greatly over time. But even if new subject matter or new uses of existing subject matter are created, the old usually continue to subsist beside the new. Existing regulation cannot be abandoned; new forms must be added: CD-ROMs have not eradicated books, nor has the internet eliminated newspapers. Every regime is under constant pressure to adapt, if not to new technology then to new commercial realities or concepts (see, eg, *National Rugby League Investments Pty Ltd v Singtel Optus Pty Ltd* [2010] FCAFC 59) or to new treaty terms. And adaptation of one regime not uncommonly has repercussions for others.

Nonetheless, review and reform of all areas of intellectual property are not often undertaken systematically in an integrated manner, a fact that has generated some criticism. Responsibility for various regimes lies with different federal ministries and departments with fluctuating powers. This is sometimes detrimental to consistent policy development, although the situation has been alleviated by the establishment of permanent university-based research bodies such as the Intellectual Property

9. See, example, Creative Commons International, Australia, http://creativecommons.org.au/; Open Source Initiative, http://opensource.org/.
10. See Advisory Council on Intellectual Property, *Patents and Experimental Use*, October 2005; Patents Act 1990 (Cth), s 119C.

Research Institute of Australia (IPRIA) and the Australian Centre for Intellectual Property in Agriculture (ACIPA). On the other hand, in early 2005, the principal law reform body for copyright law, the CLRC, was abolished, having produced many useful reports, leaving major reviews in the hands of the relevant departments or parliamentary committees: see, for instance, the review of fair use: Australian Government Attorney-General's Department, Fair Use and Other Copyright Exceptions: An Examination of Fair Use, Fair Dealing and Other Exceptions in the Digital Age, Issues Paper (2005), or the Senate Legal and Constitutional Affairs Legislation Committee, *Gene Patents Report*, September 2011. The ALRC has also undertaken law reform work, most recently the *Copyright and the Digital Economy*, Report 122, 2014. However, the recent review by the PC of intellectual property arrangements in Australia, the PC Report, does constitute a major integrated piece of work, with recommendations for reform across all fields of intellectual property, some of which have been implemented by the government: see Australian Government, *Australian Government Response to the Productivity Commission Inquiry into Intellectual Property Arrangements*, August 2017. Major recently effected or anticipated reforms are referred to throughout this text.

Unifying Factors of Varied Regimes

Unity in diversity: no general right of action

1.16 Although the various intellectual property regimes have disparate policy goals and principles, there are also unifying factors. A first point that results from the diversity of the body of law is the resulting 'pigeonholing' requirement. All the regimes that make up intellectual property law are constrained within certain boundaries. A number of 'elements' must in every case be satisfied before a court will grant relief. In other words, an applicant cannot claim general relief based on a set of facts, but must claim the breach of a specified statutory or legal right or equitable interest; this much was confirmed by the rejection of a general tort of unfair competition in *Moorgate Tobacco Co Ltd v Philip Morris Ltd (No 2)* (1984) 156 CLR 414; 3 IPR 545 and earlier in *Victoria Park Racing and Recreation Grounds Co Ltd v Taylor* (1937) 58 CLR 479, and of a general remedy for unconscionable conduct in *Australian Broadcasting Corporation v Lenah Game Meats Pty Ltd* (2001) 208 CLR 199; 54 IPR 161 (*ABC v Lenah Game Meats*). However, compare these decisions with the US position in *International News Service v Associated Press* (1918) 248 US 215; 63 Law Ed 211 where the notion of an action for unfair competition was more positively received (although the standing of that decision has been substantially eroded in recent times). This means that if every element of an action cannot be established, the plaintiff may be without a remedy, even if on one view of the facts that result may appear unfair. There is no general 'safety net' or default action.

An important example relates to breach of confidence. In *ABC v Lenah Game Meats*, the High Court confirmed that a plaintiff does not have a 'freestanding' (see at IPR 166) right to interlocutory relief. Alleged 'unconscionability' of the conduct is not sufficient in the absence of some right to final relief based on an existing action.

The ABC was not party to the trespass that had facilitated the filming of the slaughter of possums in a processing plant. Therefore, it had done no wrong that could form the basis for the granting of a remedy for breach of confidence; the recognised elements of that action had not been proven. The ABC was free to broadcast the footage, as that action could not stretch to accommodate the imposition of a restraint on it doing so.

The availability of relief may depend on the plaintiff possessing a statutory right obtained by application and examination, such as a patent, plant variety, trade mark or design right. It is important that the right is properly adapted to the subject matter and monopoly sought and the relief that may be desired. For instance, if a company seeks an exclusive right in the use or function of a new product, it must apply for a patent for an invention, not a registered design, since a registered design confers a monopoly only in the appearance and not the function of an article. (Misunderstanding of the distinctions and limitations of the registered design right in this regard may result in disappointment for plaintiff: see, eg, *Firmagroup Australia Pty Ltd v Byrne & Davidson Doors (Vic) Pty Ltd* (1987) 180 CLR 483; 9 IPR 353.) However, in the absence of some statutory right, it may be that there is still some other form of relief available. For instance, a person who uses but has not registered a trade mark (known as a 'common law mark'; commonly represented by the ™ sign) cannot bring an action on the basis of the Trade Marks Act 1995 (Cth) but may still be able to sue in passing off, a common law right. Nonetheless, that alternative strategy does not equate to the availability of a general safety net. Every element of the tort of passing off will still have to be established, no remedy being based exclusively on misappropriation, unjust enrichment, dishonest competition or some other nebulous ground of entitlement. An applicant in an infringement action may thus fail because all the recognised elements of an action are not established, but also because of the expiry of registered rights, or because restrictive entry standards (eg, novelty and inventiveness in patents law) cannot be met. Thus, intellectual property law does not provide a remedy for every perceived ill or unfairness, or for every effort or investment.

Intellectual property and property in things

1.17 At the most fundamental level, all intellectual property law is concerned with intangibles. In all regimes (although with some distinctions), intellectual property rights are separate and distinct from the rights in the underlying tangible goods that are the 'record' containing the expressed ideas, or resulting from some creative act. The bundle of rights that constitutes intellectual property in one or another regime is thus traded and commercially dealt with as a separate and distinct form of property. It constitutes (in most cases) personal property that may devolve by agreement, by will or by operation of law: see, for example, Copyright Act 1968, s 196(1); Patents Act 1990, s 13(2). The Australian National Gallery may acquire the actual 'Blue Poles' canvas by Jackson Pollock for a large sum, which will give it the right to display the canvas on its walls or put it wherever it sees fit or lend it to other galleries or sell it on. But if the gallery wants to sell postcards of the painting, it will additionally need to acquire (by assignment) ownership of the (copy-)right to reproduce the painting or obtain the copyright owner's authorisation (a licence) to make such copies.

The acquisition of property rights in get-up, common law and registered trade marks was at the core of the High Court decision in *JT International SA v Commonwealth; British American Tobacco Australasia Ltd v Commonwealth* (2012) 50 CLR 1; [2012] HCA 43. Here, the court examined whether the restrictions imposed by the Tobacco Plain Packaging Act 2011 (Cth) (the Plain Packaging Act) amounted to an indirect acquisition of property, thereby attracting the operation of s 51(xxxi) of the Constitution (which deals with the acquisition of property on just terms). The decision illustrates the wide-ranging implications of treating intellectual property as property.

The High Court conceded that the Plain Packaging Act would restrict or extinguish the tobacco companies' pre-existing rights to use their property (being a trade mark). The court found that although this could amount to a 'taking' of property, there was no resulting obligation to compensate the trade mark owners, as the Commonwealth did not acquire a benefit of a proprietary character and, further, the Plain Packaging Act did not operate to acquire any proprietary rights or interests for the Commonwealth: per French CJ at [41]–[44], Hayne and Bell JJ at [175], Crennan J at [297]–[307], Kiefel J at [353]–[372]; Gummow J agreeing with French CJ.

However, Heydon J, in his dissenting judgment, found that the Plain Packaging Act did provide the Commonwealth with the necessary control, which consequently deprived the tobacco companies of their statutory and common law intellectual property rights: at [297]–[306]. This destruction of personal property was, for the purpose of the Commonwealth, according to Heydon J, an acquisition of property: at [215]–[228]. His Honour went on to find that the Plain Packaging Act failed to provide any provision for compensation and therefore there were no just terms for the acquisition of the personal property by the Commonwealth here.

The determinants of ownership in intellectual property

1.18 As ownership of the underlying thing or material record does not determine ownership of the intellectual property, intellectual property has distinct rules that locate ownership. Two important principles come into play:

- first, rights do not arise before intangible ideas have been given some tangible expression; and
- second, mental creation rather than physical creation is the key to determining ownership.

The first principle is most important in the context of copyright (the 'idea–expression' dichotomy is a basic copyright tenet) but applies more or less in all regimes. If one person applies for a patent in an invention, another cannot turn round and say 'But I had that idea first!' and expect any legal consequences to flow from that bare assertion. Simply having an idea in mind means nothing in terms of intellectual property, but the effect may be quite different if the idea has been written down. A further requirement is that the idea will have to be expressed with *sufficient* precision to make it the identifiable subject matter of any legal claim. An overly vague idea or concept cannot be the subject of specific rights and cannot attract some remedy for misuse, but a concept need not be elaborated in all its infinite detail either. In some cases, the law has gone to considerable lengths to accommodate the interests of people who were the first to arrive at some idea, even though it is expressed as little more than a broad concept: see, for instance, in the context of formats for television shows that are the subject of confidential presentations to prospective backers, *Talbot v General Television Corp Pty Ltd* [1980] VR 224.[11]

The second basic principle is that, as a normal point of departure, intellectual property rights vest in the person who has made the creative contribution to the birth of the material — in copyright terms, the author; in patent terms, the inventor, and so on. It is mental rather than manual or technical processes that count: see, in the context of copyright, *Walter v Lane* [1900] AC 539; *Donoghue v Allied Newspapers Ltd* [1938] Ch 106. Merely providing technical or practical aid (such as recording, typing or writing down somebody else's words, or providing laboratory infrastructure) does not, as such, entitle one to participate in intellectual property rights; however, neither will merely providing broad ideas, suggestions or parameters of inquiry.

Again, this is a principle that cannot always be applied simply. In areas related to goodwill, this is particularly so. Who, for instance, is the owner of an unregistered trade mark (being a badge of origin used in relation to goods or services)? Were it the creator (designer or artist) of the mark, this would largely defeat the purpose of a trade mark, which is to indicate the origin of goods and services, which may or may not lie with that creator. More significant is the person who built up the reputation and goodwill in the mark. It is 'creating' the *goodwill* in the mark (eg, by advertising and promoting it) rather than the mark itself that is determinative of entitlement to trade mark rights and registration. Other exceptions to the general rule that creators own intellectual property rights apply by operation of statute or common law. For instance, where intellectual property is created in the course of employment, ownership commonly vests in the employer and not the employee–creator: see, for example, Copyright Act 1968, s 35.

Flexible and evolving application of rules

1.19 An important aspect of the modern law of intellectual property is that the courts, because of the evolving nature of the subject matter, must attempt to apply rules in a flexible and accommodating manner. This implies a focus on the substance rather than on the literal meaning of relevant provisions. Technology, commerce and culture constantly and rapidly change in ways that challenge existing rules and principles. For instance, the digital revolution has spawned a host of new products, such as computer programs and video games; the courts (and commerce) are faced with multiple novel questions of protection, solutions for which must often be derived from a liberal application of *existing* intellectual property rules, sometimes originally devised with quite different subject matter in mind. For instance, in *Galaxy Electronics Pty Ltd v Sega Enterprises Ltd* (1997) 75 FCR 8; 37 IPR 462, a video game, an item not expressly referred to in the Copyright Act 1968, was held to be a film, which is 'subject matter other than works' protected by virtue of Pt IV of the Act. A liberal or permissive

---

11. See also W Cornish, 'Confidence in ideas' (1990) 1(3) *AIPJ* 3–10.

approach to interpreting existing provisions concerning subsistence of rights was said to be fundamental to this area of law. Yet the terms of the statute must be respected; as Wilcox J said (at IPR 467):

> I agree with Burchett J that it would be wrong to interpret narrowly the definition of 'cinematograph film' in s 10 and s 24. These provisions were intended to cover new technologies, the emphasis being on the end product — motion pictures — rather than the means adopted to create those pictures. Nonetheless, the definition will apply to any particular new technology only if that technology satisfies the words of the definition, liberally read.

Innovation (be it commercial, technological or artistic) never ceases (as the human mind always searches for new things), and intellectual property law must attempt to accommodate this reality. In this environment, flexible extension of underlying principles, as opposed to strict adherence to rules of verbal interpretation, is preferable. The High Court has regularly expressed itself adverse to formulating or adhering to rigid 'verbal formulae'. The liberal application of flexible indicators of validity, such as those formulated in the watershed patentability case *National Research Development Corp v Commissioner of Patents* (1959) 102 CLR 252; 1A IPR 63, is preferred. Courts are also vigilant not to deny owners of intellectual property effective enforcement by an overly rigid or literal construction of the scope and extent of their granted rights. They generally do not restrict recovery to cases of literal or facsimile copying or imitation only. However, necessary as this approach may be for an effective system of intellectual property rights, it commonly calls on very fine judgments by decision-makers: where to draw the line in cases of non-literal infringement or 'resemblance and imitation', as opposed to 'identity and copying'. Illustrations of the difficulties are provided, for example, by the application of s 13 of the Copyright Act 1968 (substantial part), the standard of 'substantial similarity in overall impression' in s 19 of the Designs Act 2003 and the purposive approach to construction of patent claims (as laid down in *Populin v HB Nominees Pty Ltd* (1982) 41 ALR 471).

No guarantee of validity

1.20 Grants of statutory rights, even though preceded by formal and substantive examination, never *guarantee* legal protection. An action based on statutory rights can always be defeated by the defendant establishing that the right in question was not validly granted. For instance, a defendant in an action for infringement of a standard patent will frequently 'counterclaim for invalidity' and, if successful, will naturally escape liability. Prima facie, a statutory right is valid, which results in procedural and evidentiary advantages for a plaintiff, but, *in substance*, it is perfectly subvertible. This is partly explained by the fallibility of official examination; for instance, it would be impossible for a patent examiner in the Patent Office of IP Australia to guarantee that novelty searches performed would reveal any and all possible prior publications of an invention (or 'anticipation'). However, invalidity of a statutory right does not necessarily leave a plaintiff without a remedy. For instance, the owner of a registered mark will obtain a remedy without having to prove actual reputation or consumer deception if the mark is used without authorisation on the same goods or services as those for which it is registered. If in an action for infringement of a registered trade mark the defendant successfully counterclaims for invalidity of the registration, a remedy may still lie in passing off. But, in that case, the plaintiff will have to tender actual evidence of the reputation of the mark and of the deception of consumers.

Varied Regimes

1.21 In spite of the unifying factors in intellectual property law, it is unmistakably a very varied and disparate body of law. Some of the basic categories and divisions within intellectual property law are set out below.

Statutory and non-statutory regimes

1.22 As will already have become apparent, intellectual property law is composed of statutory and non-statutory regimes. The statutory regimes concern copyright, patents, trade marks, circuit layouts (computer chips), designs and plant breeder's rights (plant varieties). The non-statutory actions are the equitable action for breach of confidence and the common law tort of passing off. However, the latter is largely subsumed within the scope of s 18 of the Australian Consumer Law.

By virtue of s 51(xvii) (copyright, patents, designs and trade marks) of the Commonwealth Constitution, the Commonwealth Parliament has legislative power over intellectual property law. Since the field is covered by Commonwealth laws, there are no state or territory intellectual property laws. Questions do arise from time to time as to the power of the Commonwealth to legislate in less traditional areas of intellectual property law (eg, performers' rights in copyright law, and the areas mentioned at the outset of this chapter). On the one hand, the High Court has looked behind the specific terminology of s 51(xvii) to extend the intellectual property power to analogous subject matter not expressly mentioned: see the *Grain Pool* case, mentioned above at 1.1. On the other hand, s 51(xxix) (the external affairs power) now usually provides the necessary nexus, given the great expansion of treaty provisions concerning intellectual property rights.

The non-statutory actions have been devised and moulded by courts of law and equity. While not so rigidly circumscribed, such actions still only mutate slowly over time in response to changing circumstances. There is no inherent reason why non-statutory actions could not be given statutory form. As pointed out, this has in some measure occurred in relation to passing off, although the formulation of the statutory rule in s 18 of the Australian Consumer Law so broad as to cover far more than passing off alone. In certain foreign jurisdictions, misappropriation of trade secrets is governed by statute, for example in some states of the US, whereas in Australia the remedy lies in equity. The lack of statutory protection for trade secrets in Australia and most other common law jurisdictions is, at least in part, due to the fact that there are no detailed international precepts governing this area of law. All that TRIPS requires is that 'undisclosed information' benefits from protection: see art 39. That protection need not be on the basis of property rights, nor of an unfair competition tort.

The antecedents of Australian statutory regimes are found in the UK; for instance, the Copyright Act 1968 (Cth) can be traced back to the Statute of Anne 1709, and the Patents Act 1990 (Cth) to the Statute of Monopolies 1623. However, Acts dealing with modern subject matter, such as the Circuit Layouts Act 1989 (Cth), derive directly from recent treaties. The UK precursors of our statutory regimes are still of relevance: first, English cases decided when our laws more closely resembled each other, and cases dealing with matters of general principle, are persuasive in Australia; and second, in spite of the modern primacy of its international obligations, Australia still keenly observes the English example in many of its reform efforts. These days, law reformers also closely follow EU developments that are themselves determinative of, or influential on, UK law. The laws and jurisprudence of the USA and Canada have always been and remain relevant, although the divergence with US law is greater than with Canadian law.

Grant and non-grant systems

1.23 A further division among the statutory regimes is that some vest rights automatically upon creation of the relevant subject matter; for instance, once you write down an original poem, you have copyright in that poem without any further administrative requirements, registration or other formalities.

Others bestow rights only after application, examination and grant. A competent authority, IP Australia,[12] which administers the statutory application-based regimes, now also including the Plant Breeder's Rights Act 1994 (Cth), determines whether the statutory criteria are fulfilled.

Patents, registered trade marks, registered designs and plant breeder's rights can be obtained only through an application and examination process, while copyright and eligible layout rights vest automatically. It has not always and universally been the case that no formalities are required to obtain copyright protection. In the USA, until quite recently (prior to that country's accession to the Berne Convention), the © sign had to be attached to copyright works, and registration has also been required in the past. By contrast, in some countries patents have been granted without substantive examination, although never without registration.

In recent times, an intermediate form of protection has arisen in Australian law: the granting of rights without substantive examination. Innovation patents, and registered designs under the Designs Act 2003, are *granted* on the basis of formalities checks only, but can only be *enforced* once substantive examination has been requested and passed. This means that the costs of examination can be deferred to a later date, perhaps after actual exploitation has commenced. Upfront costs are a drawback of the registration model, but there are, obviously, countervailing advantages. The major *advantages* of a registration system are:

- publicity (detailed information about subject matter is available from a public register);
- clarity about ownership and other rights and interests (such as mortgages); and

12. See http://www.ipaustralia.gov.au/.

- searchability (ie, a person can avoid infringing another's rights by ascertaining the existence of rights and from whom to obtain a licence).

The major *disadvantages* are:

- cost and delay in obtaining the rights;
- the lack of ultimate certainty about validity;
- the cost to the community (the taxpayer) of maintaining an administrative system (although a system might be partly user-pays); and
- bureaucratisation and complexity, which can make life particularly difficult for small and medium enterprises.

Temporary and perpetual rights

1.24 Most intellectual property rights are of a temporary nature, except for rights in goodwill. Since a trade mark performs an ongoing informative function that is beneficial to both its owner and the consumer, it is obviously not appropriate to limit its term of validity on an a priori basis; as long as the goodwill exists, the trade mark rights should remain enforceable. Nonetheless, a registered trade mark can be removed from the register if certain statutory conditions were not or are no longer met; for example, if it is not being used or is no longer distinctive of the trade mark owner's goods or services. Arguably, the action for breach of confidence can also deliver perpetual protection for trade secrets. However, that protection is always contingent upon the information concerned remaining secret. If a third party discovers and publishes the same information, it will be in the public domain, and a remedy against disclosure or misuse will no longer be available. The obligation on a confidee not to misuse a trade secret cannot be perpetuated by contractual means once it has entered the public domain: see *Maggbury Pty Ltd v Hafele Australia Pty Ltd* (2001) 210 CLR 181; 53 IPR 1.

The subject matter of statutory rights other than trade marks reverts to the public domain after a limited term, and their effective life cannot be extended by contractual means either. A licensing agreement in relation to a patent, for instance, is not enforceable after the expiry of the statutory term of protection. The trade-off for the granting of intellectual property rights that arguably constitute a (monopoly) impost on society is that, ultimately, the subject matter of the rights is given up by its creator to the community as a whole. In any case, since so much subject matter is soon outdated and of no further commercial relevance, perpetual validity would only impose unnecessary transaction or search costs. Nonetheless, limited though the period of protection may be, it is not short: life of the author plus 70 years in copyright; 20 years from application date for a patent, and so on. Although the differing terms of protection of various rights are hard to justify precisely, they are informed by vague notions concerning the potential commercial value of certain subject matter. Thus, registered designs have a relatively short maximum term (now 10 years) because industrial design is necessarily transitory and incremental. By contrast, the longer duration of copyright may be explained by the fact that some copyright works at least (although rarely) are of a value that transcends the passage of time, and also by the greater inherent worth that people ascribe to creative works of art than to some other intangibles. Furthermore, copyrights are less comprehensive, since they are not true monopoly rights; a person who arrives at the same material independently during the term of the copyright (as may, for instance, happen in relation to musical works) is perfectly free to exploit it.

Anti-copying and monopoly rights

1.25 This leads us to a further important variation in intellectual property rights, between monopoly and anti-copying regimes. The latter are relatively limited in scope. To prove infringement, the rights owner will have to establish not only sufficient similarity but also actual copying — that the defendant derived their work from that of the plaintiff and not by independent creation. Monopoly rights are rights of action against any person who exploits the subject matter of the right, regardless of whether that person has arrived at that subject matter independently or by copying. For instance, a person who independently arrives at a patented invention will be infringing if they exploit it, even if totally ignorant of the existence of the patented invention. To some extent, the fact that patents are registered meets the concern that a person could be infringing wholly innocently. Anyone can inspect the patent register and ascertain the existence of valid patents on the subject matter they are interested in. Conversely, a copyright plaintiff may be able to point to similarities between their source work and some alleged copy, but unless the similarities are such that they warrant an inference of copying (ie, they could not be coincidental), the similarities alone are not sufficient to establish liability.

Property and non-property regimes

1.26 Although intellectual 'property' law is the common label for this area of law, we have already seen that, in fact, the word 'property' is something of a misnomer. The rights granted are — depending on the definition of 'property' — not really extensive enough to amount to property in the traditional sense. However, most of the statutes refer to bundles of rights as personal property, and they are traded as such. It is far more controversial to refer to 'property' when it comes to non-statutory actions for breach of confidence and passing off. Whether confidential information (a 'trade secret') is property is doubtful, although in contractual terms it is routinely dealt with as such. The better — and more accepted (see, eg, *Smith Kline & French Laboratories (Aust) Ltd v Secretary, Department of Community Services and Health* (1991) 28 FCR 291; 20 IPR 643) — view is that at the core of the action for breach of confidence is an obligation of conscience to respect the demands of a relationship of good faith, and not a property right in information. Similarly, in the context of passing off, although it is sometimes argued that the action protects property rights in certain well-known and distinctive aspects of a product (eg, 'a celebrity owns her image'; a trader 'owns goodwill'), the sounder analysis is that it protects commercial reputation from abuse; that is, it is about policing commercial conduct, rather than about enforcing proprietary rights in goodwill. The 'property rights in personality' approach to the law of passing off, even if well established in US merchandising cases, is not really accepted in Australia.

Overlap and dual protection

1.27 Although intellectual property law requires 'pigeonholing', as pointed out earlier in this chapter, it may well be that a single fact scenario gives rise to multiple actions in diverse regimes. The recent creation of additional and broader rights further enhances the risk of 'overlap' between regimes. In a policy sense, difficult issues of dual protection and overlap result, some of which are dealt with by the legislator, and others left to the courts to resolve. Overlap issues are the inevitable result of the absence of some broad remedy, such as for unfair competition or unjust enrichment, that could integrate all areas of the law. There would perhaps be some benefit in being able to avoid overlap issues, but on the whole the legislator has not restricted a claimant's choice of the most appropriate regime. Dual protection is also not generally prohibited.

The most significant exception to this rule lies in the relationship between copyright and designs registration. There, the Act, generally speaking, prohibits dual protection and forces manufacturers to rely on designs registration alone: see ss 73–77 of the Copyright Act 1968. Because the registered design of an article, being its shape or appearance, is often also (a reproduction of) an artistic work (a drawing or sculpture) protected under the Copyright Act, two distinct legal regimes effectively control often identical subject matter. This serves to illustrate the difficulties in identifying an incontrovertible basis for the policy distinctions that result in those different rules. But while parliament has traditionally been anxious to prevent dual copyright/designs protection, there is no such concern about the increased potential for dual trade mark/designs protection resulting from the recent inclusion of shapes and packaging of goods as signs that are registrable as trade marks under the Trade Marks Act 1995 (Cth), which was not possible under the Trade Marks Act 1955 (Cth), nor concerning dual copyright/patent protection for computer-implemented inventions that incorporate computer programs or algorithms. However, the law does force inventors to make a choice between relying on secrecy and patenting. Secret exploitation of an invention by the patentee is a ground for invalidity: see Patents Act 1990, s 18(1)(d).

Introduction to the Different Regimes

1.28 It cannot be stressed often enough that intellectual property law is a varied and wide-ranging subject covering multifarious regimes. A basic introduction to the different areas follows, so that the study of each individual regime in later chapters can be undertaken with some knowledge of the others and of the broader context of intellectual property law.

Copyright law

1.29 Copyright law is covered by the Copyright Act 1968 (Cth). There are two basic categories of protected subject matter under the Act:

- artistic, literary (which includes computer programs), musical and dramatic works — this category has the most extensive level of protection; and
- subject matter other than works, which covers (sound and television) broadcasts, films, sound recordings and published editions of works — this category is concerned with subject matter that derives from works, and enjoys less extensive protection.

While it is primarily the author who owns copyright in works, it is generally the person responsible for *the making* of the subject matter other than works who obtains copyright in it (eg, the producer of a film). Copyright in works, as a general rule, subsists for the life of the author plus 70 years, while copyright in other subject matter subsists, subject to exceptions, for 70 years from the year of making or first publication. To attract copyright protection, a work must be original, in material form (ie, expressed and contained in some record) and have some connection with Australia. The rights in works are reproduction (commonly known as copying), publication, public performance, communication to the public, adaptation and a limited rental right. Rights extend only to specific expressions and not to the ideas contained in works.

The rights in subject matter other than works are more restricted, generally extending only to facsimile reproduction or copying. Various exceptions to the exclusive rights of the owner apply, and the law prescribes different compulsory or statutory licences. Rights arise without any need for registration. Copyright may be traded as personal property by assignment or exploited by licence. The Copyright Act 1968 also provides protection to performers (as opposed to authors) and also contains provisions concerning 'moral rights'; that is, inalienable rights to attribution and to integrity (ie, against mutilation of a work). Further, the Act also contains numerous provisions concerning the infringing use of certain technologies, such as circumvention devices and decoders.

Designs law

1.30 Design rights are granted by the Registrar of Designs on the basis of an application, examination and certification procedure prescribed by the Designs Act 2003 (Cth). The 2003 Act replaced the 1906 Act and introduced substantial changes to designs law. The Act grants a monopoly in a registered design; that is, the appearance (either shape and/or ornamentation) of a handmade or manufactured article. A design must be new and distinctive to qualify for registration. A registered design may subsist for a maximum of 10 years and may be assigned or licensed. The owner of the registered design has the exclusive right to manufacture the relevant article for the term of protection. As a general rule, design and copyright protection do not operate cumulatively.

Patents law

1.31 The field of patents law is covered by the Patents Act 1990 (Cth). It provides for a complex system of application, examination and granting of either standard or innovation patents (for the time being: the PC recommended abolition of the innovation patent, a recommendation accepted by the government but not implemented at the time of writing). Patents are granted for any new and inventive technology that is useful and has some practical application. An invention can be either a product or a process, or a combination of both. The scope of the monopoly in an invention is determined by the 'claims', which must be set out in the application. The duration of a standard patent is 20 years, but the Act provides a more easily obtained alternative, the innovation patent, which requires a lower standard of inventiveness and has a maximum duration of 8 years. The patentee has the exclusive right to exploit the invention — that is, to either use a process or make or use a product that is patented — and the patentee also has exclusive commercial exploitation rights over patented products or the products resulting from the implementing of a patented process. Very few things are clearly excluded from patentability, but human beings and the biological processes of their generation are not patentable. A compulsory licence may be granted against the patentee if they do not use the patent or refuse to license its use on reasonable terms. Once the patent term expires, it cannot be extended or reinvigorated by contractual means. A patent may be assigned or licensed.

Circuit layouts (integrated circuits)

1.32 The Circuit Layouts Act 1989 (Cth) was specifically enacted to ensure that the layout of computer chips (integrated circuits) should not fall between the gaps of other regimes and fail to be protected against piracy and other forms of copying. The rights come into existence automatically upon creation of the layout of the integrated circuit, just as in copyright. The rights extend to the making of a copy of the layout, to the making of computer chips on the basis of the layout and to the making of copies of the computer chips based on the layout. To attract protection (ie, to be classed an 'eligible layout' or 'EL'), the layout must be original, in the sense of not being commonplace. The period of protection is a minimum of 10 years, and there are a number of important exceptions to the rights of the owner, most notably in the context of reverse engineering. ELs are excluded from designs registration.

Plant variety rights/plant breeder's rights

1.33 A new plant variety may be registered under the Plant Breeder's Rights Act 1994 (Cth) if it is new, uniform and stable. It may also be protected by a patent, but the granting of a patent is subject to a high standard of inventiveness. As a result, the products of traditional breeding techniques can be registered as new plant varieties but are commonly unpatentable; products of genetic plant engineering are more likely to be sufficiently inventive, and they could, in theory, attract dual protection. The person who first bred the new variety may apply for the plant breeder's right (PBR), which is granted after an administrative application and examination procedure. The registered owner of a PBR has the exclusive right to produce propagating material of the protected variety, while there are a number of exceptions, of which the 'farmer's rights' to replant seeds is the most significant. The duration of the right varies with the class of plant.

Trade marks

1.34 Trade marks can be registered under the Trade Marks Act 1995 (Cth). While unregistered, trade marks may be a sufficiently distinctive sign of a trader's business to attract protection under the action in passing off, but registration of a mark has great advantages over reliance on passing off. A trade mark can be registered even if it has not been used and has not yet established a reputation in the market. Trade marks are registered after an application and examination procedure. Basically, any sign (now including shapes, sounds or scents) that is not confusing and that can distinguish one person's goods or services from those of another as to commercial origin may be registered. That ability to distinguish either may be the result of the inherent qualities of the mark (a mark that is not descriptive of the goods is, generally speaking, distinctive) or may exist because the mark has built up recognition and reputation through actual use in the marketplace.

A mark cannot remain registered if it is not used as a trade mark, and will also be removed if it fails to remain distinctive or becomes confusing. The owner of the registered mark has the exclusive right to use it commercially as a badge of origin in connection with the goods or services for which it is registered. In the application for registration, the applicant must identify the goods or services in relation to which registration is sought and the trade mark will be used. There are a number of special categories of marks. Trade marks may now be freely traded but are usually assigned with the relevant goodwill or business; the use of the mark may also be licensed under a system of authorised user, in which case the owner must retain control over the quality of the goods or services to which the mark is attached, so that customers are not misled as to the quality of goods to which a licensee has attached the mark.

The action for passing off

1.35 The action for passing off may apply to the unauthorised use of an unregistered (or 'common law' trade mark) but, in general, protects any distinctive aspect of the plaintiff's business or image from being used in a misleading manner in commerce. The action protects against a rival trader riding on the coat-tails of another's distinctive reputation. The plaintiff will have to establish the existence of a reputation in the relevant jurisdiction, that there is a misrepresentation made by the defendant (ie, that consumers have been misled) in the course of trade as to a connection with the plaintiff's business, and that there is actual or potential damage to the plaintiff. Most recently, the common law action for passing off has been extended to merchandising cases to protect the image of celebrities against unauthorised commercial use, for instance in advertising. At the core of passing off lies proof that consumers have been misled; the action is largely subsumed under the broad terms of s 18 of the Australian Consumer Law, and in most cases both are pleaded.

The action for breach of confidence/trade secrets

1.36 The action for breach of confidence permits a confider to restrain a confidee (and sometimes third parties) from either using or publishing information that is not public and was imparted in confidence. The information may be of any kind, technical, commercial or personal, and it is not always necessary for the plaintiff to show actual monetary damage to succeed, since personal detriment may be a sufficient basis for relief (eg, the exposure of aspects of family or personal life).

The plaintiff must establish:

- that the information is not in the public domain, which is a relative concept;
- that it was imparted in a manner or in circumstances that imply that an obligation to keep it confidential attaches; and
- that there is an unauthorised use or disclosure.

Many cases revolve around either information imparted in the context of employment or government information; special considerations may apply in either case, and various exceptions exist, most notably to disclosure of trade secrets in the public interest.

Bibliography

Australian Council for Intellectual Property (ACIP), *Patents and Experimental Use*, October 2005.

A Stewart, W van Caenegem, J Bannister, A Liberman, C Lawson, *Intellectual Property in Australia*, 6th ed, LexisNexis, 2017.

C Arup, *The New WTO Agreements: Globalising Law through Services and Intellectual Property*, Cambridge University Press, 2000.

C May, *A Global Political Economy of Intellectual Property Rights: The New Enclosures?*, Routledge, 2000.

Creative Commons International, Australia, at http://creativecommons.org.au/.

D Gervais, *The TRIPS Agreement: Drafting History and Analysis*, Sweet and Maxwell, 1998.

G Hughes (ed), *Dean's Law of Trade Secrets and Privacy*, 3rd ed, Thomson Reuters, 2018.

Intellectual Property Research Institute of Australia (IPRIA), at http://www.ipria.org/.

L Bently and B Sherman, *The Makings of Modern Intellectual Property Law*, Cambridge University Press, 1999.

P Drahos, *A Philosophy of Intellectual Property*, Dartmouth, Brookfield, 1996.

P Drahos and J Braithwaite, *Information Feudalism: Who Controls the Knowledge Economy?*, Earthscan Publications, 2002.

Productivity Commission (PC), *Intellectual Property Arrangements*, Inquiry Report No 78, Canberra, September 2016 (PC Report).

S Ricketson, S Richardson, M Davison, *Intellectual Property: Cases, Materials and Commentary*, 5th ed, LexisNexis Butterworths, 2012.

S Anderman (ed), *The Interface Between Intellectual Property Rights and Competition Policy*, Cambridge University Press, 2007.

S Ricketson, *The Berne Convention for the Protection of Literary and Artistic Works*, Kluwer, 1987.

W Cornish, *Intellectual Property: Omnipresent, Distracting, Irrelevant?*, Oxford University Press, 2004.

World Intellectual Property Organization (WIPO), at http://www.wipo.int/portal/index.html.en.

World Trade Organization (WTO), 'Trade-Related Aspects of Intellectual Property Rights', http://www.wto.org/english/tratop_e/TRIPS_e/TRIPS_e.htm.

Chapter 2

Copyright: Subsistence Requirements

Introduction

The scope of copyright

2.1 Copyright is the statutory regime that touches upon the widest range of subject matter: from fine arts (eg, sculptures, paintings) to the applied and technical material (fashion, architectural plans, buildings, computer programs); from traditional dramatic arts (plays, scripts, dance, live performances) to complex entertainment products (such as computer games, videos and digital television broadcasts); from classical music through popular songs to experimental compositions (minimalism, natural music, concrete music); and from highbrow literature to commonplace creations such as anthologies, timetables and betting coupons. Whether the creation is purely artistic or commercial in intent matters not, and but for one exception (works of artistic craftsmanship: see s 10 of the Copyright Act 1968 (Cth)), the artistic merit or quality of a work is irrelevant in terms of subsistence of copyright. The Copyright Act 1968 (Cth) covers the field of copyright law, which now comprises not only the core categories of works (literary, dramatic, musical and artistic) and subject matter other than works (films, sound recordings, broadcasts and published editions) but also moral rights protection, performers' rights and a host of measures related to specific rights in, and infringement by, the use of certain technologies (eg, digital signals, circumvention of encryption, etc).

The nature and extent of protected rights and subject matter have steadily expanded over time. Partly, this has been in response to technological advances resulting in a complex set of new technology-specific rules. Other changes have resulted from Australia's membership or conclusion of international treaties and agreements. Thus, the Copyright Amendment (Moral Rights) Act 2000 (Cth), which represented a considerable policy departure for Australia, in part resulted from a reassessment of the scope of Australia's obligations under the Berne Convention for the Protection of Literary and Artistic Works (1886). Amendments concerning certain aspects of copyright on the internet resulted both from multilateral conventions (the World Intellectual Property Organization (WIPO) Copyright Treaties of the mid-1990s) and from the more recent bilateral Australia–United States Free Trade Agreement 2004 (AUSFTA).

Works and neighbouring rights

2.2 The two main categories of protected subject matter in the Copyright Act 1968 (Cth) are 'works' (Pt III of the Act) — that is, original literary, dramatic, musical and artistic works — and 'subject matter other than works' (Pt IV of the Act) — that is, films, sound recordings, sound and TV broadcasts, and published editions of works. The latter category is sometimes referred to as 'neighbouring rights', as they usually derive from or incorporate Pt III works. For instance, a film will usually incorporate a literary work (the novel), a dramatic work (the script or screenplay) and a musical work (the score of the soundtrack). While subject matter other than works is circumscribed by its technical characteristics, original Pt III works are protected by copyright irrespective of the physical or technological form in which they are expressed or the nature of the physical record in which they are contained. While Pt III copyright protects the original efforts of an identified author, the purpose of Pt IV of the Act is to safeguard the investment of technical and financial resources in producing a technologically complex product against direct copying. Consequently, the rules as to ownership, subsistence and infringement differ fundamentally between Pts III and IV.

Performers' rights

2.3 The rights granted under Pts III and IV benefit authors or makers. However, performers, whether they are copyright owners of what they perform or not, separately enjoy certain rights in their performances under the Act. These rights have not amounted to full copyrights in the past, as they are limited to rights of action in relation to the prohibition and use of unauthorised recordings. However, based on the terms of AUSFTA, performers own copyright in their sound recordings but not as yet in audiovisual recordings of their performances: see Copyright Act 1968, Pt XIA: Performers' Protection, and also Chapter 5 Copyright: Other Rights and Exceptions. They also enjoy moral rights in their performances (the right of attribution of performership and the right of integrity of performership).

Moral rights

2.4 Prior to the passing of the Copyright Amendment (Moral Rights) Act 2000 (Cth), authors benefited only from patrimonial or economic rights; that is, the exclusive rights aimed at securing an author's ability to exploit copyright material commercially. With the introduction of that Act, authors now also benefit from the inalienable, moral rights of attribution of authorship and integrity; see Copyright Act 1968 (Cth), Pt IX; *Corby v Allen & Unwin Ltd* [2013] FCA 370; *Perez v Ferandez* [2012] FMCA 2; *McCausland v Surfing Hardware International Holdings Pty Ltd* [2013] NSWSC 902 at [848]; and also Chapter 5 Copyright: Other Rights and Exceptions. These rights, in contrast to the rights in Pts III and IV (and also Pt XIA), are not economic and commercial in nature but personal and inalienable. They cannot be licensed or assigned. Whereas copyright in common law countries is traditionally based on the policy goal of securing for authors the benefits of commercial exploitation, in civil law jurisdictions, copyright is rather more based on the inherent ('personal' or 'moral') right of authors to the creations of their mind. This has resulted in the statutory expression of rights that protect the quality and status of authorship rather than exclusive commercial exploitation. These rights have only slowly found their way into common law jurisdictions, although they were recognised in the Berne Convention of 1886 from the time of the Rome revision in 1928 (art 6*bis*). Moral rights are dealt with in Chapter 5 Copyright: Other Rights and Exceptions.

International treaties relating to copyright law

2.5 Australia's international obligations in this area can be divided into three categories. First, the treaties administered by the WIPO, a United Nations agency based in Geneva, Switzerland. The most longstanding multilateral treaty within this category is the Berne Convention for the Protection of Literary and Artistic Works 1886 (after the city of Berne in Switzerland). This treaty was one of the first multilateral treaties dealing with the harmonisation of laws. Many countries have acceded to it (although the United States only in 1989) and it has been revised on a number of occasions. It sets minimum standards for copyright protection in member countries, leaving considerable scope for variation in domestic implementation. A number of other multilateral treaties also deal with aspects of copyright not covered in the Berne Convention and its revisions. Not all of them will be canvassed here. Probably the most significant are the Rome Convention 1961, dealing with the rights in films, sound recordings and performances (Rome Convention for the Protection of Performers, Producers of Phonograms and Broadcasting Organisations), and the WIPO Copyright Treaties of the mid-1990s, which deal with adaptations of copyright to the then new digital environment: the WIPO Copyright Treaty (WCT) and the WIPO Performer and Phonograms Treaty (WPPT). These treaties have been given effect in Australian law by way of the (so-called) Digital Agenda amendments to the Copyright Act 1968 (Cth). The principles of equal (or 'national') treatment and minimum standards underlie the Berne Convention.

The second category consists of the Trade-Related Aspects of Intellectual Property Rights (TRIPS) Agreement, one of the agreements establishing the World Trade Organization (WTO), successor to the General Agreement on Tariffs and Trade (GATT). The WIPO treaties provide general standards and do not have an effective mechanism to force member countries to actually incorporate treaty norms in their domestic law. The shift of intellectual property from a freestanding subject matter to an aspect of international trade in the context of the WTO overcame some of these perceived shortcomings that were said to distort international trade. TRIPS falls under the general mechanism of the WTO, which allows member countries, as an ultimate resort after various processes have been completed, to impose trade sanctions on other countries found not to be in compliance with their treaty obligations. TRIPS also imposes some additional obligations over and above pre-existing copyright treaties, and draws together obligations otherwise found in different multilateral instruments.

The third and most recent category, free trade agreements, perpetuates the trend established in TRIPS towards more detailed standards of copyright protection and effective enforcement. Treaties such as the AUSFTA perpetuate the incorporation of copyright into broader trade and commerce-related instruments. They also reach new heights in terms of detailed provisions, to the extent that the wording of the treaty and of the implementing legislation are virtually identical. There is little room for interpretation in the implementation of the treaty obligations. The reason for the level of detail is that in bilateral treaty negotiations there is not the same need for broad terms to cover disagreement and compromise over specific implementation measures between a multitude of countries. Through this mechanism, certain detailed aspects of US copyright law have found their way into Australian law, most notably in relation to safe harbour provisions for internet service providers (ISPs) and anti-circumvention rules in relation to technological protection measures. More recently, there have been more controversial attempts at supranational standard setting, in particular the Anti-Counterfeiting Trade Agreement and the Trans-Pacific Partnership Agreement. These agreements have generated substantial opposition from proponents of internet freedom, as they are perceived to seek to impose rights and obligations in relation to intermediaries such as ISPs and website hosts.

Treaties and the history of copyright law in Australia

2.6 Treaty provisions have long underpinned the development of Australian copyright law, but for a long time the most important influence on the specifics of the law was the development of copyright law in the United Kingdom. The Australian Copyright Act 1905 (Cth) reproduced the UK Copyright Act 1911. The present 1968 Act initially also reflected reforms to UK copyright implemented as a result of the Spicer Committee Report. However, more recently there have been many local reviews and amendments of copyright law, as well as a more active political and industrial interest in copyright matters. It is perhaps also the case that the growth of local copyright industries has reduced reliance on the importation of copyright material from the UK and the USA. Additional treaty obligations (eg, under the WIPO Copyright Treaties) have also directly necessitated domestic amendments. The Copyright Act 1968 (Cth) has now been amended so frequently and in so many areas that an unwieldy legislative structure has resulted.

Attempts to replace the Copyright Act 1968 (Cth) with a more streamlined Act have, to date, not met with success. The pace of piecemeal amendment continues unabated. Significant examples include the Copyright (Computer Programs) Amendment Act 1999 (Cth), the Copyright Amendment (Digital Agenda) Act 2000 (Cth), the Copyright Amendment (Moral Rights) Act 2000 (Cth) and the US Free Trade Agreement Implementation Act 2004 (Cth) (Sch 9). The fair dealing provisions of the Act have been amended to introduce more technology-specific exceptions for format and timeshifting of subject matter, and in relation to parody and commercial-scale electronic infringements: see the Copyright Amendment Act 2006 (Cth). A review into copyright and the digital economy by the Australian Law Reform Commission resulted in the publication of Report 122, which recommended further amendments, inter alia, relating to fair use. The Act was recently amended to grant the court powers to issue Orders blocking access to foreign copyright infringing websites: see the Copyright Amendment (Online Infringement) Act 2015 (Cth). The Productivity

Commission's 2016 report[1] into intellectual property in Australia has recommended further amendments, including in relation to fair use, repeal of restrictions on parallel importation of books and allowing consumers to circumvent geoblocking technology.

Literary, Dramatic, Musical and Artistic Works

Part III of the Copyright Act 1968 (Cth): copyright in works

2.7 Literary, dramatic, musical and artistic works are protected subject matter by virtue of Pt III of the Copyright Act 1968 (Cth). A number of conditions must be met. A work must:

- be expressed in material form;
- be a literary, dramatic, musical or artistic work within the meaning of the Act;
- be original; and
- have a connection with Australia.

Material form

2.8 One of the most venerable principles in copyright law is that there is no copyright in ideas or facts but only in their expression in a particular form, hence the statutory requirement that copyright works be expressed in material form. By virtue of ss 32 and 35, copyright subsists in a work made by the author. Section 22(1) provides that making a work means reducing it to writing or some other material form. By virtue of s 10, material form includes any form of storage; it does not matter whether the work is visible or not. And since the US Free Trade Agreement Implementation Act 2004, it is no longer required that a work be able to be reproduced to be 'in material form' either. Hence, a work created or stored in computer memory or some other electronic medium (eg, tape, video) has sufficient material form. This requirement that a work must be expressed in a material form implies that the exclusive right to reproduce works is also limited to reproduction in material form and does not extend to the mere extraction of ideas or implementation. As to the requirement of reproduction in material form in the digital context, see Chapter 18 Digitisation. There is no need for the expression in material form to be permanent or indestructible, but if the record is too ephemeral, then the statutory requirement may not be met.

The meaning of 'work' and public policy-based denial of copyright

2.9 A work must be reduced to material form to attract copyright and must be literary, dramatic, musical or artistic in character. But leaving those requirements aside, is there any additional limitation inherent in the word 'work'? It has sometimes been read to imply a 'substantiality' requirement or 'de minimis' rule; that is, something too small or trivial will fall outside the scope of copyright: see, for example, S Ricketson, *The Law of Intellectual Property*, Lawbook Co, 1984 at [5.61]. In *Exxon Corporation v Exxon*

1. Productivity Commission, *Intellectual Property Arrangements*, Inquiry Report No 78, Canberra, September 2016.

Insurance Consultants International Ltd [1982] Ch 119 (*Exxon*), the court held that the word 'Exxon' as such, although being 'original', was not sufficiently substantial to attract copyright (it was also not literary, since it conveyed no meaning or literary enjoyment: see 2.10 below). There is an obvious difficulty in drawing the boundary between substantial and insubstantial. In *Cortis Exhaust Systems Pty Ltd v Kitten Software Pty Ltd* (2001) ATPR 41-837; [2001] FCA 1189, Tamberlin J referred to a logo as too trivial to attract copyright as an artistic work. But in *Millwell Pty Ltd v Olympic Amusements Pty Ltd* (1999) 85 FCR 436, which concerned prize scales for gambling, the Full Court of the Federal Court did not endorse the de minimis approach, instead focusing on the fact that the prize scales afforded sufficient information to constitute a literary work. There is a justified concern about overlapping trade mark and copyright protection, but, in truth, it may be that there is no separate requirement of substantiality, and that issues sometimes considered under that heading are better considered as ones of originality; that is, whether sufficient skill, effort and judgment have been exercised in the creation of the alleged work. Nonetheless in *Fairfax Media Publications Pty Ltd v Reed International Books Australia Pty Ltd* (2010) 189 FCR 109; [2010] FCA 984 (*Fairfax Media v Reed*) at [44] Bennett J said, about a newspaper headline: 'It is, generally, too trivial to be a literary work, much as a logo was held to be too trivial to be an artistic work (*Cortis Exhaust Systems Pty Ltd v Kitten Software Pty Ltd* (2001) ATPR 41-837 at [33] per Tamberlin J), even if skill and labour has been expended on creation (*Exxon*).' See also *Volunteer Eco Students Abroad Pty Ltd v Reach Out Volunteers Pty Ltd* [2013] FCA 731 at [357].

In *Sullivan v FNH Investments Pty Ltd* [2003] FCA 323, copyright in the slogan 'Somewhere in the Whitsundays' was denied more on the basis of a lack of originality: see below 2.19 'Originality of Works'. Alternatively, it may be that the issues are more relevant to determining the character of a work. If a single word affords no information, instruction or literary enjoyment, can it be a 'literary' work? In terms of overlap, there is an arguable question as to whether an invented word with only secondary meaning acquired through advertising and promotion does not inherently afford any information and is therefore not a literary work. In the context of artistic works, the issue can also arise where a work is small but represented artistically: see, for instance, *Cortis Exhaust Systems*; *Australian Chinese Newspapers Pty Ltd v Melbourne Chinese Press Ltd* [2003] FCA 878; (2003) 58 IPR 1; and *Elwood Clothing Pty Ltd v Cotton On Clothing Pty Ltd* [2008] FCA 447 below. In the latter two cases, the distinction between literary and artistic works was at issue: see further below.

The contention that some material that is blasphemous, immoral, libellous or illegal does not attract copyright protection was firmly rejected for Australia by the majority in *Venus Adult Shops Pty Ltd v Fraserside Holdings Ltd* [2006] FCAFC 188 at [84], which concerned copyright in pornographic films:

> There is therefore no statutory basis under existing Australian copyright law for a finding that copyright does not subsist because the content of the relevant work or subject matter offends against community values or standards. That is not to say that such considerations may not inform the discretion to award particular classes of remedy but the scope of such an exercise of discretion would seem to be narrow.

Finkelstein J agreed in substance that there is no basis for the proposition that copyright does not subsist in works that are obscene or pornographic. Obviously, this case related to subject matter other than works (films), but there is no reason to suppose it would be any different for works. Where, in the past, denial of copyright on moral grounds may have occurred, times have changed, with far greater latitude concerning publication of what some may consider obscene, immoral or blasphemous material. There is a separate question of whether the copyright that subsists is enforceable. This goes to whether courts have any discretion to refuse to grant certain remedies against a party found liable in copyright infringement; as to that point, see Chapter 19 Remedies in Intellectual Property Law.

Literary works

2.10 The term 'literary work' is not exhaustively defined in the Act. However, by virtue of s 10, the ordinary meaning of the term is extended to include: '(a) a table or compilation expressed in words, figures or symbols' (whether or not in a visible form) and '(b) a computer program or compilation of computer programs': see further Chapter 18 Digitisation. A literary work is a work expressed in writing, as broadly defined within s 10: '*writing* means a mode of representing or reproducing words, figures or symbols in a visible form …' . But is anything more than an expression in writing required?

It is well established that 'literary' does not mean 'with literary merit'. Thus, in *University of London Press Ltd v University Tutorial Press Ltd* [1916] 2 Ch 601 at 608, which concerned copyright in examination papers, it was said that 'the words "literary work" cover work which is expressed in print or writing, irrespective of the question whether the quality or style is high.' Works clearly devoid of literary merit, such as betting coupons, football pools, tickets, timetables, accounting forms and prize tables, have been confirmed as literary works. However, there must be some way of distinguishing a literary work from other works. The distinguishing factor appears to be that it must convey some meaning, information or literary enjoyment. In the *Exxon* case, the earlier judgment of Davey LJ in *Hollinrake v Truswell* [1894] 3 Ch 420 at 428 was quoted with approval by Oliver and Stephenson LJJ at 144: 'Now, a literary work is intended to afford either information and instruction, or pleasure, in the form of literary enjoyment.' However, in *Fairfax Media v Reed* at [43] Bennet J pointed out that '[s]uch criteria may well describe a literary work but the mere fact that a word or sequence of words provides information or pleasure is not necessarily sufficient to constitute a literary work for the purposes of the Act.'

On the one hand, the requirement of affording literary meaning or enjoyment can be stretched. In *Express Newspapers Pty Ltd v Liverpool Daily Post & Echo Pty Ltd* [1985] 1 WLR 1089, the plaintiff newspaper distributed millions of scratch-it cards with five letters on them. Over some months, it published five-letter sequences in its paper, and the persons who could proffer a card matching one of those numbers won a prize. A rival paper published the plaintiff's letter sequences in order to promote its own publication. In the subsequent action, Whitford J held that the sequence of numbers offered information and instruction to the reader, and thus amounted to a literary work.

On the other hand, the formula of Oliver and Stephenson LJJ in *Exxon* can arguably be regarded as being more restrictive than the Act, in truth, requires. Thus, in *Apple Computer Inc v Computer Edge Pty Ltd* (1984) 1 FCR 549, Fox J cited a passage from *Copinger and Skone James on Copyright*, 12th ed, Sweet & Maxwell, 2002 [156], as 'supported by the authorities and to be applicable' (at 558):

> But so long as something in 'writing' exists, it is sufficient, and it is not necessary that what is written should express a meaning in ordinary language. Thus, there may be copyright in a list of words used as a telegraph code, or in a catalogue of type, or in a system of shorthand.

However, in this case, computer programs were at issue, something that was not then, as it is now, expressly included in the category of literary works: see Copyright Act 1968, s 10. Computer programs call for somewhat different considerations from other forms of literary works.

The difficulty inherent in the broader approach is brought to light by the cases considering the distinction between literary and artistic works. If a word or slogan is represented in a graphical style, for instance on a T-shirt, does this constitute a literary work or an artistic work? The issue of what constitutes a drawing was canvassed in two cases: *Elwood*, where an 'arrangement of principally literary material' on a T-shirt was at issue, and *Woodtree Pty Ltd v Zheng* (2007) FCR 369, where the work consisted primarily of a photograph and a few short lines of explanatory text: for the latter case, see discussion in the context of drawings at 2.14. In *Elwood* at [12] Gordon J provided a short précis of a number of other cases considering what constitutes a drawing, and said that 'the important principle in deciding whether the work is a "drawing" is whether the work at issue can be said to have a visual rather than "semiotic" function': see also *Elwood Clothing Pty Ltd v Cotton On Clothing Pty Ltd* [2008] FCAFC 197 (*Elwood* FCAFC), where this principle was confirmed on appeal. By implication, then, a literary work is one with a semiotic function; that is, with the purpose of conveying meaning rather than artistic impression or purely visual enjoyment. The special case of computer programs, included in the category of literary works by virtue of s 10 of the Act, is considered in Chapter 18 Digitalisation.

Dramatic works

2.11 The Act does not exhaustively define dramatic works but includes dumb shows (mime) and choreographic shows as well as scripts and screenplays by virtue of s 10. Such shows may be expressed as literary works (eg, in writing by way of an adapted descriptive language), but may also have sufficient material form by being recorded, for instance on film or video: see s 22(1) and (10). Thus, if an otherwise unrecorded, maybe improvised choreographic or dumb show is recorded on film, copyright will subsist in it. The copyright owner will be entitled to restrain others from reproducing the dramatic work either by replicating a substantial part of the choreography in their own performance or by making copies of the recording of the show. However, the copyright in the underlying dramatic work (novel, scenario, script, screenplay) subsists independently from the copyright in a film, which subsists under Pt IV: see s 10, which provides that a dramatic work includes a scenario and script for a film 'but does not include a cinematograph film as distinct from the scenario or script for a cinematograph film'. In the UK decision of *Norowzian v Arks Ltd (No 2)* [2000] FSR 363, an advertisement conceived of as a dramatic series of events, as distinct from the written script, the screenplay or the film, was considered to be a dramatic work fixed in material form; Merkel J in *Telstra Corporation Ltd v Royal & Sun Alliance Insurance Australia Ltd* (2003) 57 IPR 453; [2003] FCA 786 had difficulty with this notion.

What, then, is a dramatic work? Generally speaking, scenarios, plays, scripts, screenplays and so on are literary as well as dramatic works; but the concept or elements of an outdoor show or fireworks spectacle are not protected as dramatic works: see, for example, *Nine Network Australia Pty Ltd v Australian Broadcasting Corporation* (1999) 48 IPR 333; [1999] FCA 1864. What distinguishes a dramatic work is that it is intended to be performed, as was stated in *Green v Broadcasting Corporation of New Zealand* [1989] 2 All ER 1056. That case stands for the additional proposition that a dramatic work must not only be intended but also capable of being performed. Disparate elements without sufficient unity do not amount to a dramatic work. Hughie Green was the longstanding host of the British television talent quest, *Opportunity Knocks*. The salient features of that show (such as the use of a 'clapometer' and of catchphrases to address the audience and competitors) were replicated by New Zealand television without reference to Green. The Privy Council confirmed the decision of the New Zealand court that the standard elements alone did not constitute a dramatic work. By themselves, their performance was meaningless, since the greater part of the show, which gave meaning to the different stock elements, consisted of audience participation, varying from program to program.

So a collection of descriptive elements together constituting what is known as a 'format' — for example, for a TV show — is not a dramatic work, because each element is not able to be performed, and the underlying key twist or concept is only an idea and therefore not amenable to copyright. However, the courts in Australia have shown themselves somewhat unconcerned with the proper identification and classification of the works involved in format cases, tending to focus on a comparative analysis of the shows involved: see, for instance, *Nine Films & Television Pty Ltd v Ninox Television Ltd* (2005) 67 IPR 46; [2005] FCA 1404; and *Seven Network (Operations) Ltd v Endemol Australia Pty Ltd* (2015) 114 IPR 287; [2015] FCA 800.

Musical works

2.12 The term 'musical work' is not defined in any way in the current Act. Earlier legislation, the Copyright Act 1905 (Cth), referred to 'any combination of melody, and harmony, or either of them': s 4. But that is arguably too restrictive for many combinations of sounds that are today commonly regarded as being music, such as minimalist, aleatory or natural music. As with other categories of works, artistic or creative merit is not required, yet the word 'musical' implies that there is more than a mere recording of sound. That is what the ordinary or dictionary meaning of the word 'musical' suggests. Some deliberate effort to combine sounds into 'music' is required. Thus, an original arrangement or combination of recorded natural sounds may well amount to a musical work for the purposes of the Act, as well as being a sound recording under Pt IV. It does not matter that it cannot be written as a musical score.

The UK case of *Sawkins v Hyperion Records Ltd* [2005] EWCA Civ 565 explored musical works copyright in the context of a new performance edition of some scores by the composer de Lalande. The joint judgment of the Court of Appeal stated at [51]–[53]:

> [51] Patten J pointed out (at [54]) that the 1988 Act did not define what is meant by 'music'. As he observed, however, that is what this case is really about. '... the real issue which divides the parties is whether a musical work includes items such as the figuring of the bass, ornamentation and performance directions or is really limited for copyright purposes to the notes on the score, so that in the case of an existing work nothing less than significant rearrangement of, or significant additions to, the melody will create a new copyright in the edition of a musical work.'
>
> [52] I agree. I am also with the judge in rejecting Hyperion's contention that Dr Sawkins did not acquire any copyright by virtue of the considerable effort, skill and time spent by him on the task of creating the performing editions of the three works in question. To argue, as Hyperion does, that the work of Dr Sawkins is not 'the creation of new music' begs the question of what is 'music' and what amounts to 'creation' of music.
>
> [53] In the absence of a special statutory definition of music, ordinary usage assists: as indicated in the dictionaries, the essence of music is combining sounds for listening to. Music is not the same as mere noise. The sound of music is intended to produce effects of some kind on the listener's emotions and intellect. The sounds may be produced by an organised performance on instruments played from a musical score, though that is not essential for the existence of the music or of copyright in it. Music must be distinguished from the fact and form of its fixation as a record of a musical composition. The score is the traditional and convenient form of fixation of the music and conforms to the requirement that a copyright work must be recorded in some material form. But the fixation in the written score or on a record is not in itself the music in which copyright subsists. There is no reason why, for example, a recording of a person's spontaneous singing, whistling or humming or of improvisations of sounds by a group of people with or without musical instruments should not be regarded as 'music' for copyright purposes.

Note that in common parlance, 'music' may refer to a combination of musical score and lyrics or words, such as in a song or an opera, but in copyright terms the latter consist of two different works: a musical work (the score) and a literary (or dramatic) work (the lyrics or libretto). Also important is to identify precisely what the musical work is, which may require making a choice between versions. A 'hook' or most memorable portion of a work does not itself constitute a work but may be considered a 'substantial part' for infringement purposes: see *Larrikin Music Publishing Pty Ltd v EMI Song Australia Pty Ltd* [2010] FCA 29 (Jacobson J).

Artistic works

2.13 The term 'artistic work' is defined in the Act by reference to an exhaustive list of included works. In a disputed case, the relevant task is not to construe the term 'artistic work' but rather the meaning of one of the listed subcategories (painting, sculpture, drawing, etc). A careful reading of the definition in s 10 discloses two broad categories of artistic works: first, works of artistic craftsmanship that require artistic quality and, second, other artistic works that do not require artistic quality for copyright to subsist.

The latter category covers a further exhaustive list (paras (a) and (b)) of different forms of artistic expression, both two- and three-dimensional. No artistic merit or aspiration need be established to attract copyright for these types of works, and they cover material going from the mundane (technical engineering drawings, architectural plans) to the 'truly' artistic (paintings or artistic sculptures). With the exception of 'painting', the enumerated terms are further defined in s 10, although not exhaustively, but with the intention of broadening their common scope. On the whole, the courts have put this intention into effect by construing the meaning of the various terms liberally and permissively.

One illustration of this is afforded by the word 'building'. Section 10 defines the term as including a structure of any kind. In *Half Court Tennis Pty Ltd v Seymour* (1980) 53 FLR 240, a half court tennis court was said to be a building, and in *Darwin Fibreglass Pty Ltd v Kruhse Enterprises Pty Ltd* (1998) 8 NTLR 46, although without citing authority, a garden consisting of a layout including steps, walls, ponds and other structures in stone was said to have been held capable of protection as 'a structure'. In that same case, a fibreglass swimming pool was held to be a building, although the plug and mould used to manufacture it were not. Of course, the plans for a building, as well as the building itself, are protected (a 'plan' being a 'drawing' by virtue of s 10, along with diagrams, maps and charts). It is quite clear that artistic quality, merit or appeal is not the intention behind the making of these types of works.

Drawings, paintings and other works not requiring artistic quality

2.14 As stated above, the issue of what constitutes a drawing was canvassed in two cases: *Elwood* (discussed in the context of literary works above at 2.10), and *Woodtree*, where the work consisted primarily of a photograph and a few short lines of explanatory text. In *Elwood* Gordon J at [12] set out a useful précis of a number of other cases considering what constitutes a drawing as well as two principles:

> (1) whether a work will be recognized as an artistic work such as a drawing is highly fact-specific, such that no bright-line rule can be drawn; and (2) the important principle in deciding whether the work is a 'drawing' is whether the work at issue can be said to have a visual rather than 'semiotic' function.

Heerey J in *Woodtree* said that 'the essence of a drawing remains the concept of a representation of some object by a pictorial line': at [27]. This was held to be too limiting in *Elwood*, as the arrangement of lettering there considered was not a pictorial depiction but was still found to be an artistic work. The essential point was that it had visual rather than semiotic function. Rather than convey meaning or information it presented an 'an aesthetically pleasing visual "look and feel" in the same way that any picture or drawing does': *Elwood* at [16]. The bits and pieces of text ('raging bull'; 'durable by design'; 'prepared for denim') did not 'convey a coherent message as distinct from presenting a pictorial effect': at [16].

However, in *Seafolly Pty Ltd v Fewstone Pty Ltd* (2014) 106 IPR 85; [2014] FCA 321, the court simply refers to the design of the garments concerned as 'the artworks' without seemingly being concerned about the proper categorisation of the works concerned. In *The Dempsey Group Pty Ltd v Spotlight Pty Ltd* [2018] FCA 2016, the court refers to a number of artistic works (these being described as 'surface designs' of quilt covers and pillow sets) without identifying exactly what sort of work they are.

The question of copyright in logos was dealt with in *Cortis Exhaust Systems* (see above at 2.9), and was also at issue in a recent Canadian case: *Euro-Excellence Inc v Kraft Canada Inc* [2007] 3 SCR 20. This case concerned artistic work copyright in a brand or mark applied to chocolate bars. In Australia, unlike in Canada, copyright for such items associated with products or packaging cannot be relied upon to deny the right to parallel import legitimate products: see Chapter 5 Copyright: Other Rights and Exceptions. Concurrent copyright and trade mark protection was available for the logos on the chocolate bar wrapper in Canada, the logos constituting artistic works.

However, these cases must be read in their particular context, which was the artistic depiction of letters or slogans, and therefore centred on the dividing line between literary and artistic works. In different circumstances, the focus has been on the method or form of expression or production of the works rather than on function. In *Wham-O Manufacturing Co v Lincoln Industries Ltd* [1984] 1 NZLR 641, the court accepted that under the equivalent New Zealand provisions the wooden model produced for the manufacture of dies and moulds for the casting of frisbees was a sculpture and the moulds used to manufacture them were engravings (they contained patterned linear elevations). The fact that the function of the model was neither visual nor aesthetic but purely a step in a manufacturing process was not an issue. However, Australian judges have been marginally less sanguine than the New Zealand court in relation to what constitutes sculptures and engravings. Pincus J, in *Greenfield Products Pty Ltd v Rover-Scott Bonnar Ltd* (1990) 17 IPR 417 at 427, did not accept that a mower clutch assembly was a sculpture or engraving, preferring the more commonly accepted meaning of those words. This is not to say that courts in Australia will not be flexible in their interpretation: thus in *Douglas v Racing Victoria Ltd* [2019] FCCA 49 a medal was held to be a sculpture (in line with authority: see at [113]). The outcome might be different if there are underlying drawings in evidence, as was the case in *Dodson Motorsport Ltd v Logiical Performance Ltd* [2019] NZHC 918 where copyright vested in the drawings of a racing clutch assembly for Nissan sports cars, allowing the copyright owner to argue that a similar clutch assembly produced by a rival company infringed the plaintiff's reproduction right. In *Swarbrick v Burge* (2004) 138 FCR 353, a plug used in the manufacture of yachts was considered to be a sculpture, in line with *Wham-O*. Further, the Full Court of the Federal Court agreed with the decision of the trial judge that the categories of sculpture and work of artistic craftsmanship were not mutually exclusive — the plug for the yacht in this case could be both: see *Burge v Swarbrick* (2005) 149 FCR 193; 68 IPR 114; [2005] FCAFC 257 at [51]. The High Court considered only the question of what constitutes a work of artistic craftsmanship: see *Burge v Swarbrick* (2007) 232 CLR 336, discussed below at 2.15, and Chapter 6 Registered Designs.

That an artistic work may be identified by reference to the technique used to produce it does not mean that techniques or styles used in such a work are protected by copyright as such. Some artists might have a striking or innovative style or technique, but they will not be able to monopolise it by way of copyright: see *Cummins v Vella* [2002] FCAFC 218, overturning the trial decision. However, although copyright only vests in an expression in a particular visual form, in *Elwood* FCAFC the Full Court accepted that it lay in something more nebulous, that being the 'look and feel' of a work: 'the layout and the elements referred to by her Honour [Gordon J] that gave rise to the "look and feel" and resulted in the creation of an artistic work were matters of expression, not merely matters of idea or concept. The look and feel arose from the selection, arrangement and style of the elements regarded as a whole': at [76]; this look and feel approach was followed in *Seafolly* and in *Spotlight*. Three-dimensional objects or constructions may be artistic works in their own right (eg, as a building, sculpture or engraving) but may also benefit from the copyright arising in the two-dimensional underlying works (such as architectural plans, concept drawings or technical drawings). In *Plix Products v Frank M Winstone (Merchants) Ltd* [1986] FSR 608; (1985) 3 IPR 390, drawings for moulded containers designed to carry kiwifruit attracted copyright, although shape and dimension were wholly determined by technical requirements relating to the shape and size of the fruit they were to carry. The actual containers constituted three-dimensional reproductions of the drawings: see also *Vawdrey Australia Pty Ltd v Krueger Transport Equipment Pty Ltd* [2009] FCAFC 156 relating to the appearance of a trailer side assembly. The extent to which copyright in artistic works applies to functional articles has been criticised, as copyright is sometimes seen as inappropriate in areas better reserved for designs registration and patents. As will be seen below, the law generally requires reliance on designs registration to prevent the copying of manufactured objects: see the copyright–designs overlap provisions (ss 73–77); such provisions do not exist in New Zealand law, hence the outcome in *Dodson Motorsport* (above). The effect of the Australian provisions is that neither copyright in underlying two-dimensional work nor copyright possibly subsisting in an item itself can be relied upon to bring an action against product imitators in most cases, except where copyright in a work of artistic craftsmanship can be established. Fashion is an interesting example of the congruence of copyright and manufacturing: see, for example, *Muscat v Le* [2003] FCA 1540; (2003) 60 IPR 276 and further below.

Works of artistic craftsmanship

2.15 Works of artistic craftsmanship must be 'of artistic quality': see s 10. Thus, in *Cuisenaire v Reed* [1963] VR 719, the purely functional Cuisenaire set of variously coloured tubes used for the purpose of learning calculus, having no artistic merit, was not a work of artistic craftsmanship. However, the work need not be so artistic as to amount to a work of fine art; evidence of the creator's artistic intention may suffice. Traditionally, the category 'works of artistic craftsmanship' was seen as directed at products of the arts and crafts movement (without being limited to 'handicraft'); that is, functional articles made by the application of genuine craft skills and with the intention of creating an aesthetically pleasing effect. To qualify as a work of artistic craftsmanship, it was thought that the artistic input and the craft skill had to emanate from the same person: see, for example, McKeough and Stewart, *Intellectual Property in Australia*, 2nd ed, LexisNexis, 1997, p 153: 'Furthermore, the craft aspect of the work must have been supplied by the same person who provided the artistic input.' Thus, in *Burke & Margot Burke Ltd v Spicers Dress Design* [1936] Ch 400, a piece of clothing designed by one person but stitched together by another did not amount to a work of artistic craftsmanship.

In *Coogi Australia Pty Ltd v Hysport International Pty Ltd* (1998) 86 FCR 154; 41 IPR 593, however, the court held that a mass-produced item (a unique bolt of thickly textured multi-coloured fabric) can still be a work of artistic craftsmanship, irrespective of lack of manual craft skill. The requisite skill was present, according to Drummond J at FCR 169:

> There is no necessary difference between a skilled person who makes an article with hand-held tools and a skilled person who uses those skills to set up and operate a machine which produces an article. Such an article can still be a work of craftsmanship even though the creator has used a highly sophisticated computer-controlled machine to produce it, if nevertheless it is a manifestation of the creator's skill with computer-controlled machinery, knowledge of materials and pride in workmanship.

As to the question of whether the skill and artistic quality must emanate from the same person, Drummond J stated at FCR 168:

> Once it is accepted, as I think it should be, that 'works of artistic craftsmanship' are not confined to hand-made objects, there is no reason why it should be essential for such a work to be the product of the efforts of a single person, ie, of an artist-craftsman. It is enough that it satisfies the two criteria of craftsmanship and aesthetic quality.

Certainly *Coogi* seems to represent a departure from some commonly held preconceptions concerning works of artistic craftsmanship. However, Drummond J's approach was adopted in *Sheldon v Metrokane Inc* (2004) 135 FCR 34; 61 IPR 1 and also in *Swarbrick v Burge*. In *Burge v Swarbrick* (2007) 232 CLR 336; 72 IPR 235, an appeal from the Full Court of the Federal Court was allowed. The requirement of 'artistic quality' was at issue. Because of the potential to avoid the detrimental effects of the copyright/designs overlap defence, copyright owners often seek to have works recognised as 'works of artistic craftsmanship' by the court. Here, the question was whether the plug for a yacht, produced as part of the prototyping/manufacturing process, could be classed as a work of artistic craftsmanship. The High Court in joint reasons (Gleeson CJ, Gummow, Kirby, Heydon and Crennan JJ) held that this depended on the degree of artistic quality of the work. In the case before it, there was not sufficient quality, and the particular shape had been inspired by naval engineering rather than aesthetic requirements. Courts will thus have to make the judgment as to whether there is sufficient artistic intent and quality, aided by expert evidence in any given case. Generally speaking, the courts have sought to avoid being called upon to make such judgments, due to their subjective nature.

Adaptations of works

2.16 Adaptations of literary, dramatic, musical or artistic works themselves attract copyright. The owner of copyright in a work has the exclusive right to make an adaptation of the work. 'Adaptation' is exhaustively defined in s 10. To attract copyright in its own right, the adaptation must have the requisite degree of originality about it. If the author of the adaptation differs from the author of the work adapted, the term of copyright protection of the adaptation may vary from that of the work adapted.

The extent of the exclusive right to make an adaptation is considered in Chapter 5 Copyright: Other Rights and Exceptions. As to the question of whether an infringing adaptation (or reproduction) will attract copyright in its own right, see *A-One Accessory Import Pty Ltd v Off Road Imports Pty Ltd* (1996) 65 FCR 478; 34 IPR 306.

A primary connection with Australia

2.17 By virtue of s 32, a work must have a relevant connection with Australia for copyright to subsist in this jurisdiction. The section makes a distinction between published and unpublished works. An unpublished work attracts copyright in Australia (other than by operation of the Berne Convention: see 2.18) if it is made by an Australian citizen or resident. A published work will attract copyright in Australia if it was first published here or if the author was an Australian citizen or permanent resident when it was first published here. The notion of 'publication' is significant and is further defined in s 29. Only if reproductions of the whole work have been supplied to the public is there relevant publication; a public performance or exposition of a work does not amount to publication for the purpose of copyright subsistence. Section 29(5) also provides that if publication has occurred in a different jurisdiction within 30 days prior to Australian publication, the latter is still deemed to be a first publication within Australia.

Extension of copyright by virtue of international agreements

2.18 Under the regulation-making power conferred by s 184 of the Copyright Act 1968 (Cth), the provisions of the Act have been extended to apply to works whose primary connection (through publication, citizenship or residence, situation or incorporation) is with other states party to the Berne Convention for the Protection of Literary and Artistic Works (see, eg, *TS Production LLC v Drew Pictures Pty Ltd* [2008] FCA 1110; (2008) 77 IPR 587), member states of the WTO and states party to the Universal Copyright Convention that are not party to the Berne Convention nor members of the WTO: see Copyright (International Protection) Regulations 1969 (Cth) s 4; Sch 1. These provisions implement Australia's international treaty obligations. A foreign person to whom the regulations extend copyright protection will be entitled to relief in the same manner and to the same extent as if the primary connection were with Australia (the principles of national treatment and non-discrimination apply). Thus, if a certain work or subject matter is protected by copyright abroad but not in Australia (eg, because of lack of originality or because the term has expired under Australian but not foreign law), no relief is available here. The protection thus granted is reciprocal; that is, the Australian copyright owner will be entitled to relief under the copyright law of relevant treaty countries on the same basis.

Originality of Works

Only original works attract copyright

2.19 Copyright will subsist only in an original work: see s 32(1); *IceTV Pty Ltd v Nine Network Australia Pty Ltd* (2009) 239 CLR 458; 80 IPR 451;*Telstra Corporation Ltd* *v Phone Directories Co Pty Ltd* (2010) 94 FCR 142; 90 IPR 1; [2010] FCAFC 149 (*Telstra v Phone Directories*); *JR Consulting & Drafting Pty Ltd v Cummings* (2016) 116 IPR 440; [2016] FCAFC 20. What is required is originality of expression, not originality of ideas. 'Originality of expression' traditionally meant little more than that the form in which the work is expressed should originate with the author. In the leading case of *University of London Press Ltd v University Tutorial Press Ltd* [1916] 2 Ch 601 at 608–9, Peterson J expressed this as follows:

> The word 'original' does not in this connection mean that the work must be the expression of original or inventive thought. Copyright Acts are not concerned with the originality of ideas, but with the expression of thought ... The originality which is required relates to the expression of the thought. But the Act does not require that the expression must be in an original or novel form, but that the work must not be copied from another work — that it should originate from the author.

Dixon J in *Victoria Park Racing and Recreation Grounds Co Ltd v Taylor* (1937) 58 CLR 479 at 511 said:

> ... some original result must be produced. This does not mean that new or inventive ideas must be contributed. The work need show no literary or other skill or judgment. But it must originate with the author and be more than a copy of other material.

In *Elwood* at [19], the court put it as follows:

> While 'originality' for the purposes of s 32 of the Act does not require any particular level of novelty or creativity, it is still necessary to show that there has been the application of some minimum level of skill and effort to the making of the form in which the particular work is expressed: *Sands & McDougall Pty Ltd v Robinson* (1917) 23 CLR 49; *Ladbroke (Football) Ltd v William Hill (Football) Ltd* [1964] 1 All ER 465; *Kalamazoo (Aust) Pty Ltd v Compact Business Systems Pty Ltd* (1985) 5 IPR 213; *Desktop Marketing Systems Pty Ltd v Telstra Corporation Ltd* (2002) 119 FCR 491.

In *JR Consulting* the Full Court put it as follows: '[The] contemporary question is simply this: Has the author deployed personal independent skill, labour, intellectual effort, judgment and discrimination in the production of the particular expression of the work?': at [264]. The extent of skill, judgment and effort required cannot readily be defined, but the threshold is clearly low: see, for instance, the leading case of *Football League Ltd v Littlewoods Pools Ltd* [1959] Ch 637 at 651, where football league tables of fixtures were held to be original works. *Some* skill and effort on the part of the identified author is required but not too much is to be made of that requirement; the High Court in *IceTV* at [285] simply said that some 'independent intellectual effort' must have gone into the expression of the work in a particular material form.

In every case it must depend largely on the particular facts, and must in each case be very much a question of degree. Thus, in *Sullivan* there was no copyright in slogans created by the applicant without the requisite degree of judgment, effort or skill. However, in *Australian Chinese Newspapers Pty Ltd v Melbourne Chinese Press Ltd* [2003] FCA 878; (2003) 58 IPR 1, a masthead logo of a Chinese language newspaper did amount to an original artistic work. In *Elwood*, the evidence established that the plaintiff had 'expended several weeks and significant effort in creating the Design Drawings' (at [20]), and the works were thus clearly original. However, Gordon J went on to specify the 'scope of that which is protected': at [22]. This was not the underlying concept or idea 'of a central logo surrounded by a V-shaped pattern of arched text, with the distinctive feature of numbers at the shoulder level': at [23]. Instead, it was 'only a particular form of expression of the "V-shaped pattern of arched text around a central logo" idea and a particular swing tag design': at [25]. In the result, what is protected by exclusive rights is not the underlying concept or idea (as defined by the court) but the original form of expression of that idea. The requirement of originality is very closely intertwined with the notion of authorship, which the High Court in *IceTV* emphasised lies at the heart of copyright — the latter not constituting a reward for effort and investment in the generation of content, but a way of recognising the rights of an *identified* author whose unique mental activity has resulted in a work expressed in a particular form. The court in *Fairfax Media v Reed* at [30] put it as follows:

> For copyright to subsist in a work, one or more authors must have expended sufficient effort of a literary nature directed at the form of expression of the work (*IceTV* at [42] and [99]). The form of expression of the work must be the result of particular mental effort or exertion by the author/s and cannot be essentially dictated by the nature of the information.

Collections, composite works and compilations

2.20 Section 10 expands the meaning of 'literary work' to include tabulated figures, symbols or words ('tables', a word not further defined in the Act) and 'compilations', either original combinations of pre-existing literary works or listings of information such as catalogues. There is some potential overlap with artistic works copyright, which includes copyright in drawings. That term is further defined in the Act as including 'a diagram, map, chart or plan'. *Lumen Australia Pty Ltd v Frontline Australasia Pty Ltd* [2018] FCA 1807 concerned copyright in 'circuit markings', being 'the arrangement of reference designators (text and numerals) on [a] printed circuit board': at [191]. The court held that the circuit markings amounted both to a literary work as an original compilation of figures, and an artistic work as a diagram, chart or plan: at [206]. The court considered them original, seemingly because the selection and placement of the reference designators in creating the circuit markings adopted an 'approach [...] not common or widely used in the industry': at [205]. Traditionally, sufficient labour, skill or judgment must have been brought to bear (see *Football League Ltd v Littlewoods Pools Ltd* [1959] Ch 637 at 651) or, to put it in post-*IceTV* terms, that some independent intellectual effort has been expended in making the compilation. For example, in *Autocaps (Aust) Pty Ltd v Pro-Kit Pty Ltd* (1999) 46 IPR 339; [1999] FCA 1315, copyright clearly subsisted in a trade catalogue that was more than a simple listing, consisting as it did of a selection of part numbers (of a range of fuel caps) and the selection of vehicles to which those part numbers related. *A-One Accessory Imports Pty Ltd v Off-Road Imports Pty Ltd* (1996) 65 FCR 478; 34 IPR 306 also related to copyright in a spare parts catalogue. Drummond J at FCR 489 read *Ladbroke (Football) Ltd v William Hill (Football) Ltd* [1964] 1 WLR 273, where the House of Lords unanimously upheld a claim for copyright in betting coupons listing football matches and odds as standing for the proposition that:

> ... originality sufficient to attract copyright in a compilation can be found entirely in the work of selecting the material to be included in the compilation, as opposed to the work of reducing those selections to written form.

However, Drummond J also pointed out that 'skill, judgment or labour expended in the process of copying a particular work or portion of a particular work, as distinct from selecting material to be copied into a compilation, cannot confer originality': at [35].

In *Olympic Amusements Pty Ltd v Milwell Pty Ltd* (1998) 81 FCR 403; 40 IPR 180, the plaintiff had developed, with the help of consultants in mathematical statistics, 'prize scales' for poker machines. The return for players on the machines was required by law to be no lower than 85 per cent; for commercial reasons, it was not to be much higher than that if the operator of the machine was to make a reasonable return. The court held that the resulting table was an original literary work, being a table or compilation expressed in words, figures or symbols. The table consisted of a vertical listing of the different winning hands, from a royal flush downwards, with, in neighbouring columns, the amount of the prize, each column representing a different initial wager. The table resulted from complex mathematical and statistical computations and calculations, requiring considerable expertise. The presentation of the information once computed was straightforward. Wilcox J also relied extensively on *Ladbroke*, citing Lord Devlin's contention that if the object of the selection work is to create a document, then no artificial distinction can be drawn between the preparation and selection and the expression stage. He also quoted Lord Hodgson's view that it will have to be determined case by case whether the skill and effort in selection can be taken into account to determine whether an original work has been brought into existence.

In *Desktop Marketing Systems v Telstra Corporation Ltd* (2002) 119 FCR 491; 55 IPR 1, the Full Federal Court similarly held that so-called industrious collection suffices to satisfy the originality requirement. White pages of a telephone directory therefore attracted copyright. If sufficient effort could be established in the collection of material, it was thus no bar to copyright subsisting that the material was presented in an obvious manner. The US standard, as expressed in *Feist Publications Inc v Rural Telephone Service Co* 499 US 340 (1991), requiring some creativity in the making of the work, did not apply in Australia. *Desktop Marketing* had obvious implications for the protection of computerised databases, which readily attract the protection of copyright in Australia, in contrast with other jurisdictions such as the USA and the European Union. The latter has addressed the lack of copyright protection by the introduction of a sui generis non-original database extraction right: see Chapter 18 Digitisation. Because originality in the EU is interpreted as requiring a degree of creativity in expression, copyright does not extend to unoriginal databases. However, considerable investment in the compilation of principally electronic databases is therefore left vulnerable to piracy. This apparent lacuna is addressed by the sui generis database extraction right: see Directive 96/9/EC of the European Parliament and of the Council of 11 March 1996 on the legal protection of databases, and implementation laws in the various member states; for example, 'France Intellectual Property Code, Legislative Part, PART I, Literary and Artistic Property, BOOK III, General Provisions relative to copyrights, to neighbouring rights and to the rights of database producers TITLE IV, Rights of Database Producers'. Sui generis database rights have not attracted international consensus, and no multilateral instrument relating to such rights has, to date, been signed.

The copyright that subsists in a compilation — for instance, an anthology of poetry — is distinct from the copyright in the underlying parts or components (the individual poems chosen). Therefore, copyright extends only to the choice and manner of compiling the component parts; copying individual items would not normally infringe compilation copyright, but if a number of selected works are reproduced in the same sequence, there may be reproduction of a substantial part of the anthology. However, there is a risk that in this way the idea underlying the arrangement rather than the detailed execution of the arrangement is monopolised: see, for example, *Skybase Nominees Pty Ltd v Fortuity Pty Ltd* (1996) 36 IPR 529 ('Weight Watchers' programs were original compilations). The work must amount to more than the underlying idea of combining certain pre-existing material; for instance, pre-existing accounting forms: see *Kalamazoo (Australia) Pty Ltd v Compact Business Systems Pty Ltd* (1985) 84 FLR 101; 5 IPR 213. Nonetheless, the compilation must be taken as a whole, and it is not permissible to deny copyright for lack of originality in each component part.

It is important to see the limitations of copyright protection where originality is low. It lies not in the content but only in the compilation as such. What attracts copyright is the skill and effort in selecting and compiling the material in a particular form, not generating the concept behind it or the ideas, data or information contained within. In *Nine Network Australia Pty Ltd v IceTV Pty Ltd* (2008) 168 FCR 14; 76 IPR 31, the difficulties in tackling the distinction between form and content came to the fore. It is arguable that the decision on appeal strayed rather far into protecting raw data rather than the form of compilation, and the High Court finally overturned the old approach in its decision on appeal in *IceTV*. The court held that there must be evidence of some human intellectual or mental activity on the part of an identifiable author for copyright to vest. Thus, a weekly TV guide that replicated the program information from various TV stations in a predictable format was not necessarily sufficiently original (the court was actually considering infringement, but this conclusion could be inferred from its reasons). In *Telstra v Phone Directories*, the new approach was adopted by the court to deny copyright to computer-generated telephone directories, reversing the approach taken in *Desktop Marketing*. Thus, the 'industrious collection' approach traditionally adopted in common law countries has now apparently been abandoned in Australia, although it remains to be seen what will amount to sufficient evidence of intellectual activity. Lord Devlin's contention in *Ladbroke* (see above) must now be considered to be in doubt. Industrious collection of information will not suffice if there is no element of human creativity in its expression in a particular form (eg, telephone data collected and then presented in an alphabetical listing). See also Chapter 3 Copyright: Ownership and Exploitation and Chapter 4 Copyright Infringement in General.

The question of originality may also arise where a work is so simple that there is little or no choice open to the creator in the form of expression of a certain idea or concept. In *Andrew Cash & Co Investments Pty Ltd v John Porter* (1996) 36 IPR 309 (per Foster J), an interim decision, the applicant, a pawn broker, devised a pledge ticket, a document subject to certain statutory requirements and needing to be produced in quadruplicate. In determining whether copyright subsisted in the applicant's pledge ticket as a compilation, Foster J pointed out (at 312) that the applicant had 'discarded many such attempts [at producing a proper pledge ticket] and he finally produced a ticket which he regarded as one that answered the needs of his business, the needs of his customers and the requirements of the law.' Although the contents requirement of the ticket was well known, even determined by law, there were still different ways in which the ticket could be structured. The result of the exercise of the applicant's choice, even if limited, still amounted to an original work: see also *Ballieu and Poggioli v Australian Electoral Commission* (1996) 63 FCR 210; 33 IPR 494 (originality of informational parts of the Commonwealth's brochure concerning postal votes).

Originality of evolving and infringing works

2.21 The originality issue may also arise if a work evolves over time. The copyright term of works is generally limited to the life of the author plus 70 years; it is not a perpetual right. However, this limitation could be defeated by a different author making small changes to, say, a pre-existing drawing and claiming that the result is an original work for which a new copyright arises. This question was at issue in *Interlego AG v Tyco Industries Inc* [1989] AC 217 at 221ff. For complex reasons, copyright no longer subsisted in certain drawings of Lego blocks made before 1973. The question was whether some slight technical modifications made to the drawings for the blocks after 1973 and also showing dimensional specifications resulted in the making of an original work. The court held (at AC 262–3) that:

> ... skill, labour or judgment merely in the process of copying cannot confer originality. There must in addition be some element of material alteration or embellishment which suffices to make the totality of the work an original work. Of course, even a relatively small alteration or addition quantitatively may, if material, suffice to convert that which is substantially copied from an earlier work into an original work. Whether it does so or not is a question of degree having regard to the quality rather than the quantity of the addition.

On the facts, the modifications were not sufficient to confer originality upon the new drawings. In *Pokemon Company International, Inc v Redbubble Ltd* (2017) 129 IPR 1; [2017] FCA 1541, which related to infringement of the Pokemon Pikachu character, the court said at [34]:

> The requirement that the Pikachu work be an original artistic work within the meaning of s 32(1) of the Copyright Act will not be satisfied by a mere mechanical reproduction or a slavish copy of an earlier copyright work. The revision of an earlier original work, however, will attract independent copyright protection provided that the latter work has the requisite degree of originality over and above the earlier work. What is required to establish originality is that the subsequent work had some independent intellectual effort, although the work may have no literary merit, novelty or inventiveness: see *IceTV Pty Ltd v Nine Network Australia Pty Ltd* (2009) 239 CLR 458, 474, [33]; *Interlego v Croner Trading* (1992) 111 ALR 577, 608–609.

In *Husqvarna Forest & Garden Ltd v Bridon New Zealand Ltd* [1997] 3 NZLR 215; (1997) 38 IPR 513, the drawings of a chainsaw part (the 'cutter') were based on previous experimental drawings, but sufficient modifications had been made for them to amount to an original work. The changes that appeared were, apart from being visually obvious to a layperson, highly significant to the persons to whom the drawings and dimensions were addressed and who would be capable of interpreting them. Even changes that consist of additional lettering and dimensions could thus result in a sufficiently original work. In *A-One Accessory Imports*, the infringing parts catalogues were sufficiently original to attract copyright in their own right. Drummond J pointed out that a relatively small alteration or addition may quantitatively suffice to convert what was copied from an earlier work into a new and original work and 'whether it does or does not is a question of degree having regard to the quality, rather than the quantity of the addition': at FCR 488.

The question also arises when considering whether an adaptation is itself an original work. In *Redwood Music Ltd v Chappell & Co Ltd* [1982] RPC 109, copyright subsisted in an original but infringing arrangement of a musical work. In *Digga Australia Pty Ltd v Norm Engineering Pty Ltd* (2008) 166 FCR 268; 75 IPR 251, the same issue arose in the context of technical drawings produced in the context of manufacturing, here of a bobcat bucket. If drawings are copies, perhaps with minor variations, or drawings underlying a previous or outdated design, it could be that they lack originality, in that not sufficient skill, effort and judgment has been applied to their origination. They are more copies than original works. In *Digga*, the Full Court (per Lindgren J) held that the trial judge was entitled to find that the drawings in which copyright was found to subsist were the result 'of a process of origination that continued down to [the alleged date of creation of the drawings]': at [63]. In other words, previous versions were to be considered as part of a process of creating the final work. Alternatively, the later drawings could be seen as evidence of what the earlier drawings, about which there was evidence but which were not themselves produced, looked like. The question of whether the drawings were not original because they only reproduced a three-dimensional object (the bucket itself) was not addressed by Lindgren J. Whether the bucket itself constituted an artistic work was not an issue in the case. The trial court said (*Norm Engineering v Digga Australia* [2007] FCA 761 at [120]):

> When the plans in suit have a genetic footprint in earlier drawings to which the author has had regard, the degree of work, labour, skill, effort and judgment deployed in bringing the plans in suit into existence, must exhibit, as the expression of that effort, visually identifiable changes that make it plain that the drawing is a new artistic work and not simply a copy of the earlier drawings: *Interlego AG v Croner Trading Pty Ltd* (1992) 39 FCR 348; 25 IPR 65.

Note that where there is difficulty in proving originality because works are derived from, or are a version of, a pre-existing work, there may also be difficulty in proving ownership of copyright: see, for example, *TS & B Retail Systems Pty Ltd v 3Fold Resources Pty Ltd (No 3)* (2007) 158 FCR 444; 72 IPR 492.

On a final note, the scope of an author's copyright in a work may be circumscribed by that person's particular original contribution to it. For instance, where the court in *Sawkins* (see also 2.12) recognised Sawkins's copyright in the particular performing edition of de Lalande's scores, that copyright does not extend to the themes or melodies themselves that originated with de Lalande.

Subject Matter Other Than Works

Part IV of the Copyright Act 1968 (Cth)

2.22 Subject matter other than works (sometimes referred to as 'neighbouring rights') is covered in Pt IV of the Copyright Act 1968 (Cth). The various forms of subject matter are more closely circumscribed by reference to the technological or practical medium by which underlying material is exploited. They normally derive from or incorporate works (whether or not those works are (still) protected by copyright); for instance, a film is usually based on (and thus reproduces) various literary works: a novel, script, scenario or screenplay; a sound recording on a musical work: the score; and a literary work: the lyrics, etc. Entitlement to statutory rights in Pt IV subject matter results from the making of the subject matter rather than from an act of authorship. Sections 89–92 prescribe the categories of subject matter in which copyright subsists: films, sound recordings, broadcasts and published editions of works; ss 85–88 the nature of the rights that subsist in subject matter: generally these are more limited and extend only to direct derivation; ss 93–96 the copyright term: calculated from the date of publication rather than from the death of an author; and ss 97–100 the rules of ownership relating to subject matter other than works.

Cumulating rights in works and in subject matter

2.23 Copyrights in works and in subject matter other than works are cumulative, in the sense that they exist concurrently and independently of each other. This is expressly provided in s 113(1):

> Subject to subsection 110(2), where copyright subsists in any subject-matter by virtue of this Part, nothing in this Part shall be taken to affect the operation of Part III in relation to any literary, dramatic, musical or artistic work from which that subject-matter is wholly or partly derived, and any copyright subsisting by virtue of this Part is in addition to, and independent of, any copyright subsisting by virtue of Part III.

The single exception to this rule is that where copyright has subsisted in a cinematograph film, copyright that still subsists in a literary, dramatic, musical or artistic work reproduced in the film is not infringed by causing the film to be seen or heard in public after the copyright in the film has expired: see s 110(2).

Therefore, exclusive rights in the various works and in subject matter may be owned by different persons. For instance, when a sound recording of a song is produced, the producer, as owner of the master tape or record (see ss 97 and 22(3)(b)), owns copyright in the sound recording (as do the performers if it is a recording of a live performance: see s 22(3A)). But the producer's rights do not thereby extend to any works incorporated in the sound recording. The lyricist may own the rights to the lyrics of the song as a literary work and have the exclusive right to reproduce the lyrics, to broadcast them, perform them in public and so on. The composer of the music will have the same rights in the score as a musical work. So whenever a copy of the sound recording is to be made, a number of different persons must license or authorise it, each of whom may be entitled to a royalty from the subsequent exploitation of the recording. Since the term of subject matter is usually calculated from first publication, while the term of copyright for works is calculated from the death of the author, differing copyright terms must be taken into account. Some of the resulting complexity is avoided by contractual arrangements; for instance, an assignment of the relevant rights from composer and lyricist to producer for a specified term. The independent subsistence of multifarious rights in multiple parties involved in making a complex product such as a film requires close attention to 'chain of title'; that is, the party who will ultimately exploit the film commercially will require certainty that the rights of all title holders involved in the production process have been adequately dealt with either by licence or by assignment.

Subsistence of copyright in subject matter other than works

2.24 The various forms of Pt IV subject matter are defined by virtue of ss 89–92, s 10 and ss 23–24. In sound recordings and cine films, copyright subsists when they are made; that is, when sounds or visual images are embodied in an article or thing. Originality is not a requirement for any Pt IV subject matter. Sounds or images are embodied in a thing or article if the sounds or images can be reproduced from the article or thing: s 24. Video movies as well as traditional celluloid movies fall within the statutory definition. In *Galaxy Electronics Pty Ltd v Sega Enterprises Ltd* (1997) 75 FCR 8; 37 IPR 462, the definition was extended to include video games; traditional celluloid frames were not required. In *Kabushiki Kaisha Sony Computer Entertainment v Stevens* (2003) 132 FCR 31; 57 IPR 161, Sony Playstation computer games were cinematograph films as well as being computer programs under Pt III. The essential characteristic of a film is that it contains images progressing along a sufficiently predetermined path. Thus, although the moving images of a computer game are manipulated by a player, it is still a film, as the general evolution of the images is along a predetermined path, even though there will be differences in the development of each game. However, a digital representation of a spinning wheel in a poker machine was held not to be a film by Tamberlin J in *Aristocrat Leisure Industries Pty Ltd v Pacific Gaming Pty Ltd* (2000) 105 FCR 13; 50 IPR 29, since the image of rotating symbols on a poker machine wheel did not have the requisite progression or movement of the symbols themselves. In terms of when a film is complete, the court in *Krampel Newman Partners Pty Ltd v Commissioner of Taxation* (2003) 126 FCR 561 held that 'for the rights conferred by the Copyright Act to subsist in a cinematograph film like the "Feature Film", it is necessary for the making of the film to have been completed to a point where the film was capable of publication': at [52]. There must be a material embodiment or fixation of the film, and not merely in a fleeting or transitory form; thus playing a computer game on a disc does not constitute making a copy because the storage in the RAM of a DVD player or PC in the course of playing is only short-lived: see *Commissioner of Taxation v Seven Network Ltd* [2016] FCAFC 70 at [78]–[79]. A film need not be a professionally produced movie for TV or cinema release but can consist of raw footage of real events: see, for example, *Seven Network (Operations) Ltd v TCN Channel Nine Pty Ltd* [2005] FCAFC 144.

A sound recording consists of the aggregate of sounds embodied in a record, which is any device in which sounds are embodied: see s 10. A sound recording and the soundtrack of a film are two distinct things. The soundtrack of a film is part of the film and does not constitute a sound recording per se: see ss 10 and 23(1). Therefore, the maker of a film does not have an additional and concurrent copyright in respect of the soundtrack as a sound recording; however, if the soundtrack is separately recorded — for instance, pre-recorded or recorded later for release as a CD — that separate recording will constitute a sound recording under the Act. In *Phonographic Performance Co of Australia Ltd v Federation of Australian Commercial Television Stations* (1998) 195 CLR 158; 40 IPR 225, the High Court held that by virtue of s 23(1), the broadcasting of a film incorporating a sound recording as a soundtrack amounted to a broadcast of a sound recording. As well as the film copyright owners, the sound recording copyright owners were thus entitled to a licence fee when a film incorporating the sound recording was broadcast.

Broadcasts can be either radio or television broadcasts and are the only subject of copyright protection that does not require a fixed or material form. Therefore, a live TV broadcast is protected by copyright (from being recorded by an unauthorised recipient, for instance). According to s 10, 'television broadcast' means visual images broadcast by way of television and sounds broadcast for reception along with those images. In *Network Ten Ltd v TCN Channel Nine Pty Ltd* (2004) 218 CLR 273; 59 IPR 1, the High Court equated a television broadcast with a television program and rejected the notion that had been accepted in the Full Federal Court that each visual image that could be observed by a viewer constituted a television program. The meaning of the term 'television broadcast' had to be understood in context and within the broader framework of the Act. The Full Federal Court's approach would have had the surprising result that the unauthorised use of a part of a television program, however small, would have amounted to the taking of a substantial part (see s 14(1) and Chapter 4 Copyright Infringement in General). Each of the television programs identified by Channel Nine, from which Network Ten had incorporated parts in its satirical program *The Panel*, constituted a television program as discrete periods of broadcasting promoted separately. Nonetheless, in *Connect TV Pty Ltd v All Rounder Pty Ltd (No 5)* (2016) 118 IPR 133; [2016] FCA 338 the court made the point that the question of what constituted a television broadcast in *Network Ten* had been resolved by the High Court in response to the case presented by Channel Nine. The decision left open the question whether a continuous television broadcast (a concatenation of programs over a period of time) could nonetheless be considered a television broadcast under the Act, although it could not be said to be a television program. As the court put it: 'The [High] Court was not called on to determine whether or not a series of programmes, broadcast one after the other in the course of a day could individually or collectively be regarded, for the purposes of the Act, as a "television broadcast"': *Connect TV* at [36]. However, ultimately the court in *Connect TV* did not have to resolve the issue either.

Published edition copyright relates to the layout, formatting and appearance of a published work only. Publishers' investment in putting together a particular edition of a literary work is protected from facsimile copying by virtue of the exclusive right in s 88. This is of particular use where there is no copyright in the underlying work; for instance, because it has run out (eg, a new edition of the Bible). It has been held that a publication of a work in a newspaper was not a published edition of a work: *Nationwide News Pty Ltd v Copyright Agency Ltd* (1996) 65 FCR 399; 34 IPR 53 (Full Federal Court, confirming the decision of Wilcox J in *Nationwide News Pty Ltd v Copyright Agency Ltd* (1995) 55 FCR 271; 30 IPR 159).

Bibliography

A Laurie, 'Moral Rights — Have They Really Made a Difference for Copyright Owners and Users in Australia?' (2004) 57 *IP Forum* 14.

A Stewart, W van Caenegem, J Bannister, A Liberman, C Lawson, *Intellectual Property in Australia*, 6th ed, LexisNexis, 2017.

Australian Law Reform Commission (ALRC), *Copyright and the Digital Economy*, Report No 122, 13 February 2014.

F Macmillan, 'Morpheus in the Undergrowth: Copyright and Film' (2002) 49 *IP Forum* 12.

G Dalton, 'Copyright: Protecting Original Expression or the Efforts of Authors?' (2000) 11(3) *AIPJ* 129.

G Davies, N Caddick and G Harbottle (eds), *Copinger and Skone James on Copyright*, 17th ed, Sweet & Maxwell, 2016.

J McCutcheon, 'The Vanishing Author in Computer-Generated Works: A Critical Analysis of Recent Australian Case Law' (2013) 36(3) *MULR* 917.

J Pila, 'An Intentional View of the Copyright Work' (2008) 71(4) *MLR* 535.

K Stammer and M Momdjian, 'The Panel Case — Copyright in Television Broadcasts' (2004) 57 *IP Forum* 57.

M Richardon, J Gans, F Hanks, P Williams, 'Benefits and Costs of Copyright: Economic Perspective Part 1' (2000) 13(5) *IPLB* 62.

M Rimmer, 'Heretic: Copyright Law and Dramatic Works' (2002) 2(1) *QUTLJJ* 131.

M Sheargold, 'Copyright: Defining "Musical Works" in Common Law Countries' (2007) 18(2) *AIPJ* 96.

N Trevelyan, 'Copyright in Architectural Plans: What Local Governments Can and Can't Do' (2003) 1(8) *L Gov R* 117.

PW Young J, 'Copyright and the Phone Book' (2001) 75(10) *ALJ* 595.

Chapter 3

Copyright: Ownership and Exploitation

Authorship

3.1 'Copyright subsists in a literary work only by virtue of the authorship of that work by an individual or individuals.': *Telstra Corporation Ltd v Phone Directories Pty Ltd* [2010] FCAFC 149 at [1], and copyright in a work is owned by its author: Copyright Act 1968 (Cth), s 35(2). However, this basic rule is varied in the case of joint authorship and future copyright, and by specific contractual or statutory provisions by virtue of s 35(3)–(6). In other words, 'author = owner' is largely a statutory default position. But before dealing with each of the specific variations in turn, the fundamental concept of authorship requires closer scrutiny.

At one end of the spectrum, the mechanical action of reducing an expression to writing or some other material form is not to be equated with authorship. A mere scribe or 'amanuensis' is not an author; something more is required, although not necessarily much more. In *Walter v Lane* [1900] AC 539, some of the Law Lords accepted that the act of shorthand recording of speeches and subsequent transcription, correction, revision and punctuation amounted to an act of authorship (admittedly under a statute that did not expressly refer to originality). Thus, copyright subsisted in the Earl of Roseberry as the author of the speeches and a separate copyright in the shorthand writers in their reports of the speeches.

At the other end of the spectrum, merely contributing the idea or information underlying a literary or other work will not entitle a person to claim copyright as an author either: see *Donoghue v Allied Newspapers Ltd* [1938] Ch 106, in which a journalist author of abridged versions of interviews was entitled to copyright. The interviewee, Donoghue, who had merely provided information about incidents in his life, was not. *Douglas v Racing Victoria Ltd* [2019] FCCA 49 concerned the production of medals representing horseracing personalities; copyright vested in the medals as sculptures. Photographs and some instructions had been supplied to the die maker by a Mr Douglas, who claimed copyright in the medals. But the court said at [152]:

> On no view had Mr Douglas prepared the final design embodied in the medals. He agreed both that he had not drawn the final images as had appeared in those medals and that they had been Mr Forwood's work. Contrary to Mr Douglas' evidence-in-chief, he was not the person who had created the tools and dies for the pressed medal designs. He had in fact contracted that work to Mr Forwood [the die maker]. On the facts of this case, the final expression of the idea

> comprised in the dies from which the medals were cast had been Mr Forwood's and the designs embodied in those dies had been the product of his exertion, labour and activity. The final designs of those medals were embodied in the dies which had been cast by Mr Forwood. Those dies could not have been the work of Mr Douglas — he was not a tool maker. Mr Douglas had not provided final drawings to Mr Fowood with instructions to replicate them.

Ownership of copyright will result only from a contribution to the actual expression of the work that has the quality of authorship about it. In this sense, the concept of authorship is closely related to originality of expression. Some authorial skill, effort or judgment must be contributed to the manner in which a literary, dramatic, musical or artistic work is expressed. The *IceTV* case, *IceTV Pty Ltd v Nine Network Australia Pty Ltd* (2009) 239 CLR 458; 80 IPR 451, provides an illustration. The person who decided on the programming at Channel Nine — that is, which programs would be broadcast at what times — was not the author of the program guide or compilation itself. The focus was on the authorial expression of the information concerning programming in a program guide, rather than on generating the program sequence for the network itself. In *Sawkins v Hyperion Records Ltd* [2005] EWCA Civ 565; (2005) 64 IPR 627, the author of the historical scores was de Lalande, but the skill, effort and judgment Sawkins expended on producing three new performing editions made them into original works for which he had copyright. This was the case even though he had worked from what remained of de Lalande's original manuscript scores and had no intention to add a single note of his own.

Originality and authorship are correlative concepts, so a person who contributes to the expression of a work by their own intellectual activity is to be considered an author. However, novelty, inventiveness, creativity or literary ability are not required of an author.

The question of what amounts to authorship has been closely examined in the context of claims to co-authorship and co-ownership. In the English case of *Fylde Microsystems Ltd v Key Radio Systems Ltd* (1998) 39 IPR 481, the court had to determine whether a party who commissioned new software had made a contribution to the development of the new computer programs sufficient to entitle it to co-ownership of the copyright as co-authors. The commissioning party had spent considerable time and effort testing the software and identifying bugs in it, contributing substantially to the genesis of an effective program. The quality of the contribution of the putative co-author had to be examined. Did it have the character of authorship about it? Some forms of skill and expertise, even if they do contribute to the ultimate form of expression of a work, do not qualify. Laddie J adhered to the following passage from his own judgment in *Cala Homes (South) Ltd v Alfred McAlpine Homes (East) Ltd* [1995] FSR 818 at 835, a case concerning house plans: 'It is wrong to think that only the person who carries out the mechanical act of fixation is an author. There may well be skill and expertise in drawing clearly and well but that does not mean that it is only that skill and expertise which is relevant.' In *Fylde*, Laddie J saw the resolution in a two-step approach (at IPR 486): 'First it is necessary to determine whether the putative author has contributed the right kind of skill and labour. If he has then it is necessary to decide whether his contribution was big enough. The latter issue in particular is a matter of fact and degree.' In this case, the contribution of the commissioning party's employee (Barrett) was manifold: he put effort into error fixing and reporting bugs and faults; he made a functional contribution by way of setting the specification for what the software was to do; he suggested what he thought was causing some of the faults; he provided technical data on the hardware in which the software was to run; and he set parameters and timings within the software as a user. There was no doubt that the contribution he made was extensive and technically sophisticated. Nonetheless, Laddie J held that 'Although all of Mr Barrett's contributions took a lot of time and were very valuable they did not amount to contributions to the authoring of [the program].' The fact that the defendant had interchanged ideas on the software did not make him into an author; it was the plaintiff who was expert in programming, not the defendant, who was expert in the design and operation of radios in which the software was to be used. Thus, despite the extensive cooperation in the process of development of a commissioned work, the contribution of the commissioning party was too far removed from the formulation and recording of the actual expression of the program to amount to co-authorship. Clear contractual terms concerning ownership of commissioned works will prevent the kind of uncertainty that resulted in litigation in this case. It is interesting to consider these statements in the context of sequential updated versions of a computer program or package, as in *JR Consulting & Drafting Pty Limited v Cummings* [2016] FCAFC 20, where the court said at [304]:

> To the extent that each sequential update … reflects changes to the source code by addition or deletion (whether the rectification of errors or a new set of instructions to bring about a certain result) that might be regarded as, quantitatively at least, insubstantial, an inference arises from the circumstance of his authorship of the entire programs comprising QSS [Quik Series Software], over time, and his election to release, with each numerical version of QSS, the entire program as updated, to the following effect: that he has carefully considered the preceding state of the suite of programs and that the alterations, insertions or deletions are intended to be consistent with and enhancements of what has gone before. In other words, [the author] has undertaken a particular revision of the programs on each occasion as part of the whole of the work with the application of sufficient skill and judgement to make each version as updated and released an original work in its own right.

It is important to be able to identify who provided the necessary authorial input to a work, and to establish that their contribution resulted from 'independent intellectual effort' and/or 'sufficient effort of a literary nature': *Telstra Corporation Ltd v Phone Directories Pty Ltd* [2010] FCAFC 149 at [5], citing *IceTV* at [33] and [99]. Thus, because the phone directories were generated by computer, no copyright consisted in them. Contrast this with the pre-*IceTV* decision in *Desktop Marketing Systems Pty Ltd v Telstra Corporation Ltd* (2002) 119 FCR 491.

Ownership

Joint authorship and joint ownership of copyright in works

3.2 The Copyright Act expressly recognises that a given work may have multiple authors: see ss 79–83. By virtue of s 10:

> *work of joint authorship* means a work that has been produced by the collaboration of two or more authors and in which the contribution of each author is not separate from the contribution of the other author or the contributions of the other authors.

A work of joint authorship is distinct from a collective work, where the result may be a seamless whole but the contribution of each author is a separate work owned by each individually; for instance, an opera (with libretto as literary work and score as musical work). Joint owners of copyright works are tenants in common, each of whom can sue independently for an injunction or damages for a moiety. Joint authorship has often come to the fore in musical copyright cases where musical works are produced by bands or groups, and the question arises as to whether the contribution of any given member of the band has the character of authorship about it. This was at issue in the well-known Spandau Ballet case of *Hadley v Kemp* [1999] EMLR 589, the court holding that Kemp was the sole author of the band's songs. The other members of the band had performed and interpreted the songs, rather than composed and created them. The case was cited in the more recent decision of *Beckingham v Hodgens* [2003] EWCA Civ 143. There it was stressed that for joint authorship to exist, collaboration is required and each contribution must not be separate. A passage from Keating J's judgment in *Levy v Rutley* (1871) LR 6 CP 523 at 529 was cited with approval, requiring 'joint labouring in furtherance of a common design' to produce the work. Recent cases that have considered joint authorship post-*IceTV* are *Acohs Pty Ltd v Ucorp Pty Ltd* (2010) 86 IPR 492; [2010] FCA 577, *Primary Health Care Ltd v Commissioner of Taxation* (2010) 186 FCR 301; [2010] FCA 419, *Dynamic Suppliers Pty Ltd v Tonnex Pty Ltd* (2011) 91 IPR 488; [2011] FCA 362 and *Fairfax Media Publications Pty Ltd v Reed International Books Australia Pty Ltd* (2010) 189 FCR 109; [2010] FCA 984. In the latter case, the court held that the Australian authors of the body or text of articles in the *Australian Financial Review* did not produce works of joint authorship with the sub-editors who had separately devised titles for them. In *Career Step, LLC v TalentMed Pty Ltd (No 2)* (2018) 129 IPR 70; [2018] FCA 132, a number of different people had each worked on separate modules that were integrated into a single course; the court determined that those responsible for writing separate modules were all joint authors, although they had not contributed to the compilation of those modules into a single online course. The group of authors, each of whom had been identified, had been constituted for a common purpose (creating the online course) and the fact that none of the authors had worked on each and every model did not stand in the way of them all being joint authors. Authorial contribution by each of the joint authors to the *totality* of the work was not required.

Communal ownership of works

3.3 In *Bulun Bulun v R & T Textiles Pty Ltd* (1998) 86 FCR 244; 41 IPR 513, the question was whether the court should recognise some form of communal ownership of copyright, even though the Copyright Act makes no reference to it. The following passage from *Bulun Bulun v R & T Textiles Pty Ltd* (1998) 86 FCR 244 at 247 (von Doussa J) sets the scene and provides useful references:

> These proceedings represent another step by Aboriginal people to have communal title in their traditional ritual knowledge, and in particular in their artwork, recognised and protected by the Australian legal system. The inadequacies of statutory remedies under the Copyright Act 1968 as a means of protecting communal ownership have been noted in earlier decisions of this court: see *Yumbulul v Reserve Bank of Australia* (1991) 21 IPR 481 at 490 and *Milpurrurru v Indofurn Pty Ltd* (1994) 54 FCR 240 at 247; 130 ALR 659. See also *Stopping*

> *the Rip-Offs: Intellectual Property Protection for Aboriginal and Torres Strait Islander Peoples* (1994), National Capital Printing, where it was said at p 6: 'While joint authorship of a work by two or more authors is recognised by the Copyright Act, collective ownership by reference to any other criterion, for example, membership of the author of a community whose customary laws invest the community with ownership of any creation of its members is not recognised'.

In all the circumstances, the artist Mr Bulun Bulun (whose work had been infringed) owed fiduciary obligations to his people, the Ganalbingu. However, von Doussa J held (at FCR 264) that:

> … the existence of those obligations does not, without more, vest an equitable interest in the ownership of the copyright in the Ganalbingu people. Their primary right, in the event of a breach of obligation by the fiduciary is a right in personam to bring action against the fiduciary to enforce the obligation … had Mr Bulun Bulun merely failed to take action to enforce his copyright, an adequate remedy might be extended in equity to the beneficiaries by allowing them to bring action in their own names against the infringer and the copyright owner, claiming against the former, in the first instance, interlocutory relief to restrain the infringement, and against the latter orders necessary to ensure that the copyright owner enforces the copyright. Probably there would be no occasion for equity in these circumstances to impose a constructive trust.

If Mr Bulun Bulun had gone further, to deny the existence of fiduciary obligations and the interests of the parties asserting them and to refuse to protect the copyright from infringement, then the occasion might have existed for equity to impose a remedial constructive trust upon the copyright owner to strengthen the standing of the beneficiaries to bring proceedings to enforce the copyright.

An equitable interest in copyright based on a constructive trust would allow the party with the equitable interest to claim interlocutory injunctive relief. However, since Mr Bulun Bulun had fulfilled his fiduciary obligations by bringing the action under the Copyright Act, there was no basis for finding that the Ganalbingu people had an equitable interest in the work.

The government has considered addressing the lack of standing under the Copyright Act of indigenous communities as such by granting communities a conditional right of action for the breach of moral rights: see the Copyright Amendment (Indigenous Communal Moral Rights) Bill 2003 (Cth). However, this bill was never introduced into parliament, in part due to the requirement of the draft bill that the artist and community enter into an agreement before any independent rights of action could vest in the community. On a final note, in *Western Australia v Ward* (2002) 213 CLR 1, the High Court rejected the notion of copyright vesting in indigenous groups as an incident of native title. At the international level, work is continuing at the World Intellectual Property Organization Intergovernmental Committee on Intellectual Property and Genetic Resources, Traditional Knowledge and Folklore to develop treaty terms relating to indigenous traditional knowledge and traditional cultural expression.

Crown copyright

3.4 The Crown in right of the Commonwealth or a state owns copyright in original works made by it or under its direction or control: see s 176(2). Copyright will subsist in such works even if it would not were the work not made by, or under the direction or control of, the Crown; for example, if there is no legally sufficient connection with Australia: s 176(1). Similar provisions apply to subject matter other than works. The term of Crown copyright in works is 50 years from the year of first publication (or of making, in the case of artistic works). The meaning of 'under the direction or control' of the Crown was explored in *Linter Group Ltd (in liq) v Price Waterhouse* [2000] VSC 90 and more recently in *Copyright Agency Ltd v State of New South Wales* (2007) FCR 213; (2008) 233 CLR 279; 78 IPR 1, a case stated on a point of law from the Copyright Tribunal to the Full Court of the Federal Court and appealed to the High Court. The case related to survey plans made by members of the Association of Consulting Surveyors in a form compliant with certain government requirements. However, the government merely imposed certain requirements on plans of the relevant kind, and it was left to the author to determine whether or not to make them in compliance with those requirements. For a work to fall under Crown copyright, the author must be compelled or obliged to produce the work. Here, that was not the case, and the Full Court held that the plans were not Crown copyright. The government also did not determine whether or not to publish the plans, and therefore it could not be the first publisher: s 177. By virtue of ss 182B–183E, the Crown (or any person authorised by the Crown) also has a statutory licence to do anything included in copyright owned by any person for the services of the Commonwealth or state, subject to notification and on agreed terms, or in default of agreement, on terms fixed by the Copyright Tribunal: see Chapter 5 Copyright: Other Rights and Exceptions. Only these provisions, in particular s 183, were at issue in the High Court: see at [42]ff. In its report *Crown Copyright*, released in April 2005, the Copyright Law Review Committee (CLRC) recommended drastic reforms to the Crown's privileged position in relation to copyright, as the Intellectual Property and Competition Review Committee had done in its final report in 2000. The report recommended abolition of the privileged position of the Crown in relation to copyright; however, the recommendations have not been implemented to date. The CLRC was abolished soon after handing down this report, for budgetary reasons.

Statutory and contractual variation: s 35

3.5 The basic principle that ownership follows authorship (s 35(2)) may be varied by agreement or, in the absence of overriding contractual terms (by virtue of s 35(3)), by the operation of the statutory provisions of s 35(4)–(6). Those provisions relate to all works created under a contract of service (an employment arrangement) and certain works created under a contract for services (a sub-contracting or commissioning arrangement). The most significant variation relates to works made by the author in pursuance of the terms of their employment under a contract of service. The employer fully owns copyright in such works: s 35(6). However, employed journalists have more extensive rights than any other category of employees: s 35(4). In terms of commissioned works, the rule of s 35(2) is displaced, by virtue of s 35(5), in relation to portraits and so on commissioned for private or domestic purposes: see 3.8. The provisions of s 35(4)–(6) are not mandatory but can be varied by contract: s 35(3). Thus, an employee can negotiate to retain copyright in works created as part of their duties, or to obtain some of the exclusive rights, or to obtain royalties for the exploitation of a work from the employer, but if no express terms are included in the contract, the only relevant question is whether the work is created in pursuance of the terms of the contract of service. This question can be answered only by reference to the principles developed under the common law. Similarly, where the creation of a copyright work is commissioned, normally the commissioned party — that is, the actual author — owns copyright, but this can be varied by agreement.

Copyright works of employees

3.6 Principles of labour law determine whether the author is engaged under a contract of service or a contract for services: see, for instance, *Redrock Holdings Pty Ltd v Hinkley* (2001) 50 IPR 565, relating to a computer programmer who was found to be an employee despite engaging in his programming work independently: see also *Edsonic Pty Ltd v Cassidy* (2010) 189 FCR 271; (2010) 88 IPR 317. Such principles will also determine which of a number of competing entities is actually the employer of the author in question: see, for instance, *Milankov Designs & Project Management Pty Ltd v Di Latte* (2018) 129 IPR 565; [2018] WASC 14 discussed below at 3.12. If the author is an employee engaged under a contract of service, then the central issue is whether the work was made by the author in pursuance of the terms of the contract. The Copyright Act provides no further guidance on this matter, so one must turn to the cases. The essential question is, did the creation of a copyright work or works fall within the duties the employee was employed to perform? In *Stephenson Jordan & Harrison Ltd v McDonald & Evans* [1952] 1 TLR 101, an employed accountant had produced notes for the purpose of delivering lectures, which were later published in a book. His employer claimed copyright in the relevant chapters. Denning LJ pointed out that even though a person employed under a contract of service may sometimes perform services outside the contract, the employer would not be entitled to the works created in performing those extra-contractual services. He gave the example of a master at a school or a doctor employed by a hospital giving lectures orally to students. If for their own convenience the employee wrote down the lectures, it was not done under the contract of service. Morris LJ said that it had not been shown that the accountant could have been ordered to write or deliver the lectures or that it was part of his duty to write or deliver them. Therefore, the lectures were not written in the course of employment. In *Noah v Shuba* [1991] FSR 14 at 25, Mummery J approved of the narrow approach in *Stephenson* and found that the plaintiff, a consultant epidemiologist who while at home during evenings and weekends had written a guide to hygienic skin piercing, retained the copyright to the work. A temporal connection between employment and production of a copyright work is not determinative, although it may be a relevant factor in a case where the link between the copyright work and the duties of the employee is tenuous. Where employees habitually work autonomously, a temporal connection may be even less relevant: see also *Beloff v Pressdram Ltd* [1973] 1 All ER 241. The key remains to determine the exact nature and scope of the employee's duties and whether the creation of the work fell within what was required by those duties. It is only where that is the case that it can be said that an employee is adequately compensated for authoring a work by the payment of salary.

However, although the general principle is that employers own copyright in works employees had a duty to create, academic employees of universities appear to be a special case. It is at least arguable that producing written works is one of the duties of normal academic employment. However, in accordance with well-established custom, academics have dealt with their academic works as owners, entering into publishing agreements, receiving royalties and the like. The situation with regard to lecture notes and other material produced for lectures is less clear. Although, in the past, universities may have evinced little interest in asserting copyright for such materials, since they are intimately linked to the personal delivery of instruction by a lecturer, the situation may be different where lecture materials are produced for the purpose of distance or online education. Many universities have reviewed their policies concerning ownership of intellectual property of employees, including copyright: for a survey of present practices, see A Monnotti and S Ricketson, *Universities and Intellectual Property*, Oxford University Press, 2003. In the context of inventions created by employees, the validity and legal effect of university policies and statutes and their ability to vary the terms of a contract of employment were closely examined in *Gray v University of Western Australia* [2008] FCA 498: see Chapter 9 Patents: Ownership, Assignment and Licence. The reasons of the Full Court in *University of Western Australia v Gray* (2009) 179 FCR 346; 82 IPR 206; [2009] FCAFC 116 were called in aid by Moore J in *Edsonic* (at [34]) to support the principle that the existence of an employment relationship alone does not give employers ownership of employee intellectual property.

Copyright works of employed journalists

3.7 Section 35(4), in effect, amounts to an exception to subs (6), creating a narrow sub-category of employees with greater statutory rights than all other employees. However, the privileged position of journalists is reserved for employees of the print media and does not extend to television, radio or internet journalists. Journalists are seen as financially dependent on their production of copyright works, with an exceptional interest in developing individual goodwill in their works beyond the reputation of the publication for which they work. Furthermore, their conditions of employment have come to be premised on the fact that they are able to earn revenue from the exploitation of their works by certain other means (eg, by publishing collected articles in book form). As a consequence, the ownership rights of the employer (proprietor of the publication) extend to publication in the relevant newspaper, magazine or periodical and to broadcasting of the work. All other rights remain with the journalist. In *De Garis & Moore v Neville Jeffress Pidler* (1990) 37 FCR 99; 18 IPR 292 (a case also concerned with the nature and extent of the fair dealing exception), one of the questions at issue was who owned the right to license a news clipping service. De Garis was a freelance occasional contributor to a newspaper, and thus not an employee, while Moore was an employed journalist. De Garis retained full ownership of the copyright in his publications, but, as Beaumont J held, Moore retained only limited copyright under s 35(4). His works were made for publication in the *Sydney Morning Herald*, and the proprietor of the paper owned the copyright for the purposes of publication in that paper. A news clipping service, however, which entailed reproducing selected articles from certain publications for clients, did not amount to the publication of a newspaper. The words 'newspaper', 'magazine' and 'periodical' were to be given their ordinary meaning. In any case, publication in the context of s 35(4) meant only 'first publication'; that is, making public what was not previously public. The right to license the news clipping service was thus retained by Moore. A potentially more important new or further use of journalists' contributions is by online exploitation. Media owners want to provide much of the content of their existing traditional publications online. The CLRC's *Report on Journalists' Copyright* (1994) failed to make a unanimous recommendation as to who should own the right to make journalists' works available online. However, the issue has been resolved in favour of the employers. The employed journalist retains only the book publication rights and rights to reprographic royalties: see Copyright Amendment Act (No 1) 1998 (Cth), Sch 1. Thus, proprietors have the right to communicate to the public; that is, to make available online or to electronically transmit the works of the journalists they employ.

Commissioned works

3.8 When a work is commissioned — that is, created by an independent party under a contract for services rather than 'of service' — the normal rule applies; that is, the author owns copyright. However, this rule may be displaced by an assignment of future copyright, whether whole or partial. Further, the exploitation of the copyright may be subject to express or implied licences in favour of the commissioning party. For instance, if A commissions B, an architect, to produce plans for a house that A wishes to erect, then, in the absence of any express contractual provisions, although architect B owns the copyright, A will usually have an implied licence to build the house on the basis of the plans, an act (of reproduction: see s 21(3)(a)) falling within the exclusive rights of B. Section 35(5) imposes a limitation on the general rule that the commissioned party (the artist or author) owns copyright in the work concerned. In circumstances where a person, for valuable consideration, takes a photograph for a private or domestic purpose, paints or draws a portrait, or makes an engraving, the commissioning party (and not the author; ie, the commissioned party) owns the copyright. But if at the time the agreement was made, that person (ie, the commissioning party) made known, expressly or by implication, to the author of the work the purpose for which the work was required, the author is entitled to restrain the doing, other than for that purpose, of any act comprised in the copyright in the work. Thus, if A and B commission C, a professional photographer, to take their wedding photographs as mementos, unless otherwise agreed, A and B own the copyright, but C could restrain them from publishing the photos as commercial advertisements for wedding gowns.

Section 35(5), relating to ownership of copyright in certain commissioned photographs and works, was considered by a federal magistrate in *Meskenas v ACP Publishing Pty Ltd* (2006) 70 IPR 172. Particularly at issue was whether the party commissioning the portrait (of the surgeon Victor Chang) expressly made known the purpose for which it was required. If so, then the author could hold the copyright owner to that purpose. The magistrate accepted that both Victor Chang and the author wanted the portrait to be entered into the Archibald painting competition, but there was no evidence that any other specific purpose had been made known, or that entry into the Archibald was the communicated sole purpose for which the work could be used.

Future copyright

3.9 By virtue of s 197, if an author assigns copyright in a future work (ie, a work that will be created in the future) to another person (in writing and signed by the assignor), the copyright vests in that other person when the work is made. The whole or part of the future copyright can be so vested in a person other than the author. Vesting of future copyright is to be distinguished from the assignment of copyright in an existing work, which will also be effective only if done in writing and signed by the assignor: see 3.10.

Exploitation: Assignment and Licence

Assignment

3.10 Copyright may be commercially exploited by way of assignment or licence. An assignment is a transfer of ownership — see s 196(1) (copyright is personal property and is transmissible by assignment, by will and by devolution by operation of law) — while a licence is merely a grant of permission to do an act comprised in the copyright. An assignment may be partial — that is, it may be limited in time, place and/or as to the rights assigned (see s 196(2)) — but if an assignment is expressed in absolute and unlimited terms, there is no right of reversion: see *Sumner v Beyond Properties* (2003) 59 IPR 268. An agreement to assign that is not in writing and signed by the assignor does not have effect as against third parties. However, no valuable consideration is required, nor a deed: *Australian Chinese Newspapers Pty Ltd v Melbourne Chinese Press Pty Ltd* (2003) 58 IPR 1. An effective assignment may arise even though a contract does not expressly refer to the transfer of copyright; for instance, where an assignment is of goodwill or a business with all its assets with the clear intention of also conveying the copyrights of the business. Pincus J in *Greenfield Products Pty Ltd v Rover-Scott Bonnar Ltd* (1990) 95 ALR 275 at 280 said: 'It has become clear that documents which do not in terms assign copyright can suffice for the purposes of a provision such as s 196(3): *E W Savory Ltd v World of Golf Ltd* [1914] 2 Ch 566.' However, an agreement that is not in the requisite form to effect an assignment can still give rise to an equitable obligation to properly execute the assignment as between the parties. In *Gold Peg International Pty Ltd v Kovan Engineering (Aust) Pty Ltd* (2005) 67 IPR 497, the court confirmed:

> The Copyright Act does not require any specific formulation or wording for the purposes of s 196(3), but it must be apparent that the document is the assignment of the copyright itself, not a mere licence, nor conveyance of rights or property other than copyright: see *Greenfield Products Pty Ltd.*

In the same case, the relationship between legal and equitable ownership was explored. The court asserted that 'there are numerous examples where courts have been prepared to imply a condition into an agreement between the parties that the author of a copyright work will assign legal title to it when called upon to do so because equitable ownership of the copyright in the work does not belong to the author' (at [81]; the court goes on to list some of those cases). This kind of implication will arise where there is a commissioning arrangement for the preparation of copyright material (at [82]), or where a copyright work is commissioned but nothing is said about who will own the copyright (at [83]). The court then goes on to set out at length the principles that apply where parties have failed to deal with the ownership of future copyright: see also *Adams v Quasar Management Services Pty Ltd* (2002) 56 IPR 385.

Licence

3.11 A licence is the copyright owner's permission to do an act comprised in the copyright. It can be a bare licence, authorisation or permission, or a licence granted for valuable consideration; for instance, the payment of a lump sum or of royalties. The Copyright Act distinguishes between exclusive and non-exclusive licences. An 'exclusive licence' is a licence in writing signed by the owner authorising the licensee to do an act comprised in the copyright 'to the exclusion of all others', including the owner: see s 10. Only the exclusive licensee has an independent right of action: see s 119. The right of action of the exclusive licensee is concurrent with that of the owner; however, both owner and exclusive licensee are not entitled to proceed with the action, unless by leave of the court, without joining the other as plaintiff or adding the other as defendant: s 120. Clearly, in Australia, an exclusive licensee may sue an owner in infringement of copyright in relation to the rights licensed. As to the more complex situation in Canada and the United Kingdom, see *Euro Excellence Inc v Kraft Canada (Ontario)* (2007) 74 IPR 653.

It may be difficult to distinguish between an exclusive licence and an assignment, since both must be in writing and an assignment can be partial, including being limited in time; that is, with a right of reversion. Yet the distinction is important in terms of rights of action and obtaining remedies and for various other reasons. Express terms, words or denominations in an agreement are not necessarily determinative. The matter is one of construction, depending on the substance of the contract. As to the definition of an exclusive licence, see *Sega Enterprises Ltd v Galaxy Electronics Pty Ltd* (1998) 39 IPR 577. While it is clear that a non-exclusive licensee has no independent right of action in infringement relating to the work in which it holds a licence, in *MG Distribution Pty Ltd v Khan* [2006] FMCA 666, the court considered whether a non-exclusive licensee could join with a copyright owner in such an action. The court referred (at [46]) to an obiter dictum of Burchett J in *Sega Enterprises* which made an approving reference to a 'considered dictum' of Bowen CJ in Eq (as he then was) in *Young v Odeon Music House Pty Ltd* (1976) 10 ALR 153 at 161:

> [R]eferring to *Halsbury*, his Honour [Bowen CJ in Eq] said: 'I do not see why a non-exclusive licensee is not a proper plaintiff in proceedings for breach of copyright provided he joins the owner of the copyright'. The passage cited from *Halsbury* is to be found in the fourth edition, volume 9, at paragraph 880: 'A licensee, unless he is an exclusive licensee, cannot sue for infringement of copyright unless he joins the copyright proprietor as co-plaintiff in the action'.

Implied licence

3.12 Alleged infringers will frequently argue that they were entitled by an implied licence to do an act comprised in the copyright. A bare licence, in the sense of permission or authorisation, may be oral and can be implied from all the circumstances. A person who grants permission in the absence of a contract between the parties may be stopped from reneging on it. An example may be the uploading of an audio file to the internet with a simple invitation to 'enjoy the music'. The question of implied licences is also raised below in the context of parallel importation: see Chapter 5 Copyright: Other Rights and Exceptions. Even if a licence can be implied, it may be that the scope of such a licence does not cover what the defendant has done: see, for instance, *Trumpet Software Pty Ltd v OzEmail Pty Ltd* (1996) 34 IPR 481 in relation to the copyright uses impliedly licensed by the making available of shareware on the internet, and also see Chapter 18 Digitisation.

Concrete Pty Ltd v Parramatta Design & Developments Pty Ltd (2006) 229 CLR 577; 70 IPR 468 concerned an implied licensing issue involving copyright in architectural plans for a new real estate development. Because of the complexity and uniqueness of the facts and the diversity of approaches in the various judgments, it is perhaps difficult to state firmly what the case means for copyright law. Nonetheless, it is probably correct to say that the use of architectural plans that formed the basis of planning approval for the actual building by a subsequent purchaser of the land will be permitted in the absence of express terms to the contrary (see, more recently, with similar facts, *Vartzokas Architects Pty Ltd v Nazero Group SA Pty Ltd (No 2)* [2017] FCCA 1019). This is an application of the principle that a licence may be implied when there is a necessity to do so; that is, where it is 'necessary for the reasonable or effective operation of all contracts' of a particular class: see *Acohs Pty Ltd v Ucorp Pty Ltd* (2012) 95 IPR 117; [2012] FCAFC 16 at [144]–[146]. However, the implied license only arises if it is not excluded by express terms nor inconsistent with the terms of the contract. This principle was applied recently in *Milankov Designs* (see above 3.6); the key question was whether the term implied by law into this particular class of contracts (that commissioned building plans can be reproduced by way of erecting the building concerned) was in fact excluded because of inconsistency with the terms of the contract. 'The plans ... were prepared for development approval. It is necessary to consider the contract between the plaintiff and the first defendants to determine if the implication of a term that the plaintiff gave the first defendants permission or consent to use those plans for the purpose of building a house was excluded.': at [100]. On the facts, the extent of the implied licence was that the plans be used to seek building approval, and '[i]t was not an implied licence to use the plans to build a house, because that is inconsistent with the terms of the contract which provided that the plaintiff was to prepare working drawing and specification documentation' for the second stage which consisted of the actual building of the house: at [102]. Alternatively, terms may be implied in the circumstances of a particular case to give business efficacy to the contracts: *Acohs* at [147]. Another recent decision concerning the relationship between using commissioned plans for building approval, and for the actual construction of a building is *Tamawood Ltd v Habitare Developments Pty Ltd (admin apptd) (receivers and managers apptd)* (2015) 112 IPR 439; [2015] FCAFC 65. The Full Court upheld the trial judge's decision that one party had indeed granted the other a bare licence to use plans in an application for development approval, but that when the former party undertook steps to engage someone else to actually construct the buildings concerned, the licensee was no longer entitled to use the plans.

Ownership and Rights in Subject Matter Other Than Works

3.13 Initially, copyright in works vests in the author, necessarily a physical person. Copyright in subject matter other than works vests instead in the 'maker' as statutorily defined (see s 22), which can be either a physical or a corporate person (consequently, the copyright term of subject matter other than works is calculated from publication, not *post mortem auctoris*). Rather than authorial effort, it is the maker's investment, financing and organisation resulting in a finished product that warrants the granting of exclusive rights under Pt IV of the Copyright Act. Nonetheless, subsequent to the Australia–United States Free Trade Agreement 2004, performers are now also deemed to be 'makers' and thus co-owners of copyright in sound recordings (see s 22(3A)(b)), even though they only perform on those recordings and do not produce them. The government has now also bestowed on directors, as opposed to only producers (ie, persons 'by whom the arrangements necessary for the making of the film were undertaken': see s 22(4)(b)), a limited share of the copyright in films that they direct: see Copyright Amendment (Film Directors' Rights) Act 2005 (Cth), relating only to retransmisson rights. Again, this is despite the fact that directors are responsible for the artistic direction of a film rather than for the organisation and investment that result in its making. Co-ownership of copyright in Pt IV subject matter, in this case a documentary film of a youth trek along the Kokoda trail, was considered in *Seven Network v TCN Channel Nine* (2005) 146 FCR 183; 66 IPR 101. Lindgren J cited passages from Lahore, *Copyright and Designs*, Butterworths, 1996, and S Ricketson, *The Law of Intellectual Property*, 2nd ed, LawBook Co, 1999, to the effect that directors, actors, camera operators and editors, as distinct from producers, are not makers and thus not copyright owners in a film, although Ricketson expressed a more nuanced view (at [12]). In the opinion of Lindgren J, both Channel Seven and Murray, who conceived of the idea of a trip with some Australian youths to Kokoda, were responsible for making the arrangements for the production of the first copy of the camera tapes. The idea for the trip and filming it were Murray's, and he also made many of the arrangements to get the schoolboys to Kokoda, etc. Channel Seven participated by providing much of the gear and expertise required to make the documentary film itself. The project had the character of a joint venture between them, to which each had made a valuable contribution. Mr Murray's contribution was not too far removed from the production of the first copy of the film for him to be considered a 'maker' of it. As Lindgren J also pointed out, co-owners of copyright in a film, like in any other copyright material, hold as tenants in common rather than joint tenants. Each co-owner will require the consent of the other co-owner(s) to do an act comprised in the copyright or to license another for that purpose. Further in relation to who is the maker of a film or a copy of a film, see *National Rugby League Investments Pty Ltd v Singtel Optus Pty Ltd* (2012) 201 FCR 147, and *Wills v Australian Broadcasting Corporation (No 3)* (2010) 89 IPR 252; [2010] FCA 1227 (relating to music videos); as for what is a film, see *Commissioner of Taxation v Seven Network Limited* [2016] FCAFC 70.

The exclusive rights in Pt IV are more limited than rights in works, extending only to exploitation by direct technological derivation, hence the difference in terminology between the exclusive right 'to reproduce in material form' in Pt III, which extends to non-literal reproductions, and the exclusive right to 'make a copy' in Pt IV, which extends only to directly derived replication. In other words, a remedy will lie only against a person who makes an unauthorised facsimile copy (most often a 'pirated copy') of Pt IV subject matter. In *CBS Records Australia Ltd v Telmak Teleproducts Australia Pty Ltd* (1987) 17 FCR 48; 9 IPR 440, Bowen CJ held that a sound-alike of an existing sound recording did not amount to an infringing copy, the monopoly of the copyright owner extending no further than the actual embodiment of the sound recording. The other exclusive rights are to broadcast, to cause to be seen or heard in public, and to communicate to the public for films and sound recordings (see ss 85 and 86), and to make a film or sound recording of a broadcast and to rebroadcast it: see s 87. Sound recordings also benefit from a commercial rental right: see s 85.

Bibliography

A Meltzer, P Howard, P Lau, M de Alwis, 'Joint Ownership of IP — Is it the Best Option for Collaborators?' (2005) 18(3) *IPLB* 37.

A Monnotti, 'Ownership of Copyright in Traditional Literary Works Within Universities' (1994) 22 *FLR* 1.

Australian Attorney-General's Department, Aboriginal and Torres Strait Islander Commission, International Trade Law and Intellectual Property Branch, Australian Cultural Development Office, *Stopping the Rip-Offs: Intellectual Property Protection for Aboriginal and Torres Strait Islander Peoples*, Report, 1994.

B Fitzgerald, R Neville, R Jones, G Hearn, 'Cultivating the Creative Commons: Perspectives from the Creative Industries' (2006) 11(1) *MALR* 63.

C Golvan, 'Protection of Australian Indigenous Copyright — Overview and Future Strategies' (2006) 65 *IP Forum* 10.

C Morris and M Meadows, 'Indigenising Intellectual Property' (2000) 9 *Griffith LR* 212.

Copyright Law Review Committee, *Crown Copyright*, Report, 2005.

D A Ellison, 'Unauthorised Reproduction of Traditional Aboriginal Art' (1994) 17 *UNSWLJ* 327.

D Stewart, 'Protecting Privacy, Property, and Possums: Australian Broadcasting Corporation v Lenah Game Meats Pty Ltd' (2002) 30 *FLR* 177.

E Campbell and A Monotti, 'Immunities of Agents of Government From Liability for Infringement of Copyright' (2002) 30 *FLR* 459.

H Strachan, 'Employees' Work: Do You Always Own It?' (2002) 12(3) *Aust Corp Law* 24.

J Anderson, 'The Politics of Indigenous Knowledge: Australia's Proposed Communal Moral Rights Bill' (2004) 27(3) *UNSWLJ* 585.

K Tunbridge and W Chan, 'Who Owns Copyright in a Commissioned Work?' (2005) 18(4) *IPLB* 59.

M Cooley, 'Crown Copyright Update' (2005) 18(3) *IPLB* 49.

M Martin, 'Milpurrurru: What's in a Painting? The Cultural Harm of Unauthorised Reproduction' (1995) 17 *Sydney LR* 591 at 593.

M Rimmer (ed), *Indigenous Intellectual Property: A Handbook of Contemporary Research*, Edward Elgar, 2015.

N Cox, 'Copyright in Primary Legal Materials in Common Law Jurisdictions' (2008) 19(2) *AIPJ* 89.

N Hazel, 'Daring to Exploit Jointly Owned Copyright' (2006) 9(3) *IHC* 25; (2005) 18(6) *IPLB* 88.

T Catanzariti, 'I'll Tell You What I Want, What I Really Really Want' — Rights Management in Australian Films (2000) 13(4) *IPLB* 41.

V Vann, 'Copyright by Way of Fiduciary Obligation — Protection of Aboriginal Art' (2000) 5(1) *MALR* 13.

W Van Caenegem, 'Originality, Joint Authorship and Databases Post-*IceTV*' (2011) 24(6) *IPLB* 150.

Chapter 4

Copyright Infringement in General

Exclusive Rights Under The Copyright Act

4.1 The Copyright Act 1968 (Cth) grants owners not a general exploitation right but specific, enumerated rights in defined subject matter. Any claim in copyright infringement must therefore relate to an identifiable subject matter and a specific right or rights. The latter are enumerated in s 31 in relation to works and in Pt IV Div 2 in relation to subject matter other than works. Lahore[1] has rightly pointed out that if courts were swayed overly by arguments that a defendant was taking unfair advantage of a plaintiff's skill and judgment, copyright would become 'a form of protection against unfair competition rather than copying of any form of expression as such'; or as it is said in *IceTV Pty Ltd v Nine Network Australia Pty Ltd* (2009) 239 CLR 458; 80 IPR 451 [2009] HCA 14 at [52]: 'focussing on the "appropriation" of the author's skill and labour must not be allowed to distract from the inquiry mandated by the Act. To put aside the particular form of expression can cause difficulties'. In the well-known case of *Victoria Park Racing & Recreation Grounds v Taylor* (1937) 58 CLR 479; 1A IPR 308, the conduct complained of did not disclose any breach of a specific right under the Copyright Act, nor of any other intellectual property rights, although arguably the original defendant took unfair advantage of the plaintiff's efforts in organising races. There was thus no available remedy. *Nine Network Australia Pty Ltd v Australian Broadcasting Corporation* (1999) 48 IPR 333; [1999] FCA 1864 provides a more recent illustration of the limits of copyright coverage. Channel Nine applied for an injunction to restrain the ABC from broadcasting the millennium fireworks spectacular at the Sydney Harbour Bridge. In exchange for a financial contribution to the staging of the event, Sydney City Council had granted Channel Nine the status of official television broadcaster and the exclusive right to record and televise the fireworks spectacular and associated events. But it was by no means clear that the granting of exclusive rights had a firm legal basis by which others could be excluded from broadcasting the same public event. No general tort existed to assist Channel Nine, and an outdoor fireworks spectacular is not a protected copyright work or subject matter per se. Thus, the show had to be broken down into constituent parts, arguably amounting to copyright works: some stylised representations of animals and other decorative elements (in particular, a face and the word 'eternity' in copperplate script superimposed on the bridge) as sculptures or

1. J Lahore, *Copyright and Designs*, Butterworths, Sydney, 1996, ¶34, 220.

works of artistic craftsmanship, and the script for the fireworks display as a dramatic work. However, each of these gave rise to difficulties, above all the latter, and in considering the matter, Hill J was conscious of the limitations inherent in copyright law, saying at [22]: 'At the heart of the problem may well be that copyright is a monopolistic right existing not to protect ideas as such but the physical manifestation of some original literary, artistic or dramatic work.' Ultimately, no interim injunction was granted. As well as the question marks over subsistence of copyright, there was the application of ss 65–67 of the Copyright Act and the fair dealing defences to consider. Furthermore, the balance of convenience did not favour the granting of the injunction.

Thus, any finding of infringement will critically depend on, first, the subsistence of copyright in some particular work or subject matter in material form put in evidence (a question considered in Chapter 2 Copyright: Subsistence Requirements) and, second, the unauthorised doing of an act comprised within the exclusive statutory rights of the copyright owner. Furthermore, since the Copyright Act does not grant monopoly but anti-copying rights, it will be necessary to establish that the impugned material is sourced from the plaintiff's copyright work or subject matter. Independently created material, even if by some coincidence it is substantially similar to a copyright work or subject matter, cannot attract copyright infringement liability. In this sense, copyright differs from design and patent rights, where the granting of a statutory monopoly confers rights of action also in relation to independent creations that fall within the scope of the granted rights.

Liability under Pt III of the Copyright Act may arise by either 'direct' (s 36) or 'indirect' (ss 37–39) infringement. Section 36(1) reads as follows:

> Subject to this Act, the copyright in a literary, dramatic, musical or artistic work is infringed by a person who, not being the owner of the copyright, and without the license of the owner of the copyright, does in Australia, or authorises the doing in Australia of, any act comprised in the copyright.

Doing and authorising the doing of an act comprised in the copyright are separate exclusive rights of the copyright owner.

To 'authorise' is a term of art in this context, which is further explained in Chapter 5 Copyright: Other Rights And Exceptions. A breach of s 36(1) is commonly referred to as 'direct infringement', although these are not terms used in the Act itself. Sections 37 and 38 comprehend what is commonly known as 'indirect infringement' or infringement by importation (s 37; so-called parallel importation or grey marketing) or dealing (s 38). A person may be liable under both s 36 and s 38 (for direct and indirect infringement); for instance, if the person who deals in the relevant infringing articles (eg, pirated copies) also made them. A crucial distinction between direct and indirect infringement lies in the knowledge element required. Whereas liability for direct infringement (ie, doing an act comprised in the copyright) is not dependent on proof of intention to infringe or knowledge of the subsistence of copyright and of the infringing nature of the act, liability for indirect infringement can lie only if the plaintiff is able to establish that the defendant had the requisite actual or constructive knowledge concerning the infringing nature of the act(s): see ss 37(1) and 38(1). However, lack of knowledge in relation to direct infringement may have a bearing on the granting of a remedy in damages: see s 115(3).

Apart from the various forms of dealing, there is one further form of indirect infringement of copyright in works that is also subject to a knowledge requirement: permitting a place of public entertainment to be used for an infringing performance of a work: see s 39. Indirect infringement is dealt with in Chapter 5 Copyright: Other Rights and Exceptions. Copyright remedies, including the statutory presumptions concerning subsistence and ownership of copyright, are dealt with in Chapter 19 Remedies in Intellectual Property Law.

Infringement: General Principles

Substantial similarity and access

4.2 Access to the work (or 'derivation') and, in shorthand terms, 'substantial similarity' (see s 14(1)(a)) are the fundamental elements of infringement of copyright, whatever the exclusive right involved. Because copyright owners benefit only from an anti-copying and not a monopoly right, similarities in an impugned work must be shown to be derived from the plaintiff's work. Commonly, such derivation can be inferred from similarity itself, but it is not always possible to draw a firm inference without some separate additional evidence of access.

In *Ladbroke (Football) Ltd v William Hill (Football) Ltd* (1964) 1 WLR 273 at 276, Lord Reid said: 'Broadly, reproduction means copying, and does not include cases where an author or compiler produces a substantially similar result by independent work without copying.' Gibbs CJ in *SW Hart & Co Pty Ltd v Edwards Hot Water Systems* (1985) 159 CLR 466 at 472 put it as follows: 'The notion of reproduction, for the purposes of copyright law, involves two elements — resemblance to, and actual use of, the copyright work, or, to adopt the words which appear in the judgment of Willmer LJ in *Francis Day & Hunter Ltd v Bron* (1963) Ch 587 at 614 "a sufficient degree of objective similarity between the two works" and "some causal connection between the plaintiffs, and the defendants' work".'; see also Wilson J at CLR 481; Deane J at CLR 503. In *Henkel KGAA v Holdfast* [2007] 1 NZLR 577 at [43], the Supreme Court of New Zealand said:

> Proof of copying will seldom be direct; in most cases the court will rely on inference. The closer the similarity between the two works the stronger the inference is likely to be that the one was copied from the other. If the alleged infringer has had access to, and therefore an opportunity to copy, the copyright work, and the similarity between the works supports an inference of copying, it may well be appropriate for the court to conclude, on the balance of probabilities, that there was indeed copying. This of course is subject always to the evaluation of any evidence there may be that no copying actually took place.

However, sometimes access and similarity are not easily treated as distinct issues. As Greenwood J put it in *Tamawood Ltd v Habitare Developments Pty Ltd (admin apptd) (receivers and managers apptd)* (2015) 112 IPR 439; [2015] FCAFC 65 at [28], referring to *Eagle Homes Pty Ltd v Austec Homes Pty Ltd* (1999) 87 FCR 415; 43 IPR 1; [1999] FCA 138:

> However, the two elements of causal link and sufficient objective similarity 'are but aspects of "reproduction"' and it can be 'artificial to consider them separately ... where actual copying [access to and use of the copyright work] is found to have occurred': *Eagle Homes v Austec* at

[98]. That follows because a finding of copying 'can add significance to objective similarity': *Eagle Homes v Austec* at [98].

Focusing on the most fundamental 'copy'-right (ie, 'reproduction') in Pt III requires attention to the two elements of resemblance to, and actual use of, the source copyright work. The words 'reproduction' and 'reproduce' are not defined in s 10(1). However, the ordinary meaning of the words is expanded and adapted by s 21: see also s 10(3). As is indicated above, the notion of 'reproduction' is broader than the notion of 'copying' in Pt IV and extends beyond the making of facsimile copies.

Establishing access

4.3 To prove infringement of the exclusive right of reproduction in a work (see s 31(1)(a)(i)), the plaintiff may tender any relevant evidence of access to the infringed work. It may, for instance, be established that the defendant had the plaintiff's work in his or her possession; a defendant may have acquired it deliberately so as to produce a close copy. For instance, in *Seafolly Pty Ltd v Fewstone Pty Ltd* (2014) 106 IPR 85; [2014] FCA 321 the respondent, ultimately found to have reproduced Seafolly swimwear designs, admitted purchasing the garments and accessing photos of them on the internet. Alternatively, it may be that a witness can testify that a certain musical work was performed in the presence of the defendant. But it will often be unnecessary to independently prove access, because the degree of similarity between two works gives rise to an irrefutable presumption of copying (access). In other words, in many cases the similarities between two works cannot reasonably be explained by coincidence.

This is obviously so where direct facsimile or 'pirated' copies were produced, but the presumption may also assist the plaintiff where the two works compared are not absolutely identical. It may be that the differences are negligible or obviously the result of an attempt to disguise copying (resulting in a 'colourable imitation'). Additional evidence concerning the method of creating the impugned works may bring this out if the matter is more finely balanced. In other words, a finding of access may result from a combination of direct evidence and inferences drawn from similarity: see, for example, *Pacific Gaming Pty Ltd v Aristocrat Leisure Industries Pty Ltd* (2001) 116 FCR 448. The evidence may establish that in creating a new work the defendant worked from the plaintiff's material, modifying it, adding to it or subtracting from it to arrive at the impugned work. The result will not necessarily be a copyright infringement, this depending ultimately on the question of whether it is too similar to the source work or the alleged infringer has, in fact, done enough to take it outside the sphere of reproduction into the creation of a distinct original work: see, for example, *Compagnie Industrielle de Precontrainte et d'Equipment de Constructions SA v First Melbourne Securities Pty Ltd* (1999) 44 IPR 512; [1999] FCA 660.

A court may conclude that there is an inescapable inference of copying, even though accepting a defendant's/witness's evidence denying any recollection of accessing the source work. For instance, in the musical copyright case of *Francis Day & Hunter v Bron* [1963] Ch 587, Willmer LJ pointed out that 'the fact that the defendant denies that he consciously copied affords some evidence to rebut the inference of causal connection arising from the objective similarity, *but is in no way conclusive*' (emphasis added). It may be that the defendant copied the work by a process of subconscious recollection, as was accepted in *Seager v Copydex Ltd* [1967] 2 All ER 415, a case concerning a design for a carpet-gripping device and in *Bright Tunes Music Corporation v Harrisongs Music, Ltd* 420 F Supp 177 — Dist Court, SD New York 1976, concerning unconscious copying by George Harrison in the composing of 'My Sweet Lord'. In the final analysis, access is a question of fact that the court must determine on the basis of all the evidence that the parties place before it.

Indirect access

4.4 Access to the allegedly infringed copyright work need not be direct; indirect use of the plaintiff's work may also result in an infringement. Thus, it could be sufficient that an infringer who has not seen the plaintiff's copyright work has had access to some reproduction of it in a different form. For example, a defendant may only have had access to a three-dimensional article or thing based on a two-dimensional copyright work such as a plan or technical drawing: see, for example, *LB (Plastics) Ltd v Swish Products Ltd* [1979] RPC 551 and *SW Hart & Co Pty Ltd v Edwards Hot Water Systems* (1985) 159 CLR 466. In an extreme case, the defendant may only have read or heard a description of the original work: see *Plix Products v Frank M Winstone (Merchants) Ltd* [1986] FSR 608; (1985) 3 IPR 390; and *Venezuela Pty Ltd v Bright* [2017] WADC 79. In *Plix Products*, the infringer was careful not to work from the plaintiff's drawings or the actual kiwi packaging trays based on them but faithfully implemented detailed specifications representing those trays. In a musical copyright case, obviously an infringement can occur without any access to the underlying score, the defendant having heard only a musical rendition of the work.

In all such cases, a court must be vigilant not to cross the divide to affording copyright protection to an idea rather than expression. *Digga Australia Pty Ltd v Norm Engineering Pty Ltd* (2008) 166 FCR 268; 75 IPR 251 illustrates the difficulties that can be experienced when an allegation of indirect copying is before a court. Norm Engineering (Norm) alleged that Digga Australia (Digga) had infringed copyright in relation to the drawings for a scoop bucket for a bobcat. It was clear that Digga had not had access to any drawings or other two-dimensional representations of the Norm bucket. The causal link between the Norm drawings and the allegedly infringing Digga drawings and bucket was said to lie in an inspection by Digga of a Norm bucket. No copyright vested in the Norm bucket as such, as it did not constitute an artistic work. The problem facing the Full Court was that the primary judge had not clearly held that the Norm bucket was actually itself a three-dimensional copy of the Norm drawings. If the prototype Norm bucket was produced before the Norm drawings, then the Norm bucket was not a reproduction of the Norm drawings and could not constitute the causal link between the two. Lindgren J, with whom Logan and Bennett JJ agreed on the appeal, held that the various findings of fact made by the trial judge did indicate that he proceeded on the basis that the Norm bucket was a reproduction of Norm drawings rather than the other way around. However, if it were otherwise — that is, if subject drawings are held to have been produced after a prototype that they represent — then if the defendant has seen only the article itself and not the underlying drawings, no causal link can be established and there will be no infringement (unless the article attracts copyright in its own right). Generally speaking, an allegation of copying may be defeated by proof that a process of autonomous or independent creation has resulted in the impugned work, even where there is considerable similarity between the works at issue. It will be important for creators to retain preparatory works such as drafts and sketches to establish by what process they arrived at a work that happens to be similar to another work: see, for example, *Inform Design* and *Construction Pty Ltd v Boutique Homes Melbourne Pty Ltd* (2008) 77 IPR 523; [2008] FCA 912. A recent example of the question of indirect access in a copyright case is to be found in *Krueger Transport Equipment Pty Ltd v Glen Cameron Storage and Distribution Pty Ltd* [2008] FCA 803. The Full Court's reasons on the appeal in this matter, *Vawdrey Australia Pty Ltd v Krueger Transport Equipment Pty Ltd* [2009] FCAFC 156, in upholding the trial court's findings on causal connection, pointed to the significant principle that where the objective similarities are sufficiently great and the defendant had the opportunity to gain access to the source work, the onus shifts to the defendant to prove how the impugned work was created and that this did not occur through copying (at [25]).

Substantial similarity

4.5 Section 14 of the Copyright Act plays a crucial role in expanding the scope of copyright beyond literal or facsimile reproduction and infringement. The relevant part of the section reads as follows:

> In this Act, unless the contrary intention appears: (a) a reference to the doing of an act in relation to a work or other subject-matter shall be read as including a reference to the doing of that act in relation to a substantial part of the work or other subject-matter; and (b) a reference to a reproduction, adaptation or copy of a work shall be read as including a reference to a reproduction, adaptation or copy of a substantial part of the work, as the case may be.

Thus, if a substantial part of a copyright work is reproduced, prima facie there will be liability for copyright infringement; in shorthand this is sometimes referred to as 'substantial similarity' between works. The word 'substantial' is in this context a term of art. Of crucial importance in determining substantial similarity is the quality, rather than the quantity or fraction, of the total source work that the part taken represents. More generally, although the comparative test is often said to assess 'objective similarity', there need not always be visual or literary identity between a work and an alleged reproduction. The exclusive right is the right to reproduce in material form (see s 31), and s 10(1) provides that 'material form' in relation to a work 'includes any form (whether visible or not) of storage'. Furthermore, in case of conversion to or from digital form (see s 21(6)), of reproduction of literary or dramatic works in films (see s 21(1)), or where there is a three-dimensional reproduction of a two-dimensional work or vice versa (see s 21(3)), the comparison will be between visually different media.

Quality not quantity

4.6 In copyright, a quantitatively insignificant part of a source work may still be a substantial part in terms of quality; the decision in the 'kookaburra song' case (*EMI Songs Australia Pty Ltd v Larrikin Music Publishing Pty Ltd* (2011) 191 FCR 444; 90 IPR 50; [2011] FCAFC 47) is a prime example of this principle (see below 4.8). The courts have sought to assess quality in somewhat divergent ways, to some degree varying their approach depending on the category of the source work (literary, musical, artistic, etc). One approach is to have regard to the relationship of the part taken to the totality of the work: is it a material, significant, important, visually striking or essential part? Another approach is slanted more towards assessing the originality of the part: does it represent 'a substantial part of the labour, skill and judgment of the author that made the whole work "original"?': see *Tamawood Ltd v Henley Arch Pty Ltd* (2004) 61 IPR 378; [2004] FCAFC 78 at [55]. The *IceTV* decision in the High Court expresses some reservation in this regard: skill and labour is not what is protected against misappropriation; rather, what will amount to an infringement is the unauthorised taking of original expression resulting from the intellectual activity of the author. Mason CJ in *Autodesk Inc v Dyason (No 2)* (1993) 176 CLR 300 at 305 said:

> Whether a part is substantial must be decided by its quality rather than its quantity. The reproduction of a part which by itself has no originality will not normally be a substantial part of the copyright and therefore will not be protected. For that which would not attract copyright except by reason of its collocation will, when robbed of that collocation, not be a substantial part of the copyright and therefore the courts will not hold its reproduction to be an infringement. It is this, I think, which is meant by one or two judicial observations that 'there is no copyright' in some unoriginal part of a whole that is copyright.

The question of substantiality is investigated in more detail below in relation to the different categories of works.

One consequence of the fact that copyright can be infringed by the taking of a substantial part, as opposed to the whole of a work being reproduced, is that an impugned work may contain infringing and non-infringing material. A work may attract copyright in its own right while at the same time constituting a breach of copyright or of contract in relation to another person's work. In *Microsoft Corporation v PC Club Australia Pty Ltd* (2005) 148 FCR 310; 67 IPR 262; [2005] FCA 1522, it was said at [108] that:

> The applicants emphasised in that regard that the identity of the author of a copyright work for the purposes of the Copyright Act is to be determined by reference to the person who actually created the work, and not by reference to the person who might have had the legal right to create the work, and referred generally to *Wood v Boosey* (1868) LR 3 QB 223 at 229–30, in which it was held that there was a separate copyright in an adaptation owned by the author of that adaptation, despite the fact that in so doing, the author infringed copyright in the underlying work. The applicants referred for further illustration of that principle to the decision of the High Court of New Zealand in *Fiscal Technology Co Ltd v Johnson* (1991) 23 IPR 555, in which the author of an adaptation was held by Henry J to have breached a contract by creating that adaptation (as well as infringing the copyright in the underlying work). His Honour nevertheless considered that the owner of copyright in the underlying work had no proprietary rights in the adaptation made in breach of the contract (at 562–3), owing to the skill that was applied in its creation (thereby following *Redwood Music Ltd v Chappell & Co Ltd* [1982] RPC 109).

On a final note, often the question of infringement turns on whether or not the act concerned had been authorised, or fell within the scope of an existing authorisation, so that this becomes the core factual inquiry: see, for instance, *Tamawood Ltd v Habitare Developments*; see also Chapter 2 Copyright: Subsistence Requirements.

Infringement of Copyright in Literary and Dramatic Works

4.7 In literary copyright cases, the infringement may consist of the taking of parts of the actual text, and then the question is whether the part taken, irrespective of its size, is substantial in the copyright sense. Alternatively, as in dramatic work cases, the alleged infringement consists of reproducing the literary or dramatic development of the source work. Such cases commonly proceed by way of asking whether what is taken is merely an idea or information, in which case no copyright is infringed, or amounts to the reproduction of the form of expression of the idea in a particular way, in which case infringement may be found. Thus, in *Zeccola v Universal City Studios Inc* (1982) 67 FLR 225; 46 ALR 189, in the context of a claim for copyright infringement of the novel and screenplay on which the film *Jaws* was based, by the making of the Italian film *L'Ultimo Squalo*, the court rightly pointed out that 'in general there is no copyright in the central idea or theme of a story or play however original it may be; copyright subsists in the combination of situations, events and scenes which constitute the particular working out or expression of the idea or theme.' That there is no copyright in ideas is readily asserted, but where does an idea end and its expression begin? In *Telstra Corporation Ltd v Royal & Sun Alliance Insurance Australia Ltd* (2003) 57 IPR 453; [2003] FCA 786, the defendant used a striking Goggomobil car as the centrepiece of its advertisements, as the plaintiff had done in its prior ads. But Merkel J (at [44]) held that the similarities merely lay in the underlying idea rather than its expression as a series of dramatic events:

> The scripts for the two advertisements bore little resemblance to each other. The only expressions of any significance common to both scripts are those relating to the Goggomobil. Not surprisingly, there is a similar lack of resemblance between the script for the first Goggomobil advertisement and the film of the first Shannons advertisement. While the resemblances in the scripts and films relating to the Goggomobil are significant, the copying that has occurred relates more to the concept or theme employed in relation to the Goggomobil than to the expression of that concept or theme.

On the other hand, if the plot of a novel or play represents the skill, judgment and effort of the author in expressing a broad theme, concept or idea, replicating the plot may amount to the taking of a substantial part: see also *Harman Pictures NV v Osborne* [1967] 1 WLR 723 and the famous US case *Nichols v Universal Pictures Corporation* (1931) 282 US 902. However, if the only incidents of a play that are copied are stock scenes or so-called 'scènes à faire' (scenes that are common to a certain genre), there will be no infringement. As the court in *Zeccola* put it (at ALR 192):

> Originality, when dealing with incidents and characters familiar in life or fiction, lies in the association, grouping and arrangement of those incidents and characters in such a manner that presents a new concept or a novel arrangement of those events and characters. We accept that where a story is written based on various incidents which in themselves are commonplace a claim for copyright must be confined closely to the story which has been composed by the author. Another author who materially varies the incidents and characters and materially changes the story is not an infringer of the copyright.

To take the underlying format of a television show may not amount to an actionable reproduction. The format may be expressed as a literary work describing or listing the consistent elements or characteristics of a show (such as, eg, *Big Brother*). To replicate these elements in a similar show may amount only to the taking of an idea or concept, rather than a particular form of expression. The difficulty is that the actual dramatic developments during a particular episode are largely determined by the unscripted actions of participants, which are obviously not replicated in the imitation: see, for example, *Nine Films & Television Pty Ltd v Ninox Television Ltd* (2005) 67 IPR 46; [2005] FCA 1404, where *The Block* was held not to infringe copyright in *Dream Home*. In the context of factual works, infringement is not to be judged by the importance of the information that is taken but by asking whether the original way in which an author presented or 'expressed' facts has been reproduced. An interesting case is where a written work purports to be based on facts but arguably is largely fiction or an interpretation and blending of fact and fiction. *Baigent v Random House Group Ltd* [2007] All ER (D) 456 (Mar) (*The Da Vinci Code* case) was such a case. The source work, *The Holy Blood and the Holy Grail* by Baigent and Leigh, was a work of mixed fact and hypothesis whose central theme related to the supposed provenance and history of the Holy Grail and associate secret dealings. Adoption of this theme in *The Da Vinci Code*, a bestselling work of fiction by Dan Brown, was found not to constitute reproduction of expression. The similarity was at much too high a level of abstraction to trouble copyright law. The fact that some of the factual material was the same in both works was also not enough. It was possible that the information in both came from other public sources, and even if it found its way into *The Da Vinci Code* by way of Baigent and Leigh's book, the replication of facts or alleged facts, as opposed to the manner of their presentation, is not an infringement per se. Unsurprisingly, the findings of the trial court were not disturbed on appeal: *Baigent and Leigh v The Random House Group Ltd* [2007] EWCA 247. The Court of Appeal also pointed out that as a matter of law, the intention (*animus furandi*) of the alleged infringer is irrelevant. The works at issue were substantial, but as discussed in Chapter 2 Copyright: Subsistence Requirements at 2.9, something far less extensive can also amount to a literary work protected by copyright; this was, for instance, the case in *Fairfax Media Publications Pty Ltd v Reed International Books Australia Pty Ltd* (2010) 189 FCR 109; [2010] FCA 984, and also in *Budget Eyewear Australia Pty Ltd v Specsavers Pty Ltd* [2010] FCA 507. On an application for interlocutory relief, the court in *Budget Eyewear* had to distinguish between the mere copying of the idea behind an advertising campaign, or a potentially infringing reproduction of its literary expression in particular advertising material. If such material is simple and there are few alternative options to express a similar idea in words, then an alleged infringement will have to be very close in literary expression to infringe. Here the respondent had simply substituted some synonyms for certain words in the advertisement. The court's finding, that this constituted copying of a substantial part of the source work, implicitly accepted the applicant's submission that the respondent 'could have copied the idea but exercised its own imagination to express that novel concept in new and different language rather than, in its contention, "using a thesaurus" to substitute a synonym': *Budget Eyewear* at [21].

Compilations and computer programs

4.8 Literary works include compilations by virtue of s 10 of the Copyright Act. Where the original work is a compilation, one must have regard to the work as a whole rather than its component parts in order to determine substantial similarity.

In *Skybase Nominees Pty Ltd v Fortuity Pty Ltd* (1996) 36 IPR 529, the defendant allegedly reproduced the plaintiff's 'Weight Watchers' programs. While she had altered the appearance somewhat and made some slight changes, Nicholson J, relying on a relevant passage in Copinger and Skone James,[2] stated that, in the authors' view, the principle in these kinds of cases is (at IPR 541):

> ... that if one person has, with considerable labour, compiled a work from various sources which he had digested and arranged, then a defendant who instead of taking pains of researching the common sources and obtaining this subject-matter from them, simply makes use of the other's labour and adopts his arrangement, perhaps with only slight variations, thus saving himself the pains and labour which the other used, this will be an illegitimate use.

In *Desktop Marketing Systems Pty Ltd v Telstra Corporation Ltd* (2002) 119 FCR 491; 55 IPR 1, the defendant reproduced Telstra directories on CD-ROM. It did not reproduce Telstra's alphabetical arrangement of names, addresses, telephone numbers and business descriptions. Lindgren J pointed out [at 238] that the:

> ... relevant principle is that where copyright protection is attracted to a compilation of factual information by the labour of collecting, verifying, recording and assembling the data and not by reference to the form of the compilation, reproduction does not require formal resemblance, and the notion of a substantial part of the compilation is not defined by reference to its form.

There was very little labour involved in the alphabetical presentation of Telstra's data; rather, it lay in the collecting, verifying and recording of details. The defendant, by reproducing all the collected material, had appropriated that labour and was guilty of copyright infringement. However, the High Court's decision in *IceTV* effectively rejected this traditional 'industrious collection' approach. The originality of a compilation does not lie in the effort and skill of generating data or entries but in the intellectual activity that results in those data or entries being expressed in a particular form. Therefore, replication of data, even if industriously collected, does not constitute an infringement of a compilation (ie, literary work). To infringe, the impugned work must replicate an original way of compiling the material that results from an identifiable author's independent intellectual activity. The decision to deny copyright for a phone directory in *Telstra Corporation Ltd v Phone Directories Pty Ltd* [2010] FCAFC 149 results from the standard introduced by *IceTV* — that the expression of information in a particular form must result from the individual intellectual activity of a particular author or authors.

Before *IceTV*, originality in the context of infringement was said not to be the same concept as is used in the context of subsistence. Originality for subsistence purposes meant little more than that the work was not copied from elsewhere. However, since *IceTV*, courts in considering both subsistence and infringement must focus on identifying some level of creativity in expression emanating from the author's mind.

The literary works category also includes computer programs. In *Autodesk Inc v Dyason* (1992) 173 CLR 330 and *Autodesk Inc v Dyason (No 2)* (1993) 176 CLR 300, decisions of the same court, the latter concerning an application to reopen the

2. Copinger and Skone James, *Copyright*, Sweet & Maxwell, London, 1991.

case, the High Court held that in the context of computer program copyright, a part was substantial if it amounted to an 'essential' part or a 'critical' part of the computer program. Furthermore, it was not necessary that the substantial part of a computer program reproduced should itself be a computer program. The only part of the program that Dyason, in circumventing the AUTOCAD hardware lock, was found to have reproduced was a look-up table, quantitatively speaking a minuscule fraction of the overall program, and more data than command. But the court was persuaded that as the CAD package would not operate without the correct look-up table and the responses it generated, it was a vital and thus qualitatively important part of the program.

In *Cantor Fitzgerald International v Tradition (UK) Ltd* [2000] RPC 95, Pumfrey J (at [75]) criticised this aspect of *Autodesk*: 'It seems to me, with all respect, that this reasoning would result in any part of any computer program being substantial since without any part the program would not work, or at best not work as desired. It seems to me with all respect that such an approach is simplistic.' Pumfrey J (at [76]) then went on to stress that the function of copyright is to protect the relevant skill and labour expended by the author on the work. Therefore, 'a copyist infringes if he appropriates a part of the work upon which a substantial part of the author's skill and labour was extended' or, in other words, 'it is necessary to look at the substantiality of the skill and labour expended on that which is taken.' In *Data Access Corporation v Powerflex Services Pty Ltd* (1999) 202 CLR 1; 166 ALR 228, the High Court accepted that its own approach in *Autodesk* was flawed (at ALR 248):

> There is great force in the criticism that the 'but for' essentiality test which is effectively invoked by the majority in *Autodesk (No 2)* is not practicable as a test for determining whether something which appears in a computer program is a substantial part of it. For that reason, we prefer Mason CJ's [minority] opinion that, in determining whether something is a reproduction of a substantial part of a computer program, the 'essential or material features of [the computer program] should be ascertained by considering the originality of the part allegedly taken'.

Thus, the same test applies in the context of computer programs as for other kinds of works, the quality of the part taken being assessed in terms of its originality. And (at ALR 249):

> ... that being so, a person who does no more than reproduce those parts of a program which are 'data' or 'related information' and which are irrelevant to its structure, choice of commands and combination and sequencing of commands will be unlikely to have reproduced a substantial part of the computer program. We say 'unlikely' and not 'impossible' because it is conceivable that the data, considered alone, could be sufficiently original to be a substantial part of the computer program.

In *Tamawood v Henley Arch*, Wilcox and Lindgren JJ pointed out (at [54]) that the criticism in *Data Access* of the 'essentiality test' was aimed at its flaws in computer program cases:

> We do not accept Tamawood's submission that in *Data Access* the High Court intended to lay down a new test of 'substantial part'. *Autodesk* and *Data Access* concerned computer programs. Every digit in a computer program is essential to the successful operation of the program. The High Court was concerned in those cases to reject the notion that this meant that every such part also necessarily constituted a substantial part of a computer program regarded as a literary work for copyright purposes.

The focus on originality opens the door to the 'look and feel' approach, which is analogous to the approach taken in the literary work to film copying cases such as *Zeccola*.

Under that approach, copyright in a computer program may be infringed by the reproduction not only of a sequence of the source or object code (as was argued in *TICA Default Tenancy Control Pty Ltd v Datakatch Pty Ltd* [2016] FCA 815, where the amount of HTML code demonstrably copied was held to be too trivial) but also of the structure and composition of the program. If this is accepted, copyright may indirectly afford a degree of protection for the user interface of a computer program, but it is clear that it should not be taken so far as to amount to the monopolisation of the functional characteristics of a program; that is, the way it operates. Dawson J noted this in *Autodesk Inc v Dyason* at CLR 344, in criticising the trial decision of Northrop J:

> Indeed, the significance placed by Northrop J upon the function of the two locks would appear to be in disregard of the traditional dichotomy in the law of copyright between an idea and the expression of an idea.

In *EIFY Systems Pty Ltd v 3D Safety Services Pty Ltd* [2017] NSWSC 1310 the court said that it may be 'accepted, at least for the purposes of argument, that the structure, sequence or organisation of a computer program may be the subject of copyright. Arnold J said as much in *SAS Institute Inc v World Programming Ltd* [[2010] EWHC 1829 (Ch)].' The critical distinction was between the design of the program and its functionality, as stressed by Pumfrey J in *Navitaire Inc v Easyjet Airline Co* [2004] EWHC 1725 (Ch); in *EIFY Systems* functionality may well have been copied, but design not so. Nor had the layout, format and look (or 'look and feel') been reproduced: 'EIFY's case conflates the structure, sequence or organisation of the e-Induct System with the structure, sequence or organisation of the underlying computer program. It is the latter, not the former, in which copyright may subsist': *EIFY Systems* at [432]. When assessing originality, it is thus not right to focus on the functional advantage or novelty of a particular part of the source program. When the comparison is between source and object code in two programs, the key question is the originality 'with which [what was taken] expresses [the] algorithmic or logical relationship or part thereof': *Data Access* at [85]. Thus, the pseudocode analysis used to reveal similarities between two programs in *Admar Computers Pty Ltd v Ezy Systems Pty Ltd* (1997) 38 IPR 659 was misleading. Because pseudocode analysis is an abstraction of the functionality of a program, similar functionality would readily result in similar pseudocode. In an analogous manner, and as reiterated in *Metricon Homes Pty Ltd v Barrett Property Group Pty Ltd* (2008) 75 IPR 455; [2008] FCAFC 46 at [60], quoting from *Tamawood v Henley Arch*, copyright may subsist in the way a whole house plan reflects a 'combination and arrangement' of individual parts originated by an author. This was, for instance, also the decision in the kookaburra song case: see below 4.9.

Infringement of Copyright in Musical Works

4.9 Musical works go from relatively simple tunes to complex and substantial compositions. Again, the focus is on the quality rather than the quantity of what is taken. A short but striking part of a musical composition may constitute a substantial part for the purposes of copyright. In *Francis Day & Hunter v Bron* [1963] Ch 587

(*The Little Spanish Town* case), the test was said to be what the 'ordinary reasonably experienced listener' sees as the substance of the source work. Thus, a substantial part of a work may consist of only a few bars that represent the principal melodic element. But where this is the case, it must be kept in mind that it is not inconceivable that two persons arrive independently at the same or very similar musical scores; objective similarity may be misleading in some cases. In *The Little Spanish Town* case, the plaintiffs alleged that the respondents had reproduced eight bars from the musical work 'In a Little Spanish Town'. Wilberforce J at first instance had held that although there was a definite or considerable degree of similarity between the two works, there was insufficient evidence of unconscious copying. As there was no conscious copying either, he dismissed the plaintiff's case. The decision of Wilberforce J, who had the advantage of himself hearing witnesses and hearing how musical experts 'illustrated the technical evidence which they gave by demonstrations, both vocally and on the piano, a pleasure the Appeal Court had not enjoyed', could not possibly be said by the Appeal Court to be wrong: at Ch 615, per Willmer J. Ultimately, in assessing any alleged breach of the reproduction right, it is up to the court to make a comparative judgment assisted by expert evidence, if need be. In the case of musical works, the comparison may be made by way of a combination of a visual inspection of the score and an aural comparison of a performance of the two works. An Appeal Court will not lightly disturb the judgment made by the trial judge benefiting from experiencing the works first hand. In the kookaburra song case, *EMI Songs v Larrikin Music*, the question of whether an allegedly infringing work reproduced a substantial part of a source work was described as a 'kind of jury question' involving matters of impression and degree: at [71]. In contrast to *The Little Spanish Town* case, the Full Court upheld the decision of the trial judge (see *Larrikin Music Publishing Pty Ltd v EMI Songs Australia Pty Ltd* [2010] FCA 242) that the brief but oft-repeated central melodic phrase of the round 'Kookaburra Sits in the Old Gum Tree' formed a substantial part of that work.

Copying can be by a process of subconscious or unconscious recall. Such was the case in *Bright Tunes* (see above 4.3). Importantly, although aural comparison may be a crucial test of musical copyright infringement, there is a distinction between this and the test for sound recording infringement. In the latter case, where sampling has occurred, the court may assess the importance of the sampled bite to the source recording to determine whether it is a substantial part: see, for example, *Hyperion Records Ltd v Warner Music (UK) Ltd* (1991) (unreported, (Chancery Division), 17 May 1991). That is a different test from the aural comparison between source and destination works discussed above.

Infringement of Copyright in Artistic Works

4.10 The approach adopted tends to depend on the nature of the allegation in artistic work copyright infringement as well: either by way of general visual side by side comparison where an impugned work is said to be too similar overall to a source copyright work or else by way of an assessment of the importance of a specific part or aspect allegedly copied to the overall appearance of the source work. Speaking of copyright works more generally, Mason J in *Autodesk* (at CLR 305) indicated that 'the essential or material features of a [copyright] work should be ascertained by considering the originality of the part allegedly taken.' On the other hand, in relation to artistic copyright, Wilson J in *SW Hart & Co Pty Ltd v Edwards Hot Water Systems* (1985) 159 CLR 466, said in relation to a case where a part of an artistic work has been reproduced: 'whether that part can properly be described as substantial may depend upon how important that part is to the recognition and appreciation of the "artistic work" ... What is protected is the skill and labour devoted to making the "artistic work" itself, not the skill and labour devoted to developing some idea or invention communicated or depicted by the "artistic work"'. The case concerned design drawings for a hot water system — artistic works of a technical nature — hence the reference to depicting an invention in the passage just quoted. The process of assessment of the originality of what is taken is well illustrated by architectural copyright cases. Designs for suburban domestic dwellings are, generally speaking, structurally similar because of constraining parameters such as cost, average family size, building materials and techniques, and land availability. Nonetheless, project home builders invest skill and energy in giving their designs some distinguishing individuality, and cases of alleged copyright infringement of home designs (as either buildings or plans) are consequently also quite common.

In *Eagle Homes Pty Ltd v Austec Homes Pty Ltd* (1997) 39 IPR 565, both applicant and respondent were project home builders. The applicant alleged that copyright had been infringed by the publication of the respondent's advertisements containing reproductions of a substantial part of its artistic works (the floor plans) and built homes (note that by virtue of s 21(3), an artistic work in two dimensions shall be deemed to have been reproduced if a version in three dimensions is produced, and vice versa). First, on the issue of originality, Branson J concluded (at 568–9) that the source plans shared many features with a pre-existing plan. However, although copyright will not subsist in slavish copies of an earlier work, there were sufficient visual differences for the subject drawings to amount to original works in which copyright subsisted. After referring to *Beck v Montana Constructions Pty Ltd* [1964–5] NSWR 229, *Ancher Mortlock Murray & Woolley Pty Ltd v Hooker Homes Pty Ltd* [1971] 2 NSWLR 278 and *Dixon Investments Pty Ltd v Hall* (1990) 18 IPR 490 (and other architectural copyright cases), Branson J continued (at 574–5):

> So, in the case of a copyright architectural drawing which includes a feature of marked originality, a finding that that feature has been reproduced is more likely to lead to a finding of infringement of copyright than a finding of a reproduction of a commonplace feature: the reproduction of a markedly original feature will, by reason of its quality, amount to a reproduction of a substantial part of the copyright work — even where the feature comprises a relatively small part of the total copyright work. In contrast, in the case of a copyright architectural drawing which is without unusual features, the reproduction of a quantitatively [sic] greater proportion of the copyright work will be necessary to establish that a substantial part of the work has been reproduced. The subject drawings in this case did not exhibit marked originality.

It will be clear from Branson J's words that 'originality' is used here in a different sense from in the context of subsistence of copyright, as was confirmed in *Tamawood v Henley Arch* at [53].

Although quality is most often the key, quantity is not necessarily irrelevant. Wilcox and Lindgren JJ in *Tamawood v Henley Arch* at [50] said:

> But quantity may be relevant. Where the same degree of labour, skill and judgment contribute uniformly to all parts of the work, so that no part is distinguishable from any other part in this respect, it will apparently be necessary to demonstrate reproduction of a quantitatively substantial proportion of the work in order to establish reproduction of a substantial part: cf *Accounting Systems 2000 (Developments) Pty Ltd v CCH Australia Ltd* (1993) 42 FCR 470 (reproduction of 25 per cent of computer program).

For more recent examples concerning architectural copyright, see *C & J Designer Homes Pty Ltd v Robey* (2007) 207 FLR 181; *Metricon Homes*; *Barrett Property Group Pty Ltd v Carlisle Homes Pty Ltd* [2008] FCA 375; *Coles v Dormer* (2015) 117 IPR 184; [2015] QSC 224 (with an unusual fact scenario); and *Venezuela Pty Ltd v Bright* [2017] WADC 79.

In artistic copyright cases, the resemblance between works may be due rather to the selection of a similar subject or the adoption of a similar style or technique. However, there is no infringement in copying style, technique or general subject matter per se; the form of expression must be reproduced: see *Cummins v Vella* [2002] FCAFC 218. Vella's work was characterised by the application of bright colours by way of an 'impasto' technique and depiction in a 'naïve' style. These elements were adopted by Cummins when he embarked upon his own artistic career. The trial decision in favour of Vella was overturned on appeal because the trial judge focused on similarities in style and technique without undertaking a detailed examination of the similarities and differences between the works at issue.

The New Zealand Supreme Court in *Henkel KGaA v Holdfast NZ* [2007] 1 NZLR 577; (2006) 70 IPR 624, after pointing out that it is enough for the plaintiff to establish copying of a substantial part rather than the whole of the work, went on to say (at [35]–[37]):

> This can sometimes be a difficult matter of evaluation and is usually the most difficult question which arises in copyright cases. What amounts to a substantial part in an artistic work case depends more on qualitative visual impression rather than on quantitative analysis. As it has helpfully been put, what must have been copied is the essence of the copyright work. This is a subject upon which, in borderline cases, minds can reasonably differ and it is appropriate for appellate courts to give to the trial judge's assessment the degree of latitude that conventionally applies to appellate review of a discretion.

The case related to a rather commonplace drawing reproduced on packaging for a bottle of adhesive, which, in turn, was alleged to have been copied on the packaging of a competing product. The court pointed out that where the work consists of an arrangement of unoriginal elements, a trial court cannot proceed by omitting each unoriginal element of the source work and then making a judgment about what remains. Instead, the court detailed some of the differences between the two works at issue and ultimately concluded that given the low level of originality of the source work, the impugned packaging was sufficiently different in its arrangement of otherwise rather similar elements. In *The Dempsey Group Pty Ltd v Spotlight Pty Ltd* [2018] FCA 2016 also the focus was on the composition of different elements of the surface design of some quilts and pillows. These represented the 'look and feel' of the artistic work, and that had been replicated by Spotlight. There was thus a copyright infringement, although there were differences in each separate element. *The Dempsey Group* thus followed a similar approach to that adopted in *Elwood Clothing Pty Ltd v Cotton On Clothing Pty Ltd* (2008) 172 FCR 580; [2008] FCAFC 197: although the elements themselves were differently expressed, their original composition (the visually significant interrelationship between the carefully positioned elements) had been replicated. It is important in artistic works cases — in particular, where technical, engineering and architectural drawings are at issue — to remember that copyright does not extend to technical ideas and innovations reflected in such works. Thus, adopting only a functional solution found in the source work may not be reproduction of a substantial part of the expression of a work: see *Vawdrey Australia Pty Ltd v Krueger Transport Equipment Pty Ltd* (2009) 83 IPR 1; [2009] FCAFC 156.

Reproduction in Pt III and Copying in Pt IV

4.11 The Pt IV copyright owner enjoys the exclusive right to copy, rather than to reproduce, subject matter. Note the narrow meaning of the word 'copy' in Pt IV; only a facsimile copy directly derived without authorisation is an infringement. *CBS Songs Ltd v Amstrad Consumer Electronics Plc Ltd* [1988] AC 1013 held that a sound-alike or look-alike recording could not infringe Pt IV copyright. In other words, a person who produces an identical-sounding recording by imitating previously recorded performances may infringe copyright in the musical work performed, but will not infringe copyright in the pre-existing Pt IV sound recording. However, in *Sega Enterprises Ltd v Galaxy Electronics* (1996) 69 FCR 268 at 271, Burchett J pointed out that to copy in the context of Pt IV does not mean solely to reproduce in the same technological format. 'Copy' is defined in s 10(1) as 'in relation to a cinematograph film ... any article or thing in which the visual images or sounds comprising the film are embodied.' His Honour said (at [15]):

> It would be strange indeed if parliament intended the definition of 'copy' to be construed so narrowly that a representation of an animated film, which looked just like the film, would not constitute an infringement, simply because it was produced by the computer technology involved in the present case.

The technology involved reproduction in digital form of existing movies by means of object-based coding. The decision was confirmed on appeal, and the point made by Burchett J, although not required to be considered for the purposes of determining the issue, was not brought into question. The essential requirements seem to be that the copy be directly derived by some technological process, whatever that may be, from the original, and that the result looks the same as the original.

What is a substantial part of subject matter other than works, in this case television broadcasts, was sidestepped by the approach the Full Federal Court took in *TCN Channel Nine Pty Ltd v Network Ten Pty Ltd* (2002) 118 FCR 417; 55 IPR 112 to the question of what constitutes a TV broadcast. However, the High Court rejected the Full Court's determination of that issue and consequently had to remit the case back to the Full Court to consider whether a substantial part of a broadcast had been copied: *Network Ten Pty Ltd v TCN Channel Nine Pty Limited* (2004) 218 CLR 273; 59 IPR 1. A 'primarily quantitative' test, as adopted initially by the trial judge, was ruled out by the Full Court, which instead applied a test more analogous to that applied to Pt III works: *TCN Channel Nine Pty Ltd v Network Ten Pty Limited (No 2)* (2005) 145 FCR 35l; [2005] FCAFC 53. Finkelstein J at [28] identified the only proper approach by extracting from the case law the kinds of relevant questions to be asked:

> Does what has been taken amount to 'essentially the heart' of the copyrighted work; ... 'the essential part of the copyright work?'; ... 'at least an important ingredient'? ... Are the excerpts 'highlights' from the programme? Are the excerpts central to the programme in which it appeared? Does the portion used 'constitute the "heart" — the most valuable and pertinent portion — of the copyright material?'. (Citations omitted)

In relation to copyright infringement of cinematograph films, see also *Kabushiki Kaisha Sony Computer Entertainment v Stevens* (2003) 132 FCR 31 at 91–2; 57 IPR 161.

Bibliography

A Brown, 'Proof of Copying' (2000) 43 *IP Forum* 24.

A McGee and G Scanlan, 'Copyright in Character' [2003] *JBL* 470.

G Davies, N Caddick, and G Harbottle, *Copinger & Skone James on Copyright*, 17th ed, Sweet & Maxwell, 2016.

G Smith, '*Eagle Homes Pty Ltd v Austec Homes Pty Ltd* — Case Notes' (1998) 14(5) *BCL* 368.

J McCutcheon, 'Copyright Protection for Fictional Literary Characters' (2006) 67 *IP Forum* 14.

M Richardson, J Gans, F Hanks, and P Williams, 'Benefits and Costs of Copyright: Economic Perspective Part 1' (2000) 13(5) *IPLB* 62.

M Rimmer, 'Harry Potter and the Lexicon of Doom' (2008) 21(2) *IPLB* 26.

P Loughlan, 'An Issue in Architectural Copyright' (1995) 8 *IPLB* 9.

S Birchall, 'A Doctrine Under Pressure: The Need for Rationalisation of the Doctrine of Authorisation of Infringement of Copyright in Australia' (2004) 15(4) *AIPJ* 227.

S Birchall, 'Authorisation of Copyright Infringement — Is the Word "Other" an Impostor in Section 101(1A)(c)?' (2006) 66 *IP Forum* 34.

S Rebikoff, 'Restructuring the Test for Copyright Infringement in Relation to Literary and Dramatic Plots' (2001) 25 *MULR* 340.

S Stone, 'No Infringement of Copyright in Architectural Plans' (1998) 10 *IPLB* 118.

W Alstergren, 'Copyright in Architecture — Recent Developments' (2004) 17(4) *IPLB* 63.

Chapter 5

Copyright: Other Rights and Exceptions

Other Exclusive Rights

Exhaustion of rights

5.1 Chapter 4 focused primarily on the exclusive rights to reproduce works and to copy Pt IV subject matter. But, as pointed out there, the copyright owner also benefits from a number of other exclusive rights enumerated in the Copyright Act 1968 (Cth) in s 31 in relation to works and in ss 85–88 in relation to subject matter other than works. The fundamental requirements of derivation or access and substantial similarity are, naturally, preliminary requirements in relation to infringement of these rights as well. However, the copyright owner must also establish that the use made of the copyright material falls within the proper extent of one or more of those exclusive rights. In relation to Pt III works, these are the rights to publish the work, to perform the work in public, to communicate the work to the public, to make an adaptation of the work and also a limited rental right. These rights are further circumscribed by virtue of other sections of the Act, but to varying degrees, so important questions remain to be resolved by the courts. Anything a person does with, or in relation to, copyright material that does not fall within the purview of one of the exclusive rights is not actionable; for instance, the owner of a book is allowed to lend it to a friend to read, or give it away, or sell it second hand. None of these actions is comprised within the exclusive rights of the copyright owner. Whether there are any copyright-based limitations at all on the right to deal further in copies of works legitimately acquired is determined by the level of 'exhaustion of rights'. As a general principle, a copyright owner who puts copyright material into the market cannot control further physical dealings with that work, such as on-selling, exporting, etc. However, copyright owners retain, naturally, all rights of action in relation to the various exclusive copyrights; for instance, against a person who acquires a book and then photocopies it whole. The exhaustion theory is usually considered to have two limbs: national and international exhaustion. The former means that once copyright material is released into a national market, the copyright owner has no statutory rights in relation to its circulation (on-selling, etc) within the country. The latter means that once released into a foreign market, the copyright owner cannot control either circulation within that market or import into another national market. Although national exhaustion applies in all countries, positions diverge on international exhaustion. The majority do not allow 'parallel importation' or 'grey marketing' of copyright goods. In other words, the importation of legitimate copyright materials put onto the market in another country is not allowed without the copyright owner's authorisation. They do not adopt 'international exhaustion' of rights. That means the copyright owner can maintain differential pricing and conditions between separate national markets. Australia is one of those few countries that no longer exclude parallel importation by statute, in relation to most copyright materials, with the notable exception to date of paper books (an exception the Productivity Commission (PC) in its inquiry report into intellectual property in Australia (PC Report)[1] has recommended should be removed). In other words, it is legal for a distributor to purchase legitimate copyright materials overseas and import them for the purpose of sale, perhaps in competition with the copyright owner's official distributor or licensee in Australia. This is said to have the effect of engendering price competition and arbitraging in relation to legitimate copyright materials such as sound recordings in Australia. Obviously, it is always legitimate for individuals to purchase copyright materials overseas and import them for their own use; for instance, by buying an item from a foreign retail outlet or by ordering a book for personal use from a website based in another country: see further below: Parallel Importation 5.10.

Adaptation

5.2 What is comprised within the right to make an adaptation of a literary, dramatic, musical or artistic work is exhaustively circumscribed under 'adaptation' in s 10. In effect, 'adaptation' in the copyright sense comprises a narrower range of actions than its ordinary meaning might suggest. It consists of the rights to dramatisation, novelisation, translation, picturisation, to make a transcription or arrangement of a musical work and to make a version of a computer program 'whether or not in the language, code or notation in which' it was originally expressed, not being a reproduction of it. Making slight changes or adapting a copyright work for a different purpose or use is thus not an adaptation in the copyright sense unless it otherwise falls within one of the listed acts. However, the meaning and extent of the adaptation right to 'make a version of' a computer program is rather less clear than the others. The explanatory memorandum of the Copyright Amendment Act 1984 (Cth) says:

> The new definition [of adaptation] is intended to cover translation either way between the various so-called 'high-level programming languages' in which the programs may be written by humans (often called 'source code') and languages, codes or notations which actually control computer operations (often called 'machine code' or 'object code'). Thus 'adaptation' is intended, for example, to cover the compilation of a FORTRAN program to produce machine code which will directly control the operation of a computer. Languages, etc of intermediate level would also be covered.

The High Court in *Data Access Corporation v Powerflex Services Pty Ltd* (1999) 202 CLR 1; 45 IPR 353; [1999] HCA 49 stated at [109]:

> The focus on translation indicates that Parliament was concerned to ensure that the different languages in which a computer program may be expressed did not provide a means by

1. Productivity Commission, *Intellectual Property Arrangements*, Inquiry Report No 78, Canberra, September 2016.

which copying could occur and infringement be avoided on the ground that the expression in the new language was not a 'reproduction'.

The High Court thus agreed with the Full Court's view in the same case that what was meant by a version of a computer program was a translation into another language of that program; it was certainly not a program that performed the same functions but contained different code. However, by virtue of s 21(5), introduced by the Copyright Amendment (Digital Agenda) Act 2000 (Cth):

> ... a computer program is taken to have been reproduced if: (a) an object code version of the program is derived from the program in source code by any process, including compilation; or (b) a source code version of the program is derived from the program in object code by any process, including decompilation; and any such version is taken to be a reproduction of the program.

It is thus unclear how the right of adaptation relates to the reproduction right in relation to computer programs or what it adds that is not already comprised in the reproduction right: see also *Admar Computers Pty Ltd v Ezy Systems Pty Ltd* (1997) 38 IPR 659 and *Coogi Australia Pty Ltd v Hysport International Pty Ltd* (1998) 86 FCR 154; 41 IPR 593.

The publication right

5.3 The copyright owner has the exclusive right to publish the work. In the context of s 31(1), the High Court in *Avel Pty Ltd v Multicoin Amusements Pty Ltd* (1990) 171 CLR 88; 18 IPR 443 held that the words 'to publish' mean 'to make public that which had not previously been made public in the copyright territory'. The provisions of s 29 concerning when a work is deemed to have been published for the purpose of subsistence of copyright (ie, when copies are supplied to the public) were held not to operate in the context of s 31. The publication right is effectively the right of first publication and is thus not a right by which further control can be exercised over dealings in copies legitimately supplied to the public. The right of publication also does not confer a right of withdrawal of published works; in some jurisdictions this is considered to be an aspect of an author's moral rights: see Moral Rights 5.22ff. As the passage above concerning s 29 indicates, the concept of 'publication' occurs elsewhere in the Act but with a different meaning and effect. First publication will determine the starting point of the term of copyright protection for certain works and for most subject matter other than works. Publication is also relevant to the subsistence of copyright in Australia in some cases. For instance, copyright will attach to a work in Australia if it is first published here or if it is published here within 30 days from its first publication abroad pursuant to s 29(5).

The right of public performance

5.4 The public performance right is of considerable economic significance to copyright owners, particularly to the composers of musical works and the makers of sound recordings and films but also to authors of literary or dramatic works incorporated in the latter (it does not apply to artistic works). The right to perform a work in public covers not only live performance but also so-called mechanical performance; that is, performance by playing a film or sound recording of a work in public: see s 27(1) and also *Australasian Performing Right Association Ltd v Tolbush Pty Ltd* [1986] 2 Qd R 146; (1985) 7 IPR 160. Where a public performance of a film or sound recording takes place, the separately subsisting rights of the composer of the musical work; of the author of the lyrics or book, script and screenplay; and of the 'maker' of the sound recording or film (ie, the producer) are all being exercised. The authorisation (usually by contract) of every one of those copyright owners must be obtained. Mechanical performance can be by way of the placement of a radio in a public place (as to who is liable in such a situation see s 27(3) and (4)), or by way of CDs, DVDs, films, videos and so on being played in public; for instance, in cinemas or pubs, clubs and restaurants. It is important to maintain the distinction between the right of 'communication to the public' (see further below 5.6) and performance in public. Communication of a work (or subject matter) does not amount to a public performance: see s 27(2).

Broadcasting is now comprised within the right of communication to the public and thus does not constitute a public performance. For instance, if a radio is set up in a pub, the radio station will have had to acquire a broadcasting licence (ie, authorisation to communicate copyright material to the public), and the publican will require a licence to perform the work in public. The operation of these complex and multiple licensing relationships is rendered more practical by the various forms of statutory licensing schemes established or permitted under the Copyright Act: see further below.

Not every performance is a 'performance in public'. From some person singing in the shower the copyright owner cannot expect to obtain royalties. But where does the dividing line between a remunerable performance in public and other performances lie? The Act contains some specific rules that take certain performances out of the public sphere; for instance, where they take place in the classroom: see s 28. However, where no specific provision applies, recourse must be had to the principles developed in the cases. In *Telstra Corporation Ltd v Australasian Performing Right Association* (1997) 191 CLR 140; 38 IPR 294 (*Telstra v APRA*), the High Court identified a number of principles applicable to the distinction between a performance in public and performances that would not fall within the exclusive rights of the copyright owner:

1. The size of the audience is of no consequence; rather, it is the context of the performance that is determinative.
2. A performance in public may be contrasted to a performance in the private or domestic sphere; that is, it is relevant whether the audience is bound by private or other ties.
3. If the performance occurs as an adjunct or in connection with public or commercial life; that is, in a situation where the audience's public pursuits bring them together, it is a public performance.
4. Following on from the previous principle, the relevant 'public' is the group the copyright owner would otherwise contemplate as their paying public for the performance of their work.

Indeed, the court considered the last and rather broad principle the most satisfactory. The question 'Was the performance before the copyright owner's public?' was preferable to the question 'Was the performance in public or in private?'. Thus, it is not relevant that the performance is staged in a place that is arguably not accessible to the general public, such as a private club. Such an audience can still be considered to be part of 'the copyright owner's public': see *Australasian Performing Right Association Ltd v Canterbury-Bankstown Leagues Club Ltd* (1964) 5 FLR 415. In contrast, in the old case of *Duck v Bates* (1884) 13 QBD 843, a play was performed in a room at a hospital, those present being employees. This was not a public performance, since the author did not suffer any loss of income and the audience were not people who would otherwise have attended a commercial staging of a play. In *Australasian Performing Right Association Ltd v Commonwealth Bank of Australia* (1992) 40 FCR 59; 25 IPR 157, Gummow J, then of the Federal Court, held that the playing of a training video containing part of the collecting society's musical work during a training session for selected staff of the bank was a performance in public. He said (at FCR 74–5):

> The occasion of the performance was the imparting of information by the employer to its employees and the musical work was used to facilitate that process. The audience was brought together by the commercial purposes of the respondent and their public lives as employees. These are the most significant facts which, consistently with the pre-1968 case law, support the characterization of the performance of the work as one 'in public' within the meaning of s 31(1)(a)(iii) of the 1968 Act.

The commercial setting was also emphasised in *Zomba Production Music (Australia) Pty Ltd v Roadhouse Productions Pty Ltd* (2001) 53 IPR 520.

Public performance: collecting royalties

5.5 The collection of royalties in relation to the public performance of musical works, the literary works associated with musical works (lyrics) and sound recordings is administered by 'collecting societies' on behalf of copyright owners. Collecting societies such as the Australasian Performing Rights Association (APRA), representing musical and literary copyright owners, and the Phonographic Performance Company of Australia (PPCA), representing sound recording copyright owners, license performances or venues and collect royalties for all forms of live and mechanical public performance. A collecting society can bring an action in relation to unlicensed public performance: see, for instance, *Phonographic Performance Company of Australia Pty Ltd v Hairy Little Sista Pty Ltd* [2018] FCCA 2794). A licensing scheme may be approved on a reference to the Copyright Tribunal by a collecting society under ss 154–159: see, for example, *Reference by Australasian Performing Right Association Ltd* (2006) 70 IPR 211 and *Australian Hotels Association v Copyright Tribunal* [2008] FCAFC 37. The application in the first matter related to a scheme proposed by APRA relating to the performance of background music in retail and other premises with a new method of royalty calculation that was likely to result in substantial increases. The general advantages of a scheme approved by the Copyright Tribunal are explained at [9]. Tribunal-confirmed schemes are different from the statutory licences provided for elsewhere in the Copyright Act but share the same purpose of improving the practical operation of copyright in this area and earning proper returns to copyright owners: see Pts VA, VB and VC and Div 2 of Pt VII of the Act. The Tribunal has the power to set royalty rates for various uses of copyright material; see, for instance, in the matter relating to simulcasting online of radio broadcasts: *Phonographic Performance Company of Australia Ltd under s 154 of the Copyright Act 1968 (Cth)* [2016] AcopyT 2 (relying on the decision in *Phonographic Performance Company of Australia Ltd v Commercial Radio Australia Ltd* [2013] FCAFC 11, where it was held that the licence to radio broadcast certain sound recordings did not comprise the right to simulcast these via the internet, so that a separate royalty was payable for the latter).

Demands for royalty payments for the use of background music issued by collecting societies to many small businesses playing music for employees' benefit attracted public scrutiny in the wake of the decision in *Telstra v APRA*. The obligation to pay royalties appeared to be a new and unwarranted impost. An inquiry into copyright music and small business was undertaken by the House Standing Committee on Legal and Constitutional Affairs on a reference from the Commonwealth Attorney-General. The committee recommended that small businesses that employ fewer than 20 people and that play music not intended to be heard by customers or by the general public be issued with complimentary licences for public performances of copyright music in certain circumstances. This would, in effect, create a 'panel beater's exception', meaning that small workshops and so on in which music from a radio, smartphone, streaming service or digitial library is played for the benefit of employees only would not have to pay royalties to the relevant collecting societies. There is a separate question as to who should obtain authorisation for a public performance of copyright works: the organiser of the performance or the controller of the premises where the performance is to take place. As is pointed out above, permitting the use of certain venues for an infringing performance is a form of indirect infringement of copyright (s 39), and authorising, as well as actually conducting, an infringing performance is a direct infringement of copyright. As to the relationship between the different forms of infringement, see *Australasian Performing Right Association Ltd v Metro on George Pty Ltd* (2004) 64 IPR 57 (the *Metro on George* case) and see 5.9, Indirect Infringement.

As to exceptions to the public performance right, see ss 45–46 in relation to works and ss 105, 106 and 109 in relation to Pt IV copyright.

The right of communication to the public

5.6 In 2000 the pre-existing separate technology-specific broadcast and cable transmission rights were replaced by a broader technology-neutral right of 'communication to the public'. The two constituent elements are the existence of a 'communication' and that the communication be 'to the public'. The precise nature of the communications technology employed (eg, cable, microwave, fibre optic or a combination of those) to transmit material is no longer determinative, although to 'communicate' is limited by virtue of s 10 to making available online or electronically transmitting a work or other subject matter. In other words, 'communicating' a work by means of a loudhailer to strollers in a public park or by busking in the street would not constitute a communication to the public in the copyright sense because it does not involve the internet or electronic transmission; however, it would usually be a performance in public and therefore require the copyright owner's permission in any case (see above). Introduction of the right was the cornerstone of legislative attempts to adapt copyright to the internet environment: see the Copyright Amendment (Digital Agenda) Act 2000 (Cth). One significant effect of the relevant amendments was to make it clear that the uploading of copyright material onto an internet-connected server, or the connection of a computer or server with stored copyright material to the web, is an act comprised in the copyright: see Copyright Amendment (Digital Agenda) Bill 2000 revised explanatory memorandum. It is irrelevant whether the work is actually transmitted to, read by or downloaded by any internet user; that it is available to persons at remote locations to access if and when they want is sufficient. Where uploading entails the making of a copy of the work, the requirement for the copyright owner's permission would already be enlivened by the reproduction right. The pre-2000 broadcasting right and right of transmission to subscribers (cablecasting) are both forms of 'electronically transmitting' a work. As to exceptions and limitations and further comment concerning the communication right, see Chapter 18 Digitisation.

The internet is used to electronically transmit material in various ways; for instance, by uploading material to a website from which it can be downloaded or streamed; by uploading to a bulletin board, blog or shared space; by internet broadcasting or webcasting; by podcasting; or by sending an email incorporating or attaching a copyright work (eg, a sound file, picture, video). But not all of these comprise a communication 'to the public' so as to fall within the scope of the exclusive right. Similarly, some forms of electronic transmission of copyright material such as an FM radio broadcast of music are clearly 'to the public', whereas others, such as text messaging or sending a ringtone or video clip to a mobile phone, occur in the context of private communication. The High Court in *Telstra v APRA* (see 5.4) held that when Telstra transmitted music on hold to mobile phone subscribers, it was broadcasting works (the broadcast had to be 'to the public', in terms of the definition in the Act prior to the Digital Agenda amendments). Central to the question of what constituted the 'copyright owner's public' was whether the use of the works occurred in a commercial setting, and (per Dawson and Gaudron JJ at CLR 157):

> ... it is the preparedness of those who wish the music on hold to be played to bear the cost of the arrangement which provides the key, for it reveals the commercial character of the broadcast and the commercial deprivation suffered by the copyright owner. Callers on hold constitute the copyright owner's public, not because they themselves would be prepared to pay to hear the music, but because others are prepared to bear the cost of them having that facility.

Thus, Telstra was liable in relation to transmission of works, although it did not control which works were made available via the music on hold service it did not itself operate. In *Woolworths Ltd v Olson* (2004) 63 IPR 258; [2004] NSWSC 849, Einstein J relied on obiter dicta in *Telstra v APRA* that if a broadcast is received privately or domestically, it would be 'to the public' only if 'available to those members of the public who choose to avail themselves of it': at [334]. This led Einstein J to find that sending two emails to a private inbox was not a communication to the public. Naturally the transmission of documents in such circumstances does entail reproduction in the copyright sense: see *Olson*, and for instance also *Bayley & Associates Pty Ltd v DBR Australia Pty Ltd* [2013] FCA 1341.

To return to *Telstra v APRA*, that case also alerted us to the potential liability of internet service providers (ISPs) that provide access to the internet. They find themselves in an analogous situation to Telstra in the case, in that they do not control the content of material provided by subscribers on their services, but they do provide and operate the infrastructure that makes the material available or electronically transmits it. However, the Copyright Amendment (Digital Agenda) Act 2000 (Cth) introduced s 22(6), which provides that 'a communication other than a broadcast is taken to have been made by the person responsible for determining the content of the communication'. This protects ISPs from liability for direct infringement if they are not responsible for choosing the content of infringing material. The ISPs are also protected from liability for 'authorisation' by a special multifaceted regime: see s 39B of the Copyright Act 1968 (Cth) and the Copyright Legislation Amendment Act 2004 (Cth) concerning 'safe harbours' for ISPs that adhere to certain conditions. These issues are dealt with in greater detail in Chapter 18 Digitisation, as are the recommendations in this regard in the recent PC Report on intellectual property arrangements in Australia. Significant cases relating to the communication right are *Universal Music Australia Pty Ltd v Cooper* (2005) 150 FCR 1; 65 IPR 409; *Australasian Performing Right Association Ltd v Monster Communications Pty Ltd* (2006) 71 IPR 212; [2006] FCA 1806; and *IceTV Pty Ltd v Nine Network Australia Pty Ltd* (2009) 239 CLR 458; 80 IPR 451.

Lending and rental rights

5.7 People other than the initial purchaser of copyright material such as a book or CD accessing the content of a work do not usually give rise to a claim to additional royalties for the copyright owner. For instance, lending or borrowing books between friends is not subject to copyright, nor is lending a CD or DVD to a friend to listen to, nor is a copyright owner entitled to additional royalties if you read a purchased book 10 times. It is, of course, different if a friend photocopies the book to read it later or copies the DVD, CD or sound file to add to a personal collection for later enjoyment. These acts fall within the copyright sphere because they require reproduction or copying; nonetheless, in some cases, the defence of fair dealing may be available for such copying (eg, where only part of the work is copied for the purpose of study or research, or where format or time shifting of sound files is at issue). However, if the borrowing and lending are organised on a systematic level, then the commercial rights of authors or copyright owners may be affected adversely. This is addressed in two different ways. Where a book is borrowed from a public lending library, the Public Lending Rights Scheme provides limited returns to authors and publishers from such lending of books: see Public Lending Right Act 1985 (Cth). This regime stands separate from copyright. Alternatively, some commercial rental, as opposed to private lending, does now fall within copyright. Prior to the World Trade Organization (WTO) Trade-Related Aspects of Intellectual Property Rights (TRIPS) Agreement of 1994, the Copyright Act 1968 (Cth) did not recognise exclusive rights over commercial rental. However, Australia's accession to the WTO resulted in the introduction of a limited exclusive commercial rental right for copyright owners: see Copyright (WTO Amendments) Act 1994 (Cth). By virtue of s 31(1)(c) and (d), the right is restricted to literary and musical works reproduced in a sound recording and to computer programs. By virtue of s 85(1)(d), the right also extends to sound recordings themselves. In *Australian Video Retailers v Warner Home Videos Pty Ltd* (2001) 114 FCR 324; 53 IPR 242, it was held that since they were not the essential object of any commercial rental agreement, computer programs incorporated in DVDs were not covered by the rental right, even though they contributed greater user flexibility compared with traditional VHS cassettes.

Authorisation

5.8 It is a form of direct infringement for a person other than the copyright owner to authorise the doing of any act comprised in the copyright within Australia: see s 36(1). This, effectively, extends the parties that a copyright owner can sue beyond the person who actually did the act comprised in the copyright to the person who 'sanctions, approves or countenances' it: see *City of Adelaide Corporation v Australasian Performing Right Association Ltd* (1928) 40 CLR 481 at 489, 497. It might also mean that as well as a corporate entity, an individual director or employee who was in a position to permit or prevent infringing conduct can be held personally liable for authorisation: see *Sony Music Entertainment v CEL Music* (2002) 54 IPR 289 and *Microsoft Corporation v Ezy Loans Pty Ltd* (2004) 63 IPR 54. Section 36(1A) (and the equivalent s 101(1A)) sets out the matters that must be taken into account to determine whether authorisation in this sense has occurred:

1. the extent of the person's power to prevent the infringing act;
2. the nature of the relationship between the alleged authoriser and the person who did the act; and
3. whether the person took any reasonable steps to prevent or avoid the doing of the act.

The statutory formulation of the three elements, introduced by the Copyright Amendment (Digital Agenda) Act 2000 (Cth), is effectively a codification of the law as previously developed by the courts, in particular as set out in *University of New South Wales v Moorhouse* (1975) 133 CLR 1 at 10; 6 ALR 193 (*UNSW v Moorhouse*). Authorisation implies both some element of knowledge of the infringing activity (but not necessarily of its infringing nature) and a degree of actual or exercisable control over it. The latter could consist of knowing or reckless facilitation combined with a failure to police possible infringement. Thus, in *UNSW v Moorhouse*, the university was found liable for authorising copyright infringement by providing students with the means to infringe (a library and photocopiers) and failing to control or supervise what and how much they photocopied. Note the effect on this decision of the Copyright Amendment Act 1980 (Cth): see the current s 39A, which limits authorisation liability if certain conditions are met.

Express permission or formal approval of the infringement is thus not necessarily required, and inactivity can reach the point that warrants an inference of authorisation. But a person who does not know and who has no reason to suspect that copyright is being infringed does not authorise the infringement: see *Microsoft Corporation v Marks* (1995) 33 IPR 15 (affirmed in *Microsoft Corporation v Marks (No 2)* (1996) 69 FCR 144). The alleged authoriser must have some power to prevent the commission of the infringement. In *CBS Songs v Amstrad Consumer Electronics Plc Ltd* (1988) 11 IPR 1, there was no element of control over the use of the dual cassette decks once they had been sold, and no ability to prevent infringing use. Nor did the defendants purport to grant any rights. The sale of the machines thus did not amount to authorisation of infringement. Section 36(1A) was explored in the *Metro on George* case, which also usefully considers the law relating to s 39(2) (see 5.9). More recently, authorisation was at issue in the *Kazaa* case, *Universal Music Australia Pty Ltd v Sharman License Holdings Ltd* (2005) 220 ALR 1; 65 IPR 289, concerning authorisation of infringement by the supply of file-sharing software: see also *Cooper v Universal Music Australia Pty Ltd* (2006) 156 FCR 380; 71 IPR 1; [2006] FCAFC 187. *Kazaa* followed soon upon the US Supreme Court decision in *MGM Studios v Grokster* 125 S Ct 2764 (2005), which also held against the software supplier. The important underlying question is in what circumstances the supply of technology (here software) that enables copyright infringement by peer-to-peer swapping of illegal sound files amounts to 'authorisation' (or contributory infringement in the US). Wilcox J found that Sharman knew that the software was routinely used to infringe copyright and did not put in place readily available technical measures to prevent or minimise copyright infringement. Significantly, the Kazaa website encouraged users to engage in file sharing in defiance of music copyright owners. Taking all factors together, Sharman was therefore found to have authorised copyright infringement. In *Roadshow Films Pty Ltd v iiNet Ltd* (2012) 248 CLR 42, the High Court considered s 101(1A), the Pt IV equivalent of s 36(1A), and held that notices the ISP received from copyright owners concerning infringing behaviour by certain subscribers of the ISP were inadequate, and investigating their reliability was not a reasonable step the ISP could be expected to take. The ISP was thus not liable for authorising the infringements committed by its subscribers, notwithstanding the fact that some notice had been received. Authorisation in the internet context is further explored in Chapter 18 Digitisation.

In a different context, authorisation was also at issue in the New Zealand case of *Heinz Wattie's Ltd v Spantech Pty Ltd* (2005) 67 IPR 666. In that case, Spantech built a number of potato stores for Heinz. Heinz put a further store to tender and the tender was allocated to a different builder, BPM. Heinz entered into a contract with BPM and directed that the specifications were to be 'as per the existing adjacent potato stores'. These instructions amounted to a direction to BPM to copy. The specifications and instructions necessarily resulted in an infringing copy of Spantech's works. Spantech held the artistic work copyright and had not authorised the copying by BPM. Similar issues arose in *Tamawood Ltd v Habitare Developments Pty Ltd (admin apptd) (receivers and managers apptd)* (2015) 112 IPR 439; [2015] FCAFC 65, where instructions were given to construct a building in accordance with plans the copyright in which did not vest in Habitare but in the claimant Tamawood. On the facts it was clear enough that directors of Habitare were so closely involved with the giving of the instructions as to make them liable for authorisation. Thus the submission of Habitare that it did not follow that a director of a company, even a managing director or company secretary, is automatically liable for having 'authorised' an act committed by the company infringing copyright of a third party was, even if likely correct, beside the point on the facts.

Indirect Infringement

5.9 'Indirect infringement' comprises:

- infringement by importation (s 37);
- infringement by dealing in infringing articles (s 38); and
- permitting a place of public entertainment to be used for an infringing performance of a work (s 39).

Of those, ss 37 and 38 are the most significant and s 37, the parallel importation restrictions, the most controversial. As is indicated above, a person may be liable under s 36 without any knowledge of copyright or the infringing nature of conduct. Infringement may be inadvertent or where the infringer has a genuinely held belief that what was done was legitimate. However, there is no liability under ss 37, 38 or 39 without the statutory knowledge element being present. Infringement under ss 37, 38 and 39 is independent of infringement under s 36, and the two forms of infringement may be cumulated; for example, a person may be liable under s 36 by illegally copying computer programs, and also under s 38 for selling the copies. Generally speaking, only a dealing or importation in a commercial context or a distribution for the purposes of trade is an infringement of s 37 or s 38, but any distribution for any other purpose 'to an extent that affects prejudicially the owner of the copyright' concerned also amounts to infringement.

Parallel importation

5.10 Under s 37, a copyright owner (or exclusive licensee in Australia) can restrain the importation by others of legitimate copyright material that was supplied in another country, so-called 'parallel importation', or grey marketing. This provision, replicated in most foreign jurisdictions, allows international copyright owners to parcel up the global market territorially, enabling differential pricing between national markets. Parallel importation restrictions are an exception to the 'exhaustion theory'; alternatively, it is said that where statutory parallel importation restrictions are in place, there is 'no international exhaustion' because the copyright owner can control one aspect of the further dealing in goods supplied in the market: their importation into other countries. In other words, a purchaser or possessor of such goods requires the authorisation of the copyright owner to import them into another country. Under both s 37 and s 38, there is an infringement only if the dealing (with legitimate goods imported without authorisation) or importation itself occurs without the licence of the copyright owner. In *Computermate Products (Australia) Pty Ltd v Ozi-Soft Pty Ltd* (1988) 20 FCR 46; 12 IPR 487, it was stressed that 'licence' in ss 37 and 38 is used in the sense of consent or permission, not just contractual licence (at FCR 49):

> What is apparent from the foregoing is that a claim made under s 37 of infringement against an importer will fail if the importer had a bare licence not supported by consideration and non-exclusive in character.

Such a licence may be at large or may be given 'with reference to particular transactions by particular parties' (at FCR 49). A bare licence could be revoked at will, but such a revocation may be estopped where the licensee has acted on the licence. However, does the selling of legitimate copies in a foreign market, without express restrictions relating to importation into Australia, amount to an implied licence for the purchaser to import the material concerned? In the seminal case of *Time-Life International v Interstate Parcel Express Co Pty Ltd* (1976) 12 ALR 1 (see also *Computermate Products v Ozi-Soft* and *Lorenzo & Sons Pty Ltd v Roland Corporation* (1992) 23 IPR 376), it was argued that by putting the works on the market abroad, the copyright owner had granted an implied licence to a purchaser to deal with the material in any manner they saw fit after purchase. This argument was rejected by Jacobs J (at ALR 371):

> The purpose of s 37 is to make it clear that a positive licence is required. If an unrestricted sale abroad were to confer a licence under s 37, the section would in effect only be applicable where the overseas seller positively imposed a restriction. But the section does not say that importation for sale is allowed unless a restriction to that effect has been imposed. Importation is forbidden unless a licence has been given.

However, the burden of proving the absence of a positive licence, being a constituent element of s 37 and of s 38, is on the applicant for relief: see *Avel Pty Ltd v Multicoin Amusements Pty Ltd* (1990) 171 CLR 88; see also *Computermate Products v Ozi-Soft* at FCR 48. But a positive licence need not necessarily be an express licence: although it must be shown that the copyright owner positively did not intend to grant a licence to import, lack of consent may be inferred from all the circumstances of the case.

In Australia, the copyright owner's control over the parallel importation of copyright goods has been substantially eroded. As a result, copyright owners, official distributors or licensees must now compete with grey marketers or parallel importers in relation to sound recordings, computer programs and electronic literary or music items. The wind-back of parallel importation restrictions has been achieved by creating exceptions to the operation of s 37 rather than by abolishing it: see ss 44D, 44E, 44F and 112D. The most significant remaining restriction is in relation to print books: see s 44A (this does not apply to electronic musical or literary items: ss 44F and 112DA, but the restrictions also operate in relation to such things as artistic works reproduced on articles). To prevent reliance on copyright in works reproduced on labels and packaging of, for example, sound recordings or DVDs to restrain the importation of those goods themselves, further exceptions apply to 'accessories etc to imported articles': see s 44C. The parallel importation regime is distinct from the provisions that allow copyright owners to interdict the importation of infringing copyright materials.

The knowledge element in ss 37 and 38

5.11 Once the plaintiff has established the absence of a licence, each section focuses on actual or constructive knowledge with respect to the making of the article. In the context of s 37, the test is based on the statutory fiction that the articles were made in Australia; it is not relevant whether the alleged infringer knew or ought to have known that the importation was an infringement. Knowledge might be proven from an email trail: see, for instance, *Allam v Aristrocrat Technologies Australia Pty Ltd* (2012) 95 IPR 242; [2012] FCAFC 34. Even though the actual knowledge requirement had been liberally interpreted — a 'rather special meaning' was given to the relevant provision —

the Copyright Act was amended by virtue of the Copyright Amendment Act 1991 (Cth) expressly to include constructive knowledge. It now provides in s 37 (note s 38 runs along the same lines): '… if the importer knew or ought reasonably to have known, that the making of the article would, if the article had been made in Australia by the importer, have constituted an infringement of copyright.' The test is an objective one; however, Burchett J in *Raben Footwear Pty Ltd v Polygram Records Inc* (1997) 75 FCR 88 at 91; 37 IPR 417 said:

> … in my opinion, the expression used in the Australian Act does nevertheless allow regard to be had to the knowledge, capacity and circumstances of the particular defendant. An objective assessment is to be made as to whether he, not some other person, 'ought reasonably to have known'.

In *Milpurrurru v Indofurn Pty Ltd* (1994) 54 FCR 240, von Doussa J observed at [68] that knowledge 'refers to notice of facts such as would suggest to a reasonable person having the ordinary understanding expected of persons in the particular line of business that a breach of copyright was being committed: see *Apple Computer Inc v Computer Edge Pty Ltd* (1984) 1 FCR 549 at 561–562; *Kalamazoo (Aust) Pty Ltd v Compact Business Systems Pty Ltd* (1985) 84 FLR 101 at 126–127; *RCA Corporation v Custom Cleared Sales Pty Ltd* (1978) 19 ALR 123'. However, constructive knowledge goes beyond 'notice of facts'. Tamberlin J in *Raben Footwear* observed:

> Constructive knowledge focuses attention on the reasonableness of the conduct of the alleged infringer; that is, whether acting reasonably, the 'infringer' ought to have made further inquiries that would have resulted in it acquiring the requisite knowledge. The question is not simply whether there were reasonable grounds to suspect or believe, though this can be part of the exercise.

It is not necessary to prove knowledge that a particular specified person is the owner of the copyright: see *Nintendo Co Ltd v Centronics Systems Pty Ltd* (1994) 181 CLR 134. In *The Dempsey Group Pty Ltd v Spotlight Pty Ltd* [2018] FCA 2016 the court did not accept that the buyer of products (quilts and pillow covers) from a Chinese manufacturer well known to them, ought to have realised that the products they ordered had infringing artworks on them. It was reasonable of the buyer to rely on the Chinese manufacturer to warn them if any copyright issues might possibly arise in Australia when the products were imported.

Indirect infringement by permitting a place of entertainment to be used for an infringing performance

5.12 By virtue of s 39, it is an infringement of copyright to allow a place of public entertainment to be used for an infringing public performance of a work. However, there will be no liability if the alleged infringer was not aware and had no reasonable grounds for suspecting that the performance would be infringing, or if the permission to use the venue was given gratuitously or for a nominal cost: s 39(2). A 'place of public entertainment' includes premises that are made available for such entertainment only from time to time: see s 39(3). Section 39 is considered in the *Metro on George* case (see 5.5). Metro on George ran a performance venue and contracted with others who organised performances there. The question was whether Metro could itself ignore whether proper copyright licences for the performances were being obtained by a contractual clause imposing this responsibility exclusively on the performance organisers. The court held that this was not the case: by deliberately turning a blind eye, Metro had, in fact, countenanced infringing performances. In other words, Metro could not hide behind a contractual term to escape liability under s 39. Metro was also held liable for authorisation (s 36(1) and (1A)).

Brief overview of new technology-related provisions

5.13 As well as introducing the new right of communication to the public, the Copyright Amendment (Digital Agenda) Act 2000 (Cth) inserted provisions into the Copyright Act that aim to back up the self-help measures a copyright owner deploys in the new digital environment. In particular, the using, making or prejudicial provision or importation of a 'circumvention device' (or service) gives rise to both civil and criminal liability. Similar rights of action exist against persons who alter rights management information (RMI) or deal in copyright material with altered RMI: see Pt V Div 2A of the Copyright Act. As to criminal sanctions, see s 132. Some of these provisions were recently enhanced in conformity with the Australia–United States Free Trade Agreement 2004 (AUSFTA). Prior to the AUSFTA amendments, use of a circumvention device was not an infringement. Other new provisions relate to broadcast decoding devices: see Pt VAA and, in that regard, *Haddad v Foxtel Management Pty Ltd* (2008) 165 FCR 205; 75 IPR 245 and *Foxtel Management Pty Ltd v Mod Shop Pty Ltd* (2007) 165 FCR 149; 72 IPR 1.

Provisions intended to safeguard the ordinary operation of the internet from the unintended consequences of copyright have also been inserted; for instance, protection for ISPs from copyright infringement actions in certain circumstances (s 39B; Pt V Div 2AA), further amended by the US Free Trade Agreement Implementation Act 2004 (Cth), to introduce US-style 'safe harbour' provisions for ISPs), and copying that occurs in the ordinary course of operation of the internet: ss 43A and 43B. All these matters are discussed in further detail, with reference to recent recommendations for change emanating from the PC Report, in Chapter 18 Digitisation.

The Term of Copyright Protection

5.14 For a long time, the standard term of protection around the world for works remained 50 years from the death of the author (*post mortem auctoris* or PMA): see art 7(1) of the Berne Convention (also incorporated into TRIPS). However, the European Union and the United States extended the term to 70 years PMA, and Australia was brought into line by virtue of the AUSFTA. The calculation of the term varies between works and subject matter other than works. The latter do not have authors but 'makers', which can be corporate entities. The 70-year term of Pt IV material is therefore generally calculated from the end of the year of first publication. The duration of copyright protection for published works is generally 70 years from the death of the author (see s 33(2)), but works unpublished at the death of the author enjoy copyright protection for 70 years from the expiration of the calendar year in which they are first published: see s 33(3). The previously shorter term of protection for photographs (as artistic works) has now been brought into line with the term of other works, by virtue of the US Free Trade Agreement Implementation Act 2004 (Cth). One advantage of calculating the term PMA rather than from first publication is that copyright in all the works of a given author ceases at the same time, easing administration and compliance burdens. There is no perpetual or common law copyright, as was held in the old cases of *Millar v Taylor* (1769) 1B IPR 1 and *Donaldson v Beckett* (1774) 1B IPR 80. The statutory copyright created by the Statute of Anne 1709 (GB) 8 Anne c 19 was held to have extinguished any common law copyright, if such a right had existed at all: see also *Milpurrurru v Indofurn Pty Ltd* (1994) 54 FCR 240, *Bulun Bulun v R & T Textiles Pty Ltd* (1998) 86 FCR 244; (1998) 41 IPR 513 and *Attorney-General (NT) v Ward* (2002) 213 CLR 1. However, the term can effectively be indefinite while a work remains unpublished and was not published prior to the author's death. In some circumstances, publication is relevant to the calculation of the term of protection, but by virtue of the provisions of s 29, performance and exhibition are not publications for this purpose (s 29(3)), and only genuine and authorised publication will be taken into account: s 29(4), (6) and (7). The copyright term of subject matter other than works is calculated from first publication (see ss 93, 94 and 96) or making: see s 95 regarding broadcasts. As to the term of pseudonymous and anonymous works, see s 34. At the expiry of the copyright term, copyright subject matter enters the 'public domain'. Any person is at liberty to perform any act previously reserved to the copyright owner, and the term cannot be extended by contract. In other words, the contractual obligations of a licensee cease at the expiry in so far as they relate to acts comprised in the copyright. Because the term of copyright protection is long and there is no register of copyright works, it can become difficult to identify whether a work is still copyright protected and who the owner might be — the problem of so-called 'orphan works': see ALRC Report 122, *Copyright and the Digital Economy*, 2014, Chapter 13, 'Orphan Works'.

Fair Dealing and Exceptions

5.15 The exclusive rights of the copyright owner are not absolute. The Copyright Act provides that certain otherwise infringing uses of copyright materials are permissible without authorisation or compensation where they serve a dominant public purpose identified in the Act such as education, news reporting or critical comment, and have a limited impact on the copyright owner's patrimonial interests. These are the 'fair dealing' exceptions, which in recent times have attracted considerable controversy and reform proposals. The most recent of these is to replace fair dealing with 'fair use', a broader (US-style) exception which allows courts to determine whether a certain use of copyright works is for a public policy purpose that trumps copyright: see PC Report, Chapter 6 'Fair use or fair dealing — what is fair for Australia?' The Act also envisages that some aspects of copyright administration and enforcement will be conducted by 'collecting societies' that act on behalf of copyright owners to provide standard licensing terms and collect and distribute revenue. This makes the practical working of copyright possible; for instance, in relation to the public performance of innumerable musical works in commercial venues for which authorisation would otherwise have to be sought from numerous copyright owners. Further, the Act also creates exceptions in circumstances where the impact of copyright is impractical, inadvertent or inconsistent; for instance, in relation to reproductions made on web servers in the course of transmission of copyright works over the internet.

Fair dealing

5.16 A prima facie breach of s 36 may not entitle the plaintiff to a remedy if the relevant 'dealing' with the work was fair (see ss 40–42) and served a statutory purpose: research or study, criticism or review, parody and satire, or reporting the news. Whether the dealing is fair will depend not only on the quantity used but on all the surrounding circumstances of the use. Sufficient acknowledgment (meaning an acknowledgment identifying the work by its title or other description and also identifying the author; see s 10) is also required if the dealing is for the purpose of criticism or review or for the purpose of reporting the news in a newspaper, magazine or similar periodical: see ss 41 and 42(1). Analogous fair dealing exceptions apply to subject matter other than works: see ss 103A–103C. A more narrow exception exists for the purpose of judicial proceedings and the giving of legal advice: see ss 43 and 104.

The fair dealing exceptions are intended to reduce copyright barriers to education, public criticism and discussion, and the dissemination of information contained in copyright works. The provisions for subject matter other than works were considered in *TCN Channel Nine Pty Ltd v Network Ten Ltd* (2001) 108 FCR 235; 50 IPR 335; [2001] FCA 108 (*The Panel* case), which related to excerpts from rival television programs used in the show *The Panel*. The significance of the fair dealing issue in the age of the internet, pay TV and mobile telephone is illustrated by two other recent cases: *Telstra Corporation Pty Ltd v Premier Media Group Pty Ltd* (2007) 108 FCR 235; 72 IPR 89 concerning national rugby league (NRL) highlights and *Thoroughvision Pty Ltd v Sky Channel Pty Ltd* [2005] FCA 1527 dealing with films of horse racing. The Australian Law Reform Commission had already recommended that the purpose-specific fair dealing exceptions be repealed, with a broad exception for 'fair use' substituted in their place, a recommendation also adopted by the PC Report. This would bring Australian law closer to the US fair use exception which is not restricted to prescribed statutory purposes and is judicially adapted to a wide range of justifiable uses of copyright works. However, at the time of writing the Commonwealth Parliament had not yet amended the Copyright Act to introduce fair use. Its most recent amendments relating to fair dealing, in 2006, were to add a further purpose-specific exception for parody or satire (s 41A) and to introduce a narrowly circumscribed time and format shifting exception: see ss 109A and 110AA.

Fair dealing: statutory purpose

5.17 In *De Garis & Moore v Neville Jeffress Pidler Pty Ltd* (1990) 37 FCR 99; 18 IPR 292, Beaumont J held that the words 'research', 'study', 'criticism' and 'review' were intended to have their dictionary meaning. Only the purpose of the person who actually deals with the work is relevant, and that purpose must be genuine and not a surreptitious attempt to benefit from the plaintiff's copyright. In this case, the purpose of the defendant, who conducted a news clipping service on behalf of clients, was purely commercial. The defendant's copying of press articles did not itself serve any statutory purpose, even if a client required the clippings for its research. Further (at FCR 107), '[review] is the process and [criticism] is the result of the *critical application of mental faculties*' (emphasis added). Thus, there must be some genuine effort at critical analysis. The exception serves the purpose of enabling quotation in reviews and must not be a cover for colourable publication. Reporting the news is not restricted to reporting current events (see *Commonwealth v John Fairfax & Sons Ltd* (1980) 147 CLR 39 at 56; 32 ALR 485); otherwise, the dictionary meaning of 'news' indicates what is comprehended in the exception. In *The Panel* case, the trial judge Conti J held that Network Ten had not re-broadcast a substantial part of any Channel Nine television broadcast, but nonetheless went on to consider whether the fair dealing defences (in relation to subject matter other than works: see ss 103B and 103C) of criticism or review and/or reporting the news would have applied. He summarised the principles concerning fair dealing (at [66]) and found that the use Network Ten made in its *The Panel* TV show of some of the 20 extracts from Channel Nine programs would have constituted fair dealing. It was difficult in some instances to draw the line between reporting the news and entertaining, and in other cases there was little evidence of criticism and review, as opposed to satire or the lampooning of Channel Nine personalities and programs: see also *TCN Channel Nine Pty Ltd v Network Ten Pty Ltd* [2002] FCAFC 146. News includes news of sporting events. For instance, the incorporation of highlights of NRL matches is a standard form of reporting news. In *Fairfax Media Publications Pty Ltd v Reed International Books Australia Pty Ltd* (2010) 189 FCR 109; [2010] FCA 984, the question of whether copying headlines was fair dealing for reporting news in an abstraction service was at issue. The exception for parody and satire (see s 41A) has, as yet, not been judicially tested. It may be the case that some of the excerpts that were not said to serve the statutory purpose of reporting the news or criticism and review may well have fallen within this exception had it been on the statute books at the time of the decision. Some guidance may be had from the US fair use decisions concerning parody and satire. In any case, parody and satire require more than mere humour; some kind of message, criticism or comment must be imparted by the use of the copyright material.

A dealing that is fair

5.18 How much copying or use may be 'fair' is a difficult matter to determine: see *Telstra v Premier Media Group*. There is no hard and fast rule, and it is a matter of judgment and impression. The normal standards that apply in the industry (eg, broadcasting) may come into play. The quantity taken is significant but not determinative. In relation to research and study, s 40 provides quantitative parameters within which a dealing for research or study is to be taken to be fair: see ss 40(3) and 40(4) and 10(2). In relation to ss 41, 41A, 42 and 43, no quantative limits are prescribed. However, a non-exhaustive list of relevant matters to be taken into account is provided by virtue of s 40(2), so even where a larger proportion is taken, the dealing can still be fair. It is certainly possible for the taking of a relatively small proportion of source material not to constitute fair dealing. On the other hand, even reproduction of a whole work (eg, in the context of a parody: see *Clark v Associated Newspapers Ltd* (1998) 40 IPR 262) might conceivably be fair in some circumstances, although it will be a rare case where fair dealing can be called in aid of an unauthorised (first) publication of a work or part of a work. In *Commonwealth v John Fairfax & Sons*, absence of consent for publication was an important factor in determining whether fair dealing had taken place. Fair dealing is to be judged objectively by the standards of a fair minded and honest person: see *The Panel* case at [66], where the principles applying to fair dealing are usefully summarised. Whether the dealing is fair is a matter of degree, depending on all the circumstances of the case, or, as Lord Denning MR put it in *Hubbard v Vosper* [1972] 2 QB 84 at 94, 'after all is said and done, it must be a matter of impression'.

The fair dealing exceptions apply in an analogous manner to subject matter other than works. The fairness of using excerpts or highlights of films and broadcasts has arisen a number of times recently in relation to NRL highlights, horse racing clips and, of course, in *The Panel* case: see 5.16.

Fair dealing and copying of works in educational institutions

5.19 Part VB of the Copyright Act sets up a statutory licensing scheme that enables educational (and certain other) institutions to copy works on behalf of students, subject to the payment of an agreed royalty to a collecting society representing copyright owners. In *Haines v Copyright Agency Ltd* (1982) 42 ALR 549, the relationship between s 40 fair dealing and the statutory educational copying scheme (then s 53B, now replaced by Pt VB) was at issue.

The court held that the intention of the Act was that when an institution, through its teachers or lecturers, reproduces materials for students required in a course of study, the making of copies should be subject to the statutory licensing scheme and thus to the payment of equitable remuneration. Institutions could not constitute themselves as agents making reproductions on behalf of students under the fair dealing provisions without compensation for the copyright owner.

As pointed out above (5.17), for fair dealing the relevant purpose is that of the person undertaking the study or research. In *Longman Group Ltd v Carrington Technical Institute Board of Governors* (1990) 20 IPR 264, Doogue J of the High Court of New Zealand held that the making of a book of materials of which over 70 per cent was reproduced from pre-existing works for distribution to students in a technical drawing class did not amount to fair dealing for the purpose of research or private study. However, note the difference in terminology with s 40 of the Copyright Act 1968 (Cth). It was stressed — as in *De Garis & Moore* (see 5.18) — that the requisite purpose must be that of the copier and not someone else, and the purpose of the teacher here was to facilitate the teaching of the course, and use by students was only incidental to that: see also *Copyright Licence Ltd v University of Auckland* [2002] 3 NZLR 76; (2002) 53 IPR 618. So while the provision by teachers to students of photocopied materials will normally fall under the statutory licensing scheme of Pt VB, which provides for remuneration of the copyright owner, if a student photocopies works or parts of works and in the library (remaining within the parameters of s 40), this will constitute a legitimate and unremunerated fair dealing.

Neither fair dealing nor the educational licensing scheme constitutes an excuse for an education institution becoming a commercial publisher. In *Copyright Agency Ltd v Victorian University of Technology* (1995) 55 FCR 1; 30 IPR 140, the price education institutions are permitted to charge for compilations or anthologies of pre-existing works was at issue: see ss 135ZL and 135ZZH. The latter section renders the statutory licence inapplicable if the copied materials are supplied for a profit. However, the court held that the price charged for the materials could include a reasonable amount for general overheads and production costs and was not restricted to the precise cost of production of the materials.

By virtue of the Copyright Amendment (Digital Agenda) Act 2000 (Cth), the fair dealing provisions are extended in relation to the communication right, as are the library exceptions, although with relevant adaptations: see ss 10(2A), 40 and 42. Note that fair dealing is not a permitted purpose for the supply of a circumvention device within statutory parameters: see s 116A(4) and (7). For further detail and consideration, see Chapter 18 Digitisation.

Miscellaneous exceptions and licensing schemes

5.20 The Copyright Act provides some miscellaneous other exceptions to the exclusive rights of the copyright owner: see ss 74–77, relating to design/copyright overlap (discussed in Chapter 6 Registered Designs); ss 43–44D, 45–47A and 47B–47H for computer programs (discussed in Chapter 18 Digitisation); s 48 for libraries and archives; ss 65–73 for artistic works; and ss 103A–112D. By virtue of ss 109A and 111 (see also s 43C), copies made for certain forms of time shifting and format shifting are now permitted. The Act also allows for licensing schemes: voluntary licensing schemes approved by the Copyright Tribunal (see Pt VI) and statutory licensing schemes established in various ways throughout the Act.Such statutory licensing schemes established by the Act in Pt III Div 6 relate to the making of recordings of musical works; public performance of published sound recordings (s 108); the broadcast of sound recordings in certain circumstances (s 109); the copying and communication of broadcasts by educational institutions, etc (ss 135A–135ZA); the reproduction and communication of works, etc, by certain institutions (Pt VB); and retransmission of free-to-air broadcasts (Pt VC). The details of these various schemes will not be analysed here.[2]

Under the fair dealing exceptions and the other miscellaneous exceptions, a person is entitled to do an act comprised in the copyright without requiring the authorisation of the copyright owner and with no obligation to pay a royalty. The approved and the statutory licensing schemes, on the other hand, remove the need to obtain authorisation for the doing of acts comprised in the copyright, but are subject to an obligation to pay a reasonable royalty. Social policy goals (eg, in the case of the statutory licences for educational institutions or for persons with disabilities), practical considerations

---

2. For an overview, see Commonwealth Attorney-General's Department, *Fair Use and Other Copyright Exceptions, An Examination of Fair Use, Fair Dealing and Other Exceptions in the Digital Age*, Issues Paper, May 2005.

(eg, in relation to mechanical performance of sound recordings: see s 108) or economic policy (eg, in relation to the recording of musical works: Pt III Div 6) lie at the basis of the licensing schemes.

The operation of an efficient marketplace in copyright material requires some form of collective gathering of royalties by one party on behalf of all copyright owners, limiting transaction costs. Collecting societies license rights and gather royalties under the approved or statutory schemes on behalf of their members; that is, copyright owners who either license or assign the relevant exclusive rights to the society.

A number of such societies exist. The Copyright Agency administers the educational reproduction scheme and visual artists' rights over their artistic works in the context of the right of education institutions to reproduce artistic works; the APRA administers statutory licences related to the public performance, broadcasting and cable transmission of works; the Audiovisual Copyright Society (AVCS) administers the making of off-air copies by educational and other institutions; the Australian Music Publishers Association (AMPAL) and Australian Record Industry Association (ARIA) administer the statutory licence for the recording of musical works; the PPCA administers broadcast and public performance rights vested in sound recordings and music videos; and the Australasian Mechanical Copyright Owners Society (AMCOS) administers the public performance right in musical works.[3]

Collecting societies are either statutory in nature (ie, they are largely provided for by express provisions in the Copyright Act) or approved (ie, constituted under the general mechanism provided under the Act by which copyright owners can voluntarily unite, form a collecting society and seek approval for their scheme from the Copyright Tribunal).

The Copyright Tribunal, established under the Copyright Act, as well as approving schemes, performs the important function of resolving any dispute between a collecting society and those who pay royalties to it, and also sets equitable remuneration or royalty levels where parties cannot come to an agreement.

The Crown benefits from a statutory right to use copyright material for the services of the Commonwealth or a state, on terms agreed by the relevant parties, or, in default of agreement, set by the Copyright Tribunal: see ss 182B–183E. A comprehensive review of the Crown copyright provisions resulted in the last report produced by the Copyright Law Review Committee before its abolition. Note that the blank tape royalty scheme, a compulsory levy on blank tape manufacturers to compensate for loss of royalties from home copying, never became operational because it was struck down by the High Court as being unconstitutional: see *Australian Tape Manufacturers Association Ltd v Commonwealth* (1993) 176 CLR 480; 25 IPR 1. Note also the resale royalty scheme introduced by the Resale Royalty Right for Visual Artists Act 2009 (Cth), which entitles artists to a royalty of 5 per cent on the resale of certain eligible artworks sold for $1000 or more.

---

3. For further information concerning collecting societies, see S Simpson's report prepared for the Minister for Communications and the Arts and the Minister for Justice, *Review of Australian Copyright Collecting Societies*, 1995.

Other rights, remedies and offences

5.21 As well as the core exclusive rights in Pt III works and Pt IV subject matter, the Copyright Act also establishes a number of other rights and remedies. The most significant of these are the moral rights regime established by Pt IX for authors and performers, and the performers' rights regime (Pt XIA). Further, the Act also establishes separate remedies relating to certain misuses of technology: in relation to unauthorised decoders for access to encoded broadcasts (Pt VAA) and in relation to circumvention devices for technological protection measures and electronic rights management information (Pt V Div 2A). The latter are discussed in Chapter 18 Digitisation. The Act also creates a number of criminal offences; these are considered in Chapter 19 Remedies in Intellectual Property Law. The moral rights and performers' rights regimes are considered below.

Moral Rights

What are moral rights?

5.22 Moral rights are non-exploitable and inalienable rights securing the intimate connection between authors and their works. The term 'moral rights' stems from the French civilian concept of '*droit moral*', which is perhaps better translated as 'personality rights' of authors. They serve a fundamentally different purpose from the 'economic' or patrimonial rights that secure the author's exclusivity over commercial exploitation of their work. Moral rights remain with the author even if copyright is assigned in its entirety. The author can exercise moral rights irrespective of who owns the copyright. There are limits on the ability of authors to abandon or 'waive' their moral rights by way of contract. As moral rights are authors' rights, they apply in relation to all Pt III works. 'Makers' in Pt IV do not necessarily make an authorial contribution to generating 'subject matter other than works'; nonetheless, some individuals who play a potentially significant creative role in relation to the making of sound recordings and cine films are considered deserving of some of the benefits of authorship. Hence, directors, producers and screenwriters of films enjoy moral rights, as do performers under Pt XIA. Performership is thus legally recognised as a form of creative connection with recorded performances deserving of moral rights. Whatever the merits of that view, the World Intellectual Property Organization (WIPO) Performances and Phonograms Treaty (WPPT) requires recognition of moral rights in performership; introduction of all the terms of this treaty into Australian legislation was also one of the requirements of the AUSFTA. However, since a parallel treaty to the WPPT concerning audiovisual material (ie, films rather than sound recordings) was never ratified, none of the parties involved with the making of a sound recording, including the performers in their new-found capacity of 'makers' under the Copyright Act (see s 100AD), enjoys moral rights in that capacity, which has resulted in a rather lopsided situation. In other words, whereas performers recorded on sound recordings enjoy moral rights as performers under Pt XIA, they do not enjoy moral rights as makers under Pt IV. If performers were granted full authorship copyright, rather than the more limited rights of action they now enjoy under Pt XIA, a more consistent regime in terms of moral rights could result.

The main moral rights are the right of integrity and the right of sufficient attribution of authorship. Moral rights are a fundamental component of copyright law in continental European copyright (in France: *droit d'auteur*), which focuses on the concept of a work as an emanation of the personality of an author. The common law tradition is more instrumental; that is, focused on securing the owner's ability to benefit financially from copyright. Until relatively recently, moral rights protection was foreign to most common law countries, although it has been an integral part of the Berne Convention 1886 since being inserted in the 1928 Rome Revision: see art 6*bis*. In some quarters, it was felt, perhaps unjustifiably, that Australian law complied with international obligations because authors had available tortious remedies (defamation) and could secure their moral rights by contractual means. This underestimated the differences between the standards applied to defamation and in moral rights jurisprudence, as well as the difficulties faced by any plaintiff in defamation cases. It also ignored the fact that moral rights theory gives statutory support to authors who, on the whole, face considerable inequalities in bargaining power when seeking to secure the integrity of their work and recognition of their authorship in the context of commercial exploitation by others. However, the Copyright Act 1977 (UK) introduced moral rights in the UK, and Australia has now followed suit, but only since 2000. The statutory scheme is complex, as while granting moral rights it also envisages considerable derogations and limitations of those rights. It has become more common to plead both economic and moral rights infringement concurrently.

The statutory scheme

5.23 Several previous attempts to introduce moral rights legislation were unsuccessful. However, a bill was introduced in 1998 by the Howard Government and was enacted as the Copyright Amendment (Moral Rights) Act 2000 (Cth).

The Copyright Act now provides for three moral rights:

1. an author's right to be identified as the author of a work — the right of attribution of authorship: see ss 193–195AB;
2. the right of an author to take action against false attribution — the right not to have authorship of a work falsely attributed: see ss 195AC–195AH; and
3. an author's right to object to derogatory treatment of their work that prejudicially affects their honour or reputation — the right of integrity of authorship: see ss 195AI–195AW.

The rights of attribution and integrity of performership are now also recognised in the Act in relation to live (only the right of integrity) and recorded performances: see s 100AE. Only sound recordings of performances give rise to moral rights vested in the performers; there are no moral rights for performers in relation to audiovisual (film) recordings. In other words, the only moral rights subsisting in relation to film as such remain those of directors, producers and screenwriters, who are recognised as authors for the purpose of moral rights. Of course, the authors of various underlying works such as novel, script and screenplay (literary and dramatic works) and musical score (musical work) also retain moral rights as authors. These rights will all have to be dealt with by contract so that the producers of the film obtain all rights as are required to ensure the efficient exploitation of the end product.

The term of moral rights protection coincides with that of the author's economic rights; that is, generally 70 years PMA, except for the right of integrity of authorship in films, which ceases with the death of the author: see s 195AM. The underlying policy goal of moral rights provisions is to protect the rights of authors (and performers) from certain acts engaged in by those who acquire and exploit copyright in their works, as well as by infringers of their exploitation rights. However, the Australian moral rights regime effectively limits the practical effect of the granting of moral rights in a number of ways. First, if it is reasonable in all of the circumstances not to identify an author, or to subject a work to derogatory treatment, moral rights are not infringed: see ss 195AR and 195AS. Special rules that limit the rights of authors also apply to the destruction or removal of moveable artistic works or buildings: see s 195AT. Furthermore, the rights of architects in relation to buildings are limited to a right to be consulted and to make a record of the building; they cannot prevent its destruction or fundamental alteration. Second, authors can consent to an act or omission that otherwise constitutes a breach of moral rights. This means, naturally, that where an author contracts with another party concerning the assignment or licensing of copyright, they can be prevailed upon to relinquish moral rights in relation to future exploitation of a work. However, there are some limitations that mean that a blanket waiver of moral rights in broad terms will not be enforceable against an author. Authors can only consent to the doing of specified acts that breach statutory moral rights in relation to specified works, but a distinction is made between employed and other authors in terms of the scope and extent of consent: see ss 195AW, 195AWA and 195AWB. Employees can validly consent to derogations in relation to all future works generated under the contract of employment and in relation to specified works. Therefore, unlike in some other jurisdictions, there is no scope for a generalised or public and enforceable waiver of moral rights. There are also no excisions from the subject matter covered by moral rights. In the UK, computer programs do not attract moral rights protection; however, given the reasonableness, consent and employment provisions, the moral rights regime in Australia is still relatively weak. In most cases, authors will be prevailed upon to consent to the kinds of modifications and derogations that constituted established practice in particular industries before the introduction of moral rights. These limitations on moral rights must be seen in the light of the threshold tests of liability for moral rights infringement, which in themselves already pose considerable obstacles.

The rights of attribution and of integrity of authorship

5.24 By virtue of s 193, the author has the right to be identified as the author of a work ('attributed') when certain 'attributable acts' are done in relation to the work. One possible situation arises where the author has assigned or licensed (whether directly or indirectly) their copyright to another person, who then does one or more of the attributable acts in relation to the work. Alternatively, a failure of attribution can be associated with an infringing reproduction. An example is provided by *Corby v Allen & Unwin Pty Ltd* (2013) 101 IPR 181; [2013] FCA 370. The attributable acts are listed in s 194: to reproduce, publish, exhibit (for artistic works) and communicate the work to the public; as to what are 'attributable acts', see *William McCausland v Surfing Hardware International Holdings Pty Ltd* [2013] NSWSC 902. Identification of the author must be clear and reasonably prominent: see s 195AA. The inverse right of the author is the right not to have a work falsely attributed when an attributable act is done: see s 195AC. This applies, obviously, to a work with which the author has no connection but also in relation to a work of the author that has been altered by a person other than the author of the work: see ss 195AE and 195AG. The author also has the right of integrity of authorship; that is, the right not to have the work subjected to derogatory treatment: see s 195AI. This is a general right and not limited to 'attributable acts'. For instance, a sculptor's right of integrity may be infringed if their work is cut into pieces to be sold separately. Derogatory treatment of literary, dramatic and musical work is defined by virtue of s 195AJ as doing anything in relation to the work that results in a material distortion, mutilation or material alteration to the work that is prejudicial to the author's honour or reputation, or the doing of anything else in relation to the work that is prejudicial to the author's honour or reputation. For artistic works is added the exhibiting in public of the work that is prejudicial to the author's honour or reputation because of the manner and place in which the exhibition occurs: see s 195AK. Whereas the foregoing sections define what the author's moral rights are, ss 195AO–195AQ establish what amounts to infringement of those rights. Importantly, the impact of those sections is then limited by the following sections (ss 195AR and 195AS), which assert that there is no infringement if it was reasonable not to identify the work or if the derogatory treatment or other actions were reasonable. Those sections also list matters to be taken into account in determining reasonableness. Included in these, interestingly, is established industry practice, practice included in a voluntary code of practice and, in certain cases, also the expense of compliance. In *Corby*, in relation to s 195AR, the court was prepared to accept that attribution of photographs was not always done in books, in particular where photos were sourced from private collections; but on the facts there was no evidence that the failure to attribute was due to observance of any such industry practice. Some had been attributed, others not. There was also no evidence that it was too difficult to find authors — no effort had apparently been made to do so.

Further, s 195AT imposes more limitations in relation to public art works and buildings. For instance, in *Meskenas v ACP Publishing Pty Ltd* (2006) 70 IPR 172, a photograph was published by a magazine that showed Princess Mary of Denmark standing in front of a portrait painting of Dr Victor Chang by Vladas Meskenas. The magazine wrongly attributed the painting to another artist in a caption. Although the author did not own the copyright in the painting (this belonged to the estate of Dr Chang), as author he was entitled to proper attribution and also to the work not being falsely attributed. The federal magistrate held that wrongly attributing the work breached both the right to attribution (s 193) and the right against false attribution (s 195AC). He held that none of the matters referred to in s 195AR(2) relating to reasonableness was made out. Indeed, the magazine had made an attribution, albeit a wrong one. Note that the reasonableness defence does not apply to a false attribution of authorship but only to a failure to attribute authorship. The magistrate also held that the word 'falsely' as used in s 194 did not imply an element of intent; it meant simply 'objectively incorrect': at [31].

There was thus an infringement of Meskenas's moral rights, and damages had to be assessed, something for which the magistrate was unable to unearth much guidance: at [39]ff. However, damages for infringement of moral rights are, generally speaking, distinct from those awarded for the infringement of a patrimonial right; it may be that measuring damage requires some assessment of the impact on the reputation of the author due to the false or failed attribution.

To establish infringement of the right of integrity, the author must not only prove the doing of an act in relation to the work but also prove prejudice to their honour or reputation. It is unclear whether the author must establish that the act done in relation to the work is of a particular kind. The first limb of s 195AJ refers to material distortion, mutilation or material alteration, which implies an act of a certain if unquantified magnitude or impact; the second limb then refers to the doing of 'anything else' in relation to the work. In relation to artistic works, express mention is also made of public exhibition prejudicial to reputation. However, it may be that the doing of 'anything else' in relation to the work refers to ways in which a work may be performed or included in a performance, recording or film. It may be that the public performance of a musical work in a certain manner or context offensive to the author is thus included under the moral rights umbrella, whereas it does not include a material alteration, mutilation or material distortion of the work (ie, the score).

Further, the author must establish prejudice to honour or reputation. The Act provides no further guidance, but some may be had from Canadian cases that have considered analogous provisions in that jurisdiction: see, for example, *Snow v Eaton Centre Ltd* (1982) 70 CPR (2d) 105 and *Prise de Parole Inc v Guerin* (1995) 60 ACWS (3d) 390; see also the more recent decision of a federal magistrate in *Perez v Fernandez* [2012] FMCA 2. The provisions concerning moral rights of performers are analogous to those concerning authors: see 'Right of attribution of performership', s 195ABAff; 'Right not to have performership falsely attributed', s 195AHAff; and 'Right of integrity of performership', s 195ALAff.

Performers' Rights

Limited rights of action

5.25 The performing arts rely on creative contributions from different persons, yet historically in Australian copyright law, only authors were granted exclusive copyrights, and the copyright in a sound recording or film of a performance was owned by the maker, which category did not include a performer. Therefore, performers did not enjoy real copyright protection in relation to the recording and exploitation of recordings of their performances, whether sound or audiovisual. With the signing of the AUSFTA and accession to the WPPT, that has now changed in relation to performers whose performance is incorporated in a sound recording, who are now included within the concept of 'maker': see s 100AD. But in relation to performances incorporated in audiovisual form (as films), performers benefit only from the more limited rights of action bestowed by the special regime established in Pt XIA. This reluctance to grant copyright to performers persisted notwithstanding that performers' copyright was recognised in the Rome Convention for the Protection of Performers, Producers of Phonograms and Broadcasting Organizations 1961, in the form of 'neighbouring rights' to copyright, analogous to Pt IV subject matter. Performers' rights protection of a limited kind was only introduced in Australia in 1989 (Copyright Amendment Act 1989 (Cth)): see Pt XIA 'Performers protection'.

The rights there granted to performers are, for the time being at least, very limited, although there has been a gradual expansion of the rights of performers. As well as being recognised as owners of copyright in sound recordings, performers' moral rights are now also recognised. Nonetheless, rights under Pt III and Pt IV are still more extensive in critical ways than those granted to performers in Pt XIA. Naturally, an artist performing a musical, literary or dramatic work in which they own copyright in Australia will be able to rely on Pt III, and a performer in a sound recording will now also be able to rely on Pt IV. The main remaining benefit of Pt XIA, then, is in relation to live performances and in relation to audiovisual recordings of performances, where the performers do not as yet have a statutory ownership stake in the recording (film). Performers' rights are not 'real' copyrights because the performer has no statutory right to control secondary or further uses of an authorised recording of their performance. The performer has only the statutory right to authorise the making of the recording itself (with the exception of inclusion of a recording in a soundtrack for a film) or to restrain the making and exploitation of an unauthorised recording. In other words, once a performer authorises the making of a recording of a performance, they have no statutory rights in relation to further uses of that recording. The owner of the copyright in the recording can exploit it in any manner they see fit (eg, by making copies and selling them, by licensing broadcasts, etc) without requiring an additional granting or licensing of rights from the performer. The performer can, of course, rely on a contract to restrict such further uses of an authorised recording and remuneration for such uses. In other words, only contractual obligations can restrain a person authorised to record a performance from further exploiting the recording, including making and selling reproductions or communicating it to the public. There is only one exception to this rule, which is in relation to the incorporation of a sound recording as a soundtrack for a film (so-called synchronisation rights). However, as is indicated above, the AUSFTA has resulted in a performer now being recognised as a co-owner, with the other makers, of the copyright in sound recordings: see s 22(3A) and (3B) and s 116AAA. Again, it needs to be stressed that this is not the case in relation to any other Pt IV subject matter. Under the AUSFTA, Australia has also extended moral rights to performers, the provisions commencing when the WPPT came into force for Australia: see US Free Trade Agreement Implementation Act 2004 (Cth) and see Copyright Act 1968 (Cth), ss 191A and 191B; Pt IX Divs 2A, 3A and 4A; Pt IX Div 5 Subdiv B, Div 6 Subdiv B and Div 7 Subdiv B.

The structure of Pt XIA

5.26 Performers have a statutory right of action against any person who makes an unauthorised recording of their performance. Therefore, in substance, performers can be said to have the exclusive right to authorise the recording of their performances. However, some categories of recordings, including indirect recordings made for domestic or private purposes, are 'exempt recordings', which can be made without the authorisation of performers (see s 248A, the general definition section relating to Pt XIA). Under the same provision, recordings can also be made without authorisation for certain public interest purposes, analogous to the fair dealing provisions relating to Pts III and IV. A performer is a person who gives a performance. News presenting and participation in a sport or as a member of an audience are not performances under the Act (see s 248A(2)), but dance and circus or variety acts are, as is a performance of 'an expression of folklore', terms not elsewhere defined: see s 248A(1). A performer also has a right of action against a person who makes certain further uses of an unauthorised recording, but no statutory rights against such a person exist, with the exception of the so-called synchronisation right, as referred to above.

Thus, a performer may claim damages for the making of the unauthorised recording and for the sale of copies of such a recording to the public, as well as for a communication of the recording, and also obtain an injunction to restrain such further uses. Part XIA grants rights retrospectively. The beginning of the protection period is the date the performance was given, the term of protection being 20 calendar years for performances and 50 calendar years for sound recordings of a performance (eg, the soundtrack): see s 248CA. Although primarily aimed at the protection of live performances (irrespective of the presence of an audience) given on Australian soil by one or more Australian citizens or residents (see the definition of 'performance' in s 248A(1)), foreign performances are, for a large part, also protected: see ss 248U and 248V and the relevant regulations.

The WPPT 1996 requires the introduction of real copyrights for performances recorded on sound recordings but not for audiovisual performances. With the granting of ownership in sound recordings to performers, and also moral rights protection, performers' rights provisions in Australia now comply with the treaty requirements. Some commentators have lamented these greater rights, arguing that they increase transactional costs and complexity. Above all, the granting of moral rights to performers has generated controversy, with sound recordings, films and broadcasts potentially being subject to the moral rights claims of a multitude of performers. However, given the consent provisions in Pt IX (see 5.23), entertainment industry contracts will simply require all performers to consent to all possible uses of recordings of their performances.

Bibliography

Australian Law Reform Commission (ALRC), *Copyright and the Digital Economy*, Report No 122, 2014.

Commonwealth Attorney-General's Department, *Fair Use and Other Copyright Exceptions: An Examination of Fair Use, Fair Dealing and Other Exceptions in the Digital Age*, Issues Paper, May 2006.

Copyright Law Review Committee, *Report into the Jurisdictional Procedures of the Copyright Tribunal*, 2000; and Draft Report, 2000.

D Browne, 'Moral Rights: Just a Little Respect' (2000) 43 *Intellectual Property Forum* 30.

D Ellinson, 'New Moral Rights Legislation — Greater Rights for Copyright Authors' (2001) 75(7) *LIJ* 76.

D Gruzauskas, 'Performers Rights: The Right of Personality & Possibility of a Proprietary Right' (1995) 6 *AIPJ* 92.

E Adeney, 'Australia's First Moral Rights Decision: A Critical Approach to Meskenas v ACP Publishing' (2008) 19(2) *AIPJ* 74.

J Oliver, 'Copyright, Fair Dealing and Freedom of Expression' (2000) 19(1) *NZULR* 89.

K Crews, 'MDS Decision and Fair Use for Coursepacks' (1996) 9 *IPLB* 52.

L Longdin, 'Making the Most of Article 6: Parallel Importing in Australia and New Zealand' (2001) 45 *IP Forum* XX.

L Morrison and C Turner, 'Performers' Copyright in Sound Recordings After the Australia–US FTA — Mere Symbolism?' (2005) 17(10) *IPLB* 179.

M Handler and D Rolph, '"A Real Pea Souper": The Panel Case and the Development of the Fair Dealing Defences to Copyright Infringement in Australia' (2003) 27 *MULR* 381.

M McMahon, 'Commerce in (Whose?) Content — Compulsory Licensing of Copyright Works Pt I' (1997) 10 *IPLB* 49.

M Sainsbury, 'Publishing Online: Considering the Moral Rights Implications' (2006) 9 (6 & 7) *INTLB* 65.

N Hazel, 'Parallel Imports and Enforcement: Amendment to the Copyright Act' (2003) 16(1) *IPLB* 1.

P Brudenall, 'Fair Dealing in Australian Copyright Law: Rights of Access' (1997) 20 *UNSWLJ* 443.

P Loughlan, 'Parody, Copyright and the New Four-Step Test' (2006) 67 *Intellectual Property Forum* 46.

Productivity Commission (PC), *Intellectual Property Arrangements*, Inquiry Report No 78, Canberra, September 2016 (PC Report).

Senate Standing Committee on Legal and Constitutional Affairs, 'Don't Stop the Music!', *Report of the Inquiry into Copyright, Music and Small Business*, May 1998.

T Dower, 'Casting the Fair Net Further: Should Australia Adopt an Open-Ended Model of Fair Dealing in Copyright?' (2002) 20 *Copy Reptr* 4.

Chapter 6

Registered Designs

Introduction

Outline

6.1 Designs law is governed by the Designs Act 2003 (Cth). The introduction of this Act, to replace the Designs Act 1906 (Cth), brought to a close a long drawn out and controversial law reform process: see Australian Law Reform Commission (ALRC) Report No 74, *Designs*, 1996 (ALRC 74). Designs registration is closely associated with copyright law but with a far narrower ambit. Industrial designs often incorporate, reproduce or are derived from artistic works. However, while copyright law covers forms of expression ranging from the mundane and technical (eg, technical drawings, architectural plans) to the purely artistic (eg, paintings), designs law is exclusively concerned with the protection of the novel visual appearance of functional manufactured products: see the definition of 'design' in s 5 of the Designs Act 2003 (Cth) and of 'product' in s 6(1).

Designs law thus lies within the province of commerce, industry and manufacturing rather than of art. Nonetheless, often the appearance of a functional object that has been designed with consumer appeal in mind could be called 'artistic', or at least attractive. But designs law is not exclusively concerned with aesthetics, since, under Australian law, products whose shape or configuration is inspired by functional requirements are just as capable of registration by virtue of s 7(2), as are products designed for decorative effect. In fact, many designs registered and litigated in Australia are for product shapes that are largely functional. The key requirement is that the design be for a product and be new and distinctive, rather than that it be pleasing to the eye. A case concerning the provisions of the 1906 Act illustrates the point: *Polyaire Pty Ltd v K-Aire Pty Ltd* (2005) 221 CLR 287; (2005) 64 IPR 223. The design at issue in this case concerned the shape of a plastic blade constituting part of an air conditioning vent assembly. Clearly, the design choices made had little to do with consumer or aesthetic appeal.

Relationship with other intellectual property regimes

6.2 The fact that designs registration protects visual appearance, as does copyright in artistic works, could result in the role of the designs registration system being usurped by copyright. We shall see further below that in Australia (unlike in some other jurisdictions) a statutory prohibition on concurrent designs and copyright protection, and on exclusive reliance on copyright in the absence of designs registration, prevents this: see ss 74–77 of the Copyright Act 1968 (Cth).

Although the Designs Act 2003 (Cth) allows the registration of designs whose appearance is determined by functional requirements, the distinction between function and appearance is vital to an understanding of the respective roles of design registration and patent grant. Registration of a design gives the owner a monopoly only in its specific appearance and not in any of the functional advantages of the new design, even if these result from its new shape. By contrast, a patent grant does bestow a monopoly over the functionality of a new product (what it does rather than what it looks like). A choice must be made between the two protection systems, although patent and design can be cumulated as well; see, for instance, *Multisteps Pty Ltd v Specialty Packaging Aust Pty Ltd* (2018) 132 IPR 399; [2018] FCA 587 (*Multisteps v Specialty Packaging*) which concerned valid innovation patents and registered designs for plastic produce containers. The cost, threshold requirements, nature and extent of exclusive rights, terms and procedural requirements vary considerably between the two.

Where largely functional designs are at issue in infringement proceedings, the courts are usually astute to prevent, although not always expressly, design registration effectively resulting in the monopolisation of function: see, for example, *Firmagroup Australia Pty Ltd v Byrne & Davidson Doors (Vic) Pty Ltd* (1987) 180 CLR 483; 9 IPR 353 (novel design for a recessed door handle in a garage roller door: see 6.18). Courts tend to confine the registration to the specific detail of the representation(s) in the application.

Scope for design innovation and scope of protection

6.3 Since industrial design is concerned with the appearance of useful products, design choices are constrained by functional imperatives. They are also closely circumscribed by competition, industrial capacity (plant and equipment, production methods, product line-up, quality standards of the manufacturer), interoperability and compatibility, and the pursuit of mass appeal. Hence, design innovation predominantly consists of a constant process of gradual or incremental change to existing products, rather than of free and startling departures from the norm. Designs law reflects this fact in terms of both the threshold of novelty (expressed as a requirement of 'distinctiveness') and the scope of the monopoly in the face of imitations. A significant challenge for designs law is to grant a meaningful monopoly (ie, one that cannot be circumvented by minor tweaking) while recognising the incremental nature of industrial design progression. Perhaps the most important change brought by the Designs Act 2003 was to increase both the novelty threshold and the concomitant scope of protection for registered designs. Another significant change was the introduction of a process of application and registration without substantive examination.

Whereas previously under the 1906 Act a design had only to be new, with the introduction of the present Act the threshold has been specified as requiring that a design be new and distinctive: see s 15. Rather than allowing registration of designs that differ only in minor detail, registration is now reserved for designs that are not 'substantially similar in overall impression' to the prior art. However, an applicant need not establish any inventiveness or creativity in the design's development, nor that a design is for an entirely novel product. The higher validity requirement is now expressly synchronised with the test for infringement. The factors of s 19 ('factors to be considered in assessing substantial similarity in overall impression') are *mutatis mutandis* the same for comparison between the applied for designs and the prior art and between a registered design and an allegedly infringing imitation. Whereas under the 1906 Act relatively minor differences in appearance could take an impugned design outside the scope of protection of a registered design, under the 2003 Act the focus is primarily on similarity of overall impression rather than on differences of minor detail. Thus, designs with differences in the detail of appearance may still constitute infringements if they do not substantially alter the overall impression the design makes on the 'informed user'. Section 19(1) expressly requires that more weight be attached to similarities than to differences between designs.

Monopoly rights and registration

6.4 Unlike copyright, which arises without any formalities but bestows only anti-copying rights, statutory monopoly rights in a design are granted upon examination of the application. Monopoly rights are characterised by the risk of 'infringing without copying'. Whereas copyright infringement cannot occur without proven access to the source work, an independently developed design can infringe a registration if it is too similar. Whereas in Australia designs-type protection always requires examination and registration, in some other jurisdictions, notably the European Union, a limited form of protection is also afforded to unregistered designs. Monopoly rights logically go hand in hand with a public registration system. If a register gives a trader the opportunity to ascertain cheaply and effectively whether a statutory right exists, imposing liability in the absence of actual copying or even knowledge of the infringed design is justifiable. Further, in an industrial context where incremental changes to existing products can attract monopoly rights, a system that allows inspection of a register to ascertain the existence and exact scope of pre-existing monopolies has obvious advantages. It limits the risk of inadvertent infringement. A competitor can seek a licence or design around a product.

Nonetheless, the effect of registration is limited. First, since mandatory substantive examination is costly and often superfluous (eg, because the product is never actually made or never copied), the 2003 Act has introduced a system of registration without substantive examination — after a formalities check only. Substantive examination can be requested at any time after registration but is mandatory before infringement proceedings are brought. Thus, in most cases, the costs of examination (resulting in 'certification' if successful: see s 67) can be deferred or avoided altogether. Second, even upon certification, validity is not guaranteed. Thus, infringement proceedings are always potentially subject to a counterclaim for invalidity: see s 74. In this aspect, designs registration, patents and trade marks are the same — granted rights are always open to attack and removal before expiry of the maximum term of validity. To maintain these rights, occasional payment of renewal fees is also required.

The 2003 Act introduced some significant changes to designs law, the main ones being a higher novelty threshold based on a two-step test of newness and distinctiveness; a concomitant broader monopoly based on a test of similarity in overall impression;

a shorter term of protection (maximum 10 years rather than 16 years: see s 46); registration without substantive examination (formalities check only); a certification by examination requirement prior to enforcement; the option to request publication only rather than registration of a design (see s 35; this destroys novelty and prevents others from obtaining registration for the design, without requiring the applicant to proceed to registration); and an exception to infringement in relation to certain spare parts (see s 72).

By virtue of the transitional provisions, the validity and infringement tests of the 1906 Act continue to apply to designs (which had a maximum term of 16 years) pre-dating the introduction of the present Act: see ss 151(3) and 156(3). The registered designs system is regularly reviewed: note recently the review of the designs system undertaken by the Advisory Council on Intellectual Property (ACIP): see AICP, *Review of the Designs System: Final Report*, March 2015 (ACIP Report).

What can be Registered Under the Act?

Statutory definition

6.5 To be registrable under the Designs Act 2003, an application must disclose a design that conforms to the statutory definition of 'design' (s 5) and is new and distinctive (s 15(1)). If the application further satisfies the formalities check (s 39), the design will be registered. Only upon a request for certification will the design be examined for compliance with the substantive requirements. The Designs Regulations 2004 (Cth) specify the minimum filing requirements and the formalities check.

'Design': overall appearance resulting from visual features

6.6 By virtue of s 5 of the Designs Act 2003 (Cth):

> *design*, in relation to a product, means the overall appearance of the product resulting from one or more visual features of the product.

The definition articulates the fact that design rights reside in visual features rather than in functional characteristics, and that the appearance of the product in its entirety, and not some particular aspect(s), constitutes the design. Nonetheless, the applicant can draw attention to a particular novel feature by identifying it in a statement of newness and distinctiveness filed with the application, which may then be given more weight when comparison with an impugned design is called for: see s 19(2)(b) and 6.17. The exclusion from registration of 'methods or principles of construction' is inherent in the present statutory definition and follows naturally from the fact that a design is represented by visual representations in the applications (photos or drawings).

Visual features in two or three dimensions

6.7 The statutory definition of 'visual features' distinguishes between two basic categories (see s 7):

- two-dimensional features of a product: pattern or ornamentation; and
- three-dimensional features of a product: shape or configuration.

A design can naturally consist of a combination of two- and three-dimensional features. As the emphasis of the definition of 'design' is on the visual appearance of a product, its function is not part of the design, but that appearance is determined by functional requirements does not matter: see s 7(2). Furthermore, only particular visual features, and not the product as such, are protected by registration. In other words, the general impression of the design or underlying concept or function is not protected by registration. For instance, if the registered design is for a chair with a single central pillar and five horizontal support bars with rollers (as opposed to the more traditional four legs), it is only the precise way in which this technical idea is presented to the eye that is protected; not every chair with the same basic structure will fall within the scope of protection of the design. And if a design is registered for the shape of a triangular strut with the useful function of supporting a roof, the method of using triangular struts for that purpose is not monopolised by design registration.

Some features excluded from design registration

6.8 The now express statutory exclusion from design registration of feel and of materials used (see s 7(3)(a)(b)) continues an arguably outmoded approach followed in the old case law. Certain features, even though perhaps considered important innovations in contemporary design, cannot be registered. Thus, fabrics with a new and distinctive pattern can be registered, but fabrics with a new and distinctive feel cannot. Arguably, this reflects the fact that design is concerned with visual appearance. However, contrast this with the definition of 'design' in the European Community Designs Regulation ((EC) No 6/2002 of 12 December 2001), art 3: 'The appearance of the whole or a part of a product resulting from the features of, in particular, the lines, contours, colours, shape, texture and/or materials of the product itself and/or its ornamentation'. Colour or combinations of colours can be an important visual feature of a design, and colour is not excluded by s 7 of the Designs Act 2003. Although colour can be an element that contributes to the novelty of the overall pattern or ornamentation of a product, a variation in colour alone will not normally suffice to generate a novel design: see *Smith Kline and French Laboratories (Aust) Ltd's Design Application* [1974] RPC 253.

'Features judged by the eye' and 'visible features'

6.9 The Designs Act 2003 limits designs registration to *visual appearance* by virtue of the reference to a 'visible feature' in the definition of 'design' in s 5, as is elaborated in s 7. It must therefore be possible to visually perceive the features constituting the design. If a product must be broken up or destroyed to make some internal feature visible, designs registration will not be available, but visible internal features are not excluded. If use for an intended purpose renders a design feature visible, that is enough: see, for example, *Ferrero's Design Application* [1978] RPC 473, relating to a chocolate egg whose two-tone features become apparent only upon consumption. The Act expressly provides that a visible feature 'may but need not, serve a functional purpose' (see s 7(2)), but that leaves open the question of whether a design whose *every* visual feature is dictated by function is registrable. A design must result from a process of designing; that is, exercising some choice with a view to giving a product specific features of shape and/or ornamentation. Arguably therefore, a product's visual features should not be automatically and entirely determined by functional considerations. Some decisions under the old Act (see s 18 of the Designs Act 1906) addressed this point, which arguably remains relevant despite the terms of s 7(2) of the 2003 Act.

The court in *Hosokawa Micron International Inc v Fortune* (1990) 26 FCR 393; (1990) 19 IPR 531, in which the design at issue was a part of an air filter assembly, felt bound to consider the point. However, the relevant design was to be judged on the basis of the Designs Act 1906 as it stood in 1972, before the s 18 amendment of 1981 that specified that functional designs could be registered. Gummow J, basing himself on a detailed review of the history of designs legislation from the earliest UK statutes to the 1906 Australian Act, defined a purely functional design as one where functional requirements leave the designer with no other possible choice of shape or configuration. Such an alleged design did not fall within the statutory definition. His Honour's reasoning appears to be that if the appearance is solely determined by function, there can be no process of exercising a choice concerning the visual features to be applied to an article by a designer; that is, no process of designing resulting in a design. The exercising of choice and the subsequent application of the chosen features to the article are, in this approach, basic characteristics of a design under the Act; to be registrable, the design must visibly result from such a process.

Gummow J's narrow circumscription of a design solely dictated by function, if accepted, may render the exclusion of such designs largely illusory, since it is difficult to imagine a case where functional requirements leave the designer with no design choice at all. Nonetheless, and in spite of the post-1981 terms of s 18(1) of the 1906 Act, a similar approach was taken by the Full Federal Court in *Interlego AG v Croner Trading Pty Ltd* (1992) 39 FCR 348; 25 IPR 65; see also *Edwards Hot Water Systems v S W Hart & Co Pty Ltd* (1983) 1 IPR 228; 49 ALR 605 at 634–5 per Franki J, although arguably not too much should be read into this decision on this point. Note also that in *Philips Electronics NV v Remington Products Australia Pty Ltd* (1997) 39 IPR 283, Lehane J (at 298), on an application for interim relief, refers to a passage in *Dart Industries Inc v Decor Corporation Pty Ltd* (1989) 15 IPR 403 at 408 — 'If the shape exists solely to make the article work or function then it is not within the concept of a registered design' — as reflecting a well-established principle. The question was also considered in *Digga Australia Pty Ltd v Norm Engineering Pty Ltd* (2008) 166 FCR 268; 75 IPR 251, in the context of the copyright/designs overlap provisions (ss 74–77 of the Copyright Act 1968; see further below at 6.23).

Features 'judged by the eye' and 'visible features': other limitations

6.10 As is indicated above, the visibility requirement means that features that can be perceived only by other senses are not registrable, a rule now reinforced by the express exclusion of texture and feel from the ambit of the terms 'visual feature' in s 7(3)(a). It seems that designs visible only with the assistance of tools and instruments that are relevant or common to the trade are registrable now: see ALRC 74, Recommendation 21. Nonetheless, if a feature cannot be observed visually, it cannot be registered as a design.

As is suggested above, it is not required that the features of appearance are appealing to the eye, in the sense that they would influence consumer decisions, or are attractive or aesthetically pleasing or show some degree of artistic merit. Compare and contrast this with the requirement of 'artistic quality' that applies to works of artistic craftsmanship under the Copyright Act 1968 (Cth), s 10(1) definition of 'artistic work'. In *Malleys Ltd v J W Tomlin Pty Ltd* (1961) 180 CLR 120; 1A IPR 649, the court held that all that was required to justify registration was that a design should show sufficient individuality of appearance to distinguish it from the 'fundamental form' of the article. Alternatively, in *Interlego AG v Croner Trading Pty Ltd* (1992) 39 FCR 348; 25 IPR 65, Gummow J quoted with approval a passage from Lockhart J's judgment in *Dart Industries* at IPR 408:

> For a design to be protected there must be a special or distinctive appearance, something in the design which captures and appeals to the eye. To have that effect, the design must be noticeable and have some perceptible appearance of an individual character.

The term 'appeals to the eye', as used in Lockhart J's judgment above, is thus best read as 'apparent to the eye'. The features that are said to constitute the design must be sufficiently certain, distinct and individual to permit identification by an observer (sometimes this simply means that the representations included in the application must be of sufficient clarity and visible from the appropriate angle(s)). The requirement must be distinguished from ones of novelty or newness and distinctiveness under the Designs Act 2003. Those are threshold tests, calling for a comparison between the design in question and the prior art, not the identification of some inherent characteristic of the design.

Applicable to an article or product

6.11 By virtue of s 5 of the Designs Act 2003, a design refers to the appearance of a 'product', which in turn is defined as a thing that is manufactured or handmade: see s 6(1). Parts or components ('a component part of a complex product': see s 6(2)) are individually registrable as well as the 'complex product' itself; for instance, a new car model can be registered, as well as components such as wheels, facia, body panels, enhancements, etc (as to the latter, see eg, *GM Global Technology Operations LLC v SSS Auto Parts Pty Ltd* (2019) 139 IPR 199; [2019] FCA 97). Naturally occurring features or materials in their natural state are therefore not registrable designs. The Act refers to the monopoly of the design owner as the right to 'make products that embody the design': see s 10(1)(a). Generally speaking, designs registration is not relevant to immovables such as buildings; copyright is the relevant regime for architecture (see further below). Designs registration is intended for items manufactured to a design, prototype or model, and also for products manufactured in indefinite dimensions with a regular or repeated pattern, such as carpets, extrusions, and bolts of cloth or textiles. Section 6(3) of the Act thus expressly provides that features of shape or ornamentation applied to articles of indefinite extent in one or two dimensions can be registered as designs. Dimensions, proportions and pattern must be consistently repeated throughout the bolt, length, etc: s 6(3)(a)–(d); and see, for example, *Coogi Australia Pty Ltd v Hysport International Pty Ltd* (1998) 86 FCR 154; (1998) 41 IPR 593.

Under the 1906 Act, designs registration was reserved for articles whose function went beyond just carrying or presenting the ornamental features; thus, literary and artistic works as such were excluded from registration. For example, in *Edwards Hot Water Systems* at IPR 257, Franki J held that drawings as such could not be registered as a design. To remove doubt in cases where articles are largely literary or artistic, reg 11(1)(a) and (b) of the Designs Regulations 1982, based on s 17(2) of the 1906 Act, excluded articles of printing such as calendars, postage stamps, book jackets, dressmaking patterns, maps and plans, and medals. The 2003 Act confers a power to exclude *any* design by regulation (see s 43(1)(a)), not just designs that are primarily literary or artistic. Compared with the 1906 Act, only the exclusion of medals has been retained: see Designs Regulations 2004, reg 4.06(a). Additionally, certain official emblems, seals and the like, as well as 'designs that are scandalous, or might reasonably be taken to be scandalous' (see reg 4.06(d)) must be refused registration. Under the 2003 Act, purely or largely literary and artistic works are arguably registrable, but in most cases little advantage would flow from it. Stamps, book jackets and the like consist of the application of a two-dimensional artistic work to the surface of a product (rather than 'embodied' in it), and therefore even when registered as designs would not suffer a loss of copyright protection: see s 74 of the Copyright Act 1968 (Cth) and 6.23 below. The registration of a dressmaking pattern would prevent only replication of the pattern as such, not of a garment made to the pattern.

In *Re Application by Comshare Inc* (1991) 23 IPR 145, a delegate of the Registrar of Designs rejected an application for registration of a computer screen display. The approach in *Comshare* was confirmed recently in *Apple Inc* (2017) 127 IPR 191; [2017] ADO 6, the delegate stating that 'the images that appear on a display screen are not visual features of the display screen. They are manifestations of software (or in [the expert witness's] terms, operating systems or GUIs) in combination with hardware and streams of electrons': at [25]. Some other jurisdictions do provide for the registration of typefaces, fonts and branding assets (eg, the UK; the EU). Note that circuit layouts as protected by the Circuit Layouts Act 1989 (Cth) are excluded from registration as designs: see s 43(1)(c)(i–iii).

The dimensions of products appropriate for registration are not limited or restricted; for example, in *Shaklady v Atkins* (1994) 30 IPR 387, a design for an Adams class yacht was found to be registrable: see also *Swarbrick v Burge* (2004) 138 FCR 353; 61 IPR 543. However, as is indicated above, fixed buildings clearly fall within the realm of architectural copyright (in drawings and in buildings; ie, structures of any kind: see s 10). However, some 'buildings' are registrable as designs because they can properly be described as 'articles' or now 'products'; for instance, because they are 'kits' or portable: see *Re Collier & Co Ltd's Application* (1937) 54 RPC 253 and *Tefex Pty Ltd v Bowler* (1981) 40 ALR 326, in which fibreglass swimming pool units or kits were held to be 'articles'. This generates some overlap with copyright law, under which freestanding or portable structures have at times been treated as buildings under the Copyright Act 1968 (Cth): see, for example, *Darwin Fibreglass Pty Ltd v Kruhse Enterprises Pty Ltd* (1998) 41 IPR 649, where the fibreglass shell of a pool was considered to be a building, and a plug for the manufacture of the shell a 'model of a building' (see s 10): see further below 6.23. The potential for dual copyright and designs protection in this context has now largely been removed by s 77(5) of the Copyright Act: for the purpose of the overlap provisions, a 'building or model of a building does not include a portable building such as a shed, a pre-constructed swimming pool, a demountable building or similar portable building'. The creator of new structures of this kind can now rely only on designs registration and not copyright.

Under the Designs Act 2003, an application may, in certain circumstances, be in respect of more than one design: see s 22. In particular, a single application can be filed for 'one design that is a common design in relation to more than one product' (s 22 (1)(b)), which usefully includes assemblies of separate items or sets (eg, a cutlery set). The Act also provides that '[a] kit which, when assembled, is a particular product is taken to be that product': s 6(4).

The registration of components, spares and interoperable parts

6.12 The adverse effect of design registration on competition in the aftermarket for spare parts caused concern and delay in the preparations for the introduction of the 2003 Act. In particular, in relation to must-fit and must-match parts, there is little scope for the supply of substitute products if the genuine part is registered as a design, arguably resulting in unacceptably high prices. In the automotive industries, for example, designs registration allows unilateral price setting for spare and replacement parts by car manufacturers for the life of most models. The recent litigation reflected in *GM Global Technology Operations* nicely illustrates the scenario. Nonetheless the Act allows 'component parts of complex products' to be separately registered: see s 6(2). ALRC 74 recommended that applications for the registration of spare parts should be referred to the Australian Competition and Consumer Commission (ACCC) for consideration of potential anti-competitive effects; the ACCC's advice could then result in the refusal of the application: see Recommendations 165–169. However, the government chose to mitigate the monopoly effects of spare part registration by introducing a repair exception to infringement instead: see s 72. No authorisation is required to make, sell, import or use a replacement part to restore the overall appearance of a complex product: see s 72(5) 'use'. The overall appearance is restored if to a person familiar with the complex product (the 'informed user': see s 72(4)) there is no material difference between its overall appearance before and after the use of the component part. The repair defence is further considered below at 6.19 'The repair defence'.

Novelty and Distinctiveness of Designs

The two-step test

6.13 Since the purpose of a design monopoly is to encourage innovation, only designs that differ in some material respect from pre-existing designs can be registered. Lockhart J in *Conrol Pty Ltd v Meco McCallum Pty Ltd* (1996) 34 IPR 517 at 527 identified the balance that needs to be struck:

> This requirement manifests the Parliament's intention to balance or reconcile two competing elements of public policy: first, the encouragement and protection of the intellectual activity which is put into the production of industrial designs; secondly, the concern not to impede or oppress the natural development of industry.

The latter point hints at the fact that to attract monopoly rights, a new design must differ by way of more than the standard developments, variations or modifications made in the industry concerned. But since design innovation is commonly incremental, the bar cannot be set too high either. Furthermore, changes in appearance will often be constrained by existing functional or conceptual parameters. A design for a chair can be new, even though it has four legs, a back and a seat like many chairs before it. Therefore, although the underlying concept, idea or function need not be new compared with the prior art, a product's singular and specific appearance must be different enough. Formulating a standard that requires real innovation, but only in particular appearance and not in the underlying concept, and recognises the incremental and often predictable nature of design modifications, leaves little room for manoeuvre. The terminology expressing such a standard must be sufficiently precise to give real guidance to decision-makers. The Act adopts a two-step approach requiring novelty (ie, not identical to a relevant prior design) and distinctiveness (ie, substantially different in overall impression). The latter test requires attention to be directed at a different overall impression (see ss 15, 16 and 17) rather than at identifying particular detailed differences that do not have a sufficient impact on the overall appearance. The requirement of distinctiveness introduces a concept that was hitherto unfamiliar in Australian designs law, although not in other jurisdictions. In Europe, the community designs regulation employs an analogous concept of 'individual character': see art 4(1), Council Regulation (EC) No 6/2002 of 12 December 2001 on Community Designs.

Prior art and novelty

6.14 By virtue of s 15 (1), a design is registrable 'if it is new and distinctive when compared with 'the prior art base for the design as it existed before the priority date of the design'. Section 15(2) goes on to specify that publications in documentary form and through public use in Australia, as well as documentary publications outside Australia, are relevant prior art. This is known as a worldwide or global novelty test, although if the alleged 'anticipation' (ie, novelty-destroying publication) outside Australia is only by public use and not by representation in documentary form, the novelty of an Australian application is not undermined. Statutory exception is made for certain 'anticipations'; that is, publications before the priority date: see s 17 of the Designs Act 2003 and reg 2.01 of the Designs Regulations 2004. The priority date is normally the filing date of the design application: see s 27. Under the 1906 Act a person was able to obtain registration by importing a design that was not yet used or published in Australia — hardly an encouragement for local design development. Under the 2003 Act, such borrowing cannot result in valid registration in Australia if the imported design was disclosed in documentary form abroad. The concepts of prior art, priority date and what constitutes prior use or prior publication are not further discussed here. Analogous and largely interchangeable concepts are covered in the context of patents law: see Chapter 8 Patents: Novelty and Inventiveness. By virtue of s 16(1), 'A design is new unless it is identical to a design that forms part of the prior art base for the design.' The effect of this provision is to eliminate every design that is identical to a design found in the prior art. If there is some difference between the design in the application and one(s) disclosed in the prior art, then the test of distinctiveness is to be applied to determine whether the difference is material for the sake of validity.

Determining distinctiveness

6.15 The distinctiveness test (see ss 15(1), 16(2) and 19) is structured so as to provide detailed statutory guidance for a decision-maker faced with alleged prior art that is not identical to the applied for design. A design lacks the necessary distinctiveness if it is 'substantially similar in overall impression'. By virtue of s 19(1) more weight is to be given to similarities than to differences (it is often said that under the 1906 Act too much weight was given to small differences). Further, s 19 mandates factors to be considered by a decision-maker in the course of comparison; these factors apply also to assessing similarity in overall impression in infringement cases. Particularly important in assessing similarity for the sake of validity are two factors related to the nature and antecedents of the design: first, the state of development of the prior art base (s 19(2)(a)): a large body of antecedent designs and development will constrain innovation, and a relatively small variation from previous designs might therefore still suffice; and, second, the freedom of the designer to innovate (s 19(2)(d)): the more constrained the designer's choices, the smaller the difference in appearance required. In some areas, design choices will be constrained by the nature and function of the product. The ALRC also refers to factors external to the product: '[...] including the market for the product and marketing constraints': see ALRC 74 at [5.24]. If the similarities lie in one part of the design only, the amount, quality and importance of that part in relation to the design as a whole must be taken into account: s 19(2)(c). The question is ultimately one for the court but is made applying the standard (ie, through the eyes) of the 'informed user': see s 19(4); that is, a person 'familiar with the product to which the design relates' or similar products — in other words, not the eyes of a design expert (to whom differences may stand out more) nor those of a person completely unfamiliar with the kinds of product concerned. The ALRC intended the concept to be 'flexible enough to incorporate where relevant the views of consumers, experts, specialists and skilled tradespersons': at ALRC 74 [5.17].

In *Review 2 Pty Ltd v Redberry Enterprise Pty Ltd* (2008) 173 FCR 450; [2008] FCA 1588, Kenny J obtained guidance from ALRC 74 and from designs law in the UK, which adopted the concept of the informed user from European law. Kenny J concluded that the informed user was a user of articles of the sort to whom the design was directed and who was informed about 'what's around in the market' and 'alert to design issues': at [22]. The standard is said to be an objective one: see also *Review Australia Pty Ltd v New Cover Group Pty Ltd* (2008) 79 IPR 236; [2008] FCA 1589. However, Yates J in *Multisteps Pty Ltd v Source & Sell Pty Ltd* (2013) 214 FCR 323; 105 IPR 342; [2013] FCA 743 (*Multisteps v Source & Sell*) emphasised the differences between the UK and Australian statutes. The standard in Australia is of a person 'familiar with the product to which the design relates' (see s 19(4)). The word 'user' was merely a tag: at [63]. In *Hunter Pacific International Pty Ltd v Martec Pty Ltd* (2016) 121 IPR 1; [2016] FCA 796, Nicholas J simply said at [39]:

> The informed user is a notional person who is taken to be familiar with the product to which the design relates or products similar to the product to which the design relates. The

informed user will also be taken to have a familiarity with the Registered Design and the product that is alleged to infringe based upon a careful and deliberate visual inspection.

In *Multisteps v Specialty Packaging* Jagot J referred (at [85]) with approval to those words of Nicholas J, and also to the following passage from the same *Hunter Pacific* decision (at [39]):

> … the relevant comparison cannot be based upon a fleeting or casual inspection of the drawings or object in question or some 'imperfect recollection' of either of them. That is not to deny that the comparison to be undertaken is essentially impression based. I therefore respectfully agree with the following statement of Yates J in *Multisteps Pty Ltd v Source & Sell Pty Ltd* (2013) 214 FCR 323; 309 ALR 83; 105 IPR 342; [2013] FCA 743 at [55]: '... although the test is based on impression, it is not based merely on a casual comparison between designs for a given article. There needs to be a studied comparison based on the prescriptions of s 19 of the Designs Act. Thus, the notion of "imperfect recollection" — familiar in trade mark law — has no application when determining design similarity...'

It should be noted that novelty and distinctiveness examination is normally only undertaken upon a request for certification although any person can request the Registrar to examine a registered design that has not yet been certified (see s 63). At any time after certification, any person can apply to a court seeking an order revoking the registration, on any of the grounds specified in s 93. No grace period exists as yet in relation to applications for the registration of a design. In other words, if the applicant publishes the design prior to filing an application for registration of the design, the design will not be novel. The prior publication will constitute an 'anticipation'. Contrast this with patents, where a grace period now exists, which may save the application if it is made within a statutory period from publication: see Chapter 8 Patents: Novelty and Inventiveness. The ACIP Report called for the introduction of a grace period. This would be particularly advantageous for industry sectors with a short innovation cycle such as fashion. Of course, for the purpose of examination of the application, any publication or use after the priority date is to be ignored. In other words, publication after the priority date does not constitute 'anticipation'; therefore the applicant may manufacture and sell the design article without losing novelty and can advertise or publish information about it without the constraint of confidentiality.

Design Rights, Infringement and Remedies

Monopoly rights and infringement

6.16 Section 10 of the Designs Act 2003 grants monopoly rights: the owner has the exclusive right to make the product that embodies the registered design. Monopoly rights differ from mere anti-copying rights, in that independent creation is no defence. Access to the registered design need not be proven, only excessive similarity (under the 1906 Act, proof of actual copying was relevant to infringement by 'fraudulent imitation': see s 30 of the Designs Act 1906). Although as a monopoly a registered design right is thus more extensive than a right under the Copyright Act 1968, the scope of protection of a registered design is more limited than the scope of copyright for artistic works. Furthermore, in comparison, the term of protection of a registered design is relatively short: maximum 10 years under the Designs Act 2003: see s 46. Once the design is registered, the owner of the registered design may bring an action in infringement only in relation to infringements that occurred after the date of registration (as opposed to after publication of an application as in patents law). An action for infringement under the 2003 Act can be brought only in relation to a certified design (ie, a design that has undergone substantive examination rather than just the formalities check required before registration): see s 73. A person may apply for relief from unjustified threats of infringement proceedings: see s 77 (as considered in *GM Global Technology Operations*). The registered design owner has the exclusive right to make products embodying the design, and dealing with articles or products incorporating the design for the purposes of trade or business also lies within the scope of the monopoly: see ss 10 and 71.

The parallel importation of products embodying registered designs is permitted. Only the importation of an article to which the design has been applied outside Australia without the licence or authority of the person who was the owner of the registered design at the time when the design was so applied is an infringement. This is expressly stipulated in the Act: see the combined effect of s 71(1)(b) and s 71(2). Knowledge is not relevant to liability at all but is relevant to the granting of remedies. In other words, no knowledge on the part of the defendant concerning either the existence of a registration or the infringing nature of an act is required to establish liability for making or dealing commercially in an infringing design. However, the court has the discretion to reduce or refuse to award damages or an account of profits if, in relation to making or offering to make the design (so-called primary infringement: see s 75(2)(a)), the defendant satisfies the court that at the time of infringement they were not aware that the design was registered and that they had, prior to that time, taken all reasonable steps to ascertain whether a monopoly in the design existed. Reasonable steps means primarily inspecting the Register of Designs. For secondary infringement, that is, by dealing in infringing designs, the discretion is enlivened if the defendant satisfies the court that they were not aware and could not reasonably have been expected to be aware that the design was registered (see s 75(2)(b)), thus potentially providing some greater protection for unwitting retailers.

The test for infringement

6.17 Infringement is established by a visual comparison between registered and impugned designs. (By virtue of the transitional provisions of the 2003 Act, the infringement provisions of the 1906 Act continue to apply to actions relating to designs registered or applied for before the commencing day of the present Act: see s 156(3) and also s 153). The 2003 Act applies a two-tier test: either the design is identical or it is substantially similar in overall impression: see s 71(1) and (3). To determine whether two designs are substantially similar in overall impression, a court must consider the factors enumerated in s 19, the same factors as apply to the test of distinctiveness for the purpose of validity — they are considered above at 6.15. However, the effect of a 'Statement of Newness and Distinctiveness' (s 19(2)(b) and(c)) is considered here. If the statement identifies particular features as new and distinctive, then 'particular regard' must be had to those features, and 'if those features relate to only part of the design— [the decision-maker must] have particular regard to that part of the design, but in the context of the design as a whole': s 19(2)(b)(ii). Filing a statement is optional so applicants are not compelled to identify those features that render their design distinctive in appearance. Often, such statements, much like the statements of novelty or of monopoly under the 1906 Act, in fact refer to the design as a whole or to 'each feature considered separately or in combination with any other feature or features', or some similar expression.

It will be the decision-maker's task to reconcile the overarching test of similarity in overall impression with the requirement to give particular regard to certain individual features. Further, by virtue of s 19(2)(c), if only part of the design is similar to an impugned design, then regard must be had to 'the amount, quality and importance of that part in the context of the design as a whole'. The 'quality and importance' can only be visual. Again, the challenge lies in reconciling the additional weight to be attached to some visually striking feature of the registered design, with the ultimate test of substantial similarity in overall impression. It may well be that the crucial issue in most cases will be the characterisation of the 'informed user' whose mantle the decision-maker must don to arrive at a conclusion, and whether the court will accept the statements of one or another witness as more closely reflecting those of the 'informed user' than those of a witness for the other side. As to that concept, see 6.15. For an example of the approach to infringement under the 2003 Act, see *Keller v LED Technologies Pty Ltd* (2010) 185 FCR 449 and more recently *Multisteps v Specialty Packaging*; in the latter case the court points to a number of individual differences and then asserts that there is no similarity in overall impression (eg, at [95]). *Keller* concerned a rear lights assembly for motor vehicles. In the final analysis, the specific differences between the registered and impugned designs did not create a different visual appeal, nor were they prominent or particularly significant features in the judgment of the court. Most commonly the core judgment will be exactly whether differences identified in a careful visual inspection are sufficient to affect the overall impression or not. This judgment is influenced significantly by the state of development of the prior art, as s 19 now makes expressly clear. But this is not a departure from the previous law. In *Dart Industries*, Lockhart J said (at IPR 409) with regard to the degree of similarity required for a design to amount to an imitation under the 1906 Act:

> The scope of a registered design must be determined with reference to the background of the prior art at the priority date and questions of infringement and novelty or originality are connected ... Where novelty or originality is discovered in slight variations, there cannot be infringement without a very close resemblance between the registered design and the article alleged to be an infringement of the design ... Small differences between the registered design and the prior art will generally lead to a finding of no infringement if there are equally small differences between the registered design and the alleged infringing article. On the other hand, the greater the advance in the registered design over the prior art, generally the more likely that a court will find common features between the design and the alleged infringing article to support a finding of infringement.

This relative 'strength' of the registered design is the backdrop against which the court applies the tests of infringement. Under the 1906 Act, the ultimate judgment assessing overall similarity was arguably excessively influenced by the weight that often came to attach to the list of differences that resulted from the preceding detailed visual comparison. The 2003 Act attempts to avoid that trap by the express provision that greater weight should be given to similarities than to differences: see s 19(1). Note also that the comparison is with individual and identified items of prior art that are before the decision-maker, not with the prior art as a whole: see *LED Technologies Pty Ltd v Elecspess Pty Ltd* [2008] FCA 1941, *Review 2* and *Review Australia* (see above 6.15).

Infringement of registered designs with functional features

6.18 In *Firmagroup Australia Pty Ltd v Byrne & Davidson Doors (Vic) Pty Ltd* (1987) 180 CLR 483; 9 IPR 353, the court held that there were some points of similarity and some of difference between the two designs for recessed roller door locks and handles. The points of similarity were, however, features determined by function, and thus not protected by the 1906 Act. The latter expressly provided that methods or principles of construction are not designs (see s 4); in other words, adopting the method or concept or function of a registered design alone does not amount to taking a design: it is the particular appearance of the article or product that must be replicated. By virtue of s 7(2) of the 2003 Act, a visual feature may serve a functional purpose; however, similarly, this does not mean that the function the design performs is monopolised by registration — this purpose is properly served by patent law, in particular (for the time being) by an innovation patent (see *Multisteps v Specialty Packaging*, where the produce containers were the subject of registered designs and innovation patents).

It is apparent upon a comparison of representations of the two designs in *Firmagroup* that the defendant was indeed able to adopt the substantial functional idea or concept behind the recessed door handle design (which, incidentally, represented a considerable advance on the known art) with impunity. Arguably, patents protection would have been the appropriate choice for the plaintiff desiring to monopolise the functional aspects of the breakthrough design. This alternative may not be open where the design lacks the requisite degree of inventiveness for the granting of a standard patent; however, an innovation patent requires only that the invention makes a substantial (by which is meant 'real': see *Product Management Group Pty Ltd v Blue Gentian LLC* (2016) 240 FCR 85; (2015) 116 IPR 54; [2015] FCAFC 179; at [175]) contribution to the working of the invention.

It remains to be seen to what extent the 2003 Act will have an impact on the limitations of the *Firmagroup* approach under the 1906 Act. Although the statutory intention is to encompass more different designs within the scope of the registration, it may be that courts will still feel restrained in cases where recognising such wider scope would allow functionality to be monopolised. In Australia, since there is no requirement that the design appearance itself must be a factor influencing consumer choice, many registered designs are for very functional products; see, for instance, *LED Technologies* (rear lights assembly) (the appeal decision is *Keller*; *Multisteps v Source & Sell* (plastic produce containers); and *Gram Engineering Pty Ltd v Bluescope Steel Ltd* (2013) 106 IPR 1; [2013] FCA 508 (fencing panels).

The repair defence

6.19 As indicated above, the registration of designs for replacement or component parts of complex products generated considerable concern because of its potential anti-competitive effect in aftermarkets for spare parts, such as the market for HSV (Holden Special Vehicles) parts considered in *GM Global Technology*. However, s 72 of the 2003 Act introduced a repair defence to allow the production and supply of components by competitors for repair purposes without authorisation from the registered design owner. The repair defence can be invoked if a product embodying a registered design is 'used' (as is statutorily defined and further explained below) to repair a complex product so as to restore its overall appearance in whole or in part. Essential is that there is a 'repair' and that it restores the overall appearance of the complex product. The explanatory memorandum to the Design Bill 2002 points out at [107] that:

> This subclause does not provide a defence against infringement where the use of a component part embodying a design results in the enhancement of the appearance of the complex product. This approach preserves the incentive to innovate by allowing all designs of component parts of complex products to be registered if they meet the innovation threshold, without introducing any risk of subsequent anti-competitive behaviour. This enables original component parts to be protected, while the same or substantially similar component parts may be used for repairs without the risk of infringement.

The dictionary meaning of the word 'use' is extended by s 72(5) of the 2003 Act to include making, selling, importing, etc, as well as actually using a component part to make the repair (installing it). That section also provides that repair of a complex product includes replacing a part, but only where the part being replaced is either damaged or decayed or the replacement happens in the course of maintenance or is incidental to restoring or replacing a damaged or decayed component part. Only where the repair restores rather than changes or enhances the overall appearance of the complex product, either in whole or in part, will the defence operate, even if a damaged or decayed part is replaced in the process. Enhancements and additions (eg, skirts or a wing added to a car by its owner) that modify the overall appearance of the complex product are not repairs and not covered. By virtue of s 72(3), a repair is to be taken to have restored the overall appearance as a whole if there is no material difference between the appearance of the complex product immediately before and after the repair. It is to be taken to have restored the overall appearance in part if any material difference is 'solely attributable to the fact that only part of the complex product has been repaired' (ibid). For instance, if the accidentally dented boot lid of an old and decayed car is repaired by a new replacement lid, the difference in overall appearance of the car as a whole after the repair is solely due to the fact that the lid looks new compared with the car as a whole. The standard to be applied in judging restoration versus alteration of the overall appearance is that of the 'informed user'; that is, a person familiar with the complex product or with products of that sort. How to construe the 'informed user' is discussed above: see 6.15. The repair defence applies also if a replacement part only restores the appearance of a complex product in part. Sometimes, only the appearance of the area of a complex product immediately surrounding the replacement part is relevant. Again, taking a car as an example, the repair defence would apply to a damaged internal door handle if the overall appearance of the internal door panel is not materially altered by the replacement part. However, it will not always be clear to what part or extent of the overall product regard must be had.

In *GM Global Technology Operations*, HSV spare parts were sourced overseas by SSS Auto Parts (a company unconnected with GM/Holden, (SSS)) for sale in Australia. The difficulty was that some owners of regular Holden sedans (not HSV cars) were known to acquire HSV parts to enhance or change the look of their own vehicles. Such use of the spare parts imported by SSS would not be for repairs but for altering the overall appearance of the ordinary Holdens; the repair defence would not save their unauthorised importation into Australia by SSS. The Act (s 72(2)) places the onus of proving a non-repair purpose (in this case of the imporation) on the applicant (GM/ Holden). On the evidence, the court was not satisfied that GM/Holden discharged that burden. The SSS business model had always been to sell aftermarket parts for use in the repair of motor vehicles, and the importation of the HSV parts was arranged in the ordinary course of that business. Stringent repair-only policies were implemented to the supply of the parts to Australian customers. In those circumstances, it could not be said that various officers of SSS knew or ought reasonably to have known that the importation was not for a repair purpose.

Note that placing the onus to prove that a spare part is not being made, supplied or used for repair purposes is placed on the registered design owner serves a significant policy purpose; as the explanatory memorandum states at [108]–[109]:

> 108. … To place the onus on the suppliers or manufacturers of spare parts would act as a disincentive for new participants to enter the spare parts market. It would force suppliers and manufacturers of spare parts to track their entire inventory to see whether they all are being used for genuine repair purposes. 109. Nevertheless, if suppliers or manufacturers are knowingly participating in using parts for nonrepair purposes, or should have reasonably known that they are doing so, then they should not be able to hide behind the right of repair defence.

IP Australia undertook a review of the spare parts provision in 2005, noted that it had not been tested in the courts and that its effects were not likely to be felt for a considerable time, and recommended no changes: see *Review of the 'Spare Parts' Provision in the Designs Act 2003*, December 2005. The report stresses the difficulty in assessing the impact of the provision on industry. The *GM Global Technology Operations* decision has now provided some clarification concerning the operation of the repair defence. It also provides some insights into the 'unjustified threats' (s 77) provisions of the Designs Act, since SSS cross-claimed in relation to letters GM/Holden had sent to a number of businesses who were engaged in the supply of parts and who were selling HSV and VE (Holden) parts, alleging that the recipient suppliers had engaged in infringement of registered designs.

Registration and Term

Application and examination

6.20 The owner of an unregistered design may file an application for registration and the owner of the unregistered design is its author, unless the design was made in the course of employment or was commissioned: in that case, the employer or the commissioning party owns the unregistered design (see s 13; take note of the difference with copyright law in this regard: see Copyright Act 1968 (Cth), s 35(5)). The statutory provision is always subject to potential contractual variations or assignments.

Ownership of a registered design is determined by the relevant entry in the register; the law also provides for co-ownership of a registered design: see s 14. Co-owners can exercise the rights under the Act independently but require the consent of other owners to grant a licence. By virtue of s 60, a person may elect either to publish (an option that did not exist under the 1906 Act and is in fact little used if at all) or to register the design; documents relating to the application are subsequently made available for public inspection. Rights in a registered design are personal property and may be assigned in writing (signed by the assignor): see s 11. Assignments and other interests are entered or noted by the Registrar upon sufficient proof of title: see Ch 9 of the Act.

The register not only is a source of relevant information concerning ownership and interests in the design but also constitutes legal proof of such rights. Entering details of interests is of considerable importance because, unless a court directs otherwise, an instrument that has not been entered on the register does not amount to proof of title or of an interest in a registered design in a court of law (see s 119). The owner may choose to exploit the design right by authorising or licensing others to apply the design. In case of refusal to license on reasonable terms, a person can apply to the court for the granting of a compulsory licence. The applicant must establish that the product has not been made to a reasonable extent in Australia, without any satisfactory reason: see s 90.

Term and validity of a registered design

6.21 The date of filing of the application is also the commencement date of the term of validity. Under the 1906 Act, the overall maximum term was 16 years, with an initial term that expired after 12 months: see s 27A(1). Subsequent extensions for 5-year terms sought by the registered owner were subject to the right of any person to bring anticipatory matter to the attention of the Registrar (s 27A(4)). The Registrar could refuse an extension on the basis of any information that came to their notice (in which case an appeal lay to the Federal Court) or could grant the extension: s 27A(9). These provisions continue to apply to designs pre-dating the commencement of the Designs Act 2003. Such designs continue to enjoy the maximum term of the 1906 Act: see s 152(a) and (b) of the Designs Act 2003. Designs granted under the 2003 Act have a maximum term of 10 years. Old designs are taken to have been certified under the 2003 Act: see s 151(2) of that Act. But neither registration under the old Act nor certification under the present Act constitutes a guarantee of validity. Any person can apply to a prescribed court for a revocation of a registered design, but only 'after the design has been examined under Chapter 5 and a certificate of examination has been issued': see s 93(2) of the 2003 Act (this applies also to old designs, to which the grounds of invalidity of the 1906 Act nonetheless continue to apply: see s 151(3) of the 2003 Act). In any action for infringement, a defendant may also counterclaim for the rectification of the register by way of revocation of the registration of the design: s 74 of the 2003 Act. The grounds for rectification of the register by way of a counterclaim are those enumerated in s 93. At any time, any person can request the Registrar to examine a design, and the design can also be examined on the Registrar's own initiative: see s 63 of the 2003 Act.

The Relationship Between Copyright and Designs

General

6.22 Intellectual property law operates by a process of 'pigeonholing': subject matter must fit within the boundaries of one or another regime or action. In Australia, no uniform fallback action for unfair competition, unjust enrichment or similar is recognised either by statute or by the courts. But 'pigeonholing' can give rise to difficulties where subject matter may fit within several regimes. The potential cumulation of protection has become a more acute issue with the recent expansion of protected subject matter in various regimes: see, for instance, the potential overlap of copyright protection, designs and trade mark registration now that the shape and packaging of goods can sometimes be registered as a trade mark. Cumulation of protection may have anti-competitive effects and override the careful calibration of each regime. Nonetheless, no general principle of intellectual property law prevents cumulative or alternative protection; creators can opt for the form or forms of protection most suitable to their needs. For instance, a product registered as a design may also be granted a patent in relation to its functional advantages; at the same time, it may benefit from copyright protection and also be registered as a trade mark (subject to the conditions that apply in each regime). Of course, although cumulative protection may be available, each regime tends to protect different aspects of what in a commercial sense may be a single product; for example, 'function' in patents and 'appearance' in designs law. However, this is not always so clearly the case. In particular, copyright in artistic works and designs registration overlap considerably in their sphere of protection and remedies available. Both are concerned with two- or three-dimensional aspects of visual appearance and with restricting imitation.

In this area, then, the policy of the law in Australia is to severely limit the availability of copyright protection in relation to products for which designs registration is available: ss 74–77 of the Copyright Act 1968 (Cth), as amended by the Designs (Consequential Amendments) Act 2003 (Cth) ('the 2003 amendments'). The only other express statutory restriction on cumulation or choice between regimes relates to cumulative designs registration and circuit layouts protection: see s 43(1)(c) of the Designs Act 2003 ('article' does not include a circuit layout eligible for protection under the Circuit Layouts Act 1989).

Because the Copyright Act 1968 and Designs Act 2003 grant substantially similar rights (ie, an exclusive right of reproduction in two or three dimensions), it would seem that an author of a design might just as well rely on copyright in the artistic work that underlies the design (eg, a model, pattern or drawing). Indeed, it may make sense to ignore designs registration, since copyright protection has arguably greater scope, is of longer duration and does not require registration; it is also international in effect, due to the operation of the Berne Convention, while an Australian design registration has a purely municipal effect. The risk therefore exists that free choice between designs registration and copyright could render designs law largely redundant. By implication, it could therefore subvert the policy aims of the designs system: an ex ante indication of validity, publicity and searchability by way of an open register, and transactional clarity and ease of verification of ownership and interests. The relevant sections of the Copyright Act (ss 74–77) were inserted by the Copyright Amendment Act 1989 (Cth) and amended in 2003. According to ALRC 74 at [17.5]:

> The Explanatory Memorandum to the 1988 Bill states that the provisions were intended to remove copyright protection for essentially industrial products and eliminate the uncertainty and inequity caused by the overlap ... The problem that the overlap provisions were designed to address was the perceived excess of copyright protection for industrial products. Copyright protection is considered inappropriate for certain technological developments. It is argued that copyright protection for 'derivative reproductions' of artistic works is too long. Copyright and design protection are essentially different in nature and scope.

Or, as Wilcox J put it in *Hutchence v South Sea Bubble Co Pty Ltd* (1986) 6 IPR 473 at 485, 'The fundamental reasons for excepting industrial designs from the protection of copyright law are to avoid uncertainty in the industrial world and to avoid hindrance to the improvement of the design of manufactured articles.' In a sense, of course, copyright law does not leave the author with a choice. Once the work is made, copyright subsists automatically; for that reason, the overlap provisions that limit reliance on artistic works copyright if articles are produced on an industrial scale are located in the Copyright Act. It is tempting to give the overlap provisions only cursory attention, due to their complexity and apparent obscurity, but cases in which the provisions are applied are not uncommon, and the consequences of insufficient regard for the provisions can be unfortunate. For a recent and high-profile example, see, for example, *Burge v Swarbrick* (2007) 232 CLR 336; 72 IPR 235, in which a yacht designer who sought to rely on copyright in the absence of a design registration was ultimately left without a remedy. The amendments made subsequent to the introduction of the Designs Act 2003 have adapted the copyright provisions to the language of that Act. They have also addressed the absence of any defence relating to 'plan to plan' copying, which undermined the effectiveness of the previous provisions. For instance, in *Muscat v Le* (2003) 60 IPR 276, the defendants infringed copyright, not by the actual making of the garments concerned (which was pre-empted by the overlap provisions) but by the indirect reproduction of patterns and drawings used in their manufacture (actions which are now covered by the overlap provisions but were not at that time).

Operation of the overlap provisions

6.23 Drawings, sculptures and engravings, as well as buildings (as broadly interpreted), attract copyright protection as artistic works: see s 10 of the Copyright Act 1968 and relevant case law. These artistic works play a potentially significant role in the industrial design process because most industrial design items constitute reproductions of initial drawings (be they technical or artistic in nature), models (sculptures under the Copyright Act) and moulds for industrial production (arguably engravings or sculptures). Alternatively, industrial design articles or products may themselves amount to sculptures, or their ornamentation may be a drawing. Thus, copyright is a viable option for obtaining relief against unauthorised manufacture or sale of a product. It is exactly that option that the overlap provisions largely foreclose by instigating certain defences to infringement.

Where a design corresponding to an artistic work (ie, a 'corresponding design' in terms of s 74 of the Copyright Act, being a design that is a three-dimensional reproduction of an artistic work) is registered, it is not, by virtue of s 75 of the Copyright Act, an infringement of copyright to reproduce the product embodying the artistic work. The defence operates only where visual features have been incorporated into the shape or configuration of a product, not where the registered design consists solely of a two-dimensional artistic work applied to the surface of an article by way of pattern or ornamentation, or where the work, such as a logo, is not 'embodied'. For example, in *Seafolly Pty Ltd v Fewstone Pty Ltd* (2014) 106 IPR 85; [2014] FCA 321, the 'senorita' diamond pattern embroidery design was held not to be embodied in certain garments. 'Embodiment' and 'three-dimensionality' were the crucial requirements. Relevant considerations were physical and conceptual separability, whether the added features had been so applied or incorporated into the garment as to have no independent existence or ability to survive independently, and whether the added article was so interwoven into the garment's fabric as to become indistinguishable. Dodds-Streeton J had regard for these principles as rehearsed by the Full Court in *Polo Lauren Co LP v Ziliani Holdings Pty Ltd* (2008) 173 FCR 266. Thus, if a design consisting of the application of a two-dimensional artistic work to the surface of an article is registered, the design owner will be able to rely both on copyright (in the underlying, drawing, painting, photograph) and on registered design protection. The defence is limited; that is, it is not correct to say that copyright protection is lost when a design is registered. Generally speaking, the copyright owner retains a right of action in relation to all other forms of copying, even where a design in a corresponding product is registered. That includes a right of action against unauthorised drawing to drawing copying, for instance.

However, the 2003 amendments expanded the operation of the overlap provisions to forms of copying that fall outside embodiment in a product: see s 77A of the Copyright Act. By virtue of that section, copyright is now also unavailable against alleged unauthorised reproductions that occur as part of the manufacturing process in circumstances where the making of the product itself does not constitute an infringement because of the operation of the overlap provisions (ie, because of registration or industrial application of a corresponding design). This might be where the underlying artistic work has been reproduced indirectly; for instance, in the form of patterns or technical drawings used in the process of making the allegedly infringing product (see s 77A(1)) or where the infringement would otherwise occur in the making of a cast or mould for the purpose of manufacture: see s 77A(2). Thus, the outcome of *Muscat v Le* would be reversed under the new provisions, although in that case there was no registered design, and the provisions of s 77 (see below) were at issue. Section 76 ensures that the defence to copyright infringement will not apply where the design has been registered, without the knowledge of the owner of the design, by a person who was not the owner of the design for the purpose of registration.

On the basis of the foregoing alone, a copyright owner might choose not to register the design and simply rely on copyright instead. But s 77 forecloses this option by providing (subject to exceptions) that if a design is not registered but is 'industrially applied' (s 77(1)(b)) and the resulting articles have been commercially exploited (s 77(1)(c)), then copyright protection is also 'lost' in the sense of s 74. Section 77(4) allows the term 'industrially applied' to be defined by regulation. Thus, an article is to be taken to have been industrially applied if 50 or more copies have been industrially produced, or if the article is produced in lengths or pieces: see Copyright Regulations 1969 (Cth), reg 17. Regulation 17 is an inclusive deeming provision. Ultimately, in cases that fall outside the scope of the regulations, it is up to the courts to determine, in light of all the circumstances, whether an article has been industrially applied: see, for example, *Shacklady v Atkins* (1994) 30 IPR 387 (a yacht); *Pres-Form Pty Ltd v Henderson's Ltd* (1993) 26 IPR 113 (whether the making of experimental bus seats for a display amounted to industrial application); *Safe Sport Australia Pty Ltd v Puma Australia Pty Ltd* (1985) 4 IPR 120 (making of prototypes did not amount to industrial application); *Kevlacat Pty Ltd v Trailcraft Marine Pty Ltd* (1987) 11 IPR 77 (production of 40 Kevlacat Cuddy cabin boats by an industrial process amounted to industrial application); and *Gold Peg International Pty Ltd v Kovan Engineering (Aust) Pty Ltd* (2005) 67 IPR 497 (no 'system' or 'process' in the manufacture of products need be shown). The most recent consideration given to the overlap provisions in the Full Federal Court in *Digga Australia Pty Ltd v Norm Engineering Pty Ltd* (2008) 166 FCR 268; 75 IPR 251 also provides an illustration of the approach to determining whether industrial application has occurred. A further issue considered in that case is the proper approach where the design was not registrable at all: s 77(1)(d). An unregistrable design in the sense of s 77(1)(d) has been held to be a design that lacks novelty but otherwise falls within the statutory definition of a registrable design: see *Interlego AG v Croner Trading Pty Ltd* (1992) 39 FCR 348; 25 IPR 65. A design may be unregistrable in this sense because, under the Designs Act 1906, it constituted a method or principle of construction, or because functional requirements entirely determine its appearance.

Adopting this approach, if a 'design' is unregistrable not because it lacks novelty but because it does not conform to the statutory definition of 'design', copyright protection would remain available, thereby defeating the intention of limiting copyright for manufactured products. As was pointed out in the *Digga* case, the amendments introduced by the Designs (Consequential Amendments) Bill 2002 were, according to its explanatory memorandum, intended to remove the anomaly that resulted. Clause 10 of the memorandum says (as reproduced in *Digga* at [140]):

> One difficulty with the existing definition has been the meaning of the word 'design'. It has been held that the word has the same meaning as is given to it in the Designs Act 1906. The consequence is that a design that did not fall within the Designs Act definition could not be a 'corresponding design' for the purposes of the Copyright Act. As a result, these designs fell outside the reach of sections 75 and 77 of the Copyright Act and received full copyright protection. Thus drawings of utilitarian three-dimensional articles such as pump parts that are not registrable as designs (because they constitute a method or principle of construction) are entitled to copyright protection because the drawings are not 'corresponding designs'. This is an anomalous result contrary to the intention of the legislation to limit copyright

protection for utilitarian three-dimensional products. The amended definition clarifies existing policy by focussing on the three-dimensional aspects of a design.

However, s 77(2) does not apply if the design in question is excluded by regulation under s 43 of the Designs Act 2003.

Exceptions: buildings and works of artistic craftsmanship

6.24 The general rule introduced by s 77 of the Copyright Act is displaced in cases where the product embodies a building or a model of a building or a work of artistic craftsmanship: see s 77(1)(a). Note that by virtue of s 77(5) '*building or model of a building* does not include a portable building such as a shed, a pre-constructed swimming pool, a demountable building or similar portable building'. This provision was inserted into the Act to overcome the difficulties occasioned by the decision in *Darwin Fibreglass*, where a fibreglass pool transported whole on to a site where it was to be incorporated was held to be a building. Now, generally speaking, copyright will be retained only where fixed buildings are concerned; that is, for standard architectural copyright. If the building is portable, then industrial application (see above) will result in the defence to copyright infringement being available. Note that if a design is registered for a product embodying a portable building or, for that matter, for a work of artistic craftsmanship embodied in a product, the defence to copyright remains available (no exception is prescribed for such articles under s 75). In other words, for such items, alternative reliance on copyright protection is an option and is forfeited only upon registration of a corresponding design.

'Works of artistic craftsmanship' are also exempt from partial loss of copyright protection in the case of industrial application, but not exempt from the overlap provisions when a design is registered: s 75. More onerous conditions apply to categorisation as a work of artistic craftsmanship than to other artistic works. The work must combine elements of both craft skill and artistic merit. Note the significance in this context of *Coogi Australia Pty Ltd v Hysport International Pty Ltd* (1998) 86 FCR 154; 41 IPR 593, which arguably expanded the meaning of the term 'artistic craftsmanship' beyond what had been hitherto included. Since most works of artistic craftsmanship are also artistic works under the definition of 'artistic work' (s 10(1)(a) or (b) of the Copyright Act), there may appear to be little point in arguing that a certain work is a work of artistic craftsmanship. However, s 77 renders such categorisation advantageous, since the overlap provisions will not apply if a work of artistic craftsmanship is industrially applied. As to the policy behind this exclusion, ALRC 74 points out in [17.20] that 'there is a view that craft is not properly part of the concept of design'. Because classification as a work of artistic craftsmanship will allow a copyright owner to escape the effect of s 77, there have been a number of cases in which the boundaries of this category of work have been carefully scrutinised: see, for instance, *Sheldon v Metrokane* (2004) 135 FCR 34; 61 IPR 1, which concerned a new corkscrew in the shape of a rabbit. The High Court has resolved some of the uncertainty that persisted previously in *Burge v Swarbrick* (2007) 232 CLR 336; 72 IPR 235. The question was whether the plug for a fibreglass yacht, to be used in the prototyping/manufacturing process, was a work of artistic craftsmanship. The court held that this depended on the degree of artistic quality of the work; in the case before it, there was not sufficient quality. This approach causes some difficulty, since where on a scale of artistic quality a given work falls becomes a matter of fine and maybe personal judgment. On the other hand, the court's approach ignores the real difficulties that may result from extending works of artistic craftsmanship potentially to include prototypes or works produced as an integral part of a manufacturing process. Arguably, these are not inherently works of artistic craftsmanship, since they themselves are not crafted to appeal to the eye of a consumer. They are also often not made as part of a process of design in the making, arguably a critical characteristic of works of artistic craftsmanship; rather, they are made on the basis of pre-existing sketches and drawings in two-dimensional format.

On a final note, the defence obviously does not apply where the copyright material being copied onto an article is a literary work: see *Lumen Australia Pty Ltd v Frontline Australasia Pty Ltd* [2018] FCA 1807 at [225] where the 'Circuit Markings' constituted both literary and artistic works; whereas the overlap provisions operated in relation to the latter, they were of no relevance to the former.

Bibliography

A Bates, 'Artistic Works Industrially Applied: Comparison of Copyright/Designs Law in Australia and New Zealand' (1993) 17(2) *UQLJ* 247.

A Little and E Talbot, 'Sequined, Stitched, Painted, Embossed or Bedazzled: Fashion, the Designs Act and the Copyright Act' (2008) 20(9) *IPLB* 134.

Advisory Council on Intellectual Property (ACIP), *Review of the Designs System: Final Report*, March 2015 (ACIP Report).

Australian Law Reform Commission, *Designs*, Report No 74, 1996 (ALRC 74).

C Elliott, 'Form over Function — A Review of Recent Developments in Designs Law' (2005) 62 *IP Forum* 10.

C Gleghorn, 'Judging the Distinctiveness of Designs: Who is the "Informed User"?' (2008) 21(3) *IPLB* 47.

C Golvan, 'The Copyright/Design Overlap: An Appropriate Balance under the New Designs Legislation?' (2004) 59 *IP Forum* 36.

C Oberin, B Arnall, and C MacCallum, 'Protecting a Product's Shape and Appearance' (2004) 17(7) *IPLB* 109.

D Browne, 'The Shape of Things to Come: Australia's New Designs Law' (2004) 9(1) *MALR* 63.

D Watson, 'Registered Designs — Copy at Your Peril' (2006) 66 *IP Forum* 45.

J Cooke and K O'Connell, 'Rags to Riches? Changes in Australian and European Designs Laws' (2003) 14(2) *AIPJ* 65.

J Fairbairn and T Webb, 'Your Monopoly Safe? Designs and International Exhibitions' (2008) 21(1) *IPLB* 11.

L Ritson and N Hazel, 'Reform of Australian Designs Law — Designs Act 2003' (2004) 7(5) *IHC* 49.

N Cox, 'Intellectual Property Laws and the Protection of Armorial Bearings' (2001) 12(3) *AIPJ* 143.

P Baron, 'Visual Test in Registration and Infringement of Industrial Designs' (2000) 29(1) *UWALR* 39.

R Donaldson, 'Hague on the Horizon? Review of Australian Designs Law' (2006) 18(8) *IPLB* 128.

R McCormack, 'Reverse Engineering and the Overlap of Copyright and Designs — The Swarbrick Case' (2007) 71 *IP Forum* 89.

S Moore, 'Review of the Spare Parts Provision in the Designs Act' (2007) 19(8) *IPLB* 123.

W Condon and R Hoad, 'New Design Laws' (2004) 42(6) *LSJ* 42.

W Rothnie, 'The Vexed Problem of Copyright/Design Overlap' (2005) 60 *IP Forum* 33.

Chapter 7

Patents: Subject Matter

Policy Goals of the Patent System

Patents as an incentive for innovation

7.1 The Patents Act 1990 (Cth) is the contemporary source of statutory grants of temporary monopolies in the exploitation of inventions. Common usage suggests that an invention is an ingenious new practical product or process, but the concept of patentable subject matter has a long history and has become highly developed over time. Furthermore, the statutory threshold tests of novelty and inventiveness are also highly refined and, at times, complex in their application. This makes for an arcane and specialised area of the law, where, in many cases, an understanding of science and technology is a further requirement. Nonetheless, patents law covers all inventions, irrespective of the nature of the technology involved, from revolutionary breakthroughs at the scientific boundaries of modern research and development (R&D) to relatively simple mechanical inventions or small improvements to known devices. This point is further reinforced by the introduction in 2000 of a new system of protection for small or lesser inventions, the 'innovation patent', which now exists side by side with the standard patent. However, as further discussed below, the Productivity Commission inquiry report into intellectual property (PC Report)[1] recommended the abolition of the innovation patent, a recommendation the government has accepted but not acted upon.

As Lockhart J succinctly put it in *Anaesthetic Supplies Pty Ltd v Rescare Ltd* (1994) 28 IPR 383 at 397, 'The award of limited monopolies is a standard way of helping to compensate for the expense of research.' In other words, patents are a limited safeguard against free-riding. A patent reduces the risks inherent in engaging in the development of new products and processes. However, two points are worth noting here: first, a patent is available for a statutory invention whether it results from a sudden insight or from an arduous and expensive program of R&D; and, second, to what extent patents actually induce additional private investment in R&D is a fairly open question. Unambiguous empirical evidence remains hard to come by. However, there is little doubt that patents

1. Productivity Commission, *Intellectual Property Arrangements*, Inquiry Report No 78, Canberra, September 2016.

are of great importance to some high-technology industries such as pharmaceuticals, and provide an effective shield against competitors for the term of the patent (20 years). In other areas, they are seen as ineffective or unnecessary. There is considerable controversy over their utility in software development, for instance. Furthermore, since the patent monopoly is narrowly circumscribed, competitors can often invent around a patent or develop substitute products with alternative technological platforms.

In many industries, patent ownership has a relatively limited impact in isolation. Regardless of, or in association with, patenting strategies, inventive firms can stay ahead of imitators by other means; for example, because of their position as market leaders or because of imitation lag (the time it takes for imitators to catch up): see Chapter 1 Themes and Concepts in Intellectual Property Law. But whatever the true advantages of the system may be in terms of inducing invention, the granting of patents is a keystone of the intellectual property system as a whole. A further reason for this is the other main policy basis for the granting of patents; that is, that patents serve as an incentive to publish information about products and processes that may otherwise remain secret. The alternative strategy to prevent imitation of an invention is to keep it secret; however, this is costly, often impractical or impossible, and against the public interest, as valuable knowledge is withheld from society at large, thus harming the advancement of science and technology. The granting of a patent is conditional upon complete disclosure of all the details of the invention and how to put it into operation. A complete specification must '(a) disclose the invention in a manner which is clear enough and complete enough for the invention to be performed by a person skilled in the relevant art; and (aa) disclose the best method known to the applicant of performing the invention': Patents Act 1990 (Cth), s 40(2)(a)–(aa). In *Patent Gesellschaft AG v Saudi Livestock Transport & Trading Co* (1997) 37 IPR 523 at 530–1, Carr J stated the law succinctly while referring to relevant authority:

> The specification contains a full description if it makes the nature of the invention plain to persons having reasonably competent knowledge of the subject and also makes it plain, to persons having reasonable skill, how to perform the invention: *Edison & Swan Electric Light Co v Holland* (1889) 6 RPC 243 at 279; *Samuel Taylor Pty Ltd v SA Brush Co Ltd* (1950) 83 CLR 617 at 624–5. See also *AMP Inc v Utilux Pty Ltd* [1971] 45 ALJR 123 at 128 and *Valensi v British Radio Corp Ltd* [1973] RPC 337 at 377.

The law thus reflects a simple *quid pro quo*, sometimes referred to as a 'social contract': the patentee makes the invention public and in return is granted the exclusive rights to turn it to their own account for a limited term, now 20 years.

A further advantage of a patent system is that it saves transaction costs and encourages more efficient market organisation. A more or less stable market in knowledge-based goods can be structured around the relative certainty of property rights in carefully parcelled information and registered ownership. A firm can ascertain who 'owns' an invention and obtain a licence; through licensing, a patentee can organise downstream development and the application of a patented invention. A patent is personal property and can be bought and sold as clearly identified and circumscribed in the letters patent. Registration also has the advantage of providing some indication of whether an invention has some value in terms of novelty and inventiveness, even though the granting of a patent entails no guarantee of validity: see s 20 of the Patents Act 1990 (Cth) ('Validity of patent not guaranteed'). A neutral authority (the Commissioner of Patents) makes an objective assessment without reference to commercial profit potential, at the very least confirming the invention to be something that is probably not yet in the public domain. In an innovation- and knowledge-based information economy, this is highly relevant. However, from the consumer perspective, a patentee obtains a monopoly over the use of an invention, and can therefore set the terms for the supply of the invention while shielded from direct competition. This may affect the price and availability of inventions, an acute issue in relation, for instance, to some pharmaceutical drugs. The PC Report recommended that an 'objects clause' be introduced into the Patents Act that identifies the need to balance competing interests, expressed in the following terms: '... enhancing the wellbeing of Australians by promoting technological innovation and the transfer and dissemination of technology. In so doing, the patent system should balance over time the interests of producers, owners and users of technology': PC Report, Recommendation 7.1, p 33. The government decided to undertake further consultation on the matter: see IP Australia, 'Public Consultation: Introducing an objects clause into the *Patents Act 1990*', August 2017.

History of the patent system in Australia

7.2 Although advanced theoretical and economic analysis informs the evolution of patents law today, the first statutory granting of monopolies in new inventions came into existence a long time ago on the basis of rather more simple policy goals. The Statute of Monopolies of 1623, an English statute, is the organic precursor of Australian patents statutes, including the current Patents Act 1990 (Cth). Its aim was to abolish monopolies granted by the Crown in sundry trades and industries, but s 6 of the Statute made an exception for new inventions because of the perceived technological backwardness of England at that time. Similar legislation had already existed on the continent of Europe, most notably in Venice, Italy.

Section 6 of the Statute of Monopolies granted a term of exclusive exploitation rights to anyone who introduced 'any manner of new manufacture' (an invention) into the realm, either by importing it or by inventing it. From the time of the Statute, patents law in the UK grew in volume of applications and complexity, at first slowly and in a very cumbersome form, with more radical reforms following under the impetus of the Industrial Revolution. It was only in the 19th century that patents legislation, administration and implementation took on their modern forms. More recently, the rules concerning patentability, novelty and inventiveness have become more systematised. The patents law of the UK was adopted in the Australian colonies and is thus the precursor of our local law. The Paris Convention for the Protection of Industrial Property (1883) was the first international instrument dealing with some aspects of patents law, inter alia with priority dates. Today, the treaty is administered by the World Intellectual Property Organization (WIPO). Australia acceded to the treaty, as revised at Stockholm on 14 July 1967, in 1972. The treaty's most important principles relate to priority dates (the ability to file an application in another convention country within 6 months and retain the priority date of the initial domestic filing) and non-discrimination (citizens of all member countries to be in the same legal position as citizens of the country of filing).

The most significant treaty development in recent times occurred under the auspices of the World Trade Organization. The Trade-Related Aspects of Intellectual Property Rights (TRIPS) treaty contains some significantly higher mandatory standards; for instance, in relation to the patent term (20 years) and patentability of pharmaceuticals. Because the granting of patents is domestic, a person wishing to obtain a patent in a different jurisdiction must apply, pass examination and obtain a grant there. If patents are pursued in multiple jurisdictions, as is often a commercial necessity, cost and complexity will grow exponentially. The Patent Cooperation Treaty (PCT), also administered by the WIPO, allows some simplification of the patent application process in multiple jurisdictions. An applicant may file a single PCT application in Australia nominating other jurisdictions. The priority date (filing date) of the original application will apply in all nominated jurisdictions, and, through the offices of the WIPO, the application will be filed in the nominated jurisdictions after an initial WIPO examination. However, the applicant will have to pursue the domestic examination phase directly with the patent office of every nominated country, and the application must conform to the legal standards of each country where protection is sought. There is no universal patent, although the TRIPS provisions have resulted in a considerable degree of harmonisation between national systems. Nonetheless, important differences remain. The Substantive Patent Law Treaty, negotiations for which stalled in 2006, would increase harmonisation of substantive requirements to an even greater extent. However, certain controversial issues have prevented general agreement on treaty terms relating to mandatory reporting standards concerning the origin of genetic materials, the treatment of traditional knowledge and the like. The Substantive Patent Law Treaty is not to be confused with the Patent Law Treaty, signed in 2000, which concerns procedural matters.

The Australian Patent System

Filing, examination and grant

7.3 Patents law in Australia is exclusively governed by the Patents Act 1990 (Cth), which, like its predecessors, establishes an administrative system of filing, examination and granting for patents in inventions. In other words, a patent will be granted only on the basis of an application establishing compliance with objective statutory criteria. Compliance is assessed by patent examiners in the Patent Office (IP Australia), and the patent is sealed by the Commissioner of Patents. Patent Office decisions can be the subject of an internal hearing, either between the applicant and the office or involving third-party opponents. In relation to certain decisions, an application for review can be made to the Administrative Appeals Tribunal (see s 224), and, more generally, appeals lie to the Federal Court. Often, initial deficiencies in an application are dealt with by amendments suggested by an examiner at the provisional application stage. However, examination and granting do not guarantee validity, so at any time during the term of validity, a patent may still be revoked on the basis of a counterclaim for invalidity in infringement proceedings (see s 121) or on an application to a prescribed court: see s 138. A patent or specific claims may also be surrendered (see s 137) or cease before term because of the patentee's failure to pay annual renewal fees: see s 143 and also s 20. In fact, a large percentage of granted patents are not renewed for the full term. A substantial number of patented inventions are also never 'worked'; that is, made or applied in Australia. In cases of insufficient working and refusal to license on reasonable terms, however, an applicant can seek a compulsory licence from the Federal Court: see Pt 2 and Pt 3 of Ch 12 of the Patents Act 1990 (Cth).

A two-tier system: standard and innovation patents

7.4 At present, two alternatives are open to an applicant: to apply for a standard patent or an innovation patent. The PC Report recommended the abolition of the innovation patent system, and the government accepted that recommendation. However, although initially included in the Intellectual Property Laws Amendment (Productivity Commission Response Part 1 and Other Measures) Bill 2018, the measure was removed so that the government could undertake further consultations to address the needs of innovative small to medium enterprises (SMEs) before the phase-out. The measure is set to be reintroduced in 2019.

The standard patent has higher threshold requirements and a longer term (20 years) than the innovation patent, but the scope of exclusive rights is identical for both. The standard patent is by far the most common. The Patents Amendment (Innovation Patents) Act 2000 (Cth) introduced the innovation patent to replace the old 'petty patent'. The innovation patent was intended to meet the requirements of SMEs for cheap, quick and short-term protection for relatively minor advances. The maximum term of an innovation patent is 8 years: see Patents Act 1990, s 68. Although available for the same inventions as a standard patent, except for plants and animals and the biological processes for their generation (see s 18(3)), the number of claims in an innovation patent application is limited to a maximum of five. Speedy granting results from the fact that an innovation patent is granted on the basis of a formalities check only: see s 52(1). However, it can be enforced only if 'certified'; that is, examined in substance: see s 120(1A). Thus, the cost of substantive examination can be delayed or avoided altogether. In this approach, the application model is similar to the system introduced for designs applications in the Designs Act 2003 (Cth) (see Chapter 6 Registered Designs). The previous petty patent system was little used and had mainly strategic utility: see, for example, *Tidy Tea Ltd and Lyons Tetley Ltd v Unilever Australia Ltd* (1995) 32 IPR 405. One reason for preferring standard over petty patents was that virtually the same standards of novelty and inventiveness applied. However, now the government has accepted most SMEs do not obtain value from the innovation patent system, and that it imposes significant costs on third parties and the broader Australian community: *Australian Government Response to the Productivity Commission Inquiry into Intellectual Property Arrangements*, August 2017, Recommendation 8.1 (Government Response).

The innovative step

7.5 All patents must meet the core standards of novelty and some level of inventiveness. Two crucial issues determine how difficult it is to satisfy the latter: first, just how different the invention or innovation must be compared with the 'prior art' (inventions made public before the priority date: see 7.7); and, second, what exactly is the prior art the invention should be compared with: what public information must be taken into account and what can be ignored as prior art specifically for the purpose of determining inventiveness or innovativeness. As to the first aspect, the innovation patent requires only an 'innovative step' rather than an 'inventive step'. An invention does not involve an innovative step if it varies from the prior art only 'in ways that make no substantial contribution to the working of the invention': see s 7(4). Part 2.31.4.5.4 'Innovative step' of the Australian Patent Office's *Manual of Practice and Procedure* interprets this as requiring that the variation be of practical significance and not trivial, superficial or peripheral. The test focuses on a substantial improvement to the working of an invention rather than on the inventive level of the step that has brought it about, and thus differs markedly from the inventiveness requirement for standard patents. The prior art information that can be taken into account for the purpose of the innovative step requirement differs from that for inventiveness: see s 7(5). In *Delnorth Pty Ltd v Dura-Post (Aust) Pty Ltd* [2008] FCA 1225, the 'innovative step' test was judicially considered for the first time. The invention was a flexible steel roadside post that could bend and recover its previous position. The case confirms that the test for innovative step is quite different from the inventiveness test. It does not focus on whether the modification would occur to the average person in the field but on whether it has had a material, functional effect on the working of the invention. The assessment is to be made through the eyes of the 'person skilled in the art' armed with the 'common general knowledge' as it existed at the priority date, but the intellectual quality of the modification made is not relevant.[2] The test for innovative step is thus more akin to the test of novelty, in particular the gloss placed on it in *Griffin v Isaacs* (1938) 1B IPR 619: see Recommendation 2, *Review of the Petty Patent System*, Advisory Council on Intellectual Property (ACIP), October 1995. *Delnorth* contains a considered analysis of the complex method of determining the prior art for the purpose of the innovative step test: there are relevant differences with the prior art to be taken into account in the assessment of inventive step for standard patents (see s 7(5) and Chapter 8 Patents: Novelty and Inventiveness). The Full Court of the Federal Court in *Dura-Post (Aust) Pty Ltd v Delnorth Pty Ltd* (2009) 177 FCR 239; 81 IPR 480; [2009] FCAFC 81 found no error in the trial judge's approach. For an interesting comment concerning the innovative step, see J Blows and D Clark in 'Is an innovative step so easy that "any fool could do it"?' (2006) *Australian Intellectual Property Law Bulletin* 18, 8, 129ff; see also IP Australia, *Review of the Innovation Patent*, Final Report, July 2006. Cases relating to innovation patents are relatively few: see, however, *Datadot Technology Ltd v Alpha Microtech Pty Ltd* (2003) 59 IPR 402, *Masport Ltd v Bartlem Pty Ltd* [2004] FCA 591,

---

2. The concepts of the 'person skilled in the art' and the 'common general knowledge' are considered further below in relation to the inventiveness requirement for standard patents; see [8.8] and [8.9].

Aus Fence Hire Pty Ltd v Thomas (2004) 61 IPR 28; *SNF (Australia) Pty Ltd v Ciba Specialty Chemicals Water Treatments Ltd* (2012) 204 FCR 325; [2012] FCAFC 95; *Product Management Group Pty Ltd v Blue Gentian LLC* [2015] FCAFC 179; and *Encompass Corporation Pty Ltd v InfoTrack Pty Ltd* [2018] FCA 421.[3] The innovation patent is not further considered here.

Standard patents: the Patents Act 1990 (Cth)

7.6 Patents law falls within the powers of the Commonwealth Parliament, and the Patents Act 1990 (Cth) covers the field. The current Act replaced the Patents Act 1952 (Cth) and represented a major change in form with only relatively minor changes in substance. A major goal of the 1990 Act was to rewrite the statute in plain English and to make it intelligible to the uninitiated user. This was optimistic. As McMullin J pointed out in *The Wellcome Foundation Ltd v Commissioner of Patents* [1983] NZLR 385 at 398; 2 IPR 156 at 172, 'Patent law is a rather artificial, highly complex and somewhat refined subject.' Most aspects of patent applications, and certainly the drafting of the all-important patent claims, are best left to a patent attorney.

Nonetheless, the goal of making the Act (as opposed to the system) more user-friendly has been achieved to some degree. All definitions of terms are to be found in the 'Dictionary' (Sch 1) to the Act, for instance. But various other factors militate against user-friendliness. First, the transfer of much of what used to be within the body of the Act to the regulations has, in fact, necessitated more frequent cross-referencing; and, second, and more importantly, since the Act did not set out to modify the existing rules concerning patentability in any major way, some archaic terms of art were retained; for example, the core concept of 'manner of manufacture', by reference to which decision-makers determine what is patentable subject matter: see 7.13ff. In other cases, finer statutory circumscriptions were attempted; for example, in relation to 'novelty' and 'inventiveness', which are highly complex, involving multiple steps and fine judgments: see Chapter 8 Patents: Novelty and Inventiveness. Since the introduction of the 1990 Act, there have been some significant amendments. The introduction of the innovation patent has been referred to above. More recent amending Acts have sought to elevate the level of inventiveness required to obtain a standard patent by changing what prior art can be taken into account and how it can be used. This process culminated in a recommendation in the PC Report to yet again rewrite the inventiveness provisions to bring them more in line with standards overseas, in particular in Europe. These amendments are further discussed in Chapter 8 Patents: Novelty and Inventiveness. In terms of infringement, a significant amendment has introduced the so-called 'experimental use' defence: Intellectual Property Laws Amendment (Raising the Bar) Act 2012 (Cth).

---

3. The latter case may also be relevant in relation to whether computer-implemented inventions are patentable subject matter: see 7.10.

Outline of the System of Application, Examination and Grant

The priority date

7.7 The Australian system is 'first to file' (as opposed to 'first to invent'). The person who is first to file an application for a particular invention will be granted the patent, to the exclusion of all others who may, in fact, have made the invention earlier and of all later applicants for a patent for the same invention. The patents system is, in other words, 'winner takes all', because not only will the first to file get the patent but all others will be excluded from using the invention, whenever they arrived at it and whether or not they did so independently (except for a limited prior user right: see s 119). Thus, as a rule, early filing of an application is important; nonetheless, premature filing can put an application at risk, certainly where the initial filing is of a provisional application (see 7.8). The filing date is generally the 'priority date' of the application, or more precisely of a claim or claims contained in the application: see s 43. The priority date is significant also because any public disclosure of the invention after the priority date will not affect the validity of the patent — it does not constitute 'anticipation': see Chapter 8 Patents: Novelty and Inventiveness. From the priority date onwards, the applicant is thus able to exploit the invention publicly without putting the patent at risk; for instance, by selling the patented product on the open market. It is important to know that within certain parameters, the priority date of an application filed in a foreign country can apply to a later application filed in Australia: see s 43(2)(b), Chapter 8 Patents: Novelty and Inventiveness, and Pts 1 and 2 of the Act.

Provisional and complete applications

7.8 The process of applying for the grant of a patent is initiated by the filing of a patent request, accompanied by either a provisional or complete specification: see see s 29(2) and (3). Given the competitive advantages of early filing, an applicant may initially wish to file only a provisional (ie, incomplete) application, which requires no more than a disclosure of the invention that is clear and complete enough for the invention to be performed by a person skilled in the relevant art: see s 40(1). Section 40 as a whole sets out critical formal requirements with which any application must comply. A provisional application does not contain any claims, which can therefore be drafted with the requisite care during the period between the filing of the provisional application and the filing of the complete application based on it. The filing date of the provisional application will serve as the priority date of the subsequent complete application as long as the latter relates to the same invention (sometimes referred to as 'internal fair basing'). The complete application must be filed within the prescribed term from the date of filing of the provisional application. Alternatively, a complete application may be filed from the outset. As well as a formal patent request, a complete application must contain the specification and claims. The specification consists mainly of a description of the invention and what it accomplishes, accompanied by graphic material if necessary. It also contains supporting material and may explain differences between the invention applied for and the prior art (ie, pre-existing technology in the same field) and the nature of the problem that the invention overcomes.

Claims and s 40 requirements

7.9 The claims, which state the exact boundaries of what is to be monopolised by the patentee, are the critical part of the application. A complete application must 'end with a claim or claims defining the invention': see s 40(2)(b). The claims must be clear and succinct and supported by matter disclosed in the specification (see s 40(3)) — traditionally known as the 'fair basing' requirement. The claims draw a line between what is within the monopoly and what is left without. In *Populin v H B Nominees Pty Ltd* (1982) 41 ALR 471 at 475, Bowen CJ and Dean and Ellicott JJ put it as follows, with particular reference to inventions that consist of new and inventive combinations of existing elements (so-called combination patents): 'It has often been said that the claims operate as a disclaimer of what is not specifically claimed (eg, *Walker v Alemite Corp* (1933) 49 CLR 643 per Dixon J at 656).' Careful drafting of the claims is essential. As Gummow J pointed out in *Sartas No 1 Pty Ltd v Koukourou & Partners Pty Ltd* (1994) 30 IPR 479 at 497:

> A claim may be narrow in the sense that by reason of its inclusion of a large number of integers, a potential infringer may escape; but it may be a strong claim in the sense that there is a lesser likelihood of anticipation. If the patentee draws a claim which has less integers, the patentee may be in a stronger position as against an infringer, but in a weaker position to withstand an attack on novelty. That in a sense is a classical dilemma for the person drafting a patent claim.

There are commonly multiple claims relating to a single invention, going from the more general to the more specific; for standard patents, there is no limit on the number of claims allowed. As is pointed out in *ICI Chemicals & Polymers Ltd v Lubrizol Corporation Inc* (2000) 106 FCR 214; 49 IPR 513 at 543:

> ... there is nothing unusual or improper about a series of claims the first of which may be a broad claim, claiming substantially the entirety of the invention described in the body of the specification (indeed often simply repeating the terms of a consistory clause), the subsequent claims being within the territory marked out by the first (and described in the specification) but claiming smaller portions of it.

Although one often refers to the validity of a patent, in fact it is an individual claim that is valid or invalid. It may be that some of the claims of a patent are valid but others are held to be invalid. That some of the claims are invalid is not fatal to the patent as a whole. An essential statutory requirement is that the claims be 'supported by' matter described in the specification (see s 40(3)) (which may be either the provisional or the complete specification). There must, in other words, be the requisite congruence between the supporting documentation and description of the invention (possibly including a 'consistory clause' which is an opening statement of the description of an invention) and the claims based on them. The description cannot disclose one thing while the claims attempt to monopolise something else or something more. In *Grove Hill Pty Ltd v Great Western Corporation Pty Ltd* (2002) 55 IPR 257; [2002] FCAFC 183 at [170], the court pointed out that the public interest is served by not allowing the patent to claim any more than what is 'the true subject matter of the invention'. There is a further aspect to the requirement traditionally referred to as 'fair basing': the claims in a complete application must also be disclosed in the provisional application: see s 40(3). If the invention in the complete application is not supported by what was described in the provisional application, it should not benefit from the latter's earlier priority date. Sometimes, an applicant finds that the essence of the invention, when further developed after filing, reveals itself to be something different from what was disclosed in the provisional application. According to Lee, Heerey and Lehane JJ in *ICI Chemicals & Polymers* at IPR 544, 'The leading discussion of fair basing in this Court is to be found in the decision of the Full Federal Court in *CCOM Pty Ltd v Jiejing Pty Ltd* (1994) 51 FCR 260; 28 IPR 481.' See also *Coopers Animal Health Australia Ltd v Western Stock Distributors Pty Ltd* (1987) 15 FCR 382; (1987) 11 IPR 20, *Leonardis v Sartas (No 1) Pty Ltd* (1996) 35 IPR 23, *Patent Gesellschaft AG v Saudi Livestock Transport and Trading Co* (1997) 37 IPR 523 and *Abbott Laboratories v Corbridge Group Pty Ltd* (2002) 57 IPR 432. An example of fair basing issues in operation is presented by *Sartas (No 1) Pty Ltd v Koukourou & Partners Pty Ltd* (1994) 30 IPR 479 where Gummow J spelled out the basis for the fair basing requirement as between the claims and the specification (at 496):

> The questions of fair basing thus arise both in the consideration of the interrelation between the claims and the body of the specification, that is to say, from a comparison between different parts of the one document, and of the interrelation between the provisional and complete specifications. This case concerns those two aspects of the doctrine of fair basing which stem from the introduction both of provisional specifications and of claims in their modern form; see *CCOM Pty Ltd v Jiejing Pty Ltd* (1994) 122 ALR 417 at 435; 28 IPR 481. The first is that the claimed monopoly should not be wider than warranted by the disclosure to the public made in the body of the complete specification. The second is that the novelty of a claim should not be protected by a priority date given by the provisional specification if the claim is not fairly based on the disclosure in the provisional specification.

More recently, the High Court turned its mind to the question of fair basing in *Lockwood Security Products Pty Ltd v Doric Products Pty Ltd* (2004) 217 CLR 274; 62 IPR 461. The case illustrates the need to police the relationship between the claims and the specification, so that the patentee gets only what it is entitled to. If a broad new principle is disclosed in the specification, then the claims can relate to any particular embodiment or manifestation of it. But if a particular embodiment is revealed in the specification — for instance, a new combination of existing elements or 'integers' — the claims cannot extend to some broad principle. The court also reiterated the warning expressed in *CCOM Pty Ltd v Jiejing Pty Ltd* (1994) 122 ALR 417 at 4335; (1994) 28 IPR 481 (above) that no 'over meticulous verbal analysis should be undertaken' when assessing the relevant relationships. It is concerns about the complex, arcane and sometimes unexpected application of the requirement of 'fair basing' that resulted in the replacement of that terminology by the simpler requirement that claims must be 'supported by' matter disclosed in the specification by virtue of the Intellectual Property Laws Amendment (Raising the Bar) Act 2012 (Cth). The intention of the legislative change was also to require fuller disclosure in the specification, to the extent that it enables the skilled addressee to perform anything that falls within the (sometimes broader and more abstract) claims; as the Explanatory Memorandum puts it: 'The amendments address circumstances where the information disclosed in a patent specification, although sufficient to make one thing within the scope of each claim, is not sufficient to make the invention across the full scope of each claim. The changes ensure that granted patents are no broader than the invention which has been disclosed.': Intellectual Property Laws Amendment (Raising the Bar) Bill 2011, Explanatory Memorandum, Senate, 2010–2011, Outline, Schedule 1, Raising the Quality of Patents. More generally, in *Konami Australia Pty Ltd v Aristocrat Technologies Australia Pty Ltd* [2016] FCAFC 735 at [77] the terms were held to require 'a real and reasonably clear disclosure of what is claimed', citing *Lockwood Security Products* at [69].

Claims are drafted using technical terms of art and very precise language. The patent attorneys responsible for claim drafting are usually trained in the particular area of technology or science the invention relates to, and the specification and claims are generally directed at persons skilled in the particular 'art'. An example of a typical claim is provided by *Speedy Gantry Hire Pty Ltd v Preston Erection Pty Ltd* (1998) 40 IPR 543 at 546. The invention 'Improvements to Scaffolding' had 16 claims, the first of which was:

> A gantry assembly for use as a temporary pedestrian thoroughfare adjacent a site such as a construction site, demolition site or the like, said gantry assembly comprising a plurality of independently movable gantry modules, each said gantry module comprising a plurality of spaced legs, a roof assembly supported by the legs, said roof assembly having a roof panel extending between the upper ends of the legs, a side wall between adjacent legs and extending from an edge of the roof assembly to adjacent the lower ends of said adjacent legs, a pedestrian passageway extending through each said module adjacent said side wall and beneath said roof panel so that the wall and roof panel provide a protective barrier between the pedestrian passageway and the site, said roof assembly and said side wall being aligned with a roof assembly and side wall of an adjacent module to form a continuous roof assembly and side wall for said gantry.

Claims can make difficult reading, partly because they relate to technical or scientific subject matter unfamiliar to the lay reader or lawyer; see for instance, *Idenix Pharmaceuticals LLC v Gilead Sciences Pty Ltd* [2017] FCAFC 196. Nonetheless, however difficult the subject matter may be, the claims must be 'clear and succinct' by virtue of s 40(3). Claims that are not clear and succinct are said to fail because of ambiguity: see, for example, *Décor Corp Pty Ltd v Dart Industries Inc* (1988) 13 IPR 385. The requirement of s 40(2) that 'a complete specification must: (a) describe the invention in a manner which is clear and complete enough for the invention to be performed by a person skilled in the relevant art; and (aa) disclose the best method known to the applicant of performing the invention' is further considered below: see [8.13]. Generally speaking, however, patents claims and specifications are directed to 'persons skilled in the art' and not lay persons or those entirely ignorant of the knowledge and science concerned, and the requirements of s 40 must be read in that context.

Examination of the application

7.10 Upon the request of the applicant and after publication of the application in the official journal, the complete application for a patent is examined by a patent examiner, both for formal legality and for conformity with the substantive requirements of patentability. Patent examiners refer to the Australian Patent Office's *Manual of Practice and Procedure* in making a report concerning compliance with the Act. Although published (inter alia on the internet, see www.ipaustralia.gov.au), the manual is nothing but an internal administrative document for the guidance of the examiners. The Act, the Patent Regulations 1991 (Cth) and the relevant case law ultimately determine procedural and substantive rules concerning patenting. The case law is to be found in decisions on appeal from determinations by the Commissioner relating to an application, concerning revocation proceedings and concerning counterclaims for invalidity in infringement proceedings. The manual reflects the Commissioner's interpretation of the law. Unquestioned, it may be implemented over time, only to be found to have been in error once challenged in court. For instance, for many years the manual contained guidance, drawing largely on US cases, calling on examiners to reject most applications for computer-implemented inventions. As a result of *International Business Machines Corporation v Smith, Commissioner of Patents* (1991) 33 FCR 218; 105 ALR 388; 22 IPR 417 (the *IBM* case), a successful appeal against the Commissioner's rejection of an application concerning a method for producing improved curves on a computer screen, the Commissioner's approach became much less restrictive: see the current *Manual of Practice and Procedure* at 2.9.2.7. The key question now is whether the claimed invention produces a commercially useful effect; in the context of computers, this requires an algorithm to be implemented in some particular manner to produce a practical result or a useful effect; see for instance, *Encompass Corporation Pty Ltd v InfoTrack Pty Ltd* [2018] FCA 421; and further below, patentable subject matter at 7.19.

The application must be accepted if, on the balance of probabilities, the Commissioner is satisfied that the statutory criteria are complied with: see s 49(1). If not so satisfied, the Commissioner *may* refuse to accept it: see s 49(2) Under the 1990 Act, before the amendment introduced by virtue of the Patents Amendment Act 2001, the benefit of the doubt approach applied to all matters required to be examined. The Commissioner had to accept the patent request 'if the Commissioner considers that there is no lawful ground of objection [...]': s 49(1). In other words, the onus was on the Commissioner to prove the existence of any ground for rejection, rather than the applicant having to prove no such grounds existed. Franki J in *Denison Manufacturing Co v Monarch Marking Systems Inc* (1983) 1 IPR 431; 76 FLR 200 at 215 stated it as follows (under the previous Act):

> It was common ground before us that a grant should not be refused in respect of any claim upon the grounds of want of novelty or obviousness unless it appeared to the court clear that the ground had been made out. (*Montecatini Edison SpA v Eastman Kodak Co* (1971) 45 ALJR 593 at 595–6).

Or, as it was put in *Commissioner of Patents v Microcell Ltd* (1959) 102 CLR 232 at 244–5:

> [It] is well settled that the Commissioner ought not to refuse acceptance of an application and specification unless it appears practically certain that letters patent granted on the specification would be held invalid.

However, by virtue of the 2001 amendments, the benefit of the doubt test is removed in relation to questions of novelty and inventiveness. In that regard, the Commissioner must be satisfied, on the balance of probabilities, that the statutory tests have been satisfied. The 2001 amendment is aimed at increasing the standards of novelty and inventiveness and bringing them more into line with international standards. Hence, the 2001 amendment has a more stringent requirement similar to the 'balance of probabilities' requirement used in civil law matters: see ss 7 and 18.

Acceptance, opposition and rejection

7.11 The examiner reports on compliance with the provisions of the Act (see s 45); by virtue of s 49, the Commissioner then accepts or rejects the application. An appeal against the decision of the Commissioner lies to the Federal Court: see s 51. Australian patents law allows for 'pre-grant opposition'; in other words, if any party opposes the granting of a standard patent, the matter goes to an opposition hearing where the opposing party can present evidence substantiating its case that the application should be rejected. The decision of the Commissioner resulting from the hearing is open to an appeal to the Federal Court: see ss 59 (permissible grounds for opposition) and 60. An opposition may prolong the application process considerably. Note that as well as opposing the granting of a patent, any person can apply to a court to have a patent revoked after granting. In some other jurisdictions, no pre-grant opposition is possible. Opposition may be an efficient way to cull unmeritorious applications, because it allows other parties to bring certain anticipations to light. However, there is concern that the opposition procedure can be used strategically by commercial rivals to cause delay and drive up the cost of obtaining a patent: see K Weatherall, F Rotstein, C Dent and A Christie, 'Patent Oppositions in Australia: The Facts' (2011) *UNSW Law Journal* Vol 34(1) at 93. Most countries have a post-grant rather than a pre-grant opposition (or 'review') model.

Term of a patent

7.12 The application and examination process successfully completed, the patent is granted and sealed in the name of the applicant. After it is granted, the patent may lapse if the regular maintenance fees are not paid, although within certain limits a patent may be restored after lapsing. The maximum term of a patent is 20 years from the date of the patent, which, by virtue of s 65, is generally the date of filing of the complete specification. The term of a patent for a pharmaceutical substance may be extended upon application for a maximum of 5 years: see s 70, as considered in *Boehringer Ingelheim International GmbH v Commissioner of Patents* (2001) 112 FCR 595; 52 IPR 529 and *Prejay Holdings Ltd v Commissioner of Patents* (2003) 57 IPR 424; [2003] FCAFC 77; see also *Spirit Pharmaceuticals Pty Ltd v Mundipharma Pty Ltd* (2013) 216 FCR 344. The extension compensates a pharmaceutical patentee for the loss of effective monopoly term caused by the delays encountered in obtaining marketing approval for a new drug. The PC Report recommended a narrowing of the categories of pharma patents eligible for extension, but this was rejected in the Government Response to the PC Report. In a recent decision, however, the Full Court of the Federal Court has held that term extensions are not available for so-called Swiss-type claims: see *Commissioner of Patents v AbbVie Biotechnology Ltd* [2017] FCAFC 129. These claims, drafted as process steps, concern the use of a known substance in the manufacture of medication that serves a new therapeutic purpose.

Patentable Subject Matter

Manner of manufacture: proper subject matter of letters patent

7.13 The substantive requirements of patentability are found in s 18, which lies at the heart of the patent regime. The first question to be addressed is whether the subject matter described and claimed in an application is suitable for patenting or falls outside the statutory realm of invention. With the introduction of the 1990 Act, the legislator did not intend to fundamentally alter the substantive law in this regard, instead importing most existing learning concerning patentable subject matter into the new Act. It achieved this by retaining the ancient statutory terms ('manner of manufacture') and consequently also the accumulated associated case law. By virtue of s 18(1), 'a patentable invention is an invention that, so far as claimed in any claim: (a) is a manner of manufacture within the meaning of s 6 of the Statute of Monopolies'. Over centuries of judicial interpretation, both in the UK and in Australia, these terms became 'encrusted with meaning' as they were adapted to changing economic and technological conditions. In retaining this language, the legislator rejected the opportunity to modernise statutory terminology and circumscribe in more detail what is and what is not patentable. By contrast, in the UK, the term 'manner of manufacture' was replaced with the requirement that the invention be 'industrially applicable' by the 1977 UK Patents Act; in many jurisdictions, those or similar terms are commonly combined with a list of exclusions from patentability (as to the exclusions in the UK Act, see 7.14).

However, even though the archaic language was maintained, the literal meaning of the expression 'manner of manufacture' is of limited significance, as those terms have been judicially interpreted to signify a broader concept that goes far beyond the apparent strictures inherent in those terms themselves. Thus, in perhaps the most significant patent decision in the 20th century, *National Research Development Corporation v Commissioner of Patents* (1959) 102 CLR 252 (*NRDC*), the court said that the relevant inquiry is 'an inquiry not into the meaning of a word so much as into the breadth of the concept which the law has developed by its consideration of the text and purpose of the Statute of Monopolies'. The question is not whether some invention is a manner of manufacture but rather 'the right question is: "is this a proper subject matter of letters patent according to the principles which have been developed for the application of s 6 of the Statute of Monopolies?"': at CLR 269.

That approach is as applicable to the interpretation of the term 'manner of manufacture' in the 1990 Act as it was under the Patents Act 1952 (Cth), at issue in *NRDC*, or its predecessors. The Intellectual Property and Competition Review Committee, in its final report, *Review of Intellectual Property Legislation under the Competition Principles Agreement* (September 2000), noted that 'Australia has on the whole benefited from the adaptiveness and flexibility that has characterised the "manner of manufacture" test' and recommended that it be retained (at 16).

Manner of manufacture: a flexible concept

7.14 The remarkable continuity of language from 1623 to today belies the underlying elasticity of the concept of 'subject matter suitable for patenting' in light of uninterrupted technological progress. The court in *NRDC* was minded to preserve the judicial arm's flexibility in view of the scientific and technological changes it saw on the horizon. More precisely, as Dixon CJ pointed out as early as *Maeder v Busch* (1938) 59 CLR 684 at 706, 'a widening conception of a manner of new manufacture has been a characteristic of the growth of patent law'. Therefore the correct question to ask is whether the invention concerned is 'suitable for the grant of letters patent'.

With recent scientific revolutions finding their way into practical applications, that trend can only continue. The legislator chose not to interrupt the adaptive and continuous process of judicial decision-making concerning what is a patentable invention by introducing a list of exclusions as exists in other jurisdictions. For instance, in the UK, s 1 of the Patents Act 1977 (UK) provides as follows:

> (2) It is hereby declared that the following (among other things) are not inventions for the purposes of this Act, that is to say, anything which consists of (a) a discovery, scientific theory or mathematical method; (b) a literary, dramatic, musical or artistic work or any other aesthetic creation whatsoever; (c) a scheme, rule or method for performing a mental act, playing a game or doing business, or a program for a computer; (d) the presentation of information; but the foregoing provision shall prevent anything from being treated as an invention for the purposes of this Act only to the extent that a patent or application for a patent relates to that thing as such.
>
> (3) A patent shall not be granted (a) for an invention the publication or exploitation of which would be generally expected to encourage offensive, immoral or anti-social behaviour; (b) for any variety of animal or plant or any essentially biological process for the production of animals or plants, not being a micro-biological process or the product of such a process.
>
> (4) For the purposes of subsection (3) above behaviour shall not be regarded as offensive, immoral or anti-social only because it is prohibited by any law in force in the United Kingdom or any part of it.

By comparison, the only express exclusions in the Patents Act 1990 (Cth) are for human beings and biological processes for the generation of human beings: see s 18(2). The exclusion of human beings in s 18(2) was considered in *Re Whang* (2004) AIPC ¶92-031 and in *Fertilitetscentrum AB and Luminis Pty Ltd* [2004] APO 19. In that case, the deputy pointed to the limited preparatory materials available in relation to this exclusion, but nonetheless arrived at two significant conclusions: first, that human beings were in the process of generation from the moment of fertilisation to the moment of birth; and, second, that the prohibition of human beings applied to any entity 'that might reasonably claim the status of human being': at 37,917. In *International Stem Cell Corporation* [2016] APO 52 an entity produced following parthenogenic oocyte activation did not have the potential to lead to birth so the Delegate of the Commissioner held that it does not 'lie on the pathway from fertilisation to birth, and thus cannot claim the status of a human being': at [30]. Therefore the exclusion of s 18(2) did not apply. It remains to be seen how a court might approach the question. Apart from the statutory exclusions, by virtue of s 50 of the 1990 Act, the Commissioner has the discretion to refuse to accept an application for 'an invention the use of which would be contrary to law' (s 50(1)(a)) and for a food or medicine that is a mere mixture of known ingredients or for a process to produce food or medicine by mere admixture. (An example may be a sauce, salad dressing or recipe or a certain cough mixture.) In *Whang*, it was pointed out that the rarely invoked exclusion for illegality comes into play only if the main purpose or use of the invention amounts to a criminal act. It applies only in the clearest case, and *Whang* was such a case, since the invention concerned a method to create a hybrid or chimeric embryo, an act punishable by virtue of s 20 of the Prohibition of Human Cloning Act 2002 (Cth).

The effect of the *NRDC* approach perpetuated in the 1990 Act is to allow greater latitude to the courts and encourage flexible adaptation to technological change; the drawback is that important decisions of public policy with ethical, economic and social implications remain with the courts and are withdrawn from the political and parliamentary process. The difficulties inherent in courts making such decisions become apparent in cases such as *Anaesthetic Supplies Pty Ltd v Rescare Ltd* (1994) 50 FCR 1; 28 IPR 383 at 397 and *Bristol Myers Squibb Co v FH Faulding Co Ltd* (1998) 41 IPR 467 and in the Full Court (2000) 97 FCR 524. The court in the latter case had to resolve vexed questions concerning the patentability of methods of treatment of human disease; the matter has now been resolved in the affirmative by the High Court: see *Apotex Pty Ltd v Sanofi Aventis Australia Pty Ltd* [2013] HCA 50. TRIPS allows for exclusion from patentability on the grounds of morality and 'ordre public' (see art 27.2), but no such express exclusion exists in the Australian Act; contrast this with the relevant provision in the European Patent Convention (for instance, art 53), which provides:

(a) inventions the publication or exploitation of which would be contrary to 'ordre public' or morality, provided that the exploitation shall not be deemed to be so contrary merely because it is prohibited by law or regulation in some or all of the contracting states; and

(b) plant or animal varieties or essentially biological processes for the production of plants or animals; this provision does not apply to microbiological processes or the products thereof.

However, see also 7.22.

Inventions: products and processes

7.15 From the definition of 'exploit' in Sch 1, one can infer that two basic categories of claims constituting patentable inventions are envisaged; that is, either for products or for processes. Often, reference is made to 'process' or 'product' inventions, but, in fact, an invention may combine product and process claims. In terms of products, some of the main contemporary and developing patentability issues revolve around genes, plants and living organisms. In Australia, there is little doubt about the patentability of plants or organisms, whether they be of a higher or a lower order.

However, isolated and synthetically reproduced gene sequences were held not to be patentable subject matter by the High Court in *D'Arcy v Myriad Genetics Inc* [2015] HCA 35, overturning *D'Arcy v Myriad Genetics Inc* [2014] FCAFC 115 which itself had upheld *Cancer Voices Australia v Myriad Genetics Inc* [2013] FCA 65; see also ALRC Report 99: *Genes and Ingenuity: Gene Patenting and Human Health* (2004). The High Court held that a gene sequence, even if artificially (re)produced, constituted information and not an invention. In terms of processes, some of the main difficulties arise in the context of processes that do not have a clear practical or technical aspect or do not effect any physical modification; for instance, business methods. An essential requirement for all patentable inventions is that the claims are for a product or process with some practical utility, but what will be sufficiently practical is sometimes a difficult question. Nonetheless, clearly, what is claimed must be more than a theoretical idea with no practical application or use identified; thus, a discovered law of nature or a mathematical formula or algorithm per se cannot be claimed, but some specific use or application of such knowledge can be claimed as an invention. The word 'invention' as used at the outset of s 18(1) also implies some element of novelty and inventiveness inherent in the concept of suitability for patenting itself, as was clearly recognised in *Philips v Mirabella* (1995) 183 CLR 655, in which the somewhat circular language of s 18(1) ('a patentable invention is an invention that ...') was at issue: see Chapter 8 Patents: Novelty and Inventiveness.

Process patents and *NRDC*

7.16 Up until *NRDC*, an important question remained in relation to process patents (CLR at 270):

> But a question which appears still to await final decision is whether it is enough that a process produces a useful result or whether it is necessary that some physical thing is either brought into existence or so affected as the better to serve man's purpose. In some of the cases, it is suggested that the process must issue in some 'vendible matter' or a 'vendible product'.

Partly as a result of those cases, agricultural and horticultural processes (ie, methods for the cultivation of crops and plants) were consistently held not to be patentable prior to *NRDC*. The process at issue in *NRDC* did not 'issue in some vendible product', since it consisted of a method of using a known herbicide on fields to increase crop yields. In answering the question referred to above, the High Court rejected the 'vendible product' restriction (sometimes referred to as the 'Morton rules', after the judgment of Morton J in *Re GEC's Application* (1942) 60 RPC 1 at 4), which required that a process should result in the production, improvement, restoration or preservation from deterioration of a 'vendible product', and consequently found horticultural or agricultural processes to be patentable.

The court expounded a flexible and general approach to be taken to all inventions, rejecting the previous 'categorisation' approach, which required classifying an invention (eg, as 'horticultural or agricultural') and then attaching a consequence (eg, in that case, not patentable). However, the elements of the test emerge from the court's reasons in a rather piecemeal fashion. It clearly requires that an invention belongs to the practical arts (in itself nothing new: see, eg, Lindley LJ in *Lane-Fox v Kensington and Knightsbridge Electric Lighting Co* (1892) 9 RPC 413 at 416, where he points out that the Statute of Monopolies is concerned with useful arts that serve the national economy), and that if it is a method or a process, it results in an artificial state of affairs of significance to the economy or economic pursuits.

The court also said that the process should 'result in any physical phenomenon in which the effect, be it creation or merely alteration, may be observed': *NRDC* at CLR 276. Hence, the process for applying a selective herbicide to a field with cultivated crops that resulted in the destruction of weeds without directly affecting the crop (only the crop yield was altered) constituted subject matter suitable for the grant of letters patent. However, in *D'Arcy v Myriad Genetics Inc* [2015] HCA 35, French CJ, Kiefel, Bell and Keane JJ warned against treating *NRDC* as proffering a universal test. Their Honours said that the fact that an invention generates 'an artificially created state of affairs' providing economic utility does not necessarily 'mandate a finding of inherent patentability': at [21]. Most importantly, these formulae were not 'exhaustive of the concept of manner of manufacture': at [20]. Rather, NRDC warranted a 'case by case methodology' (at [23]), so that a multiplicity of factors might have to be taken into account. The essential message of the court was that a rigid application of the supposed 'test' in *NRDC* was not apt; rather, the question remains whether the invention is a proper subject of letters patent according to principles judicially developed.

Claims falling entirely outside the concept of 'invention'

7.17 Some claims fall entirely outside the concept of invention; for instance, methods of packaging and for the presentation of goods, mere presentation of information, mere instructions or schemes of operation (see, eg, *Re Rolls Royce Ltd's Application* [1963] RPC 251), or mere desiderata (the application disclosing something that it would be nice to be able to do without instructing how it can be done). Mere collocations of existing products or machines are also not patentable, but a combination patent may be valid even if each integer, when considered separately, is well known, if the combination itself has an effect that goes beyond the sum of its parts: *Welch Perrin and Co Pty Limited v Worrel* (1961) 106 CLR 588 at 611, *Minnesota Mining & Manufacturing Co v Beiersdorf (Australia) Ltd* (the *3M* case) (1980) 144 CLR 253 at 266; 1A IPR 231 and *Elconnex Pty Ltd v Gerard Industries Pty Ltd* (1991) 32 FCR 491 at 509–10; 22 IPR 551. In the *3M* case, the invention related to a new and useful type of breathable, porous, pressure-sensitive adhesive surgical tape, each element (or integer) of which was well known. Aickin J said (at CLR 266):

> The patent thus claimed is a combination patent in the proper sense of that term, ie it combines a number of elements which interact with each other to produce a new result or product. Such a combination may be one constituted by integers each of which is old, or by integers some of which are new, the interaction being the essential requirement.

Many patent applications are, in fact, for new combinations of existing or known elements. If an alleged invention amounts to a mere collocation or juxtaposition of existing elements, where the whole does not rise above the sum of the parts, it does not come within the statutory concept of invention. For instance, placing known machinery in a new order or configuration that saves production time or is otherwise more efficient does not fall within the concept of invention. There is a closely related question of obviousness relating to allegedly inventive combinations of existing elements: see, for example, *Firebelt Pty Ltd v Brambles Australia Ltd* (2002) 54 IPR 449 and see further below Chapter 8 Patents: Novelty and Inventiveness.

Furthermore, there is also a close connection with the threshold test of novelty and inventiveness, as expounded in *NV Philips Gloeilampenfabrieken & Philips Lighting Pty Ltd v Mirabella International Pty Ltd* (1995) 183 CLR 655: see Chapter 8 Patents: Novelty and Inventiveness.

Some special categories

7.18 As indicated above, the case law preceding *NRDC* largely proceeded on the basis of categorising an invention with an automatic consequence as to patentability then resulting from that categorisation. The test fashioned in *NRDC* now applies no matter what the nature or category of invention. The transition from a categorisation approach to a universal test approach for identifying patentable subject matter in *NRDC* is analogous to the development of the law of negligence before and after *Donoghue v Stevenson* [1932] AC 562. Nonetheless, the categories of invention that had been formulated prior to *NRDC* (eg, a claim for the mere presentation of information, or for a method of simply doing business, or for a discovery rather than an invention) have not entirely lost their relevance, because they can help to inform the decision whether the elements required by *NRDC* are present. Therefore, cases still explore and adopt the language of these sometimes well-established categories when considering a borderline question; but it is legitimate to do so only to the extent that the exercise informs the application of the factorial test in *NRDC*. One significant exclusion of continued application, which reflects the *NRDC* principles, is of discoveries. In *Advanced Building Systems Pty Ltd v Ramset Fasteners (Aust) Pty Ltd* (1999) 40 IPR 243; [1998] HCA 19, the majority judgments cite with approval the following passage from Carpmael,[4] '[a] clear distinction will be drawn between the discovery of one of nature's laws, and of its application to some new and useful purpose.' The majority went on to say at HCA [34]: '[W]hile discovery adds to the sum of human knowledge, s 6 of the Statute of Monopolies 1623 (UK) is concerned with a manner of new manufacture', and the court further stated that only some practical means of carrying out an idea rather than the idea itself was patentable.

Buckley J in *Reynolds v Herbert Smith & Co Ltd*, 20 RPC 123 at 126, put it as follows:

> Discovery adds only to the amount of human knowledge, but it does so only … by disclosing something … Invention also adds to human knowledge, but not merely by disclosing something. Invention necessarily involves also the suggestion of an act to be done, and it must be an act which results in a new product, or a new result, or a new process, or a new combination for producing an old product or an old result.

The same goes for products. Thus, a newly discovered but naturally occurring chemical compound as such is not a patentable invention, nor is a claim for its possible but unknown future uses. The proper application of the *NRDC* principles to determine

4. W Carpmael, *The Law of Patents for Inventions*, 5th ed, 1852, p 34.

what is suitable subject matter for patenting has recently arisen in relation to a number of loosely described categories of inventions, such as computer programs, medical treatment methods and business methods. These are separately considered below in this chapter because of their continuing significance and controversial status. They are also illustrative of the benefits and challenges inherent in the rather indefinite language of *NRDC* when it is applied to evolving areas of technology and business. There are other developments that also give rise to significant difficulties in the application of *NRDC*, such as gene patenting, but there is not the room here to go into these in further detail; however, see 7.15 above and the High Court decision in *D'Arcy v Myriad Genetics Inc*; as for the US position, see *Association for Molecular Pathology v Myriad Genetics* 569 US 12-398 (US Supreme Court invalidating Myriad's claims to isolated genes).

Non-technical methods and processes

7.19 The patentability of a process that is said to be theoretical or a discovery or belonging to the fine arts, not having a tangible, practical or technical implementation or result, arises in various contexts. One is applications for claims that describe methods of operating a computer, processes to be performed on a computer and computer programs as such; the other is so-called business method patents, a category that may also include accounting, legal and like processes. A principal difficulty for computer-implemented process or method claims is the frequent presence of algorithms, mathematical equations that, in themselves, are theoretical and thus not patentable. In the US case of *Diamond, Commissioner of Patents and Trademarks v Diehr* 450 US 175 (1981), the patent application claimed a process for moulding raw, uncured synthetic rubber into cured precision products. One step in that process involved the constant measurement of the temperature inside the mould, sending the measurements to a computer, which repeatedly recalculated the cure time using a mathematical equation and which then signalled a device to open the press at the proper time. Rehnquist J (as he then was) delivered the majority opinion of the court upholding the patentability of the process at issue:

> We view respondents' claims as nothing more than a process for moulding rubber products and not as an attempt to patent a mathematical formula. We recognize, of course, that when a claim recites a mathematical formula (or scientific principle or phenomenon of nature), an inquiry must be made into whether the claim is seeking patent protection for that formula in the abstract. A mathematical formula as such is not accorded the protection of our patent laws, *Gottschalk v Benson* 409 US 63 (1972), and this principle cannot be circumvented by attempting to limit the use of the formula to a particular technological environment: *Parker v Flook*, 437 US 584 (1978). [...] On the other hand, when a claim containing a mathematical formula implements or applies that formula in a structure or process which, when considered as a whole, is performing a function which the patent laws were designed to protect (for example, transforming or reducing an article to a different state or thing), then the claim satisfies the requirements of s 101. Because we do not view the respondents' claims as an attempt to patent a mathematical formula, but rather to be drawn to an industrial process for the moulding of rubber products, we affirm the judgment of the Court of Customs and Patent Appeals.

The Australian Commissioner for a considerable time applied a fairly restrictive approach to applications that included mathematical algorithms. Whether that approach was in conformity with the *NRDC* principles was finally considered in the *IBM* case. Burchett J constituted the Federal Court in an appeal from a decision of the Commissioner to reject a patent application filed by IBM: see *International Business Machines Corporation* [1990] APO 47. In effect, this was the first appeal to challenge the Patent Office's longstanding practice of rejecting almost all applications for computer-implemented inventions because the rules against claiming a mathematical formula could not be 'circumvented by attempting to limit the use of the formula to a particular technological environment': see above, *Diamond, Commissioner of Patents and Trademarks v Diehr* 450 US 175 (1981). IBM's application was for a method for the production of an improved curve on a computer screen and included mathematical steps. Burchett J held that the method resulted in an artificial state of affairs (the improved curve on the screen), it belonged to the practical and not the fine arts, and it was of significance in economic terms; hence, the claims concerned patentable subject matter and the application should have been accepted: the *IBM* case at ALR 393ff.

In *CCOM Pty Ltd v Jiejing Pty Ltd* (1994) 51 FCR 260; 28 IPR 481 (on appeal from the decision of Cooper J at *CCOM Pty Ltd v Jiejing Pty Ltd (No 2)* (1993) 48 FCR 41; 27 IPR 577), the invention concerned a process for producing Chinese characters on a computer screen. Cooper J held at first instance that the essence of the invention was linguistic knowledge (ie, the usual process for writing Chinese characters) that belonged to the fine and not the practical arts and was not patentable subject matter. (Although the invention was claimed in product terms, it was circumscribed by 'means for' claims, which amounts in all practical respects to a process invention.) The Full Court rejected Cooper J's reliance on identifying the essence of the invention, considering this to be an approach more relevant to the question of inventiveness than to the categorisation of subject matter as patentable. The Full Court looked at the invention as a whole, applied the *NRDC* standards and determined that because the invention was claimed in a technical embodiment, it was not merely a claim to a purely linguistic process. Even though linguistic analysis played an important part in the process, it was not claimed 'as such', the invention in fact representing a practical resolution for a practical problem. (While Latin alphabet characters A–Z easily fit on a keyboard, there are a very large number of Chinese characters.)

The ultimate result of the *IBM* and *CCOM* cases is that even computer programs, and more broadly, computer-implemented inventions, can be patented, as long as claims are limited to their application in a certain technical environment and are not too broad. As to the current practice of the Patent Office in that regard, see the Australian Patent Office's *Manual of Practice and Procedure*, 2.9.2.7 'Computer Implemented Inventions — Schemes and Business Methods' and 2.9.2.10 'Mathematical Algorithms'. However, the fact that a computer program may constitute patentable subject matter takes an applicant only so far. It will also be necessary to establish that it is both novel and inventive. This may not be the case with most run of the mill programs written with established programming techniques and languages. As to questions of novelty and inventive step, see Chapter 8 Patents: Novelty and Inventiveness.

The other issue that has been revived in the new internet environment is the patentability of non-technical processes such as business, legal or accounting methods, in particular where they are implemented using computers and network technologies over the internet. Schemes or plans for carrying on a business per se have long been considered not patentable, since they do not claim a practical or applied method as the law requires. However, the emergence of the internet and digital technology has resulted in methods of doing business being expressed as steps to be performed in a digital environment. Such processes are arguably inventions in the true sense. In the US, *State Street Bank & Trust Co v Signature Financial Group* 149 F 3d 1368 (1998) considered the question. An invention entitled 'Data Processing System for Hub and Spoke Financial Services Configuration' was found to be patentable subject matter. In Australia, the patentability of computer-based business methods was confirmed in *Welcome Real-Time SA v Catuity Inc* (2001) 113 FCR 110; 51 IPR 327, which related to the use of loyalty cards in retailing: see also Chapter 18 Digitisation. The court in that case pointed out that while methods used in business may be patentable, as was the case here because the method as a whole involved interaction of computers and data storage capabilities, this did not mean that business plans or schemes as such are patentable. The latter point is well illustrated by the rejection of applications relating to a legal procedure for the protection of a financial asset: see *Stephen John Grant* [2004] APO 11, *Grant v Commissioner of Patents* [2005] FCA 1100; 67 IPR 1 and *Grant v Commissioner of Patents* (2006) 154 FCR 62; 221 IPR 221; [2006] FCAFC 120. If an application claims a series of legal or financial steps as such, there is no patentable subject matter. *Peter Szabo and Associates Pty Ltd* [2005] APO 24; 66 IPR 370 is another valuable illustration, relating to a reverse mortgage arrangement; that is, legal steps taken to provide liquidity to asset-rich older persons. In *Grant*, a flowchart of legal steps to be taken to protect an asset from legal liability was said at the lower level not to be directed at an 'application of science or technology', as required. The Full Court did not adopt this handy formula, as it has the potential to become too restrictive in some cases, but agreed that what was claimed did not fall within the concept of invention. The US is considered to be the jurisdiction in which 'pure' business method patents are most favourably viewed. However, the Court of Appeals by majority in *In re Bilski* No 07-1130 (Fed Cir Oct 30, 2008) has now held that the US patent law required that a process is tied to a particular machine or apparatus, or else transforms a particular article into a different state or thing. The invention concerned a method of hedging risk in commodities trading. The court said: '[W]e also conclude that the "useful, concrete and tangible result" inquiry is inadequate and reaffirm that the machine-or-transformation test outlined by the Supreme Court is the proper test to apply.' As a consequence, the law in the US is largely aligned with the approach represented by *Grant* in Australia, and it cannot be said that 'business methods as such' are patentable in that country to any greater extent than they are in Australia. In fact, it might now be more difficult to obtain a computer program patent in the US than it is here.[5] The difficulties in applying the legal principles concerning computer-implemented inventions with any

5. However, for an alternative review, see A Christie, 'Some Observations on the Requirement of Inherent Patentability in the Context of Business Methods Patents' (2000) (43) *Intellectual Property Forum* 10, 16.

consistency are apparent in the contrasting outcomes of two recent cases: *RPL Central Pty Ltd v Commissioner of Patents* [2013] FCA 871, in which a 'method and system for automated collection of evidence of skills and knowledge' was held patentable, and *Research Affiliates LLC v Commissioner of Patents* [2013] FCA 71, in which claims to construction and use of passive portfolios and indexes for securities investments were held invalid (see also *Research Affiliates LLC v Commissioner of Patents* [2014] FCAFC 150 dismissing the appeal). The point of distinction may be determined by the Full Federal Court's decision in the appeal in *Encompass Corporation Pty Ltd v InfoTrack Pty Ltd* [2018] FCA 421. A single judge of the court held that a method for collecting and displaying data (including a payment step for proprietary information) did not concern patentable subject matter. Perram J held that there was no improvement to the functioning in a computer involved. By contrast, a 'method for linking a computer user to an advertising message by way of an intermediate engagement offer' was held to be patentable subject matter in *Rokt Pte Ltd v Commissioner of Patents* [2018] FCA 1988 (see in particular [205]–[208]).

Methods of human treatment

7.20 The TRIPS provisions concerning patentability permit member countries to exclude methods of human treatment from patentability: see art 27(3)(a). Obviously, with the exception of methods for the generation of human beings, which may include infertility treatment methods, there is no such exclusion in the Australian Patents Act. The question has been resolved by the courts in more recent times on the basis of *NRDC*. One of the requirements of *NRDC* is that an invention, to be patentable subject matter, must be of significance to the economy; that does not mean that it must have demonstrable commercial potential, rather that it concerns an economic pursuit. This requirement reflects a fundamental policy aim: a patentee deserves the monopoly in the invention because of its potential contribution to economic activity.

The relevance of the question is well illustrated by the issue of patentability of methods for treatment of human pathology. It is undoubted that products related to, or used in, medical treatment, such as pharmaceutical substances, adhesive surgical tape (*Minnesota Mining & Manufacturing Co v Beiersdorf (Australia) Ltd* (1980) 144 CLR 253) or apparatus for treating a chronic debilitation or illness (see the product claims in *Rescare v Anaesthetic Supplies* (1992) 111 ALR 205; 25 IPR 119), are patentable. But what about methods or processes for the treatment of illness? In *Rescare*, most of the claims of the patented invention were for an apparatus used for the control of obstructive sleep apnoea, a potentially lethal disorder, but, as well as the product claims, there were some human treatment process claims. Gummow J at first instance, as well as Lockhart J and Wilcox J in the Full Federal Court (see *Anaesthetic Supplies Pty Ltd v Rescare Ltd* (1994) 50 FCR 1; 28 IPR 383), held that methods of human treatment were an economic subject matter. In this they agreed with Barwick CJ, who said the following in *Joos v Commissioner of Patents* (1972) 126 CLR 611 at 618:

> The national economic interest in the product of good surgery — and therefore in the advancement of its techniques — if in no other respect than the repair and rehabilitation of members of the work force, including management in that grouping, is both obvious and

> may be regarded as sufficiently proximate, in my opinion, as to be capable of satisfying the economic element of an invention, if other elements are present and no impediments exist to the grant. One has only to recall the economic impact of workers' compensation, invalid pensions and repatriation costs to recognise that proximity.

But Barwick CJ, making a distinction between cosmetic and disease-related treatment processes, ultimately left open the question of patentability of a method for the treatment of disease. The *Joos* invention related to cosmetic treatment only (a process for improving strength and elasticity of keratinous material such as hair and nails). The minority judge in *Anaesthetic Supplies*, Sheppard J, disagreed with Barwick CJ obiter in *Joos* concerning treatment of pathology, or, in other words, therapeutic methods. He held (again, obiter, since the issue of validity was already decided on the basis of a lack of fair basing) that medicine and the development of medical treatment methods was not an economic but a humanitarian pursuit based on free exchange of information and assistance with appropriate treatment methods. He said (at IPR 421):

> The subject matter of all this, although it may have its commercial elements, is the treatment and relief of human suffering. It has a direct bearing on the well being of the nation.

In *Bristol-Myers Squibb Co v FH Faulding & Co Ltd* (1998) 41 IPR 467; [1998] FCA 860, Heerey J came to the same conclusion. He made the point that granting a patent in a method of medical treatment would be contrary to the essence of medicine — a non-commercial pursuit. Granting monopolies in medical treatment methods would have severe practical repercussions in clinical decision-making about appropriate treatment. As to the impact on R&D from a refusal of a patent for a method of medical treatment, Heerey J said (at IPR 481):

> It is said that the lack of monopoly patent protection will be a disincentive to investment in medical research. However, it was not suggested in argument that there is empirical evidence to support this proposition. Advances in medical science, unimaginable at the commencement of the 20th century, have been made under regimes which do not provide monopoly protection for methods of treatment. Moreover, in medical sciences there are powerful non-economic factors at work: the excitement of the search for knowledge for its own sake, hope for the betterment of mankind, and the human motivation of professional advancement and personal satisfaction.

As to arguments that it is illogical to grant patents for surgical, medical and pharmaceutical products, but not for methods of treatment, his Honour, claiming the value of experience over logic in the law, quotes Cooke J in *Wellcome Foundation Ltd v Commissioner of Patents* [1983] NZLR 385 at 388: '... there remains ... a deepseated sense that the art of the physician or the surgeon in alleviating human suffering does not belong to the area of economic endeavour or trade or commerce'. Perhaps this appeal to human emotions is not surprising, given the nature of the subject matter claimed. In *Bristol-Myers*, a method for the administration of a proved substance (Taxol) in the treatment of refractory and potentially terminal cancer was at issue.

On appeal, in *Bristol-Myers Squibb Co v FH Faulding & Co Ltd* (2000) 97 FCR 524; 46 IPR 553, methods of human treatment were held to be patentable. Finkelstein J held that methods of human treatment clearly fell within the concept of manner of manufacture. The more relevant question was whether they were 'generally inconvenient': see 7.22 below. His Honour said, at IPR 594:

> ... perhaps the most powerful argument against patenting is the idea that a patient may be denied medical treatment that she needs. It is certainly the most emotive of the arguments. It presumes that a medical practitioner may be unable to obtain the right to use a particular process, or may not be able to do so within due time, and therefore will be unwilling to undertake the process on her patients for fear of legal action.

But, at IPR 595:

> On the other side of the debate is the underlying objective of patents, namely the promotion of science and the advancement of the arts for the general welfare of the state. As a general principle there can be no doubt that patent protection is desirable to encourage new medicines and surgical methods. It is an inescapable fact that inducement is necessary to encourage the great expense that is now required to evaluate and investigate the utility of many new medical processes and surgical methods.

In the end, the substantive issue was who should properly determine the question, given the limited ability of a court of law to take evidence on the social and economic issues involved (at IPR 595):

> I do not believe that in a controversial issue such as is raised by the present argument, I would be abandoning my responsibility as a judge to follow this approach and to hold that if public policy demands that a medical or surgical process should be excluded from patentability, then that is a matter that should be resolved by the Parliament.

The issue has now been definitively resolved by the High Court in *Apotex Pty Ltd v Sanofi Aventis Australia Pty Ltd* [2013] HCA 50, which concerned the use of a known drug (leflunomide) for a new indication (the treatment of a skin disorder). The majority held that the method was patentable subject matter, only Hayne J dissenting. In *AstraZeneca AB v Apotex Pty Ltd* (2014) 226 FCR 324; [2014] FCAFC 99 the claims were directed to a method of treatment of the human body involving the administration of a pharmaceutical composition under a hitherto unknown dosage regimen for that composition. The Full Federal Court held that 'as a method of treatment of the human body, the invention as claimed is of the same general character as the invention considered by the High Court': at [366]. However, the decision arguably leaves open the possibility that some medical processes, such as surgical procedures, could yet be excluded. Note that in New Zealand, where the question was also to be resolved on the basis of the cases, the applicable Act also being silent on the matter, the opposite outcome has recently been affirmed: see *Pfizer Inc v Commissioner of Patents* [2004] NZCA 104; see also *Merck & Co Inc v Arrow Pharmaceuticals Ltd* (2006) 68 IPR 511; 154 FCR 31 and *University of Western Australia v Gray (No 20)* (2008) 76 IPR 222.

Living organisms

7.21 In relation to living organisms, TRIPS, by virtue of art 27(3)(b), permits the exclusion of 'plants and animals other than micro-organisms and essentially biological processes for the production of plants or animals other than non-biological and microbiological processes. However, Members shall provide for the protection of plant varieties either by patents or by an effective sui generis system or by any combination thereof'. Unlike in a number of foreign jurisdictions, the statutory limits on patentability of plant and animal (including human) life forms are very few in Australia: see s 18(2). Only human beings and the biological processes for their generation are not patentable by way of a standard patent in Australia.

Thus, the following are patentable in Australia:

- lower life forms (such as bacteria or other micro-organisms; see, eg, the watershed US case *Diamond v Chakrabarty* (1980) 447 US 303 to the same effect): note that, in any case, TRIPS does not permit the exclusion of micro-organisms.
- higher life forms such as new animals: a patentable animal may, for example, be one resulting from genetic manipulation. An example is the famous 'oncomouse' (a mouse genetically modified to render it unusually susceptible to the development of cancers), which was held to be unpatentable in Europe but on the basis of ordre public and morality: see art 27(2) of TRIPS and further below. By contrast, in Canada, higher life forms are not patentable subject matter, on the basis of the jurisprudence of the Supreme Court: see *Harvard College v Canada (Commissioner of Patents)* [2002] 4 SCR 45. The only 'animals' excluded by statute in Australia are human beings, and no exclusion has been fashioned by the courts.
- plant varieties: if a new plant variety is produced by traditional selective breeding techniques, it will ordinarily lack the required inventiveness for a patent; however, it is a different matter if it is produced by genetic modification. New plant varieties produced by means of traditional techniques such as crossbreeding or selective breeding may also be registrable under the Plant Breeder's Rights Act 1994 (Cth): see further Chapter 17 Sui Generis Regimes: Circuit Layouts and Plant Varieties. TRIPS requires that sui generis plant varieties protection be available if patents are not, but does not exclude both being available, as is the case in Australia.

The exclusion of 'human beings' by virtue of s 18(2) is unclear and remains untested; for instance, does the exclusion of human beings extend to parts of human beings, whether or not grown separately, and to what does the phrase 'biological processes for their generation' refer? Some consideration was given to these issues in *Fertilitetscentrum AB and Luminis Pty Ltd* [2004] APO 19, see above at 7.14. As to the patentability of human embryonic stem cells, see ALRC Report 99, *Genes and Ingenuity: Gene Patenting and Human Health* (2004), at [15.33]ff.

The Other Limbs of s 6 of the Statute of Monopolies

7.22 The term 'manner of manufacture' does not stand alone within s 6 of the Statute of Monopolies, which reads: '... any manner of new manufacture within this realm ... so as also they be not contrary to the law, nor mischievous to the state, by raising prices of commodities at home, or hurt of trade, or generally inconvenient'. This is significant because, by virtue of s 18(1)(a) of the Patents Act 1990, the term 'manner of manufacture' is to be understood 'within the meaning of s 6 of the Statute of Monopolies'. Although part of the provision appears to be inapplicable or dead letter, the exclusion of inventions that are contrary to law, and the exclusion of inventions that are 'generallie inconvenient', may still have some relevance today. The general reference to inventions 'contrary to law' in s 6 is arguably superseded by s 50(1)(a) of the Patents Act, which gives the Commissioner the discretion to refuse to accept an application for an invention 'the use of which would be contrary to law'. This is usually taken to mean contrary to criminal law or any other statutory provision or common law rule. Examples of applications rejected on the basis of illegality are rare, since it is usually taken to apply only to inventions whose sole use is contrary to law, but see *Whang* at 7.14 above. Note also the special rules and restrictions applying to inventions related to nuclear technology ('associated technology' in terms of the Act): see Ch 15 of the Act, 'Special provisions relating to associated technology'.

Of greater interest is the exclusion of inventions that are 'generallie inconvenient'. These terms of art are not to be taken at face value. Relevant case law has explored the notion, and its impact, if it exists at all, is severely restricted. The Australian Patent Office's *Manual of Practice and Procedure* says: 'There is no clear guidance as to when an invention may or may not be regarded as "generally inconvenient". Hence, examiners should refrain from taking this objection.': at 2.9.3.3. Nonetheless, claims that relate to the use or operation of existing machines in a manner for which they are designed have in the past been rejected on the basis of 'general inconvenience'; that is, impracticality. In *Re Rolls Royce's Application* [1963] RPC 251, claims for a method of flying a passenger jet airliner that conserved fuel were rejected. They would constitute a dangerous restriction on a pilot's ability to fly a plane in the safest and most appropriate manner in all circumstances. A further important illustration of the possible application of the exception is found in cases concerning the patentability of therapeutic methods of treatment for human illness. As we saw above, medicine is considered an economic pursuit, and hence medical treatment methods are considered suitable for the granting of letters patent in the sense of *NRDC*. However, in *Bristol-Myers*, Heerey J (at first instance) found that granting a patent over a method (more precisely a dosage schedule) for administering a drug (Taxol) with known anti-cancerous operation would be generally inconvenient, since it would restrict a medical doctor's clinical freedom in choosing the method most apt for the alleviation of suffering and disease. These were described by the High Court in *Apotex* as ethical considerations: at [39]. The majority on appeal disagreed with Heerey J: see above at 7.20. Finkelstein J said that if 'public policy demands that a medical or surgical process should be excluded from patentability, then that is a matter that should be resolved by the Parliament': *Bristol-Myers* at [141]. In the High Court in *Apotex*, the issue of 'general inconvenience' generated scant attention as it was not pursued by the parties. But the situation in New Zealand lends support to Heerey's approach (see, eg, *Pfizer Inc v Commissioner of Patents* [2004] NZCA 104 (28 June 2004)), and it is the case that it has sometimes been contended that the exclusion of inventions whose patenting would be 'generallie inconvenient' should be taken to represent a broader public policy restriction in Australian patents law. It was noted above that TRIPS in art 27(2) provides that:

> Members may exclude from patentability inventions, the prevention within their territory of the commercial exploitation of which is necessary to protect ordre public or morality, including to protect human, animal or plant life or health or to avoid serious prejudice to the environment, provided that such exclusion is not made merely because the exploitation is prohibited by their law.

Thus, such a reading of 'generallie inconvenient' is potentially permissable. However, while 'general inconvenience' may accommodate within its confines certain exclusions compatible with art 27, it is not by its terms restricted to them. Patent statutes in some other jurisdictions contain an express exception in the same terms as art 27(2), which supports the refusal of applications for inventions that are immoral or unethical, socially unacceptable or dangerous (see, eg, art 53 of the European Patent Convention of 1973: 'European patents shall not be granted in respect of: (a) inventions the publication or exploitation of which would be contrary to "ordre public" or morality …'); that is obviously not the case in Australia.

In the past, contraceptive devices have been held to be unpatentable in the UK and Australia under a broad morality reading of the terms of the Statute of Monopolies: see *Riddlesbarger's Application* (1936) 53 RPC 57. But in more recent times, whatever its theoretical scope might be, the real impact of the exclusion has been extremely limited so that the Patent Office's approach can hardly be gainsaid. Blanket arguments anchored in the terms of s 6, that applications for genetically altered plants and animals should be routinely rejected, both on ethical or religious bases (playing around with nature; 'owning' life) or on the basis of potential and unknown risks, have held no sway in Australian patents law and practice. Furthermore, the legislator imposed no restrictions on the patentability of life forms (other than humans) in 1990, and chose not to incorporate express public policy exclusions. In Europe, the patenting of the 'oncomouse', noted above, generated much controversy. In the end, the potential advantages of the invention in terms of medical research were found to outweigh the ethical concern about patenting a life form arguably devised to suffer debilitating illness, and the mouse patent was accepted: see *Harvard/Oncomouse* [1990] EPOR 501 at 513. However, Australian courts have historically been reluctant to engage in this kind of balancing up of public policy arguments. In any case, the issue of morality or the environmental impact of new technologies is not resolved simply by excluding them from patentability. A broader regulatory approach is required.

Bibliography

A Christie, 'Some Observations on the Requirement of Inherent Patentability in the Context of Business Method Patents' (2000) 43 *IP Forum* 16.

A McBratney, 'Problem Child in Australian Patent Law: "Fair" Basing' (2001) 12(4) *AIPJ* 211.

A Moore, 'The Requirement of Fair Basing in Australian Patent Law' (2001) 45 *IP Forum* 10.

A White, 'The Ethics — Gene Patenting and Human Health' (2004) 15(1) *AIPJ* 6.

Advisory Council on Intellectual Property (ACIP), *Report on a Review of the Patenting of Business Systems*, September 2003.

Australian Government, *Australian Government Response to the Productivity Commission Inquiry into Intellectual Property Arrangements*, August 2017 (Government Response).

B Roxborough, 'Admissions on the Face of the Specification — Practical Implications for Patent Drafting and Litigation' (2007) 68 *IP Forum* 59.

B Roxborough, 'Fair Basis — Lockwood's Implications for Patent Litigation and Drafting' (2008) 72 *IP Forum* 10.

C Arup and W van Caenegem (eds), *Intellectual Property Policy Reform: Fostering Innovation and Development*, Edward Elgar, 2009.

C Bird, 'Patenting of Business Systems — the Great Debate' (2003) 15(8) *IPLB* 109.

C Dent, 'Patent Opposition and the Constitution: Before or After?' (2006) 17(4) *AIPJ* 217.

C Lawson, 'Grant v Commissioner of Patents and Patenting Knowledge Inventions' (2008) 15(4) *JLM* 626.

C Lawson, 'Patent Privileges and the National Competition Policy — Patent Scope and Allocation?' (2005) 33(1) *ABLR* 7.

C Lawson, 'Revisiting Merits Review of Patent Application, Grant and Validity Decisions Under the Patents Act 1990 (Cth)' (2007) 14(4) *AJ Admin L* 178.

C Lawson, 'Some Economic Questions for Biotechnology Patenting in Australia' (2000) 41 *IP Forum* 10.

D Brennan, 'An Essay on the Eligibility of Business Methods for Australian Patent Protection' (2002) 13(1) *JLIS* 8.

D Catterns, 'Lockwood v Doric — Fair Basis and the High Court' (2006) 65 *IP Forum* 34.

E Gold, 'Gene Patents and Medical Access' (2002) 49 *Intellectual Property Forum* 20.

IP Australia, 'Public Consultation: Introducing an objects clause into the *Patents Act 1990*', Discussion Paper, August 2017.

J Pila, 'Inherent Patentability in Anglo-Australian Law: A History' (2003) 14(3) *AIPJ* 109.

J Pila, 'Methods of Medical Treatment within Australian and United Kingdom Patents Law' (2001) 24(2) *UNSWLJ* 420.

K Kariyawasam, S Takakura and N Ottomo, 'Legal Implications and Patentability of Human Stem Cells: Australia and Japan Compared' (2015) 10(3) *JIPLP* 198.

M Pattison, 'The Internet Starts to Take Patent Seriously' (2000) 43 *IP Forum* 10.

M Rimmer, 'The Race to Patent the SARS Virus: The TRIPS Agreement and Access to Essential Medicines' (2004) 5(2) *MJIL* 335.

P Leonard-Trewavis, 'Patent Protection and Medical Treatment of the Human Body in Australia' (2002) 15(7) *IPLB* 89.

Productivity Commission, *Intellectual Property Arrangements*, Inquiry Report No 78, Canberra, September 2016 (PC Report).

R C Dreyfuss, J Nielsen and D Nicol, 'Patenting Nature — A Comparative Perspective' (2018) 5(3) *JLB* 550.

R Macaw, 'Recent Developments Concerning the Test for Obviousness' (2001) 47 *IP Forum* 22.

T Haines, 'Are Australian Patentees Sufficiently Motivated?' (2008) 19(2) *AIPJ* 106.

T Haines, 'Patenting Legal Strategies — Does the Utility Justify the Ends?' (2005) 62 *IP Forum* 24.

W Condon, 'Patentability of Methods of Medical Treatment: Ethics, Logic and Just Plain Gut Feel?' (2000) 40 *IP Forum* 8.

W van Caenegem, 'The Technicality Requirement, Patent Scope and Patentable Subject Matter in Australia' (2002)13 *AIPJ* 41.

Chapter 8

Patents: Novelty and Inventiveness

Introduction

The threshold test of inventiveness: *Philips v Mirabella*

8.1 The Patents Act 1990 (Cth) gives effect to the well-established view that there are three principal and distinct patentability issues: patentable subject matter, inventiveness and novelty. In logical sequence, the question of whether the application discloses an invention suitable for the granting of a patent is resolved first, then the question of novelty and, finally, the question of inventiveness. Yet, as is pointed out above, an ordinary understanding of the word 'invention' implies not just a product or process but one with some inherently novel and inventive character. Therefore, there is some room for considering inventiveness and novelty within the confines of the first question. This issue came to the fore in the case of *NV Philips Gloeilampenfabrieken & Philips Lighting Pty Ltd v Mirabella International Pty Ltd* (1995) 183 CLR 655; 32 IPR 449 (*Philips v Mirabella*), where the High Court had to resolve a question of interpretation concerning the wording of the first limb of s 18(1): '... a patentable invention is an invention that ...'. The court held that since Sch 1 defines an invention as 'any manner of new manufacture ...', the provision implied that there was a threshold test that applied on the face of the application before the questions of novelty and inventiveness are examined separately by comparison with the prior art. Since the term 'manner of new manufacture ... within s 6 of the Statute of Monopolies' implied, in line with established case law, an element of inventiveness, in cases where it was apparent on the face of the application itself that this was lacking, the application failed the threshold test and should be refused without further evidence of what was contained in the prior art base and how it compared with the application: *Philips v Mirabella* at CLR 663–8. In other words, '[R]eference to the definition of "invention" in the Dictionary which constitutes Sch 1 to the 1990 Act was held to have imported into the introductory words the requirement that a manner of new manufacture for the purposes of the Statute of Monopolies should appear on the face of the specification.': see *Advanced Building Systems Pty Ltd v Ramset Fasteners (Aust) Pty Ltd* (1998) 194 CLR 171; 40 IPR 243 at 254 (*Ramset*). In *Philips v Mirabella*, the alleged invention was nothing more than a new use for an old substance whose known qualities make it suitable for that use (ie, 'the analogous use principle': the application is for the use of an old substance in a manner analogous to known uses of that substance).

It was thus clear from the description of the invention alone that the matter disclosed was not suitable for patenting, and the application should have been rejected. The 'analogous use principle' was developed under previous legislation, which, unlike the 1990 Act (see s 45), did not permit the refusal of an application by the Commissioner on the basis of want of inventiveness compared with the prior art (want of inventiveness was a basis only for revocation after granting). Such an application could instead be treated as simply not revealing an invention at all on its face, and thus be rejected anyway, rather than allowing a manifestly baseless patent to proceed, which would then be open to revocation after being granted.

In *Bristol-Myers Squibb Co v F H Faulding & Co Ltd* (1998) 41 IPR 467; [1998] FCA 860, application of the threshold test was also at issue. As in *Philips v Mirabella*, the putative invention at issue was allegedly 'nothing but a claim for the use of a known material in the manufacture of known articles for the purpose of which its known properties make that material suitable', a phrase from *Commissioner of Patents v Microcell Ltd* (1959) 102 CLR 232 quoted in *Bristol-Myers Squibb Co v F H Faulding & Co Ltd* (2000) 97 FCR 524; 46 IPR 553; [2000] FCA 316 at [19]. Well before the priority date, the drug Taxol had shown great promise in fighting cancer and, in particular, as an effective agent in the treatment of drug-refractory ovarian cancer. The trial judge held (*Bristol-Myers* (1998) at IPR 477):

> Thus the specification is not merely a claim of 'a new use of an old substance' (*Re BA's Application* (1915) 32 RPC 348 at 349; *Mirabella* 183 CLR at 661) but a claim for the same use for an old substance. Further, the specifications disclose that the claimed inventions were the product of routine testing which merely verified a hypothesis arising from analysis of reports of earlier trials: see *WR Grace & Co v Asahi Kasei Kogyo Kabushiki Kaisha* (1993) 25 IPR 481 at 497–8.

In other words, merely verifying by testing and proving an already known principle to be accurate does not amount to an invention that will pass the threshold test of *Philips v Mirabella*. However, on the facts, the Full Court in *Bristol-Myers* (2000) disagreed with the trial judge's approach, saying that his formulation overlooked two things (at IPR 565):

> One is that the claim is for a method, not a product; the other is the importance of the phrase 'nothing but' in the Microcell principle: as to both points, see *National Research Development Corp v Commissioner of Patents* (1959) 102 CLR 252, especially at 262. Taxol may, if used in accordance with the claimed invention, be used for a purpose for which its known properties make it suitable; it does not follow that the method claimed does not involve an inventive step. Nor, if the method was proved to be efficacious by a routine process of trial and error (authorities cited by his Honour have to do with how much, in order to destroy novelty, an anticipation must reveal), does it follow that the claimed invention is obvious or does not involve an inventive step: what matters is whether, to the skilled but unimaginative worker in the field, the claimed method was obvious in the sense that the worker, not necessarily seeing that the method was likely to be safe and efficacious, would have seen that it was one which justified investigation.

The threshold question was also at issue in *Ramset*, although this case concerned the 1952 Act, and in *Merck & Co v Arrow Pharmaceuticals Ltd* (2006) 154 FCR 31. *Ramset* confirms that the threshold test is not limited to the 'analogous use' exclusion; that is, to a new use for an old substance whose known qualities make it suitable for that use. In *Ramset*, the invention (being 'Lift systems for tilt-up walls') was rejected by application of the threshold test because it was clear on the face of the application that it was a mere collocation of known integers. The tenor of *Ramset* was that the category of alleged inventions that could fail the threshold test is not closed. This is further reinforced by the court's indication that some applications for patents for methods of human treatment could be rejected on the basis of the threshold test on the ground of manifest lack of inventiveness. Note that this statement in *Ramset* seems to presume that medical treatment methods are not patentable inventions, which is at odds with *Apotex Pty Ltd v Sanofi Aventis Australia Pty Ltd* [2013] HCA 50. Concerning the generalised nature of the threshold test, Padbury[1] noted that a number of commentators have suggested that 'the need for such a test [the threshold test] reflects the narrow tests for novelty and obviousness under Australian patent law'. This led her to conclude that: 'There is a good deal of initial attraction in having a ground of invalidity apart from novelty and obviousness which allows an assessment of "inventiveness"'.[2] However, as is explained below, since that time, the prior art information that can be taken into account in assessing inventiveness has been considerably expanded, broadening the 'narrow test': see Patents Amendment Act 1990 (Cth) and further at 8.9 below.

The further question is whether the threshold test is applied only by reference to the nature of the invention as described in the specification (as is the case with the analogous use subset) or also in relation to anything else that appears in or is revealed 'on the face of the specification'. For instance, reference may be made to the existence and nature of a prior patent in the specification. This issue was considered in *Bradken Resources Pty Ltd v Lynx Engineering Consultants Pty Ltd* (2007) 72 IPR 630 and also in *Apotex Pty Ltd v Sanofi-Aventis* (2009) 82 IPR 416; [2009] FCAFC 134. In *Bradken*, the following passage from the Full Federal Court's decision in *Bristol-Myers* was reproduced:

> In our view, in the light of the authorities to which we have referred, Philips stands for the proposition (as a matter of construction of the 1990 Act) that if, on the basis of what was known, as revealed on the face of the specification, the invention claimed was obvious or did not involve an inventive step … then the threshold requirement of inventiveness is not met … If however, the body of prior knowledge disclosed by the specification is insufficient to deprive what is claimed of the quality of inventiveness, then the only additional knowledge or information which will be taken into account is knowledge of information of a kind described in s 7(2) of the 1990 Act. That again, in our view, is … the only approach which does not, in practical terms, render s 18(1)(b)(ii) otiose. Of course, once that additional knowledge is taken into account, one is applying s 18(1)(b)(ii), not the opening words of s 18(1) … at FCR 536; IPR 564; see also *CSR Ltd v Rockwool International A/S* (2007) 73 IPR 294.

More recently the Full Federal Court in *AstraZeneca AB v Apotex Pty Ltd* (2014) 226 FCR 324; [2014] FCAFC 99 (*AstraZeneca v Apotex*) at [385] indicated that, in conformity with a number of precedents (including *Novozymes A/S v Danisco A/S* (2013) 99 IPR 417; [2013] FCAFC 6), what is required is 'an assessment of newness and

1. M Padbury, 'Inventiveness Apart from Novelty and Inventive Step' (1998) 9 *AIPJ* 161 at 173.
2. Ibid, p 174.

inventiveness by reference only to what is disclosed on the face of the specification'; a mere cross-reference to a document in the specification without including the substance of what it relevantly reveals may not qualify, nor will something that is not sufficiently analogous to what is claimed to deprive the latter of all inventiveness. The just quoted passages also clarify the resulting relationship between the threshold test and the tests of novelty and inventiveness. Once an application passes the threshold test because it is not, on the basis of what is disclosed in the application, so obviously lacking in inventiveness that it fails to amount to an invention in the statutory sense of that word, and it is determined that the application relates to an invention suitable for patenting, it remains to be examined whether the application recites something new compared with the prior art (s 18(1)(b)(i)) and is inventive in the light of the common general knowledge: s 18(1)(b)(ii). In contrast with the threshold test, the tests of both novelty and inventiveness connote an element of comparison, of assessment on the basis of the prior art at large, which the threshold test does not, the latter being confined to material contained in the application itself. Note that reference to the prior art that is disclosed in the application itself being made at the 'threshold stage' may motivate patent attorneys or applicants not to reveal certain relevant art in the specifications.

Novelty and inventiveness compared

8.2 The purpose of patent granting is to encourage new inventions, and no person should be granted a monopoly over an alleged invention that is, in fact, already known. Furthermore, an invention must show some inventive merit; that is, as well as not being known, it must not be an obvious thing to do or make. Thus, only inventions that are new and inventive are patentable by virtue of the Act. Section 18 requires novelty and inventiveness to be assessed separately, and, in fact, the two tests are very different in nature. As is indicated above, since the decision in *Philips v Mirabella*, application of the two tests is preceded by a threshold test of inventiveness and novelty on the face of the application. Unlike the threshold test, both the novelty test (s 18(1)(b)(i)) and the inventiveness test (s 18(1)(b)(ii)) require comparison with a wide body of 'prior art'. Generally speaking, this prior art consists of public disclosures of the invention before the priority date; that is, before the filing of an application. Such public disclosures can be either through documentary publication or through doing an act (eg, using the invention in public). They can be either by the applicant or by third parties and include, but are not limited to, disclosures in prior patent documents. Anything published after the priority date is of no consequence to the tests and cannot constitute an 'anticipation', whether it be a paper disclosure or disclosure by working the invention in public or supplying it (see s 23). The invention claimed must be novel compared with the prior art and must disclose an inventive step. The prior art information with which the claimed invention must be compared for the purposes of inventiveness was, before recent amendments (see Intellectual Property Laws Amendment (Raising the Bar) Act 2012 (Cth)), far more limited than the prior art for novelty. For the latter, any public disclosure anywhere in the world would constitute 'anticipation'. However, in assessing inventiveness in Australia, not all this prior art could be taken into account. Before the 'Raising the Bar' amendments, certain publications could not be used to undermine inventiveness. Post-2012, the prior art relevant to novelty and the prior art for inventiveness are closely aligned, but the relevant statutory language (see s 7(2) of the Patents Act 1990) remains complex. The Productivity Commission inquiry report into intellectual property (PC Report)[3] recommended further amendment to align the inventive step test more closely with the European equivalent. The draft bill proposed the following terms: 'For the purposes of this Act, an invention is taken to involve an inventive step when compared with the prior art base if the invention is not obvious to a person skilled in the relevant art.': see Pt 1 of Sch 1 of the Exposure Draft of the Intellectual Property Laws Amendment (Productivity Commission Response Part 2 and Other Measures) Bill 2019. However, the government has decided not to proceed with these amendments as yet. However, even if the prior art to be taken into account becomes more analogous for both novelty and inventiveness, the tests for each remain inherently different. The former requires a simple factual comparison (is the claimed invention the same as an alleged 'anticipation'?), whereas the latter requires a qualitative assessment of the difference between the two inventions (is the claimed invention a non-obvious step forward from the alleged anticipation?). The test of inventiveness calls on the notional 'person skilled in the art' to judge the quality of the advancement the claimed invention represents.

In *Sunbeam Corp v Morphy-Richards (Aust) Pty Ltd* (1961) 180 CLR 98; 35 ALJR 212, Windeyer J observed that the distinction between lack of novelty and obviousness was 'logically precise' and continued (at 418):

> When want of novelty was asserted, the thing or process claimed as an invention was assumed to be an invention, that is the product of the inventive faculties; but it was said that it was not now at the date of the patent, having been earlier invented and disclosed to the public. When want of subject matter, or lack of inventiveness, was asserted the thing or process claimed as an invention was assumed to be a new thing or process not previously disclosed to the public; but it was said that it was not really an invention and thus not a proper subject matter for the grant of a patent.

See also *Lockwood Security Products Pty Ltd v Doric Products Pty Ltd (No 2)* (2007) 235 CLR 173 (*Lockwood No 2*). Nonetheless, there is a danger of confusing the test of novelty and the test of inventive step when the two inventions being compared for the purpose of novelty are non-identical. Traditionally, there has been reliance in such a case on what Dixon J said in *Griffin v Isaacs* (1938) 12 ALJR 169 at 170 in referring to the test of novelty:

> Where variations from a device previously published consist in matters which make no substantial contribution to the working of the thing or involve no ingenuity or inventive step and the merit if any of the two things, considered as inventions, is the same, it is, I think, impossible to treat the differences as giving novelty.

However, under the 1952 and 1990 Acts, where novelty and inventiveness have become two clearly distinct matters, the danger implicit in Dixon J's approach is that the two tests will be conflated. There has thus been doubt about the application of Dixon J's test

3. Productivity Commission, *Intellectual Property Arrangements*, Inquiry Report No 78, Canberra, September 2016.

under contemporary patent law. Gummow J in *RD Werner & Co Inc v Bailey Aluminium Products Pty Ltd* (1989) 25 FCR 565; 13 IPR 513 at 550 said:

> In my view, in construing the grounds of opposition under the present Act [the 1952 Act] it is not an element in the objection on the ground of lack of novelty that whilst there was no anticipation in the necessary sense, nevertheless the difference in the two is to be disregarded because to come from the alleged anticipation to the alleged invention would not have involved the exercise of inventive ingenuity in the light of common general knowledge.

The test of novelty is thus rather whether the differences amount to mere mechanical equivalents; that is, if there are only minor differences with no functional implications, there will be anticipation: see also *Nicaro Holdings Pty Ltd v Martin Engineering Co* (1990) 16 IPR 545 per Gummow and Lockhart JJ. In recent cases, this has been the approach generally adopted: see, for example, Emmett J in *Speedy Gantry Hire Pty Ltd v Preston Erection Pty Ltd* (1998) 40 IPR 543 at 565: 'The prior publication must disclose all of the integers with the possible exception of the substitution of "mechanical equivalents to perform analogous purposes": *Nicaro Holdings Pty Ltd v Martin Engineering Co* (1990) 16 IPR 545 at 549; (1990) 91 ALR 513 at 517 per Lockhart J. That is to say, while it is possible that some detail may be supplied by the skilled reader of the patent, it is not permissible for an essential element not disclosed in the prior art to be supplied by common knowledge.'

Goldberg J in *MJA Scientifics International Pty Ltd v SC Johnson & Son Pty Ltd* (1998) 43 IPR 287 said:

> In order for a claim to lack novelty, the prior document must disclose all the essential integers of the claim. If it does, it is irrelevant that there are differences between the two which might be described as mere mechanical equivalents … Where the alleged anticipation does not disclose all the essential integers of the patent in suit, the fact that the skilled addressee could come from the alleged anticipation to the patent in suit without the exercise of inventive ingenuity in the light of common general knowledge does not establish lack of novelty.

This case related to a cockroach insecticide mat, 'pesticidal sheets or containers', sold under the name 'Dead End'. *MJA Scientifics*, in fact, usefully recites the steps to be taken in a novelty investigation.

The Test of Novelty

8.3 If claims in an application are anticipated (ie, the prior art information discloses them), then the application must fail, and the patent will be refused. The substance of the legal test is to be derived from the combined operation of ss 18 and 7 and the Schedule definitions of 'prior art base' and 'prior art information'. The Act requires a comparison between the invention and the 'prior art base'. The prior art base contains 'prior art information'. If the invention is publicly disclosed in the 'prior art information', it is not a new invention and not patentable. The comparison is only with information made public before the priority date. In other words, any publication or public use of the invention on or after the date of lodging of the application, either by the applicant or by a third party, is to be ignored for the purposes of the novelty test: see s 23. As to priority dates and fair basing, see Chapter 7 Patents: Subject Matter. The statutory provisions give guidance about not only which public information can be taken into account but also, to some degree, how it can be used. In particular, s 7(1) teaches the extent of 'mosaicing' that is permissible; that is, when certain separate documentary publications can be taken together to constitute one source of anticipation. Such permitted mosaicing is the exception, as normally only a single document or a single act is relevant.

The prior art information

8.4 The prior art information consists of two broad categories of material: prior publications in documentary form and prior publications by 'doing an act'. If the invention has been made publicly available in a document (in the broad sense; ie, it could be a drawing, photograph or literary description stored in any form, either traditional or on the internet or a publicly available electronic database) or by 'doing an act' anywhere in the world, the invention applied for will be 'anticipated', and the standard patent application must be rejected. The doing of an act in public is normally supported by some documentary or 'objective' evidence to that effect (eg, the tendering of an object, a contemporaneous report or photographs). However, the evidence can be exclusively that of witnesses who attest to what they saw at the time; in *Sandvik Intellectual Property AB v Quarry Mining & Construction Equipment Pty Ltd* [2017] FCAFC 138 the oral and affidavit evidence of witnesses as to their observations of the use of a certain piece of mining equipment was accepted as sufficient evidence of anticipation although it was not supported by any contemporaneous 'objective evidence'. Publications by both the applicant and by unrelated third parties will constitute anticipation, as will publications by parties who derive the information from the patentee, unless it occurs without the latter's consent: see s 24(1)(b). However, a publication by the applicant before the priority date but during the 'grace period' does not constitute anticipation. The grace period was introduced to mitigate the potentially harsh effect of inventors or applicants unwittingly destroying their ability to obtain a patent by their own actions. The 'grace period' in Australia was introduced on 1 April 2002 by regulatory amendment: see Patent Regulations 1991, reg 2.2(1A) and s 24(1)(a) of the Act. A public disclosure by the patentee must be ignored if they lodge an application within 12 months from the date of disclosure. Grace periods are not harmonised by any international instrument and thus vary across jurisdictions. Thus, a publication may benefit from the grace period in Australia but not in some other country, which limits its utility for applicants with a global patenting strategy.

A search is thus undertaken of as much of the relevant literature as the examiner (or patent attorney or applicant in preparing the application) can access. The applicant must also inform the Commissioner of the results of certain searches undertaken; for instance, by foreign patent offices: see s 45(3). However, it is, of course, impossible to access all sources of information on the subject matter of the invention: the search process is thus unavoidably imperfect. Documents that anticipate the invention may emerge during pre-granting opposition proceedings (see s 59(b) and s 60) — where a person opposing the application may bring them to the attention of the Commissioner — or, for instance, after grant on the hearing of a counterclaim for invalidity in an action for infringement: see s 121.

As noted above, by virtue of s 7, only if the invention is disclosed in a single source of information will there be anticipation. In other words, so-called 'mosaicing' — that is, proving anticipation by piecing together information from disparate sources — is not permissible. The only exception is if the invention emerges from several publications that a person skilled in the art concerned would treat as a single source; for example, because of cross-referencing or where two parts of an article are published separately, or because they are related to the same object and there is a 'reference in one [document] directing attention to another': see *Ramset Fasteners (Aust) Pty Ltd v Advanced Building Systems Ltd* (1999) 44 IPR 481 at 487. All the essential elements of the invention must be revealed in the single source. In the words of Aickin J in *Minnesota Mining & Manufacturing Co v Beiersdorf (Australia) Ltd* (1980) 144 CLR 253 at 293; 1A IPR 231 at 255–6 (the *3M* case):

> The making of a mosaic prohibited in the case of an allegation of want of novelty is the picking out of individual items of information from prior publications or prior objects and assembling them together so as to give them an appearance of unity and then alleging that such mosaic reveals the very thing claimed. That is an understandable, though not a permissible, process.

See also *Advanced Building Systems Pty Ltd v Ramset Fasteners (Aust) Pty Ltd* (1993) 26 IPR 171 at 178ff per Hill J in the Full Federal Court. Note that in relation to inventiveness, the situation is different: see further below at 8.7 Inventiveness. Other than by publication in a document, anticipation may now occur by the public doing of an act anywhere in the world, as opposed to only within Australia as previously: see Patents Amendments Act 2001 (Cth). The doing of an act may be, for example, a demonstration, the supply of goods, the use of an invention or the giving of an oral description without an obligation of confidence attaching to the listener or audience. As to whether an obligation of confidence subsists in relation to certain communications, see generally *Coco v AN Clark (Engineers) Ltd* (1968) 1A IPR 587 and Chapter 11 Breach of Confidence: Elements of the Action and see also *Fractionated Cane Technology Ltd v Ruiz-Avila* [1998] 1 Qd R 51.

But disclosure by doing an act may also be by totally unrelated parties in circumstances of which the applicant is not aware. The persons using the invention may themselves be totally unaware of its significance, the use itself appearing trivial or unrelated to systematic research or inventive activity. For example, in *Windsurfing International Inc v Petit* [1984] 2 NSWLR 196, the anticipation by use consisted of some young boys having themselves constructed, in a very amateurish fashion, a canoe with a centrally placed mast, which was sailed — if rather unsuccessfully — on a sea lake in Western Australia, a public place with no restrictions on access, by standing up and holding on to the mast, the mast being used to steer the boat, jibe and go about. As a result, the invention at stake, consisting, in essence, of the rotating and flexibly mounted central mast of a sailboard, was anticipated. Information will be publicly available only if a person to whom the information is disclosed in that person's capacity as a member of the public is free, in law and equity, to make use of the information. To prove anticipation, it is not necessary to establish that the invention was actually accessed, generally known or known to many: see, for example, *Acme Bedstead Co Ltd v Newlands Brothers Ltd* (1937) 58 CLR 689; 1A IPR 32 and *Merck & Co Inc v Arrow Pharmaceuticals Ltd* FCA Cited (2006) 154 FCR 31; 68 IPR 511. In *Sunbeam Corp v Morphy-Richards (Australia) Pty Ltd* (1961) 180 CLR 98; 1B IPR 625 at 634, Windeyer J said:

> Since the question was, 'is it new or has it been earlier disclosed?', it was immaterial whether or not it had become known to many people or to few people. A description in an obscure publication would suffice to destroy novelty, provided that it was a publication, that is to say that the document whether or not it was read generally by the public, had been available to the public: and similar considerations applied to publication by user.

See also *RD Werner and Co Inc v Bailey Aluminium Products Pty Ltd* (1989) 85 ALR 679; (1989) 25 FCR 565; 13 IPR 513 at 539–40. A document can still be publicly available even if there are restrictions on access to the document; for instance, an obligation to pay an entry fee to a library, or membership only access to a collection of materials. An anticipating disclosure may be available only in a remote place or in a foreign language: see, for example, *Dennison Manufacturing Co v Monarch Marketing Systems Inc* (1983) 1 IPR 431 (documentary disclosure).

Sufficient publication

8.5 To anticipate a claim, a prior publication must contain clear and unmistakable directions to do what the patentee claims to have invented: see *General Tire & Rubber Co v The Firestone Tyre & Rubber Co Ltd* [1972] RPC 457 at 485–6. In other words, the disclosure must be such that to a reader adopting the mantle of a skilled addressee the invention has been sufficiently revealed: see *Freeman v TJ & FL Pohlner Pty Ltd* (1994) 30 IPR 377 at 384, per Black CJ and Gummow and O'Loughlin JJ. It must also have disclosed the complete invention:

> The information comprising the prior art base must disclose to a person skilled in the relevant art all the essential features or integers of the invention the subject of the challenged patent. That information must enable the notional skilled addressee at once to perceive and understand and be able practically to apply the discovery, without the necessity of making further experiment: [see Drummond J in *Stanway Oyster Cylinders Pty Ltd v Marks* (1996) 66 FCR 577; (1996) 35 IPR 71].

In *Alphapharm Pty Ltd v H Lundbeck A/S* (2008) 76 IPR 618, Lindgren J quoted the following useful passage from the English Court of Appeal's reasons in *General Tire & Rubber* at 485–6, which his Honour said had been applied in many other cases, including *ICI Chemicals & Polymers Ltd v Lubrizol Corporation Inc* (2000) 106 FCR 214; 49 IPR 513 (*ICI v Lubrizol*):

> If the prior inventor's publication contains a clear description of, or clear instructions to do or make, something that would infringe the patentee's claim if carried out after the grant of the patentee's patent, the patentee's claim will have been shown to lack the necessary novelty, that is to say, it will have been anticipated. The prior inventor, however, and the patentee may have approached the same device from different starting points and may for this reason, or it may be for other reasons, have so described their devices that it cannot be immediately discerned from a reading of the language which they have respectively

> used that they have discovered in truth the same device; but if carrying out the directions contained in the prior inventor's publication will inevitably result in something being made or done which, if the patentee's patent were valid, would constitute an infringement of the patentee's claim, this circumstance demonstrates that the patentee's claim has in fact been anticipated. If, on the other hand, the prior publication contains a direction which is capable of being carried out in a manner which would infringe the patentee's claim, but would be at least as likely to be carried out in a way which would not do so, the patentee's claim will not have been anticipated, although it may fail on the ground of obviousness. To anticipate the patentee's claim the prior publication must contain clear and unmistakeable directions to do what the patentee claims to have invented: *Flour Oxidising Co Ltd v Carr & Co Ltd* (1908) 25 RPC 428 at 457, line 34, approved in *BTH Co Ltd v Metropolitan Vickers Electrical Co Ltd* (1928) 45 RPC 1 at 24, line 1. A signpost, however clear, upon the road to the patentee's invention will not suffice. The prior inventor must be clearly shown to have planted his flag at the precise destination before the patentee.

As to combination patents, see the *3M* case at CLR 266. If the known elements combine to produce a new result through their interaction, there is a patentable invention that may be novel if not disclosed in the prior art information. Otherwise, if there is a mere collocation, novelty is lacking because all the elements, which must then be viewed individually, are already known. There will be anticipation only if all integers of the combination are published together in a single source.

It is not permissible to claim anticipation on the basis of each individual element of a combination patent being individually known from different sources or circumstances. If the application is for a 'selection patent', it may be that the invention is novel although consisting of known elements, as long as the selection process has identified characteristics of the elements that had not been known before the priority date: see, for example, *EI Du Pont de Nemours & Co (Witsiepe's) Application* [1982] FSR 303; (1982) 1A IPR 297.

It may well be that examination reveals an identical prior published invention, either in documentary form, or by use. But there are often slight differences between the applied for invention and the alleged anticipation. A comparative test must then be applied, distinguishing an anticipation from what is, in truth, a different invention. Subject to some provisos, the 'reverse infringement test', clearly formulated in *Griffin v Isaacs* (1938) 12 ALJR 169; 1B IPR 619, is to be applied. Would the alleged anticipation amount to an infringement if the patent applied for had been granted? See, for example, *Meyers Taylor Pty Ltd v Vicarr Industries Ltd* (1977) 137 CLR 228 at 235 and see also *Nicaro Holdings Pty Ltd v Martin Engineering Co* (1990) 91 ALR 513 at 517; 16 IPR 545. A recurring proviso is that the reverse infringement test cannot be applied literally: see *Merck & Co Inc v Arrow Pharmaceuticals Ltd* (2006) 154 FCR 31; 68 IPR 511 at 537–8. The first step will be to properly construe both the prior publication and the claims of the patent: see *Aristocrat Technologies Australia Pty Ltd v IGT (Australia) Pty Ltd* (2007) 73 IPR 545. Once that is done, the reverse infringement test can be applied. Of vital importance is the fact that '... on a question of infringement, the issue is not whether the words of the claim can be applied with verbal accuracy or felicity to the article or device alleged to infringe. It is whether the substantial idea disclosed by the specification and made the subject of a definite claim has been taken and embodied in the infringing thing.': *Radiation Ltd v Galliers and Klaerr Pty Ltd* (1938) 60 CLR 36 at 51 and *Populin v H B Nominees*

Pty Ltd (1982) 41 ALR 471 at 475. "'Clear and umistakeable directions" to do what the patentee claims to have invented are necessary.': see *Imperial Chemicals Industries Pty Ltd v Commissioner of Patents* (2004) 63 IPR 476 at 488. In *Morellini v Mizzi Family Holdings Pty Ltd* [2016] FCAFC 13 it was also pointed out that an allegation of prior use must be 'strictly proved in the sense that the court determining that question must be satisfied that the proof given is sufficient in the circumstances, having regard to the gravity of the allegation': at [74], citing *Windsurfing International Inc v Petit* at 231. On a final note, whether there is anticipation will often turn on a proper construction of the claims language; as illustrated by *Kinabalu Investments Pty Ltd v Barron & Rawson Pty Ltd* [2008] FCAFC 178, where the applicable principles are well summarised at [44]–[45].

Prior claiming, exceptions and secret use

8.6 Under the 1952 Act, a separate ground of invalidity referred to as 'prior claiming' applied to anticipation by the publication of a prior patent application for the same invention. The 1990 Act subsumed the separate test of 'prior claiming' under the general novelty test: see s 7(1)(c); Sch 1 'prior art base' subparagraph (b)(ii). In other words, certain prior applications that have been published and have an earlier priority date are part of the relevant prior art. The published specification may be for the same invention and thus constitute anticipation, or it may contain information that in some other way discloses the applied for invention and thus anticipates it, without the claimed invention itself being the same: see the definition of 'prior art base' in Sch 1.

There are a number of exceptions to the general rules concerning anticipation: see s 24. By virtue of s 24(1)(a) and reg 2.2(d) of the Patents Regulations 1991 (Cth), a public use for the purpose of reasonable trial where the nature of the invention renders a public trial necessary will not defeat a patent application. The 'grace period', as is mentioned above, is also, in effect, an exception to the rules concerning anticipation.

Note, however, that secret use of the invention by the patentee before the priority date is a basis for revocation of a patent: see s 18(1)(d). Secret use in this context may be by the patentee itself or by related parties. The intention of this provision is to prevent a person from obtaining a monopoly after already having secretly exploited the invention (and thus, in effect, extending the monopoly period). Secret use in this context is to be taken as any use that secures a commercial advantage: see s 9(c), listing a number of uses that are not to be taken to be secret uses, and *Azuko Pty Ltd v Old Digger Pty Ltd* (2001) 52 IPR 75 at 116; [2001] FCA 1079. Full-scale commercial production or preparation are of course included, but it may be that even offering an invention for sale or licence, under strict conditions of confidentiality, could amount to secret use by the patentee and render the patent liable to be struck down: see *Azuko* at [131] and *Wheatley's Patent Application* (1984) 2 IPR 450. As in the context of novelty, one instance is sufficient. An inventor should thus be extremely careful not to take any steps that could confer a commercial advantage before the patent application is lodged, although secret use for the purposes of reasonable trial and experiment is permitted, as is indicated above: see s 9(a) and *Grove Hill Pty Ltd v Great Western Corporation Pty Ltd* (2002) 55 IPR 257. The key question is whether the true purpose of the use is for trial, and whether the trial is reasonable, 'in which case any collateral commercial advantage of the inventor is irrelevant': see *Coretell Pty Ltd v Australian Mud Co Pty Ltd* [2017] FCAFC 54 at [231]. By contrast, prior use by a third party if conducted secretly does not undermine any patent application, as it does not constitute anticipation. Under s 119, a person exploiting an invention at the time of filing by an unrelated applicant may continue to do so when a patent is granted by virtue of a 'prior user right'.

Inventiveness

Elements of the test

8.7 Section 18(1)(b)(ii) requires an invention to involve an inventive step. Section 7(2)–(3) and Sch 1 identify the elements of the test for inventiveness, which requires a judgment quite different from the test for novelty and allows 'common general knowledge' at the relevant time to be considered, as well as specific prior publications. Oliver LJ in *Windsurfing International Inc v Tabur Marine (Great Britain) Ltd* [1985] RPC 59 divided the inquiry into inventiveness into four steps (at 73–4):

> The first is to identify the inventive concept embodied in the patent in suit. Thereafter, the court has to assume the mantle of the normally skilled but unimaginative addressee in the art at the priority date and impute to him what was, at that date, common general knowledge in the art in question. The third step is to identify what, if any, differences exist between the matter cited as being 'known or used' and the alleged invention. Finally, the court has to ask itself whether, viewed without any knowledge of the alleged invention, those differences constitute steps which would have been obvious to the skilled man or whether they require any degree of invention.

In giving the judgment of the High Court in *Wellcome Foundation Ltd v VR Laboratories (Aust) Pty Ltd* (1981) 148 CLR 262; 1A IPR 268 at 271 (*Wellcome Foundation v VR Laboratories*), Aickin J put it as follows:

> … the question of obviousness involves asking the question whether the invention would have been obvious to a non-inventive worker in the field, equipped with the common general knowledge in that particular field as at the priority date, without regard to documents in existence but not part of such common general knowledge.

Since that passage was written, the statutory provisions have evolved, and inventiveness is no longer judged only in the light of the common general knowledge alone but also takes into account certain 'specific pieces of prior art information', as emerges from the terms of s 7(2):

> For the purposes of this Act, an invention is to be taken to involve an inventive step when compared with the prior art base unless the invention would have been obvious to a person skilled in the relevant art in the light of the common general knowledge as it existed in the patent area before the priority date of the relevant claim, whether that knowledge is considered separately or together with the information mentioned in subsection (3).

The 'information mentioned in subsection (3)' is:

> (a) any single piece of prior art information; or (b) a combination of any 2 or more pieces of prior art information that the skilled person mentioned in subsection (2) could, before the priority date of the relevant claim, be reasonably expected to have combined.

By virtue of the Patents Amendment Act 2001 (Cth), the rules concerning combining pieces of information or 'mosaicing' in the context of inventiveness were relaxed; previously, the rule concerning mosaicing was more restrictive, as it is in the context of novelty. By permitting the combining of relevant publications without restriction, the statutory change has made it easier to show that an invention is obvious; in other words, it has increased the level of inventiveness required, also taking into account that by virtue of the same Act, public use or documents published anywhere in the world can now potentially be taken into account. To that is also added the 'common general knowledge'; that is, the background knowledge of persons involved in the relevant art. The complexity of the test as set out in s 7(2) compares unfavourably with the much simpler terms used in art 56 of the European Patent Convention. The PC Report recommended adopting the European approach instead, thereby also seeking to augment the level of inventiveness required, yet another step in a long drawn-out process of statutory reform. An exposure draft bill (the Intellectual Property Laws Amendment (Productivity Commission Response Part 2 and Other Measures) Bill 2018), since withdrawn to allow further consultations, contains the following replacement for s 7(2)–(3): 'For the purposes of this Act, an invention is taken to involve an inventive step when compared with the prior art base if the invention is not obvious to a person skilled in the relevant art.'

However, for the time being the provision remains as set out earlier. The crucial question is whether the invention would be obvious to a person armed with the common general knowledge of persons skilled in the art, and then, in a next stage, further armed with knowledge of the information mentioned in subs (3). The common general knowledge can be combined with any such piece of information, or considered alone, or it could be that a claim is obvious solely in the light of one piece or a combination of pieces of prior art information.

The person skilled in the art

8.8 While a court may be assisted by expert evidence about the attributes of the 'person skilled in the art' in a particular field, the expert's judgment cannot be substituted for the judgment of the court. Ultimately, a judge must effectively 'don the mantle' of the person skilled in the art and make an objective assessment through that nominal person's eyes. The person skilled in the art (or 'skilled addressee') is the 'normally skilled but unimaginative addressee' in the area of invention; that is, a person skilled in the art but lacking inventive capacity: see, for example, *Speedy Gantry Hire Pty Ltd v Preston Erection Pty Ltd* (1998) 40 IPR 543. This does not mean that the person cannot be highly qualified and skilled: see *Britax Childcare Pty Ltd v Infa-Secure Pty Ltd (No 4)* [2015] FCA 651 (at [224]), citing *JMVB Enterprises Pty Ltd v Camoflag Pty Ltd* [2005] FCA 1474; (2005) 67 IPR 68 and *Australian Mud Co Pty Ltd v Coretell Pty Ltd* (2010) 88 IPR 270; [2010] FCA 1169. In some cases, particularly because of the high level of skill or inventiveness inherent in workers in a certain area, it may be difficult to 'model' a person skilled in the art 'lacking inventive capacity'; for instance, in biotechnology or another highly scientific area: see, for example, *Genentech Inc v Wellcome Foundation Ltd* (1988) 15 IPR 423 (DNA technology). Such a person may form part of a highly skilled and well-informed team. In other cases, the person skilled in the art may, in fact, be a team or research group: see *Minnesota Mining & Manufacturing Co v Tyco Electronics Pty Ltd* (2002) 56 IPR 248. That one or another identified person in the field testifies that the breakthrough is inventive is not necessarily relevant; it is the nominal 'person skilled in the art', as construed by the court, armed with common general knowledge and certain pieces of information, through whose eyes inventiveness must be assessed. The characteristics of the person skilled in the art will vary considerably depending on the nature and field of the invention.

Common general knowledge

8.9 A certain level of knowledge and experience must be imputed to the person skilled in the art. Such 'common general knowledge' is part of the ordinary equipment of all persons engaged in the relevant art; that is, the general background knowledge and experience that they put to use in the exercising of that branch of industry or manufacture: see, for example, *Graham Hart Pty Ltd v S W Hart & Co Pty Ltd* (1977) 141 CLR 305; 4A IPR 219. The common general knowledge stands apart from specific publications, but it may be that the person skilled in the art is considered to know certain things because such persons routinely consult certain publications (eg, a standard trade journal) or even attend a particularly significant annual conference: see, for example, *Dyno Nobel Asia Pacific Ltd v Orica Australia Pty Ltd* (1999) 99 FCR 151. Normally, what is or is not within the common general knowledge of a person skilled in the art will be the object of extensive evidence from persons active in the relevant field of endeavour. It may be directed at general background knowledge or at the question of whether the invention claimed or a clear anticipation was, in fact, already part of the common general knowledge at that time; for instance, because the product was already in circulation or had been presented in generally attended trade shows or meetings in Australia: see, for example, *Minnesota Mining & Manufacturing Co v Tyco Electronics Pty Ltd*. The crucial underlying issue will often be whether the person giving the evidence concerning common general knowledge is, in fact, a witness properly representative of the class of persons skilled in the particular art at stake: see also 8.10.

The person skilled in the art with that common general knowledge is then 'armed with' further knowledge of specific sources of information published in some form; for instance, it could be a journal article or a prior patent application: see *Bristol-Myers Squibb Co v Apotex Pty Ltd* [2015] FCAFC 2. Then the question is asked whether the invention as claimed would be obvious or not in the eyes of the skilled person. Note that the question of what forms part of the common general knowledge and what may be taken into account under the third limb of s 7 are often closely related.

The test of obviousness in operation: *Lockwood No 2*

8.10 With the 1990 Act, the Commonwealth Parliament elevated the threshold test of inventiveness by increasing the prior art information that can be taken into account and also by liberalising the manner of its use. As is indicated above, later amendments have further enhanced the level of inventiveness required. Relevant information has not been restricted to 'common general knowledge' since the 1990 Act was first introduced.

The Commonwealth has now gone so far as to allow all prior art information to be used, as in the UK.

Prior to the 'Raising the Bar' amendments, a selection process had to be applied to prior art information when considering inventiveness. This test was examined by the High Court in *Firebelt Pty Ltd v Brambles Australia Ltd* (2002) 54 IPR 449, the court endorsing the construction of the relevant s 7 adopted by Burchett J in *Tidy Tea Ltd and Lyons Tetley Ltd v Unilever Australia Ltd* (1995) 32 IPR 405, where his Honour stressed that relaxation of the rule prohibiting reliance on prior disclosures not part of the common general knowledge did not mean that in 'all circumstances such a disclosure might be used to some relevant effect': see *Firebelt* at 459. The High Court examined the old selection test in *Lockwood No 2*: see, in that regard, van Caenegem, 'Case Note — Inventiveness in Lockwood No 2' (2008) 20(1) *Bond L R* 110.

KD Kanopy Australasia Pty Ltd v Insta Image Pty Ltd (2007) 71 IPR 615 is a further good illustration of the old selective approach to prior art information. The question was whether certain US patents held not to be part of the common general knowledge could reasonably have been ascertained by the person skilled in the art in the relevant field of art. The person skilled in the art was held to be a designer/constructor in the awning, tent and shade structure business and not per se an engineer. In the absence of publications about the art, the person skilled in the art was held unlikely to have ascertained (etc) the US patents. Although with the introduction of the 'Raising the Bar' amendments, the selection issues disappear, it should be noted that due to the operation of the relevant transition provisions, the pre-amendment terms might still apply to earlier patents.

The level of inventiveness required

8.11 The next question is whether the person skilled in the art armed with the common general knowledge and specific pieces of information would consider the invention obvious or not. We have already seen that we must take the person skilled in the art as a person without special inventive talent. Whether the invention was in fact obvious to any particular real and identified person is irrelevant. The degree of inventiveness is assessed by:

1. identifying the 'inventive concept';
2. comparing that concept with what was 'known and used'; and
3. considering whether in that light the concept had some degree of inventiveness or was obvious to the person skilled in the art, as construed.

Gleeson, Gaudron, Gummow and Hayne JJ stressed in *Aktiebolaget Hassle v Alphapharm Pty Ltd* (2002) 56 IPR 129 at 138 that one need not go beyond the ordinary dictionary meaning of 'obvious'; that is, something 'very plain'. The word does not have any technical meaning. Cases have thus stressed that a scintilla of inventiveness will suffice, or that an invention is inventive enough if a person skilled in the art is 'not directly led as a matter of course' to the particular solution. The PC Report stressed repeatedly that this is a very low standard and quite out of step with the higher standard applied in Europe if not elsewhere. It therefore recommends that the Explanatory Memorandum of any Act amending the inventive step requirements should state that 'a "scintilla" of invention, or a scenario where the skilled person would not "directly be led as a matter of course", are insufficient thresholds for meeting the inventive step; [and that] the "obvious to try" test applied in Europe would in some instances be a suitable test': see PC Report, Recommendation 7.2, p 33. As the required amendments have been put on hold, it remains to be seen what will transpire in due course.

The present test has often been explained by reference to the words of Lord Herschell in *Vickers, Sons and Co Ltd v Siddell* (1890) 15 App Cas 496 at 502: whether the subject of the patent was 'so obvious that it would at once occur to anyone acquainted with the subject, and desirous of accomplishing the end'. Even if 'no smallness or simplicity will prevent a patent being good' (eg, *Meyers Taylor* at CLR 249), it must nonetheless be possible to identify some small or simple idea that is inventive. Sometimes, the question is whether it was obvious to take a certain step or direction in resolving a problem. What needs to be asked is whether experiments were 'of a routine character' to be tried 'as a matter of course'; if not, they are part of the inventive step: see *Aktiebolaget Hassle* at IPR 143. In that case, the High Court rejected the English approach, which mandates, first, formulating the invention in terms of a problem/solution, and, second, inquiring whether it would be worthwhile to try each integer of the combination to overcome the recognised problem: see also *JMVB Enterprises* (but see the PC Report's Recommendation 7.2, mentioned in the previous paragraph). *Alphapharm* concerned inventiveness under the Patents Act 1952 (Cth). The court stressed that even in relation to a combination patent, the ultimate question was simply whether the invention as claimed was 'very plain'. It was not correct to ask, where an inventor had been faced with multiple possible ways of solving a problem, whether each integer of a combination was worth trying. The question was not whether each integer was obvious but whether the combination was obvious.

It is not required to postulate an ignorant (as opposed to an uninspired) person skilled in the art. Although the perception of the true nature of a problem may supply the level of inventiveness required, where that problem is perfectly apparent, there is no inventiveness in its perception alone: see *Allsop Inc v Bintang Ltd* (1989) 15 IPR 686. However, it may be that the solution to the problem is obvious, but the problem is not itself part of the common general knowledge or revealed by s 7(3) information. In those circumstances there may yet be sufficient inventiveness: see *AstraZeneca v Apotex* at [203]ff. Alternatively, if there is a recognised problem or need, the question is whether an unimaginative person working in the field would think that the solution that the invention represents would be something worth trying in order to solve the problem: see *Coopers Animal Health Australia Ltd v Western Stock Distributors Pty Ltd* (1987) 15 FCR 382; 11 IPR 20. Whether an invention is the result of close study, experimentation and research or of some sudden lucky inspiration or insight matters not: per Aickin J in *Wellcome Foundation v VR Laboratories* at CLR 272. However, if a process of research is in evidence, the approach is to ask 'Were the experiments "part of" that inventive step claimed in the patent or were they "of a routine character" to be tried "as a matter of course"? If the latter be attributable to the hypothetical addressee of the Patent, such a finding would support a holding of obviousness.': see *Aktiebolaget Hassle* at IPR 142.

In the context of assessing sufficient inventiveness, courts consistently point out the dangers of hindsight. One must guard against the common psychological process that makes things look obvious when they have been known for a while: see, for example, *Colgate-Palmolive v Cussons Pty Ltd* (1993) 46 FCR 225. The warning about hindsight is particularly apt in the context of combination patents: see *Austal Ships Pty Ltd v Stena Rederi Aktiebolag* (2005) 66 IPR 420.

Given the highly technical and difficult nature of the many judgments ultimately required, there will be heavy reliance on expert evidence to assist the court; note, however, that a judge has the power to appoint an assessor to assist the court as an independent expert, although this does not frequently happen: see s 217 of the Patents Act 1990; *Genetic Institute Inc v Kirin-Amgen Inc (No 2)* [1997] FCA 1058. Judging obviousness is neither easy nor predictable in its outcome. The test is a multi-step one so that before the point of final judgment a considerable number of intermediate judgments will already have been made. As the High Court pointed out in *Lockwood Security Products Pty Ltd v Doric Products Pty Ltd* (2007) 72 IPR 447 (*Lockwood No 1*), inventiveness is a question of fact, one 'borne out by the evidence of experts' and 'also "one of degree and often [...] by no means easy", because ingenuity is relative, depending as it does on relevant states of common general knowledge': at IPR 461. On a final note, the inventive step must concern an invention, and not merely an elucidation or explanation of scientific mechanisms underlying a useful phenomenon already known: see *Otsuka Pharmaceutical Co Ltd v Generic Health Pty Ltd (No 2)* [2016] FCAFC 111.

Secondary indicators of inventiveness

8.12 Sometimes, the question of whether an invention is obvious is referred to as 'a kind of jury question': see, for example, *Allmanna Svenska Elektriska A/B v The Bruntisland Shipbuilding Co Ltd* (1952) 69 RPC 63 at 70 per Jenkins LJ. Therefore, all relevant circumstances can be taken into account. Thus, although, in the end, obviousness is a question of judgment through the eyes of the nominal person skilled in the art, some objective indicators of inventiveness (sometimes referred to as 'secondary' indicators) may be relevant and the subject of admissible evidence. But how persuasive is such evidence? The High Court has repeatedly issued warnings about the limited value of secondary evidence, inter alia in *Firebelt* (see 8.10 and further below). In this, it echoes similar warnings emanating from superior courts in other jurisdictions. Evidence of the course of research and experimentation, to show whether the experiments were of a routine character or were part of an inventive step, may be admissible: see *Wellcome Foundation v VR Laboratories*. It might be relevant that, despite the extent of the common general knowledge at the time, no worker in the field had reached a point equivalent to the patent: as considered in *AstraZeneca v Apotex* at [550]. Also admissible may be evidence of a long-felt need or 'want', the fact of immediate imitation of the invention, resolution of a well-known practical problem and evidence of the failure of other attempts to solve the well-known problem (see *Elconnex Pty Ltd v Gerard Industries Pty Ltd* (1992) 25 IPR 173 at 182; *ICI v Lubrizol*). Evidence of commercial success has also been proffered to assist in establishing that something was not obvious. This was one of the issues before the High Court in *Firebelt*. The evidence of commercial success tendered by the patentee was described by the court as very 'exiguous': it appeared in truth not to be directed at establishing a link with the commercial success of the claimed invention. Evidence will be required to specifically establish that there is an actual connection between the incorporation of a patented invention and the commercial success claimed for a product.

Other Grounds for Rejection, Opposition and Revocation

Remaining requirements of s 18

8.13 There are two further requirements of patentability: that the invention be useful (s 18(1)(c)) and that the invention was not secretly used by the patentee before the priority date (s 18(1)(d)). If the invention is not useful, it will 'fail for inutility'. This is not to require social, economic or commercial utility but rather that the patented invention operates as claimed or obtains the results that are claimed for it. According to the Full Federal Court in *ESCO Corporation v Ronneby Road Pty Ltd* [2018] FCAFC 46 at [232], the history of the requirement teaches that the proper course is 'to recognise, [...] that utility "depends upon" whether, by following the teaching of, in this case, the Patent Application, the result claimed is produced. That involves identifying, as a matter of construction, the promise of the invention and asking whether the invention as claimed does what it is intended by the patentee to do.' Utility has arisen as a significant issue in the context of gene patents, and the Act was amended by insertion of s 7A following the recommendation of ALRC Report 99: *Genes and Ingenuity: Gene Patenting and Human Health* (2004) to 'provide that an invention will satisfy the requirement of usefulness only if the patent application describes a specific, substantial and credible use': Explanatory Memorandum (EM), Intellectual Property Law Amendment (Raising the Bar) Bill 2011, p 44. The EM also suggests that another concern was to prevent 'speculative claiming' of gene-based inventions (at p 45). However, s 7A was not intended to displace or change the existing law on utility. A kindred question can arise in the context of the 'manner of manufacture' examination (s 18(1)(a)), since an invention must offer a material advantage of significance to the economy to be patentable. There is also a close relationship with sufficiency, as an applicant may, in fact, have failed to supply sufficient information to enable a person skilled in the art to make the invention work. The relationship between the grounds for opposition and invalidity under s 40 and the requirements of s 18 are explored in *Lockwood No 1*. As to secret use, see 8.3 above.

Remaining requirements of ss 40 and 138

8.14 Most of the requirements of s 40 are dealt with above in the passages concerning claims. The remaining requirement not there dealt with is that of sufficiency, or enabling disclosure; that is, that a complete specification must 'disclose the invention in a manner which is clear enough and complete enough for the invention to be performed by a person skilled in the relevant art': s 40(2)(a). This requirement of adequate disclosure is critical to the 'social contract' described above; that is, in return for the full disclosure of the invention, the patentee obtains a 20-year monopoly in it. In *Kimberly-Clark Australia Pty Ltd v Arico Trading International Pty Ltd* (2001) 207 CLR 1; 50 IPR 513; [2001] HCA 8 at [25], the High Court quoted the following passage from a judgment of Romer LJ in *No-Fume Ltd v Frank Pitchford & Co Ltd* (1935) 52 RPC 231 at 243:

> [I]n other words, [it is essential] that the patentee should disclose his invention sufficiently to enable those who are skilled in the relevant art to utilise the invention after the patentee's monopoly has come to an end. Such disclosure is, indeed, the consideration that the patentee gives for the grant to him of a monopoly during the period that the patent would run.

See also *Austal Ships Sales Pty Ltd v Stena Rederi Aktiebolag* [2008] FCAFC 121 at [12]. Alternatively, the disclosure is intended to benefit the further development of the practical arts, within the constraints of the patentee's rights. The specification must therefore include 'the best method known to the applicant of performing the invention' (s 40(2)(aa)), and 'in the context of s 40(2)(aa), the "invention" is the embodiment which is described and around which the claims are drawn: *Kimberly-Clark* ... at [21]': see *Dometic Australia Pty Ltd v Houghton Leisure Products Pty Ltd* [2018] FCA 1573 at [201]; the principles are usefully reiterated in *Dometic* at [200]–[208]. On the one hand, the applicant must not play fast and loose with the requirement of disclosure, but on the other hand, need not disclose more than is necessary, and a patent will often be surrounded by a penumbra of trade secrets that aid the patentee in turning the invention efficiently to account. 'Insufficiency' will be found where the specification discloses insufficient information. Section 40(2)(a) 'requires a disclosure that would enable the addressee of the specification to produce something within each claim without new inventions or additions or prolonged study of matters presenting initial difficulty' as stated in *Les Laboratoires Servier v Apotex Pty Ltd* [2016] FCAFC 27 at [48], where 'the *Kimberly-Clark* test' refers to the High Court decision in *Kimberly-Clark*.

In that case, the High Court dealt with the question of whether, to determine if an invention was fully described as required by s 40, regard had to be had to both the claims and the body of the complete specification. The court pointed out that the relevant section indicates 'that the specification must be read as a whole and that reference to the claims may dispel ambiguity or uncertainty from the body of the specification concerning the description of the invention'. The court also asserted that the addressee, for the purpose of this question, is the skilled addressee armed with the common general knowledge, not an ignorant person. Therefore, an element that would be obvious to a skilled addressee to make the invention work need not be expressly referred to. Here, the element was the use of fluid-pervious (ie, permeable) material in the construction of diapers: see also more recently *Black & Decker Inc v GMCA Pty Ltd (No 2)* (2008) 76 IPR 99 at 107:

> There is no obligation on a patentee to describe more than a single preferred form of the invention. The ground of insufficiency is not made out merely because it is said there are other ways of carrying out the invention as to which the specification is not sufficiently precise: *No-Fume Ltd v Frank Pitchford & Co Ltd* (1935) 52 RPC 231 at 248 (*No-Fume*). The test is whether the disclosure in the specification will 'enable the addressee to produce something within each claim without new inventions or additions or prolonged study of matters presenting initial difficulty': *Kimberly-Clark Australia Pty Ltd v Arico Trading International Pty Ltd* ((2001) 50 IPR 513 at 523).

On a final point, the patentee cannot be allowed to mislead. Patents obtained by fraud, false suggestion or misrepresentation can be revoked: see s 138 (3)(d) and, for example, *Pfizer Overseas Pharmaceuticals v Eli Lilly & Co* (2005) 68 IPR 1. The test is whether the false suggestion materially contributed to the decision to grant the patent even if other circumstances or causes also played a part; it must be a 'material, inducing factor': see *Warner-Lambert Co LLC v Apotex Pty Ltd (No 2)* [2018] FCAFC 26 at [150].

The relationship between refusal of the application and revocation

8.15 At the examination stage, by virtue of s 45, the Commissioner must examine the conformity of the application with s 40, as well as whether the application concerns patentable subject matter (s 18(1)(a)), and that the invention is novel and involves an inventive step, but taking into account only documentary publication and not publication through 'doing an act'. An opposition before granting may be based on the following grounds (see s 59): the invention is not a patentable invention; the nominated person is not entitled to a grant of the patent for the invention, or only in conjunction with another person; or the specification does not comply with s 40(2) or (3). Commonly, multiple grounds are advanced in opposition proceedings: for a recent example, see *Bradken Resources Pty Ltd v Lynx Engineering Consultants Pty Ltd* (2012) 210 FCR 21; [2012] FCA 944; a lack of internal and/or external fair basing is a commonly advanced ground. At the post-granting stage, in the course of revocation proceedings by virtue of s 138, the grounds for revocation are the same as for opposition — additionally, further grounds are that the patentee has contravened a condition of the patent and that the patent was obtained by fraud, false suggestion or misrepresentation. On revocation after granting, see Chapter 9 Patents: Ownership, Assignment and Licence.

Bibliography

A Fox, 'Preparation of Expert Evidence — Patent Case Provides Useful Guidance — Case Note; *Gambro Pty Ltd v Fresenius Medical Care South East Asia Pty Ltd*' (2004) 17(2) *IPLB* 34.

A Lim and A Christie, 'A Comparative Analysis of the Australian Patent Office's Examination of Biotechnology Reach-Through Patent Claims' (2007) 33 *Mon L R* 115.

C Lawson, 'Evolution of "Inventive Step" — like Elements in Australian Patent Laws' (2007) 18(3) *AIPJ* 130.

C Lawson, 'Quantum of Obviousness in Australian Patent Laws' (2008) 19(1) *AIPJ* 43.

IP Australia, *Review of Patent Grace Periods*, August 2005.

J Blows, 'The High Court Shifts on Inventive Step' (2007) 20(3) *IPLB* 34.

J S Crennan, 'Obviousness — Different Paths Through Scylla and Charybdis' (2007) 71 *IP Forum* 12.

L Livingston, 'Revocation of a Patent for Prior Secret Use by a Patentee' (2003) 14(1) *AIPJ* 5.

M Padbury, 'Inventiveness Apart from Novelty and Inventive Step' (1998) 9 *AIPJ* 161 at 173.

P Conrick, 'Taking the Hassle out of Obviousness — Measuring Inventive Step' (2004) 16(8) *IPLB* 126.

Productivity Commission, *Intellectual Property Arrangements*, Inquiry Report No 78, Canberra, September 2016 (PC Report).

W Condon and R Hoad, 'Amazing Grace: New Grace Period for Patents in Australia' (2002) 15(6) *IPLB* 73.

W van Caenegem, 'Case Note — Inventiveness in Lockwood No 2' (2008) 20(1) *Bond L R* 110.

Chapter 9

Patents: Ownership, Assignment and Licence

Ownership of Patents and Inventions

Ownership of an invention: general principles

9.1 It is important to distinguish between the situation that applies before the filing of an application for the granting of a patent and the rules of ownership applying to a granted patent. The position after granting is relatively straightforward, since the patentee (ie, 'the person for the time being entered in the Register as the proprietor or grantee of the patent' (see Sch 1, Patents Act 1990 (Cth))) owns the patent and may deal with it as the absolute owner. More complex is the question of who has rights over an invention before it is patented; in other words, who is entitled to be granted a patent over a particular invention.

As a starting principle, the inventor owns the invention for the purposes of filing an application under the Patents Act 1990 (Cth), and others can derive title only through the inventor. The Act does not define the word 'inventor', but it is well established that only a 'true and first inventor', words derived from the Statute of Monopolies, has an entitlement under the Act. This is every person who 'performed the intellectual and practical work involved in the development of the invention': see *Stack v Davies Shephard* (2001) 108 FCR 422; 51 IPR 513. French J's identification of the relevant questions at first instance in *University of Western Australia v Gray (No 20)* (2008) 76 IPR 222; [2008] FCA 498 was noted with approval by the Full Court in *University of Western Australia v Gray* 179 FCR 346; 82 IPR 206; [2009] FCAFC 116 (*UWA v Gray*) at [253]: (1) identify the 'inventive concept' of the invention as defined in the claims; (2) determine inventorship including the person responsible for the inventive concept and the time of conception as distinct from its verification and reduction into practice; and (3) determine how many contractual or fiduciary relationships give rise to proprietary rights in the invention. Several persons might make a contribution to the 'inventive concept' sufficient to be considered co-inventors within s 15(1)(a), with co-ownership of patented inventions (see s 16) resulting from such joint inventorship. The key is the quality rather than the quantity of the contribution of the purported co-inventor: see *Neobev Pty Ltd v Bacchus Distillery Pty Ltd (admin apptd) (No 3)* [2014] FCA 4 at [108]. But a person who has merely been told about the invention by the true inventor is not entitled to the patent: see *Aspiring IP Ltd v Vision*

Systems Ltd [2010] FCA 1061 at [520]; nor is a person who only contributes to the verification and reduction to practice of an invention: see *Kafataris v Davis* [2016] FCAFC 134 at [65]. If there are two or more inventors, then 'one of two inventors each responsible for a part of the invention cannot claim a patent over the total invention. That is because such a patent would confer upon him or her the benefit of that part of the invention for which he or she was not responsible.': *Stack v Davies Shephard* at IPR 518. Therefore, '[e]ach may have been entitled to a patent over his part (if it was otherwise patentable) while they both may have been entitled to a joint patent over the whole': at 522; see also *Polwood Pty Ltd v Foxworth Pty Ltd* (2008) 165 FCR 527; 75 IPR 1; [2008] FCAFC 9. But if not all parties involved were 'true and first inventors', they cannot by some arrangement create an entitlement based only on inventorship, as opposed to based on s 15(1)(b) or s 15(1)(c). The latter contemplate a right to derive title from the inventor(s) based not on inventorship but on contract or equity: see, for example, *Neobev* (a conversation allegedly giving rise to joint ownership upon certain terms). If there are two or more inventors, subject to any agreement to the contrary, the inventors become co-owners of the resulting patent, each being entitled to an equal undivided share in it: see s 16(1)(a). In the modern context of systematic and team-based research, multiple co-inventors (eg, members of a research team or group who all made an intellectual contribution to the invention) may be quite common: see, for example, *Genentech Inc v Wellcome Foundation Ltd* (1989) 15 IPR 423. The 'person skilled in the art' in complex fields may also be a team of scientists: see, for example, *Eli Lilly & Co Ltd v Apotex Pty Ltd* [2013] FCA 214 at [165]ff and *AstraZeneca AB v Apotex Pty Ltd* (2014) 226 FCR 324; [2014] FCAFC 99. In the case of co-ownership of a patent, each party is entitled to exercise the exclusive rights given by it and to retain the benefit without accounting to the others (s 16(1)(b)), but none can license or assign (an interest in) it without the consent of the others (s 16(1)(c)).

However, although only certain categories of persons may be granted a patent, by virtue of s 29 any person may apply for a patent (under the 1952 Act, only a person entitled to the granting of a patent could apply for the patent). Pursuant to s 15(1), a patent may be granted to the inventor, a person entitled to an assignment upon grant and persons deriving title from either of those. An inventor may assign the benefit of the invention, and hence the right to apply for and be granted a patent, to a third party. Although an assignment of a granted patent must be in writing to be effective against others than the parties to the agreement (see further below 9.4), no such statutory rule applies to the assignment of a right to apply for and be granted a patent. In *Camilleri v Steel Foundations Limited* [2002] QSC 397, an employee's knowledge of, and consent in, his employer applying for a patent, and his assertions to third parties to the effect that the employer owned the invention, constituted an assignment of the right to obtain the patent. The Act does not expressly provide who may be 'entitled to have the patent assigned to them'. Who is so entitled is determined by recourse to principles elaborated in the case law over time. The most frequently occurring situation of entitlement is where the inventor is an employee and makes an invention in the course of employment. The employer is then a person 'entitled to have the patent assigned to the person' (s 15(1)(b)) by the inventor once it has been granted. At the same time, the employer is entitled to apply for the patent (as any person is: see s 29) and is also a person entitled to be granted the patent in the first place by virtue of s 15(1)(b). Apart from rights derived from a contract of employment, persons other than the inventor may be entitled to an assignment of a patent where the activity resulting in the invention has been commissioned and paid for by another party. In such a case, whether the principal or the inventor is entitled to the patent will depend on the express or implied terms of each individual contract. It may be that a contract provides that certain parties, although not entitled to ownership, will benefit in some measure from the exploitation of a patent. Alternatively, a duty to assign may derive from an institutional instrument (such as a university intellectual property statute, policy or regulation), which may also establish a benefit sharing arrangement, or alternatively from a broader agreement (for instance, a joint research and development contract between commercial partners).

Employee inventions

9.2 As indicated above, and in marked contrast with legislation in some other jurisdictions, the Patents Act 1990 (Cth) contains no express reference to employed inventors, their rights or those of their employers; compare this with the Copyright, Designs and Patents Act 1988 (UK) and the German Employee Inventions Act 1975. In those countries, legislation grants employees a statutory right to benefit directly from their patented inventions, in the latter in all cases and in the former where windfall profits are derived from exploiting the patent.

No such statutory provisions exist in Australia, whether relating to employee ownership or to benefit sharing. Therefore, a combination of contractual terms and common law rules determines whether an employed inventor has a duty to assign an invention to an employer or, having obtained a patent, hold it in trust for the employer. Contracts of employment may or may not contain express terms concerning patent ownership or benefit sharing; and employees might also sign an 'acknowledgment' that an invention of theirs was made in the ordinary course of employment and belongs to their employer in its entirety: see, for example, *Reckitt Benckiser Healthcare (UK) Ltd v Glaxosmithkline Australia Pty Ltd (No 5)* [2015] FCA 486 at [209]. University employers commonly purport to incorporate the terms of intellectual property policies or statutes into contracts with academic staff, but as to the effectiveness of such arrangements, see *University of Western Australia v Gray (No 20)* (2008) 76 IPR 222; [2008] FCA 498. The trial judge found that the university's regulations had not, in fact, effected a change to the terms of employment, and therefore the rights between the parties had to be resolved without reference to them. Further, where express terms are found in the contract of employment, these have been held subject to public policy restrictions on illegal restraints of trade. Terms that favour the employer too broadly will be void and unenforceable, and thus recourse will have to be had to the nature and extent of any residual common law duty to assign. See, for example, *Electrolux Ltd v Hudson* [1977] FSR 312, where the provision was so broad as to purport to apply to any invention made by the employee, whether or not the employee was employed to invent and whether or not the invention was related to the employee's duties. Generally speaking, a person who makes an invention should enjoy the benefit of it, unless paid by another party to make it. Terms that purport to grant employers unlimited rights over inventions that an employee was neither obliged nor paid to pursue are questionable. On the other hand, if the contract of employment does not contain express terms favouring the employer, this does not mean that employees automatically get the benefit of their inventions. The common law may require the invention to be assigned, depending on the circumstances, in particular where the inventor was employed to invent: see 9.3. Note that it will be important in all cases to establish, with reference to the rules of employment law, whether an inventor is an employee or is, in fact, an independent contractor; for an interesting example of this question arising in practice, see *Kwan v Queensland Corrective Services Commission* (1994) 31 IPR 25, a decision of a delegate of the Commissioner concerning the entitlement to a patent of prisoners in relation to an invention made while in detention. They were found not to be employees and thus entitled to the patent.

The duty to assign

9.3 It is well established under common law rules that either the inventor employee or the employer solely owns the invention: see *Sterling Engineering Co Ltd v Patchett* [1955] AC 534. In other words, neither joint ownership nor a right of the employee to participate in the profits derived from exploitation of a patented invention can arise in the absence of contractual terms to that effect. The common law tends to favour the employer, on the simple policy basis that the employee's just rewards are the remuneration derived from their contract of employment. As Lord Reid expressed it at 547:

> ... at the time when he made these inventions he was employed by the appellants as their chief designer and it is, in my judgment, inherent in the legal relationship of master and servant that any product of the work that the servant is paid to do belongs to the master: I can find neither principle or authority that this rule ceases to apply if a product of that work happens to be a patentable invention.

However, the principle expressed in *Victoria University of Technology v Wilson* (2004) 60 IPR 392 at 422; [2003] VSC 299 (*VUT v Wilson*) must also be heeded:

> [...] the mere existence of the employer/employee relationship will not give the employer ownership of inventions made by the employee during the term of the relationship. And that is so even if the invention is germane to and useful for the employer's business, and even though the employee may have made use of the employer's time and resources in bringing the invention to completion. Certainly, all the circumstances must be considered in each case, but unless the contract of employment expressly so provides, or an invention is the product of work which the employee was paid to perform, it is unlikely that any invention made by the employee will be held to belong to the employer.

So the central question is whether the invention was made in the ordinary course of the exercising of the duties the employee was engaged to perform: see *Evans Deakin Pty Ltd v Orekinetics Pty Ltd* [2002] 2 Qd R 345. In other words, did the inventor have a contractual duty to pursue the making of inventions? Where a person is employed in a different capacity (eg, as a storekeeper, as in *Electrolux v Hudson*; see above 9.2) or has no duty to pursue inventions on behalf of the employer, the duty to assign may not arise if an invention is nonetheless made.

In fact, recent decisions have indicated that the question of whether an employee had a duty to undertake activities that in the normal course of affairs would result in the making of inventions should be further refined to add the rider 'of that kind'. For instance, in *VUT v Wilson* the court held that the employee was under a duty to conduct academic research of the kind that would normally result in the publication of learned papers; his terms of employment did not encompass a duty to make inventions of the kind at stake (an electronic trading system). Therefore, on this approach, he was entitled to the benefit of that invention; other aspects of the case, however, resulted in the opposite outcome. In any case, academic employed inventors are a special category: see *UWA v Gray* below, which has, in fact, overturned this aspect of *VUT v Wilson*. In *Spencer Industries Pty Ltd v Collins* (2003) 58 IPR 425, duties as a sales manager, even though requiring demonstrable knowledge of technical aspects of products sold, did not extend to a duty to make and assign patentable improvements to the product range.

However, in some cases, a particular employee's fiduciary obligations will preclude them from obtaining ownership of the invention, even though they were not employed to invent. Some high-ranking employees or directors owe a broad duty not to usurp or divert a business opportunity and turn it to their own account, and obligations in relation to some new invention that might advance the business should be seen in that light. This will be the case if the employee is concerned with the overall management of the firm or has authority for 'running the business' (in *Spencer*, the sales manager was judged not to be in such a position) or in so close a confidential relationship that the benefit of the invention should reside with the employer. In contrast, in *Fine Industrial Commodities Ltd v Powling* (1954) 71 RPC 253, the managing director of the employer company was held to hold his interest in the invention he made in trust for the employer, although he was not employed to invent. Nonetheless, in *Eastland Technology Australia Pty Ltd v Whisson* (2005) 223 ALR 123 at 136–7, it was pointed out that the case '[was] authority for the proposition that the mere fact that a person is a director or employee of a company does not disqualify a person from taking out a patent for an invention made by him during his period of service even though the invention may relate to or be useful in the company's business'. In *Eastland*, Dr Whisson invented the 'Di-Med', which had the potential to impact adversely on the development and commercialisation prospects of the technology of Eastland, of which he was also a director. However, Malcolm CJ made an important distinction, where [he] said at 137:

> I am not persuaded that Dr Whisson was obliged to stifle his creative capacity or, alternatively, hold its fruits on trust for Eastland when that is outside what was bargained for. However, if Dr Whisson wished to attempt to commercialise the Di-Med invention without Eastland's involvement, it is my view he could not have done so whilst he remained a director of Eastland.

Also relevant in a borderline case may be whether:

- the invention is related to the ordinary duties of the employee;
- the invention is related to the nature of the employer's business;
- the employer's pre-existing intellectual property rights were relied on by the inventor;

- the employee had undertaken the activities because of a specific direction of the employer; and
- the invention was made during office hours and with the employer's facilities.

However, the remedy against employees using the employer's facilities to pursue their own interests is not necessarily a constructive trust over a resulting invention in favour of the employer. Instead, the appropriate remedy against an employee who misuses the employer's resources may, depending on the facts, lie rather in damages and the like. Note, however, that employees exploiting for their personal benefit a commercial opportunity derived from an invention that comes to them in their professional capacity during the term of employment may be found in breach of fiduciary obligations. This was ultimately held against Professor Wilson, who was characterised as 'a professional employee' owing certain fiduciary obligations: see *VUT v Wilson* at [141]–[149]. At [149], Nettle J said:

> On the other hand, and subject to contract, it remains unquestionable that professional employees owe to their employers' fiduciary obligations not to profit from their position at the expense of the employer and to avoid conflicts of interest and duty [72]. Accordingly, even if an employee is generally speaking free to work for someone else, he or she must avoid work which could conflict with the interests of the employer that the employee is paid to serve [73]. Correspondingly, in the absence of full and frank disclosure and consent, a professional employee remains bound to account to the employer for gains derived as a result of the employee's fiduciary position and for opportunities of which the employee may learn in the course of employment; lest the employee otherwise be swayed by considerations of personal interest. Nothing which has occurred in the last 30 years has altered any of that.

If it were not for other factual complications, the judge would have imposed a constructive trust in favour of the employer in the circumstances: see *VUT v Wilson* at [176].

Note also the later decision in *UWA v Gray*, where, upon careful consideration by the court of the academic employee's duties and all the surrounding circumstances, the result was also unfavourable to the employer.[1] The Full Federal Court agreed with the trial judge that academics' employment contracts fall into a separate category. Universities would never own the inventions of their ongoing academic employees unless expressly provided for in the employment contract, as this would be incompatible with their freedom to publish, to set their own research priorities and to collaborate with others. The cases considered above indicate that although the law may appear at face value to favour employers, in fact, detailed judicial consideration of the precise nature of the duties and circumstances in each case, and of the connection between the invention and the nature of the employer's business, means that employers making sweeping claims to employee inventions (and other intellectual property rights) will meet with considerable difficulties. In the end, courts are fairly vigilant that employers do not get more than what they paid or bargained for. It is also apparent from the cases that courts will subject express contractual terms or intellectual property policies

1. See C Arup, 'Employee Inventions: Labour Law Meets Intellectual Property' (2008) 21 *Australian Journal of Labour Law* 208, for useful insights into this complex case.

promulgated by employers to careful scrutiny. Note also that where an employer does not lay claim to an invention to which they may be entitled, either consciously or by reason of dilatoriness, the employee is doubtless entitled to patent it, and the employer may be excluded by their own conduct from requiring a subsequent assignment of the invention or patent.

Assignments and Licences

Assignment and the register

9.4 By virtue of s 13(2) of the Patents Act 1990 (Cth), a patent is personal property and may be assigned. An assignment must be written *and* signed by assignor and assignee (see s 14). The patentee may deal with the patent as absolute owner, subject only to those rights of others that appear on the register (s 189(2)), but trusts may not be registered: s 188. However, in *Stack v Brisbane City Council* (1996) 35 IPR 296 at 299, Drummond J recognised the creation of an equitable interest in a patent as between assignor and assignee where the contractual assignment was not registered at the relevant time:

> However, the 1990 Act does not prohibit the creation of equitable interests in registered patents. Section 188 goes no further than prohibiting the inclusion in the Register of a notice of any kind of trust relating to a patent. The Act recognises that the rights comprising a patent are personal property and can be dealt with as such: see s 13(2). Equitable interests can therefore be created in patents. Section 15(1)(b) and (c) provide for the grant of a patent to, inter alia, equitable owners. The enforceability of unregistered equities in relation to patents is acknowledged by the Act: see, eg, s 189(3) and s 196(b)(ii).

Thus, equities created by an unregistered assignment can be enforced against a patentee but not against a purchaser in good faith for value: s 189(3). Section 189 does not protect a person who deals with the patentee in bad faith and with notice of fraud on the part of the patentee. An equitable interest in a patent may give, in terms of actions for infringement, some limited rights: see *Stack v Brisbane City Council.*

Licences

9.5 An important distinction is to be made between an ordinary licensee and an exclusive licensee; that is, a licensee with 'the right to exploit the patented invention throughout the patent area to the exclusion of the patentee and all other persons': see Sch 1 of the Patents Act. An exclusive licensee has the right to initiate infringement proceedings. An exclusive licence can be limited to a term shorter than the life of the patent. However, if the licence limits the extent of the rights to exploit the patented invention to less than the full reach of what is comprehended by the statutory definition of 'exploit', it is not an exclusive license. 'Exploit' is defined in Sch 1 by listing what it comprises where the invention is a product (make, hire, *sell*, etc) or a process. The concept of exploitation was considered 'indivisible' in *Bristol-Myers Squibb Co v Apotex Pty Ltd* [2015] FCAFC 2 at [105], so that a licence, even if it extends exclusivity to one or more acts listed under the Sch 1 definition of 'exploit' in the Act, cannot be considered an exclusive licence for statutory purposes. Even though this does not mean that every act comprised within the statutory meaning of the word 'exploit' must necessarily be expressly listed in an agreement for a licence to be exclusive (see *Grant v Australian Temporary Fencing Pty Ltd* (2003) 59 IPR 170) it is perhaps prudent to do so, as Novartis did to enable it to register its exclusive licence on the Register of Patents: see *Actavis Pty Ltd v Orion Corporation* [2016] FCAFC 121. *Actavis* also stands for the proposition that, provided there is no restriction, condition or limitation on the rights of the licensee itself to exploit the patent, the fact alone that the licensee undertakes to acquire patented products from the patentee does not deprive the licence of its exclusive character. If licences have been granted to other parties, then no exclusive licence would exist, and the existence or otherwise of multiple licences may therefore be the subject of contest: see, for example, *Damorgold Pty Ltd v JAI Products (No 3)* [2014] FCA 651. By virtue of s 120, only an exclusive licensee has the right to initiate infringement proceedings. Although s 187(1) of the Patents Act and reg 19.1 Patent Regulations 1991 (Cth) combined require licences to be registered, this serves the purpose of evidencing and not of constituting a licence, and therefore an exclusive licensee can sue even if the licence is not registered: see *Grant*. Where an exclusive licence reverts to the licensor at a point in time, 'statutory rights to damages or an account of profits conferred on owners or exclusive licensees of intellectual property only have effect for the period that a plaintiff in fact has the relevant status.': see *Black & Decker Inc v GMCA Pty Ltd (No 2)* (2008) 76 IPR 99 at 127. A non-exclusive licence can be for a limited time, area or form of exploitation of an invention. Such a licence need not be in writing and can be oral or implied: as to the latter, see Chapter 10 Patents: Infringement.

It would be against public policy for a patentee to be able to extend the term of the patent by contractual means, and hence by virtue of s 145, any party can terminate a contract relating to the exploitation of a patent from the moment the patent term ends. Any provision purporting to extend the term beyond the statutory monopoly period is thus rendered ineffective. Note that under s 144, restrictive dealing conditions such as tying and third line forcing in a contract relating to the sale or lease or licence of a patented invention are void: see also s 47 and s 48 of the Competition and Consumer Act 2010 (Cth).

Bibliography

A Meltzer, P Howard, P Lau, M de Alwis, 'Joint Ownership of IP — Is it the Best Option for Collaborators?' (2005) 18(3) *IPLB* 37.

A Monotti, 'Australia', in S Wolk and K Szkalej (eds), *Employees' Intellectual Property Rights*, 2015, Wolters Kluwer, The Netherlands, pp 553–91.

J Blows, 'Turf Wars: Patent Office Decides on Inventorship and Entitlement' (2008) 20(10) *IPLB* 159.

R Aarons, 'Further Analysis of Collaboration IP Ownership Structures' (2005) 18(3) *IPLB* 41.

S Gibson and V Wallin, 'Keeping Control of Intellectual and Industrial Property Assets' (2002) 76(10) *LIJ* 36.

S Harris, 'Proprietary Ownership and the Employment Relationship — Part 2' (2004) 17(5) *IPLB* 81.

W van Caenegem, 'VUT v Wilson, UWA v Gray and University Intellectual Property Policies' (2010) 21(3) *AIPJ* 148.

Chapter 10

Patents: Infringement

Rights of the Patentee and Infringement

10.1 The rights of a patentee are, by virtue of s 13 of the Patent Act 1990 (Cth), to exploit the patent and to authorise another to exploit the patent. The word 'exploit' does not have a broad and indefinite meaning. It is a term of art whose limits are closely circumscribed by the statutory definition (see Sch 1) and the relevant case law: see below 10.7. The Act envisages two forms of infringement: direct infringement by unauthorised exploitation of the patent (ie, doing an act comprised within the word 'exploit') and indirect infringement by supply: s 117. This form of infringement was first introduced with the 1990 Act.

The granting of a patent monopoly is confined to Australia: 'A patent has effect throughout the patent area [defined as Australia in Sch 1]': s 13(3). Anything done outside Australia does not infringe an Australian patent; note, however, that the rights of the patentee extend to importation, since this is an act comprised within the statutory definition of the term 'exploit'. A patentee seeking monopoly protection in other jurisdictions must lodge and prosecute an application in each of those jurisdictions. The formal aspects of a multi-nation application procedure can be simplified by way of a so-called Patent Cooperation Treaty (PCT) application, with particular advantages concerning priority date and anticipation. In an integrated global market, patents must be sought in a number of significant national markets, which adds to the expense of an effective patenting program. However, there is now increased harmony between the patent laws of many jurisdictions because of the effect of the Trade-Related Aspects of Intellectual Property Rights (TRIPS) treaty administered by the World Trade Organization. Nonetheless, certain inventions may be patentable in one jurisdiction and not in another (eg, medical treatment methods are not patentable in many other jurisdictions) and, similarly, certain acts may infringe in one country but not in another; for example, although medical treatment methods are patentable in the US, a registered physician cannot be liable in infringement of such patents. Negotiations on further harmonisation of patents law in the context of a Substantive Patent Law Treaty (as distinct from the Patent Law Treaty of 2000, which is concerned only with procedural matters) have stalled in the World Intellectual Property Organization (WIPO) Standing Committee on Patents. But patents also feature in various free trade agreements such as the China–Australia Free Trade Agreement (ChAFTA) and the Comprehensive and Progressive Agreement for Trans-Pacific Partnership (CPTPP).

When can a patentee or exclusive licensee sue for infringement?

10.2 The term of a standard patent is 20 years, calculated from the filing date of the complete specification: ss 67 and 65. For pharmaceutical patents, an extension of term can be granted for a maximum of 5 years: see Ch 6, Pt 3, s 77(2). In the case of an application for a standard patent, there is often a considerable delay between the date of the filing of the application and the granting of a patent. This is particularly so where amendments to the application are sought by the patent office, and where opposition to the granting of the patent is lodged. However, by virtue of s 57(3), an infringement that occurs at any time after the date on which the complete specification relating to an application has become open to public inspection is actionable. The patentee (or exclusive licensee) can initiate proceedings only once the patent has been granted, but a monetary award may be sought taking account of anything done after the publication of the application. Before the introduction of the innovation patent, it was strategically advantageous for the owner of an invention who was aware of imminent infringement by a competitor to apply for a petty patent rather than a standard patent, since the delay between the application for and the granting of a petty patent was much shorter (only a limited examination was performed, and no opposition before grant permitted). Thus, the patentee was able to bring an action earlier and could obtain an interim injunction to restrain the alleged infringer, as happened, for instance, in *Tidy Tea Ltd and Lyons Tetley Ltd v Unilever Australia Ltd* (1995) 32 IPR 405. The innovation patent, which replaced the petty patent, has now been slated for abolition as well; one of the reasons the Productivity Commission inquiry report into intellectual property (PC 2016 Report)[1] has recommended this, is that '[i]nnovation patents are used strategically, either to target alleged infringers of standard patents or to increase uncertainty over the scope of rights for competitors', as said to be exemplified by *Britax Childcare Pty Ltd v Infa-Secure Pty Ltd* [2012] FCA 467: see PC 2016 Report, p 239 and pp 253–6.

Infringement actions, counterclaims for invalidity and expert evidence

10.3 As has already been noted, the validity of a patent is not guaranteed: see s 20. Therefore, it is almost a matter of course for defendants to 'counterclaim for invalidity': 'A defendant in infringement proceedings may apply by way of counterclaim in the proceedings for the revocation of the patent.': s 121(1). Issues relating to s 18 (patentable subject matter, novelty, inventiveness, utility, secret use) and compliance with s 40 requirements ('fair basing', sufficiency, clarity and succinctness) are thus commonly revisited in a court of law, as well as the question of infringement itself. Often, multiple grounds of attack upon the validity of a granted patent are pursued. This results in

1. Productivity Commission, *Intellectual Property Arrangements*, Inquiry Report No 78, Canberra, September 2016.

lengthy and complex litigation whose cost is driven up by the prevalence of expert evidence. It is not uncommon for the patentee not only to suffer the disappointment of a loss concerning infringement but also to find the subject patent revoked by order of the court. In modern times, the subject matter of patents has become more scientific, particularly where chemical, pharmaceutical and medical patents or biotechnology, genetic engineering and digital technology are at issue. Litigated patents often concern highly scientific pharmaceutical inventions. As indicated previously, s 217 of the Patents Act 1990 (Cth) grants a court the power to appoint an assessor — in other words, an independent expert, rather than an expert retained by the parties — who can 'assist [the court] in the hearing and trial or determination of any proceedings under [the] Act'. In *Genetics Institute Inc v Kirin-Amgen Inc (No 2)* (1997) 39 IPR 155, Heerey J appointed an assessor, pointing out that: 'The scientific issues in this case were said by counsel opposing the appointment of an assessor to be "not difficult" … They turned out to be very difficult indeed, at least for me.': see *Genetics Institute Inc v Kirin-Amgen Inc (No 3)* (1998) 41 IPR 325 at 346. The invention at issue concerned recombinant procedures for the production of polypeptide proteins; that is, the use of recombinant DNA techniques to produce commercial quantities of erythropoietin. Heerey J's judgment is notable for its clear exposé of complex scientific concepts and processes.

Note that although expert witnesses are retained by the parties, and may at times appear partisan in their opinions, every expert's duty to the court is clear: see, for example, Federal Court of Australia, Practice Note GPN-EXPT: Expert Evidence (2016), Annexure A Harmonised Expert Witness Code of Conduct, cl 2: '2. An expert witness is not an advocate for a party and has a paramount duty, overriding any duty to the party to the proceedings or other person retaining the expert witness, to assist the Court impartially on matters relevant to the area of expertise of the witness.'

Construction of the Claims

The 'pith and marrow' and the purposive approach

10.4 The central undertaking in any patent suit is usually to determine the meaning and scope of the patent claims. A court commonly has to determine what the exact nature of the invention is and what exactly is claimed as being within the monopoly of the patentee. This is a relevant exercise both in terms of validity and of infringement, where it will also often have to be determined whether differences with an impugned product or process actually matter.

The description of the invention in the specification will, of its nature, be concrete and directed to one or a limited number of embodiments as described and/or illustrated; the claims, however, express what is claimed in more abstract language with a different purpose: not describing the invention but setting the outer limits of the monopoly sought. The choice of language in the claims is of paramount importance. That is why patent attorneys are usually retained to write them. They must arrive at language that is at once not too narrow and specific to be easily circumvented by minor modifications and also not too broad and abstract to be threatened by vagueness or ambiguity and other attacks based on s 40, or by anticipation because known things may fall within the excessively wide confines of the expressions used: see *Fisher & Paykel Healthcare Pty Ltd v Avion Engineering Pty Ltd* (1991) 103 ALR 239 at 256; [1991] FCA 434, the court reiterating dicta of Lord Upjohn in *Rodi & Wienenberger AG v Henry Showell Ltd* (1969) RPC 367. Ultimately, it is the language of the claims that courts must construe (so-called 'claims construction') to determine whether an impugned product or process constitutes an infringement, or whether certain differences take it outside the scope of the claims. In arriving at that determination, a central question for the court is often how closely to adhere to the claim's particular wording. Adhering to it with dogmatic literalism in every case risks subverting the real value of many patents. Any person, by making an insignificant or functionally inconsequential modification, would escape liability while retaining the benefit of the substance of the invention. Nonetheless, the claim terms serve the purpose of drawing the boundary between what the patentee claims is within the monopoly and what has been left without, and the specificity of the claim language can thus not simply be ignored. The patentee is at liberty to choose the particular language of the claims, and, in principle, should be held to that choice, rather than the courts rewriting them in the light of inconvenient facts. Nonetheless, in *Radiation Ltd v Galliers and Klaerr Pty Ltd* (1938) 60 CLR 36 at 51, Dixon J said:

> But, on a question of infringement, the issue is not whether the words of the claim can be applied with verbal accuracy or felicity to the article or device alleged to infringe, it is whether the substantial idea disclosed by the specification and made the subject of a definite claim has been taken and embodied in the infringing thing.

This substantive focus is referred to as the 'pith and marrow' approach (as to an early formulation of it, see *Clark v Adie* (1875) LR 10 Ch App 667). As is pointed out in *Populin v HB Nominees Pty Ltd* (1982) 41 ALR 471 at 475 per Bowen CJ and Deane and Ellicott JJ:

> It is in reliance on this approach that the courts have held that a defendant will not escape infringement by adopting what are immaterial variations, for example, by omitting an inessential part or step and substituting another part or step as its equivalent.

In *Populin*, the court stated how the pith and marrow of the invention are to be identified (at ALR 476 per Bowen CJ and Deane and Ellicott JJ):

> The essential features of the product or process for which it claims a monopoly are to be determined not as a matter of abstract uninformed construction but by a commonsense assessment of what the words used convey in the context of the then-existing published knowledge.

However, the limits of the 'pith and marrow' approach must be recognised. The substantial idea disclosed must be 'the subject of a definite claim' (see *Radiation Ltd*, above), and there will only ever be an infringement if 'each and every one of the essential integers' of a claim has been taken: see *Rodi* at 391. The relevant passage from *Rodi* is consistently reiterated: see, for example, *Fresenius Medical Care Australia Pty Ltd v Gambro Pty Ltd* (2005) 67 IPR 230, *McLaren v Industrial Roll Formers Pty Ltd* (2007) 75 IPR 187, *Alkermes Inc v Nektar Therapeutics* (2007) 75 IPR 200, *Gray v Finglen Pty Ltd* (2008) 75 IPR 610 and *Wake Forrest University Health Sciences v Smith & Nephew Pty Ltd (No 2)* [2011] FCA 1002. Naturally, that begs the question of whether or not an 'integer' or element is essential; the answer has been said to lie in distinguishing between a variation in the impugned invention that has a functional effect and one that is a mere equivalent or an immaterial variation. The difficulty with a less than literal approach, however, is that by using such concepts as 'the substantial idea', or by construing infringement by reference to 'equivalents' of what is actually claimed, the claims are freed from their moorings in the particular language chosen by the patentee. It then becomes difficult to know where to draw the line. The courts risk claim construction becoming rather a rewriting of claims to overcome some of the apparent deficiencies of the claim language or to be 'fair' to the patentee (something warned against in a number of cases): see, for example, *Clorox Australia Pty Ltd v International Consolidated Business Pty Ltd* (2006) 68 IPR 254 at 261. In this light, it is as well to keep in mind the words of Gibbs J in *Olin Corp v Super Cartridge Co Pty Ltd* (1977) 180 CLR 236; 1A IPR 197 at 204 to the effect that there will also be no infringement 'where the patentee has by the form of his claim left open that which the alleged infringer has done'.

Purposive approach

10.5 The 'purposive approach' to interpretation of specification and claims developed in the 1980s sought a middle path between literalism and the inherently indeterminate 'substantive' approach. It consolidated the rejection of literalism while developing a way to give sufficient weight to the actual wording of the claims. In *Populin* (see above 10.4), the court quoted with approval a passage from the leading English case, *Catnic Components Ltd v Hill & Smith Ltd* [1981] FSR 60 at 65: 'A patent specification should be given a purposive construction rather than a purely literal one derived from applying to it the kind of meticulous verbal analysis in which lawyers are too often tempted by their training to indulge ...'. A 'purposive construction' is one that focuses on the purpose of the document: who is it addressed to and what does it seek to impart? Therefore, the key question is whether a skilled addressee would consider that the patentee intended detailed adherence to the specific words or something less than that. In *Catnic Components*, the claims referred to a part of the invention being vertical in relation to another part; the question was whether a skilled person would take this requirement literally or take this as meaning 'vertical or one or two degrees from the vertical'. The court found that the patentee had not purposefully left out of the scope of the monopoly very slight variations from the vertical, which still performed the supportive function of the part.

The position of this 'purposive construction' adopted in *Catnic Components* and approved in *Populin* is not entirely settled in Australia, partly because it is simply not a relevant question in some factual scenarios. Gummow J in *Nicaro Holdings Pty Ltd v Martin Engineering Co* (1990) 16 IPR 545 at 560–1 thought it consistent with the pith and marrow approach; the Full Federal Court in *Rhone-Poulenc Agrochimie SA v UIM Chemical Services Pty Ltd* (1986) 12 FCR 477 used both approaches to reach its conclusions. The continuing application of the pith and marrow approach was also at issue in *KD Kanopy Australasia Pty Ltd v Insta Image Pty Ltd* (2007) 71 IPR 615 (at 622). In *PhotoCure ASA v Queen's University at Kingston* (2005) 64 IPR 314 at 356, Merkel J opted for a two-stage approach that equated the two:

> Thus, I propose to first consider the words used in the claims to ascertain whether on their primary meaning [the defendant] has made out its case of infringement and, if

> not, to apply the 'substance' or purposive approach in order to ascertain whether strict compliance with the primary meaning of the words used was intended to be a requirement of the claims.

The somewhat misleading use of 'substance' and 'purposive' as equivalents in this quote directs one's attention to the fact that the purposive test is, in the final analysis, intended to protect the substance of the invention from excessive literalism. It merely presents a somewhat more determinate technique for obtaining that objective. The purposive approach has, in a number of recent cases, come to be crystallised around the so-called 'Improver questions' from *Improver Corporation v Remington Consumer Products Limited* [1990] FSR 181 at 188–9:

> If the issue was whether a feature embodied in an alleged infringement which fell outside the primary, literal or a contextual meaning of a descriptive word or phrase in the claim ('a variant') was nevertheless within its language as properly interpreted, the court should ask itself the following three questions:
>
> (1) Does the variant have a material effect upon the way the invention works? If yes, the variant is outside the claim. If no—
>
> (2) Would this (ie that the variant had no material effect) have been obvious at the date of publication of the patent to a reader skilled in the art. If no, the variant is outside the claim. If yes—
>
> (3) Would the reader skilled in the art nevertheless have understood from the language of the claim that the patentee intended that strict compliance with the primary meaning was an essential requirement of the invention. If yes, the variant is outside the claim.

See, for instance, *Root Quality Pty Ltd v Root Control Technologies Pty Ltd* (2000) 49 IPR 225, *Baygol Pty Ltd v Foamex Polystyrene Pty Ltd* [2005] FCA 624 and *Sachtler GmbH & Co KG v RE Miller Pty Ltd* (2005) 65 IPR 605. The 'Improver questions' were reviewed by the Full Court of the Federal Court in *Fresenius Medical Care Australia*. In *Eli Lilly & Co v Apotex Pty Ltd* [2013] FCA 214 at [159], the purposive method of construction is referred to as 'now widely accepted in Australia'. However, the Improver questions may not be appropriate in every case; for instance, where the language of the claims is clear and unambiguous or where the nature of the invention does not lend itself to asking them. Nonetheless, a purposive approach remains appropriate in such cases. The Improver questions are, in the end, no more than guidelines for the resolution of that central issue: see *Kirin-Amgen v Hoeschst Marion Roussel Ltd* (2004) 64 IPR 444 per Hoffman LJ and see also *Australian Mud Co Pty Ltd v Coretell Pty Ltd* (2011) 93 IPR 88; [2011] FCAFC 121, where the Full Court makes some cautionary observations about the ubiquity of the purposive/Improver approach: at [64]–[65] and [69]–[71]. The approach can only go so far — it does not permit a deviation from the words actually used in the claims that goes too far or imports some broader idea or practical resolution found in the rest of the specification. It is the terms used in the claims that are the key, often more abstract than those found in the description of a 'preferred embodiment' in the specification, with which they cannot legitimately be conflated. The issue has also arisen in relation to an argument that a term in a claim was simply a mistake, which a skilled addressee would have realised, and a different term should thus be substituted. In *GlaxoSmithKline Consumer Healthcare Investments*

(Ireland) (No 2) Ltd v Generic Partners Pty Ltd [2018] FCAFC 71, the court posed the question as being 'whether, if the court were to also interpret the claim so as to correct the mistake, it would be re-writing the claim or merely interpreting it through the eyes of the skilled addressee in accordance with the principles to which we have referred': at [112]. It answered that question (at [139]) in the following terms:

> This is a case in which the skilled addressee's understanding of the claims, as found by the primary judge, does not make proper allowance for the function of the claims in defining the invention. Ultimately, it is for the court to decide the meaning of the claims. This is a case in which we think the language of the claim must be understood to mean what it actually says.

It should be noted that the 'purpose' referred to in *Catnic Components* was the general purpose that patent claim documents serve of informing interested parties of the true scope of a monopoly and not, as Dodds-Streeton J in *Eli Lilly* seems to imply (at [159]), the purpose of particular claims. Note that, as is suggested above, a patentee may be tempted to draft broader claims to avoid being restricted to a particular or specific form or embodiment of the invention, but this increases the risk of anticipation or ambiguity, so narrow claims may be unavoidable. In *Catnic Components*, as indicated above, reference in the claims was to the vertical juxtaposition of two elements, and the court held that the patentee had not purposefully left out of the scope of the monopoly very slight variations off the vertical. In contrast, in *Baygol*, the claims referred to a 'concrete' spacer; the court found that by the use of this word the claim had left out 'plastic' spacers, even if they performed the same function.

Using the *Baygol* invention to illustrate the drafting decision, imagine that the spacers in other materials were already known, the invention lying specifically in adopting concrete as the material. That would then require the claims to be restricted to concrete spacers. In other words, if the claim was not restricted to concrete spacers, it would fail for want of novelty. Alternatively, it may be that using spacers in the particular shape and position claimed was the invention's real step forward, and the patentee had no good reason to limit the claim language to concrete spacers only. However, since that is what, in fact, he did, and the word 'concrete' appears in the claims, it may be difficult to argue that it should be ignored and that the patentee must have intended to also include spacers in other materials. That is where the evidence of a skilled addressee may play a role. Greenwood J's reasons in *Artcraft Urban Group Pty Ltd v Streetworx Pty Ltd* [2016] FCAFC 29 at [72]–[104] are a further useful example of the purposive approach as applied to a practical difference between claim terms and an allegedly infringing product; for a more recent example, see *Nichia Corporation v Arrow Electronics Australia Pty Ltd* [2019] FCAFC 2.

Further rules of construction

10.6 In *Alphapharm Pty Ltd v H Lundbeck A/S* (2008) 76 IPR 618 at 651, the starting principle of interpretation of terms used in the specification is clearly set out:

> The hypothetical addressee of the patent is the non-inventive person skilled in the art before the priority date, and the words used in the specification and the claims are to be given the meanings that that skilled addressee would give them, both in the light of his or her own general knowledge and what is disclosed in the body of the specification: [...].

See also *Eli Lilly* (above 10.5) from [165], where the composition of the notional team constituting the skilled addressee was at issue. In *Root Quality* at IPR 236, Finkelstein J said that the skilled addressee is a person working in the art or science with which the invention is concerned or a person or team 'likely to have a practical interest in the subject matter of the invention'. If a term used in claims is of a technical or scientific nature, expert evidence may be admitted to assist the court to understand its meaning. His Honour further pointed out (at IPR 237) that:

> [T]he proper construction of the specification is a matter of law. It is, however, a task that must be undertaken through the eyes of the person to whom the specification is directed … who may give expert evidence to inform the court what is the generally accepted meaning of technical terms and also to explain how things actually work.

However, if it is an ordinary term with which all lawyers are familiar, expert evidence may be inadmissible. If the claim terms are clear and unambiguous, the rest of the specification cannot be called in aid to affect their interpretation, but if claims are unclear and ambiguous, it is appropriate to seek clarification in the specification as a whole: see *Australian Mud Co Pty Ltd v Coretell Pty Ltd (No 4)* [2015] FCA 1372. The scope of a claim may also not be confined by reference to limitations found in the body of the specification unless these are expressly or by necessary implication picked up in the claim: see *Sartas (No 1) Pty Ltd v Koukourou & Partners Pty Ltd and Nicola Leonardis* (1994) 30 IPR 479. Furthermore, a construction according to which the invention will work must be preferred to one according to which it may not do so: *Welch Perrin & Co Pty Ltd v Worrel* (1961) 106 CLR 588 at 601. Although expert evidence may be admissible in matters of clarification and construction, it is ultimately up to the court to adopt its own construction of the claims. As to a comprehensive enumeration of 'rules of construction' formulated judicially, see the judgment of Sheppard J in *Décor Corp Pty Ltd v Dart Industries Inc* (1988) 13 IPR 385 at 400, which has been oft-cited in subsequent judgments, inter alia *Pfizer Overseas Pharmaceuticals v Eli Lilly & Co* [2005] FCAFC 224 where a number of additional rules are formulated. The approach to construction of claims is also set out systematically in *Hutt v Enig Pty Ltd* (1998) 41 IPR 559 concerning a diffuser valve for fluidising powdered or granular products in hoppers and the like. See also *Minnesota Mining & Manufacturing Co v Beiersdorf (Australia) Ltd* (1980) 1A IPR 231 (the *3M* case) in relation to construction of claims of a combination patent. More recently, the approach to construction is also usefully summarised in *Sachtler GmbH & Co KG v RE Miller Pty Ltd* (2005) 65 IPR 605.

Nature of the Exclusive Rights of the Patentee

The right to exploit the invention

10.7 Once the court has determined whether the impugned invention falls within the scope of the patent claims, a further question arises: do the acts done in relation to the invention fall within the exclusive exploitation rights of the patentee as statutorily circumscribed? By virtue of s 13(1), the patentee has the exclusive right to exploit and to authorise the exploitation of the patented invention. The definition of 'exploit' in Sch 1 of the Patents Act 1990 (Cth) has a number of important features:

1. It is inclusive and not exhaustive; nonetheless, it is a detailed definition, enumerating a series of distinct activities. In the 1952 Act (and before), the monopoly of the patentee was defined by the term 'to make, exercise or vend'. The intention of the legislator in 1990 was to use plainer English yet retain all the learning surrounding those terms.
2. The definition envisages claims as falling within one of two categories — either process or product claims — although one invention may comprise both product and process claims: see, for example, *Anaesthetic Supplies Pty Ltd v Rescare Ltd* (1994) 50 FCR 1; 28 IPR 383. All or only some of the claims may be infringed.
3. The focus of the exclusive rights is on commercial use: 'Arguably, it is implicit that [the activities enumerated in Sch 1] are commercial in nature. If so, activities that are not commercial [...] may not amount to exploitation of a patent and may, therefore, be exempt from claims of infringement.': ALRC Discussion Paper 68, 'Gene Patenting and Human Health' (2003) at [14.7]. As Hardie Boys J said in *Smith Kline & French Laboratories Ltd v Attorney-General (New Zealand)* (1991) 22 IPR 143 at 149:

> If the person concerned keeps his activities to himself, and does no more than further his own knowledge or skill, even though commercial advantage may be his final goal, he does not infringe. But if he goes beyond that, and uses the invention or makes it available to others, in a way that serves to advance him in the actual marketplace, then he infringes, for the marketplace is the sole preserve of the patentee.

In that case, there was an importation of patented drug samples for the purpose of applying for marketing consent from the Minister of Health in New Zealand. Distribution was not to occur until after the plaintiff's patent had expired. The importation was held to be an infringing use. Cooke P said at 145:

> In my opinion, as a matter of the ordinary use of language, whether now or (one would suppose) in earlier centuries, to send an embodiment of the invention to a government authority for approval is plainly a use of it. Without doubt, too, Douglas acted for the commercial advantage or springboard of being more ready to launch into the market when the patent expired. This seems to me an infringement of both the letter and the spirit of the grant.

However, if initiating an application for marketing approval (ie, inclusion on the Australian Register of Therapeutic Goods) for a patented drug during the patent term amounts to exploitation, a competing generic manufacturer will have to wait until after the patent runs out to seek such approval. In effect, the patent term will hereby be extended by the time it takes for the rival to gain the necessary marketing approval after the patent's expiry. To prevent this from occurring, the Patents Act 1990 now expressly provides that certain acts done in relation to pharmaceutical patents for 'purposes connected with obtaining the inclusion in the Australian Register of Therapeutic Goods of goods' do not constitute an infringement of the patentee's rights: see s 119A and see also s 78. The exception is now extended to obtaining regulatory approval for non-pharmaceuticals as well: see s 119B.

Infringement of the exploitation right of the patentee

10.8 The definition of 'exploit' in Sch 1 of the Patents Act 1990 (Cth):

> … in relation to an invention, includes: (a) where the invention is a product — make, hire, sell or otherwise dispose of the product, offer to make, sell, hire or otherwise dispose of it, use or import it, or keep it for the purpose of doing any of those things; or (b) where the invention is a method or process — use the method or process or do any act mentioned in paragraph (a) in respect of a product resulting from such use.

Therefore, the essential rights of the patentee are:

- to work or 'exercise' the invention (eg, to implement the production process or to operate the patented machine);
- to commercially deal in an invention (eg, to sell the patented machine);
- to make the invention (eg, to assemble the patented machine); and
- if the invention is a process, to deal commercially in or work any product that is produced by implementing the patented process.

Further, importing a patented product is within the exclusive rights of the patentee, and unauthorised importation of the product of a patented process also constitutes an infringement: see *Warner-Lambert Co LLC v Apotex Pty Ltd (No 2)* [2018] FACFC 26. Note that complex issues arise where the patent claims the use of a known pharmaceutical substance for a new indication: see in that regard van Caenegem, 'Infringement of Patents for New Uses of Known Drugs: *Apotex Pty Ltd v Sanofi-Aventis & Generic Health v Otsuka & Apotex Pty Ltd v AstraZeneca AB*' (2013) 25(9) *IPLB* 187 and note the close relationship between this issue and the application of s 117: see 10.11. Few statutory limitations are placed on the exploitation right of the patentee: see further 10.12. Furthermore, although this is often a matter of degree, the attitude of the courts to any use of an invention by a defendant of a patented invention is, on the whole, strict. Suggested derogations from the patentee's monopoly not based in statutory provisions will not be readily entertained. Some instances that illustrate this include:

1. Even if a patented product is made only as a passing stage in a continuing manufacturing process, there will be an infringement, unless the making is trifling or insignificant: see, for example, *Pinefair Pty Ltd v Bedford Industries Rehabilitation Association Inc* (1998) 40 IPR 438.
2. A use of the invention for the sake of experimentation with an eye to manufacture once the patent has expired may also amount to an infringement; thus, in *Smith Kline & French Laboratories* Hardie Boys J said at 149:

   > These cases serve to delineate not only the limits of the experiment principle, but also the bounds of permissible activity, between what is and what is not use for commercial advantage. Doubtless experimentation will usually have an ultimate commercial objective; where it ends and infringement begins must often be a matter of degree.

   Note that now, in Australia, the question of the legality of experimental use has been expressly addressed by statutory amendment: see the new s 119C and see 10.2.

3. Supplying complete parts to be assembled into a patented product, where that amounts in substance to selling the whole product because of the ease of assembly, will amount to an infringement: see, for example, *Windsurfing International Inc v Petit* [1984] 2 NSWLR 196 and see **10.11**.

Nonetheless, certain acts fall outside the monopoly of the patentee: for instance, mere possession of a patented product such as, for example, by a warehouse keeper or transport company (although keeping for the purpose of commercial distribution, etc, is within the scope of the monopoly) and repairs to a patented product, unless they effectively amount to the rebuilding of the product: see *Solar Thompson Engineering Co Ltd v Barton* [1977] RPC 537.

Licence of the purchaser of a patented product

10.9 An important limitation on the rights of the patentee is sometimes said to result from the 'exhaustion theory': once the patentee puts a patented product (or a product resulting from a patented process) into the market, they cannot rely upon the patent grant to restrict the purchaser from using or dealing in the patented product in any manner. Once the product is sold, it 'passes out of the limit of the monopoly': see *National Phonograph Co of Australia v Menck* [1911] AC 336 (PC), per Lord Shaw of Dumferline at 347, quoting an 'American phrase'. Sometimes, the principle of 'non-derogation from grant' is relied on to justify the right of the purchaser to use a patented product without limitations. This principle holds that purchasers should have the full benefit of their property rights. In Australia, it is well recognised that the patentee can validly impose restrictive conditions on the use of a patented invention at the time of sale, as was recently confirmed by Burley J in *Seiko Epson Corporation v Calidad Pty Ltd* [2017] FCA 1403. However, if a patented product is sold without the purchaser's agreement to restrictive conditions, none will normally be implied. Lord Shaw of Dumferline summed up the applicable principles in *National Phonograph* at AC 353:

> … first, it is open to a licensee, by virtue of his statutory monopoly, to make a sale *sub modo*, or accompanied by restrictive conditions which would not apply in the case of ordinary chattels; secondly, that the imposition of these conditions in the case of a sale is not presumed, but, on the contrary, a sale having occurred, the presumption is that the full right of ownership was meant to be vested in the purchaser; while thirdly, the owner's rights in a patented chattel will be limited if there is brought home to him the knowledge of conditions imposed, by the patentee or those representing the patentee, upon him at the time of sale.

In *Seiko Epson* at [98] the court summarised the position as follows:

> Accordingly, there is a presumption that a sale sub modo (sale without restriction) confers an unrestricted right of use upon the purchaser or subsequent owner of the patented product, which covers at least the rights to import, use and dispose of the product. To avoid this consequence, a patentee must make a sale subject to limitations which are effective to restrict the importation, use or disposal of the product by the purchaser or successor in title to the purchaser. It must show that notice of any restriction was brought to the knowledge of the purchaser at the time of sale.

The case concerned the importation of used Epson printer cartridges which had been refilled by Calidad abroad (and the computer boards modified). The court confirmed that to repair a patented product is permitted, as long as it does not amount in reality to an unauthorised making of the patented product (it is incorrect to refer to the existence of an 'implied license' to repair, since none is required: see *Seiko Epson* at [71] quoting Lord Hoffman in *Canon Kabushiki Kaisha v Green Cartridge Co (Hong Kong)* [1997] AC 728 at [70]).

Knowledge required and remedies for infringement

10.10 The patentee or exclusive licensee can sue for infringement: see s 120(1). Liability for patent infringement requires no knowledge or intention; ignorance of the existence of a patent or of the infringing nature of an act is irrelevant. Such 'strict' liability is consonant with a registration system: a person can ascertain by inspecting a public document (the Register of Patents) whether or not a certain technology is covered by a patent, and thus whether a licence should be sought. However, innocence should not be irrelevant in terms of the remedy granted. Hence, s 123(1) grants courts the discretion not to award damages or an account of profits if satisfied that, at the date of the infringement, the defendant was not aware of and had no reason to believe that a patent was in existence; an injunction is still available in theory: see s 123(3) and also Chapter 19 Remedies in Intellectual Property Law. By virtue of s 123(2), there is a rebuttable statutory presumption that the defendant was aware of the existence of the patent if the patented product, marked as being patented, was sold or used to a substantial extent in Australia prior to the date of infringement. In this regard, s 121A is also relevant. It reverses the onus of proof in relation to the question of whether certain products have or have not been made by means of a patented process, requiring in some circumstances that the alleged infringer prove that they were not.

Infringement by Supply

An innovation introduced in the 1990 Act: s 117

10.11 The infringement by supply or 'indirect' or 'contributory infringement' provision (s 117) was an innovation of the Patents Act 1990 (Cth). The intention of the section was to permit a patentee to bring an action against a person who enabled others to infringe a process invention by the supply of the products or ingredients required to implement the process.

It was mainly targeted at the farm sector, to enable patentees to bring an action not just against every farmer who uses, for instance, a herbicide or fertiliser in accordance with a method that is patented (see, eg, the method disclosed by the patent in *National Research Development Corporation v Commissioner of Patents* (1959) 102 CLR 252 (*NRDC*)) but also — and more effectively — against the person or corporation that supplies the products that a farmer applies to crops using a process that is patented. The supplier will presumably have deeper pockets, and the need for a multiplicity of actions against every single user would be obviated. However, the operation of s 117 is not limited to farm supplies, and the majority of cases that have considered the section to date have been concerned with medical processes; nonetheless, the case of *Collins v Northern Territory* (2007) 161 FCR 549; 74 IPR 296; *Northern Territory v Collins* [2008] HCA 49 (*Collins*) was concerned with a rural commodity, as it concerned a process for extraction of oil from certain trees. Prior to the introduction of s 117, only general law principles were applicable to supply, and the courts were reluctant to impose supplier liability: see, for example, *Walker v Alamite Corp* (1933) 49 CLR 643. Section 117 was intended to overcome this by an express statutory provision. However, the initial s 117 decision of Gummow J in *Rescare Ltd v Anaesthetic Supplies Pty Ltd* (1992) 111 ALR 205; 25 IPR 119 seemed to have largely defeated the intended purpose of s 117. His Honour construed the section as applying only to a situation where the product supplied itself results from the application of a patented process. However, in *Bristol-Myers Squibb Co v FH Faulding & Co Ltd* (2000) 97 FCR 524; 46 IPR 553, the Full Federal Court rejected the approach taken by Gummow J in *Rescare*, and restored the section's intended effect. In *Leonardis v Theta Developments Pty Ltd* (2000) 51 IPR 546, Williams J treated the Full Court's decision in *Bristol-Myers* as having settled the question. The issue was not clearly addressed in the recent High Court decision in *Collins*.

In any case, by virtue of s 117(2), the supply of a product will amount to an infringement only if either one of the following conditions is satisfied:

- if the product is capable of only one reasonable use, and that use constitutes an infringement (s 117(2)(a));
- if it is not a staple product, if the supplier had reason to believe that the person to whom the product was supplied would use it for an infringing purpose (s 117 (2)(b)); or
- if the product is supplied together with instructions or inducements to use it, which specify an infringing manner of use (s 117(2)(c)).

The 'staple product' provision was analysed in *Collins*, which itself overturned the decision in *Collins v Northern Territory of Australia* (2006) 70 IPR 614. The patent concerned was entitled 'Methods of producing essential oils from species of the genus callitris'. In essence, it related to extracting oils from a mixture of bark and wood of the relevant trees. The Northern Territory issued licences to the Australian Cypress Oil Company Pty Ltd (ACOC) after the date of the patent, authorising it to take timber from Crown lands. ACOC was alleged to have used the timber to produce oil by a method protected by the patent. The majority in the Federal Court (Sundberg and Branson JJ) held that granting a licence to extract trees from a plantation amounted to a 'supply' by the Northern Territory Government (at IPR 331):

> There is no doubt that ACOC was in need of the Territory's timber. It was unable to obtain it without the Territory's consent. The Territory said ACOC could have the timber so long as it paid for it. It would grant ACOC a licence to come onto its land and take the timber. Indeed it obliged ACOC to take it. In those circumstances, in the events that happened, the Territory provided or furnished the timber to ACOC, and thus supplied it to ACOC. The timber so supplied was felled but unmilled trees of the species Callitris Intratropica.

As to whether the trees were a 'staple commercial product', the majority concluded (at IPR 332):

> However, it seems to us that a quality of such a product is that it is an item of commerce in the sense that it is ordinarily available for purchase from an entity that trades in that product. In our view, having regard to the evidence reviewed above, unmilled Callitris Intratropica trees, at least in the Northern Territory, are not a 'staple commercial product' within the meaning of s 117(2)(b) of the Act.

Definition of the class of 'product' was critical. The majority of the Federal Court considered that the relevant question was whether unmilled trees of a particular species were a staple commercial product. The majority thereby overturned the approach of the trial judge, French J (as he then was), holding that s 117 *was* applicable to the facts of the case. However, the High Court reversed the Federal Court's decision and agreed with French J that the correct question was whether millable timber in general was a staple commercial product. The answer was clearly yes, and for that reason the Northern Territory could not be found to have infringed s 117. The issue also arises in relation to the supply of drugs for a certain indication: see in that regard *AstraZeneca AB v Apotex Pty Ltd* [2014] FCAFC 99 and van Caenegem, 'Infringement of Patents for New Uses of Known Drugs: *Apotex Pty Ltd v Sanofi-Aventis & Generic Health v Otsuka & Apotex Pty Ltd v AstraZeneca AB*' (2013) 25(9) *IPLB* 187. Where the product is held not to be a staple product, then a further question is whether the supplier 'had reason to believe' it would be used for a patented purpose — this will turn on the particular facts and circumstances (eg, whether the purported purpose of the supply was realistic given the size of the putative market for it) and the nature of instructions given by the supplier (eg, to use or prescribe it for a particular medical indication and not another or others): see, for example, *Warner-Lambert Co LLC v Apotex Pty Ltd* [2014] FCAFC 59 (an appeal against an application for an interlocutory injunction).

Exemptions, Exceptions and Compulsory Licences

10.12 As indicated above, few statutory limitations are placed on the exploitation right of the patentee: s 118 in relation to use in or on foreign craft, s 119 granting protection for the rights of prior users of the invention, s 119A and s 119B permitting certain acts to obtain regulatory approval, and s 119C providing an exemption for certain experimental purposes, Ch 17 concerning the rights of the Crown and the possible granting of a compulsory licence for non-use under Ch 12.

Section 119C was inserted in 2012 and puts the experimental use exception on a secure statutory footing. Much preparatory work was done beforehand: see Advisory Council on Intellectual Property (ACIP), *Consideration of Patents and Experimental Use* (February 2004 Issues Paper; December 2004 Options Paper); ACIP Final Report, *Patents and Experimental Use* (October 2005); and also ALRC Report 99: *Genes and Ingenuity, Gene Patenting and Human Health* (2004) Ch 13 'An experimental use exception'. The exception as adopted is narrow in scope and is commonly considered to be confined to uses that would in any case not have a sufficiently commercial flavour to fall within the exploitation right.

Prior use and foreign craft

10.13 Section 118 provides a limited exemption in relation to the use of a patented invention on or in foreign vessels, aircraft or land vehicles that are only temporarily or accidentally in Australia: see also Patent Regulations 1991 (Cth), reg 11.1. This exemption is based on art 5*ter* of the Paris Convention for the Protection of Industrial Property (1883); there are no Australian cases, but see *Stena Rederi AB v Irish Ferries Ltd* [2003] RPC 36. Section 119 provides a right of continued use of a patented invention to a person who was working that invention immediately before the priority date of the patent, subject to the use being continuous and the patentee not being concerned with that working in any way: a 'prior user' right. The prior use will logically have to have been secret, since otherwise the patent will be invalid because of anticipation and non-obviousness. In *Morellini v Mizzi Family Holdings Pty Ltd* [2016] FCAFC 13 at [74] the court emphasised that 'an allegation of prior use should be strictly proved, in the sense that the court determining that question must be satisfied that the proof given is sufficient in the circumstances, having regard to the gravity of the allegation: *Windsurfing International Inc v Petit* [1984] 2 NSWLR 196 at 231, citing *Toyo Tsushinki Kabushiki Kaisha's Application* [1962] RPC 9 at 15 and *Laguerre's Patent* [1970] RPC 587 at 591, 593 and 596'. The person enjoying the prior user right may exploit the patent (s 119(1) and s 119(5)). The prior user right may be assigned (or 'transferred') in full but not licensed: see s 119(4) introduced by the Intellectual Property Laws Amendment Act 2006 (Cth). Further, 'the defence under s 119(1) is limited to the alleged infringer's own acts that exploit a product, method or process in a way that would infringe a patent. The defence does not cover the act of authorising another person to exploit the invention': see *Vehicle Monitoring Systems Pty Ltd v Sarb Management Group Pty Ltd (No 2)* [2013] FCA 395 at [103].

Compulsory licensing and crown use of a patented invention

10.14 Chapter 12, s 133ff grants any person the right to apply for a compulsory licence for a patented invention if the patentee does not work the invention sufficiently to meet the reasonable requirements of the public (as defined in s 135) in Australia. Applications, under either the present provisions or previous equivalents, are very rare, among other reasons because the statutory conditions imposed on the granting of such a licence are so onerous: see, for example, *Fastening Supplies Pty Ltd v Olin-Matheson Chemical Corp* (1969) 119 CLR 572. The Intellectual Property and Competition Review Committee, in its 'Review of Intellectual Property Legislation under the Competition Principles Agreement' (2000), recommended the repeal of s 135 and the replacement of s 133(2) with more competition-focused conditions: see p 17. The Intellectual Property Laws Amendment Act 2006 (Cth) subsequently introduced a new provision to provide for a compulsory licence to be available as a remedy if a person has contravened the anti-competitive conduct provisions of Pt IV of the Competition and Consumer Act 2010 (Cth): see s 133(2)(b). However, s 135 was not repealed. In 2013 the Productivity Commission conducted a review: *Compulsory Licensing of Patents*, the final report being released on 27 May 2013 (PC 2013 Report). It recommended replacing the 'reasonable requirements of the public' test with a 'public interest' test, and that a court when granting a compulsory licence should have regard to the public interest when specifying the terms of the licence, including remuneration. The Exposure Draft of the Intellectual Property Laws Amendment (Productivity Commission Response Part 2 and Other Measures) Bill 2019 (Cth) contains amendments relating to compulsory licensing and also Crown use, but no corresponding actual bill was introduced into Parliament during 2018, the government having other priorities.

By virtue of s 161ff, the Crown in right of a state or the Commonwealth has the right to exploit any patented invention or invention for which an application is pending. This right is not subject to the agreement of the patentee, although the Crown is obliged, pursuant to s 165, to pay the remuneration as fixed by agreement between the parties or, failing agreement, by a prescribed court.

However, as it stands, such an agreement can be made before, during or after the exploitation of the invention: the Crown does not have to wait until an agreement is struck. The Exposure Draft Bill requires, by contrast, that governments give notice to a patentee and seek a negotiated arrangement before invoking the Crown use provisions, except in emergencies. It also introduces a requirement of ministerial authorisation for invoking Crown use. The purpose of the exception is to ensure that the Crown can use inventions 'for the services of the Commonwealth or a state' (s 163(1)), which includes 'the proper provision of those services within Australia': s 163(3). It is considered to be in the public interest that the Crown should have access to all inventions, but this right is balanced by an obligation to fairly compensate the patentee. Prior to the PC 2013 Report, which considered both Crown use and compulsory licensing, ACIP published a relevant discussion paper: *Review of Crown Use Provisions in Patents and Designs Legislation* (December 2003), and subsequently a report: *Review of Crown Use Provisions for Patents and Designs* (November 2005). In this report, ACIP called for a more transparent and accountable process, recommendations with which the PC 2013 Report was largely consistent.

By virtue of s 162, a reference to the Commonwealth or a state includes a reference to an authority of the Commonwealth or a state. In *Stack v Brisbane City Council* (1996) 67 FCR 510; 35 IPR 296, Cooper J found that, under the specific statutory provisions that applied to the Brisbane City Council (BCC) in Queensland, a city council was an authority of the state and could therefore exploit patented inventions without the prior agreement of the patentee; see also *Embertec Pty Ltd v Energy Efficient Technologies Pty Ltd (No 3)* [2013] FCA 1010.

It should also be noted that under s 162(2), it is not only the departments of state of the Crown itself that can work the invention but also any other person authorised by the Crown. In *Stack v Brisbane City Council*, for instance, a third party had been contracted (and thus authorised) by the BCC to produce the water meters that incorporated the patented invention at issue. The water meters were to be used by the BCC to measure the consumption of town water provided by it to households, and the court also held that this activity was indeed 'for the services of' the Crown. However, one may question where the break line lies between a public service and a commercial activity in an increasingly deregulated environment, with the traditional provision of services by the Crown being thrown open to competition.

Bibliography

A Franklin, 'Pick a Prince — A Provocative Look at Patent Claim Construction in Australia' (2006) 67 *IP Forum* 30.

ACIP, *Patents and Experimental Use*, Final Report, October 2005.

ACIP, *Review of Crown Use Provisions for Patents and Designs* (November 2005).

Advisory Council on Intellectual Property (ACIP), *Consideration of Patents and Experimental Use*, February 2004 Issues Paper; December 2004 Options Paper.

Australian Law Reform Commission (ALRC), *Genes and Ingenuity, Gene Patenting and Human Health*, Report No 99, 2004, Ch 13: An experimental use exception.

B Sherman, 'Biological Inventions and the Problem of Passive Infringement' (2002) 13(3) *AIPJ* 146.

C Lawson, 'Public Interest Compulsory Licensing under the Patents Act 1990 (Cth): Real Incentive or a Barrier to Working?' (2008) 19(3) *AIPJ* 129.

C Oddie, 'Modifications, Morality and Law of Patent Infringement' (2000) 11(4) *AIPJ* 185.

C Smith, 'Experimental Use Exception to Patent Infringement Where Does Australia Stand?' (2003) 53 *IP Forum* 14.

Industrial Property Advisory Committee (IPAC), *Patents, Innovation and Competition in Australia*, AGPS, 1984.

IPLB, 'Contributory Infringement of a Patent — *Bristol-Myers Squibb v FH Faulding*' (2000) 13(2) *IPLB* 22.

J Hinojosa, 'The Human Genome, Property of All: Opportunities Under the ALRC Inquiry into Gene Patenting and Human Health' (2004) 26(3) *SydLR* 447.

K Weatherall and E Webster, 'Patent Infringement in Australia: Results from a Survey' (2010) 38(1) *F L Rev* 21.

Productivity Commission, *Compulsory Licensing of Patents*, Inquiry Report No 61, Canberra, March 2013 (PC 2013 Report).

Productivity Commission, *Intellectual Property Arrangements*, Inquiry Report No 78, Canberra, September 2016 (PC 2016 Report).

R Hoad, 'Compulsory Licensing of Patents: Balancing Innovation and Competition' (2003) 54 *IP Forum* 28.

R Hoad, 'Non-Literal Patent Infringement: More Honoured in the Breach than the Observance?' (2006) 17(2) *AIPJ* 121.

R Silberstein, 'Contributory Infringement of Patents: A Vexed Area of Law' (2008) 20(7) *IPLB* 105.

T Dembo, 'An Examination of the Crown Use Provisions in the Patents Act' (2007) 18(2) *AIPJ* 70.

Bibliography

Chapter 11

Breach of Confidence: Elements of the Action

Introduction

11.1 In Australia, secret information (or 'undisclosed information', as it is referred to in the World Trade Organization (WTO) treaty, Trade-Related Aspects of Intellectual Property Rights (TRIPS): see art 39) is not protected by statute or property rights. Thus, the 'owner' of a trade secret does not have a monopoly over its exploitation like they would if it were a patented invention, but only legal protection against its unauthorised use or disclosure. Where such information is commercial or technical, rather than personal, in nature, it is often referred to as a 'trade secret'. However, this is not a term of art, except perhaps in some very limited ways, in particular where employees are involved: see Chapter 12 Breach of Confidence: Defences, Remedies and Employees. An action for the unauthorised use or disclosure of confidential information lies either in contract or in equity in Australia. The equitable action for breach of confidence provides a default remedy in the absence of an express or implied contractual term or if no contractual relationship exists between the parties. In other jurisdictions, (quasi-) property rights are more accepted, and statutory provisions relating to trade secrets are not uncommon. Internationally, remedies for misuse of undisclosed information are also commonly seen as an aspect of the broader prohibition of unfair competition and dishonest commercial practice. Thus, the Paris Convention for the Protection of Industrial Property contains no express provision relating to secret information, only a more general provision (art 10*bis*) against unfair competition; art 39 of TRIPS also locates the basis for trade secrets protection in unfair competition torts. Article 39 of TRIPS provides in full:

> 1. In the course of ensuring effective protection against unfair competition as provided in Article 10bis of the Paris Convention (1967), Members shall protect undisclosed information in accordance with paragraph 2 and data submitted to governments or governmental agencies in accordance with paragraph 3.2. Natural and legal persons shall have the possibility of preventing information lawfully within their control from being disclosed to, acquired by, or used by others without their consent in a manner contrary to honest commercial practices so long as such information: (a) is secret in the sense that it is not, as a body or in the precise configuration and assembly of its components, generally known among or readily accessible to persons within the circles that normally deal with the kind of information in question; (b) has commercial value because it is secret; and (c) has been subject to reasonable steps under the circumstances, by the person lawfully in control of the information, to keep it secret.

However, a remedy for unfair competition has never been recognised by the courts in Australia, and the action for breach of confidence is not seen in that light here. Rather, the basis for a remedy for breach of confidence in Australia continues to lie in the obligation of conscionable or faithful conduct in certain relationships or interactions, or as Megarry J pointed out in *Coco v AN Clark (Engineers) Ltd* [1969] RPC 41; (1968) 1A IPR 587 (*Coco v Clark*) at 590, 'The equitable jurisdiction in cases of breach of confidence is ancient; confidence is the cousin of trust.'

Whatever the correct doctrinal basis may be, it is clear that the elements and availability of the equitable action for breach of confidence are effective to ensure Australia's compliance with its obligations under TRIPS.

The action provides default protection in relation to information, the use of which is not subject to some other form of legal restraint, contractual, statutory or otherwise. In Meagher, Gummow and Lehane, *Equity: Doctrine and Remedies*, 3rd ed, Butterworths, 1992 [4101], the authors list four reasons for the recent popularity of the equitable action for breach of confidence:

1. the short reach of existing statutory intellectual property regimes;
2. the 'delays, inconveniences and uncertainties in the operation of the patent system';
3. the lack of recognition of a tort of invasion of privacy; and
4. the High Court's decision to reject a tort of unfair competition in *Moorgate Tobacco Co Ltd v Philip Morris Ltd (No 2)* (1984) 156 CLR 414; 56 ALR 193.

Generally speaking, unlike in other regimes, the information concerned need not have particular inherent qualities, such as strict novelty or inventiveness, the only requirement being that it is sufficiently particularised and not in the public domain. Although the action for breach of confidence is of long standing, the rationale and principles underlying the action have not always been clear or unanimously accepted throughout its history. They are usually explained in two divergent ways.

First is the property approach: the basis for awarding a remedy against a person who has passed on or used confidential information without authorisation is that the plaintiff owns it. The action thus prevents misappropriation of information. Despite a degree of support at some points in history, this is not now the preferred rationale in Australian law. Second is the relationship approach: a remedy for a breach of confidence is granted to protect a relationship of good faith. The remedy is '... founded upon unconscionable action in the circumstances of a relationship between the parties': see *Titan Group Pty Ltd v Steriline Manufacturing Pty Ltd* (1990) 19 IPR 353 at 376 per O'Loughlin J.

Property, equity and contract

11.2 In *Morrison v Moat* (1852) 20 LJ Ch 513, Turner V-C cast some doubt on the importance of identifying precise grounds for awarding a remedy, simply recognising that, in the past, courts had restrained the imparting of trade secrets, saying at 522:

> Different grounds have indeed been assigned for the exercise of that jurisdiction. In some cases it has been referred to as property, in others to contract, and in others again ... as founded upon trust or confidence — meaning, ... that the court fastens the obligation upon

> the conscience of the party, …; but upon whatever grounds this jurisdiction is founded, the authorities have no doubt as to the exercise of it. [The 'property' Turner V-C was referring to was copyright, not property in a general sense.]

As indicated above, modern decisions are usually grounded in an obligation of conscience, although it is sometimes asserted that one of the bases for granting a remedy in equity is that 'equity regards information as akin to property and grants or withholds relief accordingly': see *Darvall McCutcheon v H K Frost Holdings Pty Ltd (in liq)* (2002) 4 VR 570; [2002] VSCA 85 at [56]. For a long time, a remedy for breach of confidence was associated with the existence of a contractual relationship. Only in *Saltman Engineering Co Ltd v Campbell Engineering Co Ltd* (1948) 65 RPC 203 did Lord Greene MR state clearly (although obiter) that an equitable obligation of confidence could arise independently of contract. Indeed, the key to the action for breach of confidence now is that reliance upon it properly arises where property rights, either statutory or personal, cannot be asserted, nor reliance be had on contract, nor on a broad fiduciary duty or contractual duty of fidelity (eg, as between employer and employee).

In *Saltman*, a contract did, in fact, exist, but not so in *Seager v Copydex Ltd* [1967] 2 All ER 415. The information concerning a newfangled carpet grip was revealed at the negotiation stage, so no binding contractual obligation yet existed in relation to it. Lord Denning MR asserted that the granting of relief (by way of damages) was based on the 'broad principle of equity that he who has received information in confidence shall not take unfair advantage of it': *Seager v Copydex Ltd* at 417. Alternatively, as the same judge said in *Fraser v Evans* [1969] 1 All ER 8; 1 QB 349 at 350, relief is based 'not so much on property or on contract as on the duty to be of good faith'. Arguably, courts simply treat confidences as worthy of protection in equity in the interests of harmonious social and commercial interaction, and are generally content to leave the doctrinal underpinnings somewhat vague. As Finn says, 'Perhaps the most sterile of the debates which have arisen around the subject of information received in confidence is whether or not such information should be classified as property';[1] as to a case that reflects the different approaches, see *Boardman v Phipps* [1967] 2 AC 46. In this vein, in *Moorgate Tobacco (No 2)* Deane J said (at CLR 437–8):

> It is unnecessary, for the purposes of the present appeal, to attempt to define the precise scope of the equitable jurisdiction to grant relief against an actual or threatened abuse of confidential information not involving any tort or any breach of some express or implied contractual provision, some wider fiduciary duty or some copyright or trade mark right. A general equitable jurisdiction to grant such relief has long been asserted and should, in my view, now be accepted (see *The Commonwealth v John Fairfax & Sons Ltd.* (1980) 147 CLR 39, pp 50–2). Like most heads of exclusive equitable jurisdiction, its rational basis does not lie in proprietary right. It lies in the notion of an obligation of conscience arising from the circumstances in or through which the information was communicated or obtained.

In reality, the courts' focus in the context of this equitable action is usually more on fashioning an appropriate remedy, properly adapted to the facts, than on detailed

1. See P Finn, *Fiduciary Obligations*, LawBook Co, 1977, p 131. For a more extensive treatment of the subject, see G Hughes, *Dean's Law of Trade Secrets and Privacy*, 3rd ed, LawBook Co, 2018.

doctrinal analysis of its proper legal underpinnings. In being less preoccupied with process than with results, the courts tend to gloss over doctrinal conundrums that result from founding the action on the requirement of good faith within certain relationships or exchanges. For example, courts have readily extended obligations to third parties; have assessed damages rather than an account, even without an injunction (see *Seager v Copydex Ltd* above); and have restrained the use of information that was not imparted in the context of a relationship of confidence at all but obtained by surreptitious, illegal or tortious means: see, for example, *Franklin v Giddins* [1978] Qd R 72; (1977) 1B IPR 807. The remedies granted in those situations may be more compatible with property-based thinking. In truth, the recognition of a proprietary right in confidential information or trade secrets would now require the intervention of parliament — as has happened, for example, in some states of the US, where criminal liability may also attach to misappropriation of trade secrets. Forty-seven states have adopted the Uniform Trade Secrets Act, codifying and harmonising the law of misappropriation of trade secrets. However, there is no prospect of anything similar in Australia. An alternative approach to explain the granting of remedies in the absence of any particular relationship of trust or good faith lies in unconscionability. In *Moorgate Tobacco (No 2)* at CLR 438, Deane J said the courts' intervention was based on 'the notion of an obligation of conscience arising from the circumstances in or through which information was communicated or obtained'. There is no need to refer back to actual relationships or interaction, since the courts can fix on unconscionable conduct per se and on restitution for such conduct as a wrong. Industrial espionage and third party liability can be accommodated in this manner. The difficulty is with defining what is unconscionable conduct that warrants the granting of a remedy; this may be clear if illegal conduct has resulted in the obtaining of information, but less so where a breach of privacy or a trick has been used. In any case, the tort of breach of privacy is not as yet recognised in Australia; arguably, the UK courts have gone further in that regard: see *Douglas v Hello! Ltd (No 2)* (2005) 65 IPR 449. Further, the High Court in *Australian Broadcasting Corporation v Lenah Game Meats Pty Ltd* (2001) 208 CLR 199; 54 IPR 161; [2001] HCA 63 (*ABC v Lenah Game Meats*) rejected the notion of a remedy for unconscionable acts in the absence of a recognised underlying cause of action. On a final note, although the remedy for breach of confidence is not founded on proprietary rights, trade secrets are often dealt with in trade and commerce and — in particular, in contracts — as property that can be transferred or assigned. In a sense, the protection that the law allows confidential information, gives it a proprietary character: see *Farah Constructions v Say-Dee Pty Ltd* (2007) 230 CLR 89; 236 ALR 209 at 246. That is quite different from saying that the law protects trade secrets because property rights subsist in them, something the High Court has consistently rejected: see, for example, *Breen v Williams* (1996) 186 CLR 71 at 90 per Dawson and Toohey JJ.

The equitable duty and contractual obligations

11.3 If there is a contractual relationship between two parties who have exchanged information, then the parties' duties as to its use and disclosure are governed by the terms of the contract rather than by equity. This might be a consequence of 'the fundamental rule [...] that equity will not intervene where there is an adequate remedy at law': see *Coles Supermarkets Australia Pty Ltd v FKP Ltd* [2008] FCA 1915 at [63]–[64]. However, this 'rule' was held not to apply to each and every case (eg, to deny the plaintiff an equitable remedy): see *Optus Networks Pty Ltd v Telstra Corporation Ltd* (2010) 265 ALR 281; [2010] FCAFC 21, as more recently discussed in *Antony Leslie John Woodings as liquidator of The Bell Group Ltd and The Bell Group Finance Pty Ltd v WA Glendinning & Associates Pty Ltd* [2019] WASC 54 at [55]ff.

If silent as to the parties' obligations of confidence, any secret information passing between them for the purposes of performing the contract will be subject to an implied term requiring it to be treated confidentially. In *AG Australia Holdings Ltd v Burton* (2002) 58 NSWLR 464; 58 IPR 268 at 287, the court said:

> The law recognises three different ways in which an obligation of confidentiality might arise. The first is by express provision in a contract. The second is by an implied term in a contract. The third is as an obligation recognised in the exclusive jurisdiction of equity.

To the extent that an express confidentiality agreement cannot be enforced — for instance, because it is contrary to public policy — a plaintiff can fall back on an implied term or on the equitable obligation. The question of whether a contractual obligation of confidence should be defeated 'because [it is] contrary to public policy' is discussed at some length in *AG Australia Holdings* at IPR 291–310. If the obligation of confidence relating to information exchanged in a contractual relationship arises by implication, it will generally extend only to such information as is not in the public domain; that is, confidential information as identified by the application of equitable principles: see, for example, *Ansell Rubber Co Pty Ltd v Allied Rubber Industries Pty Ltd* [1967] VR 37. Courts thus commonly conflate equity and common law in construing the extent of implied contractual obligations relating to information. Certain contractual relationships will, of course, give rise to a broader duty, which then overridingly determines the parties' obligations with respect to information. For example, within the context of a contract of employment, the employee owes the employer an implied contractual duty of fidelity. In such circumstances, the duty of an employee not to use or disclose information in certain ways may also extend to information that under equitable principles alone would not be considered confidential (ie, not secret enough to attract the granting of a remedy for disclosure or misuse). In *Maggbury Pty Ltd v Hafele Australia Pty Ltd* (2001) 210 CLR 181; 53 IPR 1, the High Court confronted a different problem: whether an express obligation to treat as secret certain information that was confidential at the time of signing the agreement could be contractually enforced after it had entered the public domain. The developer of a new kind of ironing board had entered into a written agreement to disclose relevant information to Hafele with a view to its possible commercial development. This had not come to fruition, and the information became public by way of a patent application. Hafele was found to have used the relevant information in one of its products without reference to the inventor. The court held that the contractual undertaking not to use the information could not be enforced. Once that information had entered the public domain, the contractual terms relating to the information amounted to an illegal restraint of trade.

Who has standing to sue for a breach of confidence?

11.4 Although the action for breach of confidence is not based on property rights in information, the question 'who may bring an action for breach of confidence?' may yet be rephrased usefully as 'who owns the confidential information concerned?' and thus has standing to sue. Uncertainty often arises where confidential information is produced or obtained by employees in the course of employment. As a general rule, the employer will be the owner of the information in such a case. In *Elecon Australia Pty Ltd v PIV Drives GmbH* [2010] FCAFC 56 (on appeal from *Elecon Australia Pty Ltd v Brevini Australia Pty Ltd* [2009] FCA 1327), the Full Court of the Federal Court pointed out that '... although confidential information is not property in the usual sense, it may be transferred by one person to another and the person to whom it is transferred has standing to take action to protect the confidentiality of the information.': at [35]. Therefore, courts are able to grant injunctions and equitable compensation to transferees, but it will depend on the precise facts and circumstances (when was the information obtained or produced, did it relate to the duties of the employee, and so on). If the employer owns the information, they may bring an action to restrain either the ex-employee or third parties from using or communicating the information in certain ways.

Similar issues may arise where the information is generated in the context of a contract for services rather than of service; for instance, a technical report commissioned from an expert. A contracted party who produces information for valuable consideration will have no standing to sue third parties or have any rights to restrain the commissioning party from using the information in any way they see fit, unless the contract impliedly or expressly so provides. For example, in *Fraser v Evans* [1969] 1 QB 349, a consultant was denied standing to restrain the *Sunday Times* from publishing information from a confidential report he had produced for the Greek Government. Where confidential information is sold as an object of commerce, the transferee becomes the 'owner' of the information and can sue the transferor for unauthorised use or disclosure. Yet it is not always the equitable owner who can sue; for instance, where trade secrets are licensed, it may be that the licensor can be restrained by the licensee, who is clearly not the owner of the information. As a general rule, it can also be said that it is the person who is owed the duty of confidence rather than the person who owes the duty of confidence who can bring an action for a breach: see, for example, *Finnane v Australian Consolidated Press Ltd* [1978] 2 NSWLR 435.

The Elements of the Action

The modern action: *Coco v Clark*

11.5 Megarry J's judgment in *Coco v Clark* contains the definitive statement of the elements of the modern action for breach of confidence: the information must have the necessary quality of confidence, the information must have been imparted in circumstances implying an obligation of confidence and there must be an unauthorised use or disclosure of that information to the detriment of the person who claims the confidence. But a preliminary requirement is for adequate identification (particularisation) of the information concerned. Thus in *Optus Networks Pty Ltd v Telstra Corporation Ltd* the Full Federal Court identified the following *four* essential elements:

a. the information that is said to be confidential must be identified with specificity;
b. the information must have the necessary 'quality of confidence';
c. the information was imparted in circumstances importing an obligation of confidence; and
d. there must be an actual or threatened misuse of the information by the defendant without the plaintiff's consent: at [39], citing *Smith Kline & French Laboratories (Aust) Ltd v Secretary, Department of Community Services and Health* (1990) 22 FCR 73 at 87; 17 IPR 545 (*Smith Kline & French Laboratories [No 1]*).

Gummow J in *Smith Kline & French Laboratories [No 1]* had said that '… the plaintiff must be able to identify with specificity, and not merely in global terms, that which is said to be the information in question': at FCR 87; IPR 560. Vague or abstract statements will not normally be sufficient. Dean has pointed out that the requirement of itemisation has achieved 'an importance equal to the nature of the information itself'.[2] Often, the courts will have to distinguish carefully between information that is confidential and information that is related — but separate — such as an employee's general know-how, that is not confidential. For that reason, precision is also required. The rationale is also referable to the remedy that is sought: a party subject to an order of the court relating to confidential information must be able to identify what is and what is not subject to the terms of the order. In *American Cyanamid Company v Alcoa of Australia Ltd* (1993) 27 IPR 16, the rationale is identified in terms of the proper administration of justice: 'confidential information which is sought to be protected must be described by a plaintiff with sufficient particularity to enable it to be identified and to be embodied in an order of the court granting an injunction' (at IPR 20); see also the further cases cited at that point. Sufficient precision is also required in terms of the other elements, inter alia because 'one needs to know not only what was the information conveyed but also what part of that information was not common knowledge': see *O'Brien v Komesaroff* (1982) 150 CLR 310 at 327 per Mason J in; see also *Althaus v Australia Meat Holdings Pty Ltd* [2006] 1 Qd R 493.

In *Independent Management Resources Pty Ltd v Brown* [1987] VR 605; (1986) 9 IPR 1, the court pointed out:

> The more general the description of the information which a plaintiff seeks to protect, the more difficult it is for the court to satisfy itself that information so described was imparted or received or retained by a defendant in circumstances which give rise to an obligation of confidence.

See also *Retractable Technologies v Occupational and Medical Innovations* (2007) 72 IPR 58 and *Bluescope Steel Ltd v Kelly* (2007) 72 IPR 289. The latter case illustrates the difficulties of itemising or particularising information where there is a large volume of

---

2. R Dean, *The Law of Trade Secrets and Personal Secrets*, LawBook Co, 2002, p 92.

material that was disclosed over a long period of time. In the end, the court accepted that there had been a breach, although not every item of information was itemised, and that an injunction could be appropriately framed, although it extended beyond the information itemised in the schedule of confidential information tendered by the confidor, which was, admittedly, not exhaustive. This willingness to overcome the problems of particularising large volumes of material contrasts with the approach in *Woolworths Ltd v Olson* (2004) 63 IPR 258. In that case, like in *Bluescope*, an employee was found liable for disclosing information derived from a secret development project after termination. The injunction granted was limited to information contained in identified documents, and imposed a restraint upon its disclosure 'without first giving four weeks notice to Woolworths of an intent to engage in the conduct the subject of the restraint': *Woolworths* at 334; see also *Rapid Metal Developments (Australia) Pty Ltd v Anderson Formrite Pty Ltd* [2005] WASC 255. The court gives a useful account of the requirement for, and importance of, itemisation, but also notes that a number of cases have stressed that the degree of particularisation to be required must depend on all the circumstances of the case. In particular, itemisation may not be required to the same degree if there is a risk of destroying confidentiality by doing so. In terms of the *Bluescope* type of scenario, where sheer volume of material and time elapsed make itemisation difficult, the court helpfully refers to the approach in *Re a firm of Solicitors* [1997] Ch 1, per Lightman J on p 10 at F: see *Rapid Metal Developments* at [92]. On a final point, it is well recognised that a compendium or collection of disparate items of information may be confidential, not because each item contained within is confidential but because 'the protection which equity provides in relation to confidential information should make adequate allowance for the skill, effort time and money expanded in acquiring, collating and producing the information in a readily workable and useful form': *DC Payments Pty Ltd v Next Payments Pty Ltd* [2016] VSC 315 at [60].

These judicial statements to the effect that the rule is not absolutely rigid and its application must depend on 'all the circumstances' draw attention to a broader flexibility inherent in the action for breach of confidence. Whether or not the elements are all established often depends on a close analysis of the facts and on fine judgment. Formulating an exhaustive set of rules governing the search for the elements of the action is futile, given the multifarious factual situations that can arise as far as the nature of the information is concerned — from personal information (matrimonial confidences as in *Argyll v Argyll* [1967] Ch 302 or details of family life as in *Hitchcock v TCN Channel 9* [2000] NSWSC 198) to matters of national security (*Commonwealth v John Fairfax & Sons Ltd* (1980) 147 CLR 39) to high-tech technological secrets (*Secton Pty Ltd (t/as BWN Industries) v Delawood Pty Ltd* (1991) 21 IPR 136) — but also with respect to the characteristics of the parties and their relationships and with respect to the circumstances of use or disclosure of the information. Nonetheless, the principles derived from *Coco v Clark* are now firmly established, and all the well-known elements must be present, the obligation of confidence vindicating neither a right of privacy nor a property right in disguise. In *ABC v Lenah Game Meats*, the High Court confirmed that the rules could not be relaxed to accommodate any complaint about unconscionable conduct. However justified it may seem in the circumstances, that does not fit within the constraints of the established elements. Contrast this, however, with the approach taken by the New Zealand Court of Appeal in *Hosking & Hosking v Simon Runting* [2004] NZCA 34, where the relationship between the torts of breach of confidence and invasion of privacy was analysed; see also the developments in England in this regard: T Aplin, 'Commercialising privacy and privatising the commercial: the difficulties arising from the protection of privacy via breach of confidence', in A Kur, N Lee, A Ohly, G Westkamp (eds), *Intellectual Property, Unfair Competition and Publicity — Convergences and Development*; Edward Elgar, 2014.

The Necessary Quality of Confidence

Relative secrecy required

11.6 The use or disclosure of information that is in the public domain will not be restrained on the basis of the equitable obligation of confidence — as it might well be on the basis of contract or because of the existence of a broader duty: see above. However, courts have not required that the plaintiff establish that the information is absolutely secret, merely that information not be in the public domain, or that it should have 'the necessary quality of confidence' about it. In *Attorney-General v Guardian Newspapers Ltd (No 2)* [1990] 1 AC 109 at 282, Lord Goff said that 'public domain', for these purposes, means 'no more than that the information in question is so generally accessible that, in all the circumstances, it cannot be regarded as confidential'. Hence, that information not be in the public domain does not mean that it should not be available to any member of the public anywhere. Rather, the question is whether it is available to the relevant public; that is, actually available to people interested in it or belonging to the relevant trade, rather than notionally available to any person at all. Secrecy here is also relative in the sense that whereas individual items of information are all in the public domain, the skill and effort expended in compiling them in a useful form gives the necessary cloak of confidence to the resulting compilation. The relative standard also applies to technical trade secrets. Even though a solution to a problem could be worked out from public sources, if time and effort are required to do so, the relevant information may be sufficiently secret. Unlike in patents law, it is not necessary to show that the solution was not obvious, although that may indeed indicate that it is not known more generally. If reverse engineering is required to disclose useful information about a product, this may also amount to sufficient secrecy where such information has passed between parties confidentially. Not only must the information not be in the public domain but also it must be regarded as confidential by the plaintiff. Thus, in *Autodata Limited v Boyce's Automotive Data Pty Ltd* [2007] FCA 1517 at [10]–[11], Tamberlin J said:

> [10] Objective and subjective factors are relevant when considering an application for confidentiality. The objective factor is that the information in relation to which the claim is made must possess 'the necessary quality of confidence about it': *Saltman Engineering Co Ltd v Campbell Engineering Co Ltd* at RPC 215 (per Lord Greene MR). The subjective factor is that the information must be important or significant 'not necessarily in the sense of commercially valuable ... but in the sense that the preservation of its confidentiality or secrecy is of substantial concern to the plaintiff': *Moorgate Tobacco (No 2)* 156 CLR at 438 (per Deane J) (emphasis added); see also *Thomas Marshall* [1978]

> 3 All ER at 209–210 (per Megarry V-C). Crucial to any determination of confidentiality, therefore, is a consideration of the evidence before the Court, which in this case was extremely limited, and of the nature of the information in dispute.
>
> [11] On the basis that Boyce marked the Report as 'Confidential' and that correspondence between the parties demonstrates Boyce's concern over the possibility that the information in the Report would be disclosed to the public, I am persuaded that Boyce believes that the information is important to its business and confidential in nature. The issue therefore, is whether the information, considered objectively, can be said to have the requisite degree of confidentiality.

In the absence of any evidence that the confidentiality of the information concerned had any significance to the party, it is perhaps unlikely that a court will find that it was treated as confidential, rather than being information whose use was not subject to any particular constraint. A plaintiff may have to prove that information was dealt with confidentially; for instance, by giving evidence of practical measures taken to protect it from free circulation, the inclusion of express terms in employment contracts, limited circulation of documents and proper record-keeping: see, for example, *GlaxoSmithKline Australia Pty Ltd v Ritchie* [2008] VSC 164.

Information available to a number of persons

11.7 Information may be available to a group of people but still be sufficiently secret because each of them is restrained from disclosing it by an obligation of confidence (eg, within a corporation or government department). In *Mense & Ampere Electrical Manufacturing Co Pty Ltd v Milenkovic* [1973] VR 784 at 796–8, McInerney J summed up the matters that were relevant in determining whether information was sufficiently secret when it has circulated within a business:

1. the extent to which the information is known outside the business;
2. the extent to which the trade secret was known by employees and others involved in the plaintiff's business;
3. the extent of measures taken by the plaintiff to guard the secrecy of the information;
4. the value of the information to the plaintiff and to their competitors; and
5. the amount of effort or money expended by the plaintiff in developing the information.

For a similar oft-cited statement, see also *Ansell Rubber Co Pty Ltd v Allied Rubber Industries Pty Ltd* [1967] VR 37 at 49–50. Kirby P in *Wright v Gasweld Pty Ltd* (1991) 22 NSWLR 317 at 334; 20 IPR 481 at 499 also usefully listed what courts have found relevant in determining what is confidential:

a. the fact that skill and effort were expended to acquire the information: see *Interfirm Comparison (Australia) Pty Ltd v Law Society of NSW* [1975] 2 NSWLR 104 at 117; *Wheatly v Bell* [1982]; cf *International Scientific Communications Inc v Pattinson* [1979] FSR 429 at 434;
b. the fact that the information is jealously guarded by the employer, is not made readily available to employees and could not, without considerable effort and/or

risk, be acquired by others: see *Ansell Rubber Co Pty Ltd v Allied Rubber Industries Pty Ltd; E Eorsley & Co Ltd v Cooper* [1939] 1 All ER 290 at 307; cf *Stephenson Jordan & Harrison v Mc Donald & Evans* (1952) 69 RPC 10 at 16;

c. the fact that it was plainly made known to the employee that the material was regarded by the employer as confidential: see *Printers & Finishers Ltd v Holloway (No 2)* [1965] RPC 239 at 256; *Faccenda Chicken Ltd v Fowler* [1987] Ch 117; (1985) 6 IPR 155 at 165;

d. the fact that the usages and practices of the industry support the assertion of confidentiality: see, for example, *Thomas Marshall (Exports) Ltd v Guinle* [1978] 3 All ER 193 at 209–10; and

e. the fact that the employee in question has been permitted to share the information only by reason of their seniority or high responsibility within the employer's organisation: see *Faccenda Chicken*.

See also *International Entertainment (Aust) Pty Ltd v Churchill* [2002] QSC 317, where the factors identified by Kirby P were applied to hold that information gathered and retained by fundraising contractors concerning donor history was confidential. For an example of a case where the information (embodied in architectural drawings) was not dealt with as a trade secret, see *TS & B Retail Systems Pty Ltd v 3Fold Resources Pty Ltd (No 3)* (2007) 158 FCR 444; 72 IPR 492 at 499; [2007] FCA 151.

Information not known to the relevant public

11.8 As indicated above, it may be that information is publicly available somewhere but not in an obvious or easily accessible place, or not from sources relevant circles would normally access. In some cases, such limited availability may not be sufficient to destroy confidentiality, but it depends on the precise facts. Thus, in *Franchi v Franchi* [1967] RPC 149, the invention concerned was only made public in a patent application in Belgium. But because patent agents in the UK could be expected to check foreign patent information in their professional capacity, the invention was held not to be sufficiently secret in England. Nonetheless, the strict principles that apply in patents law to destroy novelty by the slightest public availability do not apply to the same extent in the context of actions for breach of confidence: see *Interfirm Comparison (Australia) Pty Ltd v Law Society of NSW* [1975] 2 NSWLR 104 at 118–19. The matter must be judged in the light of the practices and usages of a particular industry: see *Thomas Marshall v Guinle* [1978] 3 All ER 193 at 210. Dean points out, drawing on the cases, that 'the public domain in trade secret cases is usually not the world at large but the trade in which the plaintiff competes.'[3] The same author refers to *RL Crain v Ashton* [1950] 1 DLR 601, in which it was pointed out that certain information ceased to be confidential only once it 'became known to others who were interested in the construction or sale of such [machines], that is to say, became known to the trade': at 609.

In that same case, Hogg J also points out that 'it is trite to state that a secret once disclosed is no longer a secret': *RL Crain* at 609. As a general rule, then, confidence ceases when information or ideas become public knowledge. However, becoming

3. R Dean, *The Law of Trade Secrets and Personal Secrets*, LawBook Co, 2002, p 92.

public knowledge is a matter of degree, and courts have acknowledged that relief can be given to restrain a defendant from publishing confidential information after some limited publication has occurred: see, for example, *Commonwealth v John Fairfax & Sons* at CLR 54, *Franchi v Franchi* at RPC 152–3, *Attorney-General (UK) v Heinemann Publishers Australia Pty Ltd* (1987) 8 NSWLR 341 at 374; 10 IPR 129 (*Heinemann*) and *David Syme & Co Ltd v General Motors Holden Ltd* (1984) 2 NSWLR 294 at 299. More recently, Kellam J gave consideration to the question of at what point previously private information has 'entered the public domain': see *Australian Football League v Age Company Ltd* (2006) 15 VR 419; for instance, because of coverage in the media or publication on the internet (see at 428–31). Burchett AJ, in *Artedomus v Del Casale* [2006] NSWSC 146, referred to the statement in S Ricketson and C Creswell on *The Law of Intellectual Property: Copyright, Designs & Confidential Information* vol 2, at 25.85, 'Confidentiality is not lost simply because the information is known to persons other than its originator'. Sometimes, information has not become public but has gone stale, and for that reason an injunction will be refused. In *Commonwealth v John Fairfax & Sons*, information relating to events that occurred during the 1975 Timor crisis had 'gone stale', rather than become public knowledge, by the time the action was brought, and for that reason did not attract the grant of an injunction to restrain publication.

Commercial or technical trade secrets

11.9 Where the information is technical or scientific, the crucial determinant of secrecy will often be the amount of work, effort and skill required to arrive at the information in the form in which it is claimed to be confidential. It may, for instance, be possible by trial and error and experiment, and by studying relevant literature, to arrive at the same information. Even if no special ingenuity or inventiveness is required in this process, the information may still be sufficiently confidential. However, there must be some evidence that skill, effort and expense are associated with the development of the product; for instance, computer or internet files: see *Dais Studio Pty Ltd v Bullet Creative Pty Ltd* (2007) 165 FCR 92; 74 IPR 512 at 535. It may be that commercially valuable information is used to develop a technical concept, such as the video capture card developed using confidential data concerning parts usage, profits and costings: see *Blackmagic Design Pty Ltd v Overliese* [2011] FCAFC 24.

Similarly, the fact alone that the close analysis or reverse engineering of a product that is in the public domain would reveal information that is embodied in it but is not otherwise publicly available does not mean that it is not sufficiently secret: see, for example, *Conveyor Co of Australia Pty Ltd v Cameron* [1973] 2 NZLR 38. If some skill and effort are required to reverse engineer the product, the embodied information may be secret enough. However, it may be that it is not appropriate to grant a permanent injunction in such a case, since the embodied information can be derived by any person minded to obtain it by reverse engineering. In such a case, a temporary restraint can be imposed, which deprives a defendant of the unfair 'springboard' they obtained over all others by using information in ready form in breach of an obligation of confidence: see *Terrapin Ltd v Builders' Supply Co (Hayes) Ltd* [1967] RPC 375 and Chapter 19 Remedies in Intellectual Property Law. The same point concerning information that can be derived from public sources may hold in the context of commercial trade secrets such as customer details. The fact that it is possible to ascertain who is in the market for a certain product in a certain area, by contacting all potential clients or doing market research of some sort, does not mean that the client data of a certain business containing all such information in a readily useable format are not confidential enough. What is protected is the compilation rather than the individual items contained within it.

For example, in *Schindler Lifts Australia Pty Ltd v Milan Debelak* (1989) 15 IPR 129, the question was whether ex-employees had taken confidential information, in the shape of customer lists of a lift maintenance company, in breach of an implied contractual duty. New South Wales Department of Labour and Industry records showing lift permits were freely available to the lift industry, but these departmental records did not show the owner of the building or the address to which accounts could be sent. Such information was contained in the plaintiff's customer list; thus, the list allegedly taken did contain valuable confidential information. In *NP Generations Pty Ltd v Feneley* (2001) 52 IPR 563, names, addresses and telephone numbers of landlords, compiled by an employee of a real estate agency in her address book, were held to be confidential. More recently, in *DC Payments Pty Ltd v Next Payments Pty Ltd* [2016] VSC 315 the 'Master Customer List' was considered confidential information, as it was guarded by various internal measures, it was made known to employees that it was confidential, it contained all the necessary important information, employees were only permitted to share it by reason of their seniority, and a competitor was likely to derive advantage from the knowledge contained within it: at [61]–[64]. The cases where customer lists are at issue are many and varied; it is certainly not the case that customer information in whatever form is, *ipso facto*, confidential. In other cases, the identity of suppliers is claimed to be confidential, sometimes successfully, as in *Del Casale v Artedomus (Aust) Pty Ltd* [2007] NSWCA 172, but other times not so: see *Futuretronics.com.au Pty Ltd v Graphix Labels Pty Ltd* [2009] FCAFC 2, where insufficient evidence led to the supplier's identity not being generally known.

Ideas, concepts and proposals

11.10 The cases *Fraser v Thames TV* [1984] QB 44 and *Talbot v General Television Corporation Pty Ltd* (1980) VR 224 concerning formats for television shows, and also *Seager v Copydex Ltd (No 2)* [1969] 2 All ER 718; EWCA Civ J0311-1; 1 WLR 809, where the 'germ of an idea' for a carpet grip was communicated, stand for the proposition that the existence of a fully elaborated plan or a comprehensive written record is not essential for an idea, concept or format to be protected in equity. First, what is required is that the idea or concept be sufficiently precise, both to establish whether or not it is confidential and to know whether it has some value that makes it worth protecting in equity. As Vickery J put it in *Vasco Investment Managers Ltd v Morgan Stanley Australia Ltd* [2014] VSC 455 at [275]:

> In practice, the requirement for sufficient development of the concept, also gives rise to the need for precise identification of the confidential information in question. It is necessary to identify with specificity, and not merely in global terms, that which is said to be the confidential information relied upon to found the action.

Thus an idea can be relatively undeveloped, and perhaps not even written down but simply orally communicated, and still support an enforceable obligation of confidence. Second, the concept, format or idea must not be so banal that any person could come up with it, or be common knowledge; it will have the necessary quality of confidence only if 'it is produced by somebody who applies intellectual activity to the [otherwise public] material to produce the result': *Vasco* at [278]. A concept or idea that is commonplace or utterly obvious, or something that is already known or done but in a slightly different form, does not have what is required to take it outside the public domain. Although in *Seager v Copydex Ltd (No 2)* it was held that the degree of originality of the idea need not be high (at WLR 813–14), there must nonetheless be some 'commercial twist' that takes it outside the public domain. Basing himself on *Talbot v General Television*, Hirst J in *Fraser v Thames TV* at QB 65–6 said that:

> ... to be capable of protection the idea must be sufficiently developed, so that it would be seen to be a concept which has at least some attractiveness for a television program and which is capable of being realised as an actuality ... [and that the idea must be] of potential commercial attractiveness.

Further, a 'significant element of originality not already in the public realm' was required, which may consist of a significant twist or slant to a well-known concept. By alluding to originality, Hirst J was simply referring to something that takes the idea outside the bounds of public knowledge, rather than some elevated standard of inventiveness or creativity. *Darvall McCutcheon (a firm) v HK Frost Holdings Pty Ltd (in liq)* (2002) 4 VR 570; [2002] VSCA 85 illustrates how there may be little novelty about an idea at a certain level of generality (a corporate-sponsored art collection reflecting the Sydney Olympics or Centenary of Federation), whereas a more developed concept (commissioning specific artworks from particular categories of artists that highlighted Australian life as connected with the bicentenary of Australia) was sufficiently unique to be confidential information.

In *Secton Pty Ltd v Delawood Pty Ltd* (1991) 21 IPR 136 at 155–6, where inchoate technical concepts were at issue, King J stated that mere goals or possibilities, vague mental conceptions, or untested and unproven concepts cannot amount to confidential information. In *Titan Group Pty Ltd v Steriline Manufacturing Pty Ltd* (1990) 19 IPR 353, the two elements that made up the core of the confidential information were each commonplace. But O'Loughlin J pointed out (at 379) that:

> There can be 'inventive merit in combining in one combination integers which are themselves old or the subject of common knowledge': *Harrison v Project Design Co. (Redcar) Ltd.* [[1978] FSR 81] at p 85. It is sufficient if the idea has a 'commercial twist': *Talbot v General Television Corporation Ltd.* (1980) VR 224 at 231.

The linking of a pressure control valve in a hydraulic pump system to gymnasium equipment was the relevant commercial twist in *Titan*. However, it is as well to reiterate some of the relevant points made above here. First, to attract the protection of the action for breach of confidence, information need not be inherently original or novel or inventive, as in the patents law sense; rather, establishing that an idea is novel, original or inventive may be important because it assists in proving that it is not in the public domain or public knowledge (see, eg, *Krueger Transport Equipment Pty Ltd v Glen Cameron Storage* (2008) 78 IPR 262). Second, it is important that information that is claimed to be confidential is circumscribed and identified with sufficient precision, and not just in abstract or global terms. As is pointed out above, courts will not restrain the use of information the limits of which cannot be clearly discerned, because it will not be possible to reliably determine whether or not such information is in the public domain nor to fashion a clearly bounded remedy. In other words, it will be necessary to show exactly what the idea is, and that may involve, to some degree, showing that it has some practical application and that it is therefore worthy of protection in equity. Often, there is some overlap with copyright law because an idea has been expressed in the precise form of drawing or plans (artistic works): see, for example, *TS & B Retail Systems v 3Fold Resources (No 3)*.

Trade secrets

11.11 'Trade secrets' are no more than one form of confidential information as far as the law is concerned. As McKeough and Stewart (*Intellectual Property in Australia*, Butterworths, 1991, p 107) point out, 'The better view is that "trade secret" in this context simply denotes a large subset of the range of information caught by the equitable doctrine, covering any information of a business or commercial nature which has been kept relatively secret.' In other words, in Australia, 'trade secret' is not usually a term of art, and no special significance or consequences normally attach to classification as such. In *Lansing Linde Ltd v Kerr* (1990) 21 IPR 529 at 536, Staughton LJ said that a trade secret was information that if disclosed to a competitor would be liable to cause real or significant harm to the owner of the secret. However, the term 'trade secret' is sometimes used as a term of art in the context of employment relationships to refer to that category of confidential information that an employee is not entitled to use or divulge even after the contract of employment has terminated: see Chapter 12 Breach of Confidence: Defences, Remedies and Employees.

Information Imparted in Circumstances that Imply Confidentiality

The 'reasonable person' test and the 'limited purpose' test

11.12 The second of the elements identified by Megarry J in *Coco v Clark* at IPR 590 (above at 11.5) was that 'information must have been imparted in circumstances importing an obligation of confidence'. He elaborated further, formulating a broad test to determine whether an obligation of confidence exists (at RPC 48):

> It seems to me that if the circumstances are such that any reasonable man standing in the shoes of the recipient of the information would have realised that upon reasonable grounds the information was being given to him in confidence, then this should suffice to impose upon him the equitable obligation of confidence.

Fullagar J in *Deta Nominees Pty Ltd v Viscount Plastic Products Pty Ltd* [1979] VR 167 at 193 put it in these terms:

> Would a person of ordinary intelligence, in all the circumstances of the case, including, inter alia, the relationship of the parties and the nature of the information and the circumstances of its communication, recognise this information to be the property of the other person and not his own to do as he likes with?

In other words, an obligation of confidence will not arise simply because information imparted is confidential. There must be some basis on which a recipient of information can be held liable to observe the confidence. After all, the basis of the obligation to respect confidences 'lies in the notion of an obligation of conscience arising from the circumstances in or through which the information was communicated or obtained': see *Moorgate Tobacco (No 2)* at ALR 203 per Deane J. The obligation fairly arises where the circumstances make it clear that the communication was for a limited or specific purpose, and, by implication, all other uses of the information were reserved for the confidor. Thus, the 'limited purpose' test is commonly applied to determine whether or not a duty of confidence exists; the norm is that the recipient of information is free and unfettered in its use, unless it becomes expressly or implicitly clear that it can be used or divulged only in specific ways. After all, the essential advantage of protecting confidences lies in the ability to share information for a particular purpose while retaining the exclusive right to use it for all other purposes. But although the limited purpose test may establish that a communication was in confidence, it is not the relevant or only test in all circumstances. Thus, in *Smith Kline & French Laboratories (Australia) Ltd v Secretary of the Department of Community Services and Health* (1991) 28 FCR 291; 20 IPR 643 at 655 (*Smith Kline & French Laboratories [No 2]*), the court pointed out that other factors may be relevant:

> In many circumstances, [the limited purpose test] will produce a proper result, but the circumstances in which confidential information is supplied may vary widely. To determine the existence of confidentiality and its scope, it may be relevant to consider whether the information was supplied gratuitously or for a consideration; whether there is any past practice of such a kind as to give rise to an understanding; how sensitive the information is; whether the confidor has any interest in the purpose for which the information is to be used; whether the confidor expressly warned the confidee against a particular disclosure or use of the information — and, no doubt, many other matters.

It may therefore be better to see the limited purpose test not as an overarching test but, first, as a useful rule of thumb and, second, as identifying one, albeit important, factor to be taken into account to determine whether, in the circumstances, 'a reasonable person in [the applicant's] position would have considered that he or she was not free to deal with the documents as his or her own, or could only deal with them subject to certain limiations': see *IPC Global Pty Ltd v Pavetest Pty Ltd (No 3)* [2017] FCA 82 at [210]. Note that the limited purpose test is relevant in deciding not only whether an obligation has arisen but also the extent of that obligation. As to the latter aspect, see further below at 11.15, where the facts of *Smith Kline & French Laboratories [No 2]* are further discussed.

Factors implying confidence: the nature and context of the communication

11.13 Often, the obligation will be implied from the antecedents (eg, preceding correspondence), nature and setting (eg, commercial rather than social) or conduct of the transaction or meeting during which information is imparted. Where the context of the disclosure of confidential information is commercial, the courts will not be slow to find that the circumstances gave rise to an obligation of confidence. For instance, in *Coco v Clark* Megarry J said (at RPC 48):

> In particular, where information of commercial or industrial value is given on a business-like basis and with some avowed common object in mind, such as a joint venture or the manufacture of articles by one party for another, I would regard the recipient as carrying a heavy burden if he seeks to repel a contention he was bound by an obligation of confidence.

In *Fraser v Thames TV* (see also 11.10), Hirst J thought that normal usage or custom in the industry was a factor of considerable force in deciding whether a legal obligation had arisen. Every witness from the theatre or television business agreed that it would be wrong to use a concept for a show communicated in a business-like meeting without the consent of the communicator. In fact, it was in accordance with the authorities that the 'obligation that the witnesses saw as moral is in fact also legal in character' (at QB 66).

But *Fractionated Cane Technology v Ruiz-Avila* [1988] 2 Qd R 610; (1988) 13 IPR 609 stands for the proposition that a meeting cannot retrospectively be given a commercial or professional character from which an obligation of confidence can be inferred, just because something of potential commercial value is unintentionally revealed. In this case, the appellant had learnt about the respondent's machine to dehydrate organic matter, and thought it might be used to process sugar cane for the purposes of producing useful stock feed. He asked the respondents to arrange a test processing of some sugar cane. He was present at the tests (as were the respondents), where the unexpectedly good results impressed him as to the potential of sugar cane-based stock feed. Subsequent tests of the resulting dried material confirmed the potential of the process. However, the trial judge found that what had happened on the test day did not take place in the course of a joint venture or a prospective contractual arrangement that was to govern the relationship between the parties. The appeal court agreed with the trial judge.

Fractionated Cane shows that an obligation of confidence will not automatically be attached to any information revealed in an arguably commercial context. Nor can it be so that where something interesting or commercially useful is unexpectedly revealed in an otherwise casual or unstructured setting, an obligation of confidence will be retrospectively imposed on those who have witnessed it, just because of its commercial value. Note also that not all professional meetings automatically engender a blanket obligation of confidence, all circumstances being relevant; for example, in *Esso Australia Resources Ltd v Plowman (Minister for Energy & Minerals)* (1995) 183 CLR 10, production of documents at an arbitration hearing did not necessarily imply confidence or cloak the documents with confidentiality.

Information obtained surreptitiously or illegally, deliberately or accidentally

11.14 Although, generally, the test is whether information has been imparted in circumstances of confidentiality, in many cases it can be 'a little artificial' to speak in terms of information 'being received' in circumstances that import an obligation of confidence: see, for instance, *IPC Global* where the respondent had actually *created* those documents himself in his capacity as an employee. Most importantly, a now longstanding line of cases recognise that an obligation of confidence may also arise because of the surreptitious, illegal or unconscionable manner in which information has been acquired. In other words, in *Ashburton v Pape* [1913] 2 Ch 469 at 475; (1913) 82 LJ Ch 527, Swinfen Eady LJ accepted that:

> The principle upon which the Court of Chancery has acted for many years has been to restrain the publication of confidential information improperly or surreptitiously obtained or of information imparted in confidence which ought not to be divulged.

In *ABC v Lenah Game Meats*, Gleeson CJ confirmed that 'equity may impose obligations of confidentiality even though there is no imparting of information in circumstances of trust and confidence': at [34]; see also more recently *Armstrong Strategic Management & Marketing Pty Ltd v Expense Reduction Analysts Group Pty Ltd* (2012) 295 ALR 348; [2012] NSWCA 430. In *Franklin v Giddins* [1978] Qd R 72; (1977) 1B IPR 807, the defendant had stolen budwood from 'Franklin Early White' nectarine trees in the plaintiff's orchard. The plaintiff had propagated the strain of nectarine trees over many years of selective breeding. The trees could be propagated only by grafting. The defendant was convicted of the theft of the budwood, and the plaintiff brought a civil action for breach of confidence. According to Dunn J, the budwood constituted a trade secret. It existed only in the plaintiff's orchard, and the plaintiff guarded it by exercising general surveillance over fruit-pickers and visitors and by putting it abroad that it was theirs and theirs alone. The information that the genetic structure of the wood represented was of substantial commercial value. Much time and effort had been expended by the plaintiff in evolving it, and it could not be duplicated by anybody. The plaintiff was entitled to expect that other people would respect their right of property, and electric fences and guard dogs would not be required. The defendant knew the budwood constituted a valuable trade secret, and it was unconscionable for him to use his own wrongdoing to better his position in competition with the owner and with those who consensually obtained the propagating material. The judge ordered the delivery up of the relevant trees.

A remedy will therefore be available even in the absence of an underlying relationship of confidence, as is pointed out by Gleeson CJ in *ABC v Lenah Game Meats* at IPR 171: 'But equity may impose obligations of confidentiality even though there is no imparting of information in circumstances of trust and confidence.' The action may thus be useful in combating industrial espionage; that is, where a commercial rival intentionally sets out to obtain secret information by illegal or surreptitious means. The difficulty arises of distinguishing between legitimate industrial espionage or information gathering and the kinds of activities that might warrant the imposition of a remedial restraint by the courts. Where there is clear illegality, such as the trespass or theft as in *Franklin v Giddins*, there is no real problem. However, words such as surreptitious, reprehensible, unconscionable, etc, used to categorise conduct as warranting a remedy are rather vague and difficult to delineate. *Ashburton v Pape* refers to information 'improperly or surreptitiously obtained', clearly conduct falling far short of illegality.

What can be described as 'surreptitious' or 'improper' enough for a court to impose a remedy? In this context, it should not be forgotten that the law does not protect privacy, and that a mere breach of privacy to obtain information may therefore not constitute illegality. In the absence of a distinct tort of invasion of privacy, what kind of impropriety would warrant the granting of an injunction? Certainly, in *Sullivan v Sclanders* (2000) 77 SASR 419, where a trick was used to lure a guest out of a private house so that the host could surreptitiously rifle through his bag and copy certain confidential documents, the behaviour was not illegal but was sufficiently unconscionable to give rise to a remedy in equity. By contrast, the taking of a photograph (as opposed to merely taking down written notes) of material in a file to which access had otherwise been granted, did not persuade the court that 'the information comprised in the note, including the form in which it was written, was "surreptitiously obtained" or so inherently confidential that it would be "unconscientious" for the second defendant to be relieved of respecting the plaintiff's confidentiality as its author': see *Jane Doe v Fairfax Media Publications Pty Limited* [2018] NSWSC 1996. In England, the action for breach of confidence has been extended to provide protection for privacy, but, in Australia, the law has not developed so far; see, for example, in England, *Douglas v Hello! Ltd (No 2), Mosley v Focus Magazin Verlag GmbH* [2001] EWCA Civ 1030; *Campbell v MGN Ltd* [2004] UKHL 22; 2 AC 457; and *Irvine v Talksport* (2003) 2 ER 881.

It will also be relevant whether the information was obtained deliberately or accidentally. In *Malone v Commissioner of Police of the Metropolis* [1979] 2 All ER 620, the information concerned was obtained deliberately but without consent by means of legally sanctioned phone taps. Was the information confidential and could it thus not be passed on to third parties for use in other than criminal proceedings? It was argued for the plaintiff that even if using the phone 'must be taken as implying some sort of consent to some risk of being overheard, that could not be taken to be any kind of consent to any publication to any third party' at 634. But Sir Robert Megarry VC disagreed (at 645):

> It seems to me that a person who utters confidential information must accept the risk of any unknown overhearing that is inherent in the circumstances of communication. Those who exchange confidences on a bus or a train run the risk of a nearby passenger with acute hearing or a more distant passenger who is adept at lip-reading. Those who speak over garden walls run the risk of the unseen neighbour in a tool-shed nearby. [Megarry VC gives other examples such as office cleaners or users of an office intercom.] I do not see why someone who has overheard some secret in such a way should be exposed to legal proceedings if he uses or divulges what he has heard. No doubt an honourable man would give some warning when he realises that what he is hearing is not intended for his ears; but I have to concern myself with the law, and not with moral standards. There are, of course, many moral precepts which are not legally enforceable.

However, it is not correct to say that divulging accidentally obtained information is never actionable; supporting the assertion with ample authorities, Campbell JA in *Armstrong Strategic Management & Marketing* said that 'there can sometimes be an obligation of confidence that attaches to information that is inherently confidential or private if that information is illegally or surreptitiously obtained, *or is come across in the street, or is received unsolicited*': at [100] (emphasis added). Note that in *Marcel v Commissioner of Police of the Metropolis* [1992] Ch 225, it was held that where information is extracted from a person under statutory powers, such information can be used only for the purposes for which those powers were conferred, enforceable by a private law duty of confidentiality. In *Johns v Australian Securities Commission* (1993) 178 CLR 408, the High Court approved of the decision in *Marcel*, but pointed out that the duty was one imposed by statute, not by equity; nonetheless, the equitable remedy of injunction was available to enforce the duty against a public authority.

Unauthorised Use or Disclosure

The purpose of the communication

11.15 The third element of the action is unauthorised use or disclosure of the confidential information; in other words, a breach of the equitable duty. The recipient's broad obligation is not to take unfair advantage of the information imparted. More concretely, the content of the duty is usually 'that use and disclosure of information obtained in confidence is limited to the purpose for which the information was provided': see *Elliott v Ivey* [1998] NSWSC 116 at [9]. The obligation is on the confidee to establish what use of the information is permitted, rather than what is prohibited. In other words, where a duty of confidence exists, every use is prohibited unless the confidee can establish that it is a permitted use. Two basic questions arise: first, what use or disclosure, if any, was permitted? And, second, does the impugned use or disclosure fall outside the scope of what was authorised or agreed upon?

The first question is usually resolved by identifying from its circumstances what the purpose of the communication is and therefore the limits on its permitted use. It is necessary to demonstrate that the confidee knew the purpose (eg, from express terms accompanying the communication) or ought to have inferred it from the circumstances (eg, in format cases such as *Fraser v Thames TV* and *Talbot v General Television*, it was clear from the circumstances that the purpose is evaluation of the concepts presented).

However, in *Smith Kline & French Laboratories [No 2]*, the court held that the confidor's intended purpose does not always determine the full extent of the authorised use. The dispute revolved around the use made by the Department of Community Services and Health of the information supplied by Smith Kline & French (SKF) for the purpose of evaluating certain pharmaceutical substances for marketing approval. The department wished to use the information supplied to evaluate an application by an unrelated party. Clearly, that was not the purpose for which SKF provided it. But pointing out that the government or the state acts not in the pursuit of private interests but in the general public interest, the court said (at IPR 656):

> To avoid taking unfair advantage of information does not necessarily mean that the confidee must not use it except for the confider's limited purpose. Whether one adopts

> the 'reasonable man' test suggested by Megarry J or some other, there can be no breach of equitable obligation unless the court concludes that a confidence reposed has been abused, that unconscientious use has been made of the information.

No equitable obligation was relevantly breached. The court went on to warn against too narrow a test being imposed. In this particular case, adopting the limited purpose test that the appellants put forward 'might unduly obstruct not only business and government, but also ordinary communications between people'. The court pointed out that illegal use of information and use of a kind that many people may disapprove of are two different things. There would be substantial interference with the vital functions of government, in protecting the health and safety of the community, if the appellant's submission as to the limited purpose test was accepted. The court also stated at IPR 655: 'The test of confidor's purpose will not ordinarily be appropriate where each party's interest is quite different, and known to be so.' Further, it is as well to keep in mind that the underlying obligation is not to take unfair advantage of the information. Normally, it would be unfair to use information for other than the intended purpose of its imparting, but not always. Nonetheless, SKF was unusual because one party had an incontrovertible obligation to act in the broader public interest; in a majority of cases, investigating the purpose of the communication will lead to a satisfactory result, difficult as it may be to reconcile divergent purposes of confidor and confidee in some cases.

For a close analysis of *Smith Kline & French Laboratories [No 2]* and its implications for communications with government, see T Voon, 'Breach of Confidence by Government, Smith Kline and the TRIPS Agreement — Public Interest to the Rescue' (1998) 9 *AIPJ* 66. Note that the Therapeutic Goods Administration Act 1998 (Cth) now prohibits the use, for the assessment of applications for generic pharmaceutical equivalents, of data submitted to obtain marketing approval for a new drug, for a 5-year 'data exclusivity period' from the date of approval: see s 25A. This provision derives from the Australia–United States Free Trade Agreement, which requires protection for confidential regulatory data.

Was the use or disclosure in breach of the obligation?

11.16 The prohibition is on any disclosure that does (or will) destroy the information's confidentiality, as well as on use of confidential information. As Lord Denning MR said in *Seager v Copydex Ltd*, no use may be made of confidential information 'to the prejudice of him who gave it without obtaining his consent': at 417. Whether a use or communication beyond the limits of consent has occurred will substantially depend on identifying the limited purpose of the communication. The available evidence must then be evaluated to determine whether some use or communication has in fact occurred at odds with that purpose. It may be that there is direct evidence that the plaintiff did wrongly use the information received. But it may be that inferences have to be drawn from circumstantial evidence; for instance, from the fact that the information imparted in confidence has become available from public sources, or from the similarity of the defendant's ultimate product (be it physical or, eg, a TV show format) with what was demonstrated or explained in confidence. Naturally, the confidee in receipt of information under the guise of confidence is not restrained from relying on the same information obtained from different or public sources; for instance, if at some later point the confidor makes it public or some third party independently arrives at it and publishes it. Quite commonly, the confidee will attempt to escape liability by establishing that they relied on information publicly derived, or that a 'suspiciously' similar end product was independently contrived. However, it is not necessary to show that the defendant consciously or intentionally used information received in confidence. The court might accept that a defendant genuinely thought they had independently generated something but had, in fact, made use of a confidential idea. Parallels can be drawn with copyright; in particular, the cases of *Seager v Copydex Ltd* and *Seager v Copydex Ltd (No 2)*, where it was found that unconscious or subconscious copying had occurred.

Thus, in *Fraser v Thames TV*, the court accepted that the testimony of the program producer to the effect that he did not remember being told about the concept and felt it had spontaneously generated in his mind was truthful. Yet the judge held that the producer was mistaken in this belief and that he had, in fact, subconsciously reproduced the idea that he had learnt initially from the plaintiff. As a consequence, Thames TV was liable for breach of confidence. An allegation of breach of confidence will not necessarily be defeated by showing that the ultimate product is in some way different from the product that embodied the confidential information. The relevant question is whether there is an actual misuse of the information, not the degree of similarity between the two products. Although in an action for copyright or registered design infringement, alterations may take the end result outside the scope of the exclusive rights, that is not necessarily the case in the context of breach of confidence actions: see *S W Hart & Co Pty Ltd v Edwards Hot Water Systems* (1985) 5 IPR 13 at 15–17. The wrong lies in derivation from a confidential source, not in the similarity between products per se; the latter may, however, have evidentiary value. Copyright infringement and breach of confidence are often closely intertwined in cases concerned with computer programs allegedly shared with a new employer by a departing employee: see, for example, *IPC Global, TICA Default Tenancy Control Pty Ltd v Datakatch Pty Ltd* [2016] FCA 815 and *Leica Geosystems Pty Ltd v Koudstaal (No 3)* [2014] FCA 1129.

It is common for the defendant to attempt to defeat the plaintiff's contention of a breach by tendering evidence that the information used in fact emanated from other sources, was unavailable in the public domain, was public knowledge in a certain trade or pursuit, was independently generated or entered the public domain by other means and not via the confidee: see, for example, *GlaxoSmithKline Australia Pty Ltd v Ritchie*. For instance, a defendant may tender a witness who testifies about the process of design of a contested product, or indicates how something was assembled from public sources and not from confidential information. Where the defendant is attempting to establish that the information entered the public domain independently of the confidee, whatever evidence there is may be augmented by an objective comparison. Striking similarity between the information communicated and the information that is in the public domain may well support an inescapable inference that its public availability resulted from a breach of confidence by the confidee, particularly if the confidor can establish the precise extent of the circulation of their information. For a useful exposé of the correct approach to various fact scenarios, see *Norbrook Laboratories Ltd v Bomac Laboratories Ltd* [2004] NZCA 56 at [35]–[36].

Detriment

11.17 In *Coco v Clark*, it was said that there must be 'an unauthorised use of that information to the detriment of the party communicating it': at RPC 47. However, Megarry J also mentioned that the statements of principle in some cases mention detriment whereas others do not: at 48. Significantly, the word 'detriment' is used, not 'injury' or 'damage'.

It seems well established that positive proof of actual detriment is not required. The courts base that approach on two slightly divergent views. First is that it is in the public interest that confidences be upheld: confidentiality's value to social and commercial intercourse makes it, *ipso facto*, worthy of legal protection. In other words, the obligation of conscience should always be vindicated by the courts without more. Second, the defendant needs only to contend for some minor form of detriment. On the first view, an actual or imminent breach of confidence is always detrimental per se, and a power to prevent or arrest it automatically arises; no additional detriment need be proven: see, for instance, *Attorney-General v Guardian Newspapers Ltd (No 2)* and Gummow J in *Smith Kline & French Laboratories [No 2]* at [112]:

> The obligation of conscience is to respect the confidence, not merely to refrain from causing detriment to the plaintiff. The plaintiff comes to equity to vindicate his right to observance of the obligation, not necessarily to recover loss or to restrain infliction of apprehended loss.

The second approach is subtly different. It requires some detriment to be established but accepts that hurt to feelings or embarrassment will suffice: see, for example, *Prince Albert v Strange* (1849) 2 De G & Sm 652; 13 Jur 45; 64 ER 293, referring to the risk of embarrassment. This will often be apparent from the facts of the breach alone, so only limited further inquiry will usually be required. Where commercial information is concerned, detriment will readily be inferred, but not in all cases: for instance, in *Marshall v Prescott* [2015] NSWCA 110 there was no evidence at all of actual loss suffered and therefore no actionable wrong. For the requirement of damage in cases where a plaintiff seeks an award of damages or an account of profits, see the discussion in Chapter 19 Remedies in Intellectual Property Law. Whether the two views are really distinct is debateable: see, for instance, *Attorney-General v Observer Ltd (No 2)* [1990] 1 AC 109 at 256, where arguably Lord Keith of Kinkel made reference to a bit of both:

> [A]s a general rule it is in the public interest that confidences should be respected, and the encouragement of such respect may in itself constitute a sufficient ground for recognising and enforcing the obligation of confidence even where the confider can point to no specific detriment to himself [...] I would think it a sufficient detriment to the confider that information given in confidence is to be disclosed to persons whom he would prefer not to know of it, even though the disclosure would not be harmful to him in any positive way.

It is probably correct to say that the more logical view is that since equity's policy is to enforce the observance of obligations of confidence, proof of detriment is not required: this is the view expressed by Johnson J in *Rapid Metal Developments* at [78]. This also means that in terms of *quia timet* relief, what needs to be shown is not apprehended damage or harm but apprehended breach.

Confidential government information

11.18 Establishing detriment where the confidential information is in the possession of government is, however, a more onerous requirement. The disclosure of information concerning the internal workings of government is in the public interest in a democracy. If the government brings an action for breach of confidence, it will therefore have to establish that a clear detriment to the public interest will result from publication of the information.

In *Commonwealth v John Fairfax & Sons* Mason J said (at CLR 52):

> It may be a sufficient detriment to the citizen that disclosure of information relating to his affairs will expose his actions to public discussion and criticism. But it can scarcely be a relevant detriment to the government that publication of material concerning its actions will merely expose it to public discussion and criticism. It is unacceptable in our democratic society that there should be a restraint on the publication of information relating to government when the only vice of that information is that it enables the public to discuss, review and criticise government action … Unless disclosure is likely to injure the public interest, it will not be protected.

Publication of information that merely throws light on past workings of government (the case related to 'stale' information concerning the 1975 Timor crisis and the Australia, New Zealand, United States Security Treaty), even if it is not public property, is not to be restrained by the courts: 'If, however, it appears that disclosure will be inimical to the public interest because national security, relations with foreign countries or the ordinary business of government will be prejudiced, disclosure will be restrained': at CLR 52. Mason J found support in the English case of *Attorney-General v Jonathan Cape Ltd* [1976] QB 752. The courts will sometimes be faced with a difficult balancing act between the public interest in open discussion of government affairs and the need for confidentiality to preserve the proper workings of government. Into that exercise then intrudes the matter of freedom of the press, which has also been called in aid to justify the refusal of an injunction concerning the disclosure of governmental information.

For example, in *Heinemann* at IPR 233, Kirby P cited with approval a passage from Denning J's dissenting judgment in *Schering Chemicals Ltd v Falkman Ltd* [1981] 2 WLR 848:

> Freedom of the press is of fundamental importance in our society, it covers not only the right of the press to impart information of general interest or concern, but also the right of the public to receive it. It is not to be restricted on the grounds of breach of confidence unless there is a 'pressing social need' for such restraint.

Note that not all information that is in the possession of government (in the broad sense) concerns the workings of government. Much information of a confidential nature that would not concern the public interest is passed on to government. It is only when the information is in the hands of government and concerns the workings of government in some way, or concerns a matter of public policy, that there will be, as Mason J characterised it in *Esso Australia Resources Ltd v Plowman* at (concerning confidential information disclosed during arbitration of electricity prices in Victoria), a reversal of the onus of proof: 'the government must prove that the public interest demands non-disclosure …': at CLR 30–1.

Third party liability

11.19 In the area of confidentiality that we are most concerned with in intellectual property law — that is, commercially valuable secret information — the question of third party liability is of particular relevance. Such trade secrets will often pass from a confidee to other parties. Can the confidor bring an action in breach of confidence against a third party who has information that has been passed on in breach of an obligation of confidence? Can the third party be enjoined from using it once notice of the breach is served? As a matter of principle, the law contemplates that 'in some circumstances the restraint of an apprehended or continued breach of confidence may involve enjoining third parties': see *Breen v Williams* per Gummow J at CLR 129). But the rule of thumb is that the third party will be liable only if they had actual or constructive knowledge of the breach; in other words, a recipient with knowledge is liable to be restrained by injunction in equity: see *Johns v Australian Securities Commission* (1993) 178 CLR 408 at 460; [1993] HCA 56 and *Wheatley v Bell* [1982] 2 NSWLR 544 at 550; (1982) 1A IPR 613. 'Constructive' knowledge means that the third party recipient ought to have been on notice from the circumstances that they obtained the information as the result of a breach of confidence.

Even if the third party did not have the requisite actual or constructive notice at the time of receipt of the information, they will be liable upon later notification of the breach. In the first instance, that liability may be to an injunction, but if the third party persists in using the information after notice, they may suffer liability for damages or an account of profits. The sometimes unfortunate result is that a person who has acquired information in good faith, or 'innocently', not in circumstances that gave rise to constructive knowledge of breach, may, once put on notice (eg, by a solicitor's letter) or coming to know of it, be under an obligation not to use or rely on it. It may be that the third party acquired the information 'for value'; that is, in return for valuable consideration. How can the conflicting interests of the original confidor and the third party who has made a 'bona fide for value acquisition' be reconciled? How should the courts exercise the discretion in equity to grant an injunction in such circumstances?

In *Wheatley v Bell* it was held that there is no absolute 'bona fide for value' defence; rather, all the circumstances of the case must be taken into account. The good faith and economic interests of the third party were some such factors that informed the exercising of the court's equitable discretion as to whether or not to grant an injunction; other equitable considerations, such as clean hands and so on, as well as other factual evidence, may also be relevant. In *Retractable Technologies v Occupational and Medical Innovations* (2007) 72 IPR 58, Greenwood J reviewed previous cases (at 77–79) to conclude that, as is suggested above, the outcome must depend on all the circumstances. His Honour then listed some of the circumstances that were taken as relevant by Evershed MR in *Stephenson Jordan & Harrison Ltd v MacDonald & Evans* (1952) 69 RPC 10:

> Some of the 'matters' which influenced Evershed MR in concluding that an obligation of confidence might devolve upon such a third party included discovery that the work incorporated confidential information, the breach of faith was a gross breach, publication might involve ruin of the applicant's business and the intervention of the court was sought before the incurring of any substantial expense by the publisher and, obviously enough, before publication of the work [at 79].

In *Dart Industries Inc v David Bryar & Associates Pty Ltd* (1997) 38 IPR 389 at 406, it was said that where copying of plans and misuse of confidential information had originally occurred at the hands of some party other than the respondents:

> ... a court will, in an appropriate case, grant an injunction against a person who has acquired information to which he is not entitled without any knowledge or notice of any breach of duty on the part of the person from whom he obtained the information: *Printers & Finishers Ltd v Holloway* [1965] 1 WLR 1, 7; *Butler v Board of Trade* [1971] Ch 680, 690; *Talbot v General Television Corp Pty Ltd; Wheatley v Bell* [1982] 2 NSWLR 544; *English & American Insurance Co Ltd v Smith* [1988] FSR 232.

This will certainly be the case where 'the initial wrongdoing which brought about the misuse of confidential information would be carried into effect by the third party's conduct'. In *Dart Industries*, the respondents had set up a business designing injection moulds for plastic products. The applicants were the owners of copyright and confidential information relating to the design and manufacture of Tupperware products in Australia. Drawings were found in the possession of the respondents, who had been retained by Malaysian companies to design moulds for plastic containers, that clearly reflected the applicants' drawings and confidential information. The copying and misuse happened at the hands of some party other than the respondents. But on an application before Goldberg J, an interlocutory injunction was granted against the respondents. The initial wrongdoing would be brought into effect if the respondents were allowed to continue the use of the drawings and confidential information, as it would result in the delivery to the respondents' Malaysian contractors of moulds with which they could arguably infringe the copyright and misuse the trade secrets of the applicants. Nor did the fact that some of the information used may have been public and some confidential, or that further development work had been carried out upon the confidential information, justify the denial of an injunction.

Bibliography

A McRobert, 'Breach of Confidence: Revisiting the Protection of Surreptitiously Obtained Information' (2002) 13(2) *AIPJ* 69.

C Heath and A Kamperman Sanders (eds), *Employees, Trade Secrets and Restrictive Covenants*, Wolters Kluwer, 2016.

D Lindsay, 'Playing Possum? Privacy, Freedom of Speech and the Media Following *ABC v Lenah Game Meats Pty Ltd*' (2002) 7(3) *MALR* 161.

G Hughes, *Dean's Law of Trade Secrets and Privacy*, 3rd ed, LawBook Co, 2018.

G Phillipson and H Fenwick, 'Breach of Confidence as Privacy Remedy in Human Rights Act Era' (2000) 63(5) *MLR* 660.

G Taylor and D Wright, 'Case Notes — *Australian Broadcasting Corp v Lenah Game Meats* — Privacy, Injunctions and Possums: Analysis of the High Court's Decision' (2002) 26 *MULR* 707.

J Birch, 'Breach of Confidence: Dividing the Cause of Action Along Proprietary Lines' (2007) 81(5) *ALJ* 338.

J Caldwell, 'Protecting Privacy Post Lenah: Should the Courts Establish a New Tort or Develop Breach of Confidence?' (2003) 26(1) *UNSWLJ* 90.

J Edelman, 'Assessing Damages for Breach of Confidence; *Cadbury Schweppes v FBI Foods*' [2000] *RLR* 230.

M Richardson, 'Whither Breach of Confidence: A Right of Privacy for Australia?' (2002) 26 *MULR* 381.

MULR, 'Breach of Confidence, Surreptitiously or Accidentally Obtained Information' (1994) 19 *MULR* 673.

N Moreham, '*Douglas and others v Hello! Ltd* — Protection of Privacy in English Private Law' (2001) 64(5) *MLR* 767.

P Finn, *Fiduciary Obligations*, LawBook Co, 1977, 131.

PJ McCafferty, 'Protecting Private Information Improperly or Surreptitiously Obtained from Public Disclosure: A "New Species" of Breach of Confidence? (2004) 9(3) *MALR* 205.

R Arnold, 'Circumstances Importing an Obligation of Confidence' (2003) 119 *LQR* 193.

R P Meagher, WM Gummow, JRF Lehane, *Equity: Doctrine and Remedies*, Butterworths, 2002.

T Aplin, 'Breach of Confidence and Privacy: The Impact of the Human Rights Act' (2002) 50 *IP Forum* 26.

T Aplin, L Bentley, P Johnson and S Malynicz, *Gurry on Breach of Confidence, The Protection of Confidential Information*, 2nd ed, Oxford University Press, 2012.

T Voon, 'Breach of Confidence by Government, Smith Kline and the TRIPS Agreement — Public Interest to the Rescue' (1998) 9 *AIPJ* 66.

W van Caenegem, 'Did a Former Employee Misuse Confidential Information? — Case Note: *Bluescope Steel Ltd v Kelly*' (2007) 20(6) *IPLB* 90.

W van Caenegem, *Trade Secrets and Intellectual Property: Breach of Confidence, Misappropriation and Unfair Competition*, Kluwer Law International, 2014.

Chapter 12

Breach of Confidence: Defences, Remedies and Employees

Defences

Disclosure in the public interest

12.1 In certain circumstances, there is legal justification for breaking a confidence: a defence for disclosing confidential information may be raised by a person who is otherwise under a duty of confidentiality. The defence is usually traced back to the statement in *Gartside v Outram* (1856) 26 LJ Ch 113 that there is 'no confidence in iniquity', and is therefore sometimes referred to as the 'iniquity defence' or the 'iniquity rule'. In England, a broader 'public interest defence' has been developed. However, the trend in Australia is towards rejecting that broader approach. In *Corrs Pavey Whiting & Byrne v Collector of Customs (Victoria)* (1987) 14 FCR 434 at 451ff; 10 IPR 53 at 70ff, Gummow J doubted that Gartside provided a sufficient basis for a 'public interest defence'.

In England, while initially the defence appeared to be limited to the disclosure of criminal activity, Lord Denning MR in *Fraser v Evans* [1969] 1 All ER 8 at 11 said that 'iniquity is merely an instance of a just cause and excuse for breaking confidence'. In other words, the just excuse or cause for breaking a confidence was not limited to instances of 'iniquity' but extended to cases where an overriding public interest justified it: see also the statements of that same judge in *Initial Services Ltd v Putterill* [1967] 3 All ER 145; [1968] 1 QB 396. This has resulted in a balancing approach: disclosure should not be restrained where the public interest in publication outweighs the public interest in confidentiality. As Stephenson LJ put it in *Lion Laboratories v Evans* [1984] 3 WLR 539 at 546; (1984) 3 IPR 276 at 282, 'the first public interest is the preservation of the right of organisations, as of individuals, to keep secret confidential information'. But, on the other hand, 'the duty to publish, the countervailing interest of the public in being kept informed of matters which are of real public concern, is an inroad on the privacy of confidential matters', which can be just cause or an excuse for breaking confidence. Nonetheless, Stephenson LJ issued some warnings that restrain too wide an application of the public interest test:

> … there is a wide difference between what is interesting to the public and what it is in the public interest to make known: per Lord Wilberforce in *British Steel Corp v Granada*

> *Television Ltd* [1981] AC 1096 at 1168. The public are interested in many private matters which are no real concern of theirs and which the public have no pressing need to know. Second, the media have a private interest of their own in publishing what appeals to the public and may increase their circulation or the numbers of their viewers or listeners; and (I quote from the judgment of Sir John Donaldson MR in *Francome v Mirror Group Newspapers Ltd* [1984] 1 WLR 892; [1984] 2 All ER 408 at 413) '... they are peculiarly vulnerable to the error of confusing the public interest with their own interest'. Third, there are cases in which the public interest is best served by an informer giving the confidential information not to the press but to the police or some other responsible body, as was suggested by Lord Denning MR in the *Initial Services* case and by Sir John Donaldson MR in the *Francome* case.

'Public interest defence' versus 'iniquity defence'

12.2 As is indicated in the previous paragraph, Australian cases have tended to reject the broad 'public interest' approach, although it is still commonly submitted by advocates in their cause. As Gummow J pointed out in *Corrs Pavey* at FCR 450:

> That principle [the iniquity rule], in my view, is no wider than one that information will lack the necessary attribute of confidence if the subject matter is the existence or real likelihood of the existence of an iniquity in the sense of a crime, civil wrong or serious misdeed of public importance, and the confidence is relied upon to prevent disclosure to a third party with a real and direct interest in redressing such crime wrong or misdeed.

This approach is at once wider, in the sense that rather than viewing iniquity as a defence or exception his Honour simply refused to accept that confidentiality existed in iniquity, and narrower, in the sense that it adopts the iniquity rather than the public interest approach. Other judges in Australia have tended to favour Gummow J's narrower 'iniquity defence', although they have not necessarily accepted his view that information about iniquity does not have 'the necessary attribute of confidence': see, for example, Kellam J in the passage from *Australian Football League v Age Company Ltd* (2006) 15 VR 419 at 436, quoted below at 12.3. As Gray J said in *Sullivan v Sclanders* (2000) 77 SASR 419; [2000] SASC 273 at [45]:

> However, as a matter of strict legal principle I consider the application of the iniquity rule to be the correct approach. Equitable principles are best developed by reference to what conscionable behaviour demands of the defendant rather than by balancing those demands with matters of public interest. This approach avoids the ad hoc judicial idiosyncrasy associated with deciding whether, on the facts overall, it is better to respect or override the obligation of confidence.

In other recent Australian decisions — for instance, *AG Australian Holdings Ltd v Burton* (2002) 58 NSWLR 464; 58 IPR 268 and *NRMA v John Fairfax* [2002] NSWSC 563 — scepticism has also been expressed about the UK approach. In *AG Australian Holdings*, Campbell J, having pointed out that 'the present status of a "public interest" defence in Australia in an action for breach of confidence in equity's exclusive jurisdiction is not clear', sets out the views of the supporters of a broad 'public interest' defence (at IPR [177]–[180]) and the views of those who argue there is no public interest defence: at [181]–[191]. One difficulty with the narrow view is the loose meaning of the word 'iniquity'. His Honour then goes on to consider the situation where the obligation arises not out of equity's exclusive jurisdiction but out of an implied term of a contract: see also *British American Tobacco Australia Ltd v Gordon (No 2)* [2009] VSC 77. In that context Campbell J points out that 'if the obligation being sought to be enforced is said to be an implied term in a contract, the wickedness of the conduct sought to be kept confidential is relevant to whether the implication of confidentiality is made': *AG Australian Holdings Ltd v Burton* at [195]. Since in this case there was nothing more than allegations of negligence and of misleading and deceptive conduct, the question of whether some iniquity justified ignoring an obligation of confidence did not, in fact, need to be resolved. The tide has arguably turned in favour of the narrower iniquity defence. In *British American Tobacco Australia Ltd v Gordon (No 3)* [2009] VSC 619, Kaye J, after a thorough review of the authorities (from [103]), concluded that the appropriate principles are as stated by Gummow J in *Corrs Pavey*. His Honour considered that he was not permitted by the Australian cases to apply a broader public interest defence. In the more recent case of *EF v CD* [2017] VSC 351, related to disclosure of the identity of policy informers, the court put it as follows: 'There is authority that the public interest defence is not available in Australia, although the matter has not been decided conclusively. I consider that I should apply the observations in *British American Tobacco Australia Limited v Gordon* and decide that the defence is not available.': at [37], referring to *Gordon (No 3)* at [103]–[116].

Disclosure to the proper authorities

12.3 The statement of Lord Denning in *Initial Services Ltd v Putterill* at QB [405]–[406] that 'there may be cases where the misdeed is of such a character that the public interest may demand, or at least excuse, publication on a broader field, even to the press' was prefaced by the rider that 'the disclosure must, I should think, be to one who has a proper interest to receive the information. Thus it would be proper to disclose a crime to the police; or a breach of the Restrictive Trade Practices Act to the Registrar.' Normally, it would be required that the information be disclosed to the proper authorities and not more broadly; for example, to the media. However, in some cases, of which *Lion Laboratories* was one, it is appropriate for the information, in that case about the malfunctioning of an 'intoximeter', to be made available for general public discussion. Whether this is so will depend on the facts and circumstances of each case. As to the position in Australia, in *Westpac Banking Corporation v John Fairfax Group Pty Ltd* (1991) 19 IPR 513, Powell J, who had accepted the UK 'public interest defence' as correct in Australia, also said at IPR 525:

> However, as I also sought to point out in *Spycatcher* [*Attorney-General for the United Kingdom v Heinemann Publishers Australia Pty Ltd* (1987) 8 NSWLR 341] (NSWLR at 380), a decision that, in a particular case, information might be allowed to be published, does not inevitably lead to publication to the community at large being permitted: cf and cp *Francome v Mirror Group Newspapers Ltd* [1984] 2 All ER 408; [1984] 1 WLR 892; *Lion Laboratories Ltd v Evans* [1984] 3 WLR 539.

Westpac Banking related to the disclosure in a newspaper of confidential information concerning Westpac's foreign exchange dealings, Powell J refusing to discharge injunctions restraining publication on public interest grounds. The quoted passage from Gummow J's judgment in *Corrs Pavey* (see 12.2) also emphasises 'disclosure to a third party with a real and direct interest in redressing such crime wrong or misdeed'. Perhaps the formulation of Kellam J in *Australian Football League* at VR 436 is a useful one to conclude with:

> In my view, the position advanced by Mr Marks that if information relates to an iniquity being a crime, wrong or misdeed of public importance it will not be recognised by the law as being confidential, is too wide. I accept the submission of the plaintiffs that in order to rely upon the so-called iniquity rule so as to eradicate the protection that would otherwise be granted in equity in respect of confidential information, it is necessary for the person relying upon that defence to establish that; (a) the proposed disclosure will in fact disclose the existence of or the real likelihood of, the existence of an iniquity that is a crime, civil wrong or serious misdeed of public importance; (b) that the iniquity to be disclosed is of a character of public importance, in the sense that what is to be disclosed affects the community as a whole, or affects the public welfare; and (c) that the person who is seeking to protect the confidence is so doing in order to prevent disclosure to a third party with a real and direct interest in redressing the alleged crime, wrong or misdeed.

Other defences

12.4 Disclosure may be justified because it is made under legal compulsion; for example, because of the operation of statute or by order of a court. In other words, the confidee will in some cases be able to plead compulsion as a defence against an action brought by a confider.

Remedies

Damages and accounts

12.5 Some questions concerning the granting of an injunction, the primary remedy for breach of confidence, are considered below. Other issues concerning remedies in general are considered in Chapter 19 Remedies in Intellectual Property Law. Some remarks concerning damages and accounts of profits in breach of confidence actions follow here first. Generally speaking, an account compels the defendant to hand over their ill-gotten gains, whereas damages aim to restore the plaintiff to the position they were in before the wrongful conduct occurred. Where no injunction is granted — for instance, in some cases where information has become public after initiation of the action but before trial — equitable damages (or 'equitable compensation') may be awarded: see, for example, *Seager v Copydex Ltd* [1967] 2 All ER 415; *Seager v Copydex Ltd (No 2)* [1969] 2 All ER 718; EWCA Civ J0311-1; 1 WLR 809. However, exemplary damages are not apparently available for a breach of equitable duty in Australia: see *Harris v Digital Pulse Pty Ltd* (2003) 56 NSWLR 298, reversing the decision of Palmer J on this point in *Digital Pulse Pty Ltd v Harris* (2002) 166 FLR 421; 40 ACSR 587. An award of damages will be to the extent of the diminution in value of the plaintiff's right: see *Talbot v General Television Corporation Ltd* [1980] VR 224, where Marks J usefully sums up the ways in which value can diminish (at VR 248–9); see also *Aquaculture Corporation v NZ Green Mussel Co* [1990] 3 NZLR 299, the New Zealand Court of Appeal rejecting the trial judge's decision that he had no jurisdiction to award damages in a breach of confidence action and instead assessing a substantial amount. Alternatively, an account of profits may be awarded, but, as is discussed below (in Chapter 19 Remedies in Intellectual Property Law), practical difficulties in calculating an account of profits make it an unpopular remedy in breach of confidence cases, maybe even more so than in other actions; for example, see *Peter Pan Manufacturing Corporation v Corsets Silhouette Ltd* (1962) 1B IPR 795; [1963] RPC 45, *Ansell v Allied Rubber* [1972] RPC 811 and *Halliday & Nicholas Insurance Brokers Pty Ltd v Corsiatto* [2001] NSWCA 188; [2001] ACL Rep 185 NSW 23 (concerning deduction of expenses by fiduciary in breach). The choice between an account and compensation is at the election of the plaintiff. In *Mid-City Skin Cancer & Laser Centre v Zahedi-Anarak* (2006) 67 NSWLR 569 at 626, Campbell J pointed out that:

> ... whenever an account of profits is ordered in relation to a breach of an equitable obligation, where that breach has resulted in the person in breach receiving money in consequence of both the breach of the obligation, and his or her own expenditure of time effort and skill, an allowance is ordinarily made for the value of that time, effort and skill: *Green v Folgham* (1824) 1 Sim & St 398 at 406; 57 ER 159 at 162; *Boardman v Phipps* [1967] 2 AC 46 at 104, 112; *Warman International Limited & Another v Dwyer & Others* (1995) 182 CLR 544 at 562.

See also *Bluescope Steel Pty Ltd v Kelly* (2007) 72 IPR 289; [2007] FCA 517 and *AIIB Pty Ltd v Beard* [2009] NSWSC 1001. It should be noted that Campbell J also expressed the view that an account of profits may be available even though a respondent is found to have breached an express contractual term imposing confidentiality, if, in the absence of a contractual term, equity would have imposed an equally onerous obligation: *Mid-City Skin Cancer* at [271].

Injunctions

12.6 Because the value of confidential information lies precisely in its secrecy, an interlocutory injunction granted when publication is either threatened or little progressed will often be the only effective form of relief. The matters to be addressed on an application for the granting of an interlocutory injunction are whether there is a serious issue to be tried and whether the balance of convenience supports it. Although significant, as breach of confidence matters more often go no further than the interlocutory stage, those matters will not be analysed here. However, the ordering of a permanent injunction at trial raises a number of relevant questions in trade secrets cases (ie, where not personal information but commercial and technical knowledge is at stake), which will be considered in more detail below. Commonly, a permanent injunction is of indefinite duration, but if the information later becomes public, a defendant may apply to have it dissolved. But what is an appropriate order if the confidential information has entered, wholly or in part, the public domain between the initiation of the action and the time of trial? And, also, should an injunction be granted when the confidential information has been improved upon or has become inextricably intermingled with information the confidee may rightfully use?

The springboard doctrine

12.7 If the information has become public by the time of trial, the granting of an indefinite injunction would put the unconscionable confidee at a permanent disadvantage, not only in relation to the confider but in relation to all other competitors as well. An injunction of limited duration may offer a fairer outcome in such cases, even though it in effect extends over *lawful* conduct.

The starting point in assessing the granting of an injunction at the trial stage (a 'final injunction') is the case of *Terrapin Ltd v Builders Supply Co (Hayes) Ltd* [1967] RPC 375, which gave prominence to the so-called 'springboard doctrine'. Roxburgh J said (at 391):

> As I understand it, the essence of this branch of the law, whatever the origin of it may be, is that a person who has obtained information in confidence is not allowed to use it as a springboard for activities detrimental to the person who made the confidential communication, and springboard it remains even when all the features have been published or can be ascertained by actual inspection by any member of the public.

In other words, the unconscionable confidee should not get a head start by breaching their duty of confidence; if 'a person wishes to design a product without it being alleged the person has used confidential information he must proceed through an independent design sequence and not use confidential information as a springboard to jump through the sequence': *RLA Polymers Pty Ltd v Nexus Adhesives Pty Ltd* [2011] FCA 423. The 'springboard doctrine' has been applied frequently since then, notwithstanding the obvious difficulties inherent in calculating just how long the injunction should last. The applicable principles (although derived in part from a patent matter, that being *Streetworx Pty Ltd v Artcraft Urban Group Pty Ltd (No 2)* (2015) 110 IPR 544; [2015] FCA 140) were summed up as follows by White J in *Mastec Australia Pty Ltd v Trident Plastics (SA) Pty Ltd (No 3)* [2018] FCA 99 at [21]:

> The authorities to which reference has already been made indicate that the duration of the injunction should be proportionate to the advantage obtained by the respondent; the injunction ought not to put the applicant in a better position that it would have been in had the respondent engaged in the same activity but without misuse of the confidential information; regard should be had to the availability of pecuniary remedies; and regard should be had to any adverse effects on innocent third parties.

The fact that the appropriate period of restraint can rarely be calculated with any precision has not deterred the courts from granting the injunction. The difficulties are particularly significant in cases where reverse engineering plays a role; that is, where a confidee has used information received in confidence that has since become part public because of its embodiment in a product released to the market. All other competitors are, naturally, free to access the information by reverse engineering, because, in theory at least, when a product is released into the market, embodied information that was confidential before its release is in the public domain, even if the information is difficult to extract; for example, because of encryption: see *Mars UK Ltd v Teknowledge Ltd* (1999) 46 IPR 248. Eventually, details of construction, production or manufacturing may be uncovered by various competing manufacturers. However, this process may be time-consuming and costly. Thus, the confidee who misuses information in a more readily useable form entrusted in confidence benefits in time, effort and expenditure from using it in breach of duty. The extent to which the process of reverse engineering and development would delay others in the market from producing a commercially viable product may thus assist in determining for how long such an unconscionable confidee should be placed under a disability.

Thus, in *Deta Nominees Pty Ltd v Viscount Plastic Products Pty Ltd* [1979] VR 167, Fullagar J added together the time it would reasonably take for the plaintiff to get its products (plastic drawers) on the market in substantial quantities and the time it would then take some uninformed (in the sense of a person without access to the confidential information at issue) competitor or designer to reverse engineer the product and redesign, construct and produce moulds for production of a similar item. More difficult is the situation where a product has been on the market for a while by the time the breach of confidence occurs. For instance, in *British Franco Electric Pty Ltd v Dowling Plastics Pty Ltd* [1981] 1 NSWLR 448, the defendant waited a year after a manufacturing joint venture was terminated before constructing a competing product using the confidential information at issue. The court held that, as a consequence, the defendant no longer had a relevant springboard and did not need to be restrained.

Similar issues were relevant in *Titan Group Pty Ltd v Steriline Manufacturing Pty Ltd* (1990) 19 IPR 353 (relating to pressure control valves used in hydraulic gear on gym machines). Since the plaintiff's products had been on the market for some time, it was necessary to focus on the uninformed competitor alone, who would have purchased the relevant equipment when it was commercially available. In this case, the court set the 'springboard period' at 15 months from the date on which the Titan equipment was put on tangible display and was generally available for purchase and copying. If it had not been for the existence of a patent application, the period would have been 12. During that period, the defendant (Steriline) should not have used the information it obtained in confidence. On the facts, the springboard period had expired by the time of trial, and the defendants had not enjoyed a head start by their obtaining the confidential information. The plaintiff had suffered no damage. *IPC Global Pty Ltd v Pavetest Pty Ltd (No 4)* (2017) 124 IPR 101; [2017] FCA 260 at [35] provides another example of a springboard injunction.

There is no simple rule that if the information is in the public domain because of the confider's own actions, no injunction at all will be granted. Everything depends on the circumstances: see, for instance, *Freedom Motors Australia Pty Limited v Vaupotic* [2003] NSWSC 579, where an injunction was refused because certain confidential details concerning customers were past history by the time of trial and of little significance, and also *Sun Valley Foods v Vincent* [2000] FSR 825 at 835 and *Landmark Underwriting Agency Pty Ltd v Kilborn* [2006] NSWSC 1108.

Mixed public and private information

12.8 Lord Denning MR in *Seager v Copydex* [1967] 2 All ER 415 pointed out that if there was mixed public and private information, 'then the recipient must take special care to use only the material which is in the public domain. He should go to the public source': at 417. What should the remedy be if the recipient does not? Certainly, if an indefinite injunction is imposed, this may mean that as long as the confidential information remains secret, the confidee is also restrained from using interconnected but independently developed information. This may be an excessive 'punishment' for the breach of confidence. Nonetheless, the words of Lord Denning MR impose a clear onus on the confidee. The fact that the confidee's own information, or publicly available information, is mixed up with confidential information is no excuse. The confidee will not escape their duty to the confider by developing the information until it is unrecognisable as that of the confidee. It is the actual misuse that is to be restrained, whether or not the product that ultimately results is different from or the same as the original disclosed confidentially: see, for example, *Dart Industries Inc v David Bryar & Associates Pty Ltd* (1997) 38 IPR 389 and above 12.7.

However, in terms of the remedy awarded, the respondent may be granted an allowance where they mingled profits due to a breach of duty and profits due to their own efforts. The onus is on the respondent to establish the extent of the allowance to be made for such efforts and experience and in relation to public information that may also have been used in generating a profit: see *Bluescope Steel Ltd v Kelly*. In that case, the respondent, after his retirement from Bluescope, provided information to another company as a paid consultant. Emmett J held that much of the information passed on was derived from longstanding but secret Bluescope research on which the respondent had worked. The court granted an injunction and an account of profits calculated by reference to the consultancy fees Kelly had received, while making an allowance for his own efforts and know-how. As is indicated above, the court also granted an injunction relating to all information Kelly derived from the secret research project, although the applicant had been unable to itemise everything during the proceedings.

Breach of Confidence by Employees

Confidential information in the employment context

12.9 Breach of confidence actions often relate to information generated or obtained during employment. Any contract of employment has an implied term to the effect that the employee '... shall honestly and faithfully serve his master; that he shall not abuse his confidence in matters pertaining to his service, and that he shall, by all reasonable means in his power, protect his master's interests in respect to matters confided to him in the course of his service': see *Robb v Green* [1895] 2 QB 1 at 10–11. This is the general contractual duty of fidelity or good faith of every employee — that is, 'to serve their employer faithfully'[1] — which will require regard for the employer's interests when dealing with relevant information. But the nature, extent and persistence of the employee's narrower obligation of confidence in relation to trade secrets are significantly influenced by a number of factors. During employment, the duty of confidence is absorbed within the employee's much wider duty of fidelity or good faith; the higher up an employee is in an organisation, the greater that obligation will be, extending all the way to the specific fiduciary duties owed by high-level managers. After termination

1. See B Creighton and A Stewart, *Labour Law*, 5th ed, Federation Press, 2010, at 14.14.

of employment, the restraints that may be imposed on the use of information by employers are founded on breach of confidence rather than on breach of duty of fidelity or good faith. Davies JA put it nicely in *Freedom Motors Australia Pty Ltd v Vaupotic* [2003] NSWSC 579 at [13]:

> An employee has a duty to be honest and diligent in the employer's business and not to abuse confidence in matters appertaining to his employment. However, unless it be contrary to an express term, the employee, after leaving the employment, may lawfully set up a business of the same nature as that carried on by his employer and, provided that he acts fairly, may deal with persons who were customers of his late employer, and so compete with his employer in business [references omitted]. An employee has, during his employment, an obligation of good faith towards the employer and therefore to keep confidential that which the employer considers to be confidential and desires to be kept confidential. After the employment has ceased, the obligation of good faith to the employer does not continue and the former employee must keep secret only those matters the secrecy of which a court will protect. In considering this issue, a court will take into account the general and important principle of public policy that there should be freedom of trade and that, in the public interest, persons should not be unduly restrained from carrying on their chosen occupation. The more that information can be identified as a trade secret private to the employer, the more likely it is that the secrecy will be protected by a court. The more that information can be identified as part of the general stock of knowledge which the former employee must use in carrying on his occupation, the less likely it is that the alleged confidentiality of the information will be protected.

But as Cross J pointed out in *Printers & Finishers Ltd v Holloway (No 2)* [1965] RPC 239 at 255:

> The mere fact that the confidential information is not embodied in a document but is carried out by the employee in his head is not of course, of itself a reason against the granting of an injunction to prevent its use or disclosure by him. If the information in question can fairly be regarded as a separate part of the employee's stock of knowledge which a man of ordinary honesty and intelligence would recognise to be the property of his old employer, and not his own to do as he likes with, then the court, if it thinks that there is a danger of the information being used or disclosed by the ex-employee to the detriment of the old employer, will do what it can to prevent that result by granting an injunction.

During employment

12.10 During employment, the employee's duties in relation to confidential information are subsumed by a broader contractual obligation to have consideration for the interests of the employer when dealing with *any kind* of information. In other words, turning to the press with information that is in the public domain may still amount to a breach of an employee's duty of fidelity; the manner of the disclosure and to whom exactly it is made will be significant in determining whether an employee has breached their duty of fidelity by going to the press. Further, as McKeough and Stewart pointed out: 'This duty of fidelity is a strict one. It precludes not just use or disclosure while the employment relationship subsists, but also any deliberate attempts to acquire or memorise information, even if the employee does not plan to use the information until after the employment.'[2] As a consequence, even after employment is terminated, a remedy may still be based on breach of the duty of fidelity which occurred during employment rather than of the duty of confidence. For example, an employee may have surreptitiously gained access to information to which they were not normally privy, or systematically photocopied or collected information and removed it from the employer's premises without legitimate justification. Similar principles apply in agency situations. In *Ecrosteel Pty Ltd v Prefor Printing Pty Ltd* (1996) 37 IPR 22, the defendants had surreptitiously removed customer history cards from the principal's premises and set up a business in competition with him before the date of severance of the agency relationship. The defendants, as agents, were under a fiduciary duty, which they had breached, as well as the implied contractual duty of good faith. However, the result will be different if the information has been compiled by the employee for a legitimate purpose: see, for example, *NP Generations v Feneley* (2001) 52 IPR 563, where an address book and diary legitimately compiled from the rent roll of a real estate agency were the subject of a claim for breach of confidence post-employment.

After employment

12.11 After the employment contract has terminated, the ex-employee is no longer bound by its terms, their remaining legal obligations being instead based in equity (unless there are express terms in the contract of employment relating to legal obligations after termination). As regards knowledge and information, the legal obligations of the employee are limited to confidential information *sensu stricto*. In other words, the employee is free to use other general skills, (tacit) knowledge and experience acquired on the job. This type of information is sometimes referred to as 'know-how', which is 'free' and contrasted with 'trade secrets' which 'belong' to the ex-employer, although there seems to be a degree of terminological confusion, as is alluded to in *Del Casale v Artedomus (Aust) Pty Ltd* (2007) 73 IPR 326 at 335:

> Considerations such as these have led to a distinction being drawn, in cases such as *Faccenda Chickens v Fowler* [1986] 1 All ER 617 and *Wright v Gasweld* (1991) 22 NSWLR 317; (1991) 20 IPR 481, between two classes of confidential information, one of which an ex-employee cannot use (even in the absence of contractual restrictions), and the other of which an ex-employee can use, at least unless there is a valid contractual restraint. There is some variation in the naming of these two classes. For example, there is a question whether both are properly called trade secrets, with the latter being a particular class of trade secrets which is also given the appellation 'know-how'; or whether only the former class should be called trade secrets. In either event, the latter class is often called 'know-how'.

The category of information that is confidential during employment but the use of which after termination can be only contractually restrained will include knowledge about the operation of the business.

The distinction between trade secrets and know-how goes back to the leading UK case of *Faccenda Chicken v Fowler* [1986] 1 All ER 617 at 625; [1984] ICR 589, in which trade secrets properly so called were said to be protected by the action for breach of

2. J McKeough and A Stewart, *Intellectual Property in Australia*, Butterworths, 1992, p 106.

confidence, whereas other information that was confidential only in the sense that it is protected by the duty of fidelity of the employee during employment was free to be used after termination. This is one context in which the term 'trade secret' is a term of art — categorisation as such, as opposed to as 'know-how', attracts specific legal consequences — whereas in other contexts the term is used interchangeably with, or refers to, 'confidential information' of a commercial kind: see above 11.1.

In *Wright v Gasweld Pty Ltd* (1991) 22 NSWLR 317; 20 IPR 481, the confidential information at issue related to the identity of Taiwanese suppliers of hand tools. There were approximately 3000 of these suppliers, but the employer had identified four that were reliable and operated on reasonable terms. The identity of the four suppliers was kept confidential because it had required quite an investment in time and effort to select them. The employee met a number of the suppliers while on business trips for the employer. After he left employment and set up on his own, he dealt with some of the suppliers he had dealt with while he was employed, and used information about the identity and location of suppliers in Taiwan. There was some disagreement between the members of the Court of Appeal as to whether or not the identity of the Taiwanese suppliers was confidential information. The matter was rendered more complex by the provisions of the employment contract, which contained a number of non-competition clauses or 'restrictive covenants'.

Some of the judges were led into dividing the information into three categories, after the example of *Faccenda Chicken*:

1. information that cannot be regarded as confidential at all because of its triviality or public availability;
2. information that the employee must treat as confidential (either because they are expressly told to or because it is obvious from the circumstances) but that they are free to use after their employment has terminated; and
3. specific trade secrets that are 'so confidential that, even though they may necessarily have been learned by heart and even though the servant may have left the service, they cannot lawfully be used for anyone's benefit but the master's': per Goulding J in *Faccenda Chicken* at ICR 600, as cited by Samuels JA in *Wright v Gasweld Pty Ltd* at IPR 504.

The distinction between category two and category three (in *Wright v Gasweld* above) generates logical difficulty, since it requires making a distinction by referring to degrees of confidentiality. But the categorisation serves the purpose of determining whether or not an express covenant restraining the use of certain information post-termination can be enforced at law. In *Herbert Morris Ltd v Saxelby* [1916] 1 AC 688, an oft-quoted case, one of the questions at issue was whether use of the second category of information suggested in *Faccenda Chicken* (naturally, not then identified by reference to that case) could be so restrained by a covenant, to which the answer then appeared to be 'no', as it was not a category properly classified as trade secrets.

However, in *Wright v Gasweld*, Kirby P asserted that courts should 'exercise a modest disinclination to hold that information is not confidential when parties have taken the trouble to say that it is': at NSWLR 333. Thus, the use of information in the second category could be restrained by an express covenant in the contract of employment, whereas it would not attract a remedy in equity. He also accepted the expression 'trade secret' as lying at the far end of the spectrum that runs between information, which is (at NSWLR 333):

i) publicly available or trivial;
ii) common to a particular trade or calling, even if not publicly known;
iii) confidential information properly so called; or
iv) secrets that attract equitable protection whether or not there is a contractual agreement.

A similar case to *Wright v Gasweld* is *Del Casale v Artedomus* (above 12.11). In that case, the respondent sold a type of 'Modica' stone from the Ragusa region in Italy, marketed under the name 'Isernia'. The respondent was the sole importer of Modica stone. The source of Isernia and the fact that it was Modica stone was not easily ascertained, and the respondent made efforts to conceal this information by giving it to only a few people in the organisation, including the first two appellants. The latter left Artedomus and set up a new business, which then embarked on the importation of the same stone. Hodgson JA in the NSW Court of Appeal emphasised the difficulty, which was also apparent in *Wright v Gasweld*, of isolating out this kind of information, even if it was a jealously guarded secret. Hodgson JA said at IPR 337:

> Turning to the circumstances of this case, it seems to me very difficult to separate out, from the general know-how in relation to stone acquired by Mr Del Casale and Mr Savini, as a severable piece of confidential information, the information that Isernia is modica stone. Certainly, subject to any contract that may have existed, they were entitled to compete with Artedomus in the stone business after their employment had come to an end, and they were entitled to obtain stone for that purpose from any source. They were entitled to go to a trade fair, and to look for suppliers of stone at that fair, including suppliers of stone similar to Isernia. What restraint of use of this particular piece of confidential information would require is that in doing so, they somehow blot out their knowledge that Isernia was modica stone and undertake the attempt to find similar stone under those artificial circumstances.

Note that the three-way categorisation of *Wright v Gasweld* has not met with universal approval. The majority may have adopted it in *Wright v Gasweld*, but Gleeson CJ, in the minority, treated *Faccenda Chicken* as a useful case but pointed out that 'it is not necessary to adopt in its apparent rigidity the three-fold classification of information accepted in that case [...]', referring to the Court of Appeal decision: *Wright v Gasweld* at NSWLR 329. In truth, it can hardly be said that the Court of Appeal accepted the three-way split proposed at first instance in *Faccenda Chicken*. Gleeson CJ identifies rightly that the critical distinction is between an unacceptable attempt to prevent what the plaintiff may see as an unfair competitive step and a correct attempt to protect genuinely secret or confidential information: at NSWLR 329. Young J in *TV Shopping Network Ltd v Scutt* (1998) 43 IPR 451 took a simpler approach: he regarded the information concerning possible business expansion in foreign countries as not of a confidential nature, and thus the ex-employee was free to use it. No difficult three-fold categorisation was attempted.

As to technical information, see, for example, *Secton Pty Ltd v Delawood Pty Ltd* (1991) 21 IPR 136 at 151–2, in which, before going through each item, King J set out what the plaintiffs had to prove, namely that:

1. the information concerned had the status of a trade secret (in the sense of confidential information);
2. the defendants knew of the information during their employment, either by having generated it or being informed of it;
3. it came to their knowledge under conditions of secrecy; and
4. improper use or disclosure had been made of the information since the defendants had left the plaintiff's employment.

Restrictive covenants

12.12 *Secton Pty Ltd v Delawood Pty Ltd*, one of the longest hearings in Victorian legal history, illustrates the difficulties that must be overcome in these kinds of cases. To avoid the unpredictability of distinguishing between confidential information and general skill, knowledge and experience, employers have the option of inserting express confidentiality clauses into contracts, or may prefer simply to restrict the employee's ability to compete with them at all for a period after they leave employment. As Young J pointed out in *Kone Elevators Pty Ltd v McNay* (1997) ATPR ¶41-563, 'it is extremely difficult to fashion a covenant [ie, an express confidentiality clause] which will exactly protect only that confidential information which is able to be protected and because it is difficult to predict what exact problem will emerge, it is acceptable for an employer with a legitimate interest to protect to restrain an employee from taking competing employment for a set period': at ¶43-821.

However, such covenants are, in principle, not enforceable, because they are contrary to public policy (or some such terms; as was pointed out by Williams JA, the words 'illegal', 'void' and 'unenforceable' have all been used interchangeably: see *Cedar Hill Flowers & Foliage Pty Ltd v Spierenburg* [2003] 1 Qd R 482 at 493): see *Nordenfelt v Maxim Nordenfelt Guns and Ammunition Co Ltd* [1894] AC 535. In that case, Lord Macnaghten said: '[T]he public have an interest in every persons' carrying on his trade freely [...]' — the point being that a covenant in restraint of trade prevents an ex-employee from competing not just with the ex-employer but also with every other participant in the market. However, the other limb of *Nordenfelt* is that, in exception to the general prohibition, some restraints are enforceable if they are reasonable because they are limited in scope and serve a legitimate purpose; covenants must be reasonable 'in reference to the interests of the public, so framed and so guarded as to afford adequate protection to the party in whose favour it is imposed, while at the same time it is in no way injurious to the public': at 565. The law takes a particularly strict view concerning restrictive covenants in employment contracts (less so, for instance, in contracts concerning the sale of a business with goodwill attached): 'The courts in general take a stricter and less favourable view of covenants in restraint of trade entered into between employer and employee than of similar covenants in commercial agreements (*Geraghty v Minter* [1979] HCA 42; (1979) 142 CLR 177 at 185)': per Mason P in *Woolworths Ltd v Olson* (2004) 63 IPR 258; [2004] NSWCA 372 at [38].

Nonetheless, covenants in employment contracts can be saved if they are reasonable in scope and also serve a legitimate public interest, such as protection of trade secrets (and perhaps equally so in certain relationships between an independent contractor and a principal that are analogous to employment: see *Isaac v Dargan Financial Pty Ltd ATF The Dargan Financial Discretionary Trust* [2018] NSWCA 163). The other protectable interests accepted by the courts are client connection (sometimes referred to as goodwill) and the stability of the workforce (protection against wholesale defection of groups of employees to a competitor). There must be *genuine* interests to protect. The courts are concerned to stymie employers' attempts to shield themselves from general competition by ex-employees by entering into restrictive covenants disguised as necessary for the protection of trade secrets that may not, in fact, exist. Further, 'there is obviously more freedom of contract between buyer and seller than between master and servant or between an employer and a person seeking employment', as Lord Macnaghten said in *Nordenfelt* at 566.

Restrictive covenants are unreasonable if too wide as to duration and geographical area and/or as to activities or sectors of industry from which the ex-employee is excluded. Courts have often found covenants unenforceable because they are too wide, or have read them down; restrictions must be reasonable in all the circumstances. In all states except New South Wales, the common law test is applied, which requires a restraint to be struck down rather than read down (ie, amended) by the court if it is considered unreasonable. However, employers insert cascading or ladder clauses (specifying alternative geographical and time restraints) to attempt to alleviate the risk of losing the benefit of the restraint entirely. In New South Wales, the Restraints of Trade Act 1976 (NSW) entitles a court to rewrite a restraint and substitute terms (time, extent) it considers reasonable: see, for instance, *Woolworths Ltd v Olson*, where more general principles are also discussed, and *Isaac v Dargan Financial* in particular at [66]ff. In *Commercial Plastics v Vincent* (1964) 3 WLR 820 at 826 (per Sellers, Pearson and Salmon LJJ), it was said:

> It is clear from the authorities that the plaintiffs were not entitled to impose a restriction which would prevent the defendant from using in competition with the plaintiffs the skill and aptitude and general technical knowledge acquired by him in his employment by the plaintiffs. The restriction has to be justified in this case as being reasonably required for the protection of the plaintiffs' trade secrets by preventing the defendant from disclosing confidential information imparted to him by the plaintiffs in the course of his employment.

The trade secrets must be identified and the question asked whether the restraint is reasonable to protect them or instead is too broad. For instance, in *Commercial Plastics*, although there was confidential information concerning a manufacturing process to protect, the restraint was not limited to the industry in which information might be used and not limited to similar work as carried out by the employee. Thus, a long and wide restraint might, on the other hand, be reasonable where contracts are of long duration and the employer does business over a wide area, as in *Brightman v Lamson Paragon* (1914) 18 CLR 331. For a recent example of a court considering reasonableness of a restraint, see *Genesys Wealth Advisers Ltd v Miles* [2008] NSWSC 802 and also *Hanna v OAMPS Insurance Brokers Ltd* [2010] NSWCA 267, where the so-called 'cascading' clauses (of alternative extent) are also considered.

In *TV Shopping Network Ltd v Scutt*, a prohibition on work 'in any capacity' destroyed the covenant as being unreasonable; in *Wright v Gasweld*, the court also dealt with restraint of trade clauses. But note that in *Speed Seal Products Ltd v Paddington* [1985] 1 WLR 1327 at 1331, it was said that the law will restrain the employee from unfairly securing a springboard by which to compete with their former employer. And, further, even if the covenant is void, this does not mean that the employee escapes their duty of confidence based in equity rather than in contract. The onus of proving reasonableness is on the party seeking to enforce the covenant. The ex-employer will have to establish that it has trade secrets to protect and identify them ('identifiable objective knowledge constituting the employer's trade secrets', as it is put in the headnote to *FSS Travel & Leisure Systems Ltd v Johnson* [1997] EWCA Civ 2759). Otherwise, the covenant would amount to no more than a general restraint on competition. Thus, in *Triplex Safety Glass v Scorah* [1937] 55 RPC 21 at 28, the restraint was 'seeking to do what the law will not permit, because it is seeking to prevent him using general information as distinguished from special information such as secret processes or the like which are the employer's property'. It will be apparent that it can be difficult to predict what a court may consider unreasonable. To overcome this uncertainty, employers often insert, stepwise, cascading or ladder restraints, of which an example can be found in *Cedar Hill Flowers*. However, such clauses are uncertain for the employer, and, perhaps legally, so much so that the courts will find them void for uncertainty. For further reading, see also Dent, Howe, van Caenegem, 'Restraints of Trade: The Legal Practice' (2013) 36(1) *UNSWLJ* 1. The particular difficulty in the 'common law states' (ie, not New South Wales which has the Restraint of Trade Act 1976 (NSW) to govern the matter), is that the courts generally take an all or nothing approach — they will not normally rewrite a restrictive covenant to bring it within the confines of what the court might find reasonable, as opposed to the terms actually found in the contract: see Dent et al, above). If the restraint is found to be unenforceable, the ex-employer will only have the action for breach of confidence in equity to fall back on.

Client lists

12.13 A much fought over area of employee trade secrets is client details. It is not uncommon for a recently departed employee to be accused of having taken client details that are then alleged to be confidential. But the latter is by no means always the case: see *Southern Cross Financial Group (Newcastle) Pty Ltd v Rodrigues* (2005) 66 IPR 166 per Young J at 178:

> As the textbooks say, the employer has rights in confidential customer lists and connections and it is quite clear that employees cannot take or copy a list of customers with the intention of using the list later for their own benefit. But in the absence of a valid legally enforceable restrictive covenant, an employee is entitled to rely upon any retained knowledge of the customers, their identity, requirements and so on, and this is especially the case where the ex-employee has personally dealt with the customer for some time and could reasonably be expected to recall their details in his mind [...] Again, I have been referred to previous cases which show that this sort of material is in a borderline position such as *Coco v AN Clark (Engineers) Ltd* [1969] RPC 41; (1968) 1A IPR 587 and my own decision in *Forkserve Pty Ltd v Pacchiarotta* (2000) 50 IPR 74.

Alternatively, it may be that client contact details are in the public domain as such, whereas a detailed compilation of such data in a list of existing or prospective clients of a firm is not: see *Robb v Green* (above 12.9) and *Think: Education Services Pty Ltd v Lynch* [2011] NSWSC 984. In *Halliday & Nicholas Insurance Brokers Pty Ltd v Corsiatto*, Handley JA points out that 'in business time is worth money', and the client lists that the respondent, Corsiatto, went to the trouble of obtaining surreptitiously allowed him to follow up former clients immediately. The importance and confidential nature of the lists were thus apparent from the respondent's actions: at [16]–[17]. Where protection of clients' details becomes the justification for a restraint of trade, the line between protecting a genuine trade secret and preventing competition becomes very thin. In *Weldon v Harbinson* [2000] NSWSC 272 at [70], the court reiterated what Gleeson CJ in dissent said in *Wright v Gasweld* at 330, that information as to consumer identity was 'of a low order of confidentiality', and then went on to say (also at [70]):

> A former employee's entitlement to use knowledge which the former employee remembers, and the absence of an entitlement to make notes and lists while in the employment and take them and use them, are very long established and are not open to doubt or debate. They were recognised in the judgment of Harvey CJ in Eq in *Ormonoid Roofing & Asphalts Ltd v Bitumenoids Ltd & Ors* (1930) 31 SR (NSW) 347: see particularly 354–356. In my view the plaintiff's claim to restrict the defendant's access to clients fell to be decided within these limits, and the plaintiff's claim that it should be inferred that the defendant had removed the list of customers was of very high importance in this regard.

The court later said at [72]:

> I do not accept the observations of Pritchard J in SSC&B: *Lintass New Zealand Ltd v Murphy* [1986] 2 NZLR 436 at 456: 'To my mind the distinction which seemed to have been drawn in *Robb v Green* [1895] 2 QB 1, 13 between using a written list of customers compiled while in the employment of the master, and drawing on a retentive memory for the same information, is quite unreal. There is no valid reason why a servant, endowed with a good memory, should be accorded more extensive rights of canvassing his master's customers than one who is not so blessed.' In my opinion the distinction is very well established, and is soundly based on the former employee's liberty to engage in competition, qualified by not being entitled to remove lists which are the employer's property, or to make copies or commit lists to memory which have the same effect in substance. I am not aware of any other expression of the view stated by Pritchard J.

However, as is also pointed out in *IF Asia Pacific Pty Ltd v Galbally* (2003) 59 IPR 43, an employer cannot create a trade secret by a contractual term to that effect. The effect of allowing employers to protect themselves against competition on the basis of securing client data where they are not of a special or highly confidential kind by way of a covenant would be at odds with the prohibition on employers merely protecting themselves against competition. In this case, Young J cites Gleeson CJ's more restrictive views in *Wright v Gasweld* with apparent approval, and also refers back to *Nordenfelt* and to Megaw J's view in *Printers & Finishers* [1965] RPC 239, which refers to 'matters which could be fairly regarded as trade secrets' as being appropriately protected by a covenant and nothing else. In any case, it seems now to be accepted orthodoxy that there are two forms of confidential information, as stated in *Genesys Wealth Advisers Ltd v Miles* [2008] NSWSC 802 at [45]:

> It is important to bear in mind at the outset that there are two categories of confidential information which the Courts will protect at the suit of a former employer: first, information which is of its nature so confidential or secret that the ex-employee cannot use it even if not bound by any contractual restraint; second, information which is to a degree confidential but, because it is closely linked to the know-how and experience which an employee acquires in the course of employment in a particular field, it will not be protected by the Court except where there is a valid contractual restraint on the employee. On the other hand, information which has no confidentiality, because of its triviality or because it is in the public domain, will not be protected by the Court even if it expressly described as confidential in a contractual restraint: see *Del Casale v Artedomus (Aust) Pty Ltd* [2007] NSWCA 172, at [37]–[38] per Hodgson JA; *Wright v Gasweld Pty Ltd* at NSWLR 333E–334A, 339E.

An alternative to a restrictive covenant is a non-solicitation clause. Because it does not restrict an ex-employee from working in their field of expertise *at all*, it is regarded more benevolently by courts. Normally a non-solicitation clause should extend only to a prohibition on contacting clients the employee dealt with directly in their previous employment, and that for a limited time and place. However, if it attempts to go too much further, extending to clients the particular individual never dealt with or potential clients, it may in fact amount to a covenant not to compete, in particular for those employees whose experience lies in acquiring and dealing directly with clients.

Bibliography

A Brooks, '"Fidelity" in the Post-Industrial Age: Developments in Case Law on Employee Disclosure of Confidential Information' (2002) 28 *Mon L R* 126.

A Brooks, 'The Good and Considerate Employer: Developments in the Implied Duty of Mutual Trust and Confidence' (2001) 20 *U Tas LR* 29.

A Stewart, 'Drafting and Enforcing Post-Employment Restraints' (1997) 10 *AJLL* 181.

Australian Law Reform Commission, *Serious Invasions of Privacy in the Digital Era*, Report No 123, September 2014.

B Gray, 'Ocular Sciences: A New Vision for the Doctrine of Breach of Confidence', (1999) *MULR* 9.

D Pendleton, 'Challenging Law's Traditional Refusal to Protect Information per se for Fear of Stifling Innovation, Competition' (2002) 51 *IP Forum* 32.

E Kennedy, 'Breach of Confidence in the Public Interest?' (2007) 15(4) *HLB* 33; (2006) 80(12) *LIJ* 54.

J Pizer, 'Public Interest Exception to the Breach of Confidence Action: Are the Lights About to Change?' (1994) 20 *Mon L R* 67.

K Godfrey, 'Contracts of Employment: Renaissance of the Implied Term of Trust and Confidence' (2003) 77(11) *ALJ* 764.

K Koomen, 'Breach of Confidence and the Public Interest Defence' (1994) 10 *QUTLJ* 56.

K Ries, 'Confidential Information and Media' (1999) 15 *QUTLJ* 126.

M Gronow, 'Injunctions in Breach of Confidence Proceedings' (1995) 6 *AIPJ* 246.

P Lavery, 'Secrecy, Springboards and the Public Domain' [1998] *EIPR* 93.

R Dean, 'Off the Rails — When Employees Bolt with Your Business' (2006) 80(12) *LIJ* 36.

R McNab, 'Ex-Employees: Whose Know-How?' (1993) 17(2) *UQLJ* 292.

W van Caenegem, 'Intellectual Property and Intellectual Capital' (2002) 48 *IP Forum* 10.

Chapter 13

Passing Off

The Amorphous Nature of the Passing Off Action

13.1 Over 70 years ago, dealing with the development of the action in passing off, Isaacs ACJ said that the courts had 'constantly endeavoured to keep pace with the progress of trade by adapting fundamental doctrines to advancing methods and changing circumstances': *Angelides v James Stedman Hendersons Sweets Ltd* (1927) 40 CLR 43 at 59–60. More recently, Gummow J in *ConAgra Inc v McCain Foods (Aust) Pty Ltd* (1992) 33 FCR 302; 23 IPR 193 at 246 pointed out that:

> Attempts to produce a definition of the tort [of passing-off] which is both succinct and comprehensive have had mixed success, [and] ... it is to be observed that the law of passing-off contains sufficient nooks and crannies to make it difficult to formulate any satisfactory definition in short form.

Nonetheless, courts have occasionally attempted to define the modern action comprehensively. Lord Diplock's list of five elements enumerated in the so-called *Advocaat* case was a watershed in this regard: see *Erven Warnink BV (Besloten Vennootschap) v J Townsend & Sons (Hull) Ltd* [1979] AC 731 at 742; (1979) 1A IPR 666. However, Lord Diplock's definition has been criticised as being both incomplete and too restrictive.

Whatever 'nooks and crannies' it may otherwise contain, the tort has three main elements. Per Lord Oliver of Aylmerton in the leading English case of *Reckitt and Colman Products Ltd v Borden Inc* (1990) 17 IPR 1 at 8, those elements are:

1. reputation;
2. misrepresentation; and
3. damage (actual or likely).

The modern action in passing off has, in Australia, also been substantially subsumed within the broad scope of s 18 of the Australian Consumer Law (ACL) under Sch 2 of the Competition and Consumer Act 2010 (Cth) (the old s 52 of the Trade Practices Act 1974 (Cth) (TPA); s 53 of the TPA has been replaced by s 29 of the ACL, 'False or misleading representations about goods and services'): see further below 13.6.

Policy and property

13.2 The private interests and public policy goals at stake in any action for passing off were identified by Gummow J in *ConAgra* at IPR 246:

> Within the passing-off action, there is an accommodation and adjustment of three competing interests. First, that of the plaintiff in protecting the commercial advantages flowing from his efforts and investment, secondly that of the defendant in being free to attract purchasers for his goods and services by what appears to him to be an effective means, and thirdly that of consumers in selecting between competing goods and services without the practice upon them of misrepresentations.

To this may be added the need to maintain robust competition and avoid monopolisation of common indicia of trade and commerce. Sometimes, the tort of passing off is said to confer or protect property rights in a reputation. In *Star Industrial Co Ltd v Yap Kwee Kor* (1975) 1B IPR 582 at 592, Lord Diplock stated:

> A passing-off action is a remedy for the invasion of a right of property not in the mark, name or get-up improperly used, but in the business or goodwill likely to be injured by the misrepresentation made by passing-off one person's goods as the goods of another.

However, even though Lockhart J in *ConAgra* confirmed the 'property analysis', he also stressed that the underlying rationale of passing off is to prevent wrongful commercial conduct (at FCR 340, IPR 231):

> The tort of passing-off protects the business of the plaintiff with its many facets: its assets, goodwill and reputation. It stops persons and companies gaining a commercial advantage through wrongfully taking the attributes of another's business if it causes or is likely to cause that other person's business some damage.

Thus, whereas passing off is an action that vindicates ownership of goodwill, it is not based on proprietary rights in trade indicia, although it is sometimes said that a plaintiff will have to establish a 'proprietary interest' in a name: see, for example, *Knight v Beyond Properties Pty Ltd* (2007) 71 IPR 466 at 488:

> Because the essence of Mr Knight's complaint is the use, by the respondents, of the title 'Mythbusters', and he has no statutory right to protected use of the term, he must show that he has acquired a proprietary interest in it. Because the name is, to an extent at least, descriptive he cannot do this if the name has not acquired a secondary meaning distinctively associated with him.

In other words, the 'proprietary interest' is an interest in the goodwill that attaches to a name that is sufficiently associated with the plaintiff. But only when a misrepresentation that misleads or deceives consumers can be established will a remedy be granted; misappropriation of reputation alone cannot ground an action in passing off.

Rejection of a tort of unfair competition or misappropriation

13.3 Even though the requirements of an action in passing off have grown more flexible over time, the basic elements must still be present if liability is to ensue. The High Court has rejected the suggestion that there be crafted in Australian law, either as an extension of the action in passing off or independently, a general action for unfair competition that could absorb passing off as well as other categories of unconscionable or dishonest commercial conduct: see *Moorgate Tobacco Co v Philip Morris Ltd (No 2)* (1984) 156 CLR 414 at 445; 3 IPR 545 and also the earlier case of *Victoria Park Racing and Recreation Grounds Co Ltd v Taylor* (1937) 58 CLR 479; 1A IPR 303.

Nonetheless, other courts have recognised the merit of an action less artificially constrained by the need to prove consumer deception. Pincus J suggested that the search for a misrepresentation that lies at the core of passing off imposes an artificial and arbitrary barrier to recovery in certain types of cases; for instance, those concerning misleading celebrity endorsements. His Honour suggested that the action should be expanded to include cases of misappropriation: see *Hogan v Koala Dundee Pty Ltd* (1988) 20 FCR 314; 12 IPR 508. Although redolent of good sense, that approach has not been adopted in later cases: see, for example, *Pacific Dunlop v Hogan* (1989) 23 FCR 553; 14 IPR 398. Jacob J's judgment in *Hodgkinson & Corby Ltd v Wards Mobility Services Ltd* [1994] 1 WLR 1564 puts it as follows:

> At the heart of passing off lies deception or its likelihood, deception of the ultimate consumer in particular. Over the years passing off has developed from the classic case of the defendant selling his goods as and for those of the plaintiff to cover other kinds of deception, eg that the defendant's goods are the same as those of the plaintiff when they are not, eg *Combe International Ltd v Scholl (UK) Ltd* [1980] R.P.C. 1; or that the defendant's goods are the same as goods sold by a class of persons of which the plaintiff is a member when they are not, eg *Warnink (Erven) Besloten Vennootschap v J Townend Sons Ltd* [1980] R.P.C. 29. Never has the tort shown even a slight tendency to stray beyond cases of deception. Were it to do so it would enter the field of honest competition, declared unlawful for some reason other than deceptiveness. Why there should be any such reason I cannot imagine. It would serve only to stifle competition.

However, that the tort has never shown even a slight tendency to stray beyond cases of deception is perhaps somewhat overstated. We will see below that by the application of various principles and techniques, courts have regularly awarded remedies in passing off where actual evidence of consumers being deceived is weak at best: see, for example, below 13.9.

The Evolution of the Action in Passing Off

13.4 Although the need to satisfy all the elements and respect the outer limits of the action has regularly been emphasised, certain subsidiary barriers to liability have been removed over time, resulting in what is sometimes referred to as the 'extended action in passing off'. Although in the early stages of the development of the tort the plaintiff had to show that the defendant had passed off their goods as being those of the plaintiff, it is now sufficient to show that the defendant has misrepresented the nature or existence of some connection — even if imprecise — between the goods or services of the plaintiff and those of the defendant. Further, although in the past it was a requirement that the plaintiff and the defendant be engaged in the same field of activity, *Henderson v Radio Corporation Pty Ltd* [1960] 60 SR (NSW) 576; 77 WN (NSW) 585; (1960) 1A IPR 620 stands for the proposition, now accepted without demur in Australia (and more recently in the UK: see *Irvine v Talksport Ltd* [2002] 57 IPR 621), that the plaintiff can obtain a remedy even though active in an altogether different field from that of the defendant. Thus, merchandising cases in which personalities attempt to protect their image and reputation from unauthorised commercial use have become common in Australia. Further, unauthorised commercial use of fictional characters (such as Crocodile Dundee or the Simpsons: see 13.23) or formats (such as 'Mythbusters': see *Knight v Beyond Properties Pty Ltd* (2007) 71 IPR 466 and appeal at *Knight v Beyond Properties Pty Ltd* (2007) 74 IPR 232: see further below) has also become a common cause of action. Other parties that are not active in trade or commerce in the traditional sense, such as non-trading representative organisations and non-profit associations, may also vindicate their 'promotional goodwill' or common interests through an action in passing off. The action is also sometimes said to have been extended to now also protect goodwill associated with geographical or descriptive terms: see, for instance, *Chocosuisse Union des Fabricants Suisses de Chocolat v Cadbury Ltd* [1999] RPC 826 (CA); *Comité Interprofessionnel du Vin de Champagne v Powell* (2015) 115 IPR 269; [2015] FCA 1110 (*Powell*); and see further below at 13.21.

The fact-based nature of the action in passing off

13.5 Lord Oliver, in an oft-cited passage of his speech in *Reckitt and Colman Products* at IPR 7, rightly stated that the questions that arise in passing off are generally ones of fact. Many a court has stressed that the action generally turns on its facts: see, for example, Lockhart J in *ConAgra* at FCR 327; IPR 218, as well as Gummow J at FCR 355; IPR 247; and see Beaumont, Branson and Lindgren JJ in *Vieright Pty Ltd v Myer Stores Ltd* (1995) 31 IPR 361. In practice, passing off will often turn not on one single factual parameter but on an accumulation of factors (eg, similarity in brand name, get-up and marketing). A single aspect of impugned conduct when individually regarded may appear to be of little consequence but when taken in conjunction with a number of other factual parameters may turn the case. In the final analysis, the overall impression on the putative consumer is determinative, not the effect of one or another aspect in isolation. Therefore, it is probably not right to say that a trader will have to establish an exclusive connection with a trade indicium or sign to succeed in an action for passing off. Even if it were correct to say so, it is clear that the overarching and broader s 18 of the ACL asks a broader question. For instance in *Bohemia Crystal Pty Ltd v Host Corporation Pty Ltd* (2018) 129 IPR 482; [2018] FCA 235 Burley J said at [313]: 'However, there is no requirement under the ACL to show an exclusive reputation (*Cadbury Schweppes Pty Ltd v Darrell Lea Chocolate Shops Pty Ltd* [2007] FCAFC 70; (2007) 72 IPR 261 at [99] per Black CJ, Emmett and Middleton JJ)'. The words of the court in *Cadbury Schweppes Pty Ltd v Darrell Lea Chocolate Shops Pty Ltd* (2007) 159 FCR 397; (2007) 72 IPR 261; [2007] FCAFC 70 (*Cadbury v Darrell Lea*) were as follows:

> In any event, the principles relating to passing-off do not necessarily require Cadbury to establish an exclusive reputation in relation to the use of the colour purple. More significantly, it certainly does not follow that there cannot be a contravention of the Trade Practices Act simply because Cadbury does not establish that it has an exclusive reputation in relation to the colour purple. The question is whether Cadbury can establish facts that demonstrate that a particular use by Darrell Lea of the colour purple is likely to mislead or deceive consumers into believing that there is some relevant connection between Darrell Lea and Cadbury or their respective products.

Passing Off and s 18 of the Australian Consumer Law

13.6 Cases are usually pleaded both in the common law tort of passing off and under s 18 of the ACL. Passing off is one species of misleading and deceptive conduct. Although relief under s 18 is not restricted to conduct that would amount to common law passing off (see, for instance, *Powell*, which as the court stressed on a number of occasions was not a case solely under s 18, and not in passing off), the elements and reasoning developed under that action commonly inform the analysis under the ACL. However, passing off is primarily an action regulating trade misconduct 'policed' by rival traders, with incidental benefits flowing to consumers, whereas s 18 is primarily concerned with consumer protection, with incidental benefits flowing to competitors because not only consumers but also rival traders can sue under s 18. The different policy bases of the two actions have led courts to issue warnings against conflation, as exemplified by this passage from Deane and Fitzgerald JJs' judgment in *Taco Company of Australia Inc v Taco Bell Pty Ltd* (1982) 42 ALR 177 at 197:

> Whilst, as was pointed out by Stephen J (*Hornsby Building Information Centre Pty Ltd v Sydney Building Information Centre Ltd* (1978) 18 ALR 639 at 646; 140 CLR 216 at 227) the long experience in the courts in relation to passing-off should not be disregarded and some principles which have been developed in that context may be also applicable to s 52, it is, in our opinion, important to heed his Honour's emphatic rejection on the same page of any suggestion that s 52 is no more than a statutory re-enactment of passing-off principles ... The backgrounds of s 52 and of the law of passing-off are quite different. Their respective purposes and the interests which they primarily protect are contrasting. Their areas of operation do not coincide. The indiscriminate importation into s 52 cases of principles and concepts involved in passing-off and the associated area of trade mark law is likely to be productive of error and to give rise to arguments founded on false assumptions.

However, in practice, the distinction is not so great because misrepresentation in passing off is overwhelmingly assessed by reference to the effect of the defendant's conduct on the perception of consumers. Nonetheless, Mason J rightly said in *Parkdale Custom Built Furniture Pty Ltd v Puxu Pty Ltd* (1982) 149 CLR 191 at 203:

> ... it is important to recall that s 52(1) is 'not concerned, as such, with any unfairness of competition in trade as between two traders' (*Hornsby Building Information Centre Pty Ltd v Sydney Building Information Centre Ltd* (1978) 140 CLR at 226; (1978) 18 ALR 639; cf s 5 of the United States Federal Trade Commission Act 1914). It is not directed exclusively or even primarily to situations of passing-off; it extends to any conduct that is likely to mislead or deceive as, for example, the making of negligent statements and false representations as to the quality of goods. It is not enough that conduct damages a rival trader; it must mislead or deceive or be likely to mislead or deceive members of the public in their capacity as consumers.

More recently, in *Cadbury v Darrell Lea* at [98] the Full Court said:

> There is an overlap between causes of action arising under Part V of the Trade Practices Act and the common law tort of passing off. However, the causes of action have distinct origins and the purposes and interests that both bodies of law primarily protect are contrasting.

Passing off protects a right of property in business or goodwill whereas Part V is concerned with consumer protection. Part V is not restricted by common law principles relating to passing off and provides wider protection than passing off.

Differences between s 18 and passing off

13.7 A wider spectrum of policy considerations does apply to the common law action. In particular, under s 18, there is no requirement to balance the right of a trader to control the indicia of their trade with the preservation of freedom of competition; the only relevant consideration is whether consumers are misled or deceived. While an action in passing off lies at the suit of a rival trader (broadly speaking), an action under the old s 52 of the TPA and the present s 18 of the ACL can be brought by a consumer or a rival trader: as to the latter point, see *R v Federal Court of Australia; Ex parte Pilkington ACI (Operations) Pty Ltd* (1978) 142 CLR 113 at 120–1, 128. To obtain a remedy in passing off, a rival trader must establish damage or apprehended damage ('*quia timet*'), but a s 18 action is complete once (the likelihood of) misrepresentation or deception is established — and, as well as an injunction, other non-compensatory remedies are consequently available under the ACL. Further, whereas liability under the common law of passing off may require establishing that certain recognised elements of the action have been satisfied, s 18 does not necessarily require strict adherence to the same approach. The test is an overall one, as is indicated above. For instance, in *Cadbury Schweppes*, the court said at [99]:

> Whether or not there is a requirement for some exclusive reputation as an element in the common law tort of passing off, there is no such requirement in relation to Part V of the Trade Practices Act. The question is not whether an applicant has shown a sufficient reputation in a particular get-up or name. The question is whether the use of the particular get-up or name by an alleged wrongdoer in relation to his product is likely to mislead or deceive persons familiar with the claimant's product to believe that the two products are associated, having regard to the state of the knowledge of consumers in Australia of the claimant's product.

For an action in passing off, proof of reputation in the relevant jurisdiction is essential, since the action 'is designed to protect the property and goodwill of a business': see *Hansen Beverage Co v Bickfords (Australia) Pty Ltd* (2008) 171 FCR 579; 79 IPR 174; [2008] FCAFC 181 at [35] (*Hansen v Bickfords* [2008] FCAFC 181). By contrast, s 18 is designed to protect consumers against deception. However, although proving a reputation or goodwill in the relevant jurisdiction is thus not a distinct requirement under s 18, the plaintiff will usually face considerable difficulty proving deception in the absence of a sufficient reputation. As pointed out in *Ferrari Furniture & Cabinet Makers Pty Ltd v Ferrari Furniture Pty Ltd* [2006] WASC 139 at [21], 'the principles governing liability for passing off are relevant to a true understanding of the scope and operation of s 52 (*Parkdale Custom Built Furniture Pty Ltd v Puxu Pty Ltd* and *Hornsby Building Information Centre Pty Ltd v Sydney Building Information Centre Ltd*)'. But that is not always the case to the same extent, and although, generally, where a misrepresentation is about an affiliation, connection or suggestion as to the common source or characteristics with the goods or services of another trader (in the broad sense) the courts have tended to conflate passing off and s 18, the warnings that reputation in particular may not always be relevant to s 18 must be heeded: see, for instance, *Woodtree Pty Ltd v Zheng* (2007) 164 FCR 369; 74 IPR 484; [2007] FCA 1922, where Heerey J said at [34]:

> In the court below, concentration was very much on the passing off claim. However, as the Full Court has recently pointed out in *Cadbury Schweppes Pty Ltd v Darrell Lea Chocolate Shops Pty Ltd* (2007) 159 FCR 397 at [96]–[99], the degree of overlap between the two causes of action should not obscure the important differences between them. The law of passing off protects goodwill as a species of property: *Boehringer Ingelheim Ltd v Vetplus Ltd* (2007) 73 IPR 593 at [37] per Jacob LJ, citing a passage from the judgment of Millett LJ in *Harrods Ltd v Harrodian School Ltd* (1996) 35 IPR 355 at 366. However [for] claims under the *Trade Practices Act* it is not necessary for a plaintiff to establish an exclusive reputation, or indeed any reputation at all. The question is rather whether consumers are likely to be misled or deceived by the defendant's conduct.

His Honour pointed out that, on the facts of the case, the plaintiff's pre-existing reputation was irrelevant. The goods of the plaintiff (appellant in this Federal Court appeal against a federal magistrate's decision) were packaged very similarly to those of the defendant and they appeared side by side in shops. Whether a potential purchaser when confronted with the two items was aware of the plaintiff's reputation beforehand was of no consequence to the question of whether they would be misled in that particular purchasing situation.

The matter of proving a sufficient reputation in passing off is commonly connected to the question of distinctiveness — whether the sign or term adopted by a rival trader is sufficiently distinctive of the applicant for the latter to be able to claim its exclusive use. But distinctiveness is not an essential element to address under s 18 of the ACL. In *Powell* at [223] the court pointed out that 'concepts such as "generic", "descriptive", "distinctive" and "secondary"' were often transposed from passing-off cases to s 18 scenarios between rival traders. However, it was 'altogether too simplistic to use the labels "generic", "descriptive", "distinctive" and "secondary"' in considering 'how the name Champagne would or is likely to be understood by Australian consumers'. In other words, consideration under s 18 does not necessarily have to follow the well established stages adopted in passing-off matters.

The two actions are commonly pleaded in the alternative, but this is not always the case: see, for example, *WD & HO Wills (Australia) Ltd v Philip Morris Ltd* (1997) 39 IPR 356 concerning the similarities between 'Horizon' and 'Summit' packs of cigarettes; *Vieright* concerning use of the mark FIRST; *Powell* concerning use of the term 'Champagne Jayne'; and *Bohemia Crystal*.

It has at times been held that the level of deception required is different in passing off and s 18. Confusion of consumers is said to be sufficient in passing off but not under the previous s 52 of the TPA nor under s 18 of the ACL: see, for example, *Hornsby Building Information Centre* (above 13.6). In *Parkdale Custom Built Furniture Pty Ltd v Puxu Pty Ltd* at [8], Gibbs CJ said: 'In *McWilliam's Wines Pty Ltd v McDonalds System of Australia Pty Ltd* (1980) 49 FLR 455; 33 ALR 394 it was rightly held by Smithers J and by Fisher J that to prove a breach of s 52 it is not enough to establish that the conduct complained of was confusing or caused people to wonder whether two products may have come from the same source.' Nonetheless, actual deception need not be established; all that is required is likelihood of deception. And neither in passing off nor for s 18 does the defendant need to be shown to have acted fraudulently or with 'moral obloquy': see *ConAgra*. As to remedies, an injunction is available either under the ACL or for passing off at common law, but pecuniary remedies are available in passing off only if the defendant embarked upon their activities fraudulently or for the period of the defendant's persistence after notice of the plaintiff's rights. Thus, it may be that in the same action a pecuniary remedy is not open in passing off, yet damages would be available under the ACL. Section 236 of the ACL grants a remedy in damages for what in substance may be an innocent and non-negligent misrepresentation. While fault may be relevant if not to liability then at least to remedies in passing off, statutory liability is not related to fault: see Gibbs CJ in *Parkdale* at CLR 197. Note that in the law of registered trade marks, the standard to be applied to marks that are said to be deceptively similar is that they so nearly resemble eachother as to be 'likely to deceive *or cause confusion*': see s 10 of the Trade Marks Act 1995 (Cth) (emphasis added).

The Relevance of Intention and Fraud

Intention not required

13.8 Weinberg J in *Fried v Dixie Holdings Pty Ltd* [2000] FCA 1048 at [55] pointed out that:

> ... it is of course not necessary, pursuant to s 52 of the Act, to demonstrate that they [the representations] were known or suspected to be false. Section 52 is not confined to conduct which is intended to mislead or deceive — *Hornsby Building Information Centre Pty Ltd v Sydney Building Information Centre Pty Ltd* (1978) 140 CLR 216 at 225; *Parkdale Custom Built Furniture Pty Ltd v Puxu Pty Ltd* at (1982) 149 CLR 191 at 197. A corporation which acts honestly and reasonably may, nonetheless, engage in conduct that is likely to mislead or deceive.

However, the presence of an intention to mislead ('fraud in the common law sense') is not without significance, both in an evidentiary sense and, as mentioned above, in relation to damages in passing off. Such fraud might be constituted by an original fraudulent intent or by continuing to use a mark after awareness that its use does mislead consumers.

In *ConAgra*, McCain intentionally copied the get-up and branding of ConAgra's 'Healthy Choice' pre-packed meals, sold only in the United States. Gummow J analysed the relevance of fraud (in the common law sense) to the action in passing off at FCR 364–5; IPR 256 in the following terms:

> There are various categories of case in which it will be significant if the defendant has embarked upon his activities fraudulently in the sense of the old common law cases. These categories are in addition to the class of case where there is some evidentiary assistance to be derived from those circumstances. First, the absence or presence of fraud in the common law sense will be determinative of the plaintiff's equitable rights in cases where a charge of unclean hands is made out against the plaintiff; this is because whilst the plaintiff's unclean hands ordinarily would disentitle him to relief in equity, the existence of the fraud on the part of the defendant would give the plaintiff a right to damages at law. In that action the

> equitable defence would be of no effect. The plaintiff may then have an injunction to avoid the necessity of repeated actions at law, notwithstanding the plaintiff's unclean hands. That is what is established in *Kettles and Gas Appliances Ltd v Anthony Hordern and Sons Ltd* (1935) 35 SR (NSW) 108, with reference to the analysis of *Ford v Foster* (1872) LR 7 Ch App 611, by Isaacs ACJ in *Angelides v James Stedman Hendersons Sweets Ltd* [(1927) 40 CLR 43] at 65–66. Secondly, whilst there is some authority for the view that there is no passing-off where the defendant does no more than carry on business under his own name, such user must be bona fide; *Clayton v Vincent's Products Ltd* (1934) 34 SR (NSW) 214; *Parker Knoll Ltd v Knoll International Ltd* (1962) RPC 265; *Parker and Son (Reading) Ltd v Parker* (1965) RPC 323. Thirdly, in my view, in the ordinary passing-off case (where the whole of the dispute is centred in the one jurisdiction) the failure of the plaintiff to show the existence of his reputation cannot be overcome merely by proof of a fraudulent design on the part of the defendant. The authorities bearing upon the question are collected in *Telmak Teleproducts (Australia) Pty Ltd v Coles Myer Ltd* (1988) 84 ALR 437 at 444–5. However, fraudulent conduct is important ... where the plaintiff and the defendant export their goods for sale in a foreign market and the plaintiff has no reputation with consumers in the jurisdiction in which the action is brought, although he does have a reputation in the foreign market where the goods of the defendant are sold.

Fraud must be proven if substantial damages in passing off are to be awarded, particularly where similar products are supplied but there is doubt that the defendant's similar get-up has sufficiently distinguished its own product: see, for example, *Sydneywide Distributors Pty Ltd v Red Bull Aust Pty Ltd* (2002) 234 FCR 549; 55 IPR 354; [2002] FCAFC 157 (the *Red Bull* case).

Evidentiary assistance from fraud

13.9 The class of case where there is some evidentiary assistance to be derived from those circumstances of fraud, which Gummow J refers to at the outset of the foregoing paragraph, is illustrated by the words of Dixon and McTiernan JJ in *Australian Woollen Mills Ltd v FS Walton & Co Ltd* (1937) 58 CLR 641 at 657:

> The rule that if a mark or get-up for goods is adopted for the purpose of appropriating part of the trade or reputation of a rival, it should be presumed to be fitted for the purpose and therefore likely to deceive or confuse, no doubt, is as just in principle as it is wholesome in tendency. In a question how possible or prospective buyers will be impressed by a given picture, word or appearance, the instinct and judgment of traders is not to be lightly rejected, and when a dishonest trader fashions and implements a weapon for the purpose of misleading potential customers he at least provides a reliable and expert opinion on the question whether what he has done is in fact likely to deceive.

While it is clear that a plaintiff may succeed irrespective of any intent on the part of the defendant to deceive (per Lockhart J in *ConAgra* at FCR 345; IPR 236):

> ... evidence that the defendant had a fraudulent intent may assist in establishing the requisite misrepresentation, as the court 'will not be astute to find the defendant has failed in his nefarious design': *Midland Counties Dairy Ltd v Midland Dairies Ltd* (1948) 65 RPC 429 at 435 and [a host of other cases].

It should be noted that where intention can be relevant in passing off by way of the 'principle in *Australian Woollen Mills*', it is not relevant in relation to s 18 of the ACL:

see *Spanline Weatherstrong Building Systems Pty Ltd v Tabellz Pty Ltd* [2013] FCA 1019 at [101]. Similarly, an intention to create an association in consumers' minds 'when expressed by persons "who know the field of business well", may justify the court in more readily inferring that their endeavour to create the intended association or connection would succeed': per Merkel J in *Telstra Corporation Ltd v Royal & Sun Alliance Insurance Australia Ltd* (2003) 57 IPR 453 at 472 (*Telstra v Royal & Sun Alliance*), calling in aid Tamberlin J in *Twentieth Century Fox Film Corporation v South Australian Brewing Co Ltd* (1996) 66 FCR 451; 34 IPR 225. In the *Red Bull*case (see also 13.8), the court put it as follows (at [117]):

> ... we again point out that where a trader, having knowledge of a particular market, borrows aspects of a competitor's get-up, it is a reasonable inference that he or she believes that there will be a market benefit in so doing. ... It is an available inference from those propositions that the trader, with knowledge of the market, considered that such borrowing was 'fitted for the purpose and therefore likely to deceive or confuse ...'.

The court in *Homart Pharmaceuticals Pty Ltd v Careline Australia Pty Ltd* (2017) 126 IPR 498; [2017] FCA 403 found an intention to copy; the fact that the goods whose get-up had been copied were marked with a different brand (Chéri instead of Chantelle) was neither sufficient to prove an absence of the requisite intention, nor sufficient to prevent a conclusions that s 18 of the ACL had not been breached: see *Homart* at [200]–[202].

Intention alone not enough

13.10 The factual circumstances of the case are to be taken into account in determining whether the intentional or deliberate conduct of the defendant entitles the plaintiff to relief. In *Vieright*, the Full Court, on appeal, agreed with the trial judge's conclusion that although the respondent (Myer) persisted with the use of the FIRST mark after it became aware of the applicant's use of that mark, the respondent did not set out to take advantage of the appellant's anterior reputation. The respondent knowingly adopted the mark FIRST for a new menswear line but was to use the mark on men's clothing nationwide in its stores, while the applicant's mark had been used only on women's clothing in a limited geographical area and there was no evidence of an extensive reputation. Thus, notwithstanding that the respondent paid scant regard to the effect its use of the mark would have on the business of the applicant, the latter was not entitled to relief (at IPR 370–4). The Full Court also pointed out that where the respondent proposed to use the mark in relation to women's clothing in the future the appellant was entitled to a *quia timet* injunction in relation to the proposed use on women's clothing because (at IPR 371) 'a substantial number of members of the public would probably have been misled into purchasing the respondent's goods in the belief that they were the appellant's, unless the respondent had clearly distinguished its products from the appellant's'. The same field of activity would have been involved and the same mark would have been used.

Intention to deceive and the mere intention to copy or adopt a good idea

13.11 It is important to distinguish between an intention to deceive consumers into thinking there is a connection with the plaintiff and the bare intention to adopt or copy a good idea or name: as the court put it in *Verrocchi v Direct Chemist Outlet Pty*

Ltd (2016) 247 FCR 570; [2016] FCAFC 104 at [104]: '[T]here is a distinction between an intention to copy and an intention to deceive. The former does not establish the latter. For the inference identified in *Australian Woollen Mills* to arise, the latter must be established.' Ultimately the court found that there was an intention to copy, but not an intention to deceive. In *Playcorp Group of Companies Pty Ltd v Peter Bodum A/S* (2010) 84 IPR 542; [2010] FCA 23 (*Playcorp v Peter Bodum*), the court, relying on *Australian Woollen Mills* and the *Red Bull* case, noted that the plaintiff had to prove that the adoption by the defendant of the Chambord coffee plunger features was not done merely with the intention to copy but with the intention to deceive consumers into the erroneous belief 'that they were in fact buying a Bodum or Bodum-sanctioned coffee plunger': at [153]. In *Homart* the court formulated its conclusions along the lines that 'Homart intentionally adopted a get-up for its product for the purpose of appropriating part of the trade or reputation of Careline': at [202]. Sometimes, intention will be apparent from the known circumstances; for instance, an approach to the plaintiff seeking permission to use a name is turned down, its unauthorised adoption following. In *Master Builders Association (SA) v Master Builders Advice and Helpline Pty Ltd* [2001] SASC 214, the defendant had first sought agreement to use the term 'Master Builders' in its business, but, being rebuffed, had proceeded anyway.

On the matter of fraud (in the common law sense), Lockhart J in *ConAgra* disagreed with the conclusions of the trial judge (Hill J), who found that the defendant was guilty of fraud. Lockhart J stressed that 'merely to imitate the name of another trader or his product or his get-up does not establish a case of fraud' (at FCR 352; IPR 243) (see also *Campomar Sociedad Limitada v Nike International Ltd* (2000) 202 CLR 45; 46 IPR 481; [2000] HCA 12 (*Campomar v Nike*) at [33]: 'even an imitation of one product by another does not necessarily bespeak an intention to deceive purchasers'). Lockhart J said that it was his impression that the defendant adopted as many as possible of the attributes of the plaintiff's product as was legal, not with the intention of making the consumer think that its own product was that of the plaintiff but because it was impressed by the way the plaintiff had gone about its business in the US. 'Nevertheless it seems the respondent wanted to sell its own product as a distinctive McCain product' (at FCR 353; IPR 243). Since ConAgra had no relevant reputation for 'Healthy Choice' in Australia in the first place, it would be pointless for McCain to attempt to induce consumers to think that there was some connection with ConAgra's US product.

For other recent examples of deliberate and opportunistic copying that were found not to evidence an intention to deceive but merely to indicate that the plaintiff had a good idea that the defendant had turned to their advantage, see *TGI Friday's Australia Pty Ltd v TGI Friday's Inc* (1998) 42 IPR 444; *Fido Dido Inc v Venture Stores (Retailers) Pty Ltd* (1988) 16 IPR 365; and *Just Jeans Pty Ltd v Westco Jeans (Aust) Pty Ltd* (1988) 12 IPR 403 at 406, upheld in (1988) 13 IPR 661. And as to an example where the defendant's '*intention was not to pass off the respondent's goods as those of the appellants but to take advantage of the market developed by the advertising campaign for "Solo"* [a carbonated soft drink]' (emphasis added), which was a legitimate activity, see *Cadbury-Schweppes Pty Ltd v Pub Squash Co Pty Ltd* [1981] 1 WLR 193 at 204. More recently, see also *Hansen Beverage Co v Bickfords (Australia) Pty Ltd* (2008) 75 IPR 505; [2008] FCA 406 (*Hansen v Bickfords* [2008] FCA 406), where the defendant had adopted the name

'Monster' and 'Monster Energy' for energy drinks in Australia, which was an overseas brand not marketed or intended to be marketed here by the plaintiff. Middleton J said (at IPR 551):

> In these circumstances, and despite the fact that in my view Bickfords did copy the brand of Hansen, Bickfords did not engage in fraud (in the relevant sense). Bickfords was clearly impressed by the success of the MONSTER energy drink in the United States and sought to adopt it in Australia (with some minor adaptations). Bickfords obviously perceived that the concept adopted by Hansen was a good idea, and sought to introduce it in Australia. Thus, Bickfords deliberately copied Hansen's brand, but only in Australia where Hansen had no actual sales or direct promotion, and where Hansen did not have sufficient reputation of the quality and type it now contends for in this proceeding. This was known and believed to be true by Bickfords, and Bickfords acted accordingly in its own commercial interest. The fact that Bickfords may have seized a window of opportunity to enter the market in Australia by adopting the Hansen model and brand does not detract from this conclusion.

Note that Hansen successfully appealed this decision but on a different matter relating to whether it had a sufficient reputation among the relevant consumers in Australia (the matter was then settled): see *Hansen v Bickfords* [2008] FCAFC 181.

Proof of Reputation

Goodwill, reputation, secondary meaning and distinctiveness

13.12 In passing off, the plaintiff must prove the existence of a reputation (goodwill) within the jurisdiction where the action is brought. A reputation extending over an area that is less extensive than the whole jurisdiction may still be sufficient. In this regard, a plaintiff in a passing-off action is at a disadvantage compared with a registered trade mark owner, who is not generally required to prove reputation. The reputation or goodwill need not attach to the plaintiff as such — that is, the (corporate) person with whom the product or service originates, of whose identity consumers are commonly unaware (see *Edge and Sons Ltd v Nicholls & Sons Ltd* [1911] AC 693) — but rather to the name or other distinctive attribute associated with the goods or services: see also *Change Group International PLC v City Exchange Mart Pty Ltd* [2012] FCA 1048 at [173]. The words 'goodwill' and 'reputation' represent somewhat imprecise concepts. In *ConAgra* Lockhart J recognised a property right in goodwill but also accepted that goodwill did not have an existence separate from the business: at FCR 399–401; IPR 231–2. However, he was in favour of using the word 'reputation' as opposed to 'goodwill', since that would avoid confusing associations with the notion of goodwill in other areas of the law, such as revenue law (stamp duty issues). 'Secondary meaning' and 'distinctiveness' are closely related central concepts in the context of proving sufficient reputation. The former means that the indicia (sign, brand, mark, appearance, get-up, advertising image and so on) of a trader related to goods or services have taken on an additional significance beyond their literal or primary meaning, evoking for a consumer a certain quality and consistency of commercial origin. 'Distinctiveness' is a key concept both in the law of passing off and in trade mark law. It refers to the ability of certain indicia, signs, marks, attributes or characteristics associated with the products or services of a certain trader to assist a consumer to recognise and distinguish them from those of another trader or traders. As indicated above, in relation to s 18 of the ACL there is no distinct element or requirement to prove sufficient reputation or distinctiveness — nonetheless they remain relevant considerations in the context of the overall test of consumer deception. If the applicant has little or no reputation, or effectively claims exclusive rights over descriptive terms, then it is difficult to bring home a claim under s 18. Therefore these factors will commonly receive consideration as well in the context of that section.

Reputation without business activity

13.13 For various reasons, a plaintiff may be seeking to vindicate goodwill by legal action, although no underlying business exists in the jurisdiction. For instance, the underlying business may have ceased trading. Of course, the public knowledge of the associated brand does not automatically disappear when that happens. In *Hoath v Connect Internet Services* (2006) 69 IPR 62, the continuing goodwill attaching to a domain name was at issue (at 71):

> The question then is whether, eight months after it stopped carrying on business as an internet service provider, Mortgage still had any goodwill to be protected. The defendants did not make any submissions about this. Such goodwill is incapable of subsisting independently of the business to which it is attached. However, it is a question of fact and degree at what point of time a person who ceases to carry on a business should be treated as no longer having the benefit of the goodwill which accrued from it. (*Star Industrial Co Ltd v Yap Kwee Kor t/as Newstar Industrial Co* [1976] 2 FSR 256 at 269; *Pink v JA Sharwood & Co* (1913) 30 RPC 725 at 739–740; *Thai World Import & Export Co Ltd v Shuey Shing Pty Ltd* (1989) 17 IPR 289 at 302; *Federal Commissioner of Taxation v Murry* (1998) 193 CLR 605 at 613–615). Having regard to its advertising from 1998, the level of telephone enquiries, and its favourable publicity in the 'Internet.au' magazine's annual performance comparison in May 1999, I think it likely that Mortgage would have had residual goodwill in the name 'Dragon Net' as at June 2001. I am fortified in that view by the fact that the defendants did not submit to the contrary.

Alternatively, since goodwill or reputation transcends national or state borders and geographical boundaries, even more so in the age of the internet, international travel and seamless communications, a product or service may have a reputation within a jurisdiction where it is not actually traded or available to consumers, or where the plaintiff carries on no business. In a Commonwealth of states such as Australia, this may arise as between states.

In *BM Auto Sales Pty Ltd v Budget Rent-a-Car System Pty Ltd* (1976) 12 ALR 363 at 371–2, Gibbs J, as far as the question of a local reputation in the Northern Territory was concerned, pointed out that although formally requiring some sort of business activity within the jurisdiction, both English and Australian courts had accepted that the amount of activity required might be minimal. In any case, a considerable number of prospective rental car customers in Darwin were interstate business travellers coming from states where the plaintiff's business was well established. His Honour thus accepted that there could be a sufficient local reputation even though the plaintiff had no local business activity. The point appears not to have given further difficulty in later cases, sufficient reputation not necessarily requiring evidence of business activity within the state where the action is brought: see, for example, *Dodds Family Investments Pty Ltd (formerly Solar Tint Pty Ltd) v Lane Industries Pty Ltd* (1992) 25 IPR 197; (1993) 26 IPR 261. In another case, the reputation of magazines published in two different states and using the word 'Scoop' was considered: see *Prospero Publishing Pty Ltd v Rumcoast Holdings Pty Ltd* [2000] WASCA 61. The court held that there was no need to prove reputation in every state separately to warrant the granting of a nationwide injunction.

More difficult is the question of a foreign plaintiff without Australian business activity. Can a local business be enjoined from using or adopting a mark or other indicium of trade that is associated with a foreign plaintiff whose goods or services are not traded in Australia and who does not carry on business here? Considerations of economic policy and fairness arise. Should a plaintiff who is not actually doing business here (and who has no immediate plans to enter the jurisdiction and set up a business) be able to restrain all others from using the indicia of their trade, a 'dead hand' on competition in Australia? Conversely, should a local trader be able to profit from the local reputation of a foreign brand owner simply because that owner has no commercial presence within the jurisdiction at the time? In the context of expanding international trade, the internet, global communications and travel, global reputation undeniably outruns global business activity. In an integrated world economy, appropriate resolution of the conflict between the interests of foreign and local business in any given case must depend on the precise factual circumstances and timing, rather than on the application of artificial fetters. The relevant issues have been canvassed extensively: see *ConAgra*; *Taco Company of Australia Inc v Taco Bell Pty Ltd*; *Chase Manhattan Overseas Corporation v Chase Corporation Ltd* (1985) 6 IPR 59; *Fletcher Challenge Ltd v Fletcher Challenge Pty Ltd* (1981) 1 NSWLR 196; and *Hansen v Bickfords* [2008] FCAFC 181.

In *ConAgra*, the defendants, McCain, had adopted a new line of pre-packaged, ready-to-cook meals under the name 'Healthy Choice'. The target audience was persons with a reasonable disposable income and active working lives and who were interested in health food. The defendants had adopted the product concept after observing a similar line that was for sale in the US, produced by the plaintiff. They adopted not only the same name but also a very similar livery and packaging style. However, the plaintiff's product was not for sale in Australia by either importation or local manufacture, nor was there any other form of even minimal local business activity. According to Lockhart J, there was no advantage in taking the attitude of the 'hard-line cases', mainly found in the UK law reports, that require there to be some evidence of business activity within the jurisdiction. After all, the existence of a reputation was not the only element of the tort that needed to be established; also required is evidence of deception and of damage: *ConAgra* at FCR 342–3; IPR 234. His Honour went on to say:

> … reputation within the jurisdiction may be proved by a variety of means including advertisements on television, or radio or in magazines and newspapers within the forum, it may be established by showing constant travel of people between other countries and the forum, and that people within the forum (whether residents there or persons simply visiting there from other countries) are exposed to the goods of the overseas owner.

But he emphasised (at FCR 343; IPR 234):

> ... the law of passing-off does not confer protection on the owners of goods who have no reputation in a particular jurisdiction, otherwise they would have an international monopoly with respect to the name, get-up or mark applied to their goods (and service) and may never intend to exploit it in the particular jurisdiction. It is the likelihood of deception among consumers and of damage to reputation that are the critical requirements to establish a case of passing-off and they prevent any such unauthorised international monopoly being granted to the plaintiff.

However, where the local trader deliberately and intentionally sets out to forestall the entry of a foreign brand owner into the local market, in the process filching the reputation of that foreign trader, evidence of 'fraud' (see above 13.8ff) may assist the foreign plaintiff. Such evidence must go beyond merely copying a good idea or brand name from abroad before it becomes known here: see *Hansen v Bickfords* [2008] FCA 406 (see 13.11). In that case, the defendant had also ascertained that the foreign plaintiff was not intending to enter the Australian market in the foreseeable future. The trial court and the Full Court (see *Hansen v Bickfords* [2008] FCAFC 181) disagreed on the proper approach to determining whether the applicant's energy drink had a sufficient Australian reputation. The trial court had too narrowly circumscribed the relevant class of consumers (at [48]), a key factor in determining sufficiency of reputation: some products and services are aimed at consumers in general, whereas others are directed at consumers with particular interests and characteristics. Whereas a reputation among consumers at large may be insufficient in a given case, there might be a sufficient reputation among a group of consumers more narrowly circumscribed.

Proving local reputation in the absence of local business activity

13.14 Even accepting that a passing-off action is no longer barred by a lack of local business activity, there is still a question of proof: how to establish a local reputation to the requisite standard. The plaintiff must prove that there is within the jurisdiction a sufficient or 'not insignificant' number of persons who are aware of its product or service and its relevant distinctive marks or indicia. As Lockhart J put it in *ConAgra* at IPR 237:

> For [ConAgra] to have in a practical and business sense a sufficient reputation in the forum requires something more than a reputation among a small number of persons, although the size and extent of the class may vary according to the circumstances of the case. [It did] not matter whether the persons within the relevant jurisdiction who are aware of the plaintiff's product, are resident or visitors from anywhere in the world.

His Honour did not specify what 'the circumstances of the case' were that he had in mind. On the specific facts in *ConAgra*, the advertisements published in a number of US magazines were not significant and effective, given the minuscule circulation of those magazines in Australia (many foreign magazines are published with local advertising substituted). Further, statistics of the amount of travel between the US and Australia were of little assistance because they said nothing about how many of those short-term visitors to the US would have accessed relevant advertising or shops and seen the product. Some might do so, but it was impossible to assess how many, and speculation is not evidence. Further, the tendering of affidavit evidence of some 11 persons in Australia that they were aware of the plaintiff's product was insufficient to make any extrapolation to the Australian population as a whole. Thus, even though there is, in principle, no doctrinal bar to establishing local reputation in the absence of local business activity, proving sufficient reputation within Australia will often be challenging in such circumstances.

In *Hansen v Bickfords* [2008] FCA 406, the court reiterated [at 74] that:

> … accepting that we are in the age of global communications and the extensive use of the internet, the first principal question is whether the evidence establishes that the necessary proportion of potential customers in Australia have become aware of Hansen's product so that Hansen has a sufficient reputation in the mark MONSTER ENERGY or MONSTER.

Simply pointing to the prevalence of international means of communication is not sufficient. In this case, the plaintiff pointed to the exposure of extreme sports enthusiasts to the foreign brand. But notwithstanding the international focus and appeal of such sports, that was not sufficient: 'The awareness of the target audience must be one which in a practical and business sense is such that it can be said that the Hansen product is known to the people who are the potential customers, mainly but not exclusively, young male adults.' An inference could not simply be drawn from exposure to a small band of enthusiasts to a sufficient number of young males in general (at [74]ff): see also *Natural Waters of Viti Ltd v Dayals (Fiji) Artesian Waters Ltd* (2007) 71 IPR 571 (*Fiji Waters* case). However, on appeal, the Full Court held that the correct question was not whether the required reputation existed among Hansen's target market of young males and whether Bickfords' product targeted the same group but simply 'whether a not insignificant number of persons in the Australian community, in fact or by inference have been misled or are likely to be misled even if those persons are mostly or exclusively extreme sports enthusiasts': *Hansen v Bickfords* [2008] FCAFC 181 at [48].

Competing claims to a brand name or other distinctive indicium or badge may amount to a question of resolving ownership, the owner here being the person in whom the goodwill or reputation in the common law mark or brand is vested. For instance, in *JJ Hahn Pty Ltd v Hahn Barossa Vineyards (SA) Pty Ltd* [2005] FCA 317, two branches of the same well-known winemaking family came into dispute when one who had previously marketed more abroad started to use the famous name on locally sold wines. In the *Arthur's Pizza* case, the question was who built up the goodwill: the owner or the tenant of a pizzeria: see *260 Oxford Street Pty Ltd v Premetis* [2006] NSWCA 96.

A sufficient reputation requires that a legally significant number of people within the jurisdiction are aware of the product or service and can distinguish the product or service by reference to the indicia alleged to have been misused. It is a question of fact whether there is a sufficient reputation within the jurisdiction. As suggested above, it is necessary to adequately circumscribe the group or category of people within which the products or services must have a sufficient reputation. One relevant factor is the nature and expense of the product or service. A sufficient number of people in the market for power stations, say, will be far lower than in the market for frozen prepared health food meals: see, for example, *McIlhenny Co v Blue Yonder Holdings Pty Ltd* (1997) 39 IPR 187 (the *Tabasco* case), where Lehane J held that it was proper to estimate the reputation among people in the set design trade (the business the defendant was in), as opposed to a wider group of people who may have been aware of the plaintiff's product (a peppery sauce). In terms of the final outcome, the parties' contentions as to how to circumscribe the relevant consumer group will often be critical.

A sufficient reputation: distinctiveness

13.15 As well as 'goodwill', other terms used to refer indirectly to reputation are 'secondary meaning' and 'distinctiveness': see 13.12. The former means that the marks or other indicia used by a trader have acquired, in the eyes of interested consumers, a meaning (beyond what they primarily portray) indicating their commercial origin and associated qualities. A mark, brand, sign or indicium may well have no or very little primary meaning because it is an invented rather than a descriptive or partly descriptive or otherwise meaningful word, or because it is a foreign word. On the other hand, a mark may be partially or wholly descriptive of the goods in relation to which it is used, or in some other way have primary meaning relevant to the goods. For example, the primary meaning of 'Healthy Choice' is the choice of something that is healthy; its secondary meaning is a certain food line produced by McCain: see *ConAgra*, above. Secondary meaning thus equals commercial reputation. The word 'distinctiveness' is also a key legal concept and a term of art in the law of both passing off and registered trade marks. It refers to a certain aspect of, or sign used in association with, a product or service that enables a consumer to distinguish it from others as to origin.

Cadbury-Schweppes Pty Ltd v The Pub Squash Co Ltd [1981] 1 WLR 193 stands for the proposition, although not new at the time, that the attribute misleadingly adopted by the defendant may be something other than just a name, sign, device, mark or brand; that is, it may be any aspect or other indicia of the plaintiff's business, as long as it is distinctive of that business. In that case, 'other indicia' consisted of (per Lord Scarman at RPC 490) 'other descriptive material, such as slogans or visual images, which radio, television or newspaper advertising campaigns can lead the market to associate with a plaintiff's product, provided always that such descriptive material has become part of the goodwill of that product'. In *Telstra v Royal & Sun Alliance*, the well-known actor Tommy Dysart, assuming the role of 'Mr Goggomobil' in Telstra advertisements, had become distinctive of the 'Yellow Pages'. Merkel J said (at IPR 469):

> Advertising that conjures up a brand without referring to it was described in the evidence as 'secondary' or 'suggestive' brand advertising. By such advertising images can become established and so well-known that they create an impression of association or connection to a primary brand, notwithstanding that the name of the brand does not appear in the advertisement. The symbol, logo or image is referred to as secondary or suggestive branding as its expression gives a ready impression of association or connection with the primary brand. Examples of such advertising include the Nike swoosh, McDonald's arches, the 'Ronald McDonald' character, the Coca Cola bottle and the Yellow Pages 'walking fingers' logo.

Importantly, distinctiveness can be inherent, acquired or a combination of both. The indicia of trade may be so non-descriptive, unusual or uncommon as to inherently set them apart. Or, alternatively, while not initially distinctive, they may become so over time because of constant and exclusive association with certain products or services.

Plaintiffs regularly fail to prove that the name or other aspect of their business is solely or sufficiently associated with their own products or services and hence distinctive of them. Commonly, the name or other aspect of the business is descriptive rather than distinctive. Alternatively, it is a feature other traders in the same line of business could legitimately expect to use or adopt. A sign or mark may refer to some aspect, characteristic or quality of the product or service itself: as in, for example, the leading case of *Hornsby Building Information Centre Pty Ltd v Sydney Building Information Centre Ltd* (1978) 140 CLR 216; 1B IPR 818. If there was any misconception in the minds of consumers concerning the connection between the two centres in that case, it occurred because the name was, per Stephen J at CLR 229; IPR 826, 'equally applicable to any business of a like kind, its very descriptiveness ensures that it is not distinctive of any particular business and hence its application to other like businesses will not ordinarily mislead the public'. *Hornsby* was at issue in *Melbourne's Cheapest Cars v Melbourne Street Cars* [2004] FMCA 606, the magistrate, although accepting that the words 'Melbourne's Cheapest Cars' were associated with the applicant, holding that the adoption of those words amounted only to misleading and deceptive conduct where a rival trader had also copied the colour scheme and layout of the applicant's signage; see also *RJB Wolfe Pty Ltd v Mornington Peninsula Eye Clinic Pty Ltd* [2019] VSC 27 (concerning 'Peninsula Eye Centre').

Descriptive terms, get-up or shape

13.16 It is rare that wholly descriptive names and phrases as such are found to have become sufficiently distinctive through use, because courts are vigilant not to grant a monopoly in descriptive terms, lest this amount to an unacceptable burden on competitors who legitimately want to employ them. However, unregistered marks, brands and phrases are usually positioned somewhere along a line from purely descriptive to purely distinctive, and courts have accepted that in a rare case descriptive phrases or names can become distinctive over time: see, for instance, *CPA Australia Ltd v Dunn* (2007) 74 IPR 495, where the term 'certified practising accountant' (CPA) was said to have acquired sufficient secondary meaning over time: 'the combination of those three words have a secondary meaning, namely that a person who has that designation has obtained "membership of [the applicant] which, by its tests and examinations and by its rules and requirements as to qualification, confer[s] on its members a status different from that of other members of the profession" who do not have the same qualification': at [30]. A CPA had come to mean a member of the Australian Society of Accountants and not simply a person qualified as an accountant. Distinctiveness may adhere to some ungrammatical or unusual use of terms otherwise suggestive of some quality of a product: for instance, 'blue and fresh' was an ungrammatical use of words as the name of a product: *R & C Products Pty Ltd v Hunters Products Pty Ltd* (1988) ATPR ¶40-839. The issue has recently started to arise in relation to domain names: for instance, in *Hoath v Connect Internet Services* (2006) 69 IPR 62; [2006] NSCWC 158 and in *Vendor Advocacy Australia Pty Ltd v Seitanidis* (2013) 103 IPR 1; [2013] FCA 971. However, perhaps the most striking case is *REA Group Ltd v Real Estate 1 Ltd* (2013) 217 FCR 327; 102 IPR 1; [2013] FCA 559. Despite the highly descriptive inherent character of the domain name 'realestate.com.au', the court held that by virtue of extensive promotion on a number of advertising media, a substantial number of consumers would recognise it as the trading portal of the plaintiff. But very substantial evidence of 'secondary meaning' should be required if a plaintiff is to succeed where the name or another attribute is purely descriptive rather than invented. Usually, this means that the common law mark has been used over a considerable period, consistently and prominently.

Descriptiveness is not necessarily a characteristic of a term or phrase only; it can equally apply to (an aspect of) the get-up or shape of an article that is suggestive of the nature of the article itself or of the contents. However, in *Reckitt and Colman Products* (see 13.5), the House of Lords recognised that the container of lemon juice in the shape and colour of a lemon had, over time, become so strongly associated with the plaintiff that it had become distinctive of its products. In some cases, the unregistered mark is descriptive of the nature of a business or service rather than of goods. In other cases, the question is whether get-up or packaging is standard or stands out as something striking and unusual. In *Homart* the court pointed out (at [125]) that:

> The reputation which must be proved in a case such as the present is that the get-up, packaging, shape or trade dress relied upon is associated by consumers with Careline's product. It takes a strong case to establish a reputation of this nature; *Interlego AG v Croner Trading Pty Ltd* [1992] FCA 992; (1992) 39 FCR 348 at 386 (Gummow J with whom Black CJ and Lockhart J agreed). This is because customers will not necessarily associate a get-up with the applicant's product; *Collins Debden Pty Ltd v Cumberland Stationery Co Pty Ltd (No 2)* [2005] FCA 1398 at [33]–[34] (per Lindgren J).

This would 'be more readily found where the get-up is unique or striking rather than descriptive, mundane, merely functional, or in common use': at [126] quoting Bennett J in the *Fiji Waters* case at [59]. The court found that sufficient reputation was established not only in the brand name used ('Chantelle'), but also in the get-up: at [134]. A number of similar cases have concerned Aldi generic equivalents of branded products: see, for example, *Moroccanoil Israel Ltd v Aldi Foods Pty Ltd* [2017] FCA 823; as for store-front get-up see *Verrocchi*.

For an example relating to a manufactured word, *Dodds Family Investments Pty Ltd v Lane Industries Pty Ltd* (1993) 26 IPR 261 at 271 is instructive. The term at issue was 'solar tint', which unconnected operators in different states had been using concurrently over an extended period. The court pointed out that substantial evidence of distinctiveness will be required if the designation is not inherently distinctive (the term 'solar tint' clearly referring to the process of tinting windows against sunlight). Another trader merely expressing surprise or confusion at the disputed use of the term was not sufficient evidence of distinctiveness, a question of fact that could be resolved only by adducing relevant evidence of secondary meaning; that is, that consumers associate the name substantially with the plaintiff. Note, however, that, as is pointed out above, it is not mandatory in an action under s 18 of the ACL that all the elements required for passing off are individually established. As indicated, that can also apply to the requirement of distinctiveness: see, for example, *JEM Nominees Pty Ltd v Insurance News Pty Ltd* [2008] FMCA 1227, where the federal magistrate did review the authorities on distinctiveness but then ignored the issue in concluding that the names 'InsuranceNewsAustralia.com' and 'insuranceNEWS.com.au' were so similar as to be likely to mislead or deceive. The difficulty with such an approach is that it ignores the valid arguments against allowing the monopolisation of descriptive terms by a single trader. Similarly, in *Cadbury v Darrell Lea*, the court pointed out that whether or not there is a requirement for some exclusive reputation, in this case in the colour purple used by Cadbury, as an element in the common law tort of passing off, no such requirement existed in relation to the TPA (now the ACL). Nonetheless, the trader who adopts a descriptive or telling term as a common law mark runs a risk of losing out: see, for example, *DB Breweries v Lion Nathan* [2007] NZHC 1232, where it was pointed out that the chances of some consumers being misled in their choice between two beers in very particular circumstances 'owe their genesis to the common use of the words "Summer Ale" and are a result of DB's election to choose a descriptive name ale for consumption in summer rather than a fancy name for its product: *McCain International Ltd v Country Fair Foods Ltd* [1981] RPC 69 (CA) per Templema LJ'. Another beer case related to the name 'Pacific Ale' first used by Stone & Wood (see *Stone & Wood Group Pty Ltd v Intellectual Property Development Corporation Pty Ltd* (2018) 129 IPR 238; [2018] FCAFC 29), which the court held had descriptive meaning — an association with the Pacific Ocean and also as an adjective meaning peaceful or calm. Choosing such a name engendered a risk of other traders using it descriptively (in this case, within a very different label clearly marked as emanating from Thunder Road) and thus acting within the law.

A case may also fail for lack of distinctiveness because the relevant terms or expressions, although not descriptive, are in common use, either in business or as a matter of day-to-day language: see, for example, *TGI Friday's Australia Pty Ltd v TGI Friday's Inc* (1998) 42 IPR 444, where the claim for passing off and under s 52 relating to use of the term 'TGI Friday's' failed. Terms containing a geographical reference give rise to similar difficulties. For instance, in *Hindmarsh Medical Clinic v Hindmarsh Family Practice Pty Ltd* (1997) 38 IPR 616, the court held that the name (an Adelaide suburb) carried only geographical significance — it told consumers where the medical centre was — and did not have 'sufficient secondary meaning as to entitle [the plaintiff] to assert a monopoly in the use of that geographical word': at IPR 631. The manner of proof of distinctiveness may be through individual testimony of consumers or survey evidence — subject to evidentiary and other difficulties as the latter may be. The evidence commonly given in passing-off cases that specific persons within the relevant class were led into error may be relevant but is not determinative. It is up to the court to make an objective assessment on the basis of all the evidence and the circumstances of the case.

Distinctiveness and the design and appearance of goods

13.17 A product might be distinctive in and of itself; that is, have an appearance that sets it apart. However, courts will be vigilant not to allow the role of designs registration, copyright or patent grant to be usurped by granting monopolies in the design or appearance of products through the medium of passing off. Laddie J pointed out in *Irvine v Talksport Ltd* [2002] 57 IPR 621 at 628 that passing off does not serve to protect traders against rivals selling the same or copied goods. That is not to say that the design of a product can never acquire such secondary meaning that the imitation of the design by another trader is actionable in passing off. However, imitators will rarely be liable in passing off in the absence of additional misleading factors or where they attach their own mark to an imitation product.

In the leading case of *Parkdale Custom Built Furniture Pty Ltd v Puxu Pty Ltd*, Parkdale produced and sold a range of lounge chairs under the name 'Rawhide' that was substantially identical to the respondent's well-established post and rail 'Contour' furniture range. Brennan J stressed the fact that allowing an action in passing off on the basis of similarity of goods without more would have the effect of creating a monopoly in the appearance of goods outside the existing statutory monopolies. Thus, unless Parkdale did anything additional to copying the respondent's goods that gave the impression of some connection between the goods of the defendant and the plaintiff, no liability in passing off or under s 52 of the TPA should lie: *Parkdale* at CLR 224–6; IPR 705–7. In the result, although the respondent's product was sufficiently distinctive, the fact that there was an identifying Parkdale label attached to the chairs (even though somewhat hidden), making it clear that they were not the plaintiff's, meant there was no passing off. The recent litigation concerning the Bodum coffee plunger (see *Playcorp v Peter Bodum* and the appeal decision overturning the trial court's findings, *Bodum v DKSH Australia Pty Ltd* (2011) 92 IPR 2; [2011] FCAFC 98) draws attention to difficulties a brand owner may face in proving the distinctiveness of the design features of a product where that product is always and clearly marked with a distinctive trade mark. Bodum had to prove that even where its plunger appeared without its trade mark consumers would still associate it with Bodum because of its particular features. Although the trial court held that Bodum failed in this respect, the Full Court overturned this finding, holding that there was sufficient evidence over time of Bodum drawing attention to the design features of the coffee plunger themselves for the latter to become distinctive, separately from the trade mark Bodum itself. More recently also see *Coca-Cola Co v PepsiCo Inc (No 2)* (2014) 109 IPR 429; [2014] FCA 1287 concerning Coca-Cola bottle shapes.

Misrepresentation

Deception of consumers

13.18 Liability in passing off follows from a finding that the defendant has engaged in some actionable misrepresentation. A misrepresentation in passing off means conduct on the part of the trader that results in consumers coming to an erroneous conclusion or being confused about a connection between the goods or services of that trader and those of another trader (in the context of s 18, establishing confusion alone is not enough). Thus, the existence of a misrepresentation is gauged not by reference to the views of other traders about the conduct or some inherent characteristic but on the basis of the court's objective assessment of its impact on consumers. An important part of this assessment is a careful consideration of the causal link between alleged misrepresentation and the deception. Not every case of consumer confusion can be sheeted home to the defendant: see further below. But the essential first step in establishing misrepresentation is to identify the category of consumers with reference to whom the impugned conduct is to be tested (in general, this is 'the class of consumers likely to be affected by the conduct': see *Parkdale* at CLR 199; at IPR 688–9) — in other words, to identify those to whom the allegedly misleading message is addressed; for instance, through advertising. In *Telstra v Royal & Sun Alliance*, the defendant's advertisement was shown to a large audience on commercial television. Although it was directed to motoring enthusiasts, 'the relevant class of the public likely to be affected by the conduct in question were viewers who saw the first Shannons' advertisement and were aware of the Yellow Pages 'Goggomobil' campaign. Plainly, that class "constitutes a significant segment of the public"': at [73]. Gibbs CJ in *Parkdale* held that the subsequent question then was whether reasonable persons within the class identified would be misled or deceived. The alternative approach is to ask whether a significant number of members of the class have been misled: see, for instance, *Equity Access Pty Ltd v Westpac Banking Corporation* (1989) 16 IPR 431, per Hill J at 440–1. However, in *.au Domain Administration Ltd v Domain Names Australia Pty Ltd* (2004) 61 IPR 81, Finkelstein J correctly pointed out:

> By laying down the rule that in a 'representation to the public' case the question whether conduct is misleading or deceptive is to be assessed by reference to the reaction of the hypothetical representative member of the class to whom the representation is directed, the High Court [in *Campomar v Nike*] has left no scope for the operation of the requirement that it must also be shown that a significant number of members of the class have been misled. That is, the two requirements cannot sit side by side.

In *Bohemia Crystal*, Burley J resolved the matter as follows (at [311]):

> The focus of the inquiry is on whether a not insignificant number within the class have been misled or deceived or are likely to have been misled or deceived by the respondent's conduct. If, applying the Campomar test, reasonable members of the class would be likely to be misled, then such a finding carries with it that a significant proportion of the class would be likely to be misled; *National Exchange Pty Ltd v Australian Securities and Investments Commission* [2004] FCAFC 90; (2004) 61 IPR 420 at [70] and [71] per Jacobson and Bennett JJ. The question may be put slightly differently as whether a 'not insignificant number' of 'reasonable' or 'ordinary' members of that class of the public would, or are likely to, be misled or deceived: [*Bodum v DKSH Australia*] at [204]–[210] …

In *Australian Competition and Consumer Commission v Henry Kaye and National Investment Institute Pty Ltd* [2004] FCA 1363 at [107], it was pointed out that this approach 'does not mean that the court cannot consider the diversity of the experience and knowledge within the class and other matters pertinent to members of the class'. As was pointed out by Lockhart J in *Puxu Pty Ltd v Parkdale Custom Built Furniture Pty Ltd* (1980) 43 FLR 405 at 424, this is 'including the astute and the gullible, the intelligent and the not so intelligent, the well educated as well as the poorly educated, men and women of various ages pursuing a variety of vocations'. In *Campomar v Nike* at CLR 85–7, it was held that extreme and fanciful reactions need not be taken into account.

Evidence

13.19 Ultimately the question of consumer deception is one for the court, which dons the mantle of the relevant consumer having informed itself of their characteristics as well as of the typical purchasing situation. In terms of evidence, the court will allow the testimony of actual consumers as to their own personal reaction, although this may be of only limited assistance to the court. The court might also allow survey evidence of consumers, if the usual problems of admissibility and relevance (the avoidance of leading questions in particular) that commonly face such evidence can be overcome. Further, it has become more common to call expert evidence on consumer behaviour and psychological processes. The question of admissibility of expert evidence of that type was at issue in *Cadbury v Darrell Lea*. Cadbury wanted to lead evidence not from actual consumers or from surveys of actual consumers but from experts as to how such consumers would process information about the colour purple and, in particular, what 'information processing errors' they might make. The Full Federal Court held that the trial judge erred in excluding the evidence on the basis that it addressed matters (ie, ordinary consumer behaviour) that did not lie outside the knowledge or experience of ordinary persons; the Evidence Act 1995 (Cth), s 80 does not permit exclusion on that basis. However, he could have exercised his discretion to exclude evidence with little probative value whose admission would cause a waste of time (s 135). Expert consumer psychology evidence was heard in the *Red Bull* case (and more recently also in *Moroccanoil Israel* where professors of marketing, as experts in consumer psychology, were allowed to testify).

In *Pacific Publications Pty Ltd v Next Publishing Pty Ltd* (2005) 65 IPR 58, a case concerning competing 'tweens' magazines (*Total Girl* and *Girl Power*), the evidentiary difficulties that can face an applicant became apparent. Other than 'assertion and speculation', there was no real evidence before the court as to who would be misled and exactly how (at IPR 80):

> [G]iven the age of the tween market and the absence of any evidence concerning the people who purchase magazines on behalf of tweens, these two groups would give no consideration at all to whether there is any association or affiliation between the publishers, producers or sources of the magazines or any links between the magazines so far as ownership, proprietary rights, reputation or approval are concerned.

In the context of passing off, and all the more so under s 18 of the ACL, it is the overall conduct of the defendant that is the object of scrutiny, not some isolated incident of that conduct. In other words, it will ultimately depend on the evidence about all the circumstances of the case whether a court will find the requisite misrepresentation. For instance, adopting the plaintiff's common law trade mark will not automatically amount to an actionable misrepresentation. As well as other factors, the degree of distinctiveness of the mark will need to be considered (per Barwick CJ in *Hornsby* at CLR 229; ALR 648):

> In cases of passing-off, where it is the wrongful appropriation of the reputation of another or that of his goods that is in question, a plaintiff which uses descriptive words in its trade name will find that quite small differences in a competitor's trade name will render the latter immune from action (*Office Cleaning Services Ltd v Westminster Window and General Cleaners Ltd* (1946) 63 RPC 39, at p 42, per Lord Simonds). As his Lordship said (1946) 63 RPC, at p 43, the possibility of blunders by members of the public will always be present when names consist of descriptive words — 'So long as descriptive words are used by two traders as part of their respective trade names, it is possible that some members of the public will be confused whatever the differentiating words may be.' The risk of confusion

> must be accepted, to do otherwise is to give to one who appropriates to himself descriptive words an unfair monopoly in those words and might even deter others from pursuing the occupation which the words describe.

In *Britt Allcroft (Thomas) LLC v Miller* (2000) 49 IPR 7 and *Miller v Britt Allcroft LLC* (2000) 52 IPR 419, it was held not to be legitimate for a court to examine each element of the defendant's conduct individually; rather, the cumulative effect of all of the features adopted by the defendant was to be considered. Thus, the argument that the defendant was entitled to use the common name Thomas in The Thomas Shop did not save her, given that she had also copied a number of other distinctive features of the *Thomas the Tank Engine* characters and merchandise in the fit-out and set-up of her shop. For a case with a similar fact scenario, see *Intellectual Property Pty Ltd v Mygroups Pty Ltd* [2006] FCA 15, relating to the Clark Rubber colour scheme being applied to an unlicensed shop selling foam and rubber products.

Deception must result from the defendant's actions as considered in the actual typical transactional or purchasing context, not just theoretically. It is crucial in a passing-off case to consider the details and specifics of the purchasing environment and how the transaction with a consumer would be conducted, on the basis of the available evidence. As Burchett J said in *Kettle Chip Co Pty Ltd v Apand Pty Ltd* (1993) 46 FCR 152 at 161; 27 IPR 321:

> Of course, a person who places the packets before him, side by side, can also see differences. But that is not how passing off by the imitation of another trader's mark or get-up is to be tested. In general, and more particularly in the case of an item likely to be purchased for a small price without long consideration, the comparison which must be made is between the impression of the applicant's goods retained in a customer's mind and the impression made by the sort of consideration he is likely to give to the respondent's product before purchasing it.

Thus, in *WD & HO Wills (Australia)* Davies J concluded that on the basis of the similarity between the rival cigarette packs alone, the Summit pack of the defendants would mislead and deceive customers. But cigarettes are ordinarily kept in secure areas behind counters and handed over on request, and it was unlikely that retailers and their employees would confuse the brand names 'Summit' and 'Horizon'. Therefore, in terms of s 52 (at IPR 364), 'the occasions on which mistakes would be made would be too few to satisfy the requirement of "likely" [as in "likely to mislead or deceive"]: see *Tillmans Butcheries Pty Ltd v Australasian Meat Industry Employees Union* (1979) 27 ALR 367 at 380–2, per Deane J'. However, this was not determinative of the matter. Given the similarities between the Horizon and Summit packs, and their striking lack of similarity to other packs in the market, 'a significant number of customers might think that the cigarettes come from the same source [rather than be the same] as Horizon cigarettes'. Further, there was the fact of the apparent intention of the defendants to develop a pack as close as possible to the plaintiff's. Taking all these factual circumstances together, Davies J held that if Philip Morris were to launch Summit cigarette packs in the manner proposed, its conduct would breach s 52 of the TPA. Similarly, in *Dr Martens Australia Pty Ltd v Figgins Holdings Pty Ltd* (1999) 44 IPR 281, it was important to the decision that there was no breach, that a typical purchaser of shoes would be assisted by a shop assistant, would try on the shoes and closely inspect them, and would therefore notice the defendant's brands that appeared on the shoes. It might be that experts in a particular field may be led to the conclusion that there exists a link between products, but the standard refers to the impression of ordinary consumers of a product, not, for instance, as in *Spanline Weatherstrong Building Systems*, expert installers of roof sheeting. The court found that the similarity between Spanline's 'Double-U'-shaped sheets and those of the defendant would not have been of interest to prospective purchasers of such structures, who would focus on their overall visual appeal.

Similarity in design of goods and in get-up

13.20 Normally, if goods are clearly marked as emanating from the imitator, there will be, depending on all the other circumstances, no passing off, even where the design of the goods themselves has been closely and deliberately copied. That point has already been made in the context of distinctiveness: see above. However, the imitator's branding will have to be clear and adequate to distinguish the product by source.

In *Philips Electronics NV v Remington Products Australia Pty Ltd* (1997) 39 IPR 283, the design features of the Philips triple rotary head shaver were considered to be distinctive, but there was no passing off, because the competing product that was similar in design was clearly marked 'Remington'. Similarly, in *Dr Martens*, Goldberg J also stressed that merely imitating the appearance of another trader's goods (ie, adopting the design features of the 'Doc Martens' shoe), without in any other way suggesting a connection with a rival trader, will not amount to passing off. The presence on imitative goods of the defendant's mark is normally sufficient in such circumstances to dispel any suggestion of a connection and defeat an action in passing off. A recent example is provided by *Sheldon v Metrokane* (2004) 135 FCR 34; 61 IPR 1, a case turning primarily on allegations of copyright infringement in the manufacture and sale of innovative corkscrews. The alternative argument based on breaching s 52 of the TPA by way of passing off was rejected out of hand by Conti J: 'In my opinion, however closely identical the "Pull It" corkscrew is to the "Rabbit" corkscrew ..., the different packaging of both products, in which the same are sold in Australia, is such as not to mislead consumers in Australia or potential consumers by reason of any deceptive resemblance, or of having any endorsement, approval, licence or sponsorship of Metrokane, consequential upon any conduct of S & H in the nature of passing off': at IPR 66. However, the outcome in *Bodum v DKSH Australia* was the opposite. Although the imitation product was branded 'Euroline', this, in itself, was not a very distinctive brand name and also was not found on the coffee plungers themselves but only on the packaging that would be seen less on display than at the final checkout stage. The defendant could, according to Greenwood J, easily have marked the plungers themselves with its mark, which would have been visible in the display setting. DKSH Australia had thus infringed Bodum's rights. Similarly in *Homart*, the fact that the rival product packaged and presented in very similar ways was marked 'CHÉRI' and not 'CHANTELLE' was ultimately held not to be sufficient to distinguish it enough to defeat an accusation of misleading and deceptive conduct.

It is a different matter if the resemblance is in the get-up rather than in the appearance of the goods themselves. Such was the case in *The Kettle Chip Co Pty Ltd v Apand*

Pty Ltd (1993) 46 FCR 152; 27 IPR 321 (affirmed in (1994) 52 FCR 474; 30 IPR 337), where the respondent set out not only to duplicate the characteristics of the applicant's product (potato chips) but also to give its own product the same image by replicating the packaging get-up of the successful new chips developed by The Kettle Chip Company. The respondent was found guilty of passing off. In *Parkdale* at CLR 222, at IPR 704, Brennan J said the following:

> A distinction is drawn between the get-up of goods and the copying of the actual goods. Similarity in get-up may evidence passing-off, but (statutory monopoly apart) all are free to copy the goods themselves. The distinction was stated by Fletcher Moulton LJ in *JB Williams Co v H Bronnley & Co Ltd* (1909) 26 RPC 765, at 773–4: 'The get-up of an article means a capricious addition to the article itself — the colour, or shape, it may be, of the wrapper, or anything of that kind; but I strongly object to look at anything, that has a value in use, as part of the get-up of the article. Anything which is in itself useful appears to me rightly to belong to the article itself. For instance, supposing that a firm had been, say for 20 years, the only firm to sell wooden chairs in which the natural wood was simply varnished, and not painted at all, that would not give them the slightest right to complain of a person putting on the market chairs simply varnished, even though they had been the only persons who had sold them for so long that such chairs might at first be supposed to be their manufacture. The reason is that the newcomer has not in any way imitated the get-up; he has only reproduced the article'.

As to similarities in get-up and packaging, see also *Yves St Laurent Parfums v Louden Cosmetics Ltd* (1997) 39 IPR 11 and *Parfums Christian Dior (Australia) Pty Ltd v Dimmeys Stores Pty Ltd* (1997) 39 IPR 349. Even though the get-up adopted by the defendant may be similar, the plaintiff will usually find it difficult to prove that likelihood of deception is not excluded by the defendant's use of a different brand name, such as 'LiveWire' instead of 'Red Bull' in *Red Bull Australia Pty Ltd v Sydneywide Distributors Pty Ltd* (2001) 53 IPR 481 and the appeal in the *Red Bull* case. Nonetheless, although every trader has a prima facie right to package their goods in any way considered attractive and convenient (see *Burford & Sons Ltd v Mowling & Son* (1908) 8 CLR 212), that right is subject to the proviso that the form adopted must not deceive the ordinary reasonable consumer. In *Red Bull*, the respondent 'sailed too close to the wind' by deliberately adopting the same colours and unusual shape for its energy drink can and was guilty of passing off. However, by contrast, in *Nutrientwater Pty Ltd v Baco Pty Ltd* (2010) 84 IPR 452; [2010] FCA 2, the similarities between the get-up of the two products in the 'enhanced water' market came about not because of an intention to deceive but to have a product that, although distinctive, was still 'referable to the enhanced water market': at [121].

Similar colour on packaging was also at issue in *Ricegrowers Ltd v Real Foods Pty Ltd* (2008) 77 IPR 32. In April 2007, the defendant, Real Foods, started to promote and offer for sale three varieties of flavoured thin corn cakes called 'New Corn Thins' in flow pack packaging. The plaintiff, Ricegrowers, claimed passing off or misleading and deceptive conduct in relation to the packaging and get-up of its own flavoured 'Corn Thins'. The test required the court to consider 'the effect on an ordinary reasonable shopper by conduct involving the making of a representation to the class of retail consumers shopping in a supermarket displaying a trader's packaged goods on its shelves': at IPR 46. The ordinary reasonable consumer is described as a female aged between 30 and 49 years, with some further specific characteristics: see at IPR 51. In the final analysis, the similarities between the packages (eg, the use of green) were trumped by the immediately noticeable differences and the fact that the defendant's own logo operated as a branding device appeared, and, further, 'Real Foods adopted colours and printed flow pack packaging which were in common use in the savoury biscuits category. Just because Ricegrowers was first to use these in the corn cake and rice cake subcategories did not entitle it to a monopoly of their use.': at IPR 56. The *Fiji Waters* case also concerned similarities in packaging. The defendant's 'Island Chill' packaging was alleged to share so many features with Fiji Waters' packaging that a misrepresentation arose that there was some association between the products. Again, the standard was the reasonable member of the class of prospective purchasers, without the benefit of having similarities and differences pointed out. The get-up had to be considered as a whole, and as they were relatively cheap consumer goods, it was unlikely that a consumer would engage in lengthy or detailed comparison of get-up (see at IPR 580). The court held that although most of the individual features were commonplace, the particular constellation of features adopted by the plaintiff had developed a reputation with consumers, also taking into account the level of sales and promotion of its product. Although there were some similar elements to the two bottles, these were mostly related to commonplace features used by others as well, and the overall effect was sufficiently different for there to be no infringement of the plaintiff's rights. The result was similar in relation to the striking gold packaging used for boxes of bio-placenta skincare products in *Homart*.

Misrepresentation as to the geographical origins of goods

13.21 Traders sometimes untruthfully represent that some connection exists between their goods and an area or region with an established reputation for certain products, commonly wine (see, eg, the early case of *Bollinger v Costa Brava Wine Co Ltd* [1961] RPC 116, the so-called *Spanish Champagne* case). Either individual traders from such a region who are legitimate users of the denomination of origin or their representative organisations (eg, the Union of Swiss Chocolate Manufacturers in the *Chocosuisse* case, see 13.4) have standing to sue in passing off in such circumstances. However, if the regional or geographical denomination has become, or has always been, generic — that is, associated with or identifying a certain kind of product rather than a certain region of origin — the producers of the region are deprived of the exclusive right to use the geographical reference in relation to goods emanating from that area. Consideration of the descriptive versus distinctive message emanating from a geographical term, in this case 'Persian fetta', is to be found in *Yarra Valley Dairy Pty Ltd v Lemnos Foods Pty Ltd* (2010) 90 IPR 117; [2010] FCA 1367. The term 'Persian' was said to have non-geographic relevance as evoking the exotic, as well as being vague and imprecise in a geographical sense. A similar issue arose in *Bohemia Crystal*, where the term 'Bohemia' as well as historically having geographical significance (a region in the modern-day Czech Republic) also had other connotations (of bohemianism). A further example of the distinction between the primary and secondary associations of geographical terms being considered is found in *Kosciuszko Thredbo Pty Ltd v ThredboNet Marketing Pty Ltd* (2014) 223 FCR 517; 106 IPR 434; [2014] FCAFC 87.

A more longstanding issue relates to the right to use the term 'champagne' for sparkling wines produced outside France; reference was already made above to this issue in the significant *Spanish Champagne* case. Is 'champagne' a generic word denoting sparkling wine or do consumers associate the name exclusively with wine originating within the Champagne region in northern France? See in the UK *Bollinger v Costa Brava Wine Co Ltd (No 2)* [1969] 1 All ER 561; in Australia *Comité Interprofessionel du Vin de Champagne v NL Burton Pty Ltd (t/as Freixenet Spanish Champagne Distributors)* (1981) 57 FLR 434; 38 ALR 664, also relating to Spanish champagne; and in New Zealand *Comité Interprofessionnel du Vin de Champagne v Wineworths Group Ltd* (1991) 23 IPR 435 (*New Zealand champagne* case). In the New Zealand case, the court held that New Zealanders associated the word 'champagne' with wine originating from the Champagne region, but the Australian court held that the word was associated with a certain style of sparkling wine and used generically. Australia had a fairly longstanding tradition of producing 'champagne' at the time, whereas this was not the case in New Zealand, nor had Australian champagne been imported there much before the case was brought. In the result, Australian growers were free to use the word 'champagne' for locally made sparkling wine. However, an agreement between the EU and Australia concerning the use of denominations of origin has resulted in statutory protection for European 'geographical indications' for wines: see the Australian Wine and Brandy Corporation Act 1980 (Cth), as amended by the Australian Wine and Brandy Corporation Amendment Act 1993 (Cth) and now replaced by the Wine Australia Act 2013 (Cth). For a case on the amended Act, see *Comité Interprofessionel des Vins des Côtes de Provence v Bryce* (1996) 69 FCR 450; 35 IPR 170. Australian geographical indications of origin for wines can also be registered under that legislation to enjoy the same high level of protection, as explored in *Beringer Blass Wine Estates Ltd v Geographical Indications Committee* (2002) 125 FCR 155. The Wine Australia Act 2013 also sets up an Australian system for registration of certain wine regional names (eg, Coonawarra) and imposes restrictions on the use of registered names in relation to wines using grapes grown outside their borders. Concerning the operation of the Act, see, for example, *Beringer Blass Wine Estates Ltd*.

The causal link between misrepresentation and deception

13.22 Once it has been shown that persons in a relevant class have come to an erroneous conclusion about the origins or connections of goods or services, a sufficient link must still be shown to exist between that conclusion and the conduct of the defendant. '[C]auses of confusion that are not a defendant's fault, or do not bear a sufficient connection between the impugned conduct and any confusion, must be disregarded': *Homart Pharmaceuticals Pty Ltd v Careline Australia Pty Ltd* [2018] FCAFC 105 at [82] (citing *Telstra Corporation Ltd v Phone Directories Co Pty Ltd* (2014) 316 ALR 590; 107 IPR 333; [2014] FCA 568 at [564]; *Hornsby* at CLR 228; *Flexopack SA Plastics Industry v Flexopack Australia Pty Ltd* [2016] FCA 235 at [266]–[267]; *Taco Co of Australia* at ALR 203). In other words, can the deception rightly be sheeted home to the defendant or is it due to the consumer's error, erroneous presumption or other intervening causes? If the second element in an action in passing off, 'misrepresentation', were exclusively determined on the basis of consumers' state of mind, without proper reference to the nature and character of the defendant's conduct, the outcome would be unfair to the defendant in some instances. Ultimately, the consumer's erroneous conclusion or confusion must derive from the defendant's misrepresentation and not from some other cause.

In *Campomar Sociedad Limitada v Nike International Ltd* (1998) 85 FCR 331; 41 IPR 252 (see also *Campomar v Nike*, above at 13.11), it was argued that the confusion of consumers arose from an erroneous assumption for which Campomar, owner of a registered trade mark, 'NIKE', in respect of perfumes, was not responsible. However, as we saw above, the defendant's conduct as a whole and not one aspect of it taken in isolation determines whether it is liable in passing off. Thus, the legitimacy of Campomar's registered trade mark alone could not overcome other aspects of its conduct, which amounted to passing off. It had altered the appearance of its mark to closer resemble the well-known Nike mark and had used the mark on sports fragrances, thus creating the impression of an association with the well-known sporting goods manufacturer. Given those circumstances, it was wrong to say that an assumption that the Campomar fragrances were connected to Nike International was simply an erroneous assumption on the consumer's part, not resulting from wrongful conduct on the part of Campomar but from a legitimate use of its registered mark.

Although it is necessary to establish that the defendant did cause the deception by its conduct, it is an error to presume that between misrepresentation and deception there lies a chain of causation that can simply be shown by the defendant to have been interrupted and defeated by an erroneous assumption of the consumer. This was reiterated in the trial court's decision in *Knight v Beyond Properties Pty Ltd* (2007) 71 IPR 466; [2007] FCA 70 (the *Mythbusters* case; see also *Knight v Beyond Properties Pty Ltd* (2007) 74 IPR 232; [2007] FCAFC 170), at [168]:

> [The High Court in *Campomar v Nike*] pointed out that an action under s 52 of the TP Act cannot be defeated simply by pointing to an 'erroneous assumption' because '*no conduct can mislead or deceive unless the representee labours under some erroneous assumption*' (at [104] quoting Deane and Fitzgerald JJ in *Taco Bell* 42 ALR at 200). The High Court accordingly rejected the existence or reliability of any general 'erroneous assumption' doctrine that would defeat a claim by showing that a prospective purchaser could only be misled by wrongly assuming some '*endorsement by, or other association with, the plaintiff*' (see 202 CLR at [110]). [Emphasis in original]

Were it otherwise, wherever what the defendant has done has some legitimacy about it, this could serve to establish that the confusion and deception must be the result of an erroneous assumption on the part of the consumer and can thus not amount to passing off. As is shown in *Campomar v Nike* and also in *Taco Co of Australia Inc* at ALR 200, the key is rather the degree of waywardness of the erroneous assumption. If that requirement can be met, the conclusion of a consumer that some connection exists can be shown to be due to an erroneous assumption for which the defendant is not responsible. This might, for example, be the case where, as in the *Mythbusters* case, the witnesses who laboured under the misunderstanding that there was some connection between the TV show and Mr Knight were all shown to have some particular knowledge and association with him personally. Alternatively, it might be the case where the defendant does no more than imitate or copy a rival's successful product without in any other way suggesting a connection between them. Brennan J said about this situation in *Parkdale* at CLR 225:

> If consumers or potential customers believe that all goods of a particular design are manufactured by him who first establishes a market reputation as a manufacturer of those goods, that belief is or may be erroneous. The error may be attributed to a preconceived belief that the manufacturer who first establishes a market reputation has a monopoly in the manufacture and sale of goods of that kind but, unless the manufacturer has acquired a statutory monopoly, that belief is also erroneous and the error flows from a misconception of law. A later manufacturer who does no more than exercise his freedom to manufacture and sell goods made in accordance with a design in the public domain does not mislead or deceive; and if a consumer has an erroneous preconceived belief that the first manufacturer has a monopoly, a false assumption by the consumer as to the source of the later manufacturer's goods is self-induced.

Alternatively, it may be that the reason consumers are misled is not so much due to their erroneous assumption but because their 'mental processes' were at fault (see, eg, *Siddons Pty Ltd v The Stanley Works Pty Ltd* (1991) 29 FCR 14; 20 IPR 1), in which case no liability in passing off arises either. Finally, it should be noted that there is authority to show that persons honestly trading under their own name have a defence: see, for example, *Ferrari Furniture Cabinet Makers Pty Ltd v Ferrari Furniture Pty Ltd* (2006) 69 IPR 295.

Disclaimers

13.23 The causal link between the conduct of the defendant company or entity and the confusion or deception that arises among consumers also lies at the heart of the question of the effect of disclaimers. The presence of the defendant's brand on the goods may function effectively as a disclaimer of any connection with the plaintiff's business, as was the case with the tag attached to the lounge furniture in *Parkdale* and with the imitators' own brands in the *Dr Martens* case: see 13.20. A factual issue arises as to whether the identifying label, brand or marking, or, for that matter, an express disclaimer is sufficiently prominently displayed. This question was at issue in the *Thomas the Tank Engine* case (*Britt Allcroft (Thomas) LLC v Miller* [2000] FCA 699), where a disclaimer of sorts set up within the shop was held not to be effective, since the deception of consumers was complete by then: they had entered the store. The effectiveness of an express disclaimer will depend on the context — how consumers might reasonably react to a disclaimer displayed in a traditional shop is one thing, but what about their reaction to a disclaimer on the internet? In *Kosciuszko Thredbo* the two domain names at issue were very similar: www.thredbo.com and www.thredbo.com.au. In relation to a website disclaimer, the court held as follows (at [48]–[49]):

> A consumer might easily be led to the former website thinking it was that of the appellants when doing an internet search. But in today's society the ordinary or reasonable consumer seeking accommodation, or other goods or services, on the internet will frequently click on a result in a web search thinking it is a link to a particular site, only to find when his or her browser is directed to the selected site that it is not the site of the supplier or business that the consumer wanted. The ordinary, reasonable consumer who came upon the home

> page of www.thredbo.com would have seen, depending on when he or she accessed it, the first or second disclaimer in the middle of the page. Each disclaimer appeared under a recognisable, distinctive heading 'About Thredbo.com'. It did not have the appearance, as asserted by the appellants, of being 'buried in the text'. A consumer who was concerned about the entity with which he or she was dealing could be expected to read the short text under that heading.

In some circumstances, a court may find an express disclaimer to be legally effective, although arguably the imitator's purpose of evoking an association is not defeated by it. For example, in *Sony Music Australia Ltd v Tansing (t/as Apple House Music)* (1993) 27 IPR 649, the respondents on an application for an interim injunction proposed to sell unauthorised recordings of Michael Jackson songs. On the front cover was to appear the word 'unauthorised' diagonally placed in large print and in smaller print would appear, inter alia, the words 'this live recording and its release has not been authorised by Michael Jackson or his record company'. The court held that the primary judge had rightly decided, on an application for an injunction, that there was no serious issue to be tried as to passing off or contravention of s 52. Even categorising the relevant class of consumers very widely as predominantly teenagers and people in their mid-20s, including the 'intelligent, not so intelligent and the dull' (at IPR 653), the case was most unlikely to succeed.

Merchandising Cases

Distinguishing misrepresentation and misappropriation

13.24 As we saw above, sometimes the action in passing off is described as protecting a property interest in goodwill. Usually, goodwill is traded with the underlying business, the goodwill being worthless without it, but in some cases the goodwill is the business. This is the essential characteristic of the so-called 'merchandising' cases that concern the exploitation of celebrity image or personality and fictional characters: celebrities trade in goodwill. Such cases are not concerned with a trader's illegitimate attempt to associate his or her goods or services with the competing goods or services of another. Rather, they are concerned with misrepresentations as to an association with a well-known person, image or character suggesting sponsorship, approbation or endorsement that does not, in fact, exist. Celebrities now commonly engage in the practice of licensing the use of their image, and the general public is aware of that practice; development and preservation of valuable goodwill is the essence of their 'business'. Licensees hope to derive benefit from the positive association and because the image of a celebrity acts as a hook to grab the attention of the consumer. In terms of the law, the accommodation of merchandising cases within the action for passing off was facilitated by the abandonment of the 'common field of activity' test in *Henderson v Radio Corporation Pty Ltd* [1969] RPC 218. This resulted in what has become known as the 'extended action' in passing off. As Dixon J put it in *Radio Corporation Pty Ltd v Disney* (1937) 57 CLR 448 at 457 (the *Mickey Mouse* case), 'The reason for using the names is to attract the attention of members of a public that has found pleasure and amusement in the grotesque forms and absurd antics of Disney's creatures, and at the same time to give to the goods a name or means of description at once familiar and pleasing or interesting to the possible buyer.' The inclusion of merchandising within the field of passing off and s 18 of the ACL, at the core of which lies an inquiry as to whether consumers have been misled as to the nature or existence of a connection, may seem somewhat artificial. As Pincus J pointed out in *10th Cantanae Pty Ltd v Shoshana Pty Ltd* (1987) 10 IPR 289 at 295–6:

> It appears to me a little artificial to assume that the ordinary reader is so gullible as to think these days, that (for example) the application of the name of a wellknown French clothing manufacturer to a great variety of goods necessarily implies anything about the 'origin, selection or treatment of the goods' or, to quote Dixon J [in *Radio Corporation Pty Ltd v Disney*], that it implies anything other than that the owner of the name 'must have sanctioned it'.

In other words, to suggest that, and seriously examine whether, consumers exposed to an unauthorised celebrity endorsement even think about, let alone come to some erroneous conclusion concerning, the precise nature of the relationship is not realistic. In the real world, endorsements operate and provide a competitive advantage more at a subliminal and unconscious level — hence the suggestion of Pincus J that the tort should be extended to cover not merely cases where a trader is guilty of a misrepresentation but where there is mere 'misappropriation': *Hogan v Koala Dundee* at IPR 517ff. This would, in effect, have resulted in the recognition of a tort of 'misappropriation of personality', a tort that would have established a 'right of publicity' in Australia, perhaps along the lines of relevant US law: see further below 13.25. However, courts here have rejected that approach in subsequent decisions. Nonetheless, they have had little trouble finding passing off, irrespective of imprecision about the exact nature of the misleading suggestion as to sponsorship or endorsement: see, for example, *Pacific Dunlop v Hogan*; *Hogan v Koala Dundee*; *Talmax Pty Ltd v Telstra Corporation Ltd* (1996) 36 IPR 46. Neither is the application of the tort restricted to cases of misleading association with a real person; in the *Hogan* cases it was not Paul Hogan but aspects of his fictional film character 'Crocodile Dundee' that were being misused. In *Telstra v Royal & Sun Alliance*, it was the fictional 'Mr Goggomobil' created for the Telstra ads. The considerable merchandising appeal of cartoon characters has also been recognised in the courts, as in the *Mickey Mouse* case: see above. As a recent example of an implicit recognition of the power of association ('endorsement' is not an entirely appropriate word in such circumstances) with a fictional character or popular entertainment product, *The Simpsons* case (*Twentieth Century Fox Film Corporation v South Australian Brewing Co Ltd* (1996) 66 FCR 451; 34 IPR 225) is instructive. Twentieth Century Fox was the producer of *The Simpsons* cartoons, and in virtually all instalments of the cartoon series the character Homer Simpson can be seen drinking 'Duff' beer. Tamberlin J accepted that the series had acquired substantial goodwill and reputation in Australia in relation to the characters, names and images appearing in *The Simpsons*, including the name 'Duff Beer'. South Australian Brewing (SA Brewing) produced and marketed, without authorisation from 20th Century Fox, a niche beer, calling it 'Duff' beer. The colour of the can was different from that of the cartoon can, and the word 'Duff' did not appear in the same rough handwriting and was in lower case. It was clear that SA Brewing was anxious to generate an association in the target audience's mind with the cartoon series. Tamberlin J said (at IPR 237):

> The name or word under consideration does not have to be associated with goods manufactured by the trader. In *Radio Corp Pty Ltd v Disney* (1937) 57 CLR 448 (the *Mickey Mouse* case) at 453, Latham CJ in relation to the names 'Mickey Mouse' and 'Minnie Mouse' considered that these were: '... so closely associated in the public mind, with ... Walter E Disney and his activities, that the use of either the names or the figures in connection with any goods at once suggests that the goods are "in some way or other" connected with ... Disney.'

This, together with the fact that the word 'Duff' had acquired powerful secondary meaning in Australia, was a sufficient basis for Tamberlin J's finding that SA Brewing had engaged in passing off by creating a false impression of an association with 20th Century Fox's characters.

To succeed in a merchandising case, it will be necessary to establish that the person whose image is allegedly misused actually has a sufficient reputation, attaching to some distinctive aspect of their personality (such as their name, photo, or unique symbol or device). To determine this, the characterisation of the reasonable member of the relevant class of consumers will be critical. Some personality may be well known within certain circles but not to the general public. Thus, in *Fitzgerald v 33 South Pty Ltd* [2008] FMCA 1132, a federal magistrate held that the relevant public was 'the purchasers of surfboards and the purchases (even for relatives) of surf-related products in Australia, and is predominantly composed of surfers': at [96]. With this group, Mr Fitzgerald, who had been a surf champion in the 1970s and continued to be involved with the sport, had a sufficient reputation, although the same could probably not have been said for the public at large. Further, there must be a misleading suggestion of an association, which may depend on just how clearly the image or words used without authorisation evoke a particular celebrity. Photographs may certainly suggest an association: see, for instance, *Buttrose v Senior's Choice (Australia) Pty Ltd* [2013] FCCA 2050. However, in *10th Cantanae*, the court found that the use of the common-sounding (ie, not very distinctive) name 'Sue Smith' in a television advertisement in association with images of a person who only remotely resembled Sue Smith (a television personality) did not amount to passing off or a breach of s 52 of the TPA. There must also be some suggestion of sponsorship or endorsement engendered by the juxtaposition of the defendants' goods and services and the image of the celebrity used. For an example of factual circumstances where there was found to be no such suggestion, see *Honey v Australian Airlines Ltd* (1990) 18 IPR 185. The unauthorised use of the athlete's image on a series of posters promoting participation in sport was held not to have constituted a false suggestion of sponsorship or endorsement; rather, the posters simply exalted sporting prowess.

The right of publicity

13.25 In some jurisdictions, notably in the US, the right of celebrities to control the commercial use of their image has been found to be based on the so-called right of publicity (or alternatively 'personality rights'); that is, the inherent right of persons to control the commercial use of aspects of their identity. However, that right 'has not been held to be part of the law of Australia': per French J in *Sony Music Australia Ltd v Tansing* at IPR 653–4. Nor has it been successfully argued in the UK. Vindication of the right of publicity does not require proof of consumer deception, and thus the protection of celebrities' commercial interests is much more far reaching in the

US: see Zapparoni, 'Propertising Identity: Understanding the United States Right of Publicity and its Implications — Some Lessons for Australia' (2004) 28 *MULR* 690.

Damage

13.26 Although the action in passing off is, in theory, complete once misrepresentation has been established — as well as the action under s 18 of the ACL, once misleading or deceptive conduct is proven — damage, or the likelihood of damage, will have to be shown if more than nominal damages are to be awarded. However, in most cases, it is more fruitful for a competitor to obtain an injunction to restrain the misleading behaviour and prevent the occurrence of damage and loss of market share, which may otherwise prove irreversible. If an injunction rather than damages or an account of profit is sought, the plaintiff will have to 'show irreparable injury, that is, that he has suffered injury which cannot be properly compensated by damages, or that he will probably suffer such injury': per Evatt CJ and Myers J in *Henderson v Radio Corporation* (1960) (above 13.4). There is a close connection between establishing damage and proving sufficient reputation. Usually, the damage or injury of which the plaintiff complains in an action in passing off will be in relation to loss of sales because of actual or apprehended diversion of custom or business. However, the damage complained of may also be that the goodwill of the applicant is 'adversely affected' (see *Twentieth Century Fox Film Corporation v South Australian Brewing Co Ltd* (above 13.9) in that case partly because the applicant had avoided any association with promotion of alcohol) or that the good reputation of the plaintiff is diluted because of association with inferior or shoddy products: see, for example, the *Advocaat* case (*Erven Warnink BV v J Townend & Sons (Hull) Ltd* [1979] AC 731; (1979) 1A IPR 666), where the defendant's 'Egg Flip' was of far lesser quality than the genuine Advocaat egg and brandy drink sourced in Holland, and also the *New Zealand champagne* case. Alternatively, the damage may also consist of the plaintiff being wrongfully deprived of the opportunity to sponsor, recommend or endorse products or services. Such was the damage complained of in the seminal merchandising case of *Henderson v Radio Corporation* (1960) and in *Talmax* (the *Kieren Perkins* case). The measure of damages will generally be the level of royalty forgone, although this can be difficult to estimate, since royalty fees vary widely, as in *Talmax*; contrast this, however, with *Irvine v Talksport Ltd* [2002] 57 IPR 621, where there was clear evidence that Eddie Irvine, a Formula 1 racing car driver, would not have accepted an endorsement contract for less than a specified fee of £25,000. It is not necessary to give evidence of an actual lost opportunity: see *Talmax* and *Fitzgerald* (above 13.24). It may also have to be proven by evidence that the plaintiff contemplated ever 'merchandising' their name or image; as to an example where that was not established on the evidence, see *Stringfellow v McCain Foods (GB) Ltd* (1983) 2 IPR 279. The loss of opportunity may also be in relation to expansion, diversification or brand extension: see, for example, *Lego System Aktieselskab v Lego M Lemelstrich Ltd* [1983] FSR 155 (loss of opportunity to extend the use of the Lego name to gardening equipment). Naturally, in such cases, there will have to be a finding that the distinctiveness of the plaintiff's brand is so great that consumers will tend to infer a connection even if the brand name is used on goods or services other than those with which the plaintiff has previously been concerned.

Bibliography

A Laurie, 'The Bill Sell: The Value and Effectiveness of Character Merchandising Protection in Australia' (2003) 54 *IP Forum* 12.

AIPJ, 'Protection of Geographical Indications of Wines' (1994) 5 *AIPJ* 113.

AIPJ, 'Red Bull: The Appeal', (2002) 15(4) *IPLB* 54.

B Katekar, 'Coping with Character Merchandising — Passing off Unsurpassed' (1996) 7 *AIPJ* 178.

C Kendall and T Metz, 'Ambush Marketing and the Beijing Olympics: Lessons from the Australian Experience' (2003) 55 *IP Forum* 30.

C Richards and R Berry, 'Use of a Celebrity in Advertising' (1996) 9 *IPLB* 83.

D Eliades, 'Casenote — TGI Friday's *Australia Pty Ltd v TGI Friday's Inc*' (2000) 13(5) *IPLB* 73.

D Meltz, 'These Boots were Made for Stomping — Dr Martens & the Freedom to Copy' (1999) 7 *CCLJ* 160.

D Sibraa, 'D'oh! Brewery Loses as Homer Simpson Keeps his Duff Beer' (1996) 9 *IPLB* 102.

H Stallard, J Dennis, 'Personality Rights — the Contrasting Approaches of the US and the UK' (1999) 37 *IP Forum* 16.

I Tregoning, 'What's in a Name? Goodwill in Early Passing-Off Cases' (2008) 34 *Mon LR* 75.

J Gardiner, 'It's None of Your Business!: Section 52 and the Tort of Passing Off' (1996) 4 *TPLJ* 60.

K Anker, 'Possessing Star Qualities: Celebrity Identity as Property' (2002) 11 *Griffith LR* 147.

K Hayne and J Morrison, 'Theme Restaurants Serve Up an IP Challenge' (2005) 17(10) *IPLB* 172.

L Hintz, 'Is the Beer Really Better, Drunk by Your Idol? The Duff Beer Case' (1997) 19 *Syd LR* 114.

L Taylor, 'Decision in *Campomar Sociedad, Limitada v Nike International Ltd*' (2000) 14(2) *CLQ* 14.

L Weathered, 'Trade Marking Celebrity Image: The Impact of Distinctiveness and Use as a Trade Mark' (2000) 12(2) *Bond L R* 161.

M Baldwin, 'A Passing Manoeuvre of a Different Kind: *Irvine v Talksport*' (2003) 16(5) *IPLB* 78.

O Morgan, 'Mmmmm Beeeer — Character Merchandising in Australia & Duff Beer Case — Pt II' (1997) 10 *IPLB* 23.

P Chalk, 'Cadbury Cases Continue' (2006) 19 (5 & 6) *IPLB* 81.

R Mulheron, 'Survey Evidence in Passing-Off and Trademark Litigation' (1996) 26 *QLSJ* 449.

S Bell, 'Application for Injunction to Restrain Use of 'Melbourne Inner City' (2003) 16(6) *IPLB* 97.

S Givoni, 'Half a Glass Full of Purple' (2006) 19(2) *IPLB* 17.

S Hill, 'Mr Goggomobil (Almost) Rides Again: *Telstra Corp v Royal & Sun Alliance Insurance Australia*' (2003) 19(6) *TPLB* 78.

S Sheppard, 'Manufacturers of Fiji Water Suffer Loss in Passing Off Action — Case Note; *Natural Waters of Viti v Dayals*' (2007) 23(5) *TPLB* 78.

S Stone, '*Kettle Chip Co Pty Ltd v Apand Pty Ltd*' (1998) 11 *IPLB* 22.

S Ricketson, 'Reaping without Sowing: Unfair Competition and Intellectual Property Rights in Anglo-Australian Law' (1984) 7 *UNSWLJ* 1.

S Walpola, 'Infringing 'Smell-Alikes' — Case Note; *L'Oreal SA v Bellure NV*' (2007) 19(9) *IPLB* 150.

T Catanzariti, 'Swimmers, Surfers, and Sue Smith — Personality Rights in Australia' (2002) 15(2) *IPLB* 13.

W Burnett, 'Nike — Perfume or Sports Goods?' (2001) 13(8) *IPLB* 113.

Chapter 14

Registered Trade Marks: Definition of a Mark and Distinctiveness

Introduction

Common law marks and registered marks

14.1 If a trade mark is not registered under the Trade Marks Act 1995 (Cth), the owner can rely on only the action in passing off or s 18 of the Australian Consumer Law (ACL) under Sch 2 of the Competition and Consumer Act 2010 (Cth) to obtain relief against unauthorised use. Such marks are known as 'common law marks', as opposed to 'registered trade marks'. The previous chapter demonstrates the considerable evidentiary burden that the action for passing off places on the plaintiff, who must prove the existence of a reputation in some distinct aspect of goods or a business, misrepresentation (ie, consumer deception) and (likely) damage. An action under s 18 of the ACL, although not requiring strict adherence to the elements of the action in passing off, is subject to requirements that are broadly equivalent in substance if a plaintiff is to meet the ultimate standard of consumer deception (although it is clear that no proof of damage is required).

Many actions in passing off concern a rival trader adopting another's 'trade dress' (packaging, get-up, etc), product appearance or even advertising campaign theme. However, an action in passing off can and is sometimes also brought against a trader who adopts or imitates an unregistered (or 'common law') trade mark or brand; that is, a distinctive sign associated with the plaintiff's business. This may be as an alternative or additional cause of action, even where the trade mark concerned is registered, or as the only option where it is not. Nothing prevents a trader from bringing an action in passing off or under s 18 of the ACL in relation to a trade mark that is registered. It may be that the actions of the defendant concern more than just the trade mark and extend to other forms of imitation or deceptive association. Alternatively, it may be that the unauthorised use of the trade mark relates to goods or services arguably different from those for which the mark is registered, or it may be for some other reason. However, the importance, value and tradability of marks as repositories of goodwill are reflected in the more effective protection available by way of registration under the Trade Marks

Act. There are thus considerable advantages in registering a trade mark and bringing an action based on the Trade Marks Act.

It should be noted that trade marks fall within the powers of the Commonwealth (see s 51(xviii) of the Commonwealth of Australia Constitution Act and the *Union Label Case*: *Attorney-General (NSW) v Brewery Employees' Union of NSW* (1908) 6 CLR 469). Other than on the basis of the intellectual property power, Commonwealth legislation may also rely on the external affairs power (see s 51(xxix) of the Commonwealth of Australia Constitution Act) as domestic implementation of provisions of the Paris Convention and of the World Trade Organization (WTO) Trade-Related Aspects of Intellectual Property Rights (TRIPS) Agreement (see Paris Convention for the Protection of Industrial Property, 1883, arts 6–10*ter*; TRIPS, arts 15–21). Note that the High Court has in any case adopted a broad and flexible interpretation of the intellectual property power: see *Grain Pool of WA v Commonwealth* (2000) 202 CLR 479; 46 IPR 515. Other than for ordinary trade marks, registration can also be obtained for defensive marks (Pt 17 of the Trade Marks Act), collective marks (see Paris Convention, art 7*bis*; Pt 15 of the Trade Marks Act) and certification marks (Pt 16): see Chapter 15 Registered Trade Marks: Other Requirements. Historically, trade mark registration was available only for signs used in relation to goods; however, trade marks can now be registered for services as well: see art 6*sexies* of the Paris Convention (introduced in 1958, Lisbon revision of the convention).

Advantages and disadvantages of registration

14.2 Registration of trade marks relieves some of the burdens inherent in reliance on passing off or s 18 of the ACL. First, there is no need to prove existing (local) reputation of a registered trade mark. Trade mark registration gives an automatic right of action that is national in scope, in relation to goods or services for which the mark is registered. In other words, if a registered trade mark is used by an unauthorised third party in relation to the kinds of goods or services for which it is registered, confusion or deception is presumed. Second, and in a related manner, trade mark registration may be obtained without the trade mark actually being used, as long as there is a genuine intention to use the mark; in contrast, a common law mark must be in use long enough to build up actual reputation before an action in passing off will lie. A start-up business may rely on trade mark registration while it develops goodwill by engaging in commercial use of the mark; in other words, to use passing-off terms, the action does not depend on evidence that average consumers would be misled or deceived by the use of the mark by the defendant. (Note that the ® symbol may be used only for a *registered* trade mark, while any sign used as a mark may be accompanied by ™.)

However, there are some limitations to registration. First, whereas the action in passing off can vindicate reputation adhering to any distinctive aspect of a business, including get-up, packaging or elements of appearance taken as a whole, registration is limited to a 'sign' as is arguably more narrowly defined in the Trade Marks Act: see 14.7. Second, rights to a remedy without proof of confusion or deception are limited to unauthorised use in relation to the kinds of goods or services for which the mark is registered. Note also that although a trade mark can be registered before it has been used, maintaining the mark on the register is subject to a minimum use requirement: see Chapter 16 Registered Trade Marks: Infringement.

Trade Mark Registration and Validity

14.3 The Trade Marks Act 1995 prescribes a system of application, examination and registration of marks. However, although potentially perpetual, the validity of the registration of a trade mark is not guaranteed, and the registration of a mark may thus be under attack at any time after registration, as well as being subject to opposition during the application process. In reality, only very few trade mark registrations are opposed. Commonly, removal or amendment of a mark will result from a counterclaim in infringement proceedings (if so, the plaintiff can sometimes still succeed on the basis of an action in passing off). Alternatively, an 'aggrieved person' (see s 88; a term of art discussed at 16.17) can bring an application for removal before a competent court at any time. The question of conformity with statutory requirements may thus arise during the application process or after registration, and it should be kept in mind that the substantive requirements for validity — primarily, distinctiveness and that the mark is not likely to deceive or cause confusion — remain applicable throughout the life of the trade mark.

It is also crucial to maintaining registration that the mark is actually in use as a mark; otherwise, a mark may be removed because of non-use. The requirement of continued use, or genuine intention to use at the application stage, renders the hoarding of trade marks or shadow marks difficult. A person cannot register marks intending to sell them off to legitimate potential users of the mark at some later date, or simply intending to prohibit others from using them; but see the discussion on defensive registration of marks below at 15.12.

Registration also does not result in an absolute monopoly right to use the mark. There are numerous exceptions to the exclusive rights of the trade mark owner (eg, a mark becoming generic, prior user rights, certain uses of a mark in good faith: see Chapter 16 Registered Trade Marks: Infringement). Also, the application must indicate for which goods or services, within certain predetermined classes,[1] registration is sought. The registered owner's more absolute rights are then limited to use in relation to those goods and services. Different owners may thus validly register the same trade mark but for goods or services in different classes. An owner who intends to use a trade mark for goods or services that fall into different classes may register it for goods or services in multiple classes, but use of the mark must then be maintained in each class. If the mark does not remain valid or in use in relation to goods or services in a particular class for which it is registered, it can be removed in relation to that class only. Registration of a trade mark extends only to Australia and does not confer any rights in any other jurisdiction. An applicant must therefore pursue registration individually in every country where protection is sought, just as is the case with patents. Procedurally, this is facilitated by the 'Madrid Protocol'.[2] Finally, the exclusive rights of the trade mark owner extend only to use of a trade mark as a mark; that is, as a badge of origin: see further below 16.2.

---

1. See <https://www.ipaustralia.gov.au/trade-marks/applying-for-a-trade-mark/classes-goods-and-services>.
2. See <https://www.ipaustralia.gov.au/tools-resources/publications-reports/international-trade-mark-guide>.

Recent history of trade marks law

14.4 The recent history of trade marks law has been relatively eventful. During 1994, the Labor Government published an exposure draft of a new Trade Marks Bill, which was to address some of the shortcomings and anachronisms inherent in the Trade Marks Act 1955 (Cth), so as to bring statute law into line with more modern trade mark practices and some of the stronger protection requirements of TRIPS (eg, in relation to 'well-known marks': see art 16(3)). However, the exposure bill was enacted as the Trade Marks Act 1994 (Cth) before the end of the consultation period, leaving some concerns with the draft bill unresolved. The reason for the bill's premature passage into law was the need to implement the requirements of the TRIPS Agreement by the end of 1994 for the purpose of ratification. The commencement date of the 1994 Act was 1 January 1996, but, in fact, it never did come into operation, as it was replaced during 1995 by a new Act that was substantially the same as the 1994 Act but with some important differences. The Trade Marks Act 1994 (Cth) is sometimes called in aid by courts interpreting statutory terminology in the 1995 Act: see, for example, *Kenman Kandy Australia Pty Ltd v Registrar of Trade Marks* (2002) 122 FCR 494; 56 IPR 30 at 40. The new Trade Marks Act 1995 (Cth) commenced on 1 January 1996, in effect directly replacing the Trade Marks Act 1955 (Cth) in an operational sense.

Differences between the 1955 and 1995 Acts

14.5 The Trade Marks Act 1995 (the 1995 Act) brought some important changes to trade marks law, most of which have strengthened the position of the registered trade mark owner, in line with the perceived value and importance of trade marks and brands in the contemporary marketplace. There has also been a noticeable shift in favour of applicants for registration. The adoption of a 'presumption of registrability' (see s 33) means that while previously the applicant had the onus of proving that a trade mark was registrable, the Registrar of Trade Marks must now register the mark unless satisfied that there is a sufficient statutory basis for rejecting the application; doubt is to be resolved in favour of the applicant: see Burrell and Handler, 'Rethinking the Presumption of Registrability in Trade Mark Law' (2012) 38(1) *Mon LR* 148. Trade marks have also become easier to register, because the categories of signs that may be registered have been expanded by the addition of shape, aspects of packaging, scent and colour. Further, the registration in two main classes under the 1955 Act, Part A marks and Part B marks, was abolished so that all ordinary marks are now registered in one single class. Since the lower requirements for registrability that were applicable to Part B marks, which consequently enjoyed a more limited level of protection than Part A marks, are now, in effect, applicable to all marks (the key factor is the level of distinctiveness), registration can be obtained more readily now than under the 1955 Act; by virtue of s 233 of the 1995 Act, trade marks registered under the 1955 Act continue in force, and by virtue of s 234 the grounds on which such old registrations may be challenged are limited. Finally, with the introduction of the 1995 Act, it became possible to register marks with no inherent distinctiveness; that is, on the basis of evidence of acquired distinctiveness through use alone.

Once registration is obtained, the trade mark owner's ability to obtain a remedy is also strengthened under the 1995 Act. The principle that registration of a mark gives the right of exclusive use only in relation to the same or similar goods or services as those for which it is registered has, in effect, been further attenuated under the 1995 Act. In other words, a trade mark owner is now in a stronger position where a mark is used in relation to goods and services that are not the same but are similar, or that are different from those for which the mark is registered: see s 120(2) and (3). These provisions strengthen the position of well-known marks; that is, generally, marks that are so famous that despite the fact that they are used on unfamiliar goods or services, consumers would still presume a connection with the trade mark owner.

There are other changes; for instance:

- regarding the position of licensees — the introduction of an authorised user system;
- in relation to removal of a mark from the register for non-use — the position of the owner is weakened; in other words, proving sufficient use became somewhat more onerous (although quite a low threshold still applies); and
- in relation to geographical indications of origin — the difficulties with distinctiveness are addressed to a degree.

These changes will be touched upon incidentally throughout the chapters on trade marks law.

The Statutory Definition of a Trade Mark

Basic requirements are two-fold

14.6 As with other statutory systems, the requirements for registrability of a trade mark are of two basic kinds: first, that the mark in the application for registration falls within the statutory definition of a mark (see s 17 of the 1995 Act); and, second, that certain substantive requirements are met. The principal requirements are:

- distinctiveness (s 41);
- that a mark not be deceptive or confusing (usually because of alleged similarity to an unregistered mark that had already acquired a reputation in Australia (s 60) or because of some inherently misleading quality (s 43)); and
- that a mark not be too similar to another registered trade mark (registered either for the same or for similar goods or services) (s 44).

Some further requirements, limitations and exclusions also apply and are touched upon below in relation to generic marks, marks containing prohibited signs (s 39; eg, the Australian Coat of Arms), unlawful and scandalous marks (s 42), and marks that cannot be represented graphically (see s 40). Section 17 defines a trade mark as 'a sign used, or intended to be used, to distinguish goods or services dealt with or provided in the course of trade by a person from goods or services so dealt with or provided by any other person'. For present purposes, three elements of this definition are significant: first, that the trade mark be a 'sign'; second, that it be in use or intended to be used as a mark; and, third, that its use is for the purpose of distinguishing marked goods or services of the registrant from those provided by others. The latter requirement is comprehensively addressed in s 41, which sets out the steps to be followed by a decision-maker, but distinctiveness goes to the core of the statutory definition as well.

'Signs' that may be registered as a trade mark

14.7 It has already been pointed out above that one of the major changes of the 1995 Act is the expansion of those 'indicia' or 'signs' that qualify for registration as a trade mark. The word 'sign' is defined inclusively in s 6 as including 'the following or any combination of the following, namely, any letter, word, name, signature, numeral, device, brand, heading, label, ticket, aspect of packaging, shape, colour, sound or scent'. In general, a sign will consist of either letters or a word or a device, or a more or less complex combination of both, or a word represented in a particular or striking manner. For instance, the Nike 'swoosh' is a device; the Coca-Cola sign is a partly invented word represented in a particular style and colour. The 1995 Act, recognising that a mark may be a complex combination of words (eg, a slogan), letters and/or graphic elements (eg, a label), permits registration subject to the disclaimer that the owner does not claim a monopoly in a specified part of a registered mark (eg, a complex mark may contain a common word, and the monopoly will not extend to that word on its own: see s 74).

However, the simpler and less descriptive the mark, the more effective or 'stronger' it generally is because it is more easily recognised, more distinctive and less easy to imitate or approximate without infringing the rights of the trade mark owner. Note that the definition of a 'sign' is inclusive and not exhaustive. The express inclusion in the 1995 Act of 'shapes, sounds, scents, colours and aspects of packaging' merely removes previous doubt about their registrability. Although most marks would be expected to consist of one or more of the listed signs, the definition is not exhaustive, so what may be registered (eg, a hologram or the layout of a restaurant) is ultimately determined by the need for it to function as a 'sign'.

As for the kinds of signs that have become expressly registrable under the 1995 Act — that is, shape, sound, scent and aspect of packaging — various issues arise. In relation to registration of the shape of the product, the main problem is that the product and the sign may be virtually indistinguishable. In relation to sounds and scents, the main problems relate to distinctiveness, graphical representation in the application for the purpose of examinability of the register, and infringement. These issues are referred to immediately below.

A sign used to distinguish goods or services

14.8 Because the definition of 'sign' is broad and inclusive, there is really not much that is not, prima facie, registrable as a trade mark. This throws a heavy onus on the third element of the definition — that the sign must be used or intended to be used to distinguish goods or services. This implies that the sign does not itself serve the primary purpose that those goods or services do, or act as a descriptor of them, but has the secondary purpose of distinguishing them from those provided by others. In other words, the sign must be distinctive and serve as a 'badge of origin'. If a sign is unable to perform the function of 'badge of origin', it is not a trade mark within the meaning of the Act. It was relatively clear under the 1955 Act that a trade mark was something separate from the relevant goods. It was seen as an addition whose purpose was not functional or aesthetic but to identify the commercial origin of goods. Thus, goods themselves or their packaging were not registrable as a trade mark: see *Smith, Kline & French Laboratories (Australia) Ltd v Registrar of Trade Marks* (1967) 116 CLR 628 at 639 and 640 per Windeyer J. For instance, under the 1955 Act, registration of the traditional shape of a Coca-Cola bottle was refused (see *Re Coca-Cola's Trade Marks* [1986] RPC 421), as was registration of the shape of Life Savers mints (see *Life Savers (Australia) Ltd's Application* (1952) 22 AOJP 3106). However, as a result of the express inclusion of 'shape' and 'aspect of packaging' in the 1995 Act, it can no longer be said that the mark must be separate from the goods themselves.

In *Koninklijke Philips Electronics NV v Remington Products Australia Pty Ltd* (2000) 100 FCR 90; 48 IPR 257 (*Philips*), the question of whether the shape of a product itself could now be registered as a trade mark was at issue; in particular, the shape of the triple rotary head of a shaver. The Full Federal Court held that the change in the Act had not invalidated Windeyer J's approach in *Smith Kline & French*. A mark remained 'something extra added to distinguish the products of one trader from those of another' (at IPR 268); however, that 'something' had to be 'extra' to the inherent form of the goods, and thus non-functional aspects of shape could be registered because 'the goods can still be seen as having, in Windeyer J's words, "an existence independently of the mark" which is imposed upon them': at IPR 268. In *Kenman Kandy*, the question was reconsidered by a Full Court. The shape (of a biscuit) sought to be registered was not inspired by function, as in *Philips*, but was not natural, usual or inherent to the goods. Although it was said now to be clear that even the whole shape of a product could be registered, Lindgren J agreed:

> ... with Lehane J in *Koninklijke Philips Electronics NV v Remington Products Australia Pty Ltd* (1999) 91 FCR 167 at [26], and with Burchett J (with whom Hill J and BransonJ agreed) on appeal in that case (under the same name at (2000) 100 FCR 90 at [15], that the introduction of shape trade marks was not accompanied by an intention to make a radical change in trade mark law. ... Accordingly, neither a shape 'possessed, because of their nature, by the goods' nor a shape 'that the goods must have if a particular technical result is to be obtained' is registrable, notwithstanding the omission from the 1995 Act of the express provision to that effect which had been made by s 39 of the short lived *Trade Marks Act 1994* (Cth) (No 156 of 1994) (see Burchett J, ibid).

However, in the process of reasoning, it is clear that the separation requirement that had been read into *Smith, Kline & French* no longer persists under the 1995 Act. The whole shape of a product can be registered as long as it is not a usual, functional, inherent shape or a shape that other traders would legitimately expect to be free to use for goods of that kind. In relation to the final point, see *Chocolaterie Guylian NV v Registrar of Trade Marks* (2009) 82 IPR 13; [2009] FCA 891, where a seahorse-shaped chocolate was refused registration, as it was reminiscent of a real creature, unlike the bug in *Kenman Kandy*, which was more of an imaginary creature. The question of functionality of a shape and trade mark registration was more recently at issue at the appeal court level in New Zealand: see *Fredco Trading Ltd v Miller* (2004) 65 IPR 653. Even if a shape mark obtains registration, there is a further question as to what amounts to infringing trade mark use of such a mark: see, for example, *Global Brand Marketing Inc v YD Pty Ltd* (2008) 76 IPR 161 and *Mayne Industries Pty Ltd v Advanced Engineering Group Pty Ltd* (2008) 166 FCR 312; 75 IPR 102, relating to an S-shaped 'fence dropper'; see also Chapter 16 Registered Trade Marks: Infringement. If something is an additional frolic or fantasy of shape or decoration, it can function properly as a 'sign' to distinguish those goods, rather than serving some other function. The issue of distinctiveness of shapes, including functional shapes, colours, etc, is considered at 14.11. Such marks are sometimes referred to as 'non-traditional trade marks'.

A trade mark as a 'badge of origin' under the 1995 Act

14.9 The statutory definition of a mark in the 1955 Act was:

> ... a mark used or proposed to be used in relation to goods or services for the purpose of indicating, or so as to indicate, a connection in the course of trade between the goods or services and a person who has the right, either as proprietor or as registered user, to use the mark ...

The essence of the function of a mark was thus to signal a connection between the marked goods or services and the trade mark owner or registered user with whom, or under whose control, they originate. Even under the definition of a trade mark in the 1955 Act, this was often a somewhat artificial concept. Consumers are not really aware of, or interested in, the trade mark owner, and do not tend to turn their minds to the connection at all; rather, a trade mark signifies certain qualities and consistency and also has inherent brand appeal in some cases. Nonetheless, courts saw a trade mark as a 'badge of origin' rather than of quality control, under the 1955 Act: see, for example, *Fender Australia Pty Ltd v Bevk (t/as Guitar Crazy)* (1989) 25 FCR 161; 15 IPR 257 and *Wingate Marketing Pty Ltd v Levi Strauss & Co* (1994) 28 IPR 193. That today the question of the origin of the trade-marked goods is often of no consequence to the consumer, who has no knowledge of the trade mark owner or registered user whatsoever, is well illustrated; for example, by franchising uses of trade marks. The authorised users of franchised marks (say, the marks of McDonald's) are many and varied and generally unknown to ultimate consumers. The key to consumers is that where the brand or mark appears, they can expect a consistent quality of delivery of service and of goods; this was reflected in the High Court's decision in *JT International SA v Commonwealth of Australia* (2012) 250 CLR 1; 97 IPR 321; [2012] HCA 43 at [286] per Crennan J:

> Whilst the prime concern of the Trade Marks Act is with the capacity of a trade mark to distinguish the goods of the registered owner from those of another trader, trade marks undoubtedly perform other functions. For example, a trade mark can be an indicium of the quality of goods sold under or by reference to it and it may be accepted that distinctive marks can have a capacity to advertise, and therefore to promote, sales of products sold under or by reference to them. The advertising function of a trade mark is much more readily appreciated than it once was[3], and that function may be of great commercial value.

---

3. See *Campomar Sociedad Limitada v Nike International Ltd* (2000) 202 CLR 45 at 66 [43]; *Johnson & Johnson Australia Pty Ltd v Sterling Pharmaceuticals Pty Ltd* (1991) 30 FCR 326 at 348–349 per Gummow J. See also *Kerly's Law of Trade Marks and Trade Names*, 15th ed (2011) at 10–12 [2-016]–[2-019].

Of underlying importance for any of those purposes is that consumers can recognise the trade mark and readily distinguish it from other trade marks in use for the same or similar goods or services. The definition in the 1995 Act recognises this reality. It makes no direct reference to the origin of goods or services or the owner of a trade mark but only to the ability of a mark to distinguish goods or services provided (or dealt with) by one person from those provided by another person. Notwithstanding the change in terminology, post-1995, courts have adhered to the notion of a registered trade mark as a badge of origin.

In *Top Heavy Pty Ltd v Killin* (1996) 34 IPR 282, reference was made to the new definition (more in the context of determining whether or not use of a mark by another was use of the mark as a mark, rather than in the context of whether it was registrable). Although admitting that the provisions of the 1995 Act were somewhat wider than those in the 1955 Act, Lehane J said, with reference to the law under the 1955 Act (at IPR 286), that 'The same "badge of origin" notion is plainly to be seen in the definition of "trade mark" in s 17 of the 1995 Act.' The infringement issue is further discussed in Chapter 16 Registered Trade Marks: Infringement.

Further, in *Montana Tyres Rims & Tubes Pty Ltd v Transport Tyre Sales Pty Ltd* (1998) 41 IPR 301 at 316, Wilcox J said:

> Section 17 of the *Trade Marks Act 1995* refers to a 'sign used … to distinguish goods or services dealt with or provided in the course of trade by a person from goods or services so dealt with or provided by any other person.' Despite the width of the term 'dealt with,' there is no reason to doubt that the essential purpose of a trade mark continues to be indication of the 'origin of goods.' Normally, therefore, origin of the goods will be identified by identifying the manufacturer, but in rare cases 'some other trader may have taken such an active role in selecting, or controlling the quality of, the goods as to constitute their origin, in practical terms.'

More recently, in *Christodoulou v Disney Enterprises Inc* (2005) 156 FCR 344; 66 IPR 595, Crennan J said:

> A trade mark indicates a connection in the course of trade between the goods and their source: it is a 'badge of origin': *Levi Strauss & Co v Wingate Marketing Pty Ltd* (1993) 43 FCR 344 at 361 per Lockhart J; see also Black CJ, Sundberg and Finkelstein JJ in *Coca-Cola Co v All-Fect Distributors Ltd* (1999) 47 IPR 481; (1999) 96 FCR 107 at 115–116 ('Coca-Cola Co') and Wilcox J in *Ocean Spray Cranberries Inc v Registrar of Trade Marks* (2000) 47 IPR 579 at 591 ('Ocean Spray'), citing Burchett J in *Johnson & Johnson Australia Pty Ltd v Sterling Pharmaceuticals Pty Ltd* (1991) 21 IPR 1 at 19 ('Caplets').

The result is that trade marks properly so called must be used to indicate the origin of goods or services, in the sense of who has provided or dealt with them. If they are not so used, as was the case in *Montana*, there is no use (or intended use) that can qualify as 'trade mark use' in the sense of the statutory definition, and thus such a 'mark' will not be registrable. *Woolworths Ltd v BP plc (No 2)* (2006) 154 FCR 97; 70 IPR 25; [2006] FCA 132, concerning the colour green, is illustrative of this issue. The question was whether the colour, inherently not distinctive, had acquired distinctiveness by its alleged use as a trade mark over time. The court pointed out (at [77]):

> Whether or not there has been use as a trade mark involves an understanding from an objective viewpoint of the purpose and nature of the use, considered in its context in

> the relevant trade. How the mark has been used may not involve a single or clear idea or message. The mark may be used for a number of purposes, or to a number of ends, but there will be use as a trade mark if one aspect of the use is to distinguish the goods or services provided by a person in the course of trade from the goods or services provided by any other persons, that is to say it must distinguish them in the sense of indicating origin: see *Shell Company of Australia Ltd v Esso Standard Oil (Australia) Ltd* [1961] HCA 75; (1963) 109 CLR 407 at 422–425, the *Caplets* case, *Musidor BV v Tansing* (1994) 52 FCR 363, *Coca-Cola Co v All-Fect Distributors Ltd* [1999] FCA 1721; (1999) 96 FCR 107 at 115–116 [19]–[20], *Sports Break Travel Pty Ltd v P & O Holidays Ltd* (2000) 50 IPR 51 at 57–58 [14], *Koninklijke Philips Electronics NV v Remington Products Australia Pty Ltd* at FCR 100–101 [12], *Aldi Stores Ltd Partnership v Frito-Lay Trading Co Gmbh* [2001] FCA 1874; (2001) 54 IPR 344 at 353 [22]–[23] and 365 [76].

Note also relating to the colour green, but for energy drinks, the decision in *Frucor Beverages Ltd v The Coca-Cola Co* (2018) 132 IPR 318; [2018] FCA 993, where the court similarly held that although prominent in the get-up of energy drink cans, the colour had not 'functioned as a trade mark': at [163]. In the *Montana* case mentioned above, the mark 'Montana' was also not able to distinguish the goods (tyres) bearing the mark dealt with by the Australian distributor and assignee of the mark from any other goods bearing the same mark (OHTSU or FALKEN). See also the decision on appeal: *Transport Tyres Sales Pty Ltd v Montana Tyres Rims and Tubes Pty Ltd* (1999) 43 IPR 481 (Full Court); however, on appeal, the question of the true construction of s 17 was not reconsidered.

The courts in *Kenman Kandy* and in *Philips* held that, more generally, no radical change in the law was intended by the inclusion of shape as a sign registrable as a mark, but a shape that cannot be used as a badge of origin to distinguish goods because it serves a purely functional purpose or is perceived as aesthetic, rather than serving the purpose of distinguishing the goods, cannot serve as a badge of origin: see, for example, *Re Australiana Group Holdings Pty Ltd* [2003] ATMO 32 (an ergonomically designed bottle shape).

A mark that is used or intended to be used

14.10 Competitors should be free to adopt marks that are not in actual use. Thus, maintaining a statutory monopoly in a mark is dependent on the owner or authorised user actually using the mark as a mark. Even if there has been genuine use at some stage, an extended period of non-use of a registered mark will leave the mark vulnerable to expungement for non-use: see Trade Marks Act 1995, Pt 9, ss 92–105. Such use must be either by the registered owner of the mark or by an 'authorised user' (see s 8) — ownership based on first use can be based on use by an 'authorised user', applicable principles being summarised in *Rodney Jane Racing Pty Ltd v Monster Energy Company* [2019] FCA 923 at [18]–[24]. However, as indicated above, a mark can be registered before it is in actual use (ie, before it has developed a reputation or goodwill in the market)as a sign that is 'intended to be used': s 17. Use or intended use must be in relation to the particular goods and/or services the subject of the application: see *Bauer Consumer Media Ltd v Evergreen Television Pty Ltd* [2019] FCAFC 71 (use of 'Discover Downunder' in relation to the production of television programs as opposed to the name or title of a television program); see also *Carnival Cruise Lines Inc v Sitmar Cruises Ltd* (1994) 120 ALR 495 per Gummow J. It is also required that the mark applied for coincides with the mark used for the purpose of supporting ownership and use or intention to use in relation to the application: see *Caesarstone Ltd v Ceramiche Caesar SpA (No 2)* (2018) 133 IPR 417; [2018] FCA 1096.

The ability to register a mark with only an intention to use it is an advantage over an action in passing off, which will lie only once an actual reputation can be proven (such reputation resulting from use or, at least, promotion). Naturally, a person may decide to register a mark that has been used in the market, rather than to continue to rely on passing off alone. However, the use relied upon, whether past or intended, should be use *as a trade mark*, as is indicated above. This can give rise to difficulties for shapes and colours, for instance, because their use on goods was originally or was intended to be decorative or functional and not intended to distinguish the goods from others: see, for instance, *Woolworths* and *Philips* at 14.9 and also *Mayne Industries Pty Ltd v Advanced Engineering Group Pty Ltd* (2008) 166 FCR 312; 75 IPR 102 and *Philmac Pty Ltd v Registrar of Trade Marks* (2002) 126 FCR 525; 56 IPR 452 at 467 per Mansfield J. Further, if, for instance, in a new business venture, a person has designed or chosen a mark and then registers it as a mark 'intended to be used', the intention to use the mark as a mark must be genuine and bona fide. Thus, an application to register a ghost mark (NERIT) because the mark the applicant in fact intended to use was not registrable (MERIT) may be rejected because there is no genuine intention to use the registered mark (NERIT). Alternatively, the application may be rejected or the mark expunged if the use that is made of the mark is not bona fide or good faith use but merely use for the purpose of obtaining registration and then ghost marketing the very similar commercial mark: see *Imperial Group Ltd v Philip Morris & Co Ltd* [1980] 1 FSR 146. In *E & J Gallo Winery v Lion Nathan Australia Pty Ltd* (2008) 77 IPR 69, it was held that use in good faith 'means a real as opposed to a token use in a commercial sense. It requires a "substantial and genuine" use: *NSW Dairy Corporation v Murray Goulburn Co-operative Co Ltd (No 1)* (1989) 14 IPR 26 at 45': at [190]. It was also said that a single use could be sufficient (at [189]), and, on the facts, the supply of only 59 bottles of the relevantly marked wine was enough. There was no reason to question the genuineness of the admittedly limited but repeated sales. The need for bona fide use or a genuine intention to use the mark means that marks cannot be validly registered for the sole purpose of compelling genuine users or owners of a matching common law mark to purchase the mark once registered: see also, in this regard, s 62A relating to an application made in bad faith. We shall see below that lack of a genuine intention to use a mark at the time of the application is not only relevant in terms of obtaining registration but also may affect the validity of an existing registration, since it is one of the bases for expungement: see ss 59 and 88. Use or intention to use the mark must be in Australia: *Anchorage Capital Partners Pty Ltd v ACPA Pty Ltd* (2018) 259 FCR 514; 128 IPR 255; [2018] FCAFC 6; but use does not require that trade marked goods must be present in Australia: use in marketing materials can suffice, as long as it is aimed at soliciting a supply of goods or services in Australia (here use in a slide presentation in Australia for that purpose was considered trade mark use).

The Requirement of Distinctiveness

Distinctiveness and other statutory requirements

14.11 In substance, there are perhaps two main reasons for refusing registration of a trade mark (and also for removal of a mark after registration): first, lack of distinctiveness — that is, of an ability to distinguish the goods or services of the trade mark owner from other goods or services — and, second, that the mark is confusing or deceptive in some way. These basic concepts are translated into a number of detailed rules in various sections in the Trade Marks Act 1995: see ss 41, 43, 44 and 60. Although distinct, the concepts and applicable rules relating to distinctiveness and deceptiveness do at times overlap in a complex interrelationship. Lack of distinctiveness in a mark will often result in consumer confusion; conversely, confusion caused by the use of a rival and similar mark will often affect the distinctiveness of an existing registered mark.

In *NSW Dairy Corporation v Murray Goulburn Co-op* (1989) 14 IPR 26 at 50, Gummow J (in the Federal Court) answered the question 'will not all deceptive marks lack distinctiveness?' as follows (at [83]):

> The answer is in the negative for various reasons, and the scheme of the Act has been to deal separately with each concept, but there will be cases where the concepts of lack of distinctiveness and deceptiveness tend to coalesce.

His Honour then went on to give a list of reasons for which separate treatment of distinctiveness and deceptiveness was necessary in the 1955 Act: at IPR 51. It is also important to understand at the outset that although distinctiveness and lack of deceptive or confusing implications are basic requirements, the 1995 Act in fact tolerates in some circumscribed cases the registration of marks that arguably give rise to a likelihood of some degree of confusion or deception: see, for example, the honest concurrent user provisions (s 44(3)) and see also ss 23 and 44A and others. Apart from the requirements of distinctiveness and lack of deceptiveness, there are a number of other requirements that are further discussed in Chapter 15 Registered Trade Marks: Other Requirements.

Degrees of distinctiveness and the requirements of s 41

14.12 We have seen that the requirement of distinctiveness, in a general sense, is inherent in the definition of a trade mark in s 17 of the 1995 Act. However, under that section, the relevant inquiry is whether the use or intended use of the mark is for the purposes of distinguishing goods as to their origin, rather than to serve some other purpose. It is not so much whether the relevant mark is capable of being distinctive in fact, given its inherent characteristics, its actual or intended use, the goods or services to which it relates, or its relationship to other registered or unregistered marks. This practical inquiry is undertaken by reference to the standards set in s 41. In its original form, s 41 prescribed practical steps to test distinctiveness; that is, instructions to decision-makers. However, the Intellectual Property Laws Amendment (Raising the Bar) Act 2012 (Cth) resulted in a more orthodox standard-setting provision. The change was intended to reinforce the presumption of registrability in all cases.

The purpose of a statutory monopoly over a trade mark is the protection of reputation or goodwill. In this context, the mark operates as a point of recognition for the consumer, a consistent badge that distinguishes certain goods or services from others. The essential requirement is thus that the consumers can know and recognise a trade mark and distinguish it from others. Certain trade marks will be wholly incapable of fulfilling that function. The other essential requirement is that trademarks that consist of signs that other traders legitimately expect to be able to use (ie, common or descriptive signs) should not be granted a statutory monopoly. For instance, the registered trade mark 'cheese' for cheese products would be a wholly ineffective mark. Such a descriptive term cannot serve to distinguish the products of one provider of cheese from those of another. It would also cause difficulties for other traders if it were registered to one owner. However, it may be a more distinctive and thus effective mark if it were rendered in a peculiar manner (eg, as circling a smiley face) or if it were a mark used for a totally unrelated product — say, cameras. These examples illustrate the important distinction between descriptiveness and distinctiveness. Normally, the more descriptive of the goods a word, phrase or device is, the less distinctive it is in trade mark terms. However, in the eyes of a trader, a descriptive mark has its attractions because it can convey information about or conjure up a product or service as well as serving to distinguish it as to source. Therefore, trade mark registration is commonly sought for marks with a combination of descriptive elements that evoke the product or service and non-descriptive (or invented) elements that are entirely distinctive. Nonetheless, the strongest marks are meaningless in ordinary language and non-descriptive and hence entirely and uniquely associated with one source or brand: for example, 'Exxon', 'Adidas', 'Nike' and so on. Of course, that a mark is meaningless or non-descriptive can be purely a contextual issue, rather than inherent. For instance, a foreign language term may be meaningless in the Australian context (eg, 'Nike' means victory in Greek but nothing in English), or a term may be used entirely out of context or for unrelated goods (eg, Apple as a brand of computers as opposed to apples).

As has been noted, the Act's reluctance to grant protection for descriptive marks is related to the anti-competitive effect of a monopoly in a descriptive term. Traders who wish to use the registered sign in a legitimate descriptive manner would be inhibited from doing so. Nonetheless, it is not impossible that a descriptive term or aspect (such as a basic colour) over time, through heavy use and promotion, becomes entirely distinctive of a trader's goods in consumers' eyes. But the burden on the applicant to prove exclusive association in such a case will be considerable. If others are also using the same sign in some way, it will be difficult to prove that it is distinctive of a single product or service.

In many cases, the line between descriptiveness and distinctiveness will not easily be drawn, and a fine judgment is required; for instance, the words 'moo' and 'moove' for milk products: see *NSW Dairy Corporation*. A lack of distinctiveness can also flow from the fact that a sign is in common use in relation to certain goods because it signifies something or because other traders are entitled to the benefit of its use. These are common problems for shape marks and for (pure) colour marks, but it may also be an issue for a common phrase, exclamation or expression: see, for example, *Unilever Australia Ltd v Société Des Produits Nestlé SA* (2006) 154 FCR 165; 69 IPR 255 concerning the slogan 'GO ON'.

Inherent and acquired distinctiveness

14.13 The overall standard of distinctiveness is set out in s 41(1): an application must be rejected if the mark is not capable of distinguishing the applicant's goods or service from the goods or services of other persons. The terminology under the old Act was 'adapted to distinguish'. In that regard, in *Clark Equipment Co v Registrar of Trade Marks* (1964) 111 CLR 511 at 513–14, Kitto J said:

> That ultimate question must not be misunderstood. It is not whether the mark will be adapted to distinguish the registered owner's goods if it be registered and other persons consequently find themselves precluded from using it. The question is whether the mark, considered quite apart from the effects of registration, is such that by its use the applicant is likely to attain his object of thereby distinguishing his goods from the goods of others … the question whether a mark is adapted to distinguish [is to] be tested by reference to the likelihood that other persons, trading in goods of the relevant kind and being actuated only by proper motives — in the exercise, that is to say, of the common right of the public to make honest use of words forming part of the common heritage, for the sake of the signification which they ordinarily possess — will think of the word and want to use it in connexion with similar goods in any manner which would infringe a registered trade mark granted in respect of it.

Note that '[n]evertheless, the law that developed under the distinctiveness provision in the earlier legislation (s 26 of the Trade Marks Act 1955) is applicable to s 41(2) and (3). See *MID Sydney Pty Ltd v Australian Tourism Co Ltd* (1998) 41 IPR 561 at 572 and *Blount [Inc v Registrar of Trade Marks* (1998) 83 FCR 50; 40 IPR 498] at 504': *Global Brand Marketing* at IPR 183. Note too that the current s 41(1) is the equivalent of s 41(2) as referred to in this quote.

Section 41(2) provides that a mark is to be taken not to be capable of distinguishing only if either s 41(3) or (4) applies to it. The section deals with the dividing line between distinctiveness and descriptiveness in terms of a balance between the inherent and acquired distinctiveness of a sign. The former refers to how unique, unusual, striking and unexpected the sign is in the context of its use (eg, unusual script, a neologism, unusual graphics and colour combinations); does it have an inherent meaning or significance in the way it is used? Inherent distinctiveness is a question of an objective but contextual (ie, in the context of certain goods or services) assessment of the appearance of the mark itself. Acquired distinctiveness (or, alternatively, 'actual' distinctiveness) is a different matter. The issue is not the appearance of the mark alone but how distinctive the mark has, in fact, become in the eyes of consumers — the secondary meaning and association with a particular trader or originator it has acquired by virtue of its actual use as a mark. The Act recognises that, theoretically at least, an inherently descriptive mark could, by intensive use over a period of time, become distinctive in the eyes of consumers; it can acquire sufficient secondary meaning or reputation: see s 41(3). But this will be an unusual case. In most cases, a mark has at least some element of inherent distinctiveness. Under the previous Act, it was not possible to register a mark on the basis of acquired distinctiveness alone — every mark had to have at least some degree of inherent distinctiveness — but that is no longer the case.

This requirement of 'distinctiveness on the face of the mark' in the pre-1995 law was developed in the cases, in spite of wording apparently to the contrary in the 1955 Act.

The approach was endorsed by the High Court in a number of cases: see, for instance, *FH Faulding & Co Ltd v ICI of Australia and New Zealand* (1965) 112 CLR 537 (the *Barrier Cream* case). The sometimes controversial result of this approach is highlighted by a case concerning a geographical term as a trade mark: see *Oxford University Press v Registrar of Trade Marks* (1990) 24 FCR 1; 17 IPR 509. Under the 1955 Act, the court thus implicitly accepted that a wholly descriptive mark is never capable of becoming distinctive however intense and longstanding its use and promotion in the marketplace may be. Perhaps the focus was more on the anti-competitive effect that is unavoidably inherent in allowing the registration of a mark, which must, by definition, be descriptive or commonplace. However, it was the intention of the legislator to allow the registration of some marks on the basis of actual distinctiveness under the 1995 Act, even in the absence of any inherent distinctiveness at all: see the Report of the Working Party to Review the Trade Marks Legislation, *Recommended Changes to the Australian Trade Marks Legislation*, AGPS, July 1992, Recommendation 4B. Thus, inherent distinctiveness or acquired distinctiveness or a combination of both should establish that a mark is capable of distinguishing the specified goods or services and justify registration. The applicant will have to prove the acquired distinctiveness.

In *Blount Inc v Registrar of Trade Marks* (1998) 83 FCR 50; 40 IPR 498 (concerning the mark OREGON), Branson J confirmed at FCR 61; IPR 508:

> The Act appears plainly to disclose an intention that it should no longer be the case that a trade mark which is '100 per cent distinctive in fact' should not be able to achieve registration (as to the expression '100 per cent distinctive in fact' see the *Oxford University Press* Case per Lockhart J at 511 and Gummow J at 523).

The approach in *Blount* was followed in, inter alia, *Ocean Spray Cranberries Inc v Registrar of Trade Marks* (2000) 47 IPR 579 and also in *BP plc v Woolworths Ltd* (2004) 62 IPR 545 (*BP v Woolworths*). It may, in fact, be that although a mark in theory can be registered on the basis of 100 per cent acquired distinctiveness, the threshold set in s 41 will, in reality, rarely be crossed. Therefore, in practical terms, the test of distinctiveness may have changed little from the test applied under the 1955 Act.

Proving distinctiveness

14.14 The 1995 Act is thus more favourable to trade mark owners whose marks are not, or barely, inherently distinctive but have a strong reputation. A further strengthening of the position of the applicant in this regard has come about by virtue of s 33(1) of the 1995 Act. Unlike the position under the 1955 Act, the onus is now on the Registrar to establish why the application should be rejected:

> The Registrar must, after the examination, accept the application unless he or she is satisfied that: (a) …; or (b) there are grounds under this Act for rejecting it.

Any doubt is to be resolved in the applicant's favour. In terms of distinctiveness, s 41(1) sets the general standard: if a trade mark is not capable of distinguishing the applicant's goods or services, the application must be rejected. Thus, the qualifying criterion for registration is the capacity to distinguish the applicant's goods or services, as was confirmed in *Philmac* at IPR 459 (see above 14.10). Whether the qualifying criterion is met can be broken down into a number of sub-issues:

- the extent to which the mark is inherently adapted to distinguish: s 41(2) effectively provides that only if the mark is not inherently distinctive at all (s 41(3)) or is distinctive only to some extent (s 41(4)) can it be rejected for lack of distinctiveness; therefore, a mark that is inherently wholly distinctive must be accepted for registration;
- if the mark has some inherent distinctiveness, combined with the actual use and intended use of the mark and any other circumstances, and the Registrar concludes that the mark does or will distinguish the goods or services, it must be accepted; and
- if the mark is not at all inherently adapted to distinguish, then the application can still be accepted, but only if the applicant establishes that because of the extent to which he or she has used the mark before the filing date in respect of the application it does, in fact, distinguish the designated goods or services as being those of the applicant: s 41(3). In other words, if the Registrar decides that the mark is not inherently distinctive at all, the onus will be on the applicant to show actual distinctiveness resulting from previous use as a trade mark. Note 1 to s 41 provides further clarification concerning what are marks that are not inherently adapted to distinguish — they are mostly marks that consist wholly of a sign that is ordinarily used to indicate:

  (a) the kind, quality, quantity, intended purpose, value, geographical origin or some other characteristics of goods or services; or

  (b) the time or production of goods or of the rendering of services.

In *BP v Woolworths* at [19], Finkelstein J described the prevalent test of inherent distinctiveness in Australia as a negative one, quoting the following passage from Lord Parker's judgment in *Re W and G Du Cros Ltd's Application for the Registration of Trade Marks* (1913) 30 RPC 660 at 672, where he said that it:

> ... [l]argely depend[ed] upon whether other traders are likely, in the ordinary course of their business and without any improper motive, to desire to use the same mark, or some mark nearly resembling it, upon or in connection with their own goods.

This Finkelstein J contrasted with the positive test used in the United States, where '[t]he test is whether "[its] intrinsic nature serves to identify a ... source": *Two Pesos, Inc. v Taco Cabana, Inc* 505 US 763, 768 (1992)': at [20]. The green colour at issue in *BP* was not inherently distinctive on either test (at IPR 554).

> Accordingly, for BP to succeed in its appeals it must establish two things: first, that it has used the particular shade of green as a trade mark and, second, that in the minds of the public the primary significance of that shade of green, when used in connection with the supply of petroleum products or the provision of petroleum services, identifies the source of those goods or the provider of those services as originating from a particular trader, though not necessarily from an identified trader.

This, according to the trial judge, BP was indeed able to do, on the basis that it was the only service station operator using green predominantly in its get-up, it had used the colour extensively over a long period of time and it had emphasised the colour in its advertising. Thus, customers identified BP service stations by the colour alone, irrespective of its other associated marks (see at IPR 568). However, on appeal (*Woolworths Ltd v BP plc (No 2)*), the court pointed out that the correct approach was that adopted in an earlier case (at [81]):

> In *Philmac Pty Ltd v Registrar of Trade Marks* [2002] FCA 1551; (2002) 126 FCR 525 at 548 [71], Mansfield J said that for the purposes of applying s 41(6) to a colour mark two issues needed to be addressed. The first is whether the use of the colour in the manner described in the application has, prior to the date of the application, constituted use of the colour as a trade mark. The second issue is whether the trade mark applied for does in fact distinguish the applicant's products, having regard to evidence concerning the actual use of the colour as a trade mark. We agree with that approach. Thus, s 41(6) requires specific consideration of the extent to which BP has used each of the marks applied for as a trade mark before the date of filing and whether that use was sufficient to distinguish the designated goods and services as being those of BP: *Blount v Registrar of Trade Marks* [1998] FCA 440; (1998) 83 FCR 50 at 60.

Further, 'For the purpose of s 41(6), the focus of the inquiry should be the use of the marks applied for, rather than use of colour as part of the get-up or packaging of goods generally': at IPR 45 (note that s 41(6) is the equivalent of the present s 41(3)). In terms of use, BP had used green predominantly together with yellow, and the standard of s 41(6) was therefore not met for the colour green as a trade mark alone. It is thus important to establish that the sign used was the same as the trade mark in the application, and that use was as a trade mark (and not, eg, as a decorative theme.

Unilever provides an example of difficulties with a different kind of trade mark, the slogan or part slogan GO ON. This was held not to be inherently adapted to distinguish the goods, nor had there been use establishing acquired distinctiveness before the priority date, and the intended use was not trade mark use. Hence, the registration of GO ON was removed. A further example, also in the food sector, applied to the marks 'oro' (Gold) and 'cinque stelle' (Five Star) in relation to coffee-related goods and depended on how and to what extent consumers understood these terms, which were used as trade marks: as known superlatives or of unknown terms in a foreign language: see *Modena Trading Pty Ltd v Cantarella Bros Pty Ltd* (2013) 215 FCR 16; 102 IPR 382; [2013] FCAFC 110. The High Court in the same matter held that regard should be had for the 'ordinary signification' of the mark in Australia: *Cantarella Bros Pty Ltd v Modena Trading Pty Ltd* (2014) 254 CLR 337; 109 IPR 154; [2014] HCA 48.

Cases under the 1955 and 1995 Acts

14.15 Cases regarding distinctiveness under the Trade Marks Act 1955 will remain relevant and continue to inform the analysis of the core elements of distinctiveness. Certainly, in cases other than those proceeding under s 41(3), for which there was no effective pre-1995 equivalent and which are themselves relatively rare, there is continuity in the substance of the tests, and no great change was intended with the 1995 Act. Therefore, cases under the 1955 Act provide instructive examples. Many of these relate to word marks that have some descriptive element.

For instance, in the leading case of *Mark Foy's Ltd v Davies & Co-op Co Ltd* (1956) 95 CLR 190; 1A IPR 470, the mark at issue was TUB HAPPY for clothing. Although the term vaguely suggested that TUB HAPPY clothing did not deteriorate in the wash, this idea was not obvious, and the allusion to some quality of the goods thus not sufficiently direct for the mark to be held to lack inherent distinctiveness. A more recent case, *Powell v Glow Zone Products Pty Ltd* (1996) 36 IPR 343, was resolved on the basis of the 1955 Act, in accordance with the transitional provisions of the 1995 Act (see ss 233–239). The mark in question was CAPS THE GAME, registered in respect of games and so on. The critical question was whether the word 'CAPS' was capable of being distinctive at the time the application was made (the issue was considered on the basis of a counterclaim for revocation). Sheppard J held that although the game to which the term referred was not well known in Australia at the time of the application, it was clear that 'CAPS' as a descriptive word was used extensively in the US by that time and was, in Australia at least, being used by people in the trade who had become aware of the success of the game in the US and were concerned with its potential for commercial exploitation in Australia. Because the word was a generic one describing a game (consisting primarily of collecting round, disk-like 'caps' with many different colourful images imprinted upon them), it was not inherently adapted to distinguish and henceforth could not be distinctive of the goods of the applicant: at IPR 375–9.

Also, for a run-of-the-mill example, see *Re Application by Allergan Inc* (1996) 37 IPR 638, in which the trade mark CLEAN-N-SOAK was at issue. The delegate rejected the application because CLEAN-N-SOAK was the phonetic equivalent of 'clean and soak', which was a purely descriptive term. For further examples of the test of distinctiveness in operation, the Austlii ATMO database of decisions, including oppositions, can be consulted: see also IP Australia, *Trade Marks Office Manual of Practice and Procedure*, Pt 22.

Geographical names; false denominations of origin

14.16 Geographical names or marks containing geographical references commonly give rise to difficulties in regard to distinctiveness. If there is a chance that goods of the kind for which the mark is used are made there, such marks will generally lack distinctiveness. For that reason, the application for the mark OXFORD as such was refused in the *Oxford University Press* case: see also above 14.13. The decision in that case reflected the traditional reluctance to allow such geographical marks, even where it could be proved that there was 100 per cent actual or acquired distinctiveness. An argument that the word 'OXFORD' referred in most people's minds to the university and not the town was dismissed. The key obstruction to the grant is the right of other traders, as Gummow J stated at IPR 530:

> The point is if goods of the kind in question are produced at the particular place or in the area, or if it is reasonable to suppose that such goods in the future will be produced there, other traders have a legitimate interest which is not to be supplanted by permitting any one trader to effect trade mark registration: see *Clark Equipment Co v Register of Trade Marks* at CLR 515–16.

In *Clark Equipment*, it was held that the mark MICHIGAN, in relation to heavy machinery, was not registrable, Michigan being one of the states of the US. Note that in *Bavaria NV v Bayerischer Brauerbund EV* (2009) 177 FCR 300; 81 IPR 279 [2009] FCA 428, the mark BAVARIA was registered in relation to beer brewed in Holland, not the south of Germany (see Chapter 15 Registered Trade Marks: Other Requirements 15.2).

Another example of a geographical name being refused registration under the 1955 Act, in spite of it having a very considerable reputation, is provided by *Re Application of Waterford Glass Group Ltd* (1987) 9 IPR 339. The mark WATERFORD was refused registration because the glassware concerned was actually made in that city in Ireland, and irrespective of the fact that many may be unaware of the geographical significance of the name. However, there are obviously cases where a name is either totally unknown as a place name or also has other meanings and thus would have inherent distinctiveness since it had no descriptive significance. A place name may also be combined with another word or a device element to result in a valid mark, and under the 1995 Act a term that is not inherently distinctive at all can still be registered on the basis of acquired distinctiveness alone. This was not possible under the provisions of the 1955 Act. Further, the concern that a term may be monopolised to the detriment of other traders in a region is reduced where the geographical name registered as a mark does not refer to the actual place of manufacture of the goods. Note also in this context that there is a separate defence to infringement provided by s 122 of the 1995 Act, where the person uses in good faith a registered mark to indicate the geographical origin of goods or services: s 122(1)(b)(i); see further Chapter 16 Registered Trade Marks: Infringement.

Thus, a more appropriate response by a rival trader faced with an infringement suit may be not to counterclaim for invalidity for lack of distinctiveness but to invoke the provisions of s 122, at least in cases where that rival trader actually does provide the goods or services from a place with that name. It was pointed out in *Oxford University Press*, however, that the existence of this defence does not affect the approach to be taken to the question of registrability of such a mark. For a typical example of the Trade Marks Office approach, see *Sara Lee Corporation v Bali Blue Pty Ltd* (2003) 59 IPR 619. For more recent examples relating to distinctiveness of place names, see *Blount* and *Colorado Group Ltd v Strandbags Group Pty Ltd* (2007) 164 FCR 506; 74 IPR 246. Kenny J said in relation to the mark Colorado, itself the name of a state of the US (at [29]):

> Presumably, the phrase 'inherently adapted to distinguish the designated goods from the goods of other persons' in s 41(3) of the 1995 Act is intended to be understood in light of earlier decisions under the 1955 Act, such as *Clark Equipment*. I agree with Gyles and Allsop JJ that the word 'Colorado' as applied to backpacks, bags, wallets, purses, shoes and other goods of the first appellant was not a 'fancy name' as that expression was used by Kitto J in *Clark Equipment* (at 515). It is the name of a State in the United States of America. There was evidence that the word was used to invoke adventure, ruggedness, trekking and like images associated with the State of Colorado, on account of the Rocky Mountains being there. The use of the word 'Colorado' was entirely different from the use of the expression 'North Pole' in connection with bananas, which was one of Kitto J's examples of a 'fancy name'. The use of the word 'Colorado' was not arbitrary and its use was not equivalent to a made-up word or device. I agree in substance with Allsop J that it is likely that another trader will want to use the word 'Colorado', legitimately, with regard to his goods, for the sake of the geographical reference which it is inherently adapted to make or the connotations that that geographic reference invokes. Accordingly, I agree in the conclusion of Gyles and Allsop JJ that the word 'Colorado' alone is not inherently adapted to distinguish the designated goods or services of the first appellant from the goods or services of other persons.

Yarra Valley Dairy Pty Ltd v Lemnos Foods Pty Ltd (2010) 191 FCR 297; 90 IPR 117; [2010] FCA 1367 provides a further example of the subtleties involved in determining whether a trade mark incorporating a place name is distinctive. In this case, the trade mark 'Persian fetta' was held to be not capable of distinguishing the relevant goods, because other traders should be free to use the word 'Persian'. Middleton J said: 'To choose the name Persia over Iran does not indicate an improper motive in circumstances where "Persia" is still a recognised descriptive term and has an association with fetta cheese production, and where the term "Persian" has the accepted connotations of the exotic and mystical, and where the alternative "Iranian" has negative connotations which a trader would not wish to employ': at [215]. Similar issues arose in the 'Bohemia' case (*Bohemia Crystal Pty Ltd v Host Corporation Pty Ltd* (2018) 129 IPR 482; [2018] FCA 235), as that term's significance is more historical than current in terms of geography, and also because it has other significations and therefore potential uses by competitors: bohemian in the sense of living unconventionally. The trade marks 'Bohemia' and 'Bohemia Crystal' were revoked. One difficulty was the fact that the area of Bohemia was traditionally associated with glass manufacture, the other was the inconsistency of the use and representation of the applied for marks during the period prior to the application for registration.

For a decision going the other way, partly because the trade mark concerned was not a place name *as such*, but a complex label *including* the term 'Bavaria' — illustrating the fact that the descriptiveness of one element of a mark can be overcome by its other non-desriptive components such as flourishes, colours, other terms and devices — see *Bavaria* (above). In any case the term itself was held to do little more than suggest some European origin, as opposed to origin in the German state of Bavaria (and therefore was also not held to be misleading for a beer in fact brewed in Holland).

While, in terms of distinctiveness, a place name may arguably be registered as long as it does not represent the real geographical origin of the goods or a place such goods might come from, or which has a connection in consumers' minds with such goods, the 1995 Act has also introduced provisions that make it difficult to register false or untrue denominations of origin as trade marks. These provisions were introduced in response to concerns relating to the use of the names of famous European wine regions on Australian wines: see the EU/Australia Wine Agreement and consequent amendments to the Australian Wine and Brandy Corporation Act 1980 (Cth) (now the Wine Australia Act 2013 (Cth)); as to the application of that Act, see *Comité Interprofessionnel des Vins des Côtes de Provence v Stuart Alexander Bryce* (1996) 69 FCR 450; 35 IPR 170; *BIVB v Red Earth Nominees Pty Ltd* [2002] FCA 588. Thus, a trade mark registration for certain goods can be opposed if it consists of or contains a geographical indication of origin that is false, even if consumers in Australia would be quite unaware of the location concerned: see the Trade Marks Act 1995, s 6 definition of 'geographical indication' and s 61 'Trade mark containing or consisting of a false geographical indication'; and also see the *Bavaria* decision (above).

Bibliography

A Cropley, 'The Registration of Scandalous Trade Marks' (2008) 72 *Intellectual Property Forum* 20.

A Dunlop and E Blandford, 'Shock! Horror! Registering a Scandalous Trade Mark' (2008) 21(1) *IPLB* 6.

A Ownes, '"A Rose by Any Other Name" — Foreign Language Trade Marks in a Multi-Lingual Society' (2007) 71 *Intellectual Property Forum* 21.

C Baker, 'Colourblind?' (2002) 15(7) *IPLB* 98.

C Oberin and J Mandelbaum, 'Trade Mark Snippets' (2002) 48 *Intellectual Property Forum* 26.

C Pappas, 'A Question of Distinction — Registration of Descriptive Trade Marks' (2005) 18(5) *IPLB* 81.

C Smith, 'A Real State: The Colorado Case' (2008) 20(8) *IPLB* 129.

C Smith, 'Trade Mark Protection for Product Shape — Where Does the Public Interest Lie?' (2005) 63 *Intellectual Property Forum* 32.

D Ryan, 'Geographical Indications and Trade Marks' (1998) 9 *AIPJ* 127.

G Williams, 'Are Service Marks Trade Marks? Commonwealth Power Over IP' (1995) 6 *AIPJ* 133.

I Horak, 'Make Your Mark Register' (2004) 78(9) *LIJ* 48.

IPLB, 'New World Trade Mark Regime to Test Australian Business Commitment to Innovation' (2001) 13(7) *IPLB* 87.

J Baird, 'This Mark Is So Attractive — It Should Be Free For All To Use!: An Australian Perspective on Functional Shape Marks' (2003) 52 *Intellectual Property Forum* 26.

J Eliades, 'Casenotes; *Ocean Spray Cranberries Inc v Registrar of Trade Marks*' (2000) 12(10) *IPLB* 115.

J Liberman, 'Plainly constitutional: The Upholding of Plain Tobacco Packaging by the High Court of Australia' (2013) 39 *Am J L & Med* 361.

J Luck, 'Distinctiveness, Deceptive and Confusing Marks under the Trade Marks Act' (1996) 7 *AIPJ* 97.

J Masterson, 'The Practical Value of Defensive Trade Marks' (2006) 17(4) *AIPJ* 232.

J McCutcheon, 'Monopolised Product Shapes and Factual Distinctiveness Under s 41(6) of the Trade Marks Act 1995 (Cth)' (2004) 15(1) *AIPJ* 18.

J McCutcheon, 'Rectification of the Trade Marks Register on Grounds Existing at the Time of Application to Rectify' (2002) 13(4) *AIPJ* 199.

K Trainor, 'Brand Extension — Recent Trade Marks Office Decisions' (2005) 17(9) *IPLB* 152.

L Eade, 'Along Came a Spider: *Kenman Kandy v Registrar of Trade Marks* and the Inherent Distinctiveness of Shapes of Goods Themselves' (2002) 15(7) *IPLB* 94.

L Eade, 'Puce as a Trade Mark: Acquired Distinctiveness of Colour Trade Marks' (2004) 16(8) *IPLB* 121.

L Kellie, '"What's in a Name? That Which We Call a Rose by Any Other Name Would Smell as Sweet" ... or Would it? An Overview of the Protection of Geographical Indications in Australia' (2001) 46 *IP Forum* 8.

M Arblaster, 'Shape as a Trade Mark' (2000) 40 *Intellectual Property Forum* 30.

M Davison, 'Shape Trade Marks: The Role and Relevance of Functionality and Aesthetics in Determining their Registrability' (2004) 15(2) *AIPJ* 106.

M Richardson, 'An Economic Perspective on Distinctiveness in the Trade Marks Act 1994' (1995) 6 *AIPJ* 65.

M Richardson, 'Shape Trade Marks in Australian Courts' (2001) 12(1) *AIPJ* 5.

M Richardson, 'Trade marks and Language'. (2004) 26 *Syd L Rev* 193.

M Sylvester, 'Brand Success and the Australian Commercial Fresh Fruit and Vegetable Industry: Oranges and Apples? A Guide for Intellectual Property Practitioners' (2005) 18(7) *IPLB* 97.

P Loughlan, 'Oh Yuck! The Registration of Scandalous Trade Marks' (2005) 61 *IP Forum* 38.

R Chalmers, 'Trade Marks and the Heady Wine of Metaphor: A Pilgrim's Progress' (2001) 45 *Intellectual Property Forum* 44.

S Givoni, 'Pushing the Boundaries — Scandalous Trade Marks' (2004) 17(2) *IPLB* 21.

S Hughes, 'Protection of Shape Marks in Australia: Extending the Permanent Monopoly' (2002) 49 *IP Forum* 28.

S Stern, 'Overlap Between Geographical Indications and Trade Marks in Australia' (2001) 2(1) *MJIL* 224.

S Stern, 'The Conflict Between Geographical Indications and Trade Marks or Australian Once Again Heads Off Down the Garden Path' (2005) 61 *IP Forum* 28.

S Whybrow, 'What Colour is Your Trade Mark?' (2003) 16(3) *IPLB* 42.

T Stevens, 'Applicant Not Intending to Use Trade Mark' (2008) 21(1) *IPLB* 14.

T Stevens, 'Application under S 92 for Removal of a Trade Mark Registration: The Issue of the Removal Applicant's Standing' (2006) 18(10) *IPLB* 160.

T Stevens, 'Capable of Distinguishing?' (2008) 20(8) *IPLB* 131.

W van Caenegem, 'Striking a Balance Between Protecting Commercial Reputation and Promoting Competition' (2003) 77 *ALJ* 598.

Working Party to Review the Trade Marks Legislation, *Recommended Changes to the Australian Trade Marks Legislation*, (Report), AGPS, July 1992.

Chapter 15

Registered Trade Marks: Other Requirements

Confusing or Deceptive Marks and Marks too Similar to Registered Marks

15.1 The main substantive requirement for trade mark registration under the Trade Marks Act 1995 (Cth), other than distinctiveness, is that the mark is not in some way confusing or deceptive. The object of trade marks, to provide consumers with reliable and consistent shorthand information identifying goods or services, should not be defeated by allowing registration of marks that will in fact be misleading or deceptive. In substance there are three broad categories of confusing or deceptive marks that are unregistrable:

1. marks that contain some inherently misleading representation (s 43);
2. marks too similar to registered marks for the same or similar goods or services (s 44); and
3. marks whose use is likely to confuse or deceive because of similarity to a mark that has acquired a reputation in Australia before the priority date (s 60).

Inherent deceptiveness under s 43

15.2 By virtue of s 43 of the Trade Marks Act 1995, if the use of a mark would be likely to deceive or cause confusion because of some connotation it has, the application must be rejected. A connotation is an inherent message, meaning or implication distinct from the brand message of the mark. In *Primary Health Care Ltd v Commonwealth of Australia* (2017) 260 FCR 359; [2017] FCAFC 174 at [113] it was put as follows:

> The connotation with which s 43 is concerned is a meaning secondary to that which is denoted by the subject of the application to the Registrar. In other words, the section is concerned with whether the mark the subject of the application (or a sign contained in the mark) connotes something other than a connection in the course of trade between the relevant goods or services and the person who applied (or intended to apply) it to those goods or services.

In other words, 'the "connotation" mentioned in s 43 means a "signification inherent to [the trade mark or a sign contained in the mark]", secondary to what is denoted by the application, namely, that the mark is a badge of origin of the applicant's goods or services': at [136].

There must be a reasonable likelihood that deception or confusion will result from the connotation, taking into account the nature of the goods or services in relation to which the mark is to be used and any other relevant considerations. That connotation may exist because the mark falsely suggests some quality or connection that the goods or services to which it attaches do not in fact have. In *Primary Health Care*, the court said that '[s]ection 43 ... is particularly concerned with ... ensuring that the mark indicates the trade origins of the goods or services to which it is intended that it be applied, and does not connote something else so as to be likely to deceive or cause confusion': at [135]. The question is thus whether use of the mark in relation to the goods or services for which it is registered will deceive or cause confusion because of something it signifies. In *Primary Health Care*, the applicant never provided healthcare services but instead provided medical support services to doctors; since the ordinary signification of 'primary health care' was 'first level or first contact health care', the trade mark was deceptive in the context of its intended use.

There was for some time a degree of uncertainty as to whether s 43 also applies to cases of similarity between the applied for mark and a common law (ie, unregistered) mark. That matter has now been settled. The operation of s 43 is normally confined to inherently misleading connotations alone; comparisons with other marks in use in Australia will very rarely arise anywhere other than under s 60. In *TGI Friday's Australia Pty Ltd v TGI Friday's Inc* (2000) 100 FCR 358; 48 IPR 513 at 521, Wilcox, Kiefel and Emmett JJ said:

> The case on deception and confusion sought to be made by Big Country and Friday's Australia in the present proceedings is one that falls outside the reasons specified in those sections. It does not depend upon some connotation in the registered mark, but upon its similarity to a name used by Big Country and others. So the alleged deception or confusion is not for a reason covered by section 43.

However, the connotation inherent in the mark may flow from the fact that consumers have come to associate the term concerned with, for instance, a film title (see *Twentieth Century Fox Film Corporation v Michael F Durkan* [2000] ATMO 5 (concerning BRAVEHEART) and *Twentieth Century Fox Film Corporation v Die Hard* (2001) 52 IPR 455 (concerning DIE HARD)) or a comic book and film hero (see *DC Comics v Cheqout Pty Ltd* (2013) 212 FCR 194; 101 IPR 334; [2013] FCA 478 concerning the word mark 'Superman'). See also *McCorquodale v Masterson* (2004) 63 IPR 582 concerning the trade mark 'Diana's legacy in roses': the opponents argued that the clear connotation was a connection with the late Princess of Wales, Lady Diana Spencer. Kenny J held that the words and the stylised 'D' taken together clearly connoted the Princess (at IPR 598):

> [T]he practice of licensing names and likenesses of celebrities, such as the late Princess, is now well recognised in the community. Although the Princess did not in her lifetime derive any personal profit from the use of her name and image, she plainly used (or permitted the use of) her name and image for the fundraising activities of the charitable causes that she supported. As already found, before the priority date, a relevantly significant sector of consumers knew of the Fund and its licensing and charitable activities. The goods to which the impugned mark would apply have a real connection in the public mind with the late Princess. In all the circumstances, I find that the impugned mark would not only

> directly and immediately connote the late Princess, the impugned mark would also bespeak an association with the Fund and the Estate of the late Princess. There is a real likelihood that consumers would understand that goods bearing the impugned mark are in some way sponsored or approved by the Fund or the Princess' Estate, even if they were ignorant about the specific details of the arrangements. The likelihood of this misunderstanding is sufficient to create a likelihood of confusion and deception in Australia, by reason of the connotation of the mark.

Also note that s 43 may apply where the comparison is with a mark that is registered but for different goods or services (and s 44 therefore does not apply): see *Conde Nast Publications Pty Ltd v Virginia Taylor* (1998) 41 IPR 505 (concerning the mark VOGUE), where it was argued that registration of EUROVOGUE in relation to clothes would be confusing and deceptive in light of the opponent's registration of VOGUE for magazines. The deceptive connotation may be one that suggests geographical origin where the goods for which it is registered do not necessarily originate from that place: see, for example, *Scotch Whisky Association v De Witt* (2007) 74 IPR 382 and *Scotch Whisky Association v De Witt* (2008) 75 IPR 280, where the mark GLENN OAKS was said to falsely suggest, in relation to bourbon, one of the spirits for which it was registered, that it originated in Scotland, 'glen' being a word used for 'valley' in Scotland. However, the primary judge held that, to most consumers, Glenn would appear to be a man's first name, to which no connotation of a Scottish origin adhered. In *Bavaria NV v Bayerischer Brauerbund EV* (2009) 177 FCR 300; 81 IPR 279; [2009] FCA 428, the court held that the mark BAVARIA used in relation to beer brewed in Holland and not in the German state of Bavaria (of which Munich is the capital) did not connote origin in Bavaria, as the surrounding label referred to Holland a number of times, which neutralised the Bavarian connotation. In any case, Australian consumers did not differentiate between European beers, the court found. Since the connotation the plaintiff (representing Bavarian brewers) contended for did not, therefore, exist, it was not necessary to consider the second limb of the section; that is, whether consumers would be deceived or confused in that they thought the beer originated in Bavaria.

Deceptiveness under s 60

15.3 'The purpose of s 60 is to provide protection for prior well-known marks, whether registered or not: Explanatory Memorandum to the Trade Marks Amendment Bill 2006 at [4.10(1)]': *Rodney Jane Racing Pty Ltd v Monster Energy Co* [2019] FCA 923 at [82]. Notwithstanding occasional indications to the contrary (see, eg, *Melhero Pty Ltd v Club X* (1997) 37 IPR 151), only s 60 applies to cases of deceptiveness that arise because of similarity to an unregistered or common law mark with a reputation in Australia (by way of opposition proceedings and not for ex officio examination by the Registrar; see Pt 5 of the Trade Marks Act 1995. The section will also potentially apply where there is similarity with a mark registered, but for different goods or services. The applicable general principles were recently set out in *Rodney Jane Racing* at [84]. Important to note is that a trade 'mark may acquire a relevant reputation in Australia through indirect exposure in the press, on television and on the internet': at [84(h)]; that is, actual use as a mark in relation to goods or services in Australia is not necessarily required. Whether some other mark had acquired a reputation in Australia by the relevant time is a question of fact: see, for example, *Kimberly-Clark Worldwide, Inc v Goulimis* (2008) 78 IPR 612; [2008] FCA 1415 at [46]:

> The evidence establishes that the opponent's trade mark HUGGIES has acquired a reputation in Australia. … HUGGIES is the dominant brand in the market for baby-toddler personal care items in the form of disposable nappies, liners, and ancillary items (such as wipes, cloths, and lotions). I accept the opponent's submission that HUGGIES is a household name with a substantial degree of notoriety or familiarity in Australia; HUGGIES automatically brings to mind baby-toddler personal care items, particularly nappies.

Before the amendment introduced by the Trade Marks Amendment Act 2006, s 60, by its first limb, expressly required that the mark whose registration was sought be substantially identical or deceptively similar to a mark that had acquired a reputation in Australia before the priority date of the application. However, s 60 is now 'not constrained by the concept of deceptive similarity — the words of s 60 do not refer to resemblance at all. The question is purely one of prior reputation': *Rodney Jane Racing* at [84(d)]. The section now simply requires that 'another trade mark had, before the priority date for the registration of the first-mentioned trade mark in respect of those goods or services, acquired a reputation in Australia' (s 60(a)); the separate threshold test of similarity was thus eliminated, making the test less restrictive. Whereas s 44 requires comparison between two marks, s 60 requires comparison between the applied for mark and a reputation: 'under s 60, the new inquiry centres on the reputation of the earlier mark. That reputation is critical to the opposition under s 60': *McCormick & Co Inc v McCormick* (2000) 51 IPR 102; [2000] FCA 1335 at [94]; see also *Rodney Jane Racing* at [84(a)].

Whether an applied for mark is likely to confuse or deceive because of its deceptive similarity to a mark with a predating reputation is essentially also a question of fact; the matter is to be evaluated in the light of real-world evidence about all relevant circumstances. Naturally, similarity between the marks and the extent of the reputation of the opponent's mark will play key roles. The nature of the goods and services in relation to which the respective marks are (to be) used is also relevant. The test is based on the observations and reactions of ordinary members of the public and, in particular, the class of purchasers of the goods or services in question. There must be a real, tangible danger of confusion, not a mere possibility; however, as per O'Bryan J in *Rodney Jane Racing* at [84(e)]:

> … the test for confusion under s 60 is not limited to whether consumers might think that the respective marks are the same. It is sufficient that consumers might wonder whether the respective goods might be connected in the course of trade: Explanatory Memorandum, [4.10(3)]; *McCormick* at [82]; *Southern Cross* [*Refrigerating Co v Toowoomba Foundry Pty Ltd* (1954) 91 CLR 592] at 595. It is enough if consumers might think that the product bearing the impugned mark is a variant of, or related to, an existing brand.

That was unsurprisingly the case in *Kimberly-Clark*, where the applied for mark was 'HUGGIE' MUMMY in respect of services being 'direct selling of baby-toddler's toys, videos, CDs, books, games and accessories'. For a case under the pre-2006 form of the provision, see *Health World Ltd v Shin-Sun Australia Pty Ltd* (2008) 75 IPR 478 at 496, where the situation as it would have applied under the present provision also attracts brief comment. For other recent examples, see *Tivo Inc v Vivo International Corporation Pty Ltd* [2012] FCA 252 from [300], where a detailed analysis is provided by the court, and see also *Allergan Inc v Di Giacomo* (2011) 199 FCR 126; 94 IPR 541; [2011] FCA 1540 (concerning 'No-Tox' vs 'Botox'). In *Rodney Jane Racing* the opposition was based on the alleged reputation of Monster Energy Company (MEC) trade marks, which contained the word 'monster'. The application related to marks used for wheels also including the word 'monster'. The court held that s 60 was not satisfied – the MEC marks were not the term 'monster' but 'Monster Energy' and device marks including the term 'Monster', and the term 'monster' was registered for many products in Australia; the actual Rodney Jane Racing (RJR) marks bore no resemblance to the actual MEC marks, apart from the inclusion of the word 'Monster', and the RJR marks were used for alloy wheels, for which MEC had no reputation and which invited a carefully considered purchase from a committed consumer: at [138]–[151].

Deceptiveness under s 44: similarity to registered marks

15.4 The test under s 44 concerns similarity between the trade mark in the application and prior *registered* marks. Whether or not the prior registered trade mark will prevent registration on this ground has nothing to do with prior registered mark's actual reputation in Australia. A 'mark to mark' comparison is required. The test under s 44 is a purely theoretical or notional one, which is not concerned with any actual use or reputation of the prior registered mark. As Gyles J said in *Pfizer Products Inc v Karam* (2006) 219 FCR 585; 70 IPR 599 at 611–2:

> I am by no means satisfied that it is appropriate to take reputation into account for the purposes of the comparison relevant for s 44. The orthodox view is that what is compared is the lawful use in the future of each mark across the goods for which it is registered rather than being tied to what has happened in the past (*Berlei Hestia* [*Industries Ltd v Bali Co Inc* (1973) 129 CLR 353] per Mason J at 362; *MID Sydney Pty Ltd v Australian Tourism Co Ltd* (1998) 90 FCR 236 at 245–246). Section 60 brings in reputation. I am not persuaded that what was said by French J in *Woolworths* [*Ltd v BP plc* (2006) 150 FCR 134] at [61] is sufficient to alter the test for s 44. There is support for the use of reputation in connection with infringement (*CA Henschke & Co v Rosemount Estates Pty Ltd* [(2000) 52 IPR 42] at [51]; *Caterpillar Loader Hire (Holdings) Pty Ltd v Caterpillar Tractor Co* (1983) 48 ALR 511; (1983) 1 IPR 265; (1983) 77 FLR 139 per Lockhart J at 151, Franki J at 141 and Neaves J at 163). It is not clear that, if correct, this is to be imported into s 44 (cf *NEC Corporation v Punch Video* (S) [*Pte Ltd* (2005) 67 IPR 17]).

See also *Clinique Laboratories Inc v Luxury Skin Care Brands Pty Ltd* (2003) 61 IPR 130.

Where the confusion or deception comes about because of the actual reputation in the market of a registered or unregistered mark, s 60 applies. It may be that a prior mark is registered but also used, presented or incorporated in ways that constitute common law marks: see *Kimberly-Clark* at [46]. In *Pfizer Products*, there was already a registered mark, VIAGRA. The application for the mark HERBAGRA was refused as confusing and deceptive. The decision illustrates the close interplay and partial overlapping between the various provisions in the Act, in this case ss 43, 44 and 60: see further Burrell and Handler, 'The Intersection between Registered and Unregistered Trade Marks' (2007) 35 *F L Rev* 375.

Section 44 provides that a trade mark application should be rejected if it is for a mark that is either substantially identical or deceptively similar to another registered mark registered for the same goods or services. However, s 44 expands the categories of comparison by providing that a trade mark application is also to be rejected if the mark is too similar to a mark registered in respect of *similar goods or similar services, goods closely related to services, or services closely related to goods*. There are thus two key issues in the context of s 44:

- first, the meaning of 'substantially identical or deceptively similar'; and
- second, what 'similar goods or closely related services' are.

This question is logically antecedent to the other question: see French J in *Registrar of Trade Marks v Woolworths Ltd* (1999) 93 FCR 365; 45 IPR 411 (cited below 15.5).

Substantially identical and deceptively similar marks

15.5 The terms 'substantially identical' and 'deceptively similar' have a distinct and particular meaning. The latter casts a wider net than the former, which is the more straightforward test: it requires only a side by side comparison of the two marks. In *Shell Co (Aust) Ltd v Esso Standard Oil (Aust) Ltd* (1963) 109 CLR 407, it was said at 414 that the marks are 'compared side by side, their similarities and differences noted and the importance of these assessed having regard to the essential features of the registered mark and the total impression of resemblance or dissimilarity that emerges from the comparison'. In *Singtel Optus Pty Ltd v Optum Inc* (2018) 140 IPR 1; [2018] FCA 575 the court said: 'Thus, two marks are "substantially identical" if a total impression of similarity emerges from the side-by-side comparison of the two marks, having regard to the essential features of the registered mark': at [8]. The court held at [13] that 'Optus' and 'Optum' were not substantially identical trade marks:

> Whilst there is only a single spelling difference between the two words, that spelling difference … is enough to make the words distinct from each other in that the letters 'S' and 'M' are not visually similar and also differ in sound. The different consonant endings affect how the words are pronounced and make the words aurally distinct. … [T]he visual and aural differences produced by the different last letter of each word make the marks sufficiently different to distinguish the marks on a side-by-side comparison. The different meanings which the words evoke because of their different endings underscore how the different last letters render the marks sufficiently different from each other.

For another example, in *Torpedoes Sportswear Pty Ltd v Thorpedo Enterprises Pty Ltd* (2003) 132 FCR 326; 59 IPR 318, the word 'Thorpedo', coined from the name of the well-known swimmer Ian Thorpe, was sought to be registered. The similarity with a registered device mark incorporating the word 'Torpedoes' was under consideration. Taking the totality of the characteristics of the marks into account — that is, the device features (absent from the 'Thorpedo' mark), the differences between the actual words (Thorpedo vs Torpedoes) and the aural dissimilarities (only slight differences, 'th' vs 't' and the '-es' of Torpedoes) — Bennett J was led to the conclusion that on a side-by-side comparison the two marks were not substantially identical.

The test of deceptive similarity is quite different, depending not on an objective visual/aural comparison but on the impression and recollection of the hypothetical consumer.

It raises questions of 'suggestion, connotation, impression and recollection': *Australian Chinese Newspapers Pty Ltd v Chinese Press Pty Ltd (No 2)* [2001] FCA 651 at [12]. The test is not whether consumers would actually be deceived or confused but whether they would be caused to wonder whether the two products come from the same source: see *CA Henschke & Co v Rosemount Estates Pty Ltd* (2000) 52 IPR 42 at 67–8. The term 'deceptively similar' is defined in s 10:

> … a trade mark is taken to be deceptively similar to another trade mark if it so nearly resembles that other trade mark that it is liable to deceive or cause confusion.

The following passage from *Australian Woollen Mills Ltd v FS Walton & Co Ltd* (1937) 58 CLR 641 describes the nature of the test, per Dixon and McTiernan JJ at CLR 658:

> An attempt should be made to estimate the effect or impression produced on the mind of potential customers by the mark or device for which the protection … is sought. The impression or recollection which is carried away and retained is necessarily the basis of any mistaken belief that the challenged mark … is the same. The effect of spoken description must be considered. If a mark is in fact or from its nature likely to be the source of some name or verbal description by which buyers will express their desire to have the goods, then similarities both of sound and of meaning may play an important part. The usual manner in which ordinary people behave must be the test of what confusion or deception may be expected. Potential buyers of goods are not to be credited with any high perception or habitual caution. On the other hand, exceptionally carelessness or stupidity may be disregarded. The course of business and the way in which the particular class of goods are sold gives, it may be said, the setting and the habits and observation of men considered in the mass affords the standard.

In *NEC Corporation v Punch Video (S) Pte Limited* (2005) 67 IPR 17 at 20, Branson J referred to an oft-repeated passage of French J (Tamberlin J agreeing) from *Registrar of Trade Marks v Woolworths Ltd* (1999) 93 FCR 365 at 382; 45 IPR 411:

> (i) To show that a trade mark is deceptively similar to another it is necessary to show a real tangible danger of deception or confusion occurring. A mere possibility is not sufficient. (ii) A trade mark is likely to cause confusion if the result of its use will be that a number of persons are caused to wonder whether it might not be the case that the two products or closely related products and services come from the same source. It is enough if the ordinary person entertains a reasonable doubt. It may be interpolated that this is another way of expressing the proposition that the trade mark is likely to cause confusion if there is a real likelihood that some people will wonder or be left in doubt about whether the two sets of products or the products and services in question come from the same source. (iii) In considering whether there is a likelihood of deception or confusion all surrounding circumstances have to be taken into consideration. These include the circumstances in which the marks will be used, the circumstances in which the goods or services will be bought and sold and the character of the probable acquirers of the goods and services. (iv) The rights of the parties are to be determined as at the date of the application. (v) The question of deceptive similarity must be considered in respect of all goods or services coming within the specification in the application and in respect of which registration is desired, not only in respect of those goods or services on which it is proposed to immediately use the mark. The question is not limited to whether a particular use will give rise to deception or confusion. It must be based upon what the applicant can do if registration is obtained. In respect of the last proposition, Mason J observed in *Berlei Hestia Industries Ltd v The Bali*

> *Co Inc* (1973) 129 CLR 353 at 362: 'the question whether there is a likelihood of confusion is to be answered, not by reference to the manner in which the respondent has used its mark in the past, but by reference to the use to which it can properly put the mark. The issue is whether that use would give rise to a real danger of confusion.'

Branson J, overturning the decision of a delegate of the Registrar, concluded that the applied for mark 'necvox' for automobile audiovisual equipment was deceptively similar to the registered mark NEC for computers, telecommunications, information technology and electronics.

The test rests on a comparison 'between, on the one hand, the impression based on recollection of the registered mark used in a normal or fair manner that persons of ordinary intelligence and memory would have, and, on the other hand, the impressions that such persons would get from the impugned mark as it appears in the use complained of': *Anheuser-Busch Inc v Budejovický Budvar, Národní Podnik* (2002) 56 IPR 182 at 216 per Allsop J (citations omitted). The test thus uses the ordinary consumer in a common purchasing situation as the reference point; ultimately, a judgment must be made by considering the subjective effect of the similarity of the marks on the average consumer's mind. Allsop J in *Anheuser-Busch Inc* at 216–18 analysed the authorities. He pointed out that confusion may be nothing more than perplexity or 'mixing up the minds of the purchasing public', whereas deception requires 'the creation of an incorrect belief or mental impression': at 217. In any case, 'a mere possibility of confusion is not enough, there must be proof of a likelihood': at 218. Importantly, 'the setting or surrounding circumstances for the comparison include, relevantly, how the product will be sold and promoted': at 218. In this case, visual similarity was more important than aural, since beer would commonly be bought off the shelf or by reference to a name in a restaurant liquor list. At 219, Allsop J said:

> One then compares the look and sound of the impugned mark 'Budeˇjovický Budvar' with 'Bud' and 'Budweiser'. They are all applied to beer. The customer is an English speaking Australian who buys, or wishes to consider buying, an imported beer. No particular class or age group (as long as the person is above 18) is relevant. The multi-syllabled two words of foreign and unknown meaning do not, apart from a common syllable, bear any real visual resemblance to 'Budweiser', 'Bud' or 'Budweiser King of Beers'. The reader or viewer of the label or its equivalent may notice a resemblance in the common syllable. That, however, taking the mark as it is used, is, in my view, insufficient to make it likely that buyers will be caused from a visual examination to question whether it comes from the same trade source as 'Bud' or 'Budweiser' or 'Budweiser King of Beers' or whether it is associated with any recollection they may have of those marks. The applicant's entitlement to write its marks in any fair and normal manner would enable it to use a cursive script; but none of the registered marks has, or calls for, any diacritical elements. The diacritical elements assist in distinguishing visually the words from the registered marks. I do not think that any impression or recollection of 'Budweiser' or 'Bud' taken away will cause the visual appearance of the mark 'Budeˇjovický Budvar', as used, to create any confusion or questioning as to whether the trade source of the 'Budeˇjovický Budvar' product might be the same as that of the registered marks, 'Bud' or 'Budweiser' or 'Budweiser King of Beers'.

The applicant stressed that the 'Bud' part of the mark was critical, particularly to an aural comparison, as Australians would tend to resort to that abbreviation faced with the difficulties of the Czech mark and because of their general tendency to abbreviate.

However, Allsop J was not convinced by these arguments (see at IPR 216, [141]ff) and ultimately held that the two marks taken as a whole were not deceptively similar. These parties have engaged in litigation on these issues around the world: note, for instance, the New Zealand decision in *Anheuser-Busch Inc v Budejovický Budvar, Národní Podnik and Others* [2002] NZCA 264. Generally speaking, although a mere possibility of confusion is not enough, 'the threshold for confusion is not high': see *Australian Postal Corporation v Digital Post Australia* (2013) 105 IPR 1; [2013] FCAFC 153 at [70]. In *Caesarstone Ltd v Ceramiche Caesar SpA (No 2)* (2018) 133 IPR 417; [2018] FCA 1096 the two marks were CAESARSTONE on the one hand (as a word and as a device mark) and CAESAR (as an earlier registered device mark). The application concerned registration of CAESARSTONE, and was opposed on the basis of the prior registration of CAESAR (which was rendered in a particular font and with the A and E run together: Æ). The court pointed out that 'it is recognised that deceptive similarity may be established when an impugned mark uses an "essential" or "distinguishing" feature of the mark as registered': at [678]. The consumer's imperfect recollection would be of the word CAESAR as such. Further, 'the beginning of words is more important for the purpose of distinction: see also *Johnson & Johnson v Kalnin* [1993] FCA 279; 114 ALR 215 at 221 per Gummow J. … [T]he word "caesarstone" begins with the very word and sounds that I have found to be the word recollected by the consumer when recalling the CÆSAR Device mark': at [683]. Because the word 'stone' was descriptive, the CAESAR in CAESERSTONE was dominant and distinctive. There was thus aural, visual and conceptual similarity; and for all those reasons, unprisingly the court found the two marks to be deceptively similar. It should be noted that if there has been 'honest concurrent user' of two marks, the Registrar can accept registration 'subject to any conditions or limitations that the Registrar thinks fit to impose' (see s 44(3)); in *Caesarstone* the applicant was held to have shown honesty in the relevant statutory sense: at [741]–[744]; see further below 15.7.

Similar goods or closely related services

15.6 The other issue that needs to be resolved in terms of s 44 is what 'similar goods or closely related services' are. As indicated, logically this issue is dealt with first. The Trade Marks Act 1995 limits the owner's core monopoly to the goods or services for which the mark is registered, so other providers are, theoretically, free to register the mark in relation to goods and services of a different kind. The theory underlying this approach is that the reputation of a mark is largely confined to goods or services of the kind in relation to which it is used. But it is incontrovertible that the reputation of certain trade marks extends beyond the goods or services to which the owner normally attaches them, and thus beyond the goods or services for which they are registered. The practice of so-called brand extension may in fact result in a single mark being used in relation to a wide variety of goods or services. Thus, the comparative test under s 44 is not limited to marks registered for the same goods and services, but neither does it extend to goods and services of any kind. The Act finds a middle ground by extending the test to marks registered for similar goods and closely related services, defined by s 14 as either the same as other goods or services or of the same description as the other goods or services; note that these terms also arise in the context of infringement under s 120.

Interpretation of the equivalent provision under a previous Act was at issue in *Southern Cross Refrigerating Co v Toowoomba Foundry Pty Ltd* (1954) 91 CLR 592; 1A IPR 465. The applicant (appellant in the High Court) was refused registration of the words 'Southern Cross' as a trade mark in respect of 'gas absorption refrigerators and electric refrigerators and parts thereof', later limited to domestic refrigerators. The respondent, who had opposed the registration, was registered proprietor of the trade mark 'Southern Cross' in respect of well drilling equipment, milking machines, windmills and engines. It also had trade marks on the register consisting of the device 'S' over a cross in respect of windmills and pumping machinery, tubing and milking machines. Relevant to determining whether they were the same goods or of the same description was not only the inherent character of the goods but also such matters as their respective uses and the trade channels through which they were to be sold. Their origin, their purpose, whether they were commonly produced together or distributed by the same wholesaler, whether they were sold in the same shops over the same counters to the same customer classes and whether they were regarded as belonging to the same trade, were also held to be relevant.

No single consideration is conclusive, and, obviously, the fact that goods or services are or are not in the same class for the purpose of registration is not conclusive by itself. The court was of the opinion that on the facts of the case (at CLR 607):

> The goods to be compared and their respective uses are vastly different and, though the evidence shows that in the course of marketing and distribution there may be substantial points of contact, the evidence does not lead to the conclusion that the goods of the appellant are of the same description as those of the respondent.

The considerations held to be relevant in the *Southern Cross* case are equally so under the Trade Marks Act 1995. Note that if registration is refused because of the operation of s 43 or s 44, as in the *Southern Cross* case, that does not mean the applicant cannot use the mark as an unregistered mark. However, if they do, they may be vulnerable to an action for passing off or to an action for trade mark infringement under s 120(2). This, as we shall see below, expands the rights of the registered trade mark owner beyond the goods or services for which the mark is registered to use on goods or services of a similar description, unless the defendant can establish that no deception or confusion will result from use of the (unregistered) mark. As to the question of whether goods are closely related to services, see also *Caterpillar Loader Hire (Holdings) Pty Ltd v Caterpillar Tractor Co* (1983) 1 IPR 265; *Woolworths Ltd v Registrar of Trade Marks*; and *Kimberly-Clark*, relating to the trademark HUGGIE MUMMY, opposed by Kimberly-Clark, the owner of the trade mark HUGGIES. The registration sought by the applicant was for 'services described as "direct selling of baby-toddler's toys, videos, CDs, books, games and accessories"'. The registration of Huggies was for a number of baby/toddler goods, including nappies, training pants, underpants, liners, bibs, wipes and cloths, swimwear, paper products and personal care products. The respondent's services and the opponent's goods were held to be closely related within the meaning of s 44(2)(a)(i): *Kimberly-Clark* at [28]ff.

For an interesting example as to whether goods are of the same description, see *McCormick*, where Kenny J noted at IPR 107 that:

> … the authorities establish that there are three principal factors to be considered in this regard. They are: (1) the nature of the goods, including their origin and characteristics; (2) the uses made of them, including their purpose; and (3) the trade channels through which the goods are bought and sold.

The court held that batter and herbs and spices etc were goods of the same description, since they were both added to food to enhance taste and were traded through the same channels. More recently, see *E & J Gallo Winery v Lion Nathan Australia Pty Ltd* (2008) 77 IPR 69, where beer and wine were held not to be goods of the same description. Apart from the obvious inherent differences, the goods do not have the same origin; they are sold separately, as evidenced by the separate beer and wine parts of restaurant drinks lists and the different placement in bottle shops; they are drunk in different ways; and most corporations do not combine the production of wine and beer. The point that goods were sold through entirely different trade channels also arose in *Notaras v Barcelona Pty Ltd* [2019] FCA 4 where coffee machines and coffee products were held not to be goods of the same description, and 'services such as retailing and wholesaling of coffee do not have a sufficiently close function with respect to the coffee machines, as distinct from the function of the services with respect to coffee': at [337]. In *SMA Solar Technology AG v Beyond Building Systems Pty Ltd (No 5)* [2012] FCA 1403, the court held that solar panels and solar inverters were not goods of the same description. Although the trade channels were similar, the two products performed different functions, and substitutability, although not being the whole story, was a good guide in most cases (at [75]); see also *Singtel Optus* for a detailed consideration where a multitude of goods and services in multiple classes were concerned.

Honest concurrent user

15.7 Trade mark registration is of national application, and the monopoly over use of the trade mark is granted for the whole of the Commonwealth (see Trade Marks Act 1995, s 20; as to the definition of 'use', see s 7). The honest concurrent use provisions of s 44(3) and (4) address, to some extent, the difficulties that flow from the fact that registration of a trade mark, although of national effect, may, in fact, relate to a trade mark known or used only locally or on a state or regional level. It is a regular occurrence that identical trade marks or substantially identical or deceptively similar trade marks are in use concurrently in different places in Australia without there being any overlapping goodwill or reputation and without significantly detrimentally resulting in deception or confusion. A registered owner may be honestly unaware of the use of a similar unregistered mark by another. That other user may, in turn, be acting in honest ignorance of the registered mark. Section 44(3) addresses this situation by enabling the Registrar to allow the registration for similar goods or services of a mark that is substantially identical or deceptively similar to a registered mark where there has been honest concurrent use, subject to any conditions or limitations of use that are appropriate. They may include limitation to use in a particular geographical area; for instance, a state. The criteria to be assessed to determine whether registration should be permitted pursuant to s 44(3) are rehearsed in *McCormick* at IPR 111; see also *Trident Seafoods Corporation v Trident Foods Pty Ltd* [2019] FCAFC 100; and *Caesarstone*. Furthermore, if the applicant's mark has been in continuous use before the registration of the other mark, the Registrar may not reject the application: s 44(4). See also ss 20(4), 23, and 69(1)(c).

Other Grounds for Rejecting an Application

Representation of marks and searching the register

15.8 A public register of trade marks is maintained so that the details of registered marks can be ascertained by any person wishing to use or acquire a certain mark: see ATMOSS, the Australian Trade Mark Online Search System. For the purpose of permitting record keeping, categorisation and searching, the Trade Marks Act 1995 requires that a mark be able to be 'graphically represented' to be registrable: see ss 27(3)(a) and 40. Adequate graphic representation is also essential for the ascertainment of the precise scope and features of the mark and to allow proper examination. For most marks that are devices or words, the requirement creates little difficulty. For three-dimensional marks, specific guidance is provided by the regulations for the appropriate representation, which would apply to some shape marks and packaging marks. The representation must show every relevant feature of a mark (eg, by solid lines contrasting with dotted lines). A written description may accompany the graphic representation if it is necessary to draw attention to the specific features of shape that constitute the trade mark. The introduction by 1995 Act of sounds (sound or aural marks) and scents as signs that may be registered as trade marks has added an element of complexity. How is a sound mark or a scent to be graphically represented?

By virtue of reg 4.3(7) of the Trade Marks Regulations 1995 (Cth), if a trade mark for which registration is sought contains or consists of a sign that is a colour, scent, shape, sound or an aspect of packaging, or any combination of those features, the application for registration of the trade mark must include a concise and accurate description of the trade mark. The description must not be too technical or abstruse, so that it can be understood by an ordinary consumer. A sound mark may be represented in the form of a score, but that would be difficult with a mechanical or electronically generated sound mark (eg, the engine note of a Harley Davidson or the characteristic opening sound for Microsoft Windows). A written description may be appropriate, but it must be sufficiently accurate; a recording of the sound must accompany the application but it alone is not sufficient to meet the requirement of graphic representation. Scents must also be described in words and with sufficient precision (an example is an application, now lapsed, for a beer-scented dart, which was described as comprising 'the strong smell of beer'). The regulations further provide that if the application does not adequately describe the mark, the Registrar may require a further description and 'a specimen of the trade mark': see reg 4.3(8).

Nonetheless, as indicated above in relation to sounds, a deposit of a specimen in itself would clearly not suffice in terms of s 40, and thus the requirement of an accurate description that allows the distinctiveness of the mark to be assessed will inevitably mean that only a limited number of sound and scent marks will be registrable. An additional difficulty for scent marks, where the application might consist of a literary description of a scent and a deposit, is that reg 4.3(10) requires that the representation of a trade mark in an application for registration must be of a kind and quality that ensure that the features of the trade mark will be preserved in the course of time and is suitable for reproduction. Colour trade marks may be represented by a drawing or picture of the object with the colour applied or with an accompanying swatch in the right colour, or by reference to a recognised colour matching system (eg, Pantone). In any case, in Australia, as in the United Kingdom, where registration of sound and scent marks became possible in 1994, there appear to be very few such applications. In Europe, the registration of 'olfactory' marks has been severely limited by the jurisprudence of the European Court of Justice concerning graphic representation (see *Sieckmann v Deutsches Patent-und Markenamt* (C-273/00, 12 December 2002)), and sound marks require representation as a musical score (see *Shield Mark BV v Joost Kist hodn Memax* (C283/01, 13 April 2003)). As to the Trade Marks Office practice, see IP Australia, *Trade Marks Office Manual of Practice and Procedure*, Pt 21, 'Non-traditional signs'.

Scandalous marks, marks whose use would be contrary to law and proscribed signs

15.9 By virtue of s 42, if a trade mark contains or consists of scandalous matter (ie, it is offensive) or its use would be contrary to law, the application for registration must be rejected. It is not clear what constitutes scandalous matter; reference may be had to the *Trade Marks Manual of Practice and Procedure*, Part 30, p 2. Note also in this regard the controversy, partly triggered by the *Waltzing Matilda* case, *Winton Shire Council v Lomas* (2002) 119 FCR 416; 56 IPR 72, concerning the trade marking of national Australian icons: see Advisory Council on Intellectual Property, *The Protection of National Icons*, December 2002.

As to marks whose use would be contrary to law, there are many potential grounds that can be raised under this heading; for instance, that the mark is defamatory, contains or consists of an infringing reproduction of a copyright work, or offends against a provision of the Australian Consumer Law under Sch 2 of the Competition and Consumer Act 2010 (Cth) (which superseded the Trade Practices Act 1974 (Cth)). The contemporary broad understanding of the scope of the provision finds its genesis in *Advantage-Rent-A-Car Inc v Advantage Car Rental Pty Ltd* (2001) 52 IPR 24; [2001] FCA 683. In that case, Madgwick J rejected the narrow English approach that the ground must be made out because of something inherent in the mark, in favour of an inquiry as to whether the use of the mark was potentially contrary to law (in this case, the use would have amounted to an infringement of copyright). The correct approach the Registrar should take is also explored: see at IPR 30. The illegality must arise from the trade mark itself, rather than the particular manner in which the applicant's business has been or will be arranged: see *New South Wales Lotteries Commission v Novamedia BV* (2001) 52 IPR 638. Contrary to law can include contrary to fair trading or trade practices law, and, in fact, that is the most common ground to be raised: see, for example, *Kimberly-Clark* at [48]:

> These conclusions with respect to ss 44 and 60 of the Act mean that I also accept the opponent's objection based on s 42(b) (use of the trade mark would be contrary to law). I accept that use of the respondent's trade mark would be likely to mislead and deceive consumers in relation to the supply of the nominated goods; the circumstances described above mean that some consumers confronted by the 'HUGGIE' MUMMY mark in the course of the respondent's authorised use will be likely to identify the opponent as the source of the goods or think that there is an affiliation between the opponent and the respondent's services. By reason of s 42 of the *Fair Trading Act 1987* (NSW) and s 52 of the *Trade Practices Act 1974* (Cth) this is sufficient to satisfy the requirements of s 42(b) of the Act (*Health World v Shin-Sun Australia Pty Ltd* (2008) 75 IPR 478; [2008] FCA 100 at [156]).

However, contrary to law can also refer to a breach of contract law. In *Neumann v Sons of the Desert SL* [2008] FCA 1183, Ryan J said: 'The phrase "contrary to law" in s 42 of the Act is not limited to breaches of statutory provisions. … "it appears any law at all is contemplated, statutory or otherwise.": at [31] (citation omitted). The purported exclusive use would have been in breach of contractual agreements, and therefore 'contrary to law'; see also *Harcourts WA Pty Ltd v Roy Weston Nominees Pty Ltd (No 4)* (2016) 116 IPR 269; [2016] FCA 138.

The trade mark regulations may provide that certain signs are not to be used as trade marks: see s 18 and reg 4.15. By virtue of s 39(1), applications for such marks must be rejected. Words such as 'patent' and 'copyright' and crests of arms of states and territories are proscribed by reg 4.15. An application may also be rejected if other legislation proscribes the registration of the mark concerned: for an example see s 19 of the Olympic Insignia Protection Act 1987 (Cth) as amended by s 14 of the Olympic Insignia Protection Amendment Act 2001 (Cth).

Ownership

Ownership of an unregistered mark and the right to apply

15.10 Ownership of a registered mark is determined by the particulars on the register. Identifying the person who may apply for and be granted registration of a mark in the first place is a more complex matter. By virtue of s 27 of the Trade Marks Act 1995, a person who claims to be the owner of the mark and is either using or intends to use the mark (or to license another person to use it or to assign it to a body corporate for that purpose) may apply for registration. The term 'owner' is not defined in the Act. Note that all that is required at the application stage is that a person claims to be the owner; however, that the applicant is not the owner of the (unregistered) mark is a ground for both opposition (see s 58) and cancellation: see s 88(2)(a).

It is a frequent ground of attack on a registered trade mark. In *Rodney Jane Racing* O'Bryan J set out the basic principles derived from the decisions of the Full Court of the Federal Court in *Food Channel Network Pty Ltd v Television Food Network GP* (2010) 185 FCR 9; 86 IPR 437; [2010] FCAFC 58 and *Pham Global Pty Ltd v Insight Clinical Imaging Pty Ltd* (2017) 251 FCR 379; [2017] FCAFC 83. Most relevant are the following (*Rodney Jane Racing* at [14]):

> (b) In respect of a mark that has not been used prior to the application for registration, the basis of a claim to ownership has been found in the combined

effect of authorship of the mark, the intention to use it upon or in connection with the goods and the application for registration: *Food Channel* at [52] citing *Shell Company of Australia Ltd v Rohm and Haas Company* [1948] HCA 27; (1949) 78 CLR 601 at 627 per Dixon J; *Pham Global* at [18] and [19].

(c) In respect of a mark that has been used prior to the application for registration, ownership is established by authorship of the mark and prior use: *Food Channel* at [55]; *Pham Global* at [19].

But where the mark has been used before the priority date, the person who uses the mark in commerce is the owner of the (unregistered) mark for the purpose of applying for registration. Thus, whether or not there has been use of a mark, and by whom, is a significant question. In *Winton Shire Council v Lomas* (2002) 119 FCR 416; 56 IPR 72 (see also above 15.9), the contest was 'between the respondent who was first to file and the applicants who claim to have been the first to use [the mark 'Waltzing Matilda']'. A very small amount of use before the priority date as a trade mark for the goods and services of the application 'or the same type of thing' would suffice; for instance, by identifying an actual trade or offer to trade in the goods (or services) bearing the mark, or an existing intention to offer or supply goods (or services) bearing the mark in trade. There were a few instances of a genuine intention to offer products under the trade mark in the context of the operation of the Waltzing Matilda Centre in evidence, which sufficed for the ground of opposition under s 58 to be made out. The person who used the mark before the application is also the owner (or proprietor under previous legislation) only provided there is no earlier user of that mark. Ownership in this context is not 'at large'; that is, for all purposes but in relation to the goods or services for which it has been used or is intended to be used and goods 'of the same kind': see *In re Hick's Trade Mark* (1897) 22 VLR 636 at 640. What is required is use of the mark in relation to the same 'kind of thing' or goods that are 'essentially the same' as those for which registration is sought: see *Colorado Group Ltd v Strandbags Group Pty Ltd* (2007) 164 FCR 506; [2007] FCAFC 184 at [89]–[90]; and *Accor Australia & New Zealand Hospitality Pty Ltd v Liv Pty Ltd* (2017) 345 ALR 205; [2017] FCAFC 56 at [177]–[190].

Thus, an opponent's claim to ownership may be defeated by showing that the use of the contested mark related to different goods; then, obviously, a question may arise as to whether or not certain goods are different for this purpose. An illustrative example of these issues is found in the abovementioned case of *Colorado Group Ltd v Strandbags Group Pty Ltd* (2006) 67 IPR 628 and *Colorado Group Ltd v Strandbags Group Pty Ltd* (2007) 164 FCR 506; 74 IPR 246. If the mark is inherently distinctive, then first use establishes ownership; if it is less than that, it will also be required to show that the mark is factually distinctive of the goods or services of the applicant. In this case, the Colorado Group registered the trade mark COLORADO in respect of bags, wallets, purses, backpacks, belts, clothing, boots, shoes, slippers and other footwear, among other things. But both it and Strandbags had used the mark COLORADO long before that date. One question was whether the mark had been used as part of a combination mark — significant because 'as a general rule, however, an owner of a combination mark is not the owner for trade mark purposes of the marks comprising each separate component of it: see *In re JB Palmer's Trade-Mark* (1883) 24 Ch D 504 and *Richards v Butcher* [1891] 2 Ch 522' (at IPR 246). Another issue that may be the subject of detailed evidence is who or what entity was the actual owner of the goodwill in a business at the relevant time (ie, the time of registration). This may be complicated by various transactions or contractual relationships: see, for example, *Anakin Pty Ltd v Chatswood BBQ King Pty Ltd* (2008) 79 IPR 44; [2008] FCA 1467; *Edwards v Liquid Engineering 2003 Pty Ltd* (2008) 77 IPR 115; *Miller v JLCS Pty Ltd* (2007) 158 FCR 1; 71 IPR 499; and *King Par, LLC v Brosnan Golf Pty Ltd* (2014) 106 IPR 457; [2014] FCA 795, where, inter alia, the question of prior abandonment is discussed. Note also the potential overlap between contested ownership and applications in bad faith: see further 15.11.

Application for registration of a foreign mark in Australia

15.11 A fine distinction arises in cases where a person applies for Australian registration of a foreign mark not yet in use nor registered in this jurisdiction. Ownership here is not determined by use, reputation or registered ownership in another jurisdiction. As noted above, the starting principle is that where a trade mark is not in use (which is the hypothetical situation under consideration here), the owner is the author or 'originator' of the mark who intends to use it as such, which can include a person who copied a foreign mark who intends to use it in Australia. Use or adoption of the mark in Australia by a person other than the foreign trade mark owner may thus result in the latter being pre-empted by a local, unauthorised or unconnected registration. Cases of this type are not unknown in Australia; for example, the American burger franchise Burger King was pre-empted in its use of that mark on entry into the Australian market and adopted the Hungry Jack's brand instead. This outcome may, in some cases, appear unfair to the foreign owner, although it is arguable that the existence of a foreign reputation in a mark should not amount to a dead hand on Australian firms that forever restrains them from registering such a mark here; competition and the public interest would not be served.

The courts have sought to balance the interests of the foreign trade mark owner against the public interest in freedom of local competition by various strategies. One is to accept even a minimal amount of local use of the mark as sufficient to justify a claim of ownership in Australia by the foreign trade mark owner. The difficulty with this approach is that there must be some use of the mark as a mark within the jurisdiction; that is, some use designating certain goods or services that are at least available in Australia. Thus, the mere fact that advertising for the Fuddruckers hamburger chain appeared in the *Wall Street Journal*, which was available in Australia, was not sufficient to claim ownership in this jurisdiction: see *Michael Sharwood & Partners Pty Ltd v Fuddruckers Inc* (1989) 15 IPR 188. Similarly, the sending of samples to Australia was not sufficient local use: see *Moorgate Tobacco Co Ltd v Philip Morris Ltd* (1984) 156 CLR 414; 3 IPR 545. However, actually ordering goods from abroad may indicate a sufficient intention to commercially deal in the goods locally, and thus be sufficient to establish ownership here: see *Re Yanx Trade Mark* (1951) 82 CLR 199; 1B IPR 504. Thus, a distinction must be drawn between 'use of a mark in trade and activities with respect to the mark which are preliminary to actual use of the mark': *Woolly Bull Enterprises Pty Ltd v Reynolds* (2001) 107 FCR 166; 51 IPR 149.

An alternative approach that is maybe more satisfactory because it is less artificial and more in tune with modern levels of global travel and communication, is that taken in the *Spuds Mackenzie* case, *Anheuser-Busch Inc v Castlebrae Pty Ltd* (1991) 32 FCR 64; 23 IPR

54, which focuses on distinctiveness. Davies J held that since the decisions referred to above and the even less recent but well-known *Seven Up* decision, *Seven Up Co v OT Ltd* (1947) 75 CLR 203, factual circumstances had not stood still. In *Seven Up*, registration of the mark '8Up' could not be attacked, in the absence of fraud, on the basis of lack of ownership by the applicant for registration of the mark '7Up'. In *Anheuser-Busch* Davies J said at IPR 58:

> Thus, there has been a great increase in the travel both of Australian citizens to other countries and of the citizens and residents of other countries to Australia. And the media, particularly television through satellite transmission, has become increasingly international. ... Moreover, there has been an increasing public awareness of the existence and commercial significance of character merchandising.

Having regard to the extent of use of the Budweiser brand name and the Spuds character and name worldwide, his Honour thus found that the marks as registered in Australia by Castlebrae were never capable of becoming distinctive of goods associated with Castlebrae. In other words, given the extent to which the Anheuser-Busch products were already known in Australia (although not sold) at the time of the Castlebrae registration, the Castlebrae marks could never distinguish their goods from those of Anheuser-Busch (a US corporation).

This approach, which stresses the essential element of distinctiveness as the crucial issue in a dispute between a foreign and a local trade mark owner, where the mark is well-known abroad, is more satisfactory than the artificial search for a minimal level of local exploitation of the mark. Yet it is dependent on the particular facts and the relevant evidence that the parties are able to muster, and thus may not always achieve the desired result for the foreign owner. A further strategy is to submit that the trade mark applied for by an unrelated party in Australia is misleading or deceptive because consumers who are knowledgeable about the mark, although it is not in use here, will be misled into thinking there is a connection between the mark and the owner of that same or a similar mark in another jurisdiction. However, since 2006, when s 62A was introduced, the registration of a trade mark may also be opposed on the ground that the application was made in bad faith. Although not limited to such circumstances, an allegation of bad faith might emanate from the owner of a foreign trade mark used for the same goods or services. Such was the case in *Fry Consulting Pty Ltd v Sports Warehouse Inc (No 2)* (2012) 201 FCR 565; 94 IPR 551; [2012] FCA 81. Dodds-Streeton J rejected the proposition that 'mere awareness that an overseas company owning the mark is already operating or intending to operate in Australia would amount to bad faith': at [167]. The proper question was whether the applicant's knowledge 'was such that his decision to apply for registration at the relevant date would be regarded as in bad faith by proper standards' (ibid). The court concluded that this was not such a case: at [167]–[174].

Other Kinds of Marks

Defensive registration

15.12 Under the Trade Marks Act 1995, there are three categories of special marks that serve a different purpose from ordinary marks: certification marks, collective marks and defensive marks. These categories are much less important, in terms of numbers, than ordinary marks, but are each significant in their own specific context.

Registration of a defensive mark (see Pt 17 of the Act) permits the owner of a famous mark to protect a mark against registration or use by others in relation to goods and services for which it is not registered as an ordinary mark nor used or intended to be used. In today's marketplace, where merchandising, trafficking in marks (ie, the sale of marks without attendant goodwill or business) and franchising are increasingly important, the goodwill attached to famous marks crosses the boundaries of product classification, and brand extension is commonplace. Yet a trade mark owner may not wish to extend the brand (ie, use it in relation to new or different goods or services) to non-related goods or services, for fear of diluting or attenuating the goodwill or reputation of the brand.

Defensive registration allows registration in a class or classes of goods or services without any obligation to use the mark (a mark that is not used is liable to be removed: see Pt 9 of the Act) to maintain the registration. However, such registration is available only for marks that are already registered as ordinary marks for some goods or services and that are indeed, colloquially speaking, famous. In terms of s 185(1) of the Act, this is a mark that, because of the extent of its use within the class of goods or services for which it is registered, would be construed as connecting other goods and services on which it is used with the owner of the trade mark. This requirement has been strictly interpreted by the Registrar, so only a limited number of marks have obtained defensive registration (eg, Defensive Trade Mark 192258 'Kleenex' for 'toilet soaps, perfumery, essential oils for toilet and cosmetic purposes, cosmetics and hair lotions' (Class 3)). Note that the Trade Marks Act 1995, through the mechanism of s 120, has somewhat reduced the significance of defensive registration, since it provides greater protection for well-known marks than was available under the 1955 Act: see, for example, *Pfizer Products Inc* [2004] ATMO 25, a decision concerning defensive registration of the mark VIAGRA for certain classes of goods; and see further Chapter 16 Registered Trade Marks: Infringement. However, defensive registration certainly alleviates the evidentiary burden on the well-known trade mark owner in an infringement action, which is considerable in the context of an action under s 120.

Collective trade marks

15.13 Collective trade marks are marks that are used or are intended to be used by members of an association in relation to goods or services provided or dealt with by that association: see Pt 15 of the Act. In this context, the *Union Label* case (*Attorney-General (NSW) v Brewery Employees Union of NSW* (1908) 6 CLR 469) is significant. The power over trade marks is vested in the Commonwealth Parliament by s 51(18) of the Commonwealth Constitution. The question that arose in the *Union Label* case was whether a 'Workers' Mark', as provided for by the Trade Marks Act 1905 (Cth), that, in this case, indicated that certain goods had not been handled by non-union labour, was a constitutionally valid category of registrable mark. The High Court held that it was not. It was not a trade mark, since it did not indicate that the goods originated with the owner of the mark (merely that they had passed through the hands of a certain unionised labour force). Therefore, that part of the 1905 Act providing for workers' marks was unconstitutional, since it did not relate to a trade mark and thus did not fall under the trade marks power of s 51(18). However, the similar, though broader, category of marks that has now been reintroduced under the guise of 'collective marks' in the 1995 Act ('goods or services … dealt with … by members of an association': s 162) is now constitutionally valid under the external affairs power, since collective marks are included in the Trade-Related Aspects of Intellectual Property Rights (TRIPS) Agreement of the World Trade Organization.

Certification trade marks

15.14 Certification marks are signs used or intended to be used to distinguish goods or services dealt with or provided in the course of trade and certified as to quality, accuracy, origin, material or mode of manufacture or some other characteristics from other goods or services not so certified: see Pt 16 of the Act. An example might be the Heart Foundation logo, used to certify health characteristics of foods, or the Quality Assurance logo. The 1995 Act contains provisions allowing rules governing the use of certification marks to be assessed by the Australian Competition and Consumer Commission as to competence of the approval authority and as to the public interest, notably in relation to potential anti-competitive effect or unfairness: see ss 172–183. Certification marks may serve the purpose of protecting the reputation of goods whose regional origins have come to be associated with certain qualities or characteristics: see, for instance, Certification Trade Mark 69212 'Harris Tweed'. For some examples of cases concerning certification marks, see *Benchmark Certification Pty Ltd v Standards Australia International Ltd* (2004) 212 ALR 464; ATPR 42-039; [2004] FCA 1489 and *Wilhelm Sihn jr KG v Wi-Fi Alliance* [2007] ATMO 39.

Bibliography

A Artinian, 'Opposition to Registration on the Basis of Deceptive Similarity — Case Note; *Law of the Jungle Pty Ltd v Jungle Management Pty Ltd*' (2006) 19(7) *IPLB* 111.

ABLR, 'Protection of International Business Reputation in Australia' (1994) 22 *ABLR* 345.

D Shavin, 'Famous Marks — Have They Ever had Effective Protection? Post TRIPS — Has Anything Changed?' (1999) 36 *IP Forum* 30.

J Luck, 'Distinctiveness, Deceptive and Confusing Marks under the Trade Marks Act 1995' (1996) 7 *AIPJ* 97 100.

K Everett, J McCormick, A Lang, '*Hill of Grace v Hill of Gold*' (2001) 14(1) *IPLB* 1.

L Ritchie, 'ACCC Ends the Party for Schoolies Trade Mark Owner' (2006) 18(9) *IPLB* 140.

M Handler, 'Disentangling functionality, distinctiveness and use in Australian trade mark law' (2018) 42(1) *MULR* 55.

P Loughlan, 'The Trade Mark is a Cultural Resource. (Use it to Tell a Joke or Sing A Song)' (2001) 44 *IP Forum* 22.

R Burrell and M Handler, 'A Requiem for Champagne Heidsieck: Trade Mark Use and Parallel Importation' (2016) 26 *AIPJ* 110.

R Burrell and M Handler, *Australian Trade Mark Law*, 2nd ed, Oxford University Press, Melbourne, 2016.

S Christie, 'Intent to Use Must be Settled: "Waltzing Matilda" Trade Mark Case; Case Note — *Lomas v Winton Shire Council*' (2003) 16(1) *IPLB* 9.

S Givoni, 'Brawl Over Beers' (2002) 15(3) *IPLB* 41.

S Givoni, 'Section 120(3) — The Bottling Up of Well Known Brands? Or a Level Playing Field for All?' (2000) 41 *IP Forum* 18.

S Stone, 'Case Note: *Mid Sydney Pty Ltd v Australian Tourism Co Ltd*' (1999) 11(6) *IPLB* 65.

T Stevens, 'Trade Mark Ownership and Sharp Business Practice' (2004) 17(1) *IPLB* 4.

W Pengilley, 'Coca-Cola Bottle has Trade Mark Protection' (2000) 13(1) *IPLB* 7.

Chapter 16

Registered Trade Marks: Infringement

Infringing Use of a Registered Mark

16.1 The rights of the trade mark owner are circumscribed by s 20 of the Trade Marks Act 1995 (Cth). The registered owner has the *exclusive* right to use the trade mark and to authorise other persons to use the trade mark in relation to the goods and/or services in respect of which the trade mark is registered: see also s 7. This monopoly translates into a statutory right of action in relation to unauthorised use of the mark as a mark (see s 120). We will see below that in some circumstances rights of action extend beyond the unauthorised use of the registered mark in relation to goods or services for which the mark is registered, to use on other goods. However, in the latter case, the onus on the trade mark owner is far greater and more akin to what is required under passing off or s 18 of the Australian Consumer Law under Sch 2 of the Competition and Consumer Act 2010 (Cth): see Trade Marks Act 1995, s 120(2) and (3). Note that the owner's use of a mark may be subject to conditions imposed by the Registrar upon granting (see s 33(2)), and that by virtue of s 74, an applicant or an owner of a registered trade mark may also disclaim any exclusive right to use or authorise the use of a specified part of the trade mark. By virtue of s 7, use of a trade mark means 'use upon, or in physical or other relation to' goods or services (s 7(4) and (5)); in *Nokia Corporation v Truong* (2005) 66 IPR 511, the trade mark was used in a 'physical relation' to goods, although it was not impressed upon them, where they were packed together with some other goods bearing a false trade mark. Further, aural representation of a mark can amount to use of the mark (s 7(2)), and use with additions or alterations that do not substantially affect the identity of the trade mark equates to use of the mark (s 7(1)). Therefore, attaching a trade mark to goods is within the statutory monopoly, as is using a trade mark in an advertisement or by way of any literary, graphic, radio, television or internet representation that is in relation to goods or services, as long as the use amounts to use 'as a trade mark'. An authorised use of the trade mark by a person other than the owner is taken to be a use of the trade mark by the owner: see s 8(3). An authorised use is a trade mark use under the financial or quality control of the owner: see s 8 (eg, under a licence or franchise agreement that provides for sufficient quality or financial control). Only use by the owner and/or use by an authorised user (in the statutory sense of s 8) are to be taken into account to establish sufficient use of the mark to maintain registration (see Pt 9 of the Trade Marks Act 1995 'Removal for non-use'). Use without sufficient financial or quality control as required by s 8 cannot be taken into account for the purpose of meeting the statutory use requirement; the use must also relate to the registered trade mark owner in Australia — see *Dunlop Aircraft Tyres Ltd v Goodyear Tire & Rubber Co* (2018) 262 FCR 76; 134 IPR 220; [2018] FCA 1014 where it was held that by importing and then selling aircraft tyres marked with the Dunlop/Flying D marks in Australia, Goodyear Australia was using them as trade marks.

Use of a mark as a mark

16.2 The exclusive rights of the owner extend only to 'use of a mark as a mark'. Section 120 of the Trade Marks Act 1995 provides: '(1) A person infringes a registered trade mark if the person uses as a trade mark a sign …'. To determine what use 'as a trade mark' means, reference must be made to the definition of s 17 of the Act, which circumscribes a registrable mark by reference to both formal and functional elements, as was seen above: see Chapter 14 Registered Trade Marks: Definition of a Mark and Distinctiveness. Thus, use as a trade mark is use in a manner that will be taken as indicating the commercial source or origin of goods or services. The use need not be on or in a direct physical relationship to the goods or services but might, for instance, be in advertising or promotions literature or correspondence: see, for example, *Prismex Technologies Pty Ltd v Keller Industries Pty Ltd* [2006] FCA 1504. A use that consumers interpret as indicating commercial origins falls within the traditional notion of a mark being used as a 'badge of origin'. Uses that may not fall within the sphere of 'use as a mark' are many and varied; one example is inclusion of another's mark in searchable metadata, or its purchase and use as a Google Adword. In relation to the latter, in *Veda Advantage Ltd v Malouf Group Enterprises Pty Ltd* (2016) 241 FCR 161; 118 IPR 291; [2016] FCA 255, the Federal Court held that this did not amount to 'use' of a trade mark, principally because Google AdWords are invisible to consumers. However, in *Accor Australia & New Zealand Hospitality Pty Ltd v Liv Pty Ltd* (2017) 124 IPR 264; [2017] FCAFC 56 it was held that including the trade mark 'Harbour Lights' in source code did constitute trade mark use, as it was visible to those who know what to look for and influenced search results (it was not used in a descriptive manner). Drawing the line between trade mark use and non-use (commonly descriptive use only) is often a critical issue in trade mark infringement cases other than those of simple counterfeiting.

The case establishing the basic principle (under the Trade Marks Act 1955 (Cth), which remains relevant to this issue under the 1995 Act) is *Shell Co of Australia Ltd v Esso Standard Oil (Australia) Ltd* (1963) 109 CLR 407 (*Shell v Esso*). A humanised oil drop, a registered trade mark of Esso, was used as an animated figure in a TV advertising cartoon devised by Shell, praising the qualities of its own product in a light-hearted manner. The court held that this was not use that would be seen by consumers as a means of indicating trade origin but as a way of binding together the various developments in the cartoon and to illustrate the characteristics of the product in an entertaining and captivating manner.

Generally, use of a registered trade mark is likely to amount to use 'as a mark' if the manner in which it has been employed does not serve some other purpose; for example, as a descriptive term (see 16.3), as a declaration, to meet functional requirements or to communicate some other message. For instance, in *Top Heavy Pty Ltd v Killen* (1996)

34 IPR 282, Lehane J considered the use of the trade mark CHILL OUT, registered for goods within Class 25: clothing, footwear and head gear. The court had to determine whether the use of the words 'CHILL OUT' in a decorative manner on T-shirts constituted use of a mark as a mark. Lehane J said (at IPR 286): 'Chill out has a meaning and the question is whether, used in the way the applicant used it, it indicates the trade origin of the T-shirts rather than (or at least as well as) conveying some other message to the reader.' He held that the term conveyed an exhortation to the reader to relax, rather than performing the role of a badge of origin for T-shirts. Since the mark had not acquired any secondary meaning either (ie, the term had not come to indicate anything other than its natural meaning), it could not be said that its use was as a 'badge of origin' at all. There was therefore no infringement. In *Coca-Cola Co v All-Fect Distributors (t/as Millers Distributing Co)* (1998) 43 IPR 47, the question arose of whether the applicant's two-dimensional Coke bottle contour trade mark was infringed by the importing of confectionery in the (three-dimensional) shape of a Coke bottle. The trial court held that the use of the Coke bottle shape was use as a product and was not also use as a mark, since, despite the fame of the mark, the shape of the confectionery would not be taken to indicate a connection with the registered trade mark owner: at IPR 63–6. However, the Full Federal Court upheld an appeal against the trial judge's decision: see *Coca-Cola Co v All-Fect Distributors Ltd* (1999) 96 FCR 107; 47 IPR 481.

Use as a mark or descriptive term

16.3 Often, the use of an invented term on packaging or goods will amount to trade mark use; note, however, *Johnson & Johnson Australia Pty Ltd v Sterling Pharmaceuticals Pty Ltd* (1991) 30 FCR 326; 21 IPR 1, where the use of the invented word 'CAPLET', registered as a trade mark, on the packaging of goods of a competitor was held not to be use as a badge of origin but use that was descriptive of the shape of the tablets contained in the packs. Even invented words or words used out of context can thus be taken by consumers as suggestive of some quality other than commercial origin or be descriptive to some degree. Sometimes, the mark at issue is a composite one, as in *Lift Shop Pty Ltd v Easy Living Home Elevators Pty Ltd* (2014) 106 IPR 419; [2014] FCAFC 75, where it consisted of the words 'LIFT SHOP' against a green-coloured rectangular background and flanked by a lift button. A competitor used the words 'lift shop' on its website as a search result optimisation strategy. The Full Court agreed with the trial judge that those words appearing in search results and on the respondent's web page were used 'to convey that its business was one of supplying lifts': at [46]. Neither the prominence of the words on the web page nor their positioning 'imbued them with the character of a trade mark': ibid.

In *Pepsico Australia Pty Ltd v The Kettle Chip Co Pty Ltd* (1996) 135 ALR 192; 33 IPR 161 (the *Kettle Chip* case), the question was whether the impugned use of the mark was as a badge of origin or as a descriptive term. The Kettle Chip Company was owner of the registered trade mark KETTLE, relevantly here in respect of potato chips. Its competitor launched a line extension within its 'Thins' range of potato chips, on the packet of which appeared the words 'Thins', 'Double Crunch' and 'Kettle Cooked Potato Chips' in descending order of prominence. The Full Federal Court found that the use of the word 'Kettle' was as part of a descriptive phrase: a sufficient proportion of the population would understand the use of the term to refer to cooking in a vat of oil. It was wrong to presume that most members of the public would understand the word 'kettle' to refer only to a water-boiling closed-lid kitchen appliance. Even though the word may have acquired some secondary meaning as a result of its use by The Kettle Chip Company, that did not take away from the fact that the use in this case was descriptive and not as a badge of origin. The plaintiff in this case had to some extent contributed to its own downfall by itself, at least for a time, using the word as a descriptor of its cooking method, rather than purely as a badge of origin.

In *Aldi Stores Ltd Partnership v Frito-Lay Trading Co GmbH* (2001) 54 IPR 344, the registered mark was 'Twisties', the impugned mark 'Cheezy Twists' being used on Aldi's home brand equivalent. Hill J formulated the relevant question as follows: 'Do the words "Cheezy Twists" appear as a mark for distinguishing an Aldi product from other extruded cheese snack food products in the course of trade?': at IPR 354. In Hill J's view, the words did much more than just describe the contents, a task at any rate performed by the words 'cheese-flavoured snacks', which also appeared on the packs. The presence of another mark, 'Chazoos' (Aldi's home brand for this type of snack), did not detract from this conclusion: both functioned as badges of origin, one for the whole range and the other for the particular product. Lindgren and Conti JJ basically agreed on this point. Note that the question of whether a trade mark is used as a mark depends on all the circumstances of its use — it is often a contextual question (an aspect of the relevant context is trade custom: as for instance in relation to the *Adidas* case, see further below at 16.4). As is illustrated by the *Kettle Chip* case, the trade mark owner's own actions can sometimes contribute to some other party's use not amounting to trade mark use. Furthermore, trade mark use is not usually an issue considered in isolation. Closely related questions will commonly arise, such as:

- Is the trade mark valid in the first place — if it is to some degree descriptive of the goods, is it distinctive enough?
- What is the trade mark actually used by the respondent?
- Does a statutory defence apply — for example, use in good faith, under s 122?
- Has the mark become generic — has it become descriptive of a class of goods (eg, Kleenex for paper tissues) rather than distinctive of one trader's goods, and does s 24 therefore apply?

Use as a mark: shape marks and decorative marks

16.4 As is explained in Chapter 15 Registered Trade Marks: Other Requirements, the shape of the goods themselves is no longer a priori excluded from registration as a trade mark; the issue is now primarily one of distinctiveness. Even if a shape mark makes it to registration, the question remains as to whether copying or adoption of the shape by a rival trader amounts to a trade mark use; think about the analogous question in passing off where copying by itself does not necessarily amount to an actionable misrepresentation either. There, one concern is usurping the finely calibrated role of copyright, designs and even patents by brand protection under more general rules. In this context, similar concerns are relevant.

A landmark case providing an interesting insight into the 'use as a mark' of shape marks is *Philips Electronics NV v Remington Products Australia Pty Ltd* (1997) 39 IPR 283 and *Philips Electronics NV v Remington Products Australia Pty Ltd* (1999) 91 FCR 167; 44 IPR 551 (see also Chapter 14 Registered Trade Marks: Definition of a Mark and Distinctiveness). Philips was the registered owner of a three-dimensional mark that was the shape of a triple rotary shaving head, subject to a disclaimer that the mark 'shall neither confer nor recognise any right to the use of its features as a design applied to an article of manufacture'. The shape used by Remington for the head of its rotary shaver was held to be substantially identical or deceptively similar to the registered Philips mark. Despite the disclaimer, Lehane J said at 39 IPR 289, on the application for an interlocutory injunction, that:

> ... it may be that though registration of the design does not give Philips Electronics a monopoly in the design, ownership of the mark gives Philips Electronics statutory protection against another who (without authority) not merely applies the design to goods *but does so in a way that indicates trade origin* (emphasis added).

Thus, the judge found that the argument of Philips, that the prominent display of the rotary shaver head in Remington's transparent bubble packs and in advertising material amounted to use as a badge of origin, was not hopeless, and that there was, at the least, a serious issue to be tried. On the trial of the action, Lehane J held that mere adoption of a functional shape mark could not constitute an infringement. Therefore, although mere copying might not, certain further uses (eg, prominent display of the shape in packaging or advertising) might amount to an infringement because consumers would perceive it as a trade mark type use, but not on the facts of this case: see also *Koninklijke Philips Electronics NV v Remington Products Australia Pty Ltd* (2000) 100 FCR 90; 48 IPR 257 (*Remington*), which confirmed the trial decision.

A more recent case provides an interesting example both of trade-marking practice in the modern context of registrability of shape marks and of infringement issues: see *Global Brand Marketing Inc v YD Pty Ltd* (2008) 76 IPR 161. Apart from use of a mark as a mark, this case also considers substantial identity and deceptive similarity in the shape marks context; for these issues, see further below in this chapter. The plaintiff's particular DIESEL trade marks consisted of a shape mark that was made up of a stylised letter 'D' combined with various external visual features of a shoe, including the patterned hatching of the sole and various stripes on the outside, and a separate 'Sole' mark consisting of the patterning of the sole of a shoe. Obviously, the shape mark here was of a different kind from that in the *Philips* case, including a greater number of decorative features. However, individually, many of the features were either commonplace for shoes of that kind or, indeed, functional. The court provides a useful summary of the principles at at IPR 175 and then goes on to distinguish between functional and non-functional non-descriptive features. In concluding that the 'Sole' mark was used as a mark, the court then said, at IPR 176:

> [68] YD's submission that the sole patterns are applied to provide grip, and are thus for a functional and not for a trade mark purpose, is pitched at too high a level of generality to be helpful in the present context. All soles provide some grip. The sole is inherent in the shoe itself and provides traction when a person is walking or running. Saying that the

> grip is functional is like saying that the shoe protects the foot from cuts and abrasions. In each case it is too broad a proposition. The position might have been different had there been evidence that the grip pattern provided a special quality leaving little or no room for choice. When choice is limited, it is likely that the goods or an important feature thereof will reflect the product or feature itself, as in *Mayne* [*Industries Pty Ltd v Advanced Engineering Group Pty Ltd* (2008) 166 FCR 312; 75 IPR 102] and *Remington*. In such a case function will overwhelm a trade mark purpose. In the absence of evidence to this effect, grip is in my view but a broad functional requirement. As Mr Vickery's evidence indicated, this function can be achieved by use of a variety of different patterns. In my view any functionality of the grip offered by the sole is overwhelmed by the non-descriptive aspects of the marks.

In relation to the shape mark of the overall shoe, the court said at IPR 177:

> [71] In my view the Photon and the Cube shoe are used as trade marks where the features listed in [70], especially features (a), (b), (d), (g) and (h), are combined in the shape of a shoe. The most important of these features for present purposes are the stitched YD label on both shoes, the small rounded piece at the back of the Cube shoe, and the Photon's stripe running parallel to the base of the sole. Neither the Cube's rounded piece nor the Photon's parallel strip is found on any of the shoes in evidence other than YD's shoes. Mr Vickery described the rounded piece as 'quite distinctive' and not a feature commonly used in the shoe industry. It can I think be considered a striking feature given its lack of commonality in the trade: cf [*Coca-Cola Co v*] *All-Fect* [*Distributors Ltd* (1999) 96 FCR 107; 47 IPR 481] at [25].
>
> [72] Features (c), (e), (i) and (j) in the list at [70] are either functional or in common use. Common features are like descriptive words.
>
> [73] In my view the non-functional and non-descriptive features referred to in [71] overwhelm the functional features and common features referred to in [72] and give the Cube and Photon shoes a trade mark purpose.
>
> [74] This case is not as clear cut as *Kenman Kandy* on the one hand (use) or *Mayne* and *Remington* on the other (no use). It is towards the middle of the spectrum referred to at [62] to [64], neither black nor white, but just on the use side of the grey in the middle.

These passages are reproduced here in full because they illustrate the approach of the court. The court distinguishes its approach from that in the earlier case of *Mayne Industries Pty Ltd v Advanced Engineering Group Pty Ltd* (2008) 166 FCR 312; 75 IPR 102, which related to a far simpler and more functional shape (an S-shaped 'fence dropper'), and also from the above-mentioned *Philips v Remington* case. Further examples of use of a shape mark is afforded by *Outdoor Power Products Pty Ltd v Silvan Australia Pty Ltd* [2005] FCA 1696; and more recently *Coca-Cola Co v PepsiCo Inc (No 2)* (2014) 109 IPR 429; [2014] FCA 1287. In its reasons, the court in the latter case pointed to '[t]he need to consider the setting or context in determining whether there has been the use of a sign or mark as a trade mark' (at [199]) and said that this was illustrated by the approach taken by Sundberg J in *Global Brand Marketing*. However, in this case the goods were the beverages — and therefore it was their container rather than *the goods themselves* which was the trade-marked shape. The court held that the Pepsi-Cola bottle shape would be seen by consumers as distinctive — and thus as serving a trade mark function (ie, use of a mark as a mark). However, because of that same distinctiveness, the Pepsi bottle shape was not deceptively similar to the Coca Cola bottle-shaped trade mark.

Sometimes, the distinction to be drawn is between trade mark use and decorative use rather than between a trade mark and a technical feature. This distinction arose in another case concerning shoes, *Adidas AG v Pacific Brands Footwear Pty Ltd (No 3)* (2013) 103 IPR 521; [2013] FCA 905, where Adidas's three stripes mark was at issue. Pacific Brands placed four stripes in a similar position on its sports shoes, and the question was whether this amounted to trade mark or rather decorative use. The court held that the two functions were not mutually exclusive. Here, the decorative element was not dominant, as consumers would be familiar with the fact that 'signs as identifiers are generally placed on the side of sports footwear' (this was a matter of trade usage, a relevant contextual feature), which is where Pacific Brands had placed its four stripes: at [64]. There was thus trade mark use; the question of deceptive similarity remained. The area of functional and aesthetic trade marks remains difficult and controversial. Whatever the correct approach may be to registration and infringement of such marks, the outcome of such cases remains unpredictable.

Section 120: Actionable Use of a Registered Mark

The scope of s 120

16.5 Whether the registered mark is used 'as a mark' is a key threshold question and is logically considered first. But if the answer is yes, then two further issues must be considered:

1. Is the impugned mark sufficiently similar to the registered mark?
2. Was the mark used in relation to goods or services for which it was registered?

Sometimes, there is little doubt that the sign used by the alleged infringer was the same as the registered sign; that is the case in instances of piracy and counterfeiting. However, by virtue of s 120(1), the Trade Marks Act does not confine the right of action in infringement to restraining the use of identical marks only, but expands it to cover signs that are 'substantially identical with, or deceptively similar to' the registered trade mark — as is further defined in s 10:

> For the purposes of this Act, a trade mark is taken to be deceptively similar to another trade mark if it so nearly resembles that other trade mark that it is likely to deceive or cause confusion.

Further, the impugned use may be in relation to the same goods or services for which the trade mark was registered. Here also the Act does not confine the right of action only to such use but expands it, in prescribed circumstances, to use in relation to closely related services or goods of the same description (see s 120(2)) or, if the mark is a well-known mark, even to use in relation to unrelated goods or services: see s 120(3) and (4). However, in relation to those two categories of goods, neither reputation nor deception is presumed, and the evidentiary onus on the trade mark owner is more extensive. Note further that there must be a sufficient connection between the use of the trade mark and the Australian jurisdiction — a particularly pertinent question in the age of the internet. In *Ward Group Pty Ltd v Brodie & Stone Plc* (2005) 143 FCR 479; 64 IPR 1; [2005] FCA 471 the court held that although presenting an Australian registered trade mark on a foreign website can amount to infringement, unless Australian purchasers are deliberately being targeted, and are likely to use the foreign website, there will be no infringement in this country; see also *Lamont v Malishus* [2018] FCCA 423 where the court held that the uploading on Facebook of a trade mark 'was intended by each of the respondents, at least in substantial part, to be made in, or was directed to jurisdictions that include Australia': at [132]. For that reason, the uploading of clothing with the trade mark on it constituted a use of the mark in Australia.

Identical, substantially identical and deceptively similar marks

16.6 The use of an identical mark is not actually referred to in s 120, but since s 20 grants the owner the right to the exclusive use of the mark itself, s 120 can be read as not exclusively defining all forms of infringement but rather expanding the owner's rights of action beyond unauthorised use of identical marks in relation to goods or services for which they are registered. Note also that, as mentioned above, s 7 provides that a court may decide a person has used a mark if that person has used the mark with alterations and/or additions that do not substantially affect the identity of the mark. It appears to be the case that if words are added to a mark by an alleged infringer, a court may either proceed under s 7 and determine whether the identity of the mark has been substantially affected, or proceed under s 120 and ask whether the mark, with the alterations or additions, is substantially identical or deceptively similar (thus preferring the approach in *Mark Foy's Ltd v Davies & Co-op Co Ltd* (1956) 95 CLR 190 (the *Tub Happy* case) over the approach suggested by Fitzgerald J in *Angoves Pty Ltd v Johnson* (1982) 43 ALR 349, where the mark ST AGNES was used in ST AGNES LIQUOR STORE in the suburb of St Agnes). Underlying these two alternatives is an important initial step: determining what exactly the defendant was using as a trade mark.

This question is well illustrated by *Wellness Pty Ltd v Pro Bio Living Waters Pty Ltd* (2004) 61 IPR 242. The applicant's mark was 'Living Water', inter alia registered for bottled, spring and mineral water. Bennett J held that the phrase 'Pro Bio Living Waters' on the respondent's bottled water consisted of two separate marks: 'Pro Bio' and 'Living Waters', rather than a single composite mark. The use of 'Living Waters', although in the presence of a further mark, was still trade mark use and the two marks were substantially identical. A similar issue was considered in the *Budweiser/Budvar* case: *Anheuser-Busch Inc v Budejovicky Budvar* (2002) 56 IPR 182 at 219. The terms of s 120 ('substantially identical or deceptively similar') are also found in s 44, which applies to registration of marks (see Chapter 15 Registered Trade Marks: Other Requirements) and have already been considered in that context: see also *Shell v Esso*. A recent example of the similarity tests in the context of infringement is to be found in *MID Sydney Pty Ltd v Australian Tourism Co Ltd* (*Chifley Tower* case) (1998) 90 FCR 236; 42 IPR 561. The question in the latter case was whether the mark 'Chifley Tower', registered by the owners of the Chifley Tower residential complex in Sydney, would be infringed by the use of the word 'Chifley' in connection with hotels the respondent proposed to establish. The decision on appeal contains a useful summary of principles to be applied. An example of relatively slight differences between word marks is found in *Beecham Group Plc v Colgate-Palmolive Pty Ltd* (2005) 66 IPR 273: 'MaxClean' was held not to be deceptively similar to 'Macleans': at [54]ff.

Where a composite mark is registered and only one part of the mark is alleged to have been replicated by the respondent, a judgment will be required as to whether that part is an essential part of the registered mark. In *Crazy Ron's Communications Pty Ltd v Mobileworld Communications Pty Ltd* (2004) 61 IPR 212, the Full Court overturned the trial judge's decision and held that the words 'Crazy John' were not an essential element of the applicant's trademark consisting of the words 'CRAZY JOHN' with graphics of a man atop a globe holding a mobile phone; they were just one of a number of prominent features of the mark. Thus, the finding that the two marks were deceptively similar, which had focused on comparing only the words 'Crazy John' with the impugned mark 'Crazy Ron', could not stand. A further recent example, useful because it concerns a series of marks that in the result were found to fall on either side of the fence, is *Yves St Laurent Parfums v Louden Cosmetics Ltd* (1997) 39 IPR 11, decided under relevantly similar provisions — s 8 of the New Zealand Trade Marks Act 1953. The defendant had marketed perfumes under the names Kosmos, Java, Paradise and Optimism, which according to the plaintiff were too close to its Kouros, Jazz, Paris and Opium registered trade marks. The word 'Kosmos' was found to infringe the mark Kouros: virtually nobody in New Zealand would be aware of its meaning (the ancient Greek word for young man or boy), and its significance was thus more graphical than etymological. The resemblance from that point of view was so strong that '[t]he infringement is palpable, there being not merely a likelihood but an inevitability of deceit and confusion': at IPR 22. However, OPIUM/OPTIMISM and JAZZ/JAVA fell on the other side of the fence. None of those words would, in the mind of ordinary New Zealanders, 'either graphically, etymologically or connotatively' be associated in a relevant sense. If any confusion or deception did arise, it would be due to the visible context in which the marks were used, not from any resemblance between them. The Full Court of the Federal Court in Australia addressed some of the issues in a unanimous judgment in *Starr Partners Pty Ltd v Dev Prem Pty Ltd* (2007) 71 IPR 459: see, in particular, at IPR 462–4. The appellant's mark, registered for real estate services, was 'Starr Partners' represented in a certain way against a blue background and with a star-like device in front; the respondent used the mark Star Realty also with a stylised star and against a blue background. The Full Court held the two marks to so nearly resemble each other as to deceive or cause confusion (see s 10). The essential features, which had to be compared and which consumers would retain, were the word 'star(r)' and the star device before it. The different words 'Partners' and 'Realty' would be glossed over by consumers: there was nothing striking or distinctive about the use of those words in the context of real estate services. What would be remembered were the star device and the 'star kind of word': see at IPR 464. Because the mark was the star device combined with the words, aural comparison was of little relevance in the circumstances. The Full Court criticised the trial judge for over-emphasising side-by-side comparison 'at the expense of considerations of imperfect recollection' (see at IPR 464), which lies at the heart of the test of deceptive similarity. The importance of a careful analysis of the detail and context of the impugned use for the sake of determining deceptive similarity is apparent from the decision in the *Adidas* case (see above 16.4). The set of four stripes on some of the shoe models was found to have been deceptively similar to the Adidas three stripe mark; others not. This decision is also notable for its analysis of the probative value of intention to deceive, which is analogous to its role in the context of passing off: 'where there is a finding of intention to deceive, the court may more readily infer that the intention has been or in all probability, will be effective': *Adidas* at [103], quoting from *Campomar Sociedad Limitada v Nike International Ltd* (2000) 46 IPR 481; [2000] HCA 12 at [33]. *Coca-Cola Co v PepsiCo Inc (No 2)* illustrates that it will sometimes be difficult to 'construe' what the registered mark actually is — in this case the outlines or silhouettes of the Coca-Cola bottle shape were registered. The court listed all the visual differences with PepsiCo's actual bottle and found that its three-dimensional shape was distinctive in its own right — and therefore not deceptively similar.

Use in relation to related goods or services: s 120(2)

16.7 In the *Starr Partners* case, the impugned mark was clearly used for exactly the same services as those for which the appellant's mark was registered, so liability was 'automatic' under s 120(1) once the two marks were found to be too similar. Liability under s 120(1) does not depend on proving that there has been actual or potential deception or confusion; nor can the defendant escape liability by proving that consumers were not, in fact, deceived. But the facts are not always that simple: the goods or services in relation to which the impugned mark is used are often not exactly the same but arguably related to the goods or services of registration. In that situation, liability may still lie under s 120(2).

Liability under this subsection is dependent on two conditions: first, that the goods or services in relation to which the impugned mark is used are 'of the same description' or 'closely related' to those for which the plaintiff's mark is registered (for precise terms, see s 120(2)(a), (b), (c)); and, second, the defendant in a suit under s 120(2) may escape liability if they can establish that the use of the impugned mark is not likely to deceive or cause confusion. The onus is on the defendant and is not necessarily easy to discharge. As to the meaning of the terms used in s 120(2)(a), (b) and (c), see *Southern Cross Refrigerating Co v Toowoomba Foundry Pty Ltd* (1954) 91 CLR 592; 1A IPR 465 and *Re J Lyons & Co Ltd's Application* [1959] RPC 120 at 128; and for a more recent consideration under the Trade Marks Act 1995 see the *Chifley Tower* case and also see 16.9 below. In the latter case, it was held that hotel services were not services of the same description as property management services. See also *Coca-Cola Co v All-Fect Distributors (t/as Millers Distributing Co)* (1998) 43 IPR 47, where Coca-Cola confectionery and beverages were held not to be goods of the same description; this decision was reversed on appeal in *Coca-Cola Co v All-Fect Distributors Ltd* (1999) 96 FCR 107; 47 IPR 481; [1999] FCA 1721, but on a technicality. The principles are the same as apply in the context of s 44 (see above Chapter 15 Registered Trade Marks: Other Requirements; and in particular, more recently, *Accor* (above 16.2).

On a final point, *Nokia Corporation v Truong* (2005) 66 IPR 511 illustrates the importance, as a first step, of deciding which goods (or services) are actually included in the specification; that is, for which goods or services the trade mark is actually registered. Crennan J held that neck straps were included in the word 'accessories' for telephones that the Nokia trade mark was registered for. Alternatively, if they were not the same goods, they were goods of the same description under s 120(2): they were 'goods for use as an accessory to a mobile phone or handsfree set, and … neck straps are used to hold these items and that the trade channels through which they are sold, such as mobile phone shops like those operated by the respondents, are common trade channels': at IPR 519.

Use in relation to unrelated goods or services: well-known marks under s 120(3)

16.8 The use of a registered trade mark on totally unrelated goods or services may still be actionable by virtue of s 120(3), but the option is available only in relation to a well-known mark. This provision originates in art 16(3) of the Trade-Related Aspects of Intellectual Property Rights (TRIPS) Agreement, which required stronger domestic protection for famous marks than was hitherto given in Australia. 'Dilution' is putative damage to the reputation and thus value of a trade mark in the absence of deception of consumers or actual diversion of trade, which is the case where a mark is used on totally different goods or services. As will become apparent below, whether s 120(3) is, in fact, an anti-dilution measure is controversial.

Handler argues that it is, but Australian law arguably does not provide remedies against dilution in the absence of deception, even for the most famous marks.[1] 'Well known' as used in the Trade Marks Act is a term of art with a specific meaning: see s 120(3)(a). The concept is not statutorily defined, but by virtue of s 120(4), one must take into account 'the extent to which the trade mark is known within the relevant sector of the public, whether as a result of promotion of the trade mark or for any other reason'. This indicates that the extent to which the marked goods or services are traded is not necessarily determinative; heavy promotion alone could theoretically render a mark well known.

Such universally known trade marks as Coca-Cola, Ford and Cadbury spring to mind, but s 120(4) also suggests that 'well' known does not necessarily mean 'universally' known; that is, it is implicit in s 120(4) that a mark known only to a sector of the public can still be a well-known mark. Nonetheless, it is also implicit in s 120(3) that a well-known mark is one whose attractive goodwill extends beyond the category of goods or services for which it is registered. In other words, even when it is used in relation to goods or services for which it was hitherto not registered, consumers would think there is a connection with the trade mark owner. In practice, the focus tends to be on the extent of promotion and advertising, the number of outlets or establishments, and the market share of the applicant: see, for example, *San Remo Macaroni Company Pty Ltd v San Remo Gourmet Coffee Pty Ltd* (2000) 50 IPR 321 (relating to use of the Sam Remo mark for pasta products in relation to coffee) and *Lone Star Steakhouse & Saloon v Zurcas* (2000) 48 IPR 325. The test as to whether a trade mark is well known in Australia for the purposes of infringement is related to the test concerning s 60: see *Hills Industries Ltd v Bitek Pty Ltd* (2011) 214 FCR 396; 90 IPR 337; [2011] FCA 94.

---

1. M Handler, 'Trade Mark Dilution in Australia?' (2008) *UNSWLR* 48; and M Handler, 'What Can Harm the Reputation of a Trademark? A Critical Re-Evaluation of Dilution by Tarnishment' [2016] *UNSWLRS* 41.

In that matter it was also stressed that the volume of sales of goods is not necessarily a measure of the status of the mark — it is the mark that must be well known, not the goods themselves.

However, simply proving that the mark is well known is only the first step in establishing liability under s 120(3). The plaintiff must also establish that because the mark is well known the sign would be likely to be taken as indicating a connection between the unrelated goods or services and the registered owner of the trade mark (s 120(3)(c)), and that for that reason, the interests of the registered owner are likely to be adversely affected (see s 120(3)(d)). Although there may be some overlap, one distinction between s 120(3)(a) and 120(3)(c) is that in considering the latter, the question relates to the specific goods or services in relation to which the impugned mark has been used. In practice, the cumulative requirements of s 120(3) impose a considerable onus on an applicant for relief (as is arguably appropriate where the impugned use is in relation to goods or services in which the trade mark owner does not actually trade, thus potentially amounting to an unwarranted restraint on competition). There is an interesting question here as to the relationship between the protection of a well-known mark under s 120 and defensive registration: concerning the latter, see Chapter 15 Registered Trade Marks: Other Requirements.

An advantage of defensive registration is that an action in infringement will normally lie under s 120(1), with its attendant evidentiary advantages over s 120(2) and (3). However, it seems clear that some marks would be sufficiently well known for the purposes of s 120(3) but would not be sufficiently well known to qualify for defensive registration. For an example of brand extension of a famous mark, see *Nike International Ltd v United Pharmaceutical Industries (Aust) Pty Ltd & Campomar Sociedad Limitada* (1996) 35 IPR 385 and *Campomar Sociedad Limitada v Nike International Ltd* (2000) 46 IPR 481. Although this was an application for removal of a mark, it illustrates the potential difficulties an owner of a famous mark faces in managing its brand extension decisions. (The case was concerned with the unauthorised use of the NIKE trade mark on perfumes.) In *Coca-Cola Co v All-Fect Distributors (t/as Millers Distributing Co)* (see above), it was conceded without argument by the respondent that each of the Coca-Cola trade marks were well-known marks in terms of s 120(3). Note that the common law action in passing off and s 18 of the Australian Consumer Law may provide further potential grounds for a remedy in cases where a well-known mark is used on unrelated goods or services.

Other Forms of Infringement

Second-hand goods and parallel importation: exhaustion of rights

16.9 By virtue of s 123, it is arguable that under the Trade Marks Act 1995, once legitimately trade-marked goods (or, in theory, services) have entered the market, the owner of the registered trade mark has no further statutory control over any dealings with or in those goods (the 'exhaustion doctrine'). Section 123 provides that use of a trade mark in relation to goods or services for which it is registered is not an infringement if 'the trade mark has been applied to, or in relation to, the goods by, or with the consent of, the registered owner of the trade mark'. This means that dealing in legitimately trade-marked goods within Australia and importation of trade-marked goods bearing a mark applied by or with the consent of the Australian trade mark owner can normally not infringe s 120. In other words, 'international exhaustion' applies in Australian trade marks law. Arguably, s 123 expressly provides something that, except in relation to importation, is already implicit in other provisions of the Act; it has been argued that 'use' of a mark extends only to unauthorised application of the mark in relation to goods, conduct that would have the effect of misleading consumers as to the true origin. From that point of view, even in the absence of s 123, dealing locally in goods in relation to which the mark has been applied by the trade mark owner would not infringe. This argument arose in *Brother Industries Ltd v Dynamic Supplies Pty Ltd* (2007) 163 FCR 530; 73 IPR 507 (see at IPR 518). However, in the circumstances of the case, it could not save the defendant. The latter had obtained unbranded printer drum units that had possibly been manufactured by or for the purposes of Brother, the trade mark owner, which supplied both branded drums and unbranded drums to wholesalers. The defendant obtained some of the unbranded drums overseas and sold them into Australia in packaging to which it had applied the Brother trade mark. It submitted that since the drums were made by or on behalf of Brother (which was, in fact, disputed) and were therefore sourced with that company, there was no infringing use of the trade mark. However, the court rejected this argument. It also did not accept that the consent section, s 123, could save the defendant. It held that the critical question was (at IPR 525):

> As pointed out in Davison M, Johnston K and Kennedy P, *Shanahan's Australian Law of Trade Marks and Passing Off* (3rd ed, LawBook Co., 2003) at [19.40], the '*critical issue in the context of the defence under s 123 of the Act ... is whether the registered owner in Australia has consented to the application of the trade mark to the goods*'. Although that observation was made in the context of passingoff claims, it is equally applicable to cases, such as the present case, where the registered owner of the trade mark did not apply or authorise the application of its mark to or in relation to the goods in question. Accordingly, in order to make out a defence under s 123 of the Act, Dynamic Supplies must demonstrate that the application of the 'BROTHER' trade mark was done with Brother Japan's express or implied consent. (Emphasis in original)

This the defendant, Dynamic Supplies, was unable to do.

Nonetheless, use of a mark is not restricted to applying a mark without authorisation but also extends to dealing in goods bearing an unauthorised mark, even by persons who have not applied the mark: see *E & J Gallo Winery v Lion Nathan Australia Pty Ltd* (2009) 175 FCR 386; [2009] FCAFC 27 at [58] as cited in *Paul's Retail Pty Ltd v Sporte Leisure Pty Ltd* (2012) 202 FCR 286; 95 IPR 151; [2012] FCAFC 51. There is no statutory provision concerning secondary civil liability (ie, for authorising or abetting trade mark infringement or supplying goods with infringing trade marks); general tort principles will apply: see *Louis Vuitton Malletier SA v Toea Pty Ltd* (2006) 156 FCR 158; 70 IPR 307, concerning liability of the organisers of markets for the sale of counterfeit goods by stallholders. However, note that selling falsely marked goods may constitute a criminal offence: see s 148. Although s 123 has the beneficial effect of expressly clarifying the underlying position now in relation to interpretation — as is also confirmed in *Transport Tyre Sales Pty Ltd v Montana Tyres Rims and Tubes Pty Ltd* (1999) 93 FCR 421; 43 IPR 481 (see also 16.10) — it is arguable that some of the uncertainty in specific circumstances that existed under the 1955 Act has still not been entirely removed by s 123 of the 1995 Act.

There are two principal areas of difficulty with the application of the exhaustion doctrine, one relating to dealing in legitimately trade marked goods generally and another in relation to parallel importation or grey marketing:

- first, the rights of the registered trade mark owner in relation to alterations made to legitimately trade-marked goods or to trade marks themselves after goods have entered the market; and
- second, the extent and application of international exhaustion, the question being whether the registered owner of a trade mark in Australia has really lost all its ability to control parallel imports of legitimately trade-marked goods.

As to the first question, absolute loss of control over the way other people trade in legitimately trade-marked goods does give rise to concerns for trade mark owners whose marked goods are subsequently altered and then sold on: see *Wingate Marketing Pty Ltd v Levi Strauss & Co* (1994) 49 FCR 89; 28 IPR 193. The sale of legitimately marked goods that have been detrimentally altered could dilute goodwill. In *Wingate Marketing* (a decision under the previous Act), the marked clothing was deliberately ripped and discoloured before being sold on by a second-hand dealer. Similar concerns exist about the importation of legitimately marked goods purchased abroad: such importation may traverse a multinational trade mark owner's global market segmentation strategies. Quality differentials between various national markets may result in confusion and deception of consumers who have come to associate the trade mark with certain qualities and standards that do not, in fact, apply in the jurisdiction from which goods are parallel imported. In *Scandinavian Tobacco Group Eersel BV v Trojan Trading Company Pty Ltd* (2016) 243 FCR 152; 119 IPR 247; [2016] FCAFC 91 an issue was whether s 123 applied when a trade mark previously applied to goods by or with the consent of the registered owner are removed and subsequently applied by an importer who re-packages the goods for the purpose of sale in Australia. The court was satisfied that s 123(1) applied and therefore there was no infringement; its reasons include a useful discussion of the policy background of s 123.

Nonetheless, the case of *Parfums Christian Dior (Australia) Pty Ltd v Dimmeys Stores Pty Ltd* (1997) 39 IPR 349 provides an interesting proviso to the general rule that the trade mark owner loses control over marked goods that have entered the marketplace. In that case, a discount trader offered unboxed testers of Christian Dior perfumes for sale, which Christian Dior had imported for distribution to authorised dealers as testers and which were in inferior packaging marked 'not for sale'. Branson J cited *Champagne Heidsieck et Compagnie Monopole SA v Buxton* [1930] 1 Ch 330 and *Fender Australia Pty Ltd v Bevk (t/as Guitar Crazy)* (1989) 15 IPR 257; 25 FCR 161 in support of the following proposition, accepted by both sides:

> Ordinarily a registered proprietor cannot succeed in a claim for infringement where what is being offered for sale are genuine goods upon which the registered proprietor's mark is properly used, it having been placed there as a badge of origin by the registered proprietor itself.

But her Honour then quoted a passage from Lord Wright's speech in *Aristoc Ltd v Rysta Ltd* [1945] AC 68 at 101: 'The fundamental idea of the function of a trade mark … [is] to indicate the origin of the goods, … […] The word "origin" … denotes at least that the goods are issued as vendible goods under the aegis of the proprietor of the trade mark.' Thus, on an application for an interim injunction, her Honour was led to the conclusion that there was a serious issue to be tried, at 354: '… on the basis that the second applicant, by making it clear by markings on the product that it was not for sale, has indicated that no express or implied consent is given to the use of the marks in connection with the sale of the goods'. The exhaustion theory would apply only if the goods entered the market as 'vendible goods', which the testers with their 'not for sale' markings were arguably not. (Interestingly, her Honour cited *Castrol Ltd v Automotive Oil Supplies Ltd* [1983] RPC 315 in support of this proposition. That case had to do with parallel importation and may now be of rather doubtful relevance. Nonetheless, there is little doubt that her Honour's finding in this case, that there was at least a serious issue to be tried, is well supported.) See also *Brother Industries*, above, where the sale of unmarked goods, although they were made by Brother, did not imply that another unrelated person had the right to apply the Brother marks to the goods. Brother was entitled to control the use of its marks and choose to supply some of its goods with the marks and others without; note, however, the facts and what was held in the *Scandinavian Tobacco* case.

In any case, in relation to the issue of modifications of trade-marked goods or trade marks themselves, the Trade Marks Act 1995 has expressly addressed the legitimate concerns of trade mark owners by giving the registered owner a statutory right to restrict certain specified post-sale uses. By virtue of s 121, a trade mark owner may attach a notice to trade-marked goods prohibiting:

- the making of alterations to the goods or to the mark on the goods or used in relation to goods;
- the addition of another mark; or
- using on goods or their packaging any material that is likely to injure the reputation of the goods.

If another person breaches the restrictions by doing an act that is prohibited on the notice, the owner may bring an action in infringement, subject to a good faith defence.

Parallel importation under the 1995 Act

16.10 The intention of the 1995 Act was to clearly enshrine the doctrine of international exhaustion of trade mark rights. Section 123 translates this policy into statutory terms; for general background see M Handler and R Burrell, 'A Requiem for *Champagne Heidsieck*: Trade Mark Use and Parallel Importation' [2016] *UNSWLRS* 40.

In *Montana Tyres Rims & Tubes Pty Ltd v Transport Tyre Sales Pty Ltd* (1998) 155 ALR 489; 41 IPR 301; [1998] FCA 708 and *Transport Tyre Sales Pty Ltd v Montana Tyres Rims and Tubes Pty Ltd* (1999) 93 FCR 421; 43 IPR 481; [1999] FCA 329, the Federal Court had an opportunity to consider the impact of s 123 and the related question of the appropriate form of an assignment of a trade mark by an international trade mark owner to a local (exclusive) distributor for the purported purpose of restricting parallel importation.

Japanese tyre manufacturer Ohtsu assigned its Australian-registered trade marks (OHTSU and FALKEN) to its local Australian distributor (TTS), who had become concerned about parallel importation of Ohtsu tyres sourced in Singapore. The Registrar recorded the assignment, not having been informed that Ohtsu and the local assignee had also executed a reassignment option deed. The business of assignee and assignor continued just as before the assignment; that is, Ohtsu continued to mould the trade mark into the tyres in Japan, and the distributor did not add to or alter the tyres at all. The purpose of the assignment was to enable the local assignee to bring an action against a parallel importer (Montana) of Ohtsu tyres, who sourced legitimately marked tyres mostly in Singapore. Once the marks in Australia were assigned by Ohtsu to TTS, s 123 would not operate, since the marks would not have been applied by the post-assignment owner. Montana refused to accede to some of the assignee's demands, resulting in the present action. The trial judge, Wilcox J, held that the Australian registered marks (OHTSU and FALKEN) would not suggest a connection with the assignee of the marks but rather a continued connection with the assignor (Ohtsu) in Japan. The latter had not caused any disassociation from the original connotation of the mark and remained the registered owner of the mark in other jurisdictions, as well as having the right to reacquire the mark in Australia. The marks were thus incapable of distinguishing the goods distributed by the assignee from those distributed by others.

In other words, when a local distributor becomes the local registered owner of a mark, there must be a clear disassociation from the original significance (ie, goods originating with the assignor) to support the conclusion that the mark has become exclusively distinctive of the local distributor's goods or services. (As to the circumstances under which a trade mark may be used so as to effect a statement about the identity of a distributor as opposed to a manufacturer, see *Major Brothers v Franklin and Son* [1908] 1 KB 712.) His Honour also pointed out that the Registrar would probably not have registered the assignment if aware of the deed of reassignment. He also held that as the marks connoted a connection with Ohtsu, they also caused confusion or deception within the meaning of s 43 (s 88(2)(c) thus did not apply): see *Montana* (1988) 155 ALR at 498ff; 41 IPR at 311ff. However, the Full Court disagreed on the question of the assignment of the marks, accepting it as formally valid. Having come to that conclusion, the Full Court was obliged to consider the issue of infringement. Determinative of that question was the meaning and impact of s 123, and the court interpreted that section as enshrining the international exhaustion theory in Australian trade marks law. But the importation of the trade-marked goods by Montana did not amount to an infringement, since the marks had been applied by Ohtsu before assignment of the trade mark rights in Australia to TTS, and s 123 thus applied. However, as Dwyer and Yates point out:[2]

> No mention is made [in the judgment of the Full Court], however, of the rationale of preventing deception and confusion of the public in this context, and, as a result, the reasoning underlying the judgment does not appear to allow an exception in a situation where the imported genuine goods are in fact of a lesser quality or safety standard than the domestic genuine goods.

As to the restrictions that can be imposed in cases where the imported goods, although genuinely marked, are of a different quality than those supplied via authorised

2. See J W Dwyer and D L Yates, 'Montana Case — its Legal and Commercial Implications' (1998) 9 *AIPJ* 200.

distributorships (eg, because they come from a market with different product standards), one option open to the trade mark owner would be to argue that the grey marketing of such goods is misleading or deceptive, as the goods have different qualities than the consumer would expect. Alternatively, the question might arise as to what exactly the trade mark owner has actually allowed, authorised or licensed in relation to the marking of, and dealing in, the goods: see, for example, *Paul's Retail* above 16.9. For a further illustration of the difficulties and complexities that can result from the relationship between different parties in various jurisdictions with an interest in a trade mark and trade-marked goods and services, see *Dunlop* above 16.1.

Importation of goods bearing infringing marks

16.11 Section 123 applies only where a trade mark has been applied by or with the consent of the registered owner. Importation of goods bearing trade marks applied without the authorisation of the owner is, naturally, an infringing act: see, for example, *Sony Entertainment Australia Pty Ltd v Saleh* [2001] FCA 717 and *Playboy Enterprises International Inc v You Tao Hong* (2004) 63 IPR 533. Cases such as these illustrate the process involved under ss 131–43 of the Act, which allow the registered trade mark owner to restrain the importation of goods bearing infringing marks. The trade mark owner can choose to put the Customs CEO on notice concerning the anticipated importation of infringing goods. The Customs CEO is then empowered to seize imported goods that infringe or appear to infringe the registered trade mark. The trade mark owner (the 'objector') must initiate an action for infringement within 10 days from the date of the seizure of goods by Customs; failing this, Customs may release the goods to the importer. Normally, security in the amount of the anticipated costs to the Commonwealth will be required. The Customs CEO may release or refuse to seize the goods if satisfied, because of information that has come to their knowledge, that there are no reasonable grounds for believing that the notified trade mark has been infringed. The court hearing the infringement action may order the person giving the notice to pay damages if unsuccessful to the owner of the imported goods for the loss or damage suffered due to the seizure of the goods.

The Trade Marks Act 1995 makes no provision for security for damages that the importer of goods suffers if goods are seized but no action for infringement is brought. However, the period during which the goods remain seized is only 10 days, and the Customs CEO can, in any case, release goods earlier if satisfied that there are no reasonable grounds for believing that the trade mark has been infringed by the importation of the goods: s 136(3). Once the action in infringement is brought, the court may make orders in relation to the goods held by Customs.

Exceptions and Defences

Certain uses of trade marks in good faith

16.12 As is discussed above, only unauthorised use of a mark *as a mark* constitutes infringement; that is, use as a badge of origin. Either the application of an infringing mark or a dealing in goods bearing an infringing mark may be actionable. However, some specified trade mark uses do not constitute an infringement, even though the use may well fall within the scope of infringement. Section 122(1)(a)–(g) of the Trade Marks Act 1995 provides that the use in good faith of certain kinds of marks does not infringe: principally, use of a personal or business name or of some descriptive or informative term indicating quality, kind, purpose, origin and so on of the goods or services. Use 'in good faith' (previously known as 'bona fide use') means 'honest' use: *Baume & Co Ltd v AH Moore Ltd* [1958] RPC 226. The defendant must show that they acted honestly 'and without any ulterior motive': *Johnson & Johnson* (above 16.3 per Gummow J at FCR 353–4. An example of a good faith descriptive use of a mark is provided by *Australian Postal Corporation v Digital Post Australia* (2013) 105 IPR 1; [2013] FCAFC 153 (see at [71]ff). In adopting for its business the name 'Digital Post Australia', the respondent chose terms that were descriptive of its services, without seeking to associate itself with Australia Post or 'to "leverage" any of its brands': at [57]. In *Anakin Pty Ltd v Chatswood BBQ King Pty Ltd* (2008) 79 IPR 44; [2008] FCA 1467, s 122(1)(b)(i) was at issue, which provides as follows: '(1) In spite of section 120, a person does not infringe a registered trade mark when: … (b) the person uses a sign in good faith to indicate: (i) the kind, quality, quantity, … geographical origin, or some other characteristic, of goods or services; …'. The respondent gave evidence that the name 'Chatswood BBQ King' was chosen because it had previously been used for the sale of Chinese roast meats; the word 'King' signified top quality; and the business was located in Chatswood. However, the court did not accept the respondent's account concerning his choice of the name, and concluded that he chose it to benefit from the reputation of the applicant's restaurant. He had thus not acted in good faith. Use in good faith requires a finding of absence of ulterior motive: see *Angoves Pty Ltd v Johnson*. In *Wellness* (see above 16.6), Bennett J said at [43]:

> The requirement for the use to be in good faith imports an absence of intention to make use of the goodwill which has been acquired by another trader. The resemblance between the registered trade mark, of which the first respondent was aware and the name of the first respondent does not prevent the use being bona fide provided that there was an honest belief that no confusion would arise and if there were no intention of wrongfully diverting business … Evidence of such an honest belief is necessary to establish 'bona fide use' … (Citations omitted)

Absence of good faith cannot necessarily be inferred from the striking similarity between two marks: see, for example, *Geoffrey Inc v Luik* (1997) 38 IPR 555 concerning the Toys-R-Us mark. Whether the mark has been used in good faith must be determined taking into account all the circumstances of the case; for instance, in *Sterling Pharmaceuticals Pty Ltd v Johnson & Johnson Australia Pty Ltd* (1990) 18 IPR 309, the defence was not made out, because Johnson & Johnson used the mark 'Caplets' deliberately after receiving advice concerning its registration and the potentially infringing nature of its use, and in circumstances where the use was shown to be part of an international strategy to render the mark generic. Thus, a defence of good faith will be difficult to sustain if the evidence discloses deliberate copying of other aspects of a business, such as the restaurant menus in *Noodle Box Pty Ltd v Dave's Noodle Box* (2002) AIPC ¶91-816; [2002] FCA 579. Where s 122 permits use of a mark for a certain purpose (eg, to indicate that an accessory is to be used with trade-marked goods), the defence must be borne out by the precise circumstances of the use.

In *Nokia Corporation v Mai* (2003) 59 IPR 413, the defence of s 122(1)(c) in relation to use of the Nokia mark on accessories failed because of the absence of words such as 'for use with' a Nokia phone. It is obvious that in many cases where good faith use is in issue it will be equally open to the defendant to cross-claim for the removal of the mark from the register or to argue that the impugned use is not use as a trade mark. That also applies in the case of s 122(d), use of a mark for the purposes of comparative advertising. The remaining three defences (s 122(e), (f), (g)) are concerned with the extent of the actual or potential rights of plaintiff and defendant. A registered trade mark is not infringed where:

- the person exercises a right under the Trade Marks Act 1995;
- the court is of the opinion that the person would be able to obtain registration for the mark; or
- the act is not an infringement, because of a condition or limitation to which the registered trade mark is subject.

In relation to the adoption of a shape for goods that turns out to be registered as a shape mark, where the court held that the defence would have been made out if the conduct had been held to be infringing in the first place, see *Mayne Industries* (concerning an S-shaped fence dropper; see also 16.4). In relation to a corporation using its own name in good faith (s 122(1)(a)(i)), see *Anchorage Capital Partners Pty Ltd v ACPA Pty Ltd* (2018) 259 FCR 514; 128 IPR 255; [2018] FCAFC 6 at [207]. As far as s 122(1)(fa) is concerned, which provides that there is a defence to infringement where the court 'is of the opinion that [the infringer] would obtain registration of the ... deceptively similar trade mark in his or her name if the person were to apply for it', see also *Anchorage*, and *Sensis Pty Ltd v Senses Direct Mail and Fulfillment Pty Ltd* [2019] FCA 719 at [42]ff.

Other defences: prior use; generic trade marks; goods previously produced under patent

16.13 By virtue of s 124, where a person has continuously used an unregistered trade mark, either from a time before the registration of the substantially identical or deceptively similar mark or from before a registered owner or user of the mark first used the mark, whichever is earlier, the registered mark is not infringed by the use of a substantially identical or deceptively similar unregistered mark. The defence may extend to use in a certain area within Australia only if the prior use was only in that area: see s 124(2). The prior use exception extends to use on similar and closely related goods and services (in accordance with s 14, similar goods includes identical goods). It does not appear to apply where the registered mark is a well-known mark in an action under s 120(3). Presumably, it would be impossible for the plaintiff to establish the matters required to be proven under s 120(3) if there were evidence of some concurrent use of the mark by another person in Australia. A defendant may often have a choice between asserting prior user rights or counterclaiming for invalidity on the basis that the registration of the plaintiff's mark is not valid because it is not distinctive (given the market use of a similar unregistered mark on similar goods), because it is deceptive or confusing or because the defendant is the actual owner of the mark. For an example of prior use of an identical trade mark, see *EOS Australia Pty Ltd v Expo Tomei Pty Ltd*

(1998) 42 IPR 277. The prior use must have been continuous for the relevant period in Australia: *Anchorage* at [221].

A further defence is afforded by s 24, which relates to trade marks that have become generic or, in the precise terms of s 24(1), in circumstances where a trade mark 'becomes generally accepted within the relevant trade as the sign that describes or is the name of an article, substance, or thing' (eg, a 'kleenex', for a tissue; to 'google', to perform an internet search). From the date on which the sign first becomes generic, the registered owner no longer has the exclusive right to use the mark in relation to the goods or services to which it refers.

In *Powell v Glow Zone Products Pty Ltd* (1997) 39 IPR 506, a case relating to the registered mark CAPS THE GAME, the operative part of the mark being CAPS, the Full Court found that, on the facts, the word 'CAPS' had been used generically subsequent to registration, depriving the applicant of his exclusive rights. The use of the word 'CAPS' to describe the game had become widespread in the trade, existed among customers for the product 'no matter who was the manufacturer, distributor or vendor of it' (as the trial court put it, see *Powell v Glow Zone Products Pty Ltd* (1996) 36 IPR 343 at 377) and was well known and established. See also *FH Faulding & Co Ltd v Imperial Chemical Industries (ICI)* (1965) 112 CLR 537: use of the term 'SAVLON, a barrier cream' was not an infringement, because the registered trade mark BARRIER had become generic.

Note that we are considering here a defence that is distinct from a counterclaim for invalidity; cancellation of a mark or removal of an entry will be ordered only in cases where the trade mark becomes generic due to some degree of blameworthy conduct on the part of the registered owner. Such blameworthy conduct (ie, conduct of the trade mark owner that contributed to the mark becoming generic in an otherwise avoidable manner) need not be established for s 24 to come into operation.

Finally, s 25 provides an excuse where a trade mark relates to an article formerly manufactured under patent: see, for example, *Mayne* (above 16.4).

Maintaining the Validity of a Registered Trade Mark: Ongoing User Requirements

The non-use application

16.14 One of the main principles inherent in trade mark registration is that no person should be permitted to monopolise a trade mark by registration without also using it, and this applies to all classes of goods or services for which it is registered individually. We have seen that either the trade mark must be in use or the registered owner must have a genuine intention to use the trade mark at the time of the application, for every class for which the trade mark is registered. To maintain the registration after acceptance, use must continue and must be sufficient. However, this does not mean that there are no unused trade marks on the register; after registration, the Registrar is not required ex officio to remove unused marks or to investigate whether they are being used. It also does not mean that there can never be an interruption or period of non-use, as is explained further below. Use in terms of infringement and in terms of ownership are closely related: a party might meet an allegation of infringement by establishing that it had in fact used the mark before the applicant applied to have it registered. That prior use can then be the basis for a finding that the alleged infringer is in fact the owner of the mark for the purpose of registration: see, for example, the facts in *Anchorage* (where it was also found that trade marks appearing on promotional slides sent to potential investors in Australia amounted to sufficient trade mark use to support a claim to ownership for the purpose of registration in this country).

Removal of a trade mark for non-use may occur upon the written request of the owner (s 84) or removal may result from an application to the Registrar by any person: s 92(1); the Registrar may refer the application to a prescribed court for determination (s 94). The relevant use must be of the registered mark itself and not some other mark or modification or composition. Once an allegation of non-use is made in a non-use application, the onus shifts to the owner of the mark to establish relevant use. This reversal of the onus of proof was an important innovation of the Trade Marks Act 1995. The owner is referred to as the 'opponent' in the relevant sections in the Act, because they oppose the non-use application: s 100.

There are two bases for a non-use application:

1. On the day of the application for the registration of the mark, the owner did not have the intention in good faith, either personally or by another, to exploit the trade mark in relation to the goods or services for which it was registered, and has not in fact done so within the prescribed parameters before the filing date of the non-use application: see s 92(4)(a).
2. The trade mark has not been used in good faith for any 3-year period ending 1 month before the filing of the non-use application: see s 92(4)(b).

By virtue of s 92(2), an application for removal for non-use can be either in relation to all the goods or services for which the mark is registered or for any one of those goods or services. In *McHattan v Australian Specialised Vehicle Systems Pty Ltd* (1996) 34 IPR 537 at 543, Drummond J had this to say concerning the non-use provisions of the 1995 Act in this context:

> The statute now makes clear that a mark can be limited by an order made on a non-use application to exclude goods in respect of which the mark was originally registered, but in respect of which specific goods the proprietor has not used his mark, while leaving his registration otherwise intact. Just as it was well-established by authority that s 23 of the 1955 Act conferred a discretion not to remove or limit a registered mark even though relevant non-use was shown — see *Carl Zeiss Pty Ltd's Application* (1969) 122 CLR 1 — so does s 101 of the *Trade Marks Act 1995* (Cth) confer a discretion not to remove a mark from the Register or limit a registered mark to exclude from its scope specific goods in relation to which the registered proprietor of the mark has been unable to prove relevant use of his mark. In these respects, the liability of a registered mark to removal or limitation is much the same under both the 1955 and the 1995 Acts.

No great level of use is required: see *Moorgate Tobacco Co Ltd v Philip Morris Ltd (No 2)* (1984) 156 CLR 414; 3 IPR 545 and *Settef SpA v Riv-Oland Marble Co (Vic) Pty Ltd* (1987) 10 IPR 402. Nonetheless the use made of the mark must be 'as a trade mark': see *Anchorage*. However, proof of a bare intention to use a mark during the relevant period is not sufficient unless the owner 'so acted to show that it has gone beyond investigating whether to use the mark and beyond planning to use the mark and has got to the stage where it can be seen objectively to have committed itself to using the mark, ie, to carrying its intention to use the mark into effect': see *Woolly Bull Enterprises Pty Ltd v Reynolds* (2001) 107 FCR 166; 51 IPR 149 at 161. In *E & J Gallo Winery v Lion Nathan Australia Pty Ltd* (2010) 241 CLR 144; [2010] HCA 15, the High Court held that where an overseas producer places a trade mark registered in Australia on goods that are then sold by the overseas purchaser in the Australian market, the trade mark owner has 'used' the mark in this country. Thus, despite the fact that the sales of 'Barefoot' branded wine bottles were very few, and the trade mark owner neither knew of them nor knowingly projected them into the market here, there was sufficient trade mark use.

The authorised user

16.15 It is, prima facie, the registered owner who must use the mark for the purpose of maintaining registration; however, the 1995 Act extends the category of legally effective use to use made by an 'authorised user'. An important issue in trade marks law is how to permit the exploitation of trade marks by persons other than the owner without the mark becoming deceptive or misleading as to the origin and qualities of the goods or services or without it losing distinctiveness associated with the actual owner's use. If a registered trade mark is a badge of origin, indicating that the goods or services originate with the owner of the trade mark, and the goods or services in fact originate with a licensee, this indication may be misleading. And if both licensee and owner use the mark contemporaneously, the mark may cease to be distinctive of the goods of the owner of the mark and become (partly) associated with the licensee. Normally, such consequences can be avoided by the registered owner retaining some control over the use made of the mark by the licensee. The 1955 Act employed a system of user registration, but upon repeal of that Act that system was replaced with an 'authorised user' system that does not rely on registration of the user. By virtue of s 8, an authorised user is a person who uses the mark under the control of the trade mark owner. Control in this context is defined as *including* quality control over the goods and services provided by the user and/or financial control over the user's relevant trading activities (sufficient control may, however, be established in other ways). It is clear that authorised users may be persons other than franchisees or licensees (eg, subsidiaries).

For present purposes, it is important that, by virtue of s 7(3), use of the mark by an authorised user qualifies as relevant use for the purpose of the non-use application provisions. In other words, such applications will be defeated by showing sufficient use of the mark by another person, as long as the owner can prove the requisite degree of control over that other person's activities. Furthermore, an authorised user may bring an action in infringement if the owner refuses or neglects to do so, in which case the owner must be joined.

Other Requirements for Maintaining Registration: Grounds of Invalidity

Validity of a registered trade mark

16.16 The registration of a trade mark does not guarantee its validity (the 1995 Act removed the system of 'prescriptive validation' under the 1955 Act, which meant that the grounds for invalidity of a registered mark were reduced after a number of years of registration). A trade mark represents 'living goodwill', which evolves and changes with the use of the mark in a real market; hence, if the mark ceases to fulfil its function (distinguishing goods and services) or becomes in some way misleading, it should not remain on the register. However, although some reasons for removal will and can arise only by reason of the use made of the mark after registration, others will relate back to a failure to meet the requirements for registration at the time of the original application. The validity of the registration of a trade mark may be attacked either by way of a specific application to the court or the Registrar or by way of a counterclaim in an infringement action. The former category of application will usually be made by a competitor with similar goods or services; such a person may well have opposed the initial registration unsuccessfully or may not have opposed the registration but now attacks it for reasons of invalidity that can arise only after registration. It should be noted that in any application to remove a trade mark from the register, the Registrar has a right to appear. However, most commonly, the validity of a trade mark is attacked by way of a counterclaim in an infringement action, the defendant in such an action automatically being a person aggrieved in terms of s 88 (see below 16.17).

Bases for removal of a mark from the register

16.17 The question of removal of a mark for invalidity is complex, in that the bases for removal are many and varied. *NSW Dairy Corporation v Murray Goulburn Co-op* (1989) 14 IPR 26 (on appeal, (1990) 171 CLR 363; 18 IPR 385) illustrates the many issues that may arise. Removal for non-use has already been canvassed above. The picture is further complicated by the fact that, besides a counterclaim for invalidity, there are other options open to a defendant in an infringement action; for instance, pleading use in good faith or that the mark has become generic. The core provision concerning cancellation of a registered mark or removal of an entry in the register wrongly made or remaining is s 88. The application under this section can only be made by an 'aggrieved person'. This term is not to be ascribed a special or technical meaning and concerns a person with a real interest in having the marks removed 'and thus would include any person who would be, or in respect of whom there is a reasonable possibility of his being, appreciably disadvantaged in a legal or practical sense by the mark remaining on the Register': *Unilever Australia Ltd v Karounos* (2001) 113 FCR 322; 52 IPR 361 at 371. An obvious example is a person who is involved in legal proceedings concerning the mark or who has received a letter demanding cessation of allegedly infringing use of a mark, as in *Unilever*. However, in *Kraft General Foods Inc v Gaines Pet Foods Corp* (1995) 31 IPR 439, it was held that the mere fact of being an applicant for a similar trade mark is not sufficient. A person aggrieved is also more than a mere busybody or morally aggrieved person: see, for instance, *Ellis's Trade Mark* (1904) 21 RPC 617, where it was held that the Society of Friends (the Quakers), who are concerned with combating alcoholism and other addictions, had no standing to apply for the removal of the QUAKER trade mark, which remained on the register for spirits. See also *Kowa Company Ltd v NV Organon* (2005) 66 IPR 131. Most importantly, a registration may be cancelled upon the application of an aggrieved person because at the time the application for registration was made it contained a prohibited sign or could not be represented graphically; because the trade mark was not distinctive, was scandalous or its use was contrary to law; because it was likely to deceive or cause confusion; or because it was too similar to an already registered mark (the same grounds as for rejection of the application).

Further, a mark may be cancelled because, at the time of the application for rectification, the mark is deceptive or confusing, not because of a connotation of the mark (s 43) nor because it is too similar to a registered mark (s 44) nor because it is substantially identical or deceptively similar to another mark that before the priority date of the application had a reputation in Australia (s 60) — but for some other reason. The grounds for cancellation are to be found in s 88(2)(a)–(e). The Act recognises that rectification of the register should not be allowed to result from the efforts of an assiduous infringer. Hence, by virtue of s 89, the registered owner can establish to the satisfaction of the court that the reason for rectification did not arise through any act or fault of their own. Under the 1955 Act, much case law arose on this point, since there was no clear equivalent to the present provisions of s 89(1)(c). The debate centred around the requirement for 'blameworthy conduct' on the part of the registered owner and how this term was to be interpreted: see, for instance, *NSW Dairy Corporation v Murray Goulburn Co-op* for an analysis of this question. The issue that now arises under the new provisions is whether the term of s 89(1), 'any act or fault of the registered owner', will be interpreted along the same lines as the term 'blameworthy conduct' under the 1955 Act. This question also arises where an application for cancellation is made on the basis of s 87, which provides for the cancellation of a trade mark (or removal or amendment of an entry relating to it) that has become generic: see also ss 24 and 25.

In *Powell v Glow Zone Products Pty Ltd* (1996) 36 IPR 343 at 378, Sheppard J alluded to the question of blameworthy conduct in the context of the 1955 Act. The registered owner did not fail to give the alleged infringer proper and prompt notice, nor did the failure to carry through an application for an interim injunction amount to blameworthy conduct. The fact that the registered owner referred to his product as 'CAPS', which was also the registered trade mark, was not blameworthy conduct either. All he was doing was what everyone else in the trade was doing as well; that is, using the word 'CAPS' generically.

Concerning s 89 of the 1995 Act, see *Nettlefold Advertising Pty Ltd v Nettlefold Signs Pty Ltd* (1997) 38 IPR 495. Concerning removal see also *Campomar Sociedad Limitada v Nike International Ltd* (1998) 85 FCR 331; (1998) 41 IPR 252; *Campomar Sociedad Limitada v Nike International Ltd* (2000) 202 CLR 45; 46 IPR 481; *Montana Tyres Rims & Tubes Pty Ltd v Transport Tyre Sales Pty Ltd* (1998) 41 IPR 301 and *Transport Tyre Sales Pty Ltd v Montana Tyres Rims and Tubes Pty Ltd* (1999) 93 FCR 421; 43 IPR 481; *Le Corden Bleu BV v Cordon Bleu International Lte* (2000) 50 IPR 1 and *Esselte Meto International Produktions GmbH v Mita Industrial Co Ltd* (2000) AIPC ¶91–610.

Bibliography

A Andreazza, 'Barefoot Gets the Boot: Trade Mark Infringement and Removal for Non-Use' — Case Note (2008) 21(5) *AIPLB* 85.

A Baker, 'Application for Removal of Trade Marks for Non-Use Fails — *Pioneer KK v Pioneer Computers*' (2007) 20(4) *IPLB* 62.

A Rahmatian, 'Trade Mark Infringement as a Criminal Offence' (2004) 67(4) *MLR* 670.

AIPJ, 'Gray Privateers Sink into Black Market: Parallel Imports & Trade Marks' (1990) 1 *AIPJ* 72.

C Lee, 'When an Ex-Distributor Accuses You of Trade Mark Infringement' (2003) 16(6) *IPLB* 96.

C Oberin, B Arnall, and C MacCallum, 'Protecting a Product's Shape and Appearance' (2004) 17(7) *IPLB* 109.

D Eliades, 'Trade Marking of Shapes Under Australian Legislation' (2002) 15(3) *IPLB* 33.

D Lisbon, 'The "Use As A Trade Mark" Requirement In Keyword Search Advertising' [2018] *WAStuLawRw* 3.

F Mostert and T Stevens, 'Protection of Well-Known Trade Marks on Non-Competing Goods' (1996) 7 *AIPJ* 76.

H Stallard and J Dennis, 'Personality Rights — the Contrasting Approaches of the US and the UK' (1999) 37 *IP Forum* 16.

J Bosland et al, 'Trade Mark and Counterfeit Litigation in Australia' (2006) 4 *IPQ* 347.

J McCutcheon, 'Rectification of the Trade Marks Register on Grounds Existing at the Time of Application to Rectify' (2002) 13(4) *AIPJ* 199.

J W Dwyer and D L Yates, 'Montana Case — its Legal and Commercial Implications' (1998) 9 *AIPJ* 200.

J W Dwyer and D L Yates, 'The Montana Case on Appeal Dealing with "Parallel Importers"' (1999) 10 *AIPJ* 111.

K Weatherall, 'The Consumer as the Empirical Measure of Trade Mark Law' Modern Law Review (2017) Vol 80 Iss 1, 57.

M Handler, 'Trade Mark Dilution in Australia?' (2008) *UNSWLR* 48.

M Handler, 'What Can Harm the Reputation of a Trademark? A Critical Re-Evaluation of Dilution by Tarnishment' [2016] *UNSWLRS* 41.

M Handler and R Burrell, 'A Requiem for *Champagne Heidsieck*: Trade Mark Use and Parallel Importation' [2016] *UNSWLRS* 40.

M Gonsalves, 'Dilution Down Under: The Protection of Well-Known Trademarks in Australia' (2006) 28(3) *EIPR* 174.

N Weston and M Davison, 'Groundless Threats of Trade Mark Infringement Proceedings' (2000) 11(3) *AIPJ* 151.

P Dyrberg and M Skylv, 'Does Trade Mark Infringement Require that the Infringing Use be Trade Mark Use and if so, What is 'Trade Mark Use'?' (2003) 25(5) *EIPR* 229.

P Knight, 'The Rights of Trade Mark Owners to Prevent Importation of Goods Legitimately Made Overseas' (2005) 18(4) *IPLB* 53.

R Burrell, 'The Requirement of Trade Mark Use: Recent Developments in Australia' (2005) 16(4) *AIPJ* 231.

R Cutler and T Webb, 'Trade Mark Infringement: Who Can Provide Consent?' (2008) 20(7) *IPLB* 115.

S Birchall, 'Groundless Threats in Trade Marks and Copyright Law: Policy, Legislation and Cases' (2005) 18(2) *IPLB* 26.

S Givoni, 'Trade Mark Case With a Twist' (2001) 14(6) *IPLB* 69.

S Stern, 'Trade Mark Counterfeiting — The Australian Problem' (2007) 71 *IP Forum* 68.

S Stone, 'Case Note: *Mid Sydney Pty Ltd v Australian Tourism Co Ltd*' (1999) 11(6) *IPLB* 65.

Chapter 17

Sui Generis Regimes: Circuit Layouts and Plant Varieties

The Circuit Layouts Act 1989 (Cth)

The statutory scheme

17.1 The microprocessor, consisting of integrated circuits on a silicon base, executes a computer's functional commands. A concern emerged in the late 1980s that the design of the layout of the circuitry was not effectively protected against piracy. Designs of integrated circuits were expressly excluded from registration under the Designs Act 1906 (Cth) (see s 4(1) definition of 'article') and continue to be so under s 43(1)(c)(i) of the Designs Act 2003 (Cth). However, it was always doubtful whether an express exclusion was actually necessary, certainly under the Designs Act 1906 (Cth) but also in other jurisdictions. Nor does copyright apply to an integrated circuit as such, although it might apply to the underlying 'plan' of the layout. To remedy the apparent gap in protection, the US Congress passed sui generis legislation, the Semiconductor Chip Protection Act 1984. Subsequently, a multilateral treaty was concluded at a diplomatic conference in Washington: the World Intellectual Property Organization (WIPO) Washington Treaty on Intellectual Property in Respect of Integrated Circuits, 26 May 1989. Protection of the layout of semi-conductor chips is now also an international obligation under the World Trade Organization (WTO) Trade-Related Aspects of Intellectual Property Rights (TRIPS) Agreement: see arts 35–38.

Australia introduced statutory protection by virtue of the Circuit Layouts Act 1989 (Cth). The Act provides sui generis, automatic, copyright-style, limited term protection for 'eligible layouts' (ELs). An EL is defined as an original circuit layout, the maker of which was, at the time the layout was made, an eligible person, or one that was first commercially exploited in Australia or another eligible foreign country: see s 5. Protection under the Australian statute thus extends to a layout that was neither made nor published in Australia or by an Australian citizen or resident. For instance, a circuit layout first commercially exploited (ie, sold, let for hire or otherwise distributed by way of trade, etc: see s 8) in Japan or the United States (both eligible foreign countries) will be protected in Australia under the Act. As to other aspects of 'commercial exploitation', see further below in this chapter. By virtue of s 5, circuit layout 'means a representation, fixed in any material form, of the three-dimensional location of the active and passive elements and interconnections making up an integrated circuit'.

An integrated circuit is defined in the same section as 'a circuit, whether in a final form or an intermediate form, the purpose, or one of the purposes, of which is to perform an electronic function, being a circuit in which the active and passive elements, and any of the interconnections, are integrally formed in or on a piece of material'. In *Lumen Australia Pty Ltd v Frontline Australasia Pty Ltd* [2018] FCA 1807 the issue was whether a printed circuit board assembly (PCBA), described as 'a circuit comprising a series of components such as capacitors, resistors, diodes, transistors and semi-conductor chips' was an integrated circuit. The court held that the printed circuit board — a board that connected electrical components including active elements (transistors and semi-conductor chips) and passive elements (resistors, capacitors and diodes) — was not an 'integrated circuit' as the active and passive elements were not 'integrally formed in or on a piece of material' as required by the definition of integrated circuit: at [308].

The relevant characteristics of the statutory scheme were identified by Northrop J in *Centronics Systems Pty Ltd v Nintendo Co Ltd* (1992) 39 FCR 147 at 147–8; 111 ALR 13 at 15–16:

> [The Circuit Layouts Act] creates rights in the nature of intellectual property rights and which are described as EL [eligible layout] rights. The Act contains many technical expressions, but in essence EL rights are rights conferred on the owner of an original circuit layout which can be described as the drawing of a plan, in a material form, for an integrated circuit, the purpose of which is to perform an electronic function and being a circuit in which the active and passive elements, and any of the interconnections, are integrally formed in or on a piece of material. An integrated circuit is the device made in accordance with a circuit layout. Thus, there is a similarity between the drawings of a plan prepared by an architect for the construction of a building and a circuit layout prepared for the construction of an integrated circuit. The EL rights apply both to the circuit layout and to an integrated circuit made in accordance with the circuit layout. Integrated circuits form part of electronic equipment such as computers and electronic games.

Subsistence of rights in an EL is 'copyright-like' because it is not conditional upon registration or any other formalities. If the EL is original and in material form, and the necessary jurisdictional connection exists, exclusive rights automatically subsist. 'Originality' under the Circuit Layouts Act 1989 differs from the statutory concept in copyright: by virtue of s 11, a circuit layout shall be taken not to be original if its making involved no creative contribution by the maker or it was commonplace at the time it was made. The maker of the EL is the owner of the statutory rights unless it is made in the course of employment, in which case the employer is the owner: see s 16. The maker of an EL is the person who first 'fixed it in material form', which includes making and storing it on a computer; if a computer is so used, the person who used the computer is considered the maker: see s 10. EL rights are also copyright-like in that the Act grants anti-copying rights rather than monopoly rights.

Exclusive rights in an eligible layout

17.2 By virtue of s 17, the owner of the EL rights has the following exclusive rights during the protection period of the layout:

- to copy the layout, directly or indirectly, in a material form;

- to make an integrated circuit in accordance with the layout or a copy of the layout — an integrated circuit made in accordance with a layout includes an integrated circuit made in accordance with a substantial part of a layout (see s 13(c)); and
- to exploit the layout commercially in Australia.

In other words, rights extend both to 'plan to plan' copying and to making a three-dimensional reproduction in the form of an actual processor on the basis of a two-dimensional plan or representation of the layout. Reproduction of an integrated circuit from a chip containing an EL may also infringe the owner's rights, since the integrated circuit in the chip would constitute a copy of a circuit layout: see s 17(b). The 'protection period' of an EL is (s 5):

> ... the period beginning on the day on which the layout was made and ending: (a) if the layout is first commercially exploited within 10 calendar years after the calendar year in which the layout was made at the end of the tenth calendar year after the calendar year in which the layout was first commercially exploited; and (b) in any other case at the end of the period of 10 calendar years after the calendar year in which the layout was made.

Infringement of the exclusive right to exploit the layout commercially in Australia (ie, by dealing in rather than by copying an EL) is subject to a knowledge element: see s 19(3) (as examined in *Nintendo Ltd v Centronics Systems Pty Ltd* (1994) 181 CLR 134; 28 IPR 431) and also s 20 concerning 'innocent commercial exploitation', as discussed at 17.3. In this respect, also note that, by virtue of s 27, damages are unavailable in certain cases of innocent infringement. By virtue of s 8(1)(c), commercial exploitation includes importation 'for the purposes of sale, letting for hire, or other distribution by way of trade'. It may thus appear that parallel importation of circuit layouts (ie, the importation of legitimate copies of layouts obtained in a different jurisdiction) is an exclusive right of the owner of the EL rights. However, the effect of s 24(1) is that an authorised (ie, legitimate) computer chip first put on the market by the EL owner may be freely imported into Australia; in other words, parallel importation is permitted. Furthermore, it may be that because of the operation of s 19 or s 20, or for other reasons (eg, because the Act does not, or no longer does, cover a certain layout), even the importation of an unauthorised computer chip does not constitute an infringement in a particular case. An apparent alternative option then would be to rely on copyright in a copyright work incorporated in the chip, such as a computer program (a literary work): see ss 37 and 38 of the Copyright Act 1968 (Cth). However, the provisions of s 24(2) preclude this option: if the importation of the EL is not an infringement, then the importation of the work stored on the EL is, by virtue of that section, not an infringement either. For example, importation of a gaming device containing an unauthorised reproduction of a computer chip does not constitute an infringement of copyright in a computer program: see further *Avel Pty Ltd v Wells* (1992) 36 FCR 340; 23 IPR 353 and *Galaxy Electronics Pty Ltd v Sega Enterprises Ltd* (1997) 75 FCR 8; 37 IPR 462. In other words, copyright in a work embedded in a computer chip cannot be relied on to prohibit importation.

'Innocent commercial exploitation' and other exceptions

17.3 The legislative policy underlying s 20, as stated in *Nintendo Ltd v Centronics Systems Pty Ltd* at CLR 154, is:

> ... to make special provision for circumstances in which it would be unjust to impose liability for infringement on a person who innocently acquires and subsequently deals with an unauthorised integrated circuit. One can readily envisage circumstances in which an ordinary person who innocently acquires, and subsequently commercially deals with, an item of electronic equipment would have no means of knowing or ascertaining that some concealed integrated circuit in the article was an unauthorised copy of an eligible circuit layout in which EL rights subsist.

An obvious example is an innocent purchaser and on-seller of a video game console who, even if they took the machine apart, would not have been able to ascertain in accordance with which EL the incorporated integrated circuit was made. The effect of the *Nintendo* decision has been said to be that the defendant will be liable for infringement by commercial exploitation only if they knew or ought reasonably to have known who the owner of the EL rights was, and that owner had not licensed the defendant to exploit the layout. Apart from this limitation on liability, various other statutory exceptions to infringement are prescribed:

- s 21 'copying for private use';
- s 22 'copying for research or teaching purposes';
- s 23 'evaluation or analysis'; and
- s 25 'copying for purposes of defence or security'.

The exception in s 23 is of particular relevance with respect to reverse engineering. It allows the making of a copy or copies of a layout for the purpose of evaluation and analysis, and provides that the making of an original circuit layout on the basis of the evaluation or analysis carried out with the use of the copy or copies of a layout does not constitute an infringement. In *Lumen* in obiter, the court drew the relevant distinction as follows: 'If it were necessary to decide this issue, I would conclude that Vision Taiwan sought to replicate the Lumen PCBA for the purpose of supplying a substitute product; I would not be satisfied that it made a copy for the purpose of evaluation or analysis': at [317]. An interesting parallel can be drawn with the provisions introduced by the Copyright Amendment (Computer Programs) Act 1999 (Cth) relating to the reverse engineering of computer programs: see Copyright Act 1968 (Cth), s 47Bff. Note that if circuit layouts were protected by way of registration as designs, none of these exceptions would apply.

Plant Varieties: The Plant Breeder's Rights Act

Introduction

17.4 By virtue of art 27(3)(b) of TRIPS, member countries may exclude plants from patent protection; however, any country that does so must provide an effective sui generis system of protection. Such sui generis protection usually takes the form of plant variety rights or 'plant breeder's rights' (PBR) protection, such as is provided by the Plant Breeder's Rights Act 1994 (Cth) (PBR Act). The Act was most recently amended by the Intellectual Property

Laws Amendment (Productivity Commission Response Part 1 and Other Measures) Act 2018 (Cth), inter alia in relation to the granting of additional damages, unjustified threats of infringement, and giving exclusive licensees rights of action. In Australia, both patents and PBRs are available, since plants are not here excluded from patentability. Australia is also a UPOV Convention country; that is, it is a signatory to the International Convention for the Protection of New Varieties of Plants (the UPOV Convention), adopted in Paris in 1961 and revised in 1972, 1978 and 1991. The UPOV Convention as revised in 1991 entered into force with respect to Australia on 20 January 2000. The PBR scheme in Australia conforms to the 1991 revision of UPOV. It obliges Australia to provide protection for new plant varieties. The option is thus open in Australia to either apply for a plant patent or register a new plant variety under the PBR Act. Where new plant varieties are obtained by more traditional methods of cross-breeding and selective breeding, the PBR Act will usually be the proper choice, as the patenting requirement of inventiveness will usually be difficult to meet. Rather than having to prove an inventive step in the development of a new plant, as well as its utility, an applicant can obtain a PBR for a plant produced by thoroughly well-known or traditional methods, as long as the plant variety obtained is new (ie, varies in one or more morphological characteristics from previous varieties: see further below 17.5) and is 'distinct, uniform and stable' (DUS). There is no requirement that the variety be agronomically advantageous or demonstrate utility of some sort. Plant patents are significantly harder to obtain than a PBR: whereas PBRs number in the thousands, plant patents are few.

Despite the fact that there are some important differences as to conditions for the granting and extent of rights between patents and PBR protection, and the fact that plant variety rights are not mentioned in the Commonwealth Constitution's intellectual property head of power (s 51(xviii)), the High Court in *The Grain Pool of WA v The Commonwealth* (2000) 202 CLR 479; [2000] HCA 14 had little difficulty in finding that PBR protection is sufficiently analogous to patent protection to fall within the scope of the intellectual property power of the Commonwealth Parliament. By virtue of the 2002 amendments to the PBR Act (see the Plant Breeder's Rights Amendment Act 2002), the rights in a PBR were strengthened. However, there are still significant derogations from grantees' rights, most importantly the farm-saved seed exemption and the breeding exemption. The former permits farmers to retain and use seeds produced by protected varieties for replanting in subsequent seasons; the latter permits a protected variety to be used in the development of a new variety; for instance, by using it for cross-breeding. Therefore, PBR rights are significantly more constrained than patent rights, of which there are very few derogations. This reflects traditional farming and breeding methods and matches a less onerous threshold test for subsistence. A 2010 report by the Advisory Council on Intellectual Property (ACIP), *A Review of Enforcement of Plant Breeder's Rights*, Final Report, illustrates the ongoing concerns about the enforcement and effectiveness of the PBR system. However, note the Explanatory Memorandum of the 2002 Amendment Bill, which is more confident in this regard.

The Plant Breeder's Rights Act 1994: subject matter and novelty

17.5 The PBR scheme is administrative in nature, based on application, examination (which includes breeder test plantings) and grant. The scheme is administered by the Registrar of PBRs, who maintains a register of plant varieties. The Plant Breeder's Rights

Office is situated within IP Australia. As indicated above, the subsistence requirements reflect the terms of the 1991 revisions of the UPOV Convention. The subject matter of a PBR is any plant variety that is distinctive, uniform and stable (the DUS criteria; see s 43(1)(b)–(d)). All new varieties of plant, fungal and algal species and transgenic plants are eligible for protection. Distinctiveness is assessed by reference to the physical (or 'morphological') characteristics of the plant variety. As the report of the expert panel convened by the Registrar of PBRs, *Clarification of Plant Breeding Issues Under the Plant Breeder's Rights Act 1994* (the 2002 Report), points out at p 20:

> While at least one clear difference is required to qualify for protection, economic/ aesthetic/performance/values are not, *per se*, relevant for PBR protection. *PBR is primarily a registration scheme based on perceived 'physical difference(s)' (eg a morphological, phonological or physiological difference) that distinguishes the candidate variety from all others.* The difference may result in characteristics that have no agronomic value relevant to the registration process. (Emphasis in original)

The plant variety must be distinguishable from all commonly known varieties (see further below in this paragraph) by at least one such characteristic. The defining characteristics must be heritable: the basic parameters of PBR-protected plant varieties are uniform characteristics stable across generations and across all plants within the variety; no heterogeneity is tolerated. Breeders must conduct formal comparative trials to establish the distinctness, uniformity and stability of a new variety, in relation to which applicants have to engage the services of an accredited qualified person. As well as being DUS, a plant variety must also have a breeder, which, in essence, amounts to a requirement that it has been 'bred' in the statutory sense. Breeding includes both selective propagation so as to enable the development of a new plant variety and discovery: see s 5. However, a commonly known variety cannot be 'discovered' in the statutory sense. It is the breeder who is entitled to the granting of a PBR over a new and DUS plant variety (see s 43(1)(a)), and for the plant variety to be 'discovered', the breeder has to come upon it independently rather than obtaining it from some other person.

Selective propagation as a breeding technique requires comparison between the alleged new plant variety and the parents or population from which it is developed, showing a clear difference in at least one characteristic; for instance, coming across a mutant branch on a plant and propagating a variety from that branch would amount to 'breeding' under the PBR Act. However, as well as being available for new varieties bred in a traditional manner, a PBR is also an available option (as may be a patent) for plants derived by more modern breeding techniques such as gene insertion. Examples and clarification in relation to the word 'breeding' are available in the 2002 Report.

As indicated above, the new variety must have at least one different characteristic in comparison with all varieties 'whose existence is a matter of common knowledge' and thus be distinct. As is pointed out in the 2002 Report at p 10, 'In situations where the source population/parent is also the most similar variety of common knowledge, breeding and distinctiveness can be tested and satisfied simultaneously.' The onus is on the applicant to establish that a plant variety is different from some source population in which it was found, and they will have to provide, as part of the material description, as well as particulars of distinguishing characteristics also evidence of the comparative trials (test growings) referred to above (see s 34). Novelty in the context of a PBR requires that before the application date the variety has 'not been exploited or has been only recently exploited' (see s 43(1)(e)) in Australia. In *Sun World International Inc (formerly Sun World Inc) v Registrar, Plant Breeder's Rights* (1998) 87 FCR 405; 42 IPR 321, minimal sales were held to amount to an 'exploitation', and it is clear that a grower cannot offer the variety for sale for the purpose of cultivation. However, by virtue of the 2002 amendments (see above), certain sales made in the process of development are now excluded from constituting an anticipation.

Exclusive rights and derogations

17.6 The term of PBR protection is calculated from the day of granting and is 25 years for vines and trees and 20 years for any other variety: see also *Elders Rural Services Ltd v Registrar of Plant Breeder's Rights* (2012) 95 IPR 229; [2012] FCAFC 14. The grantee has the exclusive right to produce, reproduce or condition propagating material and deal commercially in the material, including importing and exporting it (see s 11). By virtue of s 3, 'propagating material' in relation to a plant of a particular plant variety means any part or product from which, whether alone or in combination with other parts or products of that plant, another plant with the same essential characteristics can be produced. As pointed out in the note to s 11, 'In certain circumstances, the right conferred by this section extends to essentially derived varieties (see section 12), certain dependent plant varieties (see section 13), harvested material (see section 14) and products obtained from harvested material (see section 15).' Prior to the 2002 amendments, s 18 exempted any dealing in the material for the purpose of food etc, but the decision in *Cultivaust Pty Ltd v Grain Pool Pty Ltd* (2005) 147 FCR 265; 67 IPR 162 made it apparent that the limiting effect of this provision tended to render the grantee's rights nugatory. Therefore, s 23 provides instead for the exhaustion of the grantee's rights once the propagating material (seed) has been sold, except for the right to further reproduce or to export the material. The concept of the 'essentially derived variety' (EDV) is an important feature of the scheme, resulting from the fact that under the PBR Act it is not an infringement of the breeder's rights to use a protected plant variety for the purpose of further breeding (eg, by cross-breeding).

The 'Declaration of an EDV' allows a line to be drawn between illegal copycat activity resulting in what is no more than an EDV and such legitimate further breeding to produce a new variety from a protected plant variety, as is permitted under the PBR Act. A breeder can apply to the Registrar to have a certain variety declared an EDV; by virtue of the Intellectual Property Laws Amendment (Productivity Commission Response Part 1 and Other Measures) Act 2018 (Cth) amendments, a non-PBR-protected variety can now also be declared as an EDV. An EDV must be predominantly derived, have the same essential characteristics and have no important (ie, more than cosmetic) differentiating features (see s 4). The 2002 Report explains at p 22:

> …'important' would probably be taken to denote significant changes that affect performance, value or place in the market. For example, purple anthers in wheat, which do not affect performance or value of the crop, might fall into the category of a cosmetic feature.

> ... The current provisions of the PBRA regarding essential derivation go further than the relevant UPOV 1991 provisions by: 1. Defining 'essential characteristics' as 'heritable traits ... that contribute to the principal features, performance or value of the variety' (see PBRA section 3(1)); 2. Requiring that important differences (more than cosmetic) must be demonstrated if the second variety is *not* to be regarded as an EDV; and 3. Stipulating that the PBR Office should make decisions in relation to a declaration that a variety is essentially derived. (Emphasis in original)

In substance, although it arises in the context of infringement (ie, in determining the scope of the PBR), the test of essential derivation applies a novelty standard. Adverse claims that a variety is an EDV can be defeated by establishing that important differences do exist between the two. The 2002 Report points out that the category of EDV is narrow (at p 20):

> Real progress in plant innovation — which must be the goal of intellectual property rights — relies on access to the latest improvements and new variation. As a general rule, the easier the access, the more incremental breeding is promoted.
>
> Incremental breeding refers to the breeding of an unlimited series of new varieties with each subsequent variety being bred from, and relying heavily on, the characteristics of the previous varieties. The differences between the previous and subsequent variety can be large, small or very small, with the latter being the most common. ...
>
> Any proposition to strengthen the first breeder's power by extending EDV to all incrementally bred varieties (and not just copies) would go to the fundamentals of the PBR system, with profound implications for the community of breeders, for consumers and for Australia's national interests. ...
>
> In the context of PBR, incremental breeding is associated with 'freedom to operate' (more formally known as the 'breeder's exemption', or the 'research exemption'), which prescribes free access to PBR varieties (see PBRA section 16) for the purpose of research or breeding a new variety and, in virtually all (non EDV) cases, the commercialisation of that new variety.

The grantee has the exclusive right to produce and reproduce the propagating material of the variety: see s 11(a). However, this right is attenuated by the 'farmer's rights' exemption, which allows farmers to gather seed from plantings of a protected variety and reuse it for sowing: see s 17. However, the farmer's right is subject to s 14, which extends the PBR to harvested material in circumstances where the grantees have not had a reasonable opportunity to exercise their rights. Farmers can use only the farm-saved seeds for their own purposes and are not allowed to on-sell them to other farmers. The 1991 revision of UPOV made the farmer's rights exception optional for the first time; previously, it constituted a core aspect of international plant variety protection norms. Under the European Community plant variety rights system, the farmer pays a royalty on saved seeds. The ACIP recommended no change to the s 17 farm-saved seed provisions: see ACIP, *A Review of Enforcement of Plant Breeder's Rights*, Final Report, 2010. The exception allowing use of the protected variety for breeding purposes (see s 16) means that a PBR cannot block the continued improvement of plant varieties, effectively preserving a public domain of available lines for further breeding purposes. There is an important concern in relation to the exception of s 16. The same variety can masquerade as a variety in the derivation of which a protected variety has legally been used but which is supposedly new. However, this concern is alleviated by the option of seeking a declaration of an EDV as is explained above. Another significant exception applies to acts done 'for private, experimental or breeding purposes' (see s 16), which is further supported by the requirement of reasonable public access to plant varieties covered by a PBR (see s 19). Note that the validity of a PBR is not guaranteed. In any action for infringement under the PBR Act, the defendant can counterclaim for revocation of the right: see s 54 and also s 50, 'Revocation of PBR'.

Bibliography

A Christie, *Integrated Circuits and their Contents: International Protection*, LBC Information Services, Sydney, 1995.

Advisory Council on Intellectual Property (ACIP), *A Review of Enforcement of Plant Breeder's Rights*, Final Report, 2010.

AIPJ, 'Infringement Found under Circuit Layouts Act' (1992) 3 *AIPJ* 184.

B Browne and B Muir, 'Subordinating Plant Breeder's Rights Against Australia's Interests' (2008) 20(9) *IPLB* 144.

C Lawson, 'Patents and Plant Breeder's Rights Over Plant Genetic Resources for Food and Agriculture', (2004) 32 *FL Rev* 107.

C Turner, 'Sale of Imported Video Game Machines Held to Infringe Circuit Layouts Act' (1994) 15 *QldLawyer* 41.

G Chin, 'Technological Change and Australian Constitution' (2000) 24 *MULR* 609.

M Rimmer, 'Franklin Barley: Patent Law and Plant Breeders' Rights' (2003) 10 *MurUEJL* 40.

Report of the Expert Panel on Breeding, *Clarification of Plant Breeding Issues under the Plant Breeder's Rights Act 1994*, December 2002 (the 2002 Report).

Chapter 18

Digitisation

Introduction

The digital revolution

18.1 The 'digital revolution' has affected every intellectual property regime. The development of computers has given rise to the creation of entirely new statutory objects of intellectual property protection, such as computer programs (or software) and integrated circuits (computer chips). Existing intellectual property rights, in particular copyright, were ill adapted to the digital revolution and the internet, which caused the convergence of disparate modes of expression, recording and distribution of subject matter into a uniform digital language and integrated global distribution network. Digitisation has exponentially increased the ease of creation, modification, reproduction and distribution of all information (whether expressed in literary, artistic or any other form) and allows users to interact with material, blurring the previously clearer distinction between creators and users. It has spawned a new area of ubiquitous technological and commercial innovation, which has an ongoing impact on various areas of intellectual property law, be it patents (internet-based inventions), copyright or trade marks law (eg, domain names protection). The rate of technological and commercial innovation based on digital technology has increased exponentially, resulting in acute pressure on the legal system to adapt to constantly evolving factual parameters. Furthermore, the internet, as a supranational virtual jurisdiction without borders, has struggled to come to terms with the predominantly national reach of intellectual property laws. For an example of the internet's impact on registered trade marks in multiple jurisdictions, see *Ward Group Pty Ltd v Brodie & Stone Plc* (2005) 143 FCR 479; 64 IPR 1; and on copyright and trade marks, see *Hells Angels Motorcycle Corporation (Australia) Pty Ltd v Redbubble Ltd* (2019) 140 IPR 172; [2019] FCA 355.

The impact on intellectual property law

18.2 It is impossible to examine every intellectual property question that has arisen as a result of the digital revolution and the internet; in any case, the list is constantly evolving. Some of these topics are dealt with in the previous chapters; for instance, statutory protection for integrated layouts or computer chips, which was introduced with the Circuit Layouts Act 1989 (Cth), is dealt with in Chapter 17 Sui Generis Regimes: Circuit Layouts and Plant Varieties. The following topics will be subjected to some closer scrutiny in this chapter, without attempting to provide exhaustive coverage of all the ways in which intellectual property law and the digital world interact.

First, computer programs: copyright law now accommodates software as literary works, but a patent may also be an option if the computer program amounts to, or is comprised in, an invention. Patents law has also had to adapt to the emergence of other computer-implemented and internet-related inventions. Second, digitisation has given birth to entirely new forms of expression, such as electronic databases, computer games, multimedia and websites/screen displays, which may or may not be accommodated within the framework of copyright law. Third, the operation of the internet has spawned new technical reproduction and distribution practices, which on the one hand implicate copyright unintentionally, and on the other hand reduce the level of copyright owners' control. This has encouraged amendments, including legal measures that support the technological protection measures (TPMs) (mostly encryption) deployed by content owners. And, last, trade marks law and the law of passing off have had to accommodate both the creation of new signs incorporating goodwill on the internet (domain names) and their coexistence with 'analogue' marks. Each of these broad areas can be broken down into a host of more specific legal issues. In relation to each topic, Australian law is the principal focus below, but many of the relevant problems occur within supranational cyberspace and have multi-jurisdictional ramifications. Clarification of the Australian legal position may be of little consequence if the other party or parties, although their activities have an impact within the country, are located in foreign jurisdiction(s) outside the effective reach of a local complainant.

Computer Programs

Subsistence of copyright in computer programs

18.3 *Apple Computer Inc v Computer Edge Pty Ltd* (1983) 1 IPR 353 (and *Computer Edge Pty Ltd v Apple Computer Inc* (1986) 161 CLR 171; 6 IPR 1) was the first case in Australia to address the intellectual property status of computer programs. The court cast doubt on the notion that a computer program in object code (machine readable) amounted to a literary work. Where it is in source code, it constitutes a literary expression that is human readable. But that cannot be said for object or binary code, which is only machine readable. The Commonwealth Parliament responded by expressly accommodating computer programs within the Copyright Act 1968 (Cth): see the Copyright Amendment Act 1984 (Cth). Further amendments relating to computer programs then followed in 2000: see the Copyright Amendment (Digital Agenda) Act 2000 (Cth), which inserted a new definition of 'computer program' into s 10 of the Copyright Act. By virtue of that section, a computer program now means 'a set of statements or instructions to be used directly or indirectly in a computer in order to bring about a certain result'. Other consequential amendments were also made.

Whatever their code or notation, computer programs have a literary element, particularly when expressed in human-readable or source code: they are constructed in a computer language, and to a person skilled in the art they convey information and instruction. Yet in object code, they are not made for the purpose of informing or giving literary enjoyment to human beings as are other literary works but to make computers operate (although, in theory, it is possible to 'view' stored object code using various devices, which makes object code understandable to a small group of software engineers). Computer programs are thus unlike any other copyright subject matter, and 'difficulties … arise from accommodating computer technology protection to principles of copyright … but the Act now expressly requires such an accommodation': *Data Access Corporation v Powerflex Services Pty Ltd* (1999) 202 CLR 1; 45 IPR 353 at 360–1. In light of the functional nature of computer programs, there is potential overlap with patents.

Alternatively, given the fact that computer programs are functional, novel and inventive, claims to computer programs that otherwise satisfy the criteria of the Patents Act 1990 (Cth) are proper subject matter for letters patent if they have the effect of controlling computers to operate in a particular way, achieving 'an end result which is an artificially created state of affairs of utility in the field of economic endeavour': *National Research Development Corporation v Commissioner of Patents* (1959) 102 CLR 252 at 275–7; 1A IPR 63 (*NRDC* case). The appropriateness and limitations of the categorisation of computer programs as literary works can justifiably be questioned. A sui generis regime may have allowed better adaptation to the special nature of software, but international developments pre-empted this from happening. However, there are now so many distinct provisions relating only to computer programs within the Copyright Act that a virtual sui generis regime has been created within the Act's broader confines. Some of the general principles of copyright law are largely displaced or at least of doubtful application when it comes to computer programs.

The Copyright Act requires that there be 'a set' of 'statements or instructions' for computer program copyright to subsist. The High Court has held that therefore single reserved words of a computer language do not amount to a computer program as such: see *Data Access* at IPR 361:

> [W]hether a Reserved Word is a 'computer program' within the meaning of the definition depends on whether it is an 'expression … of a set of instructions … intended … to cause a device having digital information processing capabilities to perform a particular function'. However, each of the Reserved Words is a single word; none is a set of instructions in the Dataflex language. Further, none of the Reserved Words intends to *express, directly or indirectly, an algorithmic or logical relationship between the function desired to be performed and the physical capabilities of the 'device having digital information processing capabilities'.* (Emphasis added)

However, although a computer program differs from all other works because it has a functional purpose, it may also include non-functional parts (sometimes referred to as 'data'). The present statutory definition refers to 'statements or instructions', and the old definition to 'a set of instructions (whether with or without related information)'. This led Gaudron J in *Autodesk Inc v Dyason (No 2)* (1993) 176 CLR 300 at 329 to distinguish between 'data' and 'commands':

> [G]iven ordinary usage and given that it has never been suggested that the expression 'set of instructions' in the definition of 'computer program' in s 10 of the Act is a technical or art term, it is, in my view, clear that that expression directs attention to an entire instruction or, more accurately, an entire set of instructions, and not merely those parts that consist of bare commands.

Data may form an integral part of a computer program because 'in many cases it will be necessary for instructions to be accompanied by related information if those devices are to perform quite ordinary computer functions', as Gaudron J also pointed out (at CLR 329).

Thus in *Autodesk (No 2)* the look-up table, although consisting entirely of nonfunctional data, was a substantial part of the security program Widget-C for the purpose of infringement. (It should be noted that in the later decision in *Data Access* the High Court cast serious doubt on the approach to infringement of computer program copyright adopted in *Autodesk (No 2)*: see 18.4.) A data feature integral to the function and operation of a computer program, such as a look-up table, must be distinguished from a database stored on a computer, data from which may be retrieved by means of a separate and distinct computer program: see, for example, *CA Inc v ISI Pty Ltd* (2012) 95 IPR 424; [2012] FCA 35 at [115], where the court considered the different approaches to infringement that may be called for depending on whether copyright material is a computer program or a literary work other than a computer program. The court also held that a 'macro' qualified as a computer program, even if the result in a computer was brought about indirectly by the participation of other macros in the process: see at [146]. In *Coogi Australia Pty Ltd v Hysport International Pty Ltd* (1998) 86 FCR 154; 41 IPR 593, the computerised knitting machines at issue were operated by means of a computer program that included graphs representing knitting patterns. The graph and control program together constituted a computer program, as it was the clear legislative intention (as confirmed in *Autodesk*) that the latter may include material other than instructions or commands for a computer. The graph 'though in one sense only data' was as much the source of signals that made the computer perform a function as was the control program. However, if the database and the computer program are separate entities, then the question may arise as to whether the database is sufficiently original to attract copyright as a literary work other than a computer program; the answer to this question is now substantially determined by the principles that emerged from the High Court's reasons in *IceTV Pty Ltd v Nine Network Australia Pty Ltd* (2009) 239 CLR 458; 80 IPR 451; [2009] HCA 14, as applied in *Telstra Corporation Ltd v Phone Directories Co Pty Ltd* (2010) 194 FCR 142; 90 IPR 1; [2010] FCAFC 149 (see below at 18.11). As for the question of originality of computer programs as such, it is common that they evolve incrementally over time and that many versions are thus produced. In *JR Consulting & Drafting Pty Limited v Cummings* (2016) 116 IPR 440; [2016] FCAFC 20 at [304] the court found that the author had:

> ... carefully considered the preceding state of the suite of programs and that the alterations, insertions or deletions are intended to be consistent with and enhancements of what has gone before. In other words, [the author had] undertaken a particular revision of the programs on each occasion as part of the whole of the work with the application of sufficient skill and judgement to make each version as updated and released an original work in its own right.

The statutory definition that predated the Copyright Amendment (Digital Agenda) Act 2000 (Cth) referred to a set of instructions for 'a device having digital information processing capabilities'; the present Copyright Act refers simply to 'a computer'. This includes devices whose principal function is other than data processing, as was confirmed in *Coogi*. The function of the Coogi XYZ computer program at issue was to cause a computerised knitting machine to create a fabric knitted in the form of the Coogi XYZ design. An essential element of the Coogi XYZ program was data in the form of a graph, as distinct from instructions or commands. The graph and the control program together comprised the 'computer program', since the then applicable statutory definition referred to instruction 'with or without related information': see also *Autodesk* at CLR 329–30 per Gaudron J.

Drummond J rejected the contention that the then provision should be read down to say that the set of instructions must be intended to cause a device that has digital information processing capabilities to perform a digital information processing function. His Honour, in *Coogi* at FCR 182, referred to the Explanatory Memorandum to the 1984 Act:

> This states (in para 21) that the phrase 'to cause a device … to perform a particular function' is intended to make clear that the device is one the performance of which is ultimately controlled by the 'expression … of a set of instructions', ie by that which constitutes the computer program, whatever may be the function of the particular device; in para 22, it is said that the intention of the phrase 'having digital information processing capabilities' is to make clear that devices which only process information by analogue methods are excluded and that this phase is intended to include devices which 'though considered as a whole might not be information processors, nevertheless have some such capability'. The Memorandum gives a computerised ignition system as an example of such a device.

As is indicated, the present statutory definition does not refer to a 'device having digital information processing capabilities' but to a 'computer'. However, this change was not intended to narrow the scope of the definition, so the above is still applicable. The word 'computer' is not further defined in the Copyright Act.

Infringement, reverse engineering and exceptions

18.4 The copyright owner has the exclusive right to make a reproduction or an adaptation of a computer program. This gives rise to the 'reverse engineering' conundrum, one illustration of the uneasy fit of computer program copyright. Commonly, source code is not distributed with object code and is not published. The only method to learn the ideas, design, structure, architecture or key algorithms of a program is by reverse engineering (or decompilation or disassembly); that is, the process of turning object code into source code. That process, if unauthorised, constitutes the making of an infringing reproduction or adaptation: copying into different languages, codes or forms of notation are clearly intended to fall within the exclusive rights of the copyright owner: see s 21(5). This effective prohibition on reverse engineering renders the ideas or information underlying the program inaccessible to parties other than the copyright owners or licensees. This is arguably an attenuation of the basic copyright principle that exclusive rights extend only to forms of expression and not to the ideas or information underlying or incorporated in a work. Further, it places an obstacle in the way of coupling interoperable products (or applications) with a copyrighted computer program (such as an operating system). A further problem is that ordinary operation of a computer program may implicate acts comprised in the copyright (eg, reproduction in random access memory (RAM)).

These issues are addressed by the exceptions inserted into the Copyright Act by the Copyright Amendment (Computer Programs) Act 1999 (Cth). The exceptions are expressed in narrow and specific terms. Thus, s 47B(3) provides that copies made in the course of operating the program for the purpose of studying underlying ideas or function do not infringe. In terms of reverse engineering, s 47D ('Reproducing computer programs to make interoperable products') allows a legitimate owner or licensee to reproduce or adapt the program for the purpose of obtaining information necessary to enable the independent making of another program or article to connect or be used together with or interoperate with the original or any other program. This interoperability exception applies only if the information required was not previously readily available (see s 47D(1)(e)) and only to an extent reasonably necessary to obtain the information and produce the interoperable program: see s 47D(1)(c) and (d). However, note that *Centrestage Management Pty Ltd v Riedle* (2008) 170 FCR 298; 77 IPR 550 stands for the proposition that there is no statutory obligation to provide the source code under s 47D. More generally, by virtue of s 47B(1)(a), a statutory exception now applies to the reproduction of a program 'made in the course of running a copy of the program for the purposes for which the program was designed'. In *Microsoft Corporation v Business Boost Pty Ltd* (1999) 47 IPR 607, Tamberlin J held that there was at least a serious issue to be tried as to whether the copying into the RAM of a computer in the course of operation in fact constituted an infringement (prior to the amendments). This significant issue also arose in *Australian Video Retailers Association Ltd v Warner Home Video Pty Ltd* (2001) 114 FCR 324; 53 IPR 242 and *Kabushiki Kaisha Sony Computer Entertainment v Stevens* (2003) 132 FCR 31; 57 IPR 161; [2003] FCAFC 157: see further below at 18.13 and 18.18.[1] Section 47C permits the making of a back-up copy of a legitimate computer program. This section (as well as s 47F) was at issue in *Racing & Wagering Western Australia v Software AG* [2008] FCA 1332. This case concerned software for a mainframe computer; both the express terms of the contract and the terms of s 47C were held to permit the making of a back-up copy of the complex and extensive program. Reproducing a computer program to correct errors (s 47E) and for security testing (s 47F) is also permitted.

Infringement by doing an act comprised in the copyright: s 36

18.5 The High Court's first opportunity to consider infringement under s 36 in relation to computer programs came in *Autodesk Inc v Dyason (No 1)* (1992) 173 CLR 330. Copyright in an Autodesk computer-aided design (CAD) program was protected by a hardware lock against unlicensed simultaneous use on multiple workstations. The hardware lock was a practical alternative to a restrictive multiple-user licence and supposedly more effective against cheating. For every workstation copy required for simultaneous use, a purchaser had to acquire an Autodesk hardware lock, which operated as follows. A part of the CAD program called Widget-C sent a certain bit

---

1. The trial decision is *Kabushiki Kaisha Sony Computer Entertainment v Stevens* [2001] FCA 1379, the Full Federal Court decision is *Kabushiki Kaisha Sony Computer Entertainment v Stevens* [2003] FCAFC 157 and the High Court decision is *Stevens v Kabushiki Kaisha Sony Computer Entertainment* (2005) 224 CLR 193; [2005] HCA 58.

sequence of randomly generated digits to the hardware lock, which was plugged into the back of the computer on which the software package was installed. Unless the hardware lock returned the correct sequence to Widget-C, the CAD program would not operate. The defendant, Mr Dyason, managed to circumvent the hardware lock. By using an oscilloscope, he worked out the correlation between the ingoing and outgoing streams of electrical impulses between Widget-C and the hardware lock. He made a substitute for the Autodesk lock, which replicated the sequence required. This device was sold at a considerable discount.

Ultimately, the High Court found that in the process of making his own substitute lock, Mr Dyason had reproduced the look-up table of Autodesk's Widget-C program, which consisted of a 117-bit sequence. This was the referencing table that the Widget-C program used to check the accuracy of the signals returning to it from the hardware lock, permitting the CAD program to continue to operate. The 117-bit sequence was only a minute fraction of the total program; it was in no way 'original', since it was randomly generated; and it was associated data rather than an actual functional or command part of the program (the definition of computer program then referring to a 'set of instructions whether with or without related information'). Nonetheless, the court held that it was a 'substantial' part (see s 14(1)) because it was an essential part of the program: without it the program would not function at all. The copyright in the program had thus been infringed.

In its reasons in the *Autodesk (No 1)* decision the court, not surprisingly, dismissed the notion that similarity of function was a relevant indicator of substantial similarity in a copyright case: copyright protects expression in some code or notation, not function. However, although the facts of *Autodesk (No 1)* were unique and narrow, there was considerable disquiet at the implications of the High Court's view that every essential or 'critical' part of a program is a substantial part in the copyright sense. Although it is well established that a small fraction of a work can still amount to a 'substantial part', since the required focus is on quality not quantity, this approach appeared to displace the traditional emphasis on the originality of the part taken. Note that the High Court's reasoning resulted in a rare application, ultimately rejected, to reopen the matter after judgment to hear further argument on the point that finally decided the case: see *Autodesk (No 2)*. The High Court appeared to adopt a narrow and literal approach to infringement, focusing on finding an identical bit sequence in the infringing program. But since virtually every bit sequence of a computer program is essential to its normal functioning, no matter how small or unoriginal, the scope of protection was potentially very wide. The approach in *Autodesk (No 2)* also had important implications for interoperability and compatibility of computer programs.

Unsurprisingly, the essential part doctrine was therefore criticised in some subsequent decisions; for instance, *Cantor Fitzgerald International v Tradition (UK) Ltd* [2000] RPC 95, per Pumfrey J (see below 18.6).

In *Data Access*, the High Court took the opportunity to revisit the question and moved away from the *Autodesk* doctrine. The relevant part of the judgment at IPR 373–4 is instructive in full:

> [84] There is great force in the criticism that the 'but for' essentiality test which is effectively invoked by the majority in Autodesk (No 2) is not practicable as a test for determining

whether something which appears in a computer program is a substantial part of it. For that reason, we prefer Mason CJ's opinion [in the minority in *Autodesk*] that, in determining whether something is a reproduction of a substantial part of a computer program, the 'essential or material features of [the computer program] should be ascertained by considering the originality of the part allegedly taken'.

[85] In order for an item in a particular language to be a computer program, it must intend to express, either directly or indirectly, an algorithmic or logical relationship between the function desired to be performed and the physical capabilities of the 'device having digital information processing capabilities'. It follows that the originality of what was allegedly taken from a computer program must be assessed with respect to the originality with which it expresses that algorithmic or logical relationship or part thereof. The structure of what was allegedly taken, its choice of commands, and its combination and sequencing of commands, when compared, at the same level of abstraction, with the original, would all be relevant to this inquiry.

[86] That being so, a person who does no more than reproduce those parts of a program which are 'data' or 'related information' and which are irrelevant to its structure, choice of commands and combination and sequencing of commands will be unlikely to have reproduced a substantial part of the computer program. We say 'unlikely' and not 'impossible' because it is conceivable that the data, considered alone, could be sufficiently original to be a substantial part of the computer program.

[87] It follows that we are unable to agree with the approach to determining 'substantiality', which the majority took in *Autodesk (No 1)* and *Autodesk (No 2)*. Because of the importance of the question, we think that the court should reopen the question of what constitutes a substantial part of a computer program. To depart from the reasoning in the Autodesk cases does not necessarily mean that the outcomes in those cases were wrong. In our view, the look-up table in Widget-C was merely data and was not capable of being a substantial part of the AutoCAD program unless the data itself had its own inherent originality. However, re-opening the reasoning in the *Autodesk* cases does not require the court to express a view on whether the look-up table in that case had its own inherent originality.

It is clear that the High Court's approach to infringement of copyright in computer programs is now more closely aligned to the approach taken in relation to other kinds of works; that is, the originality of the part taken is the principal consideration in determining whether it amounts to a 'substantial' part for the purpose of infringement. To what extent does that part reflect the independent skill and labour of the author–programmer?

A further question in *Data Access* concerned the Huffman compression table. The Dataflex Huffman table was a literary work, it being an original 'table' stored on a computer (see s 10(1) definition of 'literary work'). The allegedly infringing program, PFXplus, had to be able to compress and decompress Dataflex files, and vice versa, when standard compression was used. The default Huffman compression table used in Dataflex had to be replicated precisely. The defendant, Dr Bennett, the author of PFXplus, refrained from finding the relevant file by a process of decompilation so as to avoid copyright infringement. Instead, he followed a more complex series of steps to achieve the desired result. Nonetheless, the defendant was held to have reproduced it because (at IPR 381):

[t]he fact that Dr Bennett used an ingenious method of determining the bit string assigned to each character does not make the output of such a process any less a 'reproduction' than if Dr Bennett had sat down with a print-out of the table and copy-typed it into the PFXplus program.

The High Court then went on to point out the practical consequences of this finding in relation to the Huffman compression table (at IPR 381):

> The finding that the respondents infringed the appellant's copyright in the Huffman table embedded in the Dataflex program may well have considerable practical consequences. Not only may the finding affect the relations between the parties to these proceedings, it may also have wider ramifications for anyone who seeks to produce a computer program that is compatible with a program produced by others. These are, however, matters that can be resolved only by the legislature reconsidering and, if it thinks it necessary or desirable, rewriting the whole of the provisions that deal with copyright in computer programs.

To some degree, the concerns expressed by the High Court are met by the introduction of the new reverse engineering exceptions (s 47B ff), which are considered above.

The emphasis in an action for unauthorised reproduction is quite properly on the quality of what is taken, but the question arises as to at what point the quantity of copying becomes relevant. Logically speaking, there will be no infringement if a large but commonplace or unoriginal part of a program is copied. Yet, in *Accounting Systems 2000 (Developments) Pty Ltd v CCH Australia Ltd* (1993) 42 FCR 470; 27 IPR 133, the court accepted that when a large proportion (eg, 25 per cent or more) is reproduced, it may be fair to infer that a qualitatively, not just quantitatively, important part has been reproduced. It is the proportion of the infringed program taken that is relevant, not the fraction of the infringing program made up by the part taken. In other words, no amount of additional work on a program that incorporates an illegally copied part will compensate for the infringement. By contrast, the court in *TICA Default Tenancy Control Pty Ltd v Datakatch Pty Ltd* [2016] FCA 815, while accepting that copyright might be infringed by reproduction of only a limited sequence of source or object code, held that the amount of HTML code demonstrably copied in the instant case was too trivial.

An important underlying issue in computer program infringement cases is to define correctly where a computer program starts and finishes; in other words, when a part of a computer program or package in truth constitutes a separate computer program in its own right; for instance, was Widget-C simply a part of the relevant literary work (the AutoCAD program in the *Autodesk* cases) or a literary work itself?. The High Court in *Data Access* left this question unresolved. The answer has obvious implications for the question of whether a substantial part of a program has been reproduced. The Full Federal Court in *Powerflex Services Pty Ltd v Data Access Corporation (No 2)* (1997) 75 FCR 108 said that whether a component part of a computer program is itself a computer program for the purposes of the Copyright Act is a question of fact. However, it also said that if a particular set of instructions is functionally separate from the entirety of the program, there is no difficulty in treating that set of instructions as being a literary work separate from the balance of the program. The High Court found no statutory basis for this but agreed (at IPR 378) that:

> If the segment of the larger program in question can be said to have a function which is not merely one of the functions in the set of functions performed by the larger program, but is a separate and distinct particular function, it may be that this segment can be properly viewed as a computer program in and of itself.

Unfortunately, this is not particularly enlightening. The question was considered more recently in *Dais Studio Pty Ltd v Bullet Creative Pty Ltd* (2007) 74 IPR 512. The court rejected an approach focusing on functional integration between different parts or components, drawing inferences from the statutory definition of a computer program: 'a thing might be used to bring about a certain result notwithstanding that it is but a component in a collection or sequence of things which together bring about the result': at IPR 522–3. This is a rather permissive view of when a component part of a greater program can itself constitute a program and should benefit claimants. However, it is worth noting that the language of paragraph [39] (at IPR 526) in fact does seem to focus on functional separation in substance, although the court, as is indicated, arguably rejected that approach in principle. *Dais Studio* was referred to in *CA Inc v ISI Pty Ltd* (above, 18.3) where the court had to consider the relationship between various macros and determine whether an individual macro could constitute a computer program, notwithstanding the fact that it had to interact with other macros to cause a computer to function.

Design, structure or architecture of computer programs

18.6 In *Data Access*, the High Court did not have the opportunity to consider whether the unauthorised reproduction of the overall structure, design or architecture of a program (the 'look and feel' or non-textual elements) can amount to an infringement in a manner analogous to the taking of the plot structure of plays or other literary works. However, the court did say at [85]: 'The structure of what was allegedly taken, its choice of commands, and its combination and sequencing of commands, when compared, at the same level of abstraction, with the original, would all be relevant to …' determining whether a substantial part was reproduced: see above.

An opportunity to determine the question of reproduction of program structure or architecture did present itself to the UK Patents Court in *Cantor Fitzgerald International v Tradition (UK) Ltd.* The plaintiffs, CFI, carried on business as inter-dealer brokers (IDBs) in bonds in London. They owned copyright in a bond brokering computer system, which caused bid particulars to be displayed on screen and enabled dealers to input details and effect deals. Some of its programming employees left to work for Tradition, a rival IDB company. It took them two months to write the Tradition system using the same family of VAX computers and the same programming language, VAX Basic, as the CFI system. The programmers admitted having a copy of the CFI software source code available to them. An expert's analysis revealed that copied code represented between 2 and 3 per cent of the system by number of lines. There were similarities and differences between the systems at the 'architectural' level (ie, in program design and structure) but 'no more than can be accounted for by the fact that both systems were written by the same programmers' (at RPC 102; elsewhere referred to as the programmer having a 'natural order'). Pumfrey J emphasised the importance of the quality of the part allegedly taken, determined by the skill and effort employed in the making of that part. It seems to be generally accepted that the 'architecture' of a computer program is capable of protection if a substantial part of the programmers' skill, labour and judgment went into it. However, in this context, 'architecture' is a vague and ambiguous term. It may be used to refer to the overall structure of the system at a very high level of abstraction; that is, at the level of ideas rather than expression. At that level, adopting it would not amount to copyright infringement. However, at a more detailed level, it could.

The word 'architecture' may also be used to describe what Jacob J, in *Ibcos Computers Ltd v Barclays Mercantile Highland Finance Ltd* (1994) 29 IPR 25, called program structure. In that case, functions that the parties agreed would have to be carried out by any system had been allocated between various programs in a particular manner. Jacob J identified a relevant copyright in the 'compilation of (the plaintiff's) programs': at IPR 38. Although the claim in copyright in this case was not based on any copying at either of these levels of abstraction, it is clearly arguable that similarity at the design, structural or architectural level may amount to a reproduction of a substantial part in an appropriate case: see also *SAS Institute Inc v World Programming Ltd* [2010] EWHC 1829 where Arnold J held that copyright may extend to the 'structure, sequence and organisation' of a program: at [232]. The key is to locate what is copied at the level of protected expression rather than abstract idea, conceptual approach or function; in that sense, there is an analogy with the issues surrounding the copying of the 'plot' in dramatic work infringement cases. Whether or not that is actionable depends critically on the level of detail with which the 'plot' is described. In *Navitaire Inc v Easyjet Airline Co* [2006] RPC 111; [2004] EWHC 1725 (Ch), the court rejected copyright protection for the 'business logic' or 'look and feel' of a computer program and did not accept the plot analogy. In *Karum Group LLC v Fisher & Paykel Financial Services Ltd* [2014] NZCA 389, the question of whether copyright subsisted in 'non-literal' elements of a computer program was considered: see at [98]–[116], the court reviewing some of the English and US authority in this field. More recently in *EIFY Systems Pty Ltd v 3D Safety Services Pty Ltd* [2017] NSWSC 1310 at [412] the court said that '[i]t may be accepted, at least for the purposes of argument, that the structure, sequence or organisation of a computer program may be the subject of copyright', pointing out that Arnold J said as much in *SAS Institute*. However, the court went on to point out that 'the distinction that his Lordship drew between the design of the program on the one hand and its functionality on the other is critical': at [413]. The plaintiff's case based on structure and organisation; layout, format and look; or 'look and feel' ultimately failed, the court usefully reviewing relevant precedent: at [411]–[432]. As there was no evidence before the court comparing the source or object codes of the two 'online induction systems' at issue, there was no breach based on reproduction of actual code either. The case illustrates that there is no copyright in 'computer systems' as such, they having to be broken down into their constituent parts to mount a case (also including, for instance, as in this matter, photographs as artistic works, and potentially other Pt III or Pt IV material that might have been individually reproduced); see also *StatusCard Australia Pty Ltd v Rotondo* [2009] 1 Qd R 559; (2009) 78 IPR 625 (below 18.14).

Also note that in *Admar Computers Pty Ltd v Ezy Systems Pty Ltd* (1997) 38 IPR 659 it was held that pseudocode analysis could not be used to prove copyright infringement by reproduction of the design and programming logic. Because pseudocode is an abstraction of the functionality of a program, two programs might easily be shown to have similar pseudocodes because they have similar functions. This would be akin to considering functional similarity as an indication of reproduction or adaptation, which is not appropriate. In looking at the structure and design features in a non-literal infringement case, the court was restricted to 'analysing the contents and arrangement within the four corners of the literary work': at IPR 670. Thus, a careful line must be drawn between similarities that result from programs performing the same functions and the actual copying of architecture, structure or compilation of programs at a level that constitutes the taking of expression rather than an idea.

Infringement by importation and dealing (ss 37 and 38)

18.7 There may be little an owner of copyright in computer programs can do about widespread private or domestic infringements practised by individuals or even within businesses or organisations. However, the chances of detection and effective legal action against distributors of illegally made or pirated software are slightly better. In 2003, the Act was amended to legalise the parallel importation of computer programs: see Copyright Amendment (Parallel Importation) Act 2003 (Cth) and s 44E of the Copyright Act 1968. However, under the new provisions, the onus to prove that the imported program is legitimate is on the importer: see Copyright Act, s 130B. The copyright owner cannot circumvent the provisions by relying on copyright in accessories to the computer program (see ss 44C, 102C, 10(1) 'accessory'; 10AD). As to infringing installation and supply of software on computers, see, for example, *Microsoft Corporation v Atifo Pty Ltd* (1997) 38 IPR 643, *Autodesk Australia Pty Ltd v Cheung* (1990) 17 IPR 69 and *Microsoft Corporation v Goodview Electronics Pty Ltd* (2000) 49 IPR 578, a case in which price discrepancy was taken to indicate constructive knowledge. Note also that computer programs may be protected by TPMs against infringement; in that case, the anti-circumvention provisions may come into play: see, for example, *Stevens v Kabushiki Kaisha Sony Computer Entertainment* below at 18.18.

Shrinkwrap, clickwrap, browsewrap and shareware licences

18.8 The owner of copyright in a computer program can restrict permitted uses by way of an express direction or licence at the time of purchase of the copy of the program. However, the effectiveness of such practices depends on the enforceability of licensing conditions imposed at the point of sale and purchase of computer software. Shrinkwrap or clickwrap licences attempt to impose conditions on the purchaser or licensee of software (or other copyright material) by construing the opening of the wrapping of a computer pack or an 'I agree' mouse click as acceptance of terms. Browsewrap licences are used by websites and deem browsing to constitute acceptance of their terms. Licence terms may restrict the purchaser to commercial as opposed to private or domestic use, or vice versa, disclaim warranties, deny users the authority to make back-up copies, modify or resell the software, decompile it and so on. Note that, in terms of Pt II Div 4A of the Copyright Act, the only statutory exception that can be derogated from by agreement is s 47B(1) and (2): see s 47H. Any contractual term purporting to exclude the effect of the exceptions in s 47B(3), s 47C, s 47DS, s 47E or s 47F is without effect. The extent to which other statutory provisions can be derogated from by contractual agreement is considered in detail in the Copyright Law Review Committee's (CLRC) *Report on Copyright and Contract*, 2002 ('CLRC Contract Report'). But are shrinkwrap licences enforceable? Typically, there is no contractual relationship between the copyright owner and the software purchaser — no consideration passes between them — but only between purchaser and retailer or reseller. Construing the vendor as the copyright owner's agent is usually, certainly in the case of ordinary consumer software, not consistent with the facts and circumstances. However, it may be that the purchaser of a copy of a work becomes a licensee of the copyright owner because using the work involves acts comprised in the copyright. However, the terms and conditions of such a licence may not have been brought to the notice of the customer, normally becoming apparent to a purchaser only after the bargain has concluded.

However, in *ProCD Inc v Zeidenberg*, 86 F3d 1447 (1996), none of these concerns impressed the 7th Circuit US Court of Appeals. The court held the terms of a shrinkwrap licence enforceable, finding that Zeidenberg's conduct constituted acceptance of ProCD's offer to license its goods. Having enjoyed an opportunity to review the licence terms, Zeidenberg had chosen to use the software. The court reached its conclusions on the basis of economic policy rather than on the basis of established principles of contract law. According to the CLRC Contract Report, subsequent US decisions have 'been mixed'. Although commonly used, the status of shrinkwrap licences remains uncertain in Australia, as there has been no judicial consideration of the matter. However, it may be that certain conditions in shrinkwrap licences are now so commonplace that consumers have a general knowledge of the kinds of restrictions they impose. Such conditions can then be used to construe the confines of a bare licence rather than to construe the terms of a contractual licence to which the consumer never agreed. The inclusion of conditions in the shrinkwrap licence then serves to clarify the intention of the copyright owner as to the extent of any bare licence. The situation concerning clickwrap licences is, in many ways, different, since agreement can be sought before purchase of the software is completed, and there is more commonly a direct contractual relationship between copyright owner and consumer. Important will be that unusual terms are effectively brought to the attention of the purchaser so as to secure clear agreement to them. In relation to usual or well-known terms agreement may be more readily inferred or assumed.

The provision of 'shareware' — computer programs made freely available on the internet — is now common. In some cases, shareware is made available with no express conditions attached (consideration often being required to access or use some other product provided by the shareware supplier). In other cases, shareware is supplied on a trial basis, either under an honour system (where the user pays a licence fee from expiry of the evaluation period) or with some mechanism so that the program is disabled after a fixed term (usually 30 days) unless a licence agreement is executed with the provider. Sometimes, a basic version of a program is made available for free, but a more advanced version must be purchased. The confines of an implied licence attached to shareware made available on the internet were examined in *Trumpet Software Pty Ltd v OzEmail Pty Ltd* (1996) 34 IPR 481. Heerey J held that a shareware licence was a bare licence and not a contractual licence. The 'analogous doctrine of implied contractual terms as expounded by the Privy Council in *BP Refinery (Westernport) Pty Ltd v Shire of Hastings* (1977) 180 CLR 266 at 283; 16 ALR 363 at 376' was the most appropriate basis for construing the terms and conditions of the licence: at IPR 499. Analogy with a contract was appropriate because the ultimate aim was for the shareware licence to mature into a contract if evaluation proved positive. OzEmail had distributed Trumpet's shareware as a promotion pack with certain magazines. Heerey J saw evaluation as the central purpose of shareware. A distributor who further distributed shareware without the express consent of the copyright owner, even if for profit or together with other software, did not breach the terms and conditions implied by analogy where shareware was made freely available on the internet. By exposing the product to more potential contractual licensees, the further distribution should be to the advantage of the copyright owner. However, the purpose of evaluation was defeated if the program was altered in any way before its further distribution. In this case, the program had been altered to reroute users to OzEmail as an internet service provider (ISP) and to largely obscure the notification of Trumpet's rights to payment from users who decided to keep the software. Thus, Heerey J held (at IPR 500) that 'even if any licence in favour of OzEmail had not been revoked, OzEmail breached conditions of the licence by the changes it made to the Trumpet Winsock 2.0B program'. (It was arguable that the general licence, which did not restrict distribution, was revoked since Trumpet had refused permission to OzEmail to distribute copies of the program as part of its promotional campaign.) The case is an interesting exploration of the conditions of new licensing arrangements that typically, but not exclusively, arise with internet distribution; in fact, it will often also be that such shareware is distributed with new computers or with other paid-for programs. Shareware allows traders to overcome the difficulty that a computer program package, once the wrapping is off, is not readily returnable if found wanting, as Heerey J pointed out.

There is some disagreement as to the proper approach to implied licences in copyright. Should the terms be construed, along the lines of Heerey J's decision in *Trumpet Software*, on the basis of an analogy with contract (by reference to the factors in *BP Refinery (Westernport) Pty Ltd*, as confirmed by the High Court in *Codelfa Construction Pty Ltd v State Rail Authority of NSW* (1982) 149 CLR 337; [1982] HCA 24) or by statutory implication? The overriding requirement under the contractual analogy approach is that the intention of the parties be identified and given effect. By virtue of the business efficacy rule, no term will be implied if the contract is effective without it. The alternative approach is to construe a term as being implied not by interpretation of contractual terms but by law. This approach is logically appropriate in cases where there is no contractual relationship but only a bare permission, licence or authorisation — as is arguably the case with shrinkwrap licences: see above. Many of the cases relating to implied terms, such as the older case of *Beck v Montana* [1964] NSWR 229 and the more recent cases of *Devefi Pty Ltd v Mateffy Perl Nagy Pty Ltd* (1993) 37 IPR 477 and *Concrete Pty Ltd v Parramatta Design and Developments Pty Ltd* (2006) 70 IPR 468, revolve around implying a licence to build or complete a building on the basis of copyrighted architectural plans. In such cases, a contract-based approach applying the *Codelfa* principles may well be appropriate. In cases where there is no agreement of any kind between the parties that can form a framework for implying terms, the aim of which is to give efficacy to the broader contract (ie, where there is no contract or the parties are in a pre-contractual stage), there is little point to a contract-based approach.

Software: patents versus copyright

18.9 Copyright subsists in original computer programs, as discussed at the outset of this chapter. However, an anti-copying right offers only limited exclusivity, and copyright extends only to the form of expression of the program in a certain language, code or notation. It does not cover functionality or the result or effect of operating a computer program. The statutory exceptions relating to computer programs (ss 47B–47H of the Copyright Act 1968; see above) further limit the scope of computer program copyright. Patenting of software, and of computer-implemented inventions in general, is an attractive alternative (a standard patent or an innovation patent, which has a lower inventiveness threshold). While copyright is not an exclusive right over the way a program operates, a patent aims precisely at the monopolisation of functionality. Constituting a real monopoly, a patent also denies even inventors who arrive at the same invention independently the right to use it: thus, software developers must always be alert to possible rights of patentees. Since the computer industry is disparate and diversified, this is a significant imposition. In contrast, copyright protection allows software developers to create computer programs without concern for other people's rights, as long as they do so independently (ie, without access and copying). Arguably, this encourages a diversified and competitive market for software applications. But patents also have advantages for competitors, since compulsory publication reveals the details of the operation of an invention. Under copyright law, reverse engineering is a prima facie infringement, making information about the operation of a computer program more difficult to access legally, although limited decompilation exceptions have now been introduced: see s 47H of the Copyright Act and above at 18.4. The examinable register of granted patents also enables competitors to assess their legal rights, identify a patentee (as a potential licensor) and avoid infringement of exclusive rights.

However, patenting of computer programs involves considerable transaction costs. A worldwide patenting program is expensive. Although stringent novelty and inventiveness requirements have to be satisfied at the application stage, the validity of a granted software patent is not guaranteed, and its value therefore remains uncertain to a degree. Patent protection is also shorter term than copyright; this may be more appropriate in a period of rapid technological advances. The result of the growth of software patenting will be an increase in cross-licensing and cross-infringement between holders of computer-related patent portfolios.

Computer programs: patentable subject matter?

18.10 A global trend has seen increased acceptance of computer-implemented inventions in general as appropriate subject matter for the granting of a patent. In the US, the decision in *State Street Banking Co v Signature Financial Group Inc* 149 F 3d 1368, 47 USPQ 2d 1596 (Fed Cir 1998) confirmed the position earlier expressed in *Re Alappat* 33 F 3d 1526 at 1544, 31 USPQ 1545 (Federal Circuit 1994) that the presence of an abstract idea or theoretical computation in the form of a mathematical algorithm was no bar to the granting of a patent if it was claimed as part of a practical application (*State Street Banking* at F 3d 1373, *Alappat* at F 3d 1544, 1577). In Australia, see *Welcome Real-Time v Catuity Inc* (2001) 51 IPR 327 (*Catuity*) and *Grant v Commissioner of Patents* (2006) 154 FCR 62; 69 IPR 221; [2006] FCAFC 120, as discussed in Chapter 7 Patents: Subject Matter. However, that a claimed method or system includes computing hardware or processing steps alone will not confer patentability: see *Research Affiliates LLC v Commissioner of Patents* (2014) 227 FCR 378; 109 IPR 364; [2014] FCAFC 150 and *Commissioner of Patents v RPL Central Pty Ltd* (2015) 238 FCR 27; 115 IPR 461; [2015] FCAFC 177 which related to computer-implemented business methods. A process or method that is not of an applied or technical nature in itself will not be magically transformed into patentable because it is claimed as a series of steps to be performed on or by a computer. The difficulty lies in drawing the line. Thus a 'method for linking a computer user to an advertising message by way of an intermediate engagement offer' was held to be patentable subject matter in *Rokt Pte Ltd v Commissioner of Patents* (2018) 139 IPR 1; [2018] FCA 1988 (see in particular at [205]–[208]); whereas in *Encompass Corporation Pty Ltd v InfoTrack Pty Ltd* (2018) 130 IPR 387; [2018] FCA 421 Perram J held that a method for collecting and displaying data did not concern patentable subject matter: there was no improvement to the functioning in a computer involved.

By contrast the application at issue in *Catuity* (above) clearly concerned patentable subject matter, as the claims were limited to practical steps being performed on computers in overcoming a technical problem. In the same manner, computer programs are patentable subject matter in Australia if the steps claimed belong to the practical arts and result in an 'artificial state of affairs' (see *NRDC*; the Australian Patent Office's *Manual of Practice and Procedure* [2.9.2.7]). If some technical effect is achieved, such as the improved curve on a computer visual display unit in *IBM Corporation v Smith* (1991) 33 FCR 218, there is little difficulty. Furthermore, where computer-implemented inventions do little more than adapt existing real-world knowledge, processes or solutions to a digital environment, they may be vulnerable to an allegation of either lack of novelty or obviousness. Even if certain algorithms present a non-obvious solution to a computing problem, only specific applications of an algorithm are patentable, not the algorithm itself. As a result, a novel application of an algorithm contained within a patented invention may not infringe the granted patent reciting that algorithm.

Programming solutions using existing languages and programming structures also would rarely be inventive or novel enough. Further, comprehensive novelty searches face considerable practical difficulties because of the disparate nature of software development; as a result, granted software patents may be vulnerable to legal challenge for lack of novelty.

Database Rights

Electronic database rights in Australia

18.11 Databases, in the sense of collections or compilations of data, exist in many different forms. However, the development of electronic (digital) databases has enabled storage of thus far unseen amounts of data in a format adapted to flexible search, selection and retrieval with software tools, as well as artificial intelligence (AI) applications. A database is a valuable commodity, and compilers seek legal protection against unauthorised use, extraction or access. Can copyright serve this purpose?

The level of originality determines whether or not copyright subsists in a given database. Copyright protection should be available only for those databases in which an author has invested such intellect, skill and effort as to entitle them to exclusive rights. A further determinant of copyright protection is whether the database qualifies as a work, most likely a literary work. Arguably, as is discussed below, databases containing data ordered or structured only for the purpose of effective retrieval by software programs may not fall into this category. Other jurisdictions have provided statutory sui generis database extraction rights for non-original databases that do not attract copyright protection. Such regimes give owners exclusive rights not over the actual information stored but in relation to the investment in the assembly and manner of composition of the database. No such statutory rights outside copyright exist in Australia. In relevant international forums, Australia has maintained that databases have adequate legal protection here, given that the low originality threshold makes copyright protection available for a majority of databases. However, this position has become less tenable with the decision of the High Court in *IceTV*.

The threshold in Australia was, until recently, very low, proof of 'industrious collection' being sufficient, and white pages of a telephone directory therefore being copyright-protected: see *Desktop Marketing Systems Pty Ltd v Telstra Corporation Ltd* (2002) 119 FCR 491; 55 IPR 1. However, this approach was undermined by the more recent decision in *IceTV*, which emphasised the need for an authorial imprint, the effect of independent intellectual activity. The resulting refusal of copyright protection for white pages in *Telstra Corporation Ltd v Phone Directories Co Pty Ltd* was the unsurprising consequence, the court also stressing that a literary work must have a human author (and not computer systems alone). The standard is now comparable with that in the US, where in *Feist Publications Inc v Rural Telephone Service Co* 499 US 340 at 345 (1991), the Supreme Court said that 'to qualify for copyright protection, a work must be original to the author … Original, as the term is used in copyright, means only that the work was independently created by the author (as opposed to copied from other works), and that it possesses at least some minimal degree of creativity.' It is now also analogous to the standard applied in civil law jurisdictions in Europe, which is more akin to the US standard.

It is the European Union that has led the way with the introduction of a new 'database extraction right' for non-original databases. European Directive 96/9/EC of 11 March 1996 on the legal protection of databases defines 'database' as 'a collection of independent works, data or other materials arranged in a systematic or methodical way and individually accessible by electronic or other means'. Legal protection is afforded against unauthorised extraction and/or reutilisation of the whole or a substantial part of the contents of a database. The protection lasts for 15 years from the date of completion of the database and protects the maker of the database who shows there has been a qualitatively and/or quantitatively substantial investment in the obtaining, verification or presentation of the contents. Some exceptions are prescribed; for example, in relation to teaching or scientific research. By contrast, the passage of non-original database legislation through the US Congress has met with resistance because of concerns about monopolisation of information content. Several measures have been introduced but have failed to pass: the Database Investment and Intellectual Property Antipiracy Act (1996) HR 3531, 104th Cong (1996); the Consumer and Investor Access to Information Act, HR 1858, 106th Cong (1999); the Collections of Information Antipiracy Act HR 354, 106th Cong (1999); a 'bill to prohibit the misappropriation of certain databases' produced jointly by the House Commerce and Energy Committee and the House Judiciary Committee in 2003 (HR 3261); and a 'bill to prohibit the misappropriation of databases while ensuring consumer access to factual information' 2004 (HR 3872).

In Australia, the CLRC, in its *Report on Computer Software Protection*, 1995, recommended that consideration of the introduction of database rights in non-original databases be deferred until after consideration of the EU Database Directive, but the adoption of that directive in 1996 did not result in any active consideration of that model here. Consideration of the EU Directive (which came into force on 1 January 1998) is nonetheless important, as it contains a reciprocity clause; that is, data provided by another country and used in Europe will be protected only if that country has equivalent database protection. A World Intellectual Property Organization (WIPO) treaty on intellectual property in respect of databases was considered but not adopted by a WIPO diplomatic conference in December 1996. The relevant World Trade Organization (WTO) Trade-Related Aspects of Intellectual Property Rights (TRIPS) Agreement provision is art 10(2), which provides:

> Compilations of data or other material, whether in machine readable or other form, which by reason of the selection or arrangement of their contents constitute intellectual creations shall be protected as such. Such protection, which shall not extend to the data or material itself, shall be without prejudice to any copyright subsisting in the data or material itself.

Databases that attract copyright as original compilations — for instance, commercial catalogues, dictionaries and encyclopaedias, precedents, anthologies and books of materials — will naturally do so whether in analogue or digital format. However, copyright protection for an original database has its limitations: only the particular arrangement and presentation of material that reflects the intellectual activity of an identifiable author or authors is protected by compilation copyright and not the contents or individual items as such; it is a 'thin' form of copyright. Merely taking or extracting information from an original database or some individual item or entry does not amount to an infringement of copyright. A substantial part of a compilation will have to be a part in which the structure and organisation imparted on the data by the author are apparent. Generally, infringement is likely to result only if a considerable proportion of an original database is reproduced, usually by some direct means of facsimile copying or extraction.

Hyperlinks

18.12 A hyperlink is a link to an internet location (URL) embedded in either 'a piece of text that is differentiated from regular text on a computer's screen by a special colour or formatting such as underlining' (a hypertext reference link or HREF link) or a graphical element from another source incorporated in a website (an in-line image or IMG link). IMG links appear automatically within a website: interface users need not click on a link. The URL appearing on screen is that of the website on which the image is displayed, not the URL of the image. As Jane states: 'A browser accessing a web document containing an IMG link will automatically retrieve the images from their original sources and incorporate them into the website's onscreen display.'[2] HREF links, however, require the user to click on the highlighted text, which will direct them to another location. Ideally, reasonable protocols requiring adequate acknowledgment and so on should be observed when any kinds of links are used. Unauthorised linking into another website, above all when done by means of unacknowledged embedded links, frames and IMGs, is a threat to the economic interests of the owner of the linked site. It allows a browser to bypass advertising and site promotion: see, for instance, *Shetland Times Ltd v Wills* (1996) 37 IPR 71, *Washington Post Co v TotalNEWS Inc* 97 Civ 1190 (SDNY) and *Ticketmaster Corp v Tickets.com*, 99-7654, US District Court, Central District of California, Los Angeles, 27 March 2000. In terms of competition between website proprietors, linking into a website enables the linking site:

1. to avoid the cost of establishing a website itself;
2. to divert advertising revenue; and
3. to divert custom.

In the US *Ticketmaster* case, the customer clicked on the HREF 'buy this ticket from another online ticketing company' on the Tickets.com site and was then instantly transferred to the inside web page of Ticketmaster (bypassing the home page) relating to the particular event in question. The customer could then buy the tickets (from Ticketmaster, not Tickets.com) online. The interior web page contained the Ticketmaster logo alerting customers that they were dealing with Ticketmaster not Tickets.com.

The inapplicability of copyright to this kind of overt HREF linking was succinctly expressed by Hupp J in the *Ticketmaster* decision: '... hyperlinking does not itself involve a violation of the Copyright Act (whatever it may do for other claims) since no copying is involved. The customer is automatically transferred to the particular genuine web page of the original author. There is no deception in what is happening. This is analogous to using a library's card index to get reference to particular items, albeit

2. See A Jane, 'Hyperlink Technology and the WWW — Trying on the "Coat of Copyright"' (1999) 36 *IP Forum* 14.

faster and more efficiently.' Although where embedded and unacknowledged links are used there is arguably deception in what is happening, this has little relevance to the question of copyright infringement. No reproduction takes place if a customer is directed to the linked site. However, incorporating text from a linked website (such as a news headline, as in the *Shetland Times* case above) in an HREF hyperlink may constitute reproduction of a substantial part of a copyright work. In Australia, the reproduction of headlines and titles (which could be in the form of hyperlinks) was considered in *Fairfax Media Publications Pty Ltd v Reed International Books Australia Pty Ltd* (2010) 189 FCR 109; [2010] FCA 984 (*Fairfax Media v Reed*); see Chapter 3 Copyright: Ownership and Exploitation.

The communication to the public right, like the reproduction right, will not normally be infringed by incorporating on a website a link to an unconnected server containing an infringing sound file. In *Universal Music Australia Pty Ltd v Cooper* (2005) 150 FCR 1; 65 IPR 409, the court held that it was rather the person who uploaded the file itself onto a server who was responsible for the communication. However, including hyperlinks to infringing material may amount to authorisation of copyright infringement. Although mere facilitation and knowledge of likely infringement do not constitute authorisation, in *Cooper*, the defendant's website was designed and organised to facilitate copyright infringement, which could thus be said to have been approved by him. The defence of s 112E of the Copyright Act 1968 (Cth) did not apply, because Cooper had not merely provided the facilities used by another to infringe but had encouraged and structured the infringements that occurred by providing a well-organised website with multiple links to other servers with infringing sound files available for download. The *Cooper* decision is extensively quoted in *Pokemon Company International, Inc v Redbubble Ltd* (2017) 129 IPR 1; [2017] FCA 1541; see also *Hells Angels* (above 18.1).

Computer Games, Websites and Screen Displays

Computer games

18.13 Computer games are a relatively new digital product combining functional, expressive and interactive elements. Certain component parts may attract intellectual property protection; for example, the processor as an eligible layout under the Circuit Layouts Act 1989 (Cth), incorporated computer programs as copyright works or as computer-implemented inventions under the Patents Act 1990, or the graphic elements as artistic works. The creative skill and effort engaged in the selection and combination of the disparate component parts in an integrated interactive product appear to be largely unprotected, since the Copyright Act 1968 (Cth) makes no express provision for computer games as such. However, in *Galaxy Electronics Pty Ltd v Sega Enterprises Ltd* (1997) 75 FCR 8, the Full Federal Court upheld Burchett J's decision at first instance (see *Sega Enterprises Ltd v Galaxy Electronics Pty Ltd* (1996) 69 FCR 268) that video games involving computer-generated images were cinematograph films within the meaning of ss 10 and 24 of the Copyright Act. The games concerned were *Virtual Cop* and *Daytona USA*. Except for the opening and closing sequences, the events depicted on screen from screening to screening depended on the player's input. Unless all the players' responses were perfectly correct, the sequences would differ every time. However, there was a limit to the objects, scenes and sounds available to be screened in response to the player's inputs. The game consisted of a sophisticated computer program, different artistic works in the form of characters and scenes, sound effects, music and simple dialogue. All the aural and visual elements of the game were stored in the form of mathematical coordinates translated by the software into actual images on screen. Wilcox J (with whom Lindgren and Lockhart JJ agreed) endorsed Burchett J's view that visual images that had been devised by the creators were embodied in the computer program and were capable, by the use of the program, of being shown as moving pictures. The way in which they were embodied was of no significance. Although the visual appearance may vary with each play, there had been a treatment of an article or thing to embody specific sounds and images within it so that the sounds or images were capable of being reproduced from that article or thing: see s 24 of the Copyright Act. The visual images and sounds that could appear were within limited parameters, which resulted from the embodiment of specific visual images and sounds within the program. There appears to be little relevant difference between what was here referred to as a video game and what is now commonly referred to as a computer game. However, there are limitations as to how far the approach in *Galaxy* can be extended. In *Aristocrat Leisure Industries Pty Ltd v Pacific Gaming Pty Ltd* (2000) 105 FCR 153; 50 IPR 29, Tamberlin J, while accepting that the Copyright Act should be given a liberal rather than a literal and technology-specific interpretation, doubted that the electronic simulation of the traditional rotating symbols on a gaming machine had the requisite movement and progression to constitute a cinematograph film. Further, cinematograph films are subject matter in Pt IV, which means that only direct and facsimile technological derivation can amount to an infringement. Producing an analogous game independently will not — in that case the other alternatives are to consider the computer game as a computer program, or as a computer program combined with other works (eg, artistic works), but then see the issues raised above under 'Computer Programs' at 18.3ff.

In *Kabushiki Kaisha Sony Computer Entertainment v Stevens* (2003) 132 FCR 31; 57 IPR 161, it was argued that the computer games concerned were either computer programs or cinematograph films under the Copyright Act that were being reproduced or copied in the course of playing the games. The submission was that playing a computer game generates temporary copies of a computer program, or of other works or subject matter making up the game, in the RAM of a computer. The same can be said when a sound or video file (eg, an MP3 file) is played on a media player. However, Lindgren J, with whom French J agreed, came to the same conclusion (although obiter) as the trial judge: no substantial reproduction of a computer program or copying of a cinematograph film occurred in the RAM in the process of playing the computer games concerned (he derived guidance from *Australian Video Retailers Association Ltd v Warner Home Video Pty Ltd* and *Microsoft Corporation v Business Boost Pty Ltd* (2000) 49 IPR 573). Two obstacles stood in the way: first, the requirement that a reproduction be in material form (ie, in a form from which it could itself be reproduced, which was arguably not possible with transient copies in the RAM) and, second, the requirement that any putative copying or reproduction in the RAM be of a 'substantial part' of the source program or subject matter. However, as to the first point, the inclusion of s 10(5) and (6) subsequent to the Australia–United States Free Trade Agreement 2004 (AUSFTA) overturned the *Sony* decision, but the effect of these new provisions is mitigated by s 43B, 'Temporary reproductions of works as part of a technical process of use'. Note, however, s 43B(2), which excludes the operation of the section where the work used is itself infringing.

Websites and screen displays

18.14 Websites or other interactive or functional screen displays are, in effect, a collection of different categories of works and subject matter tied together by computer programs. Although a combination of pre-existing literary and artistic works may be regarded as a compilation, and thus a literary work by virtue of s 10, it would stretch normal understanding to so categorise products that also incorporate computer programs, musical works, sound recordings and films. Further, despite the decision in *Galaxy*, and keeping in mind the limitations imposed in *Aristocrat Leisure*, it seems unlikely that the category 'cinematograph film' could apply to websites. The dynamic appearance and interactivity of a website or screen display may be based on the particular functionality of underlying software: for this, computer program copyright, patents or circuit layout rights may provide some protection. Note also that designs registration is not applicable to computer screen images or appearance. In *Re Applications by Comshare Inc* (1991) 23 IPR 145, an application for designs registration of a screen display was refused. The design features were subordinate to the literary and artistic content, and designs appearing on a computer screen were held not to amount to a design for the appearance of that screen. *Apple Inc* (2017) 127 IPR 191; [2017] ADO 6 stands for the same proposition because '[t]he images that appear on a display screen are not visual features of the display screen. They are manifestations of software … in combination with hardware and streams of electrons': at [25]. It may also be that the relevant 'features' are too variable in nature and therefore do not fit in the designs regime. Visual features must also be able to be appreciated when the product is 'at rest'. Some other jurisdictions do provide for the registration of typefaces, fonts and branding assets (eg, the UK; the EU). Note that circuit layouts as protected by the Circuit Layouts Act 1989 are excluded from registration as designs: see s 43(1)(c)(i–iii).

The remaining alternative is to rely on various forms of copyright in some constituent parts(s). But *StatusCard Australia v Rotondo* illustrates some of the difficulties with this approach. Many of the aspects of a computer interface are ephemeral or 'evanescent' and constantly changing and/or are completed by the actions of the user rather than the creator of the underlying backbone or skeleton. In *StatusCard*, the court stripped out all the aspects of the interface that were generated by particular use of the display at any given time, being left with a rather bare framework in which the program would display racing-related data, depending on the user's choice of commands or inputs. That framework could be a table and thus a literary work by virtue of s 10 of the Copyright Act; however, leaving out the variable elements left very little, just some lines and coloured panes, which could hardly amount to a table. Furthermore, it was not likely to be sufficiently original; in this regard, Chesterman J doubted the correctness of *Kalamazoo (Aust) Pty Ltd v Compact Business Systems Pty Ltd* (1985)

84 FLR 101. The alternative, that the boxed lines constituted an original drawing, was also rejected, since insufficient effort and deliberation had gone into the choice of lines and colours used.

Digital Distribution of Copyright Materials

The internet

18.15 While computers generated a new uniform medium of creative expression, linking computers through the internet also produced a revolutionary new channel for the distribution of the various categories of copyright works and subject matter. The implications of this phenomenon of 'copyright convergence' in the digital environment were first canvassed in *Highways to Change: Copyright in the New Communications Environment*, Report of the Copyright Convergence Group (CCG), 1994. The most substantial reform proposal to emerge from the CCG Report and from the WIPO Copyright Treaty, 1996 (WCT), was enacted in the Copyright Amendment (Digital Agenda) Act 2000 (Cth) (the Digital Agenda Act): the hitherto separate broadcast and cable transmission rights were subsumed in a new technology-neutral right of communication to the public, adapted to also cover internet-based distribution. The new right of communication to the public was accompanied by incidental amendments that circumscribe the role of copyright law on the internet. The basic elements of the WCT copyright reform model were as follows:

1. the introduction of a broad right of 'communication to the public'; that is, of making copyright material available for individuals to access at remote locations by technological means, whatever the precise nature of the technology involved: a 'technology-neutral' right; see art 8 of the WCT;
2. legal support for efforts of owners to secure copyright by technological means, by both civil actions and criminal sanctions, in relation to the circumvention of security and record-keeping technologies such as encryption, electronic rights management information (ERMI), watermarking and so on: see arts 11 and 12 of the WCT;
3. limiting and clarifying the potential copyright liability of ISPs for infringing material stored on or passing through their servers, with little obligation to 'police' the copyright status of such material: see agreed statement concerning art 8 of the WCT;
4. ensuring that copyright does not obstruct the technical operation of the internet, by providing exceptions for copying and other theoretical breaches of copyright law that occur in the course of transmission, use and automatic storage of copyright material: see agreed statement concerning art 10 of the WCT, permitting creation of specific digital exceptions in addition to extending existing exceptions to the digital environment; and
5. extending established exceptions (eg, fair dealing) to the digital environment: see art 10 of the WCT and agreed statement relating to art 10 of the WCT.

The WCT treaty allows signatories a fair degree of latitude in implementing these basic treaty obligations in national legislation and in making provision for exceptions and derogations. (Note that although the main focus of the Digital Agenda Act is on the internet, it also contains a number of provisions relating to computer programs: see also above in this chapter.)

The House of Representatives Standing Committee on Legal and Constitutional Affairs (the HRSCLCA) published a comprehensive report with 38 recommendations in November 1999: the Advisory Report on the Copyright Amendment (Digital Agenda) Bill 1999. The bill's approach was to apply existing copyright principles to the digital environment by analogy. However, during the course of its inquiry into the bill, the HRSCLCA came to realise that 'the digital environment could not be likened to the print environment in all respects': Advisory Report at [1.23]. The HRSCLCA also agreed with the Attorney-General's Department and the (then) Department of Communications, Information Technology and the Arts that 'in some areas the new legislation is entering into uncharted waters ... new technologies and business models for the online trade of copyright material are still evolving': at [1.10]. The committee 'became aware that it was indeed entering into uncharted waters, equipped with only a priori arguments from opposing interests': at [1.11]. As a result, the committee supported a proposed review of the legislation in three years' time, which the government committed to (see the Explanatory Memorandum of the Copyright Amendment (Digital Agenda) Bill 2000, Regulation Impact Statement, [7]). The review commenced on 1 April 2003 and concluded in 2004: see the Digital Agenda Act Review and Recommendations, January 2004. However, the conclusion of the AUSFTA intervened, the government claiming that the 2004 report informed the process of implementation of the AUSFTA copyright provisions in Australia. The AUSFTA contained some detailed provisions concerning copyright law, which are reflected in the subsequent amendments to the Copyright Act 1968: see the US Free Trade Agreement Implementation Act 2004 (Cth) and the Copyright Legislation Amendment Act 2004 (Cth). More recently, the Australian Law Reform Commission (ALRC) was tasked to investigate whether the current exceptions and statutory licences in the Copyright Act 'are adequate and appropriate in the digital era': see ALRC Report 122, *Copyright and the Digital Economy*, February 2014. Its most significant recommendation was for the fair dealing and private use exceptions to be subsumed under a proposed new and flexible 'fair use' defence. That same recommendation can also be found in the Productivity Commission report of 2016 on intellectual property (PC Report)[3] which points out that '[l]ooking forward in a digital age, the independent analysis also found that prescription (fair dealing) can be more of a liability and flexibility (fair use) an asset': at p 165. A fair use exception would also address the problem that 'Australia's current exceptions for fair dealing are too narrow and prescriptive, do not reflect the way people today consume and use content in the digital world, and do not accommodate new legitimate uses of copyright material': ibid. The main goal pursued by the change would be to better accommodate certain transformative uses of copyright material in the digital age. At the time of writing the government was still reviewing the mooted introduction of a fair use exception.

3. Productivity Commission, *Intellectual Property Arrangements*, Inquiry Report No 78, Canberra, September 2016.

The right of communication to the public

18.16 The core provisions of the Digital Agenda Act reflect the WCT approach:

- the new right of communication to the public, encompassing the old broadcast and cable transmission rights;
- fair dealing and library exceptions adapted to the digital environment and to the right to communicate to the public;
- criminal sanctions and civil actions in relation to the supply of circumvention devices and in relation to ERMI;
- limitations of ISP liability for copyright infringement; and
- the introduction of exceptions for temporary reproductions in the course of the ordinary operation and use of the internet.

The AUSFTA later resulted in significant amendments concerning circumvention devices, rendering illegal not only the making and supply but also the use in certain circumstances of circumvention devices and services and also in relation to ISPs (or service providers (SPs) under the current Copyright Act; see Pt V, Div 2AA 'Limitation on remedies available against service providers') with the introduction of safe harbour provisions in relation to copyright liability.

The right to communicate to the public is further defined in s 10(1): 'communicate' means 'make available online or electronically transmit (whether over a path, or a combination of paths, provided by a material substance or otherwise) a work or other subject-matter'. 'To the public' means to the public within or outside Australia. The right is technology neutral and applies to all works and subject matter, with the exception of published editions. The word 'online' is not further defined. The right encompasses the uploading of works or subject matter onto a server, which makes them available for downloading by a member of the public, irrespective of whether such downloading or accessing actually occurs. Subsequently, it has been held that merely incorporating links in a website to infringing material stored on a different and unconnected server does not amount to making that material available to the public: see *Cooper* (above at 18.11). However, it will be different for those who provide file-swapping services or software such as Napster, an early provider of such a service in the US. Napster was found liable for the US equivalent of authorisation liability; that is, contributory copyright infringement: see, on appeal, *A&M Records, Inc v Napster, Inc*, 239 F Supp 3d 1004 (9th Cir 2001); see also *MGM Studios, Inc et al v Grokster, Inc* 545 US (2005). In Australia, the question of whether providing file-swapping software whose operation is not controlled by the provider can amount to authorisation of copyright infringement arose in *Universal Music Australia Pty Ltd v Sharman License Holdings Ltd* (2005) 222 FCR 465; 65 IPR 289; (2005) FCA 1242. Section 101(1A) of the Copyright Act sets out the factors to be considered in determining authorisation liability in relation to infringement of copyright in sound recordings (the rights in s 85(1) of the Act). In relation to the application of s 112E, the court held that '[i]f the most that can be said against Sharman is that it has provided the facilities used by another person to infringe copyright, Sharman is not to be taken to have authorised the infringement': at [396]. However, that left open the possibility of finding Sharman guilty of authorisation for reasons other than merely providing facilities via the Kazaa file-sharing system. Here, if Sharman had not provided the facilities for file-sharing, there would have been no Kazaa file-sharing at all; further, Sharman had a financial interest in ever-increasing levels of file-sharing and knew that the files shared were subject to copyright. There was also evidence of positive acts encouraging copyright infringement: Sharman's website promotion of Kazaa as a file sharing facility and exhortations to share files and their promotion of the 'Join the "File-Sharing" Revolution' movement, which conveyed the idea that it was 'cool' to defy record companies by sharing files. The notices on the website about Sharman not condoning copyright infringement were, in the circumstances, clearly ineffective and not intended to be effective in the first place. Therefore, Sharman was held liable for authorisation of copyright infringement. In other words, the copyright owner's action against Sharman as an 'intermediary' was effective. The significance of this victory in the more general war against illegal file-sharing across the globe is a different matter. However, even systems such as BitTorrent, not originally developed for illegal file-sharing purposes, are increasingly coming under pressure from copyright owners. As well as 'making available', the right also encompasses the actual dispatch of copyright materials over the internet if they are 'to the public'. Sending a private email containing or attaching copyrighted material is not a transmission 'to the public': see *Woolworths Ltd v Olson* (2004) 63 IPR 258; [2004] NSWSC 849 at 344ff. Whether the distribution of materials over the internet is by wired or wireless technology or a combination of both makes no difference.

The fair dealing and library exceptions in the digital environment

18.17 Much of the disagreement concerning the digital agenda amendments came to be centred around the Digital Agenda Bill's adaptation of the fair dealing and library exceptions to the digital environment. In his second reading speech relating to the 1999 version of the bill, the Attorney-General stated: 'As far as possible, the proposed exceptions replicate the balance struck in the print environment between the rights of owners of copyright and the rights of users.'[4] The Digital Agenda Act provided that existing fair dealing exceptions apply to the new communication right, while providing further clarification on some matters. For example, in relation to the research and study exception (Copyright Act, s 40), a 'reasonable portion' (see s 10(2)) of a work in electronic form is redefined in a manner appropriate to works in digital form. Existing exceptions for library copying are also adapted in relation to electronic reproduction and communication of copyright material, although the ability of libraries to reproduce and deal with works in electronic form is somewhat restricted so as to preserve the economic rights of copyright owners in the internet environment: see ss 49 and 50. The Copyright Act also contains exceptions for private copying and format and time shifting: see Chapter 5 Copyright: Other Rights and Exceptions and *National Rugby League Investments Pty Ltd v Singtel Optus Pty Ltd* (2012) 201 FCR 147; 95 IPR 321; [2012] FCAFC 59 (recording of television broadcasts for viewing at a more convenient time).

---

4. *Hansard*, 2 September 1999, p 7428.

TPMs, ERMI and broadcast decoding devices

18.18 The Digital Agenda Act introduced civil remedies and criminal sanctions for the making, importation or supply of circumvention devices. The AUSFTA amendments extended the remedies to cover acts of circumvention as well. Prior to the Copyright Amendment Act 2006 (Cth), by virtue of s 10 a circumvention device was defined as meaning a device with only a limited commercially significant purpose or use other than the circumvention, or facilitating the circumvention, of any effective TPMs. 'Circumvention service' had an equivalent meaning. A TPM included copy control and access control devices (which can be hardware or software), as by virtue of s 10(1), as it then stood, a TPM meant:

> ... a device or product, or a component incorporated into a process, that is designed, in the ordinary course of its operation, to prevent or inhibit the infringement of copyright in a work or other subject-matter by either or both of the following means:
>
> (a) by ensuring that access to the work or other subject matter is available solely by use of an access code or process (including decryption, unscrambling or other transformation of the work or other subject-matter) with the authority of the owner or exclusive licensee of the copyright;
>
> (b) through a copy control mechanism.

This now superseded definition was interpreted strictly in the *Sony Modchip* case: see *Stevens v Kabushiki Kaisha Sony Computer Entertainment* (2005) 224 CLR 193; [2005] HCA 58. Where a measure inhibited only the making of illegal copies but did not directly prevent it, it was held not to amount to a TPM. This limitation was overcome by the amendments introduced by the Copyright Amendment Act 2006 that now make a distinction between an 'access control technological protection measure' and 'technological protection measure' proper. The present definition of 'technological protection measure' in s 10 is as follows:

> (a) an access control technological protection measure; or
>
> (b) a device, product, technology or component (including acomputer program) that:
>
> (i) is used in Australia or a qualifying country by, with the permission of, or on behalf of, the owner or the exclusive licensee of the copyright in a work or other subject matter; and
>
> (ii) in the normal course of its operation, prevents, inhibits or restricts the doing of an act comprised in the copyright but does not include such a device, product, technology or component to the extent that it:
>
> (iii) if the work or other subject matter is a cinematograph film or computer program (including a computer game) controls geographic market segmentation by preventing the playback in Australia of a non-infringing copy of the work or other subject matter acquired outside Australia; or
>
> (iv) if the work is a computer program that is embodied in a machine or device restricts the use of goods (other than the work) or services in relation to the machine or device.

See also the definition in the same section of 'access control technological protection measure', which refers to a device, product, technology or component that in the normal course of operation controls access to a work or other subject matter. Under the current definition, that it inhibits infringement is now sufficient for a measure to constitute a TPM under the Act. However, a measure aimed at implementing region coding (ie, whereby a legitimate copy bought in a foreign market cannot be used for its intended purpose here) is expressly excluded from being a TPM under the Act. Doing an act that results in the circumvention of an access TPM in circumstances where a person knows or ought reasonably to know that the act would have that result is now also a breach of the law (see s 116AN). With these 2006 amendments, the approach in Australia now no longer diverges with respect to actual circumvention, as opposed to supply etc, from the provisions of the Digital Millennium Copyright Act 1998 (US) that prohibit circumvention per se. Australian law is now also more consistent with the European approach, which has recently shifted to prohibit use as well as making and supply.

There are, however, significant exceptions provided for by the Copyright Act 1968, in relation to both manufacture, etc, and acts of circumvention. In terms of the latter, by virtue of s 116AN(4)–(9), doing an act that results in circumvention of an access control TPM is not actionable where the act is done for various purposes (interoperability, encryption research, computer testing, online privacy, law enforcement and national security, certain purposes of libraries and acts prescribed by regulation). In terms of manufacture and supply, by virtue of s 116AO(3)–(6), similar exceptions apply. Further, by virtue of 116AO(2), limitations are imposed on liability that results only from promoting, advertising or marketing a circumvention device. By virtue of s 116AP, parallel provisions apply in relation to circumvention services. By virtue of s 116AQ, the remedies of injunction, damages, account of profits and orders for destruction are available. Sections 116B–116D impose liability for removing or altering ERMI and various forms of dealing in works whose ERMI has been removed or altered. ERMI is defined in s 10(1) as information in electronic form associated with works or subject matter that identifies it and its author or copyright owner or indicates the terms of use of such work or subject matter. As to criminal liability in relation to circumvention of TPMs and ERMI, see ss 132APA–132AT. These provisions apply where the person does the illegal act with the intention of obtaining a commercial advantage or profit. Various defences apply.

Providers of pay television services use encoding to protect their broadcast signals from being siphoned off by those who have not paid to receive the service. The Copyright Act provides protection against unauthorised access to encoded broadcasts, both by way of remedies against those who deal in unauthorised decoders and against the gaining or providing of unauthorised access to encoded broadcasts: see Pt VAA. These provisions have been at issue in a number of cases: see, for example, *StatusCard* (see above at 18.13); *Haddad v Foxtel Management Pty Ltd* [2008] FCAFC 11; *United Broadcasting International Pty Ltd v TV Plus Int Pty Ltd* (2007) 71 IPR 353; *Amalgamated Television Services Pty Ltd v Foxtel Digital Cable Television Pty Ltd* (1996) 66 FCR 75; 34 IPR 274; and *Sportsvision Australia v Tallglen Pty Ltd* (1998) 38 IPR 294. In terms of criminal liability for making unauthorised decoders available, see *De Lorenzo v Director of Public Prosecutions (Cth)* [2017] VSCA 270.

Liability of service providers

18.19 The decision in *Telstra Corporation Ltd v Australasian Performing Rights Association* (1997) 191 CLR 140; 38 IPR 294 highlighted the fact that telecommunications carriers and service providers are exposed to a risk of copyright liability in relation to the communication of content that they themselves have not selected. In line with the WIPO treaties, the Copyright Act now imposes primary liability in relation to doing acts comprised in the copyright on content providers (website proprietors) and not on service providers: see s 22(6). In terms of technical copies or reproductions made on servers controlled by an internet service provider (ISP), s 43A provides that temporary reproductions made in the course of communication over the internet do not infringe copyright; see also s 111A, the equivalent provision in relation to subject matter other than works. However, although only the content provider is liable in relation to doing acts comprised in the copyright, an ISP could be held liable for authorising the doing of such acts under certain circumstances. With this in mind, ss 39B and 112E provide that a carrier or carriage service provider (effectively an ISP) is not taken to have authorised infringement of copyright in audiovisual items (as defined in s 100A) merely because it provides facilities used in the making of a communication. In *Cooper* (above at 18.11), the court applied the factors enumerated in s 101(1A). An ISP hosted Cooper's website and had the power to take it down. It actively cooperated in the establishment, operation and maintenance of the website. The court was satisfied that ISP staff were aware of the extent of traffic to the website. The ISP was thus guilty of infringement by authorisation; the protection of s 112E did not apply, per Tamberlin J (at IPR 436):

> Accordingly, within the meaning of s 112E it could not be said that they were doing no more than 'merely' hosting the website involved in the present circumstances. Where a host is on notice of an irregularity and deliberately elects not to investigate the operation and contents of a site and turns a blind eye to such indications, even having regard to the possible indication afforded by the title of the website, then, in my view, there are additional factors called into play beyond merely hosting the site.

The position of an ISP who received notice of copyright infringement on its servers remained somewhat unclear until by virtue of the AUSFTA, US-style 'safe harbour' provisions were introduced into the Copyright Act: see s 116AAff. Those provisions have recently been amended (by way of the Copyright Amendment (Service Providers) Act 2018 (Cth)) to extend the protection to all 'service providers' rather than only carriage service providers; see Pt V, Div 2AA. Section 116AA(1) describes the purpose of the Division as being 'to limit the remedies that are available against service providers for infringements of copyright that relate to the carrying out of certain online activities by service providers. A service provider must satisfy certain conditions to take advantage of the limitations'. Section 116ABA defines a 'service provider' so as to include, but not be limited to, a carriage service provider (an ISP). Since the passage of the 2018 amendments, educational, disability, library, archival and 'key cultural institutions' are also included as relevant service providers. The PC Report in fact recommended that '[t]he Australian Government should expand the safe harbour scheme to cover not just carriage service providers, but all providers of online services': at pp 566–7). This would effectively extend protections to service providers such as Google.

If the service provider as defined observes certain conditions, the carrying out of certain specified activities will not attract the granting of any remedies other than a court order to terminate an account or disable access to infringing material or to references to infringing material or 'some other less burdensome but comparably effective nonmonetary order if necessary': see s 116AG. The application of the safe harbour provisions was potentially under consideration in the *iiNet* case (*Roadshow Films Pty Ltd v iiNet* (2012) 248 CLR 42; [2012] HCA 16), but in the final analysis it was not necessary to rely upon these provisions. Instead, the High Court held that there was no authorisation liability, since it was not reasonable to expect an ISP to act upon a copyright notice sent to it in relation to an alleged copyright infringement by a subscriber: see *iiNet*; see also Chapter 5 Copyright: Other Rights and Exceptions.

As is indicated above, s 43A (and also s 111A) is intended to remove liability for any temporary reproduction or copy made as part of the technical process of making or receiving a communication. According to the explanatory memorandum, this should remove browsing or simply online viewing of copyright material (which also includes sounds) from the scope of the reproduction right. Thus, the reproduction in a form of permanent storage on the browsing computer would amount to an infringing reproduction (eg, downloading a sound file or saving a document available at a website); but any reproduction that occurs automatically and for technical reasons in the course of looking at or listening to a work or subject matter stored at a remote website would not; see also s 43B. According to the explanatory memorandum, s 43A should also remove liability for reproductions or copies made in the course of certain 'caching'. However, 'caching' is a compendious term that covers a number of different actions, from the automatic saving of temporary internet files on the browsing computer to the retention of a copy of accessed material on a website on the browser's ISP to mirror sites being set up on an ISP. Most of these types of caching, with the possible exception of the automatic storage of temporary files on the browsing computer, would arguably not be made as part of the technical process of making or receiving a communication, and would thus not be excepted. However, under the new 'safe harbour' provisions, caching is a protected activity if it falls within the definition of that term under s 116AB (this definition applies only to the 'safe harbour' provisions; ie, Pt V, Div 2AA): '*caching* means the reproduction of copyright material on a system or network controlled or operated by or for a carriage service provider in response to an action by a user in order to facilitate efficient access to that material by that user or other users'.

The US Digital Millennium Copyright Act contains provisions in relation to expedited subpoenas. This permits court clerks to issue subpoenas directing ISPs to disclose the name and contact information of a subscriber based on a 'good faith' allegation of copyright infringement. There is no legislation on expedited subpoenas in Australia, perhaps because the issue of privacy of ISP subscribers is contentious. However, in the case of *Sony Music Entertainment (Australia) Ltd v University of Tasmania* [2003] FCA 929, Sony sought to access university records to identify infringers who Sony alleged used the university's computer networks for reproduction and communication of MP3 files, infringing copyright in Sony's music and sound recordings. The University of Tasmania resisted disclosing the information based on privacy reasons.

The Federal Court agreed to grant the orders on certain conditions, such as preserving confidentiality and privilege.

The *IInet* decision effectively removed the option for copyright owners to shift liability from individual subscribers to ISPs, as explained above. However, a new weapon was added to their armoury in 2015 by the introduction of amendments (see s 115A) that mean copyright owners can seek injunctive relief against ISPs in order to block access to certain overseas-based websites that have the primary purpose of infringing or facilitating the infringement of copyright. Further amendments in 2018 expanded the powers of the court in this regard, inter alia by expanding the target to websites that have the 'primary effect' as well as the primary purpose of infringing etc, and by bringing online search engine providers (such as Google) within the ambit of s 115A. Copyright owners can now seek injunctions against online search engine providers to prevent them from providing search results referring to infringing online location(s). Such orders are now relatively commonplace; see, for example, *Fairfax Media v Reed*; *Foxtel Management Pty Ltd v TPG Internet Pty Ltd* (2017) 126 IPR 579; [2017] FCA 1041; *Roadshow Films Pty Ltd v Telstra Corporation Ltd* (2016) 248 FCR 178; 122 IPR 81; [2016] FCA 1503 and (2019) 132 IPR 1; [2019] FCA 885.

Bibliography

A Davidson, 'Peer-to-Peer File Sharing Online' (2005) 25(5) *Proctor* 37.

A Davidson, 'Shrinkwrap, Clickwrap and Browsewrap Contracts' (2003) 23(9) *Proctor* 26.

A Hoyle, 'Intellectual Property in Digital Age: Does Napster Experience Point the Way Forward, or Simply Add to Confusion?' (2000/01) 11(2) *JLIS* 216.

A Roy, *Australian Domain Name Law*, Thomson Reuters, 2016.

Australian Copyright Council, *A Comparative Study of Library Provisions*, 2001.

B Fitzgerald, 'The Playstation Mod Chip: A Technological Guarantee of the Digital Consumer's Liberty — Copyright Menace/Circumvention Device?' (2005) 10(1) *MALR* 85.

B Melhem, M Al-Abweh, H Halous, 'Re-Conceptualising Moral Rights in the Digital Era' (2008) 72 *IP Forum* 44.

C A Vernon, 'Current Problems in the Copyright Act Regarding Computer Software', (1998) 2 *JLIS* 205.

C Lawson, 'Patenting Health Related Databases and Information in Australia' (2005) 17(1) *BondLR* 58.

Copyright Law Review Committee (CLRC), *Report on Computer Software Protection*, 1995, Ch 14.

CLRC, *Report on Copyright and Contract*, 2002.

D Clapperton, S Corones, 'Unfair Terms in "Clickwrap" and Other Electronic Contracts' (2007) 35 *ABLR* 152.

D Neve, 'Australia's New Rules Permitting Parallel Importation of Software' (2003) 14(3) *AIPJ* 167.

D Sullivan, 'Idea/Expression Dichotomy: Application to Architectural Plans and Computer Software' (2002) 76(6) *ALJ* 389.

D Webber, 'Case Note — PlayStation Held not to Include a Technical Protection Measure' — *Kabushiki Kaisha Sony Computer Entertainment v Stevens*' (2002) 13(4) *AIPJ* 228.

G Hughes and A Sharp, *Computer Contracts Online*, Thomson Reuters.

J R Finklestein, 'Protection of Intellectual Property in Cyberspace: Jurisdictional Issues' (2001) 47 *IP Forum* 8.

K Stammer, 'Protection of Information Databases: *Telstra Corporation Limited v Desktop Marketing Systems Pty Ltd*' (2001) 46 *IP Forum* 30.

K Weatherall, 'On Technology Locks and the Proper Scope of Digital Copyright Laws — Sony in the High Court' (2004) 26(4) *SydLR* 61.

L Gamertsfelder, 'Re-engineering Circumvention Device Provision of Copyright Act — Case Note; *Kabushiki Kaisha Sony Computer Entertainment v Stevens*' (2003) 16(7) *IPLB* 110.

M Coco, 'Anti-circumvention: New Song and Dance Routine' (2001) 12(4) *AIPJ* 199.

M Cooper, '*Microsoft Corp v Business Boost Pty Ltd* — Casenote' (2000) 12(7) *IPLB* 79.

M Garlick, 'Ups and Downs of the Napster Revolution' (2000) 13(3) *IPLB* 25.

M J Davison, *The Legal Protection of Databases*, Cambridge University Press, 2003.

M Jones, 'Patents and the Software Industry' (1999) 37 *IP Forum* 20.

M Napthali, 'Unauthorised: Some Thoughts upon the Doctrine of Authorisation of Copyright Infringement in the Peer-to-Peer Age' (2005) 16(1) *AIPJ* 5.

M Paphazy and P Francis, 'Case Note — *Concrete Pty Ltd v Parramatta Design & Developments Pty Ltd*' (2007) 20(1) *IPLB* 5.

M Richardson, 'Downloading Music Off the Internet: Copyright and Privacy in Conflict?' (2002) 13(1) *JLIS* 90.

N Bogle, 'Does Black and White Make Gray? A Critical Analysis of the Legal Regime Governing Digital Music Sampling' (2005) 61 *IP Forum* 10.

P Green, '"Free" Software and Trade Mark Infringement' (2000) 42 *IP Forum* 46.

P Knight, 'Is Receipt of Source Code an Implied Term of an Assignment or License of Custom Software? — Case Note; *Centrestage Management Pty Ltd v Riedle*' (2008) 21(4) *IPLB* 60.

R Chalmers, 'The Digital Agenda: Whose Agenda?' (2000) 40 *IP Forum* 18.

R Evenden, 'Copyright Protection of Data and Databased in Australia' (2001) 44 *Comp&L* 27.

R Gay, 'Is Copyright Protection Being "Chipped" Away?' (2002) 15(5) *IPLB* 57.

R Kunkel, 'Recent Developments in Shrinkwrap, Clickwrap and Browsewrap Licenses in the United States' [2002] *MurUEJL* 34.

R Pascoe and Mia G, 'Is Forwarding an Email an Infringement of Copyright? Impact of Digital Agenda Act on Email' (2001) 13(10) *IPLB* 136.

S Gethin, 'Case Comment: *Kabushiki Kaisha Sony Computer Entertainment v Stevens*' (2002) 50 *IP Forum* 50.

S Givoni, 'Pushing the Boundaries of Copyright: Protection of Databases' (2003) 15(8) *IPLB* 113.

S Heindl, 'Australian ISPs Singing their Own Song on Illegal File Sharing?' (2008) 11(6) *INTLB* 86.

S Holthusen, 'Napster Decision: Implications for Copyright Law in Digital Age' (2001) 21(2) *UQLJ* 245.

S Lewis, 'The Formation and Enforceability of Shrinkwrap, Clickwrap and Browsewrap — A Comparative Analysis' (2003) 14(4) *AIPJ* 208.

S McConnel, 'Napster Case: Which Way Would the Balance of Interests Fall in Australia?' (2001) 6(4) *MALR* 297.

S Ricketson, 'Databases — Tool of the Information Age' (1999) 36 *IP Forum 12.*

W Adams, 'Beyond Trade Mark and the Public Domain: Allocating Property Rights in Domain Names' (2003) 52 *IP Forum* 10.

Chapter 19

Remedies in Intellectual Property Law

Introduction

19.1 This chapter examines some issues in remedies that commonly arise in intellectual property matters. The examination is selective and unavoidably glosses over some of the important differences between the various regimes, in the availability of remedies, in the calculation of compensation and in the choice of appropriate relief.

The various topics that will be examined are:

- interlocutory injunctions;
- Anton Piller Orders;
- the choice between, and calculation of, damages and accounts of profits;
- additional damages;
- conversion damages in copyright law; and
- actions for unjustified threats of legal proceedings.

Even these select topics give rise to far more issues than can be comprehensively addressed within the confines of this text. The Anton Piller Order, an ex parte order akin to a private search warrant, is the main interim order covered below. Its practical importance in intellectual property cases and its unique characteristics warrant more detailed attention. Interlocutory injunctions are also touched upon; however, because the tests for the granting of interlocutory *inter partes* injunctions are universal, only certain aspects of particular relevance to intellectual property law will be examined more closely.

The two principal monetary remedies in most intellectual property cases are damages and accounts of profits. They have fundamentally different conceptual bases and modes of calculation; one is compensatory, the other restitutionary in character. The different methods of calculation that have been applied, the typical difficulties that are encountered in performing such calculations and factors relevant to an effective choice of remedy are examined below. As to the remedy of damages, the peculiarity of additional damages traditionally available in copyright and since 2003 for designs law breaches, but now also for patent and trade mark infringements, attracts some further attention below.

Although the focus of this chapter is on litigation and judicial remedies, litigation is very much a last resort in intellectual property disputes, being unusually uncertain and expensive.[1] First, with all regimes, there is the initial question of the uncertain validity or existence of the right claimed; frequently, this is a difficult matter and is a focus of litigation. Second, often many fine judgments are required in intellectual property cases, the outcome of which may be difficult to predict (see, eg, the complex and refined test of inventiveness in patents law, or similarity in overall impression in designs law). Third, courts often require expert assistance in intellectual property matters, which renders the expense of litigation ever more prohibitive. Partly for those reasons, intellectual property disputes are rarely fully litigated. Many disputes are settled, are resolved by other alternative dispute resolution methods or are arbitrated (this is particularly the case with international contractually based intellectual property disputes). Intellectual property disputes commonly arise as a matter of urgency. Disputes that are dealt with at the interlocutory stage frequently rest there; that is, they do not go on to a full trial of the issues. As a result, reports on decisions on interim applications, although they do not consider all relevant legal issues to the full extent, take on added importance in terms of informing the study of the law of intellectual property.

But not all legal work in the area of intellectual property consists of dispute resolution and litigation. Much of it concerns management of an intellectual property portfolio; that is, the effective protection, commercialisation, licensing and exploitation of rights; and the development of an intellectual property strategy. Proactive intellectual property portfolio management will prevent the occurrence of disputes in the future (eg, by providing clear agreements concerning ownership of jointly produced intellectual property). It will also assist a party if a dispute does arise. Of the relevance of commercial strategy in managing intellectual property, the *Tidy Tea* case provides an illustration: *Tidy Tea Ltd v Unilever Australia Ltd* (1995) 32 IPR 405; see also *Samsung Electronics Co Ltd v Apple Inc* (2011) 217 FCR 238; [2011] FCAFC 156 (*Samsung v Apple*).

Statutory presumptions, notice of rights and onus of proof

19.2 Various statutory presumptions assist claimants in intellectual property cases. For instance, by virtue of s 126 of the Copyright Act 1968 (Cth), copyright is presumed to subsist in the work or subject matter to which an action relates unless that question is specifically put in issue by the defendant. In other words, the plaintiff party will not need to prove this unless the defendant puts it to proof on the matter. Giving adequate notice of the existence and ownership of intellectual property rights is an important aspect of their management, and proper notification has practical and legal consequences. For instance, in accordance with s 127 of the Copyright Act, where the name of an author appears on copies of a work, it is to be presumed that that person is the author and that the work was not made under the terms of a contract for service, whether or not as a journalist. The onus will thus be on the defendant

1. See L Toohey, 'Rights, Remedies and Relationships: Resolving Disputes through Mediation' (2003) 55 *IP Forum* 24.

in a copyright infringement case to prove the opposite, as the case may be. Similar statutory presumptions benefit publishers (see s 128 and see also ss 129, 130 and 131) and there are further presumptions where an author is dead and relating to sound recordings and films. A similar provision, but with more limited effect, also appears in the Patents Act 1990 (Cth). Section 123(2) provides that a defendant is to be taken to have been aware of the existence of a patent if the patented products, marked so as to indicate that they are patented in Australia, were sold or used in Australia to a substantial extent before the date of the infringement. The defendant's knowledge that a patent existed is, of course, not relevant to liability, but if the defendant was not aware that a patent existed, the court has the discretion not to award damages or an account of profits: see s 123(1). The claimant is also sometimes assisted by a statutory reversal of the onus of proof: see, for instance, s 121A of the Patents Act 1990 (defendant to prove in some cases that products were not made by a patented process) and ss 130A–130C of the Copyright Act 1968 (defendant to prove that an imported copy is a non-infringing copy).

Interlocutory Injunctions in Intellectual Property Cases

19.3 Intellectual property disputes often result in an application for interim relief, primarily for interlocutory injunctions to restrain allegedly infringing conduct, whether actual or anticipated (*quia timet*). Timely, if temporary, measures may prevent the total destruction of the value of intellectual property rights and irreversible damage, as well as forestalling expensive and uncertain trials. This is particularly so in the case of confidential information (see, eg, *Howden Australia Pty Ltd v Minetek Pty Ltd* [2019] FCA 981) and of rights over goodwill; that is, in the context of registered trade marks, passing off and s 18 of the Australian Consumer Law. The granting of an interlocutory injunction is discretionary, and the factual parameters of each case vary so widely that it is unhelpful to attempt to formulate detailed rules that predict the outcome of an application. The most current High Court statement of the test is to be found in *Australian Broadcasting Corporation v O'Neill* (2006) 227 CLR 57; [2006] HCA 46 (*ABC v O'Neill*), the significant precursors being *Beecham Group Ltd v Bristol Laboratories Pty Ltd* (1968) 118 CLR 618; [1968] HCA 1, and *Australian Broadcasting Corporation v Lenah Game Meats* (2001) 208 CLR 199; [2001] HCA 63 (*ABC v Lenah Game Meats*).

In recent times, the gravamen of the test has arguably shifted away from the 'serious question' or 'prima facie case' requirement to focus more on the balance of convenience; the question of irreparable harm is normally addressed in the consideration of balance of convenience: *Samsung v Apple* at [61] per Dowsett, Foster and Yates JJ (see further below). Nonetheless, there must be some legal or equitable right that could ground the granting of final relief at trial; the unconscionability alone of what the respondent proposes to do 'cannot be used to conjure up a right to interlocutory relief where there is no right to final relief': *ABC v Lenah Game Meats* at [17] per Gleeson J. To obtain interim relief, the applicant will have to convince the court of an arguable case (ie, that there is a serious issue to be tried). In *ABC v O'Neill* at CLR 82–3, Gummow and Hayne JJ treated the requisite degree of seriousness of the question to be tried and the probability of success at trial as amounting to substantially the same thing. Both were dependent on 'the nature of the rights [the plaintiff] asserts and the practical consequences likely to flow from the order he seeks' (at CLR 82). In *Howden Australia* at [30] the core question was nicely stated as follows:

> Has [the applicant] established a sufficient or 'some' likelihood of success to justify, in the circumstances, the preservation of the status quo pending the trial having regard to the nature of the rights [the applicant] asserts and the practical consequences likely to flow from the order it seeks?

In intellectual property cases, the fact that the validity of statutory property rights is not guaranteed adds a further level of uncertainty, which could affect the exercising of the court's discretionary power to grant an interim injunction. Commonly, the applicant will counterclaim that the patent or other right is invalid, a matter that the court will have to consider when evaluating the strength of the applicant's case. Gummow J in *Martin Engineering Co v Trison Holdings Pty Ltd* (1988) 81 ALR 543; 11 IPR 611 set great store by the increased stringency both of the statutory standards of patentability and of the examination procedures for standard patents, at least under more modern patent Acts. His Honour pointed out that more modern decisions in Australia (such as *Peter Pan Electrics Pty Ltd v Newton Grace Pty Ltd* (1985) 8 FCR 557) have brought practice into step with the changed patents law, rendering obsolete the former rule of practice, which inspired a reluctance to grant interlocutory injunctions in patent cases. However, Gummow J did indicate that registered designs may be a different case, since '[t]he administrative procedures in respect of the registration of designs have remained at a more rudimentary level than has come to pass with standard patents': at ALR 549; IPR 617.

In *Aktiebolaget Hassle v Biochemie Australia Pty Ltd* (2003) 57 IPR 1; [2003] FCA 496, the fact that the patent at issue had been found valid by the High Court in previous proceedings against a different party was an advantage to the applicant, although that did 'not of itself preclude [the respondent] from showing that there is merit in the ground on which it alleges the Patent is liable to be revoked': at [30]. The respondent had in any case, on the construction of the claims contended for by the applicant, an arguable case based on a lack of fair basing. The judge also called in aid a number of cases as authority for the proposition that '[t]he fact that this is a patent case does not displace or qualify the fundamental principles which govern applications for interlocutory injunctions generally': at [30]. The proper approach to interlocutory applications in patent cases was recently considered by the Full Federal Court in *Samsung v Apple*; that decision is now commonly cited in other intellectual property rights-related matters also. The court overturned the trial judge's decision (see *Apple Inc v Samsung Electronics Co Ltd* (2011) 93 IPR 441; [2011] FCA 1164) because her Honour gave too much weight to the unwillingness of one of the parties to accept an accelerated trial and because she failed to assess Apple's case for infringement to determine whether there was a prima facie case of sufficient strength. The court pointed out (at [87]) that since the 'grant or refusal of interlocutory injunctive relief was going to have the practical consequence of deciding Apple's claims for final injunctions and thus deciding the commercial fate of the Galaxy [tablet], Apple was required to demonstrate a relatively strong case'. Nor had the trial judge, in deciding whether Apple was entitled to relief on the balance of convenience, taken account of the strength of its case. The Full Court also held that Samsung had failed to make out a prima facie case for invalidity. In the circumstances, the injunction was lifted and Samsung was able to sell its tablets. More recently in *Sanofi-Aventis Deutschland GmbH v Alphapharm Pty Ltd* (2019) 139 IPR 409; [2019] FCAFC 28 at [14] the Full Court reiterated the principle enunciated in *Janssen Sciences Ireland UC v Alphapharm Pty Ltd* [2017] FCA 1399 and *Interpharma Pty Ltd v Commissioner of Patents* (2008) 79 IPR 261; [2008] FCA 1498 in the following terms:

> The approach in *Interpharma* and *Janssen* is clear. A case for invalidity which is merely arguable, of itself, does not undermine the existence of a prima facie case of infringement which has otherwise been found to exist. However, a sufficiently strong case of invalidity may well qualify the conclusion that there is a prima facie case of infringement at all.

A further difficulty arises where there is a counterclaim for infringement; for instance, of the respondent's closely related patent: see the discussion of this type of situation in *Interpharma* at [17]. The judge's conclusion as to this aspect of the consideration is instructive (at [63]):

> Questions of whether an invention involves an inventive step in the light of common general knowledge as at the priority date are notoriously difficult, where approached many years subsequently. Evidence of the kind which is presently before the court stops a deal short of permitting me to express even a provisional view as to how those questions will be resolved at trial. Invalidity is for the cross-respondent to prove. The material upon which it relies manifestly leaves considerable scope for argument. To the extent that I am otherwise of the view that the cross-claimants have established a prima facie case of infringement with respect to the process patent, I am not prepared to qualify that view by reason of the prospect that that patent might be invalid for want of an inventive step.

In the context of copyright, in *Wrangler Apparel Corp v Classic Boots Australia Pty Ltd* (1997) 38 IPR 19; [1997] AIPC ¶91-352 it was said that claims for interlocutory relief should also be treated the same as any other, the strength of the prima facie case requiring careful assessment, which might include consideration of any defences, such as in relation to the design/copyright overlap: see, for example, *Grace v Beaulieu of Australia Ltd* (2004) 60 IPR 540; [2004] FCA 265. Note that bringing a dispute before a court entails the risk of exposing for all to see the 'weakness' of the claimed right, particularly at the interlocutory stage, where questions of validity are exposed but ultimately left unresolved.

Apart from the issue of validity of the right asserted by a plaintiff or applicant, both facts and law are often complex in intellectual property cases. Although the issues need not be resolved at the interlocutory stage, a court must at least develop a sufficient understanding to allow it to determine whether the applicant's prima facie case has been made out and there is a probability of success at trial. An illustration of the complexities sometimes confronting a court at the interlocutory stage is provided by a case with curious facts involving the well-known brand Christian Dior Parfums (Dior), *Christian Dior (Australia) Pty Ltd v Dimmeys Stores Pty Ltd* (1997) 39 IPR 349, where the value of goodwill was at stake. Dior filed an application for an interlocutory injunction restraining Dimmeys from selling in its stores unboxed 'tester' bottles of 'Poison' and 'Tendre Poison', two perfumes. Somehow, Dimmeys had obtained a quantity of the tester bottles that Dior provided in less upmarket packaging to its licensed retail stores for use within shops. Dimmeys advertised them for sale in leaflets and inside shops. As far as trade marks law was concerned, it was at least an arguable case that the testers had been marked 'not for sale' and had not been sold or authorised for sale. There was thus no implied or express consent to use the trade-marked goods and thus the trade mark in the manner that Dimmeys had used it. Dior feared not so much damage to its market share but damage to its reputation for quality. Such damage could neither easily be estimated in monetary terms nor adequately compensated. The balance of convenience thus justified the granting of the injunction. Even though the legal question at issue in the case was subject to considerable uncertainty, since the trade marks had been legitimately attached, there was at least an arguable case, the claim could not be called frivolous or vexatious and the decision to grant the injunction was thus warranted as the only possible effective measure. (The question of whether damages would be an adequate alternative to an injunction is to be distinguished from the requirement of security for damages that the applicant must provide prior to the granting of an injunction. Such security provides assurance that if the applicant who was successful at the interim stage fails at the trial, the damage suffered by the respondent who has, as it turned out, unfairly suffered the restriction of an injunction can be compensated.) A further example of the kinds of complex issues that must be assessed is found in *Samsung v Apple*. Because, given the commercial realities at the time, the court decision concerning interim relief will often determine the matter in fact, the legal issues require careful consideration, but the interlocutory hearing is nonetheless urgent and not a full trial of the issues. Courts are loath to see interlocutory applications and hearings used to frustrate normal court processes such that the opportunity to fully ventilate their case is denied to the parties. It should also be noted that the strength of the plaintiff's submission is not only relevant to whether there is a serious issue but also is a factor in determining the balance of convenience. It must be remembered that if the interlocutory injunction is refused, the applicant can still make out a case for damages at the trial.

Irreparable harm and the balance of convenience

19.4 In *Aktiebolaget Hassle v Biochemie Australia Pty Ltd*, Sackville J said at [31]:

> Whether there is a sufficiently serious question to be tried and whether the balance of convenience favours [the applicant] are not issues to be considered in strict isolation. The strength, or weakness, of the case can affect the balance of convenience …

In that case, the application for interlocutory relief was ultimately dismissed; more recently see *Samsung v Apple* at [61] per Dowsett, Foster and Yates JJ. In *Tooheys Pty Ltd v Coopers Brewery Ltd* [2003] FCA 148, Tamberlin J also pointed out that the strengths and weaknesses of the applicant's case were relevant to the balance of convenience question.[2] Tooheys New was a well-established brand when the rival brewer began to

2. See also D Millen, 'Good as New? Beer, Brand Names and Section 52 — Case Note; *Tooheys Pty Ltd v Coopers Brewery Ltd*' (2003) 11(4) *TPLJ* 253 and W Pengilley, 'Passing Off: 'New' Beer, Fat Blasters and Fat Terminators' (2003) 19(1) *TPLB* 10.

market Coopers 'New Draught' and 'New Light'. There was some evidence that the word 'New', although an ordinary adjective, had acquired a secondary meaning in its use as a noun, and because of extensive advertising and promotion had become a Tooheys brand. But *Tooheys*' case as to the use of the word 'New' by Coopers was not by any means unanswerable; nonetheless, there was 'a serious question to be tried … However, it is not a sufficiently strong [question] of itself, to compel the exercise of the discretion on the balance of convenience in favour of the applicant': at [25]. On the balance of convenience question, Tooheys made the traditional submission that the maintenance of the status quo favoured the granting of an injunction. However, the word 'New' was at least partly descriptive in nature, and Coopers gave evidence that it would abandon its use once the market for the product was established. Coopers would also stand to incur significant detriment if forced to abandon use of the word in its campaign launching the new products, which was already underway, and, geographically, the markets for Coopers products (predominantly South Australia) and Tooheys beers (predominantly outside South Australia) did not coincide. Hence, Tamberlin J held at [29]:

> In my view the balance of convenience favours refusal of the injunction sought. The evidence before me does not satisfy me that Tooheys would suffer substantial damage to its reputation nor any other detriment which are not compensable in damages or which outweighs the hardship to Coopers if an immediate injunction is not granted.

In *AB Hassle v Pharmacia (Australia) Pty Ltd* (1995) 33 IPR 63, at 76–7, Ashley J pointed out that there has been a tendency to treat the requirement of irreparable injury as going to the balance of convenience. However, in *ABC v O'Neill* (see above), the High Court clearly reiterated that this remains a separate issue, and in *Hexal Australia Pty Ltd v Roche Therapeutics Inc* (2005) 66 IPR 325; [2005] FCA 1218, the Federal Court also emphasised that fact. In any case, whether the plaintiff would suffer irreparable injury that cannot be compensated by damages granted at trial if an interlocutory injunction is refused is a significant factor in intellectual property matters. In *Hexal Australia*, Roche was not able to demonstrate that unless an injunction was granted it would suffer irreparable harm for which damages would not be adequate compensation. The court accepted that if the patent at stake was ultimately found to be valid, the loss suffered by Roche and any profits Hexal might make would be easily quantifiable. In other circumstances (eg, trade secrets cases), the potentially irreversible destruction of the value of intellectual property may favour prompt judicial intervention (as, for instance, in *APT Technology Pty Ltd v Aladesaye* [2014] FCA 966), but the potential negative impact on the activities of a defendant who as yet has not been found guilty of any breach and whose business may well be wholly destroyed by the prohibition favours caution. Ultimately, it is important to remember that the balance of convenience question commonly amounts to a choice between two evils; that is, there will usually be detriment suffered by one or other party, whether or not the injunction is granted. The courts will not — and cannot — look for a solution that results in no harm to either party. In *Wrangler Apparel Corp v Classic Boots Australia Pty Ltd* (1997) 38 IPR 19 at 33 Lehane J aptly said: 'the process of weighing the balance of convenience assumes that the unsuccessful party, whichever it is, will suffer prejudice.' In any case the weighing up by the court is a discretionary matter, and therefore the preferred option of the judge below will not readily be disturbed by an appeals court. In *Sanofi-Aventis* at [5] the Full Federal Court provided this salutary reminder:

> … [W]hile [all the relevant discretionary considerations] were 'quite evenly balanced' they weighed in favour of the refusal of interlocutory relief having regard to [the primary judge's] evaluation on the available evidence that Sanofi's loss would be more readily able to be calculated and compensated by damages if no interlocutory injunction were granted than the harm Alphapharm would suffer if an interlocutory injunction were granted … Faced with orthodox reasoning of this kind, in relation to the making of an order which is discretionary and based on evaluative judgments about which reasonable minds may differ, Sanofi's allegations of error have no inherent attraction for appellate intervention. Sanofi's appeal grounds and submissions lend further weight to the impression that the application for leave is an attempt to re-run the entirety of the application before the primary judge under the guise of a multiplicity of alleged errors which, on analysis, dissolve into nothing more than dissatisfaction with the primary judge's evaluation of all of the relevant circumstances.

Calculated and deliberate actions of the respondent

19.5 Apart from the relative strength of the applicant's right (of which the lapse of time since registration may be an indication), the course of conduct of the respondent is also a relevant consideration on an interlocutory application. In the *Tidy Tea* case the deliberate conduct of the respondent ultimately played against it. Burchett J had to consider an application for an interlocutory injunction to restrain the marketing of a squeezable teabag. The first applicant was the registered owner of a petty patent and was the licensor of the second applicant, who was exclusive licensee of the petty patent and whose associated company, Lyons Tetley Australia Pty Ltd, distributed the squeezable teabags in Western Australia and planned to expand distribution nationwide. This was a battle of the brands over a new product: the applicant's brand, 'Tetley', on the one hand, and the respondent's brand, 'Lipton', on the other. The respondent was an opponent to the granting of a standard patent for the invention, the application for a petty patent being a divisional application of the standard patent application. The only reason the applicant lodged the petty patent application was to be able to bring infringement proceedings as soon as possible. (No opposition to the granting of a petty patent being possible, it could be sealed quickly and proceedings commenced; infringement of a standard patent may occur from the moment of the publication of the complete specification, but an action lies only from the time of granting; because of opposition and other factors, there may be a considerable lapse of time between both.) The two distributors attempted to establish market share as quickly as possible, given that once market share is established, it is not easily dislodged by a competitor, certainly not in the fairly generic market for teabags. Knowing of the applicant's patent application, therefore, the respondent embarked on its own marketing and distribution campaign to pre-empt the effect of the granting of the patent and grab market share. The applicant wished to prevent such a fait accompli unfolding by its application for the interim injunction. On the balance of convenience, the court gave 'substantial weight to the consideration that the respondent deliberately took the applicant's innovation, knowing of the claim that this was an invention entitled to protection': *Tidy Tea* at IPR 415. Also, his Honour quoted a passage from Ipp J's judgment in *George Laurens (WA) Pty Ltd v Laurens & Co Australia Pty Ltd* (1994) 16 ATPR ¶41–329 as relevant in the case before him: '[T]he defendant proceeded with its conduct in the full knowledge that it would face an application by [the plaintiff] for an injunction. It becomes difficult then for the defendant to rely on losses [caused as a consequence]': *Tidy Tea* at IPR 416. In other words, the respondent's argument that it would face substantial losses if the injunction prevented its market expansion plans was to be discounted because of its calculated conduct. The interlocutory injunction was granted. For a more recent case considering conduct entered into with 'eyes wide open' and 'disingenuous dealing', see also *Interpharma* (above) at [77].[3] In *Samsung v Apple* at [191]ff, the court reviews the cases concerning the relevance of knowledge of the infringed right. A relevant factor is whether in all the circumstances of the case (including, for instance, the 'strength' of any intellectual property right at issue) the alleged infringer ought reasonably to have stopped the allegedly infringing conduct. However, the issue paled into insignificance for the court compared with the strengths and weaknesses of each side's case and the 'equality of likely detriment': at [196]. On the other hand, the knowledge of the respondent may also go to establishing that there is a serious issue to be tried. In *Beecham Group PLC v Colgate-Palmolive Pty Ltd* (2004) 64 IPR 45; [2004] FCA 1335, the promoters of the new MAXCLEAN trade mark for tooth brushes were, on the evidence, well aware of the impact its introduction could have on the rival MACLEANS brand. Their awareness could, on the authorities, be taken to indicate that an adverse impact was indeed more likely to eventuate, which helped to establish that there was indeed a serious issue to be tried in relation to consumer deception.

Anton Piller Orders: Preservation of Evidence

19.6 A further challenge facing a plaintiff in the initial stages of an intellectual property dispute is that a defendant who becomes aware of contemplated or impending legal action can often destroy the evidence of infringement with great ease and speed. The risk of destruction of incriminating evidence can effectively be forestalled by the execution of an ex parte order allowing the obtaining of relevant evidence from the defendant's premises or control and its secure keeping: the so-called Anton Piller Order, now also referred to as Search (and Seizure) Orders. Anton Piller Orders have become commonplace since the 1970s, when the order was initially handed down by judges of the Chancery Division in the UK. They serve the limited purpose of preserving evidence that is at particular risk. The order permits entry onto private premises for the purpose of the preservation of evidence that is in the hands of an alleged infringer and that is vulnerable to destruction or removal. The practice of granting the order was confirmed, and guidelines for its terms and execution formulated, in *Anton Piller KG v Manufacturing Processes Ltd* [1976] Ch 55. The order is granted ex parte; that is, without the respondent(s) being present or able to make submissions, so that the

3. In general, concerning interlocutory injunctions in intellectual property cases, see G S Clarke, 'Interlocutory Injunctions in Intellectual Property Cases — Principles and Practice' (2007) 69 *IP Forum* 10.

destruction of evidence by an alerted party can be prevented. The court is thus entirely reliant on the information provided by the applicants in determining whether or not and on what terms to grant the order. The terms of the order, although they may vary, usually entitle a surprise search of premises to be conducted by the successful applicants, under strict constraints, for the items of evidence identified in the order. The order entitles the applicants to take away the specified items and to peruse and preserve them for evidentiary, and not normally any other, purposes. The order may also enable the applicant to obtain information concerning both suppliers and clients of the suspected infringer, as revealed by documentation found on the premises; a useful example of an order and the reasons for granting it is *Brooks Sports Inc v Paul's International Pty Ltd (No 1)* [2011] FCA 999 and see also *(No 2)* [2011] FCA 1000. The purpose of the order is not to serve as a 'mere investigatory tool' for applicants but to preserve evidence where there is a real risk that evidence may be secreted or destroyed: see *Jemella Australia Pty Ltd v Internet Marketing Pty Ltd* (2008) 75 IPR 59; [2008] FCA 13 at [10]–[13]. Unsurprisingly, courts are vigilant to ensure strict adherence to the letter of the order, open and honest disclosure by the applicant and conscientious conduct on the part of legal advisers. In *Memory Corporation PLC v Sidhu (No 2)* [2000] 1 WLR 1443 at 1459–60, Mummery LJ said:

> It cannot be emphasised too strongly that at an urgent without notice hearing for a freezing order, as well as for a search order or any other form of interim injunction, there is a high duty to make full, fair and accurate disclosure of material information to the Court and to draw the Court's attention to significant factual, legal and procedural aspects of the case. It is the particular duty of the advocate to see that the correct legal procedures and forms are used; that a written skeleton argument and a properly drafted order are prepared by him personally ... and that at the hearing the Court's attention is drawn by him to unusual features of the evidence adduced, to the applicable law and to the formalities and procedure to be observed.

Since the concern that leads to the ex parte application is the risk of destruction or removal of evidence if the respondents are alerted to the applicant's actions, the order is commonly applied for in cases concerning video tapes, CDs, audio tapes, merchandising products, computer programs, decoding devices and now also illegal sound files. The number of these applications has grown as those industries have expanded and diversified: see, for instance, cases relating to illegal dealings with broadcast decoding devices (see s 135AN of the Copyright Act 1968): *Sky Channel Pty Ltd v Darcy's Tavern Pty Ltd* [2003] FCA 19 and *Sky Channel Pty Ltd v Yahmoc Pty Ltd* (2003) 58 IPR 63; [2003] FCA 401, where Allsop J thought the granting of the order appropriate, given the ease with which the very small smart card used to decode the applicant's signals could be removed or hidden.[4] Commonly, the applicant wants to target so-called fly-by-night or dishonest operators with only a temporary abode and cash-based transactions and who are alert to the ways and means of avoiding detection and effective prosecution of a claim against them. But that is by no means always the factual scenario, since intellectual property, given the ease and speed with which it can

---

4. For a more detailed discussion, see H Strachan, 'Broadcast Decoding Devices: Actions by Sky Channel' (2003) 16(4) *IPLB* 50.

be made and undone, lends itself to many different shades of infringing conduct. So, for instance, it has become more commonplace to execute an Anton Piller Order against an ex-employee alleged to have breached the employer's confidence: see *Woolworths Ltd v Olson* (2004) 63 IPR 258; [2004] NSWSC 849; *Austress Freyssinet Pty Ltd v Joseph* [2006] NSWSC 77; *Visy Board Pty Ltd v D'Souza (No 3)* [2008] VSC 572; and also *Berg Engineering Pty Ltd v Tivity Solutions Pty Ltd* [2019] QSC 68. The legal issues are not always clear cut: see, for example, *Allam v Aristocrat Technologies Australia Pty Ltd* (2012) 95 IPR 242; [2012] FCAFC 34.

Constraints on the granting of an Anton Piller Order

19.7 Concerns about observance of strict constraints in the granting and execution of the order were expressed by the courts early on. In *Anton Piller KG*, the UK Court of Appeal examined the basis for the order, Lord Denning MR holding that it lay in the inherent jurisdiction of the court (since there was no other basis) and that, as there was only scant old precedent concerning the question, it fell to the Court of Appeal to decide its legitimacy 'on principle' (at 61):

> It seems to me that such an order can be made by a judge ex parte, but it should only be made where it is essential that the plaintiff should have inspection so that justice can be done between the parties: and when, if the defendant were forewarned, there is a grave danger that vital evidence will be destroyed, that papers will be burnt or lost or hidden, or taken beyond the jurisdiction, and so the ends of justice be defeated: and when the inspection would do no real harm to the defendant or his case. Nevertheless, in the enforcement of this order, the plaintiffs must act with due circumspection. On the service of it, the plaintiffs should be attended by their solicitor, who is an officer of the court. They should give the defendants an opportunity of considering it and of consulting their own solicitor. If the defendants wish to apply to discharge the order as having been improperly obtained, they must be allowed to do so. If the defendants refuse permission to enter or to inspect, the plaintiffs must not force their way in. They must accept the refusal, and bring it to the notice of the court afterwards, if need be on an application to commit [for contempt].

Lord Denning MR's last words refer to the important distinction between an Anton Piller Order and a search warrant: the person(s) executing the order has no right to force entry or to enter premises against the will of the respondents or persons in charge of premises. Lord Denning MR continued at 61, identifying a further reason to permit entry on the basis of the order:

> [The order] serves to tell the defendants that, on the evidence put before it, the court is of opinion that they ought to permit inspection nay, it orders them to permit and that they refuse at their peril. It puts them in peril not only of proceedings for contempt, but also of adverse inferences being drawn against them; so much so that their own solicitor may often advise them to comply. [The court was prepared to sanction the granting of such orders], but only in an extreme case where there is grave danger of property being smuggled away or of vital evidence being destroyed.

As Ormond LJ said at 62, 'The proposed order is at the extremity of this court's powers. Such orders, therefore, will rarely be made, and only when there is no alternative way of ensuring that justice is done to the applicant.'

Most of the contemporary elements of the order are apparent from the extract quoted above and have not varied much since. The principal trend has been for the courts to become progressively more alert both to the adequacy of the factual basis for granting the order and to precise adherence to the terms of the order in its execution. As Bryson J noted about the Federal Court in *EFG Australia Ltd v Kennedy* [1995] NSWSC 58 at [9], 'This court has responded with caution to applications for Anton Piller discovery, and the caution with which such applications are received has, if anything, increased with the passage of years and the accumulation of experience.' Courts have often expressed reservations and sometimes regrets about being in the difficult position of having to decide whether or not to grant the order, demonstrating an ambivalent attitude because of its harshness and the ex parte nature of the hearing. An Anton Piller Order will normally be granted only subject to the filing of an action against the respondent. The Anton Piller Order is usually used in circumstances where the normal procedures of discovery (or 'disclosure') are likely to be subverted; it would therefore be extremely unusual to grant the order once the respondents have been served with initiating documents; but see the exceptional case of *Microsoft Corporation v Goodview Electronics Pty Ltd* (1999) 46 IPR 159 (*Microsoft v Goodview*), where the order was refused in such circumstances. However, an Anton Piller Order is for the preservation of specified items of evidence in the custody of the applicant's solicitors and not for the purpose of applicants perusing seized materials themselves with the aim of facilitating discovery or provision of particulars: see *Metso Minerals (Australia) Ltd v Kalra (No 3)* [2008] FCA 1201 at [36]; and also more recently *Findex Group Ltd v McKay* [2019] NSWCA 93. It is for that reason that the evidence seized is released only to the applicants themselves for perusal with the specific consent of the court. Nonetheless, the same implied undertakings that apply to a solicitor to whom documents are produced on discovery in civil litigation apply to a solicitor obtaining the order and conducting the search under it: see also *Home Office v Harman* (1983) 1 AC 280 about the implied undertakings of a solicitor concerning discovered documents.

Evidence for the granting of an Anton Piller Order

19.8 The evidence on an application will be limited in nature and extent, since the whole purpose of the order is to obtain the evidence of infringement in the first place. Most often, it will consist of affidavit material and/or, for instance, submitting 'trap purchases' of the impugned goods. For example, in *Milcap Publishing Group AB v Coranto Corp Pty Ltd* (1995) 32 IPR 34, the order was granted on the basis of affidavits in which the applicants expressed their belief that the respondents were selling pirated video cassettes. 'The allegation of copying was expressed in the form of a belief rather than putting forward any direct evidence to that effect': at IPR 35. Taking a bare assertion, even if under oath, as evidence, unavoidable as that may be, is naturally a source of concern for the courts. Thus, in *International Entertainment New Zealand (No 2) v Lewis* (1998) 42 IPR 162 at 168, Bryson J said:

> It must always be remembered that when deciding to grant such an application [for an Anton Piller Order] the court places itself for relevant information wholly in the hands of an interested party whose motivations and interests could well obscure from that party what needs to be done to comply with the obligation of frank disclosure. Competitive

> rivalries are often at work …, and the prospect of delivering a heavy and disruptive first blow on a business rival who does not know of the existence of the litigation is a temptation and distraction from which an applicant may not be able to free itself … Courts must distinguish genuine applications from those that are motivated rather, whether consciously or not, by a desire to disrupt a competitor's business. What is more, they must do it in entire reliance on the applicant who may be so motivated. It is in that light that the duty of frank and full disclosure of all relevant facts, both in favour and against the applicant's case, and the applicant's duty to err on the side of caution, is constantly emphasised in the cases.

Mala fides and inadequate disclosure are possible grounds for setting aside or discharging an order obtained ex parte; a duty of candour applies: see *Australian Football League v Hard On Sports Pty Ltd* [2012] VSC 475. The standard of disclosure in ex parte applications is high: *uberrima fides* is required 'and the party inducing the Court to act in the absence of the other party, fails in his obligation unless he supplies the place of the absent party to the extent of bringing forward all the material facts which that party would presumably have brought forward in his defence to that application': see *Thomas A Edison Ltd v Bullock* (1912) 15 CLR 679. In the words of the court in *Milcap Publishing Group* at IPR 367, 'Whether, if that disclosure had been made, the Anton Piller Order would not have been granted, is not something I can say. To be material, a fact does not have to be such as would have caused the application to be refused.' A matter is material if it is one that the court would take into account in making the order; that is all. In *Universal Music Australia Pty Ltd v Sharman License Holdings Ltd* (2004) 205 ALR 319; 59 IPR 299; [2004] FCA 183 (the Kazaa file-sharing litigation: see Chapter 18 Digitisation), an application for setting aside Anton Piller Orders relating to computer records for non-disclosure was thus dismissed. The court emphasised that the fact that a witness (a solicitor) was unaware of certain facts concerning equivalent proceedings in the US did not excuse him in the face of an allegation of non-disclosure if he need only have asked about them to find out. However, the non-disclosure was held to be immaterial: the information would not have affected the decision about the Anton Piller Order. In *Berg Engineering* (19.6 above) the court gave very careful consideration to the factors to be taken into account in an application to discharge a search order, inter alia in circumstances of material non-disclosure. Even if the non-disclosure *is* material, discharging the order is not *automatically* required: see *Dart Industries Inc v David Bryar & Associates Pty Ltd* (1997) 38 IPR 389 at 419. Thus, in *MG Distribution Pty Ltd v Khan* (2006) 230 ALR 352; [2006] FMCA 666, although the federal magistrate accepted that the court had been misled to some extent about the nature of the applicants' ownership or rights in the relevant films, a variation of the terms of the order was more appropriate 'though of course at the trial of the action further material may become evident which may lead to significant orders in relation to damages and/ or costs which will be dealt with at the trial': at [64].

Contents of an Anton Piller Order

19.9 For an example of a search order, see *Brooks Sports* 19.6 above. The order usually consists of a number of prohibitory clauses ordering the respondents to restrain from certain acts that allegedly infringe the applicant's intellectual property rights; for example, to be restrained from infringing the copyright in, further using, reproducing, adapting, exhibiting, distributing or otherwise dealing with the following (a list of computer programs): see *JC Techforce Pty Ltd v Pearce* (1996) 138 ALR 522; 35 IPR 196. The order's execution is normally to be supervised by an independent solicitor, other than a solicitor for the applicant: see Federal Court Search Orders Practice Note (GPN-SRCH) and see the remarks of Branson J in this regard in *Microsoft v Goodview* at [27]ff. Such a solicitor acts as an independent witness and can mediate disputes between the parties at the premises that are to be searched. The order identifies the persons who shall execute the order, and the premises where the order may be executed. It must specify what may be searched (eg, computer hardware and software, databases and documents in the possession, custody and control of the respondents) and list specified items that may be removed into the custody of the solicitors for the applicants; further examples may be found in *JC Techforce* and in *Polygram Records Pty Ltd v Monash Records (Aust) Pty Ltd* (1985) 10 FCR 332; 6 IPR 423. A number of other matters will usually be covered in the order.

Adherence to the terms of the order

19.10 Concerns have been raised about the use of the order to enable an unwarranted general fishing expedition: 'The Court must, in my view, be careful to avoid the extraordinary jurisdiction of the Court to make an Anton Piller Order from being subverted to a mere investigatory tool for applicants or indeed, from being used for any purpose other than the preservation of vital evidence pending the hearing and determination of a proceeding.': per Branson J in *Microsoft v Goodview* at [26]. The removal of materials that were not specified in the order has resulted in judicial criticism. A case in point is *JC Techforce*, although the taking of additional materials did not there result in the setting aside of the order. The judge held that although materials were taken that should not have been, the order had been executed in good faith and not oppressively. The execution of an Anton Piller Order is most often stressful for all concerned, and this was clearly in Branson J's mind when commenting on what had transpired during the execution of the order in *JC Techforce*: 'It is not disputed that the execution of the Anton Piller Order took place in a highly charged atmosphere. In view of the order this is hardly surprising.' Her Honour went on to point out that in such circumstances, with neither of the respondents being lawyers, their conduct could not be held against them in a legal sense (at ALR 526; IPR 201): 'The fact, as I find, that no steps were taken by or on behalf of the respondents, or any of them, to oppose the removal from the premises of documents [not specified in the order] is not, in my view, in the circumstances which prevailed … to be equated to a consent freely given for the removal of each document.' It was the responsibility of the applicants' solicitors to ensure that the carrying out of such an order was 'meticulously carefully done and with the fullest respect for the defendant's rights' in every regard. Her Honour quoted a passage from *Columbia Picture Industries Inc v Robinson* [1987] 1 Ch 38 in support, where, at 62–3, Scott J said: '… given the nature of Anton Piller Orders and the circumstances of surprise and shock which almost always attend their execution, there is a very real danger in allowing the executing solicitors to go outside the terms of the order in reliance on an alleged consent on the part of the respondent.' Even if the applicants came across items that allegedly belonged to them, extreme caution should be shown.

Normally, materials seized are handed into the custody of the solicitors for the applicant; they are not to be put at the disposal of, kept or used by the applicants in person unless the order specifically allows this, as is indicated above. The applicant (as opposed to the applicant's lawyers) does not have automatic access to what has been seized: see *Metso Minerals (Australia) Ltd v Kalra (No 3)*. Nor should the seized materials be released to third parties unless there are special circumstances justifying this: see, for example, *Visy Board Pty Ltd v D'Souza (No 3)*, refusing release of seized material to the police. As to the exceptional circumstances in which documents obtained in the execution of an Anton Piller Order may be used for purposes other than the proper conduct of the proceeding, see *Dart Industries Inc v David Bryar & Associates Pty Ltd*. The aim of the order is to secure evidence, not to allow the business of the applicant to continue with the help of what is found in the respondent's possession, no matter how strong the claim to ownership of the applicant may be. A related requirement is the making and keeping of adequate inventories of the materials seized, so they can be properly tracked. Take, for instance, the example of a situation where a respondent has been accused of taking original customer records; an applicant may want them back for use in the applicant's business. In *Specifier Publications Pty Ltd v Long* (1997) 40 IPR 91, a solicitor had undertaken to make an inventory of all the items removed from the premises and to retain them in his custody at all times subsequent. The solicitor was charged with contempt for failing to comply with these undertakings. The court pointed out that estoppel of a party was irrelevant as a test for compliance by a solicitor with an undertaking given to a court: the opinion of the respondents as to the adequacy of the list prepared, given at the scene, was thus not relevant. Copious material had been taken, and no attempt to detail it on the inventory was made. (For instance, one item read 'multi-coloured bag of materials for future and from past issues to "Specifier" to staff and editorial notes'; another 'box of 2 black and 2 red folders of old contracts'.) The judge said (at IPR 100):

> This was only a colourable attempt, a gesture towards preparing an inventory, and could not be described as or understood by a reasonable person to be an inventory of goods … The burden of practicalities and of complying with undertakings connected with an Anton Piller Order falls on those who wish to have it carried out, and if it is impractical, they should not carry it out; they should not depart from their undertakings.

The solicitor had also broken his undertaking to seize and remain in control of the goods at all times, preserving them for the purpose of evidence. Instead, they were spirited away by the applicants, who claimed ownership rights in them and whose purpose was to obtain them to carry on their own business. As a result of the solicitor's failure to comply with the undertakings, the whole exercise had gone disastrously wrong, requiring further court action to reclaim the goods in question. The solicitor was found in contempt, a serious consequence illustrating the risks and responsibilities attendant upon applying for and executing an Anton Piller Order.

Practical aspects

19.11 As we saw above, there are severe practical constraints upon the execution of the order. The solicitor must ordinarily execute the order during normal trading hours.

Upon being served, the respondents must be given an opportunity to contact a solicitor who can subject the order to critical examination. If appropriate, the solicitor for the respondents will arrange for an application to be made to the court for discharge of the order. The order as served must be attached to the affidavits forming the basis for its granting; it may be that they are incomplete or contain inaccurate information, a possible basis for discharging the order. Or it may be that there is another deficiency with the order or its execution; for example, if it is executed at premises other than those specified in the order.

There is a period of delay, concerning to the applicants, during which the parties wait for the solicitor of the respondents to arrive at the scene. This may provide opportunity to erase materials from computers, so the consent or agreement of the respondents or persons in charge of the premises may be sought to devise a manner of ensuring that this does not happen while the search proper is still not started. Forced entry is not allowed at any time, nor is equivalent oppressive conduct that may result in entry being gained — excessive threats and so on. In *JC Techforce*, the independent solicitor was accused of oppressive conduct, in that he allegedly said that the respondent would be in contempt unless he permitted access to the documents and computers on the premises immediately, before the respondent's solicitors had arrived. It was also said that he had threatened to call the police if not allowed to execute the order. Such conduct would arguably be oppressive, but in this case the judge decided that the conduct of Mr Simpson, by his own, unchallenged report, had in fact been perfectly appropriate and that he had not expressed himself in the terms alleged. It is certainly the case that it may be prudent to have police in attendance at the execution of the order, but only to make sure that no breaches of the peace occur at the time. The police have no role to play in the execution of the order itself; for example, in forcing persons occupying the premises to comply with the order: at ALR 524; IPR 199.[5]

The privilege against self-incrimination

19.12 Increasing criminalisation of intellectual property law is a contemporary trend. For example, for certain infringements of the Trade Marks Act 1995 (Cth) and the Copyright Act, a term of imprisonment up to five years may be imposed. Infringement of intellectual property rights is increasingly a matter of public rather than only private law. Public authorities (the Australian Federal Police and Commonwealth prosecutorial services) are obliged to mount criminal investigations and prosecutions of individuals suspected of infringement: see, for example, *Holder v Searle (No 2)* (1997) 78 FCR 430; 39 IPR 343.

If a claim of privilege against self-incrimination can be raised as a basis for refusing compliance with the order, what does it extend to? Only to documents, as was held in *Rank Film Distributors v Video Information Centre* [1981] FSR 363, or also to the common targets of Anton Piller Orders, such as tapes, masters, plates and others? The civil

5. As to further practical information concerning the execution of Anton Piller Orders, see M Gawler, 'Making Anton Piller Orders Work' (April 1997) *LIJ* 42 and B Fitzmaurice, 'Protecting Intellectual Property with Anton Piller Orders' (2002) 15(7) *IPLB* 103.

action is still the primary remedy by which individual intellectual property owners obtain redress. It would be a perverse result if, by including criminal penalties that are intended to reinforce their position, the private remedies are rendered less effective by a defendant's broad right to claim privilege. But the penalties for infringement, as indicated above, are potentially severe, and the likelihood of prosecution, although maybe not great, is no longer as remote as before. It has been said that if there is a real or appreciable risk of prosecution, or if the risk is not too remote and the possible charges too trivial, then the privilege may be invoked in the circumstances of a civil action. As well as in the context of an Anton Piller Order, this could relate to other evidence-gathering procedures, such as discovery, but it is obviously not uncommon that certain dishonest conduct would attract both the execution of an Anton Piller Order and criminal prosecution. A balance must be struck, either by way of assessing the actual chances of prosecution and the gravity of the potential consequences for the defendant or, as was done in *Warman International Ltd v Envirotech (Australia) Pty Ltd* (1986) 11 FCR 478; 6 IPR 578, by making the execution of the order conditional upon an undertaking by the applicant not to use the evidence for the purpose of criminal prosecutions.[6] In any case, both courts and commentators are generally of the opinion that intellectual property law is mainly concerned with civil rights, and the privilege should therefore not be too readily supported in law: see *Busby v Thorn EMI Video Programmes Ltd* [1984] 1 NZLR 461; (1984) 2 IPR 304 and also *Authors Workshop v Bileru Pty Ltd* (1989) 88 ALR 211; 16 IPR 661. More recently, in Australia, see *Websyte Corporation Pty Ltd v Alexander (No 2)* [2012] FCA 562, where there was a prosecution under the Crimes Act 1958 (Vic) in relation to unauthorised computer access by former employees, and prosecution under the Copyright Act was also 'on the cards'. A stay of the civil proceedings was granted until determination of the criminal proceedings, because of a real risk of prejudice. In the United Kingdom, the ability to claim the privilege in intellectual property cases has been abolished by statute: see Supreme Court Act 1981 (UK), s 72; as to the application of the Act, see *Coca-Cola v Gilbey* (1995) 33 IPR 650. If a respondent claims privilege in any particular item, the order can provide that it be placed in the hands of the supervising solicitor.

Other ex parte orders

19.13 Apart from Anton Piller Orders, so-called 'Mareva' injunctions (or 'Freezing orders'), preventing the removal of assets, are also relevant to intellectual property cases: see, for example, *Cardile v LED Builders Pty Ltd* (1999) 73 ALJR 657; 162 ALR 294 and *Universal Music Pty Ltd v Sharman License Holdings Ltd* [2005] FCA 1587, litigation in which Anton Piller Orders were also granted. A further ex parte order with special relevance to intellectual property law is known in Australia and the UK as a 'representative order' and in New Zealand as a 'John Doe order'. The common distinguishing element of such orders is that they are granted ex parte against unknown defendants or against a known defendant representing a class of unknown defendants against whom the order can then be enforced. The order operates much like an Anton

6. See also W Kelcey, 'Offence Provisions of the Copyright Act 1968 — Do They Protect or Punish?' (1995) 6 *AIPJ* 229.

Piller Order, in that it is executed by the appellants and their solicitors. It is subject to the sanction of contempt of court for non-compliance against those respondents that fall within the category of persons described within the order. The order allows the obtaining of evidence of infringing acts and allows the applicants to obtain information from the unnamed parties concerning names and addresses and so on, so that they can be identified. The order may be used against bootleggers who sell infringing copies at musical performances, for instance, and who often do not have a permanent place of business or are otherwise hard to identify or locate. For some examples of representative orders, see *Tony Blain Pty Ltd (t/as ACME Merchandising) v Jamison* (1993) 41 FCR 414 (sale of merchandise outside Metallica concert venues); in the UK, *EMI Records Ltd v Kudhail* (1983) 4 IPR 513 (sale of pirate cassettes). At least one individual in the group must be identified and named in a representative order. Further, if the names or correct names of the other members of the 'group' are not known, to enable execution against them, some identity of interest amongst the group of persons engaged in the infringing activity must be shown, or at least 'fairly close ties of organisation'. In the *Tony Blain* case, the application was based on evidence that a more or less organised group of persons had engaged in the sale of unauthorised merchandise at previous Paul McCartney concerts, which showed a generic likeness to a further series of concerts by the group Metallica, which were to take place shortly: see *Tony Blain Pty Ltd v Splain* [1994] FSR 497. See also *Stacey Brothers Plumbing Pty Ltd v Waterco Ltd* [2009] FCA 438, relating to a representative order against a franchisee representing others in relation to patent infringement.

Damages

Compensatory, restitutionary and punitive remedies in general

19.14 All intellectual property regimes allow for an award of compensatory damages as a remedy. Even in the context of the equitable action for breach of confidence, although the primary remedy is an injunction, courts have not hesitated to award damages or 'equitable compensation' (although not exemplary damages: see *Harris v Digital Pulse Pty Ltd* (2003) 56 NSWLR 298; 197 ALR 626). As well as ordinary compensatory damages awards, the Copyright Act 1968, the Designs Act 2003, the Patents Act 1990 and the Trade Marks Act 1995 also provide for an award of additional damages — see further below. Alternatively, in most cases, a plaintiff can elect an account of profits rather than damages. The two remedies are quite distinct, damages being compensatory by nature, while an account is restitutionary, accounting for the profit made by the infringer rather than for the damage suffered by the plaintiff.[7] Below we deal in more detail with the characteristics of both remedies and with the question of an appropriate choice between the two.

---

7. See also D Miller, 'Restitutionary and Exemplary Damages for Copyright Infringement' (1996) 14 *Aust Bar Rev* 143.

Award of damages available as of right

19.15 It is said that, in copyright, damages are available as of right, and the legal position is often considered to be the same in all statutory regimes. Courts have treated damages for breach of statutory intellectual property rights as analogous to common law damages, rather than equitable damages (or 'equitable compensation'). In *Robert J Zupanovich Pty Ltd v B & N Beale Nominees Pty Ltd* (1995) 59 FCR 49; 32 IPR 339, Carr J said (at FCR 65; IPR 355): 'I respectfully agree with Sheppard J's observation in *LED Builders [Pty Ltd v Masterton Homes (NSW) Pty Ltd* (1994) 54 FCR 196; (1995) 30 IPR 447] concerning the discretion to order an account of profits and also with his Honour's conclusion [at IPR 466] that so far as damages are concerned, there cannot be any room for the exercise of a discretion.' Thus, normally, the award of damages is not subject to equitable principles such as laches or delay (note, however, that all statutory regimes provide a prescription period within which an action must be brought). The award of equitable damages (or 'equitable compensation') for breach of confidence, on the other hand, is subject to the court's discretion (which, in practice, means subject to the application of well-established equitable principles), although in many cases the equitable remedy will be subsidiary to a remedy for breach of contract: see the discussions in this regard in *Streetscape Projects (Australia) Pty Ltd v City of Sydney* [2013] NSWCA 2. However, treating the award of common law-type damages in statutory regimes as being 'as of right' must be reconciled with the actual wording of the relevant provisions: see, for instance, s 115(2) of the Copyright Act 1968 '... the relief that a court *may* grant ... includes ... either damages or an account of profits.'

The same word 'may' is used in the Designs Act 1906 and in the Trade Marks Act 1995, s 126, the Patents Act 1990, s 122 and the Circuit Layouts Act 1989 (Cth), s 27(1). Drummond J in *A-One Accessory Imports Pty Ltd v Off Road Imports Pty Ltd (No 2)* (1996) 66 FCR 199; 34 IPR 332 was willing to ignore the problem (at FCR 201–2; IPR 335):

> Even if the remedy, by way of damages, provided for by s 115(2) of the [Copyright] Act is created by a form of words that suggests it too is discretionary relief, I do not consider there is any justification for not adopting, by way of analogy, the rule at law that a person whose legal rights have been interfered with is entitled to damages even though he may be, by reason of his own conduct, disentitled to equitable relief. While the grant of the remedies provided for by s 115(2) by way of injunction and an account of profits should be governed by applying, by analogy, the equitable rules applicable to the grant of those kinds of relief, I do not think that there is a discretion to deny a copyright owner who has established an infringement of his copyright the remedy by way of damages also provided for by the section: see *LED Builders Pty Ltd v Masterton Homes (NSW) Pty Ltd* (1994) 54 FCR 196.

See also Carr J in *Robert J Zupanovich Pty Ltd v B & N Beale Nominees Pty Ltd* at FCR 65: 'If an owner makes a claim for damages and proves damage there is no room for the exercise of discretion.' Arguably, the statutory terms could be interpreted as conferring a power on the courts to grant any of the various remedies referred to in the relevant sections, as is indicated in *Review Australia Pty Ltd v Innovative Lifestyle Investments Pty Ltd* (2008) 166 FCR 358; [2008] FCA 74 at [33]:

> For my own part, I consider that the words 'the relief may include' do no more than introduce an identification of the range of remedies that would be available to a court in accordance

> with well-established principles. In the case of par (b) of s 75(1), the remedies identified are damages or an account of profits. Each is a description of a remedy with which the general law is familiar. Putting to one side the special case of damages in equity, the remedy of an award of damages has traditionally been treated as non-discretionary in the sense that, if the wrongful act of the plaintiff causes damage to the defendant, damages should be awarded. I do not accept that the way in which s 75(1) of the *Designs Act* is expressed is intended to make an award of damages discretionary, as though it were analogous to an equitable remedy.

In any case, if an award of damages is available as of right as a general rule, various statutes create a discretion not to award damages in cases of innocent infringement. An injunction then remains available, but, being an equitable remedy, is only ever granted at the discretion of the court. In some cases, an account of profits remains available in cases of innocent infringement but in others not.

Innocent infringement

19.16 If the award of damages were available as of right in cases where the infringer was not actually or constructively aware of the infringing nature of their conduct or of the existence of intellectual property rights, a person acting in ignorance and good faith could be liable for substantial compensation.[8] Certainly in regimes without any organised system of registration and publication, this may be harsh in the circumstances of the case, hence the courts' statutory discretion not to award compensatory damages. The precise wording of the relevant provisions in the various regimes varies. Under s 115(3) of the Copyright Act 1968, if the infringer was 'not aware and had no reasonable grounds for suspecting that the act constituting the infringement was an infringement [the plaintiff is] not entitled ... to any damages ...'. Section 27(3) of the Circuit Layouts Act 1989 (Cth) has analogous wording to that of the Copyright Act, whereas s 75(2) of the Designs Act 2003 (Cth) places a higher onus on a defendant to establish innocence for primary than for secondary infringement. Section 123(1) of the Patents Act 1990 provides:

> ... a court may refuse to award damages, or to make an order for an account of profits, in respect of an infringement of a patent if the defendant satisfies the court that, at the date of the infringement, the defendant was not aware, and had no reason to believe, that a patent for an invention existed.

Thus, under the designs and patents legislation, a court retains the discretion to award damages in cases of innocent infringement, while in the copyright and circuit layouts legislation, a court is 'not entitled' to award damages in similar circumstances of innocence. Further, under the Copyright Act, the plaintiff arguably remains entitled to an account of profits subject to equitable principles, whether or not the infringement was innocent, while under the Patents Act and the Designs Act 2003 the court may refuse to award either damages or an account of profits. However, the test of 'innocence' is more demanding in patents and designs legislation than in copyright and circuit layouts laws (even more so given the statutory presumptions of s 123(2) of the

8. See also S Gilchrist, 'Australia — Copyright — Innocent Infringement' [1996] 8 *EIPR* D-225.

Patents Act). Note that under the Copyright Act, the award of conversion damages under s 116 is not affected by the provisions of s 115; however, s 116(2) provides that in certain circumstances of innocence, the plaintiff is not entitled to a pecuniary remedy under the section. The Trade Marks Act 1995 simply provides that a court may grant damages or an account at the option of the plaintiff, and makes no special provision for innocent infringement: see s 126(1)(b). However, these remedies are not available in certain circumstances where the defendant has made a non-use application: see s 127. 'Innocent infringement' can arise in many factual circumstances, such as in relation to importation of infringing goods produced overseas, but it will not protect a party who continues to sell infringing items despite being put on notice: see *The Dempsey Group Pty Ltd v Spotlight Pty Ltd* (2018) 138 IPR 190; [2018] FCA 2016.

Calculation of compensatory damages

19.17 The overarching goal of damages is to compensate for the loss suffered; in other words, to restore the plaintiff to the position they were in before the infringement occurred or if the infringement had not occurred: see *General Tire and Rubber Co v Firestone Tyre and Rubber Co Ltd* [1976] RPC 197 at 212 per Lord Wilberforce. Besanko J, citing *General Tire*, put it as follows in *Futuretronics.com.au Pty Ltd v Graphix Labels Pty Ltd (No 2)* (2008) 76 IPR 763; [2008] FCA 746 at [10] (*Futuretronics*):

> In relation to the claim for damages under s 115(2) of the [Copyright] Act, the Court, in awarding damages for infringement of copyright, will have regard to similar considerations as attend the award of damages in tort: *General Tire & Rubber Co v Firestone Tyre and Rubber Co Ltd* [1976] RPC 197. The purpose of an award is to compensate the plaintiff for the loss suffered as a result of the defendant's infringement: *Bailey v Namol Pty Ltd* (1994) 53 FCR 102 at 110–111.

See also *Facton Ltd v Rifai Fashions Pty Ltd* (2012) 199 FCR 569; 95 IPR 95; [2012] FCAFC 9 at [14]–[20].

Nonetheless, although the principle is common to both torts and intellectual property law, different considerations apply in intellectual property cases. In *Bailey v Namol Pty Ltd* (1994) 53 FCR 102; 30 IPR 147, it was said that there is no rigid rule equating compensatory damages in tort with ordinary damages for copyright infringement. In many intellectual property matters, the starting point for the measure of damages is an apparently precise legal formula. For example, in copyright cases, it is said that the measure of damages is the depreciation caused by the infringement to the value of the copyright as a chose in action: as per Lord Wright in *Sutherland Publishing Co Ltd v Caxton Co Ltd* [1936] Ch 323 at 336; All ER 177. However, detailed investigations on the basis of the facts of the actual case commonly result in the court concluding that:

- no precise legal formula is in fact applicable;
- the formula is so general as to be bereft of real meaning; or
- the formula provides little more than a vague starting point for the actual calculation.

Sometimes, no specific method of calculation can realistically be applied; nonetheless, if damage there is, then damages there will be. In *Enzed Holdings Ltd v Wynthea*

Pty Ltd (1984) 57 ALR 167 at 183 Sheppard, Morling and Wilcox JJ said: 'If the court finds damage has occurred it must do its best to quantify the loss even if a degree of speculation and guess work is involved. Furthermore, if actual damage is suffered, the award must be for more than nominal damages. … We emphasise, however, that the principle applies only when the court finds that loss or damage has occurred. It is not enough for a plaintiff merely to show wrongful conduct by the defendant.' The result is inspired by an appreciation of what is fair in the circumstances rather than by mathematical correctness: for an example in the context of copyright, see *Fortuity v Barcza; Fortuity v Skybase Nominees* (1995) 32 IPR 517. The 'reasonable sum' thus arrived at may then be discounted on account of the vagaries of commerce that the exploitation of the rights by the plaintiff is subject to; for a further example of damages 'at large', see *Autodesk Australia Pty Ltd v Cheung* (1990) 94 ALR 472; 17 IPR 69, also a copyright case. The difficulties of calculation of damages, by whatever general measure, are not restricted to copyright: for an example in the context of both copyright and confidential information, see *Interfirm Comparison (Aust) Pty Ltd v Law Society of NSW* (1975) 6 ALR 445 and *Fortuity*. In cases of breach of confidence, the measure of damages is said to be either the value of the information wrongly taken or a reasonable sum for its use, depending on the circumstances; both general measures are not easily firmed up into concrete figures. The same can be said of the value of goodwill in the context of, for instance, merchandising cases such as *Talmax Pty Ltd v Telstra Corporation Ltd* (1996) 36 IPR 46; [1997] 2 Qd R 444 (the *Kieren Perkins* case) where the court had to put a value on a loss of opportunity as a form of damage suffered (as can be additional to the loss of a royalty forgone by unauthorised use of a person's image: see eg *Fitzgerald v 33 South Pty Ltd* [2008] FMCA 1132) which by its very nature is difficult to quantify; see also further below.

However, although courts often make an award in the absence of much concrete and specific evidence going to the calculation of a particular sum, it is essential to establish that some damage has occurred. There was no such admissible evidence (the court dismissing the expert's evidence proffered about the diminution of the value of the trade mark) concerning actual loss or damage in *Bing! Software Pty Ltd v Bing Technologies Pty Limited (No 1)* (2008) 79 IPR 454; [2008] FCA 1760, because the activities of the respective parties were well removed from each other. Collier J (at [123]) referred to the passage from *Enzed Holdings* quoted above in support of her decision to grant only an injunction. To warrant a monetary award, even if the value of the damage is difficult or near impossible to ascertain, there must at least be *some* evidence that actual damage has occurred (such as some diminution of value of a mark or loss of trade). However, in the absence of evidence of any real damage, an award of nominal damages is sometimes said to be warranted to vindicate the invasion of an applicant's proprietary rights: see, for example, *MJA Scientifics International Pty Ltd v SC Johnson and Son Pty Ltd* (1998) 43 IPR 275 at 281 per Sundberg J and *Futuretronics*. Loss of reputation 'sounds in compensatory damages', which may be awarded under s 115(2) of the Copyright Act: see *Facton* at [25]; and *Geneva Laboratories Ltd v Prestige Premium Deals Pty Ltd (No 5)* (2017) 122 IPR 279; [2017] FCA 63. Finally, it may be that even though compensatory damages are quite low, a more substantial sum is awarded in additional damages.

Calculation of damages: licence fee approach

19.18 In copyright, as was mentioned in the previous section, damages are commonly said to be the measure of the depreciation that the infringement causes to the value of the copyright as a chose in action: see *Sutherland Publishing* and, for example, *International Writing Institute v Rimila Pty Ltd* (1994) 30 IPR 250. But this measure of damages is criticised as frequently as it is put forward in the cases, and in itself offers little practical guidance; further, it is usually said not to be the only possible measure of damages: see *Autodesk Australia Pty Ltd v Cheung* and *Milpurrurru v Indofurn Pty Ltd* (1994) 54 FCR 240; 30 IPR 209. A common route followed in copyright, as well as in other matters, is to equate the depreciation in the value of the intellectual property right, and thus the injury to the plaintiff, with the value of licensing fees forgone because of the infringement. This is a course beset by theoretical difficulties, particularly where the plaintiff did not actually license the product to anyone: see, for example, *Catnic Components Ltd v Hill & Smith Ltd* [1983] FSR 512. In some factual circumstances, the putative licence approach is so artificial as to be inapplicable because, for instance, the plaintiff would never have granted a licence or because the defendant would never have bought a licensed copy: see *Autodesk Australia Pty Ltd v Cheung* and *Columbia Pictures Inc v Luckins* (1996) 34 IPR 504. In other words, the licence fee approach is appropriate only if it can be inferred that consumers would have bought genuine products if they had not acquired infringing copies: see *Adidas-Salomon AG v Turner* (2003) 58 IPR 66; [2003] FCA 421. If the estimated 'loss of licence fee approach' is not to be applied, alternative methods must be devised that are appropriate to and reflective of the actual facts and circumstances of the case: see, for instance, *Microsoft Corporation v Atifo Pty Ltd* (1997) 38 IPR 643.

One analogous method is to approach the estimation in terms of the value of the plaintiff's lost opportunity to profit from the exploitation of their rights due to the actions of the defendant. If the overarching aim of compensation damages is to put the plaintiff in the position they would be in if the infringement had not taken place, this is clearly an appropriate measure of damages. When that measure is adopted, a risk of confusion with the remedy of an account of profits arises: in an account of profits, the issue is not the loss made by the plaintiff but the profit made by the defendant. As Windeyer J pointed out in *Colbeam Palmer Ltd v Stock Affiliates Pty Ltd* (1968) 122 CLR 25 at 32, 'what a plaintiff might have made had the defendant not invaded his rights is by no means the same thing as what the defendant did make by doing so'. Further, calculating the value of a lost opportunity to make profits presents obvious practical problems. In the context of passing off, for instance, what is the effect of the plaintiff's image being used without consent? It may be two-fold: first, a loss of their own opportunity to exploit that image by licensing either the defendant or third parties; and, second, attenuation of goodwill by the unauthorised and uncontrolled exploitation of the image, resulting in a loss of value in terms of future exploitation. In the *Kieren Perkins* case (*Talmax*; see also *Fitzgerald*, above), assessment of damages was at issue. Kieren Perkins, a swimmer, and his management company brought an action alleging unauthorised use of his image in advertising. On appeal, the Full Federal Court overturned the decision of the trial judge, who had dismissed the claim in passing off and for breach of the Trade Practices Act 1974 (Cth), and consequently had to assess damages. There was no suggestion that the reputation of the famous swimmer had been adversely affected, the damages claim being based on the diminished (not lost; there were other merchandising opportunities, notably with Telstra's main competitor, Optus) opportunity to commercially exploit name, image and reputation. According to the court, what was called for was (at IPR 53):

> ... an assessment of the possible extent to which Mr Perkins' commercial advantage was generally diminished and of the possibility that he lost the chance of a particular opportunity of exploitation of that advantage. Where there has been an actual loss of some sort, the common law does not permit difficulties of estimating the loss in money to defeat an award of damages [from *Sellars v Adelaide Petroleum NL* (1994) 179 CLR 332 at 349]. On our assessment, the damages related to the possibilities to which reference has been made should be set at $15,000.

The court acknowledged the difficulties inherent in quantifying damages in this kind of case. It pointed out that little evidence supported the assessment either of a specific lost opportunity or of any specific financial award that would be appropriate. The respondents led only evidence showing that Perkins had already undertaken some appearances for Optus and that he received substantial but very variable sums of money for permitting his name, image and reputation to be used. In theory, the court set the level of damages at an amount roughly related to sums mentioned before it and inspired by a general sense of what might be fair in the circumstances; in practice, the court unavoidably engaged in some informed guesswork. The often unpredictable level of damages awards in cases such as this results from the real practical and evidentiary difficulties encountered in calculating the value of a lost opportunity.

Similar difficulties, but in the context of copyright infringement, arose in *Bailey v Namol Pty Ltd*: the opportunity to secure a contract in a tendering process was frustrated by the copyright infringement (which allowed the infringer to secure the contract instead). The measure of damages was the sum that the applicant would have received under the contract that was frustrated, including a measure of profit. Even where there was only a loss of an opportunity or a chance of securing a contract due to an infringement, that loss can thus be compensated.

It should be noted that in cases where there is no estimable pecuniary or commercial loss due to the use made of a copyright work, damages have been awarded for the loss of freshness: see *Prior v Lansdowne Press Pty Ltd* [1977] VR 65 at 70 and *Milpurrurru* at FCR 276; IPR 243; and for the effect on the reputation of the artwork concerned see *TS & B Retail Systems Pty Ltd v 3Fold Resources Pty Ltd (No 3)* (2007) 158 FCR 444 at 496 per Finkelstein J and *Prior v Sheldon* (2000) 48 IPR 301 at 321–2 per Wilcox J. In *Prior*, one joint author whose ownership had not been recognised sued another in copyright. The loss of recognition of authorship resulted in a loss of possible future commissions from film and TV producers and thus quantifiable damage: see, however, *Futuretronics* for a contrasting result. In terms of loss of reputation, also note the potential significance of damages for an infringement of the moral right of integrity or attribution: in relation to quantification, see *Meskenas v ACP Publishing Pty Ltd* (2006) 70 IPR 172; [2006] FMCA 1136. Compensatory damages have also been awarded or said to be available for other forms of non-pecuniary harm in copyright cases where a special relationship exists between the work and the author(s): see, for example, *Milpurrurru*, where aboriginal artworks had been reproduced, without authorisation, on carpets manufactured in and imported from Vietnam, causing the artists grave cultural harm within their communities. Normally, of course, 'in the commercial context of our market economy' (*Milpurrurru* at FCR 277; IPR 244), s 115(2) damages are concentrated 'upon aspects of monetary loss likely to flow from the impaired commercial potential of the copyright': at FCR 277; IPR 244.[9] But, at FCR 277; IPR 244:

> The assessment of damages under s 115(2) may include compensation for personal suffering, for example, for insulting behaviour: *Beloff v Pressdram Ltd* [1973] 1 All ER 241 at 268; and for humiliations: *Nichols Advanced Vehicle Systems Inc v Rees* [1979] RPC 127 at 140. In the present case the infringements have caused personal distress and, potentially at least, have exposed the artists to embarrassment and contempt within their communities if not to the risk of diminished earning potential and physical harm.

In those circumstances, compensatory damages were available for those injuries. Note that similar circumstances may give rise to an award of additional damages (see further below in this chapter).

Conversion damages in copyright

19.19 By virtue of s 116 of the Copyright Act 1968, a court can award conversion damages — but note that by virtue of s 116(2), conversion damages are not available in cases of innocent infringement. In effect, s 116(1) and (1A) set up a legal fiction: a plaintiff can bring an action in detention or conversion in relation to an infringing copy or a device used or intended to be used for making infringing copies, as if the owner of the copyright had been the owner of the infringing copy since the time the copy was made, or the owner of the copyright had been the owner of the device since the time when it was used or intended to be used for making infringing copies. Damages (s 115) and conversion damages (s 116) are quite distinct, as Lord Wright MR explained in *Sutherland Publishing* (at All ER 180–1):

> Both are claims for a wrong, each wrong being different from the other. The former is for a wrong done to an incorporeal right, copyright, the latter is for conversion of particular chattels, the infringing copies. The measure of damages is different. In the latter case the measure is the value of the copies, which by force of the statute are deemed to be the property of the plaintiff, from the mere fact of being brought into existence; whereas in the other case, the measure of damage is the depreciation caused by the infringement to the value of the copyright, as a chose in action. It was strenuously contended that where the infringement consisted in the multiplication and sale of copies of a work, the damages under the two sections would overlap and the injustice of giving double compensation would be committed. It may be true that in some cases there may be an overlapping of the damages under the two sections, but, as I have already explained, there are two separate and diverse causes of action, each of which must receive appropriate consideration when it

9. See also J Gibson, 'Justice of Precedent, Justness of Equity: Equitable Protection and Remedies for Indigenous Intellectual Property' (2001) 6(4) *AILR* 1 and C Golvan, 'Protection of Australian Indigenous Copyright: Overview and Future Strategies' (2006) 18(10) *IPLB* 154.

> comes to the question of damages ... It must be left to the good sense of the tribunal which assesses the damages to avoid giving excessive damages.

However, the matter is no longer simply left to 'the good sense of the tribunal' under the present s 116 in Australia. Section 116(1B) provides that any relief granted by a court in an action for conversion or detention is in addition to any relief that the court may grant under s 115, but s 116(1C) now specifies that a court is not to grant conversion or detention damages if the relief under s 115 is, in the opinion of the court, a sufficient remedy. This was the conclusion reached by the court in *Elwood Clothing Pty Ltd v Cotton On Clothing Pty Ltd* (2009) 81 IPR 378; [2009] FCA 633 from [42], because it deemed damages under s 115 to be sufficient: see also in a like vein *Seafolly Pty Ltd v Fewstone Pty Ltd* (2014) 106 IPR 85; [2014] FCA 321. Conversion damages and compensatory damages are thus not mutually exclusive awards, but the courts will be alert to prevent double dipping: see, for example, *Milpurrurru* at FCR 274–5; IPR 241–2. The remedy of conversion damages has been called draconian[10] and was the subject of a Copyright Law Review Committee (CLRC) inquiry, chaired by Sheppard J.[11] The CLRC report accepted 'the harshness with which the section operates' (p 14), but did not recommend its repeal. It saw the conferral upon courts of a wide discretion to determine whether it is appropriate to order delivery up or to award conversion damages in a particular case as appropriate and a preferable reform. The CLRC report thus recommended that 'the remedies of conversion damages and an action for detention be no longer available to the owners of copyright as of right; rather the two remedies, although retained in the Act, should be discretionary' (Recommendation 1). The CLRC report also made some more specific recommendations. Section 116 was amended accordingly by the Copyright Amendment Act (No 1) 1998 (Cth). It requires a court, in deciding whether to grant conversion damages and any amount payable, to take into account numerous factors, namely:

1. where the goods deemed to be converted are infringing copies, the extent to which the goods consist of material that infringes copyright, the value the copyright adds to the goods, and its severability from them (see s 116(1E));
2. where the goods deemed to be converted are infringing copies, certain expenses incurred by the defendant in relation to production or acquisition of the goods (see s 116(D)(a) and (b));
3. the sufficiency of the remedies for damages for infringement provided in s 115 of the Act (see s 116(1C)); and
4. any other matter the court considers relevant (see s 116(1D)(c)).

The flexible relationship between s 116 in its current guise and s 115 is illustrated by *Boyapati v Rockefeller Management Corporation (No 2)* (2008) 78 IPR 600; [2008] FCA 1375. The respondents were found to have infringed copyright in practice exam questions for an undergraduate medicine and health sciences admission test. The court said, at [14]:

> I accept that, as the applicants maintain, the provision to a student of an infringing copy of an Icarus College practice exam was an actionable conversion, the measure of damages

10. See *Cornish on Intellectual Property*, 2nd ed, Sweet & Maxwell, London, 1989, p 30.
11. See Copyright Law Review Committee, *Report on Conversion Damages*, July 1990.

> being the market value of the exam. So calculated, conversion damages may be awarded under s 116. The applicants accept that, on this analysis, damages under s 115(2) would be confined to indirect losses, such as the diminution of goodwill or any loss associated with the failure to enhance goodwill or reputation: see *TS & B Retail Systems Pty Ltd v 3Fold Resources Pty Ltd (No 3)* (2007) 158 FCR 444 at 496 per Finkelstein J and *Prior v Sheldon* (2000) 48 IPR 301 at 321–22 per Wilcox J. This would apparently prevent any overlap of the kind that s 116(1C) is intended to avoid.

The court may order delivery up where the infringing goods have not been disposed of, and may not be willing to order damages where goods are to be so delivered: see, for example, *Milpurrurru* at [134].

Assessment of conversion damages

19.20 The measure of damages is the value of the goods converted at the time of the conversion (in other words, at the time the infringing copies were made): see *Caxton Publishing Co Ltd v Sutherland Publishing* Co [1939] AC 178. As to the process of calculation of conversion damages, see *Autodesk Inc v Yee* (1996) 68 FCR 391 and *Polygram Pty Ltd v Golden Editions Pty Ltd* (1997) 76 FCR 565; 38 IPR 451. Reference should also be made to the new s 116(1D) mentioned in the previous paragraph. Normally, the wholesale price of the goods will be taken as the basis for the assessment. Note that Lockhart J held in *Polygram Pty Ltd v Golden Editions Pty Ltd* that interest should be awarded on damages in so far as they were compensatory only. In *Microsoft Corporation v CT Group (Australia) Pty Ltd* [1997] AIPC ¶91–355, Burchett J stressed that where an award is somewhat arbitrary, the court should take care not to err on the high side: at 39,689. The assessment is to be made on a realistic basis. Thus, in *Autodesk Inc v Yee*, it was held that the conversion value should not be calculated as if the infringing copies were legitimate copies: the market in which the (counterfeit) copies were actually traded and sold should be taken into account in assessing the amount of conversion damages. The result was a much reduced award, the plaintiff having claimed the value of legitimate copies in the legitimate market, as opposed to heavily discounted black market copies. As to the expenses to be taken into account in the calculation of conversion damages, see *Microsoft Corporation v Auschina Polaris Pty Ltd* (1996) 36 IPR 225. Note also that the measure of conversion damages will be reduced if the subject matter converted itself contains copied parts, since conversion damages are awarded on the basis that the infringing article is deemed to be the property of the copyright owner: see, for example, *A-One Accessory Imports Pty Ltd v Off Road Imports Pty Ltd (No 2)* (above [9.15]), where the work infringed consisted of a catalogue of parts, which was made up of original sections and sections reproduced from existing catalogues.

Often, the goods converted (as a matter of statutory fiction) contain both infringing and non-infringing material. The whole article is deemed to have been converted, even though the copyright infringement may be only one aspect of it (see, eg, *Infabrics Ltd v Jaytex Shirt Co Ltd* [1982] AC 1; [1981] 2 WLR 646 where T-shirts bearing infringing copyright works were treated as the articles converted: see also s 10 definition of 'infringing copy'). However, in accordance with s 116(1E), various factors may be taken into account to determine whether damages should be granted and in what amount, where only part of an article consists of infringing material. *Polygram Pty Ltd v Golden Editions Pty Ltd* is a case predating the introduction in 1998 of s 116(1E). The case related to a package of two compact discs and of two cassettes embodying the works of Cat Stevens and of Donovan. The applicants' only claim for copyright rested with the Cat Stevens disc and cassette. However, Lockhart J pointed out at FCR 571; IPR 457 that it was well established, where the infringing and non-infringing material cannot be severed, that:

> ... the court will find that it was the making of both components that constituted an infringement of a work, and therefore the infringing copy consists of both components. In such a case the copyright owner is entitled to damages that represent the value of the whole goods; *Infabrics Ltd v Jaytex Ltd* [1982] AC 1; [1981] 2 WLR 646 [in that case the goods were a T-shirt with an infringing drawing that could not be severed] and *Brine* [*WH Brine Co v Whitton* (1981) 37 ALR 190; (1981) 55 FLR 440; in that case the goods were soccer balls bearing certain marks and devices that were the property of the applicant in the case] are two examples.

However, in this case, although the two compact discs were sold in the one package, they were made separately and were physically severable. As a consequence, the relevant 'infringing copy' for the purpose of s 116 was the Cat Stevens CD and not the whole package. However, where no severance was possible, the result of the pre-1998 provisions could be quite harsh, since conversion damages related to the value of the whole article even if the infringing material constituted only a small part of it.

In contrast, s 116(1E) now provides:

> If the infringing copy is an article of which only part consists of material that infringes copyright, the court, in deciding whether to grant relief and in assessing the amount of damages payable, may also have regard to the following:
>
> (a) the importance to the market value of the article of the material that infringes the copyright;
>
> (b) the proportion the material that infringes copyright bears to the article;
>
> (c) the extent to which the material that infringes copyright may be separated from the article.

In *Sony Entertainment (Australia) Ltd v Smith* (2005) 64 IPR 18; [2005] FCA 228 (*Sony v Smith*), the application of this current section was at issue. There was no evidence of the relative importance of the infringing tracks to the market value of the CD; they were only a small portion of the total and they could not be separated. The latter were competing factors between which a fair balance was to be struck. Jacobson J at [149] said: 'It seems to me that in striking the appropriate balance, the starting point should be the proportion of the infringing tracks to the whole but an amount should be added to recognize the impossibility of severance. I therefore propose to increase the proportion by 100 per cent, that is to say, I will double the percentage which would otherwise flow from the proportion of the infringing tracks on each CD.' In terms of the application of the current s 116(1C), Jacobson J held that damages under s 115 were not sufficient because the respondents had not fully disclosed documents that would enable damages to be properly calculated, and because it was inappropriate to assess damages under s 115, as it was unlikely the applicants would ever have granted the licences sought: at [119]–[121]. The judge also considered the relationship between conversion and additional damages, saying at [150]: 'There is usually a punitive element in an award of conversion damages because the verdict operates as a forced sale but any further punitive aspect should be determined in the application for additional damages under s 115(4).' More recently, see also *Boyapati v Rockefeller Management Corporation (No 2)*, above.

Additional damages

19.21 The power to award additional damages, going beyond compensation, allows the courts to have regard to flagrancy, particular aggravating circumstances of an infringement, and the need for deterrence in intellectual property cases. Additional damages may be awarded under the Designs Act 2003, s 75(3), under the Copyright Act 1968, s 115(4), under the Patents Act 1990, s 122(1A) and now also under the Trade Marks Act 1995, s 126(2). The wording differs between the various provisions. Under s 115(4) of the Copyright Act, a court may award such additional damages as it considers appropriate in the circumstances if it is satisfied that it is proper to do so with regard to:

- the flagrancy of the infringement and the need for deterrence;
- the conduct of the defendant after the infringement;
- any copying from analogue to digital form;
- benefit shown to have accrued to the defendant by reason of the infringement; and
- all other relevant matters.

Section 122(1A) of the Patents Act is expressed in relevantly similar terms, as is s 126(2) of the Trade Marks Act, whereas s 75(3) of the Designs Act simply provides that '[t]he court may award such additional damages as it considers appropriate, having regard to the flagrancy of the infringement and all other relevant matters.' As for a matter in which the additional damages provisions of a number of regimes arose, see *Geneva Laboratories Ltd v Prestige Premium Deals Pty Ltd (No 5)* where both copyright and trade mark infringements were flagrant, deceptive and occurred over a long period of time, the conduct of the respondents being uncooperative and obstructive. Note that there are some differences with UK law in the statutory provisions concerning additional damages. In *Bailey v Namol Pty Ltd*, the court held that Australian courts, when awarding additional damages, are not constrained by the restrictions imposed in the UK upon the awarding of exemplary damages by *Rookes v Barnard* [1964] AC 1129. That UK decision does not represent the common law in Australia: *Australian Consolidated Press Ltd v Uren* (1967) 117 CLR 221. Section 115 clearly allows courts considerable discretion to award additional damages in copyright in circumstances of flagrancy. Flagrancy has usually been interpreted as a deliberate course of conduct on the part of the infringer in the full knowledge of the rights of the plaintiff, or conscious disregard for the rights of the plaintiff. Deliberate dissimulation and dishonesty (eg, by altering records) may also contribute to a finding of flagrancy, as may a determination to put plaintiffs to proof on all possible matters of evidence. However, the conduct of the defence in proceedings may go to costs rather than additional damages, the court having the option of awarding indemnity costs in cases of egregious conduct of the proceedings: see, for example, *Futuretronics*. Mere knowledge of the infringement is not sufficient; a degree of *mala fides*, a calculated disregard of the plaintiff's rights or cynical pursuit of benefit is required: see *Prior v Lansdowne Press Pty Ltd* (1975) 29 FLR 59; 12 ALR 685. Those ingredients were lacking in *International Writing Institute v Rimila Pty Ltd*: there had been no clandestine activity nor disregard for the personal impact of the infringement. See *Futuretronics* at [17]ff for some useful general observations concerning the award of additional damages and see also *Dynamic Supplies Pty Ltd v Tonnex International Pty Ltd (No 3)* (2014) 107 IPR 548; [2014] FCA 909 where the applicable principles are usefully summarised at [37]–[53]. In *Futuretronics*, the infringements of copyright were held to be 'flagrant'. In *Milpurrurru* the directors of the defendant had been served with notice of the Aboriginal copyright owner's objections, and still continued the infringement even after court proceedings were commenced, thus their conduct warranted the award of additional damages. In *Sony v Smith*, no regret was expressed about the infringements, proof was in no way facilitated and no intention not to infringe in the future was expressed (in contrast with the otherwise similar case of *Universal Music Australia Pty Ltd v Miyamoto* (2004) 62 IPR 605; [2004] FCA 982).

The court in *Sony v Smith* marked its strong disapproval of the fact that the unauthorised inclusion of sound recordings on a remix CD had been accompanied by threats of physical violence if the requisite licences were not granted, by a large award of additional damages: A$500,000. In fact, considerable amounts have been awarded as additional damages, even where the compensatory damages award was small (the two may be cumulated). Thus, in *Microsoft v Goodview*, additional damages of A$500,000 were also awarded, and in *Microsoft Corporation v TYN Electronics Pty Ltd (in liq)* (2004) 63 IPR 137; [2004] FCA 1307, the award was for A$700,000 but against two respondents: see also the table in M Hall, 'Additional Damages under s 115(4) of the *Copyright Act 1968*' (1995) 13(1) *Copyright Reporter* 22 at 26. There is no rule that additional damages should be proportionate with or should normally be the same or less than compensatory damages: see *Raben Footwear Pty Ltd v Polygram Records Inc* (1997) 75 FCR 88; (1997) 37 IPR 417.[12] In that case, the court reiterated that additional damages are the subject of a broad general discretion and are not to be fettered in any arithmetical or mechanical way. It is also sometimes said that the award must be adequate to 'mark the disapproval of that conduct' (*Bailey v Namol Pty Ltd* at [45]), which could, depending on the circumstances, also require the assessment of a substantial amount. The statement highlights the fact that the award of additional damages is punitive rather than compensatory, and that the need for deterrence, for instance of a developing widespread practice, can also inflate the award: see, for example, *Universal Music Australia v Hendy Petroleum* (2003) 59 IPR 204; [2003] FMCA 373. Additional damages are not to have the effect of granting the applicant both damages and a disguised account of profits: 'In this case it seems that the appellants advanced a case in which they sought both damages and an account of profits. They did so by claiming the profits made by the respondents as additional damages. That course was in our opinion impermissible, and led to the error made by the primary judge in awarding $11,000 by way of additional damages pursuant to s 115(4)': *Facton* at [21].

12. See also J Dwyer, '*Raben Footwear Pty Ltd v Polygram Records Inc*' (1997) 8 *AIPJ* 166.

Nonetheless, the third element of s 115(4), 'all other relevant matters', has, in effect, opened the way for additional damages awards that arguably, in truth, compensate for non-traditional forms of harm such as cultural harm (or 'culturally based harm' — see *Milpurrurru* at FCR 279; IPR 246) and being held up to ridicule or contempt in the community or part of the community. Harm to feelings or embarrassment may also fall under this category, although compensatory damages are available for harm to reputation (see above 19.3 and 19.18). In *Milpurrurru* it was held at FCR 277; IPR 244 that '[l]osses resulting from tortious wrongdoing experienced by Aborigines in their particular environments are properly to be brought to account: *Napaluma v Baker* (1982) 29 SASR 192; *Weston v Woodroffe* (1985) 36 NTR 34, and *Dixon v Davies* (1982) 17 NTR 31.' Another matter that has been taken into account under the third heading is an allowance for the fact that compensatory damages may not have compensated certain instances of likely but undetected infringement: see, for example, *Autodesk Australia Pty Ltd v Cheung*. Nonetheless, additional damages awards are not dependent on the adequacy or otherwise of compensation damages: see *Flags 2000 Pty Ltd v Smith* (2003) 59 IPR 191 [2003] FCA 1067.[13] Occasionally, there has been mention of the possible impact that illegality (eg, of selling certain adult material) might have on the award of additional damages; the Full Federal Court in *Venus Adult Shops Pty Ltd v Fraserside Holdings Ltd* (2006) 157 FCR 442; 70 IPR 517; [2006] FCAFC 188 did not entirely rule this out (at [114]); see also *Zero Tolerance Entertainment Inc v Venus Adult Shops Pty Ltd* [2007] FMCA 155 and *Vivid Entertainment v Digital Sinema Aust Pty Ltd* (2007) 209 FLR 212; [2007] FMCA 157.

For an example of an award of additional damages in a designs action, see *Review Australia Pty Ltd v New Cover Group Pty Ltd* (2008) 79 IPR 236; [2008] FCA 1589, in which additional damages were awarded because of continued copying after formal notice: see also *Review 2 Pty Ltd v Redberry Enterprise Pty Ltd* (2008) 173 FCR 450; [2008] FCA 1588. In relation to trade marks, see *Geneva Laboratories Ltd v Prestige Premium Deals Pty Ltd (No 5)*; to patents, see *Coretell Pty Ltd v Australian Mud Company Pty Ltd* (2017) 250 FCR 136; 124 IPR 210; [2017] FCAFC 54, and *H Lundbeck A/S v Sandoz Pty Ltd* (2018) 137 IPR 408; [2018] FCA 1797, where a claim was rejected. Note that in passing-off cases, exemplary damages may be awarded: see, for example, *Taleb v GM Holden Ltd* (2011) 94 IPR 459; [2011] FCAFC 168; and *Lumen Australia Pty Ltd v Frontline Australasia Pty Ltd* [2018] FCA 1807.

The Account of Profits

Accounts of profits as a discretionary remedy

19.22 As has already been stated, the account of profits is a different remedy altogether from an award of damages. The aim of an account of profits is the restitution of gains made by the defendant from the infringing exploitation of the plaintiff's rights. Thus, an account prevents an infringer from remaining unjustly enriched; that is, retaining

13. For a case note, see C Lee, 'Copyright Infringement of Aboriginal Flag — Case Note; *Flags 2000 Pty Ltd v Smith*' (2004) 16(8) *IPLB* 125.

profits that it would be unconscionable for it to keep. If common law damages are claimed and proved then (subject to s 115(3) of the Copyright Act 1968), an applicant is entitled as of right to those damages. That is not the case with the statutory remedy of an account of profits, which is awarded subject to discretionary considerations based in equity. However, as the High Court noted in *Warman International Ltd v Dwyer* (1995) 182 CLR 544 at 559; 128 ALR 201 at 210, 'Although an account of profits, like other equitable remedies, is said to be discretionary, *it is granted or withheld according to settled principles*. It will be defeated by equitable defences such as estoppel, laches, acquiescence and delay.' (Emphasis added).[14] As for the question of delay, it is sometimes said that a plaintiff should not be tempted by the existence of the remedy of an account of profits to allow a defendant to continue a course of infringement, then to turn round and claim the profits resulting from the defendant's endeavours as a remedy. If a court sanctioned such behaviour, it would amount to allowing a compulsory licence. In *Warman International Ltd*, their Honours said at CLR 559; ALR 210: 'The conduct of the plaintiff may be such as to make it inequitable to order an account. Thus a plaintiff may not stand by and permit the defendant to make profits and then claim entitlement to those profits.' On the other hand, normally, delay alone will not impose a bar on the remedy, as some element of detrimental reliance will have to be shown. Despite what the High Court said in *Warman International Ltd*, the 'settled principles' must be flexibly applied. Thus, for example, in *A-One Accessory Imports Pty Ltd v Off Road Imports Pty Ltd (No 2)*, the court took into account the fact that the applicants' work contained so much pirated material that it would have been inequitable to treat them as authors of the entire work, and an account would therefore have been an equally inequitable remedy. Drummond J, at FCR 201; IPR 335, applied the 'clean hands' principle in these circumstances and spoke of 'dirt on the applicants' hands, constituted by their extensive copying of the works of others', which justified denying either an injunction or an account of profits. Note that an account must fairly reflect the profits gained; thus, if it is too difficult to determine profits (eg, where the defendant has contributed substantial time, energy and skill to the making of the profits), a court should probably refuse the remedy. On the particular facts of *Fortuity*, concerning copyright infringement in Weight Watchers programs, Heenan J stated that 'the difficulties involved in the procedure do not justify the making of any … order for taking an account.' He therefore decided to award damages instead. On the other hand, as was pointed out by the Full Federal Court in *Liquideng Farm Supplies Pty Ltd v Liquid Engineering 2003 Pty Ltd* (2009) 175 FCR 26; 79 IPR 437; [2009] FCAFC 7 at [36]:

> … the Court must do the best it can on the *whole* of the material before it. While it is generally not appropriate to 'speculate' or 'guess' without foundation, the exercise calls for allowance to be made for lack of precision where, as in the present case, the available material is incomplete, inexact and generalised. (Emphasis in original)

14. See also P Sugden, 'Account of Profits: Some Guidelines for Assessment' [1996] 12 *EIPR* 692; L Aitken, 'Account or Compensation in the High Court' (1995) 69 *ALJ* 782; and P Hastie, 'Restitution and Remedy in Intellectual Property Law' (1996) 14 *Aust Bar Rev* 6.

Calculation

19.23 Finn has observed that 'save in the very simplest of cases, accounts are burdensome, expensive, and usually unrewarding'.[15] Nonetheless, note that an account may have some collateral advantages, in that it will reveal information that may be of interest to the plaintiff in a business or competitive sense. The major difficulty with the remedy is accurate and fair calculation of profits. The complexity of the calculation, both conceptually and in practical accounting terms, often makes the remedy less attractive than it seems at first glance and involves considerable expense. Nonetheless, an account of profits can be an attractive remedy in some cases. It can result in the plaintiff being enriched over and above what it could itself have achieved, rather than merely compensated as with an award of damages. The aim of the remedy is to get the infringer to account for the actual profits, no more, no less, and regard should be had to substance over form. Commercial accounting methods can be of assistance, although 'mathematical exactitude is generally impossible': see *Dart Industries Inc v Decor Corporation Pty Ltd* (1993) 179 CLR 101 at CLR 111; 116 ALR 385; 'a judicial estimation of the available indications' (*General Tire* at WLR 826, cited in *Liguideng* at [36]) is commonly required. It is inappropriate for a court to 'simply award the gross revenue as profits with an arbitrary discount': *Liguideng* at [42]. The court must do its best with the figures available on the evidence, even if these are inexact, incomplete and inconsistent. The benefit of any doubt should go to the party wronged, and any profit properly attributable to the infringement should be accounted for; although rejected on the facts in *Polyaire Pty Ltd v K-Aire Pty Ltd* (2012) 96 IPR 101; [2012] SASC 75, that could extend to a portion of the salary of managing director of the infringing company.

The information concerning costs is uniquely within the control of the infringer, and that party will have to produce evidence to substantiate deductions. These may be individual costs directly related to the production, sale and delivery of particular items, or it may be a proportion of general overheads (eg, administration, plant and equipment); the onus will be on the infringer to establish how much of such costs should be attributed to the infringing sales. In *Dart Industries Inc v Decor Corporation Pty Ltd*, the High Court tackled some difficult issues as to the appropriate approach: first, if the infringer produces both infringing and non-infringing articles and, second, if the article does not infringe in its entirety but only in some aspect or another.[16] As to the second question, the key is to identify the reason for production or sale of the product; if the product would not have been produced but for the infringing element, then the profit from the sale of the whole item is to be accounted for: see also *Colbeam Palmer Ltd* at CLR 43 per Windeyer J. Or, as Lindgren J put it in *LED Builders Pty Ltd v Eagle Homes Pty Ltd* (1999) 44 IPR 24 at 48; [1999] FCA 584 at [87], 'a distinction is to be drawn between cases in which the infringement is in respect of the essential feature of a product that generates the profit and other cases.' In *Dart Industries Inc*

15. See P D Finn, *Fiduciary Obligations*, LBC Information Services, Sydney, 1977, [384].
16. See also L Bently, 'Account of Profits for Infringement of Copyright' (1990) 3 *EIPR* 106; P Blayney and M Wyburn, 'The Remedy of an Account of Profits in a Patent Infringement Action: The Difficulties in Determining a "True" Product Cost' (1994) 5 *AIPR* 77.

v Decor Corporation Pty Ltd, the sealable plastic containers included an infringing push-button sealing mechanism, the rest of the item being 'legitimate'. The infringer produced a host of other plastic products that did not infringe any other person's rights. What characterised the infringing product was the push-button lid, without which this particular container would never have been produced at all; thus, profits from the sale of the container as a whole had to be accounted for. (If, on the other hand, on the facts of a given case, the product concerned was not produced solely because of the incorporation of the infringing part, some apportionment will have to be made.) In *Tenderwatch Pty Ltd v Reed Business Information Pty Ltd* (2008) 78 IPR 329; [2008] FCA 931, a Mr Walltz engaged in unauthorised 'blatant and wholesale' copying of a manual belonging to the applicant in delivering some workshops in relation to tender opportunities. The court held that absent the infringing use and distribution of the original manual, he would not have been able to take up the opportunity of delivering the workshops. As the infringement was fundamental to his presentation of the workshop, the 'gross revenue received by him should be the starting point for the calculation of profit': at [16].

In *Black & Decker Inc v GMCA Pty Ltd (No 5)* (2008) 79 IPR 450; [2008] FCA 1738, there were two infringing products, profits having been made on one but losses on the other over several years. The court cited with approval a passage from the judgment of Laddie J in *Celanese International Corp v BP Chemicals Ltd* [1999] RPC 203 at [33]:

> The general proposition that nothing is payable to the plaintiff if the defendant's business is loss-making ignores the possibility of a case in which those loss-making activities can realistically be treated as a sequence of separate and self-contained businesses where profits made on one are obliterated by losses on others so that, looked at as a whole, the profits attributable to infringement are hidden. In such a case it may be possible to disentangle the profits made on the infringing business and order them to be paid to the plaintiff notwithstanding the losses made elsewhere. It was not suggested that any such analysis was possible on the facts of this case.

The court in *Black & Decker* then went on to say at [13]:

> The present case is a straightforward one and consistent with the hypothetical example discussed by Laddie J. GMCA made a profit on some infringements but a loss on others. It should disgorge the profits it made. It would be ironic in the extreme if GMCA could take the benefit of its own infringing conduct in respect of T2 by setting off the losses made in such activity against the profits on the T1 infringements which it is required to disgorge to Black & Decker.

While establishing individual cost items directly related to the infringing articles is relatively straightforward, the apportionment of general overheads is not. As a general rule, the infringer is at liberty to establish that various categories of overheads are attributable to the obtaining of profits, and in what proportion the overheads should be allocated. However, certain things may be excluded: in *Liquideng* (at [46]), the court said that '[i]t is well-settled law that an infringing party cannot claim remuneration or director's fees for carrying on the infringing activities: see *Le Plastier & Co Ltd v Armstrong Holland* (1926) 26 SR (NSW) 585 at [593]; *Tenderwatch v Reed Business*

Information Pty Ltd [2008] FCA 931 at [17]–[19].' Similarly, in *Tenderwatch*, Heerey J said at [18]:

> It would be wrong in principle to allow [the infringing copyist] Mr Walltz a deduction for the time he had spent working up his presentation with aid of Tenderwatch's original manual. This would be tantamount to making a copyright owner pay an infringer for the time and effort spent in infringement. As was said in *Sheldon v Metro-Goldwyn Pictures Corp* 106 F 2d 45 (1939) at 51 'a plagiarist may not charge for his labour in exploiting what he has taken'.

Dart Industries Inc v Decor Corporation Pty Ltd stands for the proposition that while general overheads should be allowed, they must be appropriately and realistically attributed and apportioned; for example, the allocation of overheads could reflect the infringing product's contribution to overall revenue. However, where the infringing product is a 'sideline' (ie, uses up excess capacity), no allocation of fixed overheads will be allowed, because these would be incurred in any case. Nonetheless, although in such a case profit that would have been made from producing an alternative, non-infringing product (the so-called 'opportunity cost') cannot be deducted, it is allowable to attribute (as a cost) to the infringing product a proportion of the general overheads that would have sustained the lost 'opportunity'. The principles that emerged from *Dart Industries Inc v Decor Corporation Pty Ltd* are usefully summed up in point form in *Apand Pty Ltd v The Kettle Chip Co Pty Ltd* (1999) 43 IPR 225 at 240 per Heerey J, a decision on appeal against the decision of Burchett J: *The Kettle Chip Co Pty Ltd v Apand Pty Ltd* (1998) 83 FCR 466; 40 IPR 481. These two decisions relate specifically to the calculation of the account of profits (as to the substance of the passing-off issue, see *The Kettle Chip Co Pty Ltd v Apand Pty Ltd* (1993) 46 FCR 152; 27 IPR 321 and *Apand Pty Ltd v The Kettle Chip Co Pty Ltd* (1994) 52 FCR 474; 30 IPR 337 and Chapter 13: Passing Off at [13.20]).[17] Regarding the related trade mark decisions, see *The Kettle Chip Co Pty Ltd v Pepsico Australia Pty Ltd (t/as Frito Lay Australia)* (1995) 132 ALR 286; 32 IPR 302 and *Pepsico Australia Pty Ltd (t/as Frito Lay Australia) v The Kettle Chip Co Pty Ltd* (1996) 135 ALR 192; 33 IPR 161.

In *Apand Pty Ltd v The Kettle Chip Co Pty Ltd* (1999) 43 IPR 225 (Full Court), the trial judge had found that the defendants were liable in passing off when they marketed 'Country Kettle' chips under the Smith's brand, in competition with the plaintiff's Kettle Chips. The judge ordered an account and the Full Court discussed the appeal against the method of calculation and allowance for overheads used. In accordance with general principle, the defendant (Smith's) bore the onus of establishing the incurring of particular costs and the reasonable allocation of such costs to the production of the infringing item. Applying *Dart Industries Inc v Decor Corporation Pty Ltd*, 'opportunity cost', as such, could not be deducted (ie, the profit forgone by not pursuing a different product option), but a reasonable amount representing a proportion of the costs that would have been incurred pursuing the alternative could be deducted. On the evidence, in producing the infringing 'Country Kettle' chip, Smith's had forgone the opportunity of continuing the production of 'Smith's Classic', which had been the product initially

17. For an analysis on this case, see S Stone, '*Kettle Chip Co Pty Ltd v Apand Pty Ltd*' (1998) 11 *IPLB* 22.

launched to counteract the entry into the market of 'Kettle Chips'. That predecessor had in fact achieved only 23 per cent of the sales that 'Country Kettle' achieved for Smith's (a figure augmented to 30 per cent by the trial judge to allow for potential future improvement had the line been continued). The infringing Country Kettle chips accounted for 3.88 per cent of Smith's total sales, and thus Smith's argued that it should be allowed to deduct 3.88 per cent of total general overheads. However, if that had been allowed, the infringer would have benefited from its own wrongdoing, and thus the amount proposed by Smith's as a general overheads deduction was, for a number of items, reduced by 70 per cent by the court. After all, if Smith's had continued to produce the non-infringing product, it would only ever have recovered 1.164 per cent (30 per cent of 3.88 per cent) of its general overheads by the sale of that line. Smith's recoupment of 3.88 per cent of its general overheads, rather than 30 per cent of 3.88 per cent of those overheads, would only have been due to the fact that its sales were driven up by its decision to switch production to a product that passed off The Kettle Chip Company's product. Thus, if the infringer had been allowed the full 3.88 per cent of general overheads, it would have benefited from its infringement of The Kettle Chip Company's rights. The outcome in this case proves two things: every calculation of profits and of allocation of costs and overheads will turn on its particular facts and will not lightly be overturned on appeal, and the arguments and the factual evidence often being complex, the outcome can rarely be accurately predicted. For a further example of the same issues at play, see *LED Builders Pty Ltd v Eagle Homes Pty Ltd* (1999).

In the *Kettle Chip* case, the defendant's business was sold pending the proceedings for passing off, which resulted in the granting of an account of profits. Arguably, the infringer had made a capital profit on the sale of its business, part of which was attributable to the infringing product. Since the matter had never before been decided, the court returned to first principles and stressed that it had been repeatedly stated in the leading cases that the object of an account was to 'make the infringer give up its gains in order to prevent its unjust enrichment': per McHugh J in *Dart Industries Inc v Decor Corporation Pty Ltd* at CLR 123 and see also *Colbeam Palmer Ltd.* In the trial judge's opinion (*The Kettle Chip Co Pty Ltd v Apand Pty Ltd* (1998) 40 IPR 481 at 490 per Burchett J), 'the distinction between capital and revenue profits is not of significance for the purpose of the taking of an account of profits in an action for passing off. The account relates to all profit by the wrongful conduct in question.' Thus, the defendant had to account for the part of its capital profit attributable to the infringing product. The court calculated the capital profit made due to the infringing Country Kettle brand by reference to the proportion of total sales of the business represented by the infringing product line (2.4 per cent). Interest was also awarded on both the capital and revenue profits. The Full Court agreed that capital profits should be accounted for as long as there was a connection between wrongful conduct and the profit made, and saw no reason to disturb the trial judge's findings as to the calculation of the capital profits.

The choice between an account of profits and damages

19.24 A party entitled to relief *must* make an election between either damages or an account of profits. The authorities are clear to that effect: see *Aristocrat Technologies*

Australia Pty Ltd v DAP Services (Kempsey) Pty Ltd (in liq) (2007) 71 IPR 437; [2007] FCAFC 40 [at 24]. Some of the disadvantages of accounts of profits and of damages have become apparent from the discussion above: in many cases, neither allows for precise calculation nor for a predictable outcome.[18] The court will often be reduced to making a rough estimate if damages are 'at large', because there is neither a clear basis nor a starting point for a calculation. Accounts have the appearance of greater precision, but, in reality, precise calculation is beset by accounting difficulties and evidentiary problems. It may well be that a plaintiff will have a reasonable expectation of a greater award from an account of profits than from damages. In terms of damages, the effect of the infringement may well be minimal; the success of the infringer in turning a profit from the intellectual capital concerned may be far greater than the plaintiff could ever have achieved. Accounts may have collateral advantages, in that the process of discovery, for the purposes of calculation of the award, could reveal information of commercial interest to the plaintiff. However, other factors may favour a claim in damages; for instance, because the courts consider the remedy of an account to be discretionary, in the sense that it is subject to the normal equitable principles, while damages are said to be 'as of right'.

A further factor influencing the election to be made by the plaintiff between the two remedies is that additional damages in copyright are available only with compensatory damages and not with an account of profits. The terms of s 115(4) — '... the court may, in assessing damages for the infringement, award such additional damages as ...' — tend to suggest that additional damages are not available if the plaintiff opts for an account.[19] It is clear enough that the plaintiff is not entitled to have both damages and an account of profits; they are inconsistent remedies, and an election must be made prior to judgment. In *Island Records Ltd v Tring International PLC* [1996] 1 WLR 1256, Lightman J aptly formulated the principles applicable to making an election between an account of profits and damages (at WLR 1258–9):

1. A plaintiff can only obtain judgment for either an account or damages and not both.
2. Once judgment has been entered for one or the other remedy, the right to the other is forever lost.
3. A party should not be made to make an uninformed election and should have access to readily available information to determine their probable entitlement prior to making the election.
4. The election must not be unreasonably delayed to the detriment of the defendant.[20]

The last two points are connected: as is pointed out in *LED Builders v Eagle Homes Pty Ltd (No 4)* (1998) 38 IPR 107, election would be meaningless if it were not an 'informed

18. See also MJ Leeming, 'When Should a Plaintiff Take An Account of Profits?' (1996) 7 *AIPJ* 127.
19. See further M Hall, 'Additional Damages Under s 115(4) of the *Copyright Act 1968*' (1995) 13(1) *Copyright Reporter* 22, as confirmed by Lindgren J in *LED Builders Pty Ltd v Eagle Homes Pty Ltd* at [221].
20. See also P McDermott, 'Election of Account of Profits' (1996) 70 *ALJ* 540.

election'. This does not necessarily mean that a plaintiff has the right to pursue both remedies and make an election when the final figures on both are determined by the court. At the very least, the plaintiff should not be forced to make an election before the process of discovery has been completed or properly and effectively completed: see in this regard *SBO Pictures v Kaos Shop Pty Ltd* [2006] FMCA 82. Lindgren J's reasons in *LED Builders Pty Ltd v Eagle Homes Pty Ltd* (1996) 36 IPR 293; [1996] 972 FCA 1 quote, with approval, the words of Lightman J in *Island Records Ltd*:

> … a party should in general not be required to elect or be found to have elected between remedies unless and until he is able to make an informed choice. A right of election, if it is to be meaningful and not a mere gamble, must embrace the right to readily available information as to his likely entitlement in case of both the two alternative remedies. It is quite unreasonable to require the plaintiff to speculate totally in the dark as to whether or not the sum recoverable by way of damages will exceed that recoverable under an account of profits.

The issue of timing of the election arose in *Dr Martens Australia Pty Ltd v Bata Shoe Co of Australia* (1997) 145 ALR 233; [1997] AIPC ¶91–351. Goldberg J made a distinction between a case such as the one before him, where the issues of liability and remedies were to be heard together, and one where they were heard separately, which commonly occurs in intellectual property cases. As his Honour pointed out (at AIPC 39,658), 'It is clear … that the decision in *Island Records Ltd* … was only concerned with the issue of election after liability was established.' Goldberg J disagreed with Lindgren J in *LED Builders v Eagle Homes Pty Ltd* (at AIPC 39,660):

> None of the cases referred to by his Honour in my respectful opinion support the proposition that the election cannot be made either at the conclusion of the evidence in an 'all issues' hearing or in the second stage of a 'split' hearing. [His Honour cited some cases in support of his proposition.] In my view, an applicant cannot be compelled to insist upon an election being made before the commencement of trial and, consistently with the cases to which I have referred, in my opinion the applicant is entitled to delay making an election at least until all the relevant evidence is in. If the trial is not split, this means that an applicant will have to call evidence to deal with both damages and an account of profits, as will the respondents. If the trial is split then the issue will not arise until after the determination of liability, as is exemplified in a number of cases to which I have already referred.

See also *Edwards v Liquid Engineering 2003 Pty Ltd* (2008) 77 IPR 115; [2008] FCA 970, a matter related to election and calculation in a non-split trial concerning trade mark validity and infringement.

Actions for Unjustified Threats

19.25 When considering risks and benefits of litigation and threats of litigation, the so-called 'unjustified threats' provisions common to the various intellectual property Acts are very relevant. The upshot of those provisions, which will be examined in some further detail below, is that if a letter of demand is sent to a suspected infringer, or threats of legal action are more generally advanced, the statute permits the recipient to force the hand of the sender by obliging them to file an action. The provisions also allow the defendant to recover damages if the threat proved unjustified in subsequent proceedings and disrupted the defendant's business. The relevant statutory provisions are Copyright Act 1968, ss 202 and 202A; Patents Act 1990, s 128; Trade Marks Act 1995, ss 129 and 130; and Designs Act 2003, ss 77–81. All these provisions have a similar structure: if a person is threatening to bring an action in infringement, any person aggrieved by that threat can bring an action to obtain a declaration from a court that the threat has no basis, an injunction restraining further threats and, importantly, damages to compensate for the injury that the person aggrieved has sustained because of the conduct of the defendant. The aim of the copyright provision (s 202) was referred to by Bennett J in *Nine Network Australia Pty Ltd v IceTV Pty Ltd* (2007) 73 IPR 99; [2007] FCA 1172 at [232]:

> The history of the section suggests that it was concerned to deter unjustified threats themselves, threats that did not result in infringement proceedings or could not be justified by actual infringement; threats made to 'frighten away competitors or to damage such persons less directly, by threatening to sue their customers or suppliers as joint tortfeasors' (S Ricketson and C Creswell, *The Law of Intellectual Property: Copyright, Designs & Confidential Information* (Lawbook Co., subscription service) at [2.195]; *Avel Pty Ltd v Intercontinental Grain Importers Pty Ltd* (1996) 65 FCR 154 at 159)). It is a right extended to the threatened person not generally available to those threatened with an action for a civil wrong.

Normally, an action for unjustified threats will not be successful either if the court finds, in hearing the application of the person aggrieved, that the facts on the basis of which the threats are offered constitute infringement or if a person in a position to do so actually initiates and pursues an action in infringement against the person threatened. Keifel J in *Advance Data Integration Pty Ltd v ADI Ltd* (2004) 138 FCR 520; [2004] FCA 731 remarked on the oddity of the situation where the legislation provided relief to the person threatened but then prevented the remedy from being pursued if proceedings for infringement were brought, in this case by the trade mark owner; nonetheless, that was the clear intention of s 129(5) of the Trade Marks Act 1995.[21] Note that the right to bring an action for unjustified threats lies against the person who issued the threats, who is not necessarily the actual owner of the intellectual property right at issue. As to who may bring an action, the Designs Act 2003, Trade Marks Act 1995 and Patents Act 1990 refer to any person aggrieved without more; the Copyright Act 1968 refers to a person aggrieved, whether the person making the threats is or is not the owner of the copyright or an exclusive licensee. A person aggrieved is not necessarily the person to whom the threats were addressed. Rather, it is any person adversely affected. A remedy for unjustified threats is granted on a discretionary basis: see *GM Global Technology Operations LLC v SSS Auto Parts Pty Ltd* (2019) 139 IPR 199; [2019] FCA 97 (considering the provisions under both the Copyright Act and the Designs Act).

21. For an analysis, see N Weston and M J Davison, 'Groundless Threats of Trademark Infringement, Proceedings: How to Avoid Getting Court' (2000) 11(3) *AIPJ* 151.

What amounts to a threat of legal proceedings?

19.26 The Patents Act 1990 and Copyright Act 1968 specify that the threat need not be made by way of a private letter or letter from a solicitor: see s 128(1) of the Patents Act 1990: 'Where a person, by means of circulars, advertisements or otherwise ...'. Section 202(1) of the Copyright Act 1968 uses the same terms; see also s 77(2) of the Designs Act 2003. The different terms of the Trade Marks Act 1995 have nonetheless been interpreted in the same way since the 19th century. The Copyright Act, by virtue of s 202(2), further specifies that mere notification of the existence of a copyright does not constitute a threat of an action or proceeding; the same is provided *mutatis mutandis* by virtue of s 80 of the Designs Act. A plaintiff must first establish that a threat has been made in Australia. In the context of s 128 of the Patents Act, it was said in *U & I Global Trading (Australia) Pty Ltd v Tasman-Warajay Pty Ltd* (1995) 60 FCR 26; 32 IPR 494 that the test to be applied to determine whether there was a threat in terms of the Act was whether the language would convey to any reasonable person that the author of the letter intended to bring proceedings for infringement against the person said to be threatened; direct words to the effect that action would be taken were not necessary: at FCR 32–3; IPR 501. In other words, as Crennan J pointed out in *JMVB Enterprises Pty Ltd v Camoflag Pty Ltd* (2005) 67 IPR 68 at [209], '[a] threat may arise without a direct reference to infringement proceedings.' Although (as Crennan J also pointed out at [209]) 'a communication merely notifying a person of the existence of a patent or a patent application, together with a statement that any suggestion that the recipient is entitled to replicate the invention is not maintainable, or a communication seeking confirmation that no improper or wrongful use or infringement of the patent has come to the recipient's attention is not a threat ...', a general public notification that certain actions will be regarded as infringements and that action will be taken if they occur *will* amount to an actionable threat: see, for example, *S W Hart & Co v Edwards Hot Water Systems* (1980) 47 FLR 377; 30 ALR 657. As to distinguishing damage due to the unjustified threats from other forms of damage, see *Avel Pty Ltd v Intercontinental Grain Exports Pty Ltd* (subnom *Avel Pty Ltd v Intercontinental Grain Importers Pty Ltd*) (1996) 145 ALR 533; [1996] AIPC ¶91–227 and see also *Cowan v Avel Pty Ltd* (1995) 58 FCR 154; 32 IPR 96 concerning threats issued to customers of the alleged infringer and damages suffered as a consequence. As to whether a court has a discretion not to grant a declaration or an injunction, even where a prima facie case for relief under unjustifiable threats provisions (in this case in the Patents Act 1990) is made out, see *Bradken Resources Pty Ltd v Lynx Engineering Consultants Pty Ltd* (2008) 78 IPR 586; [2008] FCA 1257 at [39]ff.

Bibliography

B Fitzmaurice, 'Protecting Intellectual Property with Anton Piller Orders' (2002) 15(7) *IPLB* 103.

C Golvan, 'Protection of Australian Indigenous Copyright: Overview and Future Strategies' (2006) 18(10) *IPLB* 154.

C Lawson, 'The interlocutory Injunction Dilemma in Patent Infringement and Invalidity Disputes' (2010) 21 *AIPJ* 73.

Copyright Law Review Committee (CLRC), *Report on Conversion Damages*, July 1990.

Cornish on Intellectual Property, 2nd ed, Sweet & Maxwell, London, 1989.

D Miller, 'Restitutionary and Exemplary Damages for Copyright Infringement' (1996) 14 *Aust Bar Rev* 143.

D Spalding, 'Culpable Copying: The Criminal Offence Provisions of the *Copyright Act 1968*' (2003) 54 *IP Forum* 38.

G S Clarke, 'Interlocutory Injunctions in Intellectual Property Cases — Principles and Practice' (2007) 69 *IP Forum* 10.

G Taylor and D Wright, 'Case Notes — *Australian Broadcasting Corp v Lenah Game Meats* — Privacy, Injunctions and Possums: Analysis of the High Court's Decision' (2002) 26 *MULR* 707.

H Strachan, 'Broadcast Decoding Devices: Actions by Sky Channel' (2003) 16(4) *IPLB* 50.

Harvard Law Review, 'The Criminalization of Copyright Infringement in the Digital Era' (1999) 112(7) *Harvard LR* 1705.

J Dwyer, '*Raben Footwear Pty Ltd v Polygram Records Inc*' (1997) 8 *AIPJ* 166.

J Gibson, 'Justice of Precedent, Justness of Equity: Equitable Protection and Remedies for Indigenous Intellectual Property' (2001) 6(4) *AILR* 1.

K Addo, 'Kazaa, "Anton Piller" Orders and the Current State of Play' (2005) 18(1) *IPLB* 14.

L Aitken, 'Account or Compensation in the High Court' (1995) 69 *ALJ* 782.

L Bentley 'Account of Profits for Infringement of Copyright' (1990) 3 *EIPR* 106.

L Toohey, 'Rights, Remedies and Relationships: Resolving Disputes through Mediation' (2003) 55 *IP Forum* 24.

M Hall, 'Additional Damages Under s 115(4) of the *Copyright Act*' (1995) 13(1) *Copyright Reporter* 22.

M J Leeming, 'When Should a Plaintiff Take an Account of Profits?' (1996) 7 *AIPJ* 127.

N Weston and M J Davison, 'Groundless Threats of Trademark Infringement, Proceedings: How to Avoid Getting Court' (2000) 11(3) *AIPJ* 151.

P Blayney and M Wyburn, 'The Remedy of an Account of Profits in a Patent Infringement Action: The Difficulties in Determining a "True" Product Cost' (1994) 5 *AIPR* 77.

P Hastie, 'Restitution and Remedy in Intellectual Property Law' (1996) 14 *Aust Bar Rev* 6.

P McDermott, 'Election of Account of Profits' (1996) 70 *ALJ* 540.

P Sugden, 'Account of Profits: Some Guidelines for Assessment' [1996] 12 *EIPR* 692.

S Gilchrist, 'Australia — Copyright — Innocent Infringement' [1996] 8 *EIPR* D-225.

S Harris, 'Stringent Approaches to Counterfeit Couture: *Louis Vuitton v D & L Design*' (2003) 16(5) *IPLB* 73.

S Stone, '*Kettle Chip Co Pty Ltd v Apand Pty Ltd*' (1998) 11 *IPLB* 22.

T Cockburn, 'Interlocutory Injunctions: Restraining Publication of Unlawfully Obtained Information' (2002) 23(2) *QldLawyer* 40.

W Kelcey, 'Offence Provisions of the *Copyright Act 1968* — Do They Protect or Punish?' (1995) 6 *AIPJ* 229.

Index

References are to paragraph numbers

Related LexisNexis Titles

Collins & Forrest, *LexisNexis Study Guide: Intellectual Property Law*, 2nd ed, 2014, ISBN 9780409336245

LexisNexis Legislation Series: Intellectual Property Collection, 2019, ISBN 9780409350197

Ricketson et al, *Intellectual Property: Cases, Materials and Commentary*, 6th ed, 2019, ISBN 9780409348613

Roy, *Quick Reference Card: Intellectual Property*, 2011, ISBN 9780409329353

Stewart et al, *Intellectual Property in Australia*, 6th ed, 2018, ISBN 9780409345780